2024 RELEASE

Human Communication

Scott Titsworth
Ohio University

Angela M. Hosek
Ohio University

McGraw Hill

1 2 3 4 5 6 7 8 9 LWI 29 28 27 26 25 24

ISBN 978-1-266-35674-2 (bound)
MHID 1-266-35674-6 (bound)
ISBN 978-1-264-89234-1 (loose-leaf)
MHID 1-264-89234-9 (loose-leaf)

Senior Product Development Manager: *Dawn Groundwater*
Product Developer: *Victoria DeRosa*
Content Project Managers: *Sherry Kane, Vanessa McClune*
Manufacturing Project Manager: *Nancy Flaggman*
Design: *Beth Blech*
Content Licensing Specialists: *Carrie Burger*
Cover Image: *Top to bottom: George Rudy/Shutterstock; Gstockstudio/123RF; Jose Luis Pelaez Inc/Blend Images LLC; Andriy Popov/123RF; Odua Images/Shutterstock; Jacob Ammentorp Lund/Ammentorp/123RF*
Compositor: *Aptara®, Inc.*

Library of Congress Cataloging-in-Publication Data
Names: Titsworth, Scott, editor. | Hosek, Angela M., editor. | Pearson,
  Judy C., editor. | Nelson, Paul E. (Paul Edward), 1941- editor.
Title: Human communication / Scott Titsworth, Ohio University, Angela M.
  Hosek, Ohio University, Judy C. Pearson, North Dakota State University,
  emeritus, Paul E. Nelson, North Dakota State University, emeritus.
Description: 2024 Release. | New York, NY : McGraw Hill LLC, 2024. |
  Includes index.
Identifiers: LCCN 2023029174 (print) | LCCN 2023029175 (ebook) | ISBN
  9781266356742 (hardcover) | ISBN 9781264892341 (spiral bound) | ISBN
  9781265432843 (ebook) | ISBN 9781264894987 (ebook other)
Subjects: LCSH: Communication.
Classification: LCC P90 .H745 2024 (print) | LCC P90 (ebook) | DDC
  302.2/24–dc23/eng/20230621
LC record available at https://lccn.loc.gov/2023029174
LC ebook record available at https://lccn.loc.gov/2023029175

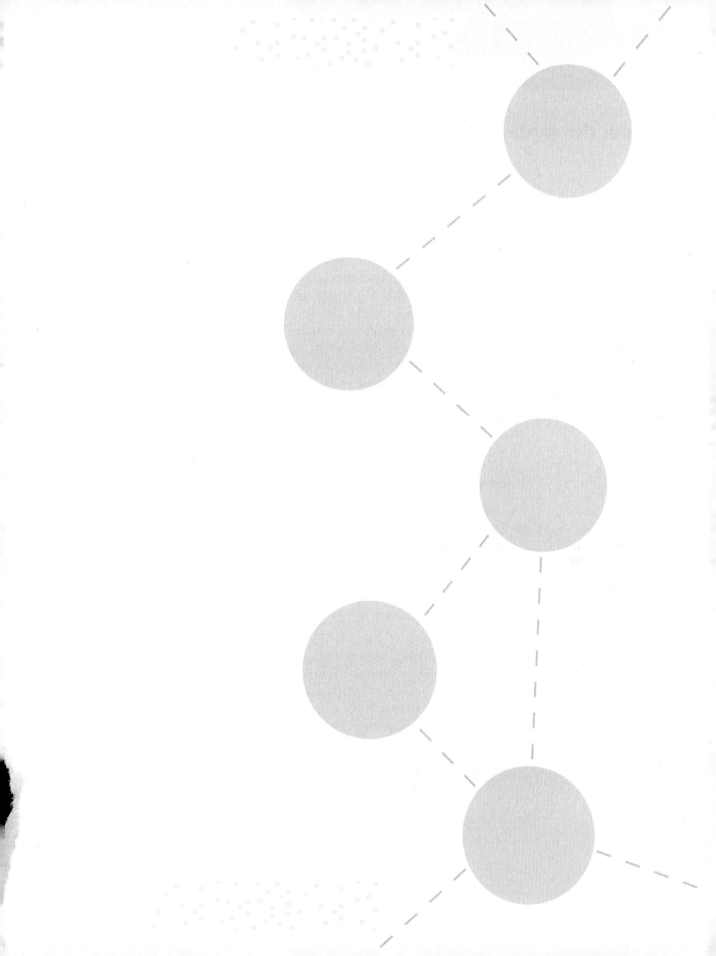

From the Authors

Current social and economic realities confront all of us with unprecedented change. In many fields and professions, entire landscapes of jobs will change; socially and politically we will continue to confront polarizing views; technology will alter how we connect with other humans and carry out the daily tasks of life. Through such change, communication will remain a constant necessity of personal and professional success. We are hopeful that this course will be a vibrant step in your journey to using communication when navigating such change in your world.

Your life is punctuated with critical moments in which communication plays an important role. Whether you are talking to a potential employer during a job interview, a loved one about an important issue facing your family, or an instructor about an assignment, what you say and how you say it can dramatically shape the outcome of an interaction. Our goal in writing *Human Communication* is to help you feel confident in any situation. We want you to have the knowledge, skills, and attitudes necessary to be a successful communicator.

We want you to be ready to

- **Communicate** effectively in novel and uncertain situations
- **Assess** who you are talking to and establish common ground
- **Listen** effectively and respond appropriately
- **Practice** the skills appropriate to a variety of relationships and cultures
- **Adapt** your communication using technologies that enhance, express, and transmit your messages
- **Speak** with confidence and clarity on important topics

Human Communication draws on the best available research to help you develop the knowledge you need to communicate effectively in a variety of situations. The research-based theories we present in this text, coupled with the street savvy you have developed over the course of your life, will equip you with a strong foundation for reading situations, acting appropriately, and adapting your communication behaviors.

— *Scott Titsworth*
— *Angela M. Hosek*

brief contents

contents

Chapter 2 Perception, Self, and Communication 30

Chapter 3 Language and Meaning 54

Part 2   Communication Contexts

Chapter 6   Interpersonal Communication   124

Chapter 14   Informative Presentations   334

Chapter 15   Persuasive Presentations   352

McGraw Hill Connect: An Overview

McGraw Hill Connect™ offers full-semester access to comprehensive, reliable content and learning resources for the Communication course. Connect's deep integration with most learning management systems (LMSs) offers single sign-on and deep gradebook synchronization. Data from Assignment Results reports synchronize directly with many LMSs, allowing scores to flow automatically from Connect into school-specific grade books, if required.

Evergreen

Content and technology are ever-changing, and it is important that you can keep your course up to date with the latest information and assessments. That's why we want to deliver the most current and relevant content for your course, hassle-free.

Titsworth and Hoseck's *Human Communication* is moving to an evergreen delivery model, which means it has content, tools, and technology that are current and relevant, with updates delivered directly to your existing McGraw Hill Connect® course. Engage students and freshen up assignments with up-to-date coverage of select topics and assessments, all without having to switch editions or build a new course.

Writing Assignment

Available within McGraw Hill Connect®, the Writing Assignment tool delivers a learning experience to help students improve written communication skills and conceptual understanding. Assign, monitor, grade, and provide feedback on writing more efficiently and effectively.

Instructor's Guide to Connect for *Human Communication*

When you assign **Connect** you can be confident—and have data to demonstrate—that the students in your course, however diverse, are acquiring the skills, principles, and critical processes that constitute effective communication. This leaves you to focus on your highest course expectations.

TAILORED TO YOU. Connect offers on-demand, single sign-on access to students—wherever they are and whenever they have time. With a single, one-time registration, students receive access to McGraw Hill's trusted content.

EASY TO USE. Connect seamlessly supports all major learning management systems with content, assignments, performance data, and SmartBook, the leading adaptive learning system. With these tools you can quickly make assignments, produce reports, focus discussions, intervene on problem topics, and help at-risk students—as you need to and when you need to.

Human Communication SmartBook

A Personalized and Adaptive Learning Experience with Smartbook®. SmartBook with Learning Resources is the leading adaptive reading and study experience designed to change the way students read and master key course concepts. As a student engages with SmartBook, the program creates a personalized learning path by highlighting the most impactful concepts the student needs to learn at that moment in time and delivering learning resources—videos, animations, and other interactivities. These rich, dynamic resources help students learn the material, retain more knowledge, and get better grades.

Enhanced! With a suite of learning resources and question probes, as well as highlights of key chapter concepts, SmartBook's intuitive technology optimizes student study time by creating a personalized learning path for improved course performance and overall student success.

Reader/eBook. Alongside SmartBook, there is also Connect eBook for simple and easy access to reading materials on smartphones and tablets. Students can study on the go without an internet connection, highlight important sections, take notes, search for materials quickly, and read in class. Offline reading is available by downloading the eBook app on smartphones and tablets, and any notes and highlights created by students will be synced between devices when they reconnect. Unlike SmartBook, there is no pre-highlighting, practice of key concepts, or reports on usage and performance.

Hundreds of Interactive Learning Resources. Presented in a range of interactive styles, *Human Communication* learning resources support students who may be struggling to master, or simply wish to review, the most important communication concepts. Designed to reinforce the most important chapter concepts—from nonverbal communication cues and critical thinking skills to workplace interviewing techniques and organizing presentations—every learning resource is presented at the precise moment of need. Whether video, audio clip, or interactive mini-lesson, each of the approximately 200 learning resources was designed to give students a lifelong foundation in strong communication skills.

More than 1,000 Targeted Question Probes. Class-tested at colleges and universities nationwide, a treasury of engaging question probes—new and revised, more than 1,000 in all—gives students the information on communication they need to know, at every stage of the learning process, in order to thrive in the course. Designed to gauge students' comprehension of the most important *Human Communication* chapter concepts, and presented in a variety of interactive styles to facilitate student engagement, targeted question probes give students immediate feedback on their understanding of the material. Each question probe identifies a student's familiarity with the instruction and points to areas where additional remediation is needed.

Informed by the Latest Research. The best insights from today's leading communication scholars infuse every lesson and are integrated throughout *Human Communication*. For example, Chapter 1 includes new research from the International Journal of Business Communication that supports the importance of communication in reducing the anxiety associated with the sudden shift to remote work, and Chapter 4 includes recent research from Robert Sternberg regarding the ways in which the COVID-19 pandemic caused adaptations of our nonverbal behaviors.

Fresh Examples Anchored in the Real World. Every chapter of *Human Communication* opens with a vignette exploring communication challenges in our everyday lives. For example, Chapter 11 opens with a discussion of Arnold Schwarzenegger's recent speech on the war in Ukraine. Dozens of new examples that demonstrate essential elements of the communication process appear throughout, such as the ways in which the COVID-19 pandemic have affected our nonverbal and digital communication. Whether students are reading the text, responding to question probes, or reviewing key concepts in a learning resource, their every instructional moment is rooted in the real world. McGraw Hill research shows that high-quality examples reinforce academic theory throughout the course. Relevant and contemporary examples coupled with practical scenarios—reflecting interactions in school, the workplace, and beyond—demonstrate how effective communication informs and enhances students' lives and careers.

An Emphasis on Creativity. The feature box *Communicating Creatively* illustrates ways in which originality—including effective collaboration strategies, emphasizing one's personality, and using music to boost a message—can be used to augment the communication skills addressed in the chapters.

communicating creatively

Can Rituals Drive Creativity?

Blogger Priyanka Gupta challenges the notion that creativity happens through flashes of unexpected insight. Gupta's blog, titled Creative Routine and Rituals—How to Dream and Create Consistently, explains how rituals allow people to free their mind from distractions and be receptive to creative ideas. Rituals allow artists of all types to flow into a creative process that helps them optimize work habits, think clearly and freely, and learn how to bring ideas into outcomes. An artist may begin by arranging brushes on a work-surface or a musician may warm up by playing the same scales before practicing. Because communication involves creativity, think about the routines you use to be ready for certain communication interactions. Do you carefully consider your clothing for particular situations? Do you have a routine for practicing presentations? Do you rehearse what you want to say before talking about something important with a family member or friend? How can you use this understanding of rituals and creativity to improve how you approach a variety of communication situations?

Source: Gupta, P. (2022). Creative routine and rituals: How to dream and create consistently. *On My Canvas.* www.onmycanvas.com/creative-routine-rituals/

communicating with agility

Steps for Managing Unconscious Bias

Identifying unconscious bias in ourselves typically requires a shift in how we normally think about our behaviors and how we talk with others. The following are four ways you can begin to manage unconscious bias in your own life:

1. **Personal awareness**. Conduct a self-examination to identify your beliefs and values that can lead to unconscious bias.

2. **Acknowledgment**. Recognize the ways in which you could have or have engaged in unconscious bias in the past.

3. **Empathy**. Actively listen to people who are different from yourself and seek to understand their views and experiences.

4. **Education**. Increase your knowledge about how unconscious bias impacts your communication. Ask others to challenge you when they notice you are engaging in unconscious biases.

Source: Adapted from Bucknor-Ferron, P., & Zagaja, L. (2016). Five strategies to combat unconscious bias. *Nursing*, *46*(11), 61–62.

A Focus on Agility. New to this revision, the *Communicating with Agility* feature box presents strategies for adapting to various communication situations, including adopting a growth mindset in challenging circumstances, managing unconscious bias, using flexible modes of communication, adjusting to working remotely, persuading on emotionally charged topics, and adapting presentations to enhance audience engagement.

Annotated Student Outlines and Examples Speeches. The example outlines in the Organizing Presentations chapter help students understand the outlining format. The Informative Presentations and Persuasive Presentations chapters include compelling example student speeches on contemporary topics. Each speech models how a speaker can increase audience members' awareness of an issue, integrate sources and other supporting material, and organize the message to help listeners better understand a topic.

Tips for Embracing Diverse Cultures. To help students navigate the communication challenges of a multicultural society, *Engaging Diversity* boxes offer guidance on topics such as nonverbal cues, disabilities, bilingualism, new technologies, and provocative speech.

Guidance for a Lifetime. The end-of-chapter feature, *Be Ready . . . for What's Next*, stresses the lifelong application of communication skills and how mastery of these skills can help students in other classes, the workplace, and life.

Video Capture Powered by GoReact

With just a smartphone, tablet, or webcam, students and instructors can capture video of presentations with ease. Video Capture Powered by GoReact, fully integrated in McGraw Hill's Connect platform, doesn't require any extra equipment or complicated training. All it takes is five minutes to set up and start recording! Create your own custom Video Capture assignment, including in-class and online speeches and presentations, self-review, and peer review. With our customizable rubrics, time-coded comments, and visual markers, students will see feedback at exactly the right moment, and in context, to help improve their speaking, presentation skills, and confidence!

Video Capture includes the following features:

- Time-coded feedback via text, video, and audio
- Visual markers for short-hand, repetitive comments
- Customizable rubrics
- Asynchronous video
- Synchronous screen capture and video ("Live Event")
- Group assignment/presentation
- Presenter split screen for visual aids or presentation decks
- Customizable rubrics
- Self and peer review
- Time-coded feedback with text, video, and audio
- Customizable in-line comment markers
- Rubric placement and comment box next to video for easier grading
- Mobile recording and uploading
- Improved accessibility
- Deep integration with most Learning Management Systems via McGraw Hill's Connect

Data Analytics

Whether a class is face-to-face, hybrid, or entirely online, McGraw Hill Connect provides the tools needed to reduce the amount of time and energy instructors spend administering their courses. Easy-to-use course management tools allow instructors to spend less time administering and more time teaching, while reports allow students to monitor their progress and optimize their study time.

- The **At-Risk Student Report** provides instructors with one-click access to a dashboard that identifies students who are at risk of dropping out of the course due to low engagement levels.

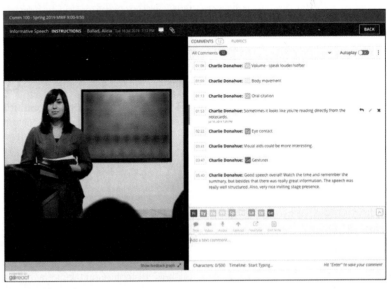

lucadp/Shutterstock

- **The Category Analysis Report** details student performance relative to specific learning objectives and goals and levels of Bloom's taxonomy.
- The **SmartBook Reports** allow instructors and students to easily monitor progress and pinpoint areas of weakness, giving each student a personalized study plan to achieve success.

Classroom Preparation Tools

Whether before, during, or after class, there is a suite of *Human Communication* products designed to help instructors plan their lessons and to keep students building upon the foundations of the course.

Powerpoint Slides. The PowerPoint presentations for *Human Communication* provide chapter highlights that help instructors create focused yet individualized lesson plans.

Test Bank. The Test Bank is a treasury of approximately 1,000 examination questions based on the most important communication concepts explored in *Human Communication*.

Available within Connect, Test Builder is a cloud-based tool that enables instructors to format tests that can be printed, administered within a learning management system, or exported as a Word document of the test bank. Test Builder offers a modern, streamlined interface for easy content configuration that matches course needs, without requiring a download. Test Builder enables instructors to:

- access all test bank content from a particular title.
- easily pinpoint the most relevant content through robust filtering options.
- manipulate the order of questions or scramble questions and/or answers.
- pin questions to a specific location within a test.
- choose the layout and spacing.
- add instructions and configure default settings.

Test Builder provides a secure interface for better protection of content and allows for just-in-time updates to flow directly into assessments.

Instructor's Manual. Written by the authors, this comprehensive guide to teaching from *Human Communication* contains activities and worksheets for each chapter.

Remote Proctoring & Browser-Locking Capabilities. Remote proctoring and browser-locking capabilities, hosted by Proctorio within Connect, provide control of the assessment environment by enabling security options and verifying the identity of the student.

Seamlessly integrated within Connect, these services allow instructors to control the assessment experience by verifying identification, restricting browser activity, and monitoring student actions.

Instant and detailed reporting gives instructors an at-a-glance view of potential academic integrity concerns, thereby avoiding personal bias and supporting evidence-based claims.

Polling. Every learner has unique needs. Uncover where and when you're needed with the new Polling tool in McGraw Hill Connect®! Polling allows you to discover where students are in real time. Engage students and help them create connections with your course content while gaining valuable insight during lectures. Leverage polling data to deliver personalized instruction when and where it is needed most.

Support to Ensure Success

- **Implementation Team**—Our team of Implementation Consultants are dedicated to working online with instructors—one-on-one—to demonstrate how the Connect platform works and to help incorporate Connect into a customer's specific course design and syllabus. Contact your Learning Specialist to learn more.

- **Learning Specialists**—Learning Specialists are local resources who work closely with your McGraw Hill learning technology consultants. They can provide face-to-face faculty support and training.

- **Digital Faculty Consultants**—Digital Faculty Consultants are experienced instructors who use Connect in their classroom. These instructors are available to offer suggestions, advice, and training about how best to use Connect in your class. To request a Digital Faculty Consultant to speak with, please email your McGraw Hill learning technology consultant.

CONTACT OUR CUSTOMER SUPPORT TEAM

McGraw Hill is dedicated to supporting instructors and students. To contact our customer support team, please call us at 800–331–5094 or visit us online at http://mpss.mhhe.com/contact.php.

Content Changes

New and updated material in *Human Communication* reflects the latest research in the field, as well as McGraw Hill's research identifying the skills and topics students find most challenging.

Chapter 1: Updated research, statistics and examples; integrated analysis of video-chat technologies and other unique communication situations caused by the COVID-19 pandemic; new discussion of retweeting as an example of the principle that communication involves choices; new feature box analyzing the role of rituals in driving creativity; updated information and examples related to online communication; and a new Communicating with Agility feature box on changing communication channels.

Chapter 2: Updated research, statistics, and examples; revised sections on identity factors to discuss spaces on campuses that specialize in identity; new section on mental health and well-being and the relationship to the self and perception; and a new Communicating with Agility feature box on adopting a growth mindset.

Chapter 3: New analysis of commonly understood statistics presuming a binary distinction between verbal and nonverbal communication to better represent the holistic nature of meaning-making; new discussion of how COVID-19 forced creative use of nonverbal communication; new examples of how nonverbal communication is used in online and virtual environments; and a new Communicating with Agility feature box on names and pronunciation.

Chapter 4: New discussion of ways in which the COVID-19 pandemic caused us to adapt nonverbal communication behaviors; new research on the effects of using emojis in workplace communication; and a new Communicating with Agility feature box on synchronizing facial expressions.

Chapter 5: Updated statistics and examples of how people listen while using social media; new discussion on how podcasts are becoming a substantial opportunity for practicing listening and critical thinking; new research exploring generational differences in listening habits and practices; updated analysis of research on how touch can be used as a form of feedback; and a new Communicating with Agility feature box on listening with curiosity.

Chapter 6: Updated statistics on trends related to forming and maintaining interpersonal relationships; new analysis on how COVID-19 forced people to be creative about how they formed and maintained relationships; and a new

Communicating with Agility feature box on using flexible modes of communication to interact with others.

Chapter 7: New chapter title and focus on inclusive communication; a new section on diversity and equity; a new section on theories related to inclusive communication; a new Sizing Things Up box on communication accommodation and age; a new Communicating with Agility box on ways to manage unconscious bias; a new section on microaggressions; new discussion of challenges towards inclusive communication and strategies for building inclusive behaviors; and an updated *Be Ready ... For What's Next* box to outline ways to get involved with people with different social identities.

Chapter 8: Updated coverage on group organization and interaction; new discussion about the impact of the COVID-19 pandemic on groups and teams; new examples of technology tools groups can use; and a new Communicating with Agility feature box on agile leadership.

Chapter 9: Substantial updates to emphasize common workplace communication skills and practices; new opening vignette illustrating how students experience entries into multiple organizations; new section on organizational assimilation that analyzes specific communication strategies and skills that promote successful entry into an organization; and a new Communicating with Agility feature box on hybrid organizations.

Chapter 10: Updated research findings and analysis of brainstorming and surveying interests; and a new Communicating with Agility feature box on the ways in which the COVID-19 pandemic impacted how we frame messages.

Chapter 11: New opening vignette on Arnold Schwarzenegger's speech about Ukraine; new analysis of common mistakes by speakers that diminish perceived competence; updated research on improving credibility; updated discussion of misinformation and source verification; augmented explanation and examples of several types of supporting material; and a new Communicating with Agility feature box on communicating statistics.

Chapter 12: New opening vignette on gentrification; expanded discussion of nonlinear thinking, particularly as it relates to new and emerging digital communication technology; updated references to reflect current APA style; and a new Communicating with Agility feature box on using AI.

Chapter 13: Addition of the remote delivery method and its unique characteristics; updated research on verbal and non-verbal delivery behaviors; revised tables and charts; and a new Communicating with Agility feature box on adapting to remote work.

Chapter 14: Revised examples and research throughout; and a new Communicating with Agility feature box on adapting presentations to enhance audience engagement.

Chapter 15: Revised examples and research throughout; and a new Communicating with Agility feature box on emotion and persuasion, which focuses on *how* we argue rather than *what* we argue.

acknowledgments

The authors wish to extend a very sincere thank you to the many colleagues who assisted in the revision of *Human Communication*. Many of our communication faculty colleagues and students have provided feedback, both formal and informal, about how to improve both the substance and feel of this book. Such insight is critical, and we are very appreciative of your time and expertise. We are forever grateful to Judy Pearson, Paul Nelson, and Lynn Harter, who were co-authors on previous revisions of this book. Your voices, spirit, and commitment to students are, and will forever be, integral parts of this project.

Reviewer Names

Chara Bowie, *College of Health Care Professions, McAllen, Texas*

Braze Brickwedel, *Tallahassee Community College*

Kelsey Burrell, *Kean University*

Joan R. Cartwright, *Palm Beach State College*

Lori Crane, *Palm Beach State College*

Kim Copeland, *Palm Beach State College*

Allison Edgley, *Kean University*

Laura Farrell, *Kean University*

Meghan O'Connor Gill, *Kean University*

Dianne Hargrove, *CHCP Online*

Ronald Hochstatter, *McLennan Community College*

Annalise Knudson, *Kean University*

Kara Laskowski, *Shippensburg University*

Sharon Martin, *Palm Beach State College*

Jason Molloy, *Kean University*

James Rowland, *Palm Beach State College*

Sarah Smitherman, *Tallahassee Community College*

Rachael Tiede, *Dallas College, North Lake Campus*

Olivia Vogt, *North Dakota State University*

Janice Webber, *Palm Beach State College*

We are also indebted to the outstanding team of McGraw Hill colleagues who contributed their time and talent to this revision. Sarah Remington and Dawn Groundwater provided critical guidance as we developed a vision. Your wisdom and pragmatic approach provided us with confidence, while your enthusiasm and vision instilled excitement! There are many other individuals who worked on several essential aspects of this project, including Sherry Kane, Carrie Burger, Vanessa McClune, and Beth Blech. Thank you for being part of the *Human Communication* team!

We were particularly blessed to work with a delightful editor, Victoria DeRosa. Victoria was a true collaborator on this project. Her eye for detail, insightful suggestions, understanding of our vision, and commitment to be inclusive to students was evident in the work she did with us. We are so thankful to have had you with us on this journey!

Finally, we are reminded that book projects are family endeavors. Scott would like to thank Lynn Harter for providing a creative sounding board and unending support for this project. Thanks also to Emma, Jasper, and Cleo for their love and fun diversions from the computer! Angela would like to thank her partner, Timothy, for his faith in her talents, and their children, Lillie, Ayden, Genevieve, and Luke for their laughter, love, and inquisitive minds.

Human Communication

introduction to human communication

When you have read and thought about this chapter, you will be able to

1. state reasons why the study of communication is essential.

2. define communication.

3. name the components of communication.

4. explain some principles of communication.

5. explain how the contexts of communication differ from each other.

6. list goals for improving yourself as a communicator.

In this chapter you will learn about the importance of communication in your everyday life. You will find that communication is the foundation on which you build your personal, social, and professional life. You will also learn about communication on a deeper level, including the terms, processes, and contexts of communication.

The week of September 5, 2020, was an important week in Athens County, Ohio. The Alexander High School Spartans were scheduled to play the Athens High School Bulldogs in both football and soccer for games that would be pivotal in the district championship race. Typically, players and fans for both schools, separated by only a few miles, would focus on competition to the point of polarizing the entire southern part of the county into those who bleed red for the Spartans or green for the Bulldogs.

Amanda Lasure is a survivor of childhood cancer and now uses athletic activism as a platform to raise awareness and help others battling the disease.

Scott Titsworth

September is also Childhood Cancer Awareness month. Both schools had recently witnessed cancer affect students in their respective districts, so under the leadership of athletic directors, coaches, and players, both schools chose to emphasize the color gold to highlight their goal of raising awareness of childhood cancer.

Student athletes, parents, and community members created banners with gold ribbons to place on light poles throughout town, staffed tables where individuals could purchase donated "#TurnItGold" shirts to wear at games, and held silent auctions to raise funds. Lynn Harter, a local organizer of the TurnItGold activities, stated in a personal interview with one of your authors, "Both off the field and on the field, these athletes are demonstrating the power of coming together to compete for something larger than a game or match. They are using their stage to tell others what they think is important—helping their classmates and raising awareness about this disease that affects hundreds of thousands of children annually in the U.S."

Using athletic activism and other communication strategies, students, parents, administrators, and community members partnered with the Houston-based #TurnItGold Foundation to raise thousands of dollars to support local families with children facing cancer. Their success was facilitated by a multifaceted communication effort involving groups of people using compelling messages to unify competitors during what could have been a polarizing week. Communication has power to promote social and personal successes, and that is what we hope you will learn from this course.

The Study of Communication Is Essential

Communication is central to your life. Effective communication can help you solve problems in your professional life and improve relationships in your personal life.[1] In fact, the field of communication studies is on the rise in terms of popularity, degrees earned, and undergraduate majors. Data reported by the National Center for Education Statistics show that communication is the eighth most popular major nationally and that the number of students graduating with a bachelor's degree in the major has grown by 62% from 2010 to 2020.[2] This should not be surprising, given that a recent survey of corporate recruiters identified communication skills as the most important skill that employers look for in the hiring process.[3]

In 2014, *The Huffington Post* noted that studying communication is timely because, as a discipline, communication studies is at the very center of substantial changes in our personal, professional, and social lives resulting from our increased reliance on mobile and digital technology.[4] That advice has only grown in importance. Recent events like the global pandemic, economic volatility, political and social polarization, and the continued expansion of digital and mobile technologies have only magnified the importance of understanding how communication works and of being skilled when communicating.

Understanding communication theory, research, and applications will make a substantial difference in your life and in the lives of people around the world.[5] A quick daily review of social media highlights the importance of communication principles. Communication is central to resolving disputes between nations as well as family members; communication is vital to effective local, regional, and national economies; communication is the primary tool through which organizations of all types engage customers, employees, and collaborators. Effective communication may not solve all the world's problems, but better communication practices can help us solve many of them. A strong understanding of communication, theory, and research is critical to effective communication.

Regardless of your personal interests and goals, the ability to communicate effectively will enhance and enrich your life. Learning about communication will help you know how to be ready to communicate. Studying communication comprehensively offers the following seven advantages:

1. *Studying communication can improve the way you see yourself.* Communication is the single way that we learn about who we are and find ways to develop our own sense of self. Through our communication with others, or *inter*personal communication, we begin to understand how others see and relate with us. Then, through our own thoughts, or *intra*personal communication, we begin to develop self-awareness and perhaps even take steps to alter how others perceive us. People who do not understand the communication process and the development of self-awareness, self-concept, and self-efficacy may not see themselves accurately or may be unaware of their own self-development. Knowing how communication affects self-perception can lead to greater awareness and appreciation of the self.

Learning communication skills can improve the way you see yourself in a second way. As you learn how to communicate effectively in a variety of situations—from interpersonal relationships to public speeches—your self-confidence will increase. In a recent study of more than 2,500 students, researchers found that after taking a course emphasizing communication skills, students reported substantial improvement in their ability to express themselves verbally and nonverbally across a variety of personal and professional situations.[6] In short, your success in interacting with other people in social situations and your achievements in professional settings will lead to more positive feelings about yourself.

2. *Studying communication can improve the way others see you.* You can control your own behavior to a considerable extent, which will lead to positive outcomes with others. Your interactions can be smoother and you can achieve your goals more easily as you manage the impression you make on others. See Chapter 2 for more on self-presentation and identity management.

You can improve how others see you a second way. Generally, people enjoy communicating with others who can communicate well. Compare your interactions with someone who stumbles over words, falls silent, interrupts, or chooses to not turn their camera on during an online meeting to your interactions with someone who gives consistent nonverbal feedback, listens when you speak, reveals appropriate personal information, and smoothly takes turns talking with you during conversation. Which person do you prefer? Most of us prefer competent communicators. As you become increasingly competent, you will find that others seek you out for conversations, assistance, and advice.

3. *Studying communication and engaging in effective communication behaviors can improve your relationships with others.* The field of communication includes learning about how people relate to each other and about what type of communication is appropriate for a given situation. Most people value human relationships and find great comfort in friends, family, and community. Within these relationships we learn about trust, intimacy, and reciprocity.

Human relationships are vital to each of us. From the time that we are babies, our relationships with others give us a sense of safety, connection, and satisfaction. In fact, we tend to thrive when we have rich interpersonal relationships with friends and family at an early age. Into adulthood, interpersonal relationships continue to nurture us in our education, in our careers, and during times of change in our family structures. Although the strength and quantity of our relationships naturally change over time, they always remain a vital component of our sense of well-being.

We learn about the complexity of human relationships as we study communication. We learn, first, that other people in relationships are vastly different from each other. We learn that they may be receptive or dismissive toward us. We learn that they may behave as if they were superior or inferior to us. We learn that they might be approachable or highly formal.

We also learn that our interactions with others may be helpful or harmful. Communicators can share personal information that builds trust and rapport. The same personal information can be used outside the relationship to humiliate or shame the other person. Whereas some relationships enhance social support, others are riddled with deception and conflict. Interactions are not neutral.

We learn that people create the reality of their relationships through communication. Families, for example, love to tell stories of experiences they have had when on vacation, when moving across the country, or when some particularly positive or negative event occurred. Indeed, they often take turns "telling the story." Couples, too, create and tell stories of their lives. Couples' stories may be positive as the couple emphasizes their feelings of belongingness and their identity as a couple. On the other end of the spectrum, stories may be highly negative as people deceive others with information that allows them to cover up criminal acts, such as drug use, child abuse, or murder.

Human relationships are complex. As you study communication, you will clarify the variables involved in relationships—the people, the verbal and nonverbal cues provided, the effect of time, the nature of the relationship, and the goals of the participants. You will be ready to engage in relationships with an understanding of the communication process.

People who receive communication-skills training experience greater relational satisfaction than those who don't.[7,8] The link between communication skills and life satisfaction is strong. The connection holds true in health contexts,[9] including situations in which family members are experiencing life-threatening illnesses.[10] For example, couples' communication during early stages of cancer diagnoses impacts their levels of intimacy and adjustment.

• Effective communication strengthens family connections across generations.

LightField Studios/Shutterstock

4. *Studying communication can teach you important life skills.* Studying communication involves learning important skills that everyone will use at some point in life, such as critical thinking, problem solving, decision making, conflict resolution, team building, media literacy, and public speaking.[11] Our visual literacy is improved as we understand the technical and artistic aspects of the visual communication medium.[12] The increasing focus on visual and social media requires us to attend to how communication skills are at work in these contexts.

Studying communication early in your college career can enhance your success throughout college. Consider the centrality of oral communication to all of your college classes. You

• Studying communication will give you skills to be effective in both face-to-face and online communication situations.

Kateryna Onyshchuk/ Shutterstock

are regularly called on to answer questions in class, to provide reports, to offer explanations, and to make presentations. In addition, both your oral and written work depend on your ability to think critically and creatively, to solve problems, and to make decisions. Most likely, you will be engaged in group projects in which skills such as team building and conflict resolution will be central. The same skills will be essential throughout your life.

5. *Studying communication can help you recognize how communication affects your community, nation, and world.* Few nations have a bill of rights that invites people to convey their opinions and ideas, yet freedom of speech is essential to a democratic form of government. Being an engaged citizen in a democratic society means knowing about current issues and being able to speak about them in conversations, in speeches, and through the media; it also involves being able to critically examine messages from others.

Our understanding of communication shapes our political lives. Mass communication and communication technology have sharply altered the way we consume and use information as part of the political process. Today many more people have the opportunity to receive information than ever before and through more channels than ever before. Think about how you get information about local, national, and global issues. Do alerts from the CNN app ping your phone? Do you have apps such as Flipboard or Apple News aggregate information from newspapers, magazines, and online outlets organized around your speci-fied interests? Perhaps you watch news or other informative channels on YouTube. In many ways, the methods through which you consume media determine the amount and frequency of the information to which you have access. Through mass media, and speci-fically social media, people in remote locations are as well informed as those in large urban centers. The public agenda is largely set through the media. Pressing problems are given immediate attention. McCombs notes, "The agenda-setting role of the mass media links journalism and its tradition of storytelling to the arena of public opinion, a relationship with considerable consequences for society."[13]

Whereas some people may feel more enfranchised by advances in communication technology, particularly social media, to advocate their positions, others feel more alien-ated as they become increasingly passive in the process. Face-to-face town meetings were the focus of democratic decision-making in times past, but today people receive answers to questions, solutions to problems, and decisions about important matters from tweets, Facebook messages, and Instagram posts.

Social media has become the most important tool for communicators engaging in political discussions and other forms of public dialogue. According to a recent survey from Pew Research Center, just over half of Americans have been engaged in civic dia-logue or discussion using social media in the past year.[14] Also, as noted by an article in *The New Yorker*, entire social movements have been created and sustained through social media. For instance, the #BlackLivesMatter movement was initiated in July 2016 and continues to sustain itself through its prominent hashtag.[15] Have you expressed dissent or agreement about political issues using social media? How did the people in your life react to your posts or involvement? Have your friends or family members been involved in movements that were organized through social media?

Although democracy is indelibly tied to our freedom of speech, we must also rec-ognize that such freedoms sometimes create discomfort. Research reported in *Psychology Today* noted that between 1992 and 2016 the United States had become substantially more polarized.[16] **Polarization** occurs when people divide into groups that seemingly share very little common ground, such as political parties. Although we often observe polarization around politics, polarization can emerge around any number of topics: public versus charter schools, Ohio State versus Michigan, immigration, gun control, vaccines, global warming, and so on.[17] Such polarization has implications for how we communicate. When people talk face to face, social norms guide certain politeness behaviors that promote civility; however, on social and broadcast media, those norms are increasingly nonexistent (if not completely reversed to emphasize incivility).[18] Regardless of whether you are communicating face to face, through a video app, or through social media, communication training can help you develop the skills necessary for you to have a positive impact on the democratic processes in your local and broader community.[19]

By studying communication, you will be more effective in shaping your own messages while at the same time carefully listening to messages from others. You will be a better consumer of information. All of these skills are important for promoting rigorous but civil debate, and in fact, they are the basis for democratic decision-making.

As educators, we firmly believe in the importance of public discussion, debate, and advocacy. At the same time, we feel that communication should follow principles of civil-ity and hope that you will use your study of communication to advocate for outcomes that benefit all, even those with whom you disagree. Because polarization and its effects

polarization
The division of people into groups that have conflicting views, per-spectives, or ideologies and very little common ground.

on communication behaviors is so evident in our current culture, we will return to this theme periodically throughout the book.

6. *Studying communication can help you succeed professionally.* A look at job postings, such as those found online, will give you an immediate understanding of the importance of improving your knowledge and practice of communication. The employment section of a newspaper or website has entries such as these:

- "We need a results-oriented, seasoned professional who is a good communicator and innovator," reads one posting for a marketing manager.
- Another posting, this one for a marketing analyst, reads, "You should be creative, inquisitive, and a good communicator both in writing and orally."
- A posting for a training specialist calls for "excellent presentation, verbal, and written communication skills, with ability to interact with all levels within organization."

Employers want to hire people who are competent communicators. A recent study noted that exemplary communication skills include being dependable, documenting points, and being able to adapt to audiences, whereas unacceptable workplace communication traits include being defensive, aggressive, and deceptive.[20] You may believe that some professions are enhanced by communication skills but that many are not. However, professionals in fields such as accounting, auditing, banking, counseling, engineering, industrial hygiene, information science, public relations, and sales have all written about the importance of oral communication skills.[21] More recently, professionals in engineering,[22] science,[23] farming and ranching,[24] education,[25] and the health field[26] have stressed the importance of communication skills for success in these fields. The variety of these careers suggests that communication skills are important across the board.

Communication skills are crucial in your first contact with a prospective employer. By studying communication, you can enhance your interviewing skills. Further, human resource interviewers note that oral communication skills, in general, significantly affect hiring decisions.[27] One recent survey of over 700 employers indicated that effective communication is vital to career success and that they are finding many college graduates lacking such skills.[28] Another study showed effective communication skills are associated with higher wages for workers in a variety of job settings.[29] Taking this course and being able to persuasively explain how it has prepared you to be an effective communicator will set you apart from other job applicants and help you achieve professionally.

What communication skills are employers seeking? Employers view your written and oral communication competencies, your ability to listen and analyze messages, and your ability to relate well with others as essential job skills.[30] The vital importance of these skills was highlighted for all of us as the COVID-19 pandemic forced a shift from in-person work to remote work. Research suggests that effective communication was critical in reducing anxiety for individuals as they navigated the constantly changing effects of the pandemic in schools, workplaces, and communities.[31] As you begin to improve your communication skills, and consequently your appeal to potential employers, you should concentrate on skills such as listening (Chapter 5) and speaking clearly, succinctly, and persuasively, which you can read more about in Chapters 3, 13, and 15. In many professional settings, group and team-based communication is especially important, particularly as organizations make increasing use of teams working from different locations and using communication technology to connect.[32] Many workplace practices, like teamwork and problem solving, are also improved through effective interpersonal communication skills,[33] which you can learn about in Chapter 6. Public-speaking skills are important in most professions because employees are often required to give talks and presentations.[34] You will have an opportunity to improve your writing skills as you prepare outlines and manuscripts for public speeches, which you can learn more about in Chapters 14 and 15. Ultimately, the content and skills in this course will prepare you to be ready to communicate in ways that matter for your professional career.

7. *Studying communication can help you navigate an increasingly diverse world.* As you stroll through a mall, deposit money in a bank, or work at your job, odds are that about one in every five people you come into contact with will speak English as a second language. According to the 2017 American Community Survey, conducted by the U.S. Census Bureau, nearly 22% of respondents speak a language other than English in their home.[35] The increasingly diverse population of the United States means that multilingual communication encounters are, for most of us, the norm rather than the exception. Learning how to communicate in today's world, whether English is your first language or not, requires an understanding of communication and culture and how those two concepts are related.

As you develop an understanding of basic communication concepts and learn how to apply those concepts in everyday interactions, you will be better equipped to bridge language and cultural barriers and promote effective interpersonal relationships, teamwork, and digitally mediated communication.

Defining Communication

Now that you have considered why learning how to communicate is important, you should know exactly what the term means. Over the years, scholars have created hundreds of definitions of communication. How they define the term can limit or expand the study of the subject. In *Human Communication,* we will adopt a broad definition of communication that is applicable to many different situations and contexts in which people interact.

Communication comes from the Latin word *communicare,* which means "to make common" or "to share." The root definition is consistent with our definition of communication. We define **communication** as the process of using messages to generate shared meaning. Communication is considered a **process** because it is an activity, an exchange, or a set of unfolding behaviors. Communication is not an object you can hold in your hand; it is an activity in which you participate. David Berlo, a pioneer in the field of communication, probably provided the clearest statement about communication as a process:

> If we accept the concept of process, we view events and relationships as dynamic, ongoing, ever changing, continuous. When we label something as a process, we also mean that it does not have a beginning, an end, a fixed sequence of events. It is not static, at rest. It is moving. The ingredients within a process interact; each affects all the others. . . .[36]

In stating that communication is a process, we mean that you cannot look at any particular communication behavior as a snapshot and fully understand what is happening. Suppose that you were in a coffee shop and observed an interaction between a customer and a server. The customer asks for a double-shot espresso, and the barista responds by asking, "Sure you don't want a latte?" The customer responds by saying, "Definitely no," to which the barista says, "Wow, must be a bad day." On its face, this interaction could seem somewhat abrupt—maybe even inappropriate. But, if the customer is a regular, the barista might know that this is an unusual order, inferring that the need for an extra jolt of caffeine is indicative of a hectic day for the patron. In this example, the communication interaction started well before the actual behaviors you observed. Those behaviors were part of an ongoing process of communication between the customer and the barista. How

communication
The process of using messages to generate shared meaning.

process
An activity, an exchange, or a set of behaviors that occurs over time.

the customer responds to the "bad day" comment, perhaps with annoyance or with a story about what is going on, will further influence that unfolding communication process.

Messages include verbal and nonverbal symbols, signs, and behaviors. When you smile at another person, you are sending a message. Public speakers might spend days choosing just the right words and considering their bodily movements, gestures, and facial expression. During a group meeting you might signal respect for another person's statement, nodding your head while they speak. As a communicator, you attempt to use these verbal and nonverbal behaviors to create and provide a message to others.

meaning
The intent of a message by the sender and the interpretation of a message by the receiver.

People hope to generate common meanings through the messages they provide. **Meaning** is the intent of a message by the sender and the interpretation of a message by the receiver. Consequently, meaning is both assigned and negotiated with each person in a communication interaction. When you communicate, you might intend for a certain meaning to be represented in your messages, but there is also the meaning that others perceive from your message. We communicate more effectively when our intended meaning and others' perceived meaning of our messages are similar. During a presentation by classmates, you might smile to indicate agreement only to later learn that the speakers thought you were laughing at them; in that situation, meaning was not shared effectively. What we say and do can be communication only if the meaning of what we intend is generally shared with the other person. In the same classroom example, a smile accompanied by a quiet clap of the hands might make your intended meaning more apparent to your classmate. Of course, communication cannot be perfect, so 100% shared meaning is rarely achieved. Yet, maximizing such shared meaning is one of the goals of this course.

• Understanding emerges from shared experience.
BaanTaksinStudio/Shutterstock

During the process of communication, we naturally attempt to negotiate meaning with others. Understanding the meaning of another person's message occurs more easily when the two communicators elicit common meanings for words, phrases, and nonverbal codes. For instance, during class, you might raise a hand to have a professor clarify the meaning of a term. During a conversation with a friend, you might use a shake of the head to indicate that you are not following their point. In both examples, you used commonly understood verbal or nonverbal symbols to provide feedback and negotiate meaning with another person. This negotiation is constant, and it means that the process of communication is continually unfolding as we attempt to share common meaning with others. Much of what you will learn in this course is intended to help you make that negotiation easier and more natural.

Components of Communication

The definition of communication that you just learned points out that the process of communication can be divided into specific components that are part of the process. The components of communication are people, messages, channels, codes, encoding and decoding, feedback, noise, and situation.

source
A message initiator.

receiver
A message target.

PEOPLE

People are involved in the human communication process in two roles—as both the sources and the receivers of messages. A **source** initiates a message, and a **receiver** is the intended target of the message. Individuals do not perform these two roles independently; instead, they are the sources and the receivers of messages simultaneously and continually.

The people with whom we communicate are diverse. They are of different ages and genders and perhaps from different cultural backgrounds. Each of these characteristics associated with diversity can influence the process of communication as people attempt to negotiate the meaning of messages.

MESSAGES

The **message** is the verbal and nonverbal form of the idea, thought, or feeling that one person (the source) wishes to communicate to another person or a group of people (the receivers). In any specific interaction between people, that interaction may contain multiple messages expressed by each participant. Messages include the symbols (words and phrases) you use to communicate your ideas, as well as nonverbal codes such as facial expressions, bodily movements, gestures, physical contact, and tone of voice. Messages may be relatively brief and easy to understand or long and complex. Some experts believe that real communication stems only from messages that are intentional, those that have a purpose. However, we believe that some messages can be unintentional. For example, you may not intend to show your emotions during a meeting, but your facial expressions and tone of voice might tip off others that you are angry or anxious. These unintended messages add potentially important information to the communication interaction.

CHANNELS

The **channel** is the means by which a message moves from the source to the receiver of the message. Think about how you communicate with your family. In some situations you are face-to-face and use your voice to send messages through sound waves. In other situations you might talk over the phone, send a text message with emojis, or post a short video. Each of these examples illustrates how the same communicators—you and your family—can use multiple channels to send messages. Of course, the channel used can potentially influence the meaning assigned to the messages. For instance, what are the implications of breaking up with a partner via text or Instagram as opposed to a face-to-face conversation?

CODES

A computer carries messages via binary code on cable, wire, or fiber; similarly, you converse with others by using a code called "language." A **code** is a systematic arrangement of symbols used to create meanings in the mind of another person or persons. Words, phrases, and sentences become "symbols" used to evoke images, thoughts, and ideas in the minds of others. If someone yells "Stop" as you approach the street, the word *stop* has become a symbol that you are likely to interpret as a warning of danger.

engaging diversity

Gender Differences in Social Media Use

Because social media is so common in our lives, we tend to assume that everyone generally uses social media in the same way. However, recent research suggests that for online discussions, some differences in behaviors may exist between men and women. In topically focused online discussion groups, men tend to make posts that provide information, while women tend to focus more on relationship building. Women in online discussion groups tend to post about positive emotions more frequently than do men, though both men and women tend to shy away from negative emotions when posting. These behavioral differences between men and women illustrate how cultural differences can affect how we typically communicate. At the same time, these differences are only general tendencies of broad groups and should not be assumed to be true of any particular individual.

Source: Sun, B., Mao, H., & Yin, C. (2020). Male and female users' differences in online technology community based on text mining. *Frontiers in Psychology, 11.* doi: 10.3389/fpsyg.2020.00806.

message
The verbal and nonverbal form of the idea, thought, or feeling that one person (the source) wishes to communicate to another person or a group of people (the receivers).

channel
The means by which a message moves from the source to the receiver of a message.

code
A systematic arrangement of symbols used to create meanings in the mind of another person or persons.

communicating
with agility

Changing Channels

For nearly all of us, the COVID-19 pandemic caused shifts from in-person to fully remote interactions for school, work, and even interpersonal relationships. As we experienced those disruptions, we were forced to be agile in how we adapted our messages based on which channel of communication was available. For example, Nancy Duarte, a prominent speaker and design-thinker known for her minimalist approach to slides during in-person presentations, adapted her presentations during the pandemic by creating visually rich presentations and using dramatic vocal variety to keep remote listeners engaged with her message. We must not only be agile in adapting our message to specific listeners and situations, but we must also be agile in adapting our message to the primary communication channel that we are using.

Source: Duarte, N. (23 August, 2022). Tips for remote presenters. *Duarte*. www.duarte .com/presentation-skills-resources/tips-for-remote-presenters/

Verbal and nonverbal codes are the two types of code used in communication. **Verbal codes** consist of symbols and their grammatical arrangement. All languages are codes. **Nonverbal codes** consist of all symbols that are not words, including bodily movements, the use of space and time, clothing and other adornments, and sounds other than words. *Nonverbal* codes should not be confused with *nonoral* codes. All nonoral codes, such as bodily movement, are nonverbal codes. However, nonverbal codes also include oral codes, such as pitch, duration, rate of speech, and sounds such as "eh" and "ah."

ENCODING AND DECODING

If communication involves the use of codes, the process of communicating can be viewed as one of encoding and decoding. **Encoding** is the process of translating an idea or a thought into a code. **Decoding** is the process of assigning meaning to that idea or thought. Think about the process you go through when ordering pizza with friends. In response to the typical question of "What do you want?" how often is "I like anything" provided in response? When ordering the pizza, do you take free rein to order a large pie with anchovies, extra onions, and jalapeños? Probably not. You probably know not to interpret "I like anything" too literally. During communication, our use of codes to encode and decode often requires additional explanation to arrive at solid shared meaning. That's why feedback is so important to the communication process.

FEEDBACK

Feedback is the receiver's verbal and nonverbal response to the source's message. Ideally, you respond to another person's messages by providing feedback so that the source knows the message was received as intended. Feedback is part of any communication situation. Even no response, or silence, is feedback, as are restless behavior and quizzical looks from students in a classroom. It is through feedback that communicators negotiate meaning in the process of communicating. Silence could signal disagreement. A raised eyebrow could imply a lack of understanding. A simple word—"Fantastic!"—could show excitement in response to another person's idea or the complete opposite, if the tone suggests sarcasm. Because we are simultaneously senders and receivers of messages, we are constantly providing feedback to others in an attempt to negotiate meaning.

NOISE

In the communication process, **noise** is any interference in the encoding and decoding processes that reduces the clarity of a message. Noise can be physical, such as loud sounds; distracting sights, such as a piece of food between someone's front teeth; or an unusual behavior, such as someone standing too close for comfort. Noise can be mental, psychological, or semantic, such as daydreams about a loved one, worry about the bills, pain from a

verbal codes
Symbols and their grammatical arrangement, such as languages.

nonverbal codes
Messages consisting of symbols that are not words, including non-word vocalizations.

encoding
The process of translating an idea or thought into a code.

decoding
The process of assigning meaning to the idea or thought in a code.

feedback
The receiver's verbal and nonverbal response to the source's message.

noise
Any interference in the encoding and decoding processes that reduces message clarity.

---

tooth, or uncertainty about what the other person's words mean. Noise can be anything that interferes with receiving, interpreting, or providing feedback about a message.

SITUATION

The final component of communication is the **situation**, the location where communication takes place. Later in the chapter you will learn about six different contexts for communication, ranging from interpersonal to mass communication. Each context provides a different type of situation in which you communicate. For instance, a conversation between two people tends to be less formal, whereas a public speech before hundreds might be more formal. The relationship between people could also affect the situation. You communicate with your boss differently than with your coworkers. Even the channel can influence the situation—face-to-face communication might be more personal than some forms of social media. The situation combines other elements of the communication process to influence the overall tone of the interaction.

We should recognize that the communication situation is influenced by broader events. Think about how the COVID-19 pandemic changed the communication channel from face-to-face to remote and how the use of masks changed how we could interpret facial expressions. Earlier in this chapter you learned how society is becoming more polarized. Think about how such polarization influences communication situations. Are there certain topics that you would intentionally avoid when speaking to a large audience? Have you observed how certain hats, ribbons, flags, and other symbols seem to carry more polarized meanings than ever before? Have you recently been involved in a face-to-face conversation and wondered how that interaction might find its way onto a social media post? Each of these examples illustrates how broader societal forces impact specific communication situations.

building behaviors

Current Behaviors 360 Feedback

Write down at least three communication skills you think you regularly do well in your daily conversations with others. Next, list three communication skills you need to improve on over the course of this term. Now ask at least three people from different social groups in your life to answer the same questions about you. For example, you could pick a friend, a sibling, and a parental figure. How do their answers compare to yours? Based on your personal assessment and those of the people who answered your question, what are the top two communication behaviors you want to focus on improving? Let the people in your life know you are working on these skills; their support will encourage you to practice and improve.

situation
The location where communication takes place.

Communication Principles

A definition of communication may be insufficient to clarify the nature of communication. To explain communication in more detail, we consider some principles here that guide our understanding of communication.

COMMUNICATION BEGINS WITH THE SELF

How you see yourself can make a great difference in how you communicate. In any particular conversation, interaction, speech, or group meeting, you communicate with others based on your sense of yourself. If you perceive yourself to be an extrovert, you will likely be outgoing in such encounters; if you perceive yourself as an introvert, you might be more quiet and withdrawn. Therefore, how you perceive yourself will influence how you communicate with others. You should remember, however, that no single instance of communication is truly isolated. Why would you perceive yourself to be extroverted or introverted? Most likely, that self-perception grew because of your interactions with others over time. Although each communication interaction begins with the self, it is also connected to your previous communication experiences in important ways.

As human beings, our sense of self is always changing, and consequently, so are our approaches to communication. Our understanding of the world is limited by our experiences. John Shotter, a former communication professor at the University of New Hampshire, suggests that we cannot understand communication through external, abstract, and systematic processes. Instead, he describes communication as a "ceaseless flow of speech-entwined, dialogically structured, social activity."[37] In other words, communication is participatory; we are actively involved and relationally responsive in our use of communication.

Suppose you have a roommate or co-worker who is from another country. Over the course of your interactions, you may feel challenged by the belief systems, values, perspectives, and behaviors of your roommate. More specifically, if you impose rules of communication and other behaviors based only on your previous experiences, there may be very little chance of a successful relationship. However, if you are able to move beyond your previous views and allow your perceptions of communication and other behaviors to become products of new interactions, you might learn to communicate in interesting and effective ways. That might sound abstract, but have you ever had a close friendship where you used nicknames and had sort of a secret code to talk? In that relationship you allowed new norms to develop. Could you use that same approach with others to avoid misperceptions, polarizing statements, and even conflict?

You are the center of your own communication behaviors. As we will explain, you have many choices to guide your communication with others. You construct your own messages, you choose channels to use, and you develop your own unique style. Consequently, understanding yourself as a communicator and developing skills to adapt and improve your communication behaviors is essential to your growth in personal, professional, and social interactions.

COMMUNICATION INVOLVES OTHERS

Although communication begins with the self, communication also involves others. Famous philosopher George Herbert Mead pointed out that our sense of self is developed in and through communication, starting early in our childhood.[38] Through verbal and nonverbal symbols, a child learns to accept roles in response to the expectations of others. Take the example of Simone Biles, who has amassed 32 Olympic and World Championship medals in gymnastics. Biles, who was recently awarded the Presidential Medal of Freedom,[39] often points to the messages and encouragement of her adoptive parents as sources of success and determination. In a 2018 commentary written by Biles for CNN, she stated, "When I was far too young to know it, others around me saw that I had a gift for gymnastics. Without their encouragement and support, I would have never been a gymnast."[40] Simone's example shows how positive, negative, and neutral messages from others all play a role in how you determine who you are, even at a young age. Her example also illustrates how those messages, and your sense of self, can change over time.

You may be aware of how important your peers are to your academic career. Students report that peers provide support for a variety of reasons: they allow you to vent about teachers and classes; provide you with information about assignments, classes, and other academic matters; offer positive statements that build your self-esteem and sense of worth; and make statements that motivate you to attend class, to do your homework, and to generally succeed at your work. Other people are essential to how you feel about yourself during college and throughout your life.

dialogue
The act of taking part in a conversation, discussion, or negotiation.

Communication itself is probably best understood as a dialogic process. A **dialogue** is simply the act of taking part in a conversation, discussion, or negotiation. As we take part in dialogue, we are constantly creating meaning, interpreting meaning, assessing whether common meaning is achieved, and adapting communication behaviors as necessary. Essentially, dialogue is another way of thinking about the set of behaviors that make

• Understanding can emerge from dialogue.

Kristy-Anne Glubish/Design Pics

communication a process. Our understanding of communication occurs not in a vacuum but in light of our interactions with other people.[41]

In a more obvious way, communication involves others in the sense that a competent communicator considers the other person's needs and expectations when selecting messages to share. The competent communicator understands that a large number of messages can be shared at any time, but sensitivity and responsiveness to the other communicators are essential. In short, communication begins with the self, as defined largely by others, and involves others, as defined largely by the self.

COMMUNICATION HAS BOTH A CONTENT AND A RELATIONAL DIMENSION

All messages have both a content and a relational dimension. When you form a message to another person, that message has content. For instance, in a workplace situation you might say to a coworker, "One of us needs to take returned items back to the shelves. They are piling up." The content of that message is clear: something needs to be done. A relational dimension also exists in that communication. Notice how the phrase "one of us" does not establish that one person is in charge of the other. Think about how that message might be different if said by a manager. When we communicate, we convey both the content of a message and also cues about the relationship among the communicators. Although we often think about the content of a message as being most important, there are situations in which the relational dimension might carry prominence. Think about classroom situations in which you had to work in a group with peers you had not met before. Much of the initial communication involves group members establishing an effective working relationship to work toward the assigned objectives.

COMMUNICATION INVOLVES CHOICES

Communication is far more than simple information transmission. Communication involves choices about the multiple aspects of the message: the verbal, nonverbal, and behavioral aspects; the choices surrounding the transmission channels used; the characteristics of the speaker; the relationship between the speaker and the audience; the characteristics of the audience; and the situation in which the communication occurs. A change in any one of these variables affects the entire communication process.

The fact that communication involves choices has powerful implications, and it also involves risk. Consider your use of texting and social media. Research reported by the Pew Research Center reveals that more than 60% of political tweets by adults in the United States are actually retweets of posts made by others.[42] What are the implications of retweeting political posts? Are you fully endorsing the message of the original post? Are you responsible for the accuracy of such tweets when you retweet them? Does such behavior result in robust public dialogue over important topics? Many of us engage in these behaviors across social media platforms, but we rarely think about the implications of those behaviors. However, we are making an explicit choice to communicate with others through such retweets, and those choices involve the same risks as statements we make in public speeches, meetings, or conversations with others. With social media, those risks may be even greater because there is a nearly permanent digital record of our choices.

COMMUNICATION QUANTITY DOES NOT INCREASE COMMUNICATION QUALITY

You might believe that a course on communication would stake claims on the importance of increased communication. You may have heard leaders or coaches say, "What we need is more communication." However, greater amounts of communication do not necessarily lead to more harmony or more accurate and shared meanings. Sometimes people disagree, and more communication can actually increase conflict. Other times people have very poor listening or empathy skills and misunderstand vast quantities of information. Have you ever been in a class where the teacher used far too many PowerPoint slides? High quantities of poorly crafted communication can be much less effective than carefully planned concise statements.

COMMUNICATION IS PERVASIVE

Although communication involves choices and more communication is not necessarily better communication, communication is pervasive and occurs almost every minute of your life. In other words, communication spreads to all aspects of your life. If you are not communicating with yourself (thinking, planning, reacting to the world around you), you are observing others and drawing conclusions about their behavior. If people yawn while you are talking, you may believe that they are bored with your message. If friends fail to like your social media post, you may assume they are mad. We are continually gleaning meanings from others' behaviors, and we are constantly behaving in ways that have communicative value for those with whom we communicate.

COMMUNICATION CANNOT BE REVERSED

Once you say something, it cannot be unsaid. Because communication cannot be reversed, you should use sound judgment and think before you speak or write. Part of the polarization we witness in political discourse occurs because some candidates and elected officials attempt to land rhetorical punches before thinking about potential ramifications. Such lack of planning can damage credibility, diminish the effectiveness of valid arguments, and create turmoil that can even lead to violence.[43]

Possible negative effects of poorly crafted communication are not limited to political figures, however. Social media has created platforms through which previously private, if not intimate, details are regularly made public. A 2018 national survey by CareerBuilder.com found that 70% of employers research potential job candidates on social media sites, 48% monitor the social media of current employees, and 34% of employers have fired or reprimanded employees because of social media posts.[44] Negative effects of social media are also observed in romantic relationships. Another recent study reported that romantic partners often feel retroactive jealousy when reviewing each other's social media sites.[45] You might conclude that it is best to just erase yourself from social media. However, potential employers also report that they are less likely to interview a person if they cannot find an online presence.[46] The lessons here are clear. Whether you are speaking in public, posting on social media, or having a casual conversation with a friend, your communication with others remains part of how others perceive you.

Communication Contexts

Communication occurs in a **context**, a recurring pattern of behaviors that typically take place in similar settings. Communication occurs between two friends, among five business acquaintances in a small-group setting, and between a lecturer and an audience in a packed auditorium. Each of these is a different context because the pattern of behavior is different, as is the setting. At many colleges and universities, the communication courses are arranged by context: interpersonal communication, interviewing, small-group communication, public speaking, and mass communication. Across these contexts of communication there are key similarities and differences. Although the process of making shared meaning might be consistent from one context to another, they differ greatly in terms of the number of people involved, the formality expected by communicators, and the opportunity for feedback.

context
A recurring pattern of behaviors and actions that typically take place in similar settings.

intrapersonal communication
The process of using messages to generate meaning within the self.

INTRAPERSONAL COMMUNICATION

Intrapersonal communication is the process of using messages to generate meaning within the self. Intrapersonal communication is the communication that occurs within your own mind. Think about a situation at work in which you have an ongoing conflict with coworkers. When talking with them in meetings, you likely engage in dialogue with yourself trying to anticipate how they will react to your statements or actions. So, if you say to them, "Great job on that presentation," you might ask yourself if they will interpret your comment as patronizing, even if you were trying to be totally authentic. That internal questioning illustrates how we use intrapersonal communication to try to create and infer meaning when we communicate with others.

Intrapersonal communication occurs, as this example suggests, when you evaluate or examine the interaction that occurs between yourself and others, but it is not limited to such situations. This form of communication occurs before and during other forms of communication as well. For instance, you might argue with yourself during a conversation in which someone asks you to do something you do not really want to do: before you accept or decline, you mull over the alternatives in your mind.

• Intrapersonal communication occurs in our reflections.

John Lund/Drew Kelly/Sam Diephuis/Blend Images LLC

communicating creatively

Can Rituals Drive Creativity?

Blogger Priyanka Gupta challenges the notion that creativity happens through flashes of unexpected insight. Gupta's blog, titled Creative Routine and Rituals—How to Dream and Create Consistently, explains how rituals allow people to free their mind from distractions and be receptive to creative ideas. Rituals allow artists of all types to flow into a creative process that helps them optimize work habits, think clearly and freely, and learn how to bring ideas into outcomes. An artist may begin by arranging brushes on a work-surface or a musician may warm up by playing the same scales before practicing. Because communication involves creativity, think about the routines you use to be ready for certain communication interactions. Do you carefully consider your clothing for particular situations? Do you have a routine for practicing presentations? Do you rehearse what you want to say before talking about something important with a family member or friend? How can you use this understanding of rituals and creativity to improve how you approach a variety of communication situations?

Source: Gupta, P. (2022). Creative routine and rituals: How to dream and create consistently. *On My Canvas.* www.onmycanvas.com/creative-routine-rituals/

Intrapersonal communication also includes such activities as solving problems internally, resolving internal conflict, planning for the future, and evaluating yourself and your relationships with others. Intrapersonal communication—the basis for all other communication—involves only the self.

Each one of us is continually engaged in intrapersonal communication. Although you might become more easily absorbed in talking to yourself when you are alone (while walking to class, driving to work, or taking a shower, for instance), you are likely to be involved in this form of communication in crowded circumstances as well (such as during a lecture, at a party, or with friends). Think about the last time you looked at yourself in a mirror. What were your thoughts? Although intrapersonal communication is almost continuous, people seldom focus on this form of communication.

Indeed, not all communication experts believe that intrapersonal communication should be examined within communication studies. The naysayers argue that communication requires two or more receivers of a message, and since there are no receivers in intrapersonal communication, no communication actually occurs. They reason that intrapersonal communication should be studied in a discipline such as psychology or neurology—fields in which experts study the mind or the brain. Nonetheless, intrapersonal communication is recognized by most scholars within the discipline as one context of communication for you to know and understand.

INTERPERSONAL COMMUNICATION

interpersonal communication
The process of using messages to generate meaning between at least two people in a situation that allows mutual opportunities for both speaking and listening.

dyadic communication
Two-person communication.

When you move from intrapersonal to interpersonal communication, you move from communication that occurs within your own mind to communication that involves one or more other people. **Interpersonal communication** is the process of using messages to generate meaning between at least two people in a situation that allows mutual opportunities for both speaking and listening. Like intrapersonal communication, interpersonal communication occurs for a variety of reasons: to solve problems, to resolve conflicts, to share information, to improve perceptions of oneself, or to fulfill social needs, such as the need to belong or to be loved. Through our interpersonal communication, we are able to establish relationships with others that include friendships and romantic relationships.

Dyadic and small-group communication are two subsets of interpersonal communication. **Dyadic communication** is simply two-person communication, such as interviews with an employer or a teacher; talks with a parent, spouse, or child; and interactions among strangers, acquaintances, or friends. Although dyadic interpersonal communication is typically face-to-face, we increasingly rely on various forms of social media and other communication technologies to create and maintain highly fulfilling interpersonal relationships. **Small-group communication** is the interaction among three to nine people working together to achieve an interdependent goal. Small-group communication occurs in families, work groups, support groups, religious groups, and study groups. Communication experts agree that two people are a dyad and that more than two people are a small group if they have a common purpose, goal, or mission. Disagreement exists regarding the maximum number of participants in a small group, though some experts suggest that the upper limit for true group communication is 10 people. Technology also poses questions for communication scholars to debate: for instance, does a small group have to meet face-to-face? That teleconferences can involve small-group communication is uncontroversial, but what about discussions in chat rooms on the Internet? See Chapter 8 for more on this topic.

small-group communication
Interaction among three to nine people working together to achieve an interdependent goal.

PUBLIC SPEAKING

Public speaking is the process of using messages to generate meanings in a situation in which a single speaker transmits a message to a number of receivers, who give nonverbal and sometimes question-and-answer feedback. In public speaking, the speaker adapts the message to the audience in an attempt to achieve maximum understanding. Sometimes virtually everyone in the audience understands the speaker's message; other times many people fail to understand.

public speaking
The process of using messages to generate meanings in a situation in which a single speaker transmits a message to a number of receivers.

Public speaking is recognized by its formality, structure, and planning. You probably are frequently a receiver of public speaking in classes, at convocations, and at religious services. Occasionally, you also may be a source (for example, when you present in class, explain a new procedure in front of coworkers, or make an argument in favor of reducing the cost of higher education for students). Public speaking most often informs or persuades, but it can also entertain, introduce, announce, welcome, or pay tribute.

MASS COMMUNICATION

Mass communication is the process of using messages to generate meanings in a mediated system, between a source and a large number of unseen receivers. Mass communication always has a transmission system (mediator) between the sender and the receiver. You are engaging in forms of mass communication when you post a video on YouTube, write for a campus newspaper, or talk about a song on a podcast. Mass communication is often taught in a college or university department of mass communication, radio and television, or journalism.

mass communication
The process of using messages to generate meanings in a mediated system, between a source and a large number of unseen receivers.

People who study mass communication may be interested in the processes by which communication is transmitted, and therefore they study the diffusion of information. Alternatively, they may be interested in the effects of media on people and study persuasion or how public opinion is created and altered. Mass communication has become of increasing interest today because of the expanded opportunities for communication through new technologies. Today many students are interested in **media convergence**, or the way that technology is unifying what were formerly separate channels for communication. Now, when you want to listen to news, watch movies, or enjoy music, you do not use separate mediums such as newspapers, television, and radio. Your smartphone and similar devices have converged those traditional forms of media into one easily accessible portal.

media convergence
The unification of separate channels of communication through new communication technology.

ONLINE COMMUNICATION

The **online communication** context, or Internet, typically allows social media sites, gaming sites, and similar technologies to help people stay connected with close friends, acquaintances, and others with whom they share similar interests. If you are using Snapchat, Instagram, or almost any other interactive online resource, you are likely engaging

online communication
Use of the Internet, particularly social media and other networking resources, to carry out communication with others.

sizing things up

Communication Skills in Context

We communicate in a variety of contexts. To improve your skill as a communicator, you should assess your own communication skills in each of the general communication contexts so that you can identify your strengths and areas for growth. Read each of the following questions carefully, and respond using the following scale:

1 = Strongly disagree
2 = Disagree
3 = Neither agree nor disagree
4 = Agree
5 = Strongly agree

1. I can use communication to solve conflicts with friends.
2. I am able to express my ideas clearly when working in a group.
3. I am comfortable when giving public speeches.
4. I can use the Internet to locate highly reputable information.
5. Other people tell me that I am a good speaker.
6. My friends tell me that I am a good listener.
7. Others listen to my opinions in group meetings.
8. I am skilled at communicating with others online.
9. I am good at delivering speeches.
10. I can effectively lead groups to discuss problems.
11. I make friends easily.
12. I am skilled at using computers to communicate with others (for example, using Skype, instant messaging, chat rooms, and other communication tools).

Note: This list has no "right" or "wrong" answers. It simply provides an overview of your communication skills at the beginning of the course. You might want to complete the survey again at the end of the course to determine whether your scores have changed. A guide for interpreting your responses appears at the end of the chapter.

technological convergence
The consolidation of voice, data, video, audio, and other channels of communication through smartphones and other devices.

synchronous communication
The instantaneous sending and receiving of messages, as occurs in face-to-face or some text-message interactions.

in communication through that site. Many video games allow you to interact with fellow players. Since the early 2000s, social media sites have created an unprecedented convergence of technology related to communication. **Technological convergence** has occurred as voice, data, video, audio, and other channels of communication have become consolidated into online communication tools. Whereas the telephones of our grandparents' generation provided one option for communication, the smartphones of today contain potentially limitless options for how we can send and receive messages with other people.

As a context for communication, the Internet is unique because of its versatility. First, online communication is mobile. Provided that you have a smartphone, a tablet, or even a smart watch, you can use social media virtually anywhere. Another characteristic of the Internet is that it can facilitate all types of communication ranging from dyadic interactions to mass-mediated messages. A simple tweet about your evening, intended perhaps for close friends, has the potential to go viral and reach thousands. As of 2022, the current record for likes on a tweet is from Chadwick Boseman's account, with more than 7.1 million likes and more than 1.9 million retweets.[47] Chadwick Boseman was an American actor known for his highly acclaimed portrayal of Thurgood Marshall in *Marshall* and the superhero Black Panther in the Marvel Comics franchise. Sadly, the record-breaking tweet from Boseman's account was the official announcement of his death from cancer.

Finally, online communication can be both synchronous and asynchronous. **Synchronous communication** occurs when there is instantaneous sending and receiving of messages, such as in face-to-face or Snapchat interactions. **Asynchronous communication** occurs when there is a brief or substantial delay in interaction. Suppose that you listen to a favorite podcast and later tweet your thoughts to the host about something that you heard. That example illustrates a form of asynchronous communication. Because online communication can be synchronous or asynchronous, communicators may encounter some situations in which the prestructuring of messages is required, such as carefully thinking out a post for a discussion board, and other situations in which prestructuring is virtually impossible, such as engaging in a two-way video chat.

In one sense, communication through social media sites simply replicates what we do in other communication contexts. Some scholars argue that the differences between face-to-face interaction and online interaction have become increasingly irrelevant as both technology and our comfort in using digital tools have advanced. Certainly our experiences with the COVID-19 pandemic suggest that we can conduct business, take

Table 1.1 Differences Among Communication Contexts

Contexts	Number of People	Degree of Formality or Intimacy	Opportunities for Feedback	Need for Prestructuring Messages	Degree of Stability of the Roles of Speaker and Listener
INTRAPERSONAL COMMUNICATION	1	Most intimate	Complete feedback	None	Highly unstable; the individual as both speaker and listener
INTERPERSONAL COMMUNICATION Dyadic Communication	2	Generally intimate; interview is formal	A great deal of feedback	Some	Unstable; speaker and listener alternate
Small-Group Communication	Usually 3 to 10; may be more	Intimate or formal	Less than in intrapersonal communication but more than in public speaking	Some	Unstable; speakers and listeners alternate
Public Speaking	Usually more than 10	Generally formal	Less than in small-group communication but more than in mass communication	A great deal	Highly stable; one speaker with many listeners
Mass Communication	Usually thousands	Generally formal	Usually more	Almost totally scripted	Highly stable; on-air speakers, invisible listeners
Online Communication	2 to millions	Intimate or formal	None to a great deal	None to totally scripted	Unstable to highly stable

classes, and maintain relationships using robust online technologies. However, there is also worry that reliance on virtual meetings has actually increased social isolation among families, friends, and communities.[48] Regardless of which view is correct, online communication has become one of the most important and pervasive communication tools in our lives. In fact, Cambridge Dictionary selected as the "people's word of 2018" the term *nomophobia*, which is "the fear or worry at the idea of being without your mobile phone or unable to use it."[49]

Table 1.1 provides a visual summary of the various contexts discussed here. As you review the table, note how things such as the number of people, the degree of formality, and the need for structure vary across the contexts of communication.

Goals of Communication Study

You learned the importance of studying communication at the beginning of this chapter. As we end our introduction to the topic of communication, we want to encourage you to set goals for yourself as a communicator. We believe that great communicators are able

asynchronous communication Interactions in which there is a small or even substantial delay, as occurs with email or discussion board posts.

to positively impact their own lives, as well as those of the people around them, thus contributing to the greater good of society. It is our hope that through this class you will find ways to improve your skills and knowledge as a communicator. That improvement must start by setting goals. Although you should carefully consider your personal goals and objectives as a communicator, three broad goals to get you started are to become a competent communicator, to become an ethical communicator, and to become knowledgeable about communication theory and research.

PRACTICING COMMUNICATION COMPETENCE

communication competence
The ability to effectively exchange meaning through a common system of symbols or behavior.

Communication competence is simply the ability to effectively exchange meaning through a common system of symbols or behavior. As you will learn in this course, communication competence is not necessarily easy to achieve. Communication competence can be difficult because your goals and others' goals may be discrepant. Similarly, you and those with whom you communicate may have a different understanding of your relationship. Cultural differences may cause you to view the world and other people differently. Indeed, different perspectives about communication may themselves create problems in your interactions with others. As you read this text, you will learn about the multiple variables involved in communication, and you will become more competent in your communication.

Although communication competence is the goal, the complexity of communication should encourage you to be a student of communication over your lifetime. In this course you will begin to learn the terminology and the multiple variables comprised in communication. Though you will not emerge from the course as an expert, you should see significant changes in your communication abilities. The professional public speaker or comedian, the glib TV reporter, and the highly satisfied spouse in a long-term marriage make communication look easy. However, as you will learn, their skills are complex and interwoven with multiple layers of understanding.

COMMUNICATING ETHICALLY

ethics
A set of moral principles or values.

The second goal in studying communication lies in its ethical dimension. **Ethics** may be defined as a set of moral principles or values. Ethical standards may vary from one discipline to another, just as they differ from one culture to another. The standards within the communication discipline are derived from Western conceptions of communication, democratic decision making, and the ideologies of people in the communication discipline.

Within the communication discipline, the National Communication Association (NCA) has created a set of ethics guidelines.[50] You may wish to search online and read these guidelines for communication behavior and consider the extent to which they are true in your life. As you listen to politicians, activists, and people with opposing views, consider how these ethical principles are violated.

Communication professionals believe that people should be open, honest, and reasonable. They affirm the First Amendment to the Constitution of the United States of America, which guarantees freedom of speech. They agree that respect for other people and their messages is essential. They acknowledge the need for access to information and to people. Finally, they view responsible behavior as important.

• The First Amendment is a cornerstone of our Democracy and the field of communication.
zimmytws/123RF

UNDERSTANDING COMMUNICATION THEORY AND RESEARCH

Theory and *research* are two commonly used words that cause eye rolls and strike fear among thousands of college students across the world. We want to make a case for you to think differently. Theories are nothing more than stories. Good theories provide clear narratives of how things work. In communication, we develop theories—some simple and some not so simple—to understand the causes, processes, and effects of communication. Whereas your common sense works in many situations, it is not infallible. How often have you made an error in judgment? What happens when you encounter a new type of situation, such as participating in a group-based job interview or communicating with someone from a very different culture? Does common sense always work in these situations?

In this book we use research findings and theories to help you better understand communication. These theories are based on social-scientific research conducted in real situations. Using social-scientific methods, researchers systematically observe people communicating, summarize patterns in what they observed, and then draw conclusions about how those patterns might be generalized into a theory about communication.

Your goal should be to understand these theories and research findings so that you can apply them to your own life. By making those connections, you will have a greater knowledge base from which to plan your communication, and you will become a more effective communicator. Common sense works in situations for which you are very familiar, but knowledge of theories provides you with a playbook for the type of new and unique situations that will increasingly confront you as you add new chapters to your life.

In becoming a competent and an ethical communicator and becoming more knowledgeable about communication research and theory, you will be ready to grow as a communicator. However, you should also set more specific and personal goals. As you read each chapter, your intention should be to use the information to improve at least one aspect of your communication. Communication is at the core of your current and future successes—challenge yourself to get better at it.

Communication Skills and Your Career

People take communication courses for a variety of reasons. At many colleges and universities, communication is taught as part of a general education program. Of course, many students enter their college or university with the intention of majoring in some aspect of communication; other students find their way to communication after they start college. Regardless of why you are in the class, understanding the variety of career pathways in communication is important.

The communication field covers many subfields, including public relations, advertising, business communication, journalism, corporate training, health communication, and marketing. Some students use their communication degree to keep many potential career tracks open to them, whereas others combine their degree with highly specialized minors or certificates to pursue specific career paths. We have seen our former students who majored in communication go on to become chief information officers, the CEO of an international produce growing company, a public information officer at the Pentagon, a local news reporter, an event planner for an international nonprofit, and many other successful career pathways. Below are examples of contemporary jobs held by communication graduates:

Field	Job Examples
Human/Speech Communication	Salesperson
	Teacher
	Corporate Trainer
	Event Planner
	Campaign Manager
	College Recruiter
	Fundraiser
	Public Information Officer
	Attorney
	Human Resources Administrator
	Nonprofit Manager
	Government Lobbyist
Media and Entertainment	Audio Engineer
	Videographer/Photographer
	Multimedia Reporter
	Augmented Reality Designer
	Broadcast Engineer
	Publicist
	News Anchor
	Screenwriter
	Film Critic
	Talent Manager
	News Producer
	Filmmaker
Technical Specialties	Public Relations Strategist
	Web Designer
	Public Health Officer
	Data Analyst/Visualizer
	Digital Designer
	Social Media Analytics Researcher
	App Developer
	Advertising Project Manager
	Creative Director
	Network Administrator
	Forensic Media Analyst
	Animator

Although new graduates are likely to find jobs in a variety of entry-level positions, individuals with communication degrees frequently find that advancement comes quickly. Some communication graduates take advantage of graduate school, professional school, or other postgraduation opportunities to advance their careers. Regardless of the career field, effective communication skills are essential, and through this course you will learn communication theories and skills that will have practical effects on your personal life, on your involvement with your community, and in your career.

be ready... for what's next

Communication Growth as a Lifelong Process

Take a few moments to envision what you define as success. Perhaps it is a certain type of job or a significant relationship with another person that would make you feel successful. For many of us, success is defined along multiple dimensions, both personal and professional. Whatever your definition, communication is the most important skill that will help you achieve your goals. So, the question is, how do you develop the skills needed for success?

Although your communication class is a starting point for developing skills necessary for success, you must develop a commitment to lifelong learning. Below are several strategies for enacting that commitment:

1. *Challenge yourself.* Great communicators do not shy away from challenging communication situations. Find opportunities to communicate as a leader in student organizations, seek out situations in which you can give public speeches, and consider taking other communication classes so that you can gain additional knowledge. Challenging yourself to become a better communicator means that you will embrace many learning opportunities with increasing levels of difficulty.

2. *Be centered.* If you challenge yourself by communicating outside your comfort zone, you will likely make some mistakes. Speeches will not always go as well as you would like, and some people may not connect with you interpersonally. But don't give up. These outcomes are inevitable and part of the learning process. To benefit from these experiences, you must have a clear understanding of what you value. If your objective is to act with integrity, to challenge yourself, and to constantly work toward improving, you can react to these situations with grace and maturity.

3. *Be reflective.* To learn from your experiences, you must be willing to reflect with honesty on how you did, what went well, and what you would improve upon next time. Using a journal, keeping well-organized notes, and actively seeking feedback from others are all strategies that can help you grow as a communicator.

Your growth as a communicator started well before this class, and it will continue long after. Although you will learn many techniques, principles, and theories of effective communication over the course of this term, your true growth as a communicator will stem from an attitude of continual improvement. Your personal and professional future has many possible pathways, and communication will play a critical role in how you navigate those options.

Chapter Review & Study Guide

Summary

In this chapter you learned the following:

1. Communication is essential because
   - understanding communication can improve the way people view themselves and the way others view them.
   - people learn more about human relationships as they study communication and learn important life skills.
   - studying communication can help you become aware of how communication affects events in your community, state, nation, and world.
   - an understanding of communication can help people succeed professionally.
   - studying communication can help you learn to navigate an increasingly diverse world.
2. Communication is the process of using messages to generate shared meaning between people.

3. The components of communication are people, messages, channels, codes, encoding and decoding, feedback, noise, and situation.
4. The principles of communication include the ideas that
   - communication begins with the self.
   - communication involves others.
   - communication has both a content and a relational dimension.
   - communication involves choices.
   - an increased quantity of communication does not necessarily increase the quality of communication.
   - communication is pervasive.
   - communication is irreversible.

5. Communication occurs in intrapersonal, interpersonal, public, mass, and online communication contexts. The number of people involved, the degree of formality or intimacy, the opportunities for feedback, the need for prestructuring messages, and the degree of stability of the roles of speaker and listener all vary with the communication context.

6. The goals of your study of communication should be to

   • practice communication competence.

   • communicate ethically.

   • understand communication theory and research.

7. Studying communication can help you find a career in various sub-fields, such as human communication, media and entertainment, and technical communication specialties. Good communication skills help new job recipients advance quickly in their careers.

Key Terms

Asynchronous communication
Channel
Code
Communication
Communication competence
Context
Decoding
Dialogue
Dyadic communication
Encoding
Ethics

Feedback
Interpersonal communication
Intrapersonal communication
Mass communication
Meaning
Media convergence
Message
Noise
Nonverbal codes
Online communication

Polarization
Process
Public speaking
Receiver
Situation
Small-group communication
Source
Synchronous communication
Technological convergence
Verbal codes

Study Questions

1. Communication is considered a process of using messages to generate meaning because it is

   a. an activity or exchange instead of an unchanging product.
   b. a tangible object.
   c. something with a beginning, a middle, and an end.
   d. static.

2. Understanding another person's messages does not occur unless

   a. the speaker uses nonverbal messages.
   b. common meanings for words, phrases, and nonverbal codes are elicited.
   c. the listener asks questions.
   d. both parties use verbal and nonverbal symbols.

3. The process of translating an idea or a thought into a code is known as

   a. communicating.
   b. decoding.
   c. encoding.
   d. deciphering.

4. Which communication principle considers variables such as verbal, nonverbal, and behavioral aspects; the channel used; and audience characteristics?

   a. Communication has a content and a relational dimension.
   b. Communication begins with the self.
   c. Communication involves others.
   d. Communication involves choices.

5. In online communication, _____ communication has delayed responses from the other person.

   a. antisocial
   b. asynchronous
   c. altruistic
   d. synchronous

6. Which of the following statements is accurate about online communication?

   a. The maximum number of people in online communication is five to nine.
   b. Online communication is unstable in the roles of participants.
   c. Online communication can reach as few as two people.
   d. Online communication does not allow for feedback.

7. Which of the following is defined as the ability to effectively exchange meaning through a common system of symbols, signs, or behavior?

   a. dyadic communication
   b. communication competence
   c. message
   d. feedback

8. Ethical standards within the communication discipline have been created by the
   a. National Communication Association.
   b. American Communication Association.
   c. Communication Administration.
   d. Public Speaking Administration.

9. Which of the following statements was identified as an advantage of comprehensively studying communication?
   a. It allows you to find a job very easily.
   b. It enhances your chances of selling questionable products to unknowing customers.
   c. It allows you to multiply the number of friends you have on social networks.
   d. It improves the way you see yourself.

10. When you respond to a speaker with a verbal or nonverbal cue, you are
   a. giving feedback.
   b. not communicating.
   c. providing noise.
   d. using a metaphor.

Answers:
1. (a); 2. (b); 3. (c); 4. (d); 5. (b); 6. (c); 7. (b); 8. (a); 9. (d); 10. (a)

Critical Thinking

1. In this chapter you learned that broader events at the local, regional, national, or even international level can affect the process of communication in specific situations. Identify a broader event that has affected your own communication with friends, family, or colleagues. How did that event impact how you framed messages to others and/or decoded what other said to you?

2. Think of your online communication. How do you use online communication in your daily life (that is, for school, personal use, or work)? Does digital and social media serve as a ritual for how you conduct your daily communication activities? Analyze what role digital and social media play in your personal communication choices.

Sizing Things Up Scoring and Interpretation

Communication Skills in Context

This chapter introduces the concept of communication competence. The survey you completed measures your competence. Each question in the survey asks you to indicate how effectively you can communicate within a particular context of communication (for example, friendships or online communication); some questions also target specific purposes for communicating (for example, resolving conflict). You can use this scale either as a global Communication Competence Scale, in which case you should average your answers for all questions to achieve an overall score, or as a way of analyzing particular communication contexts or processes. This latter approach would involve analyzing your responses to each statement. If your overall average or response to any individual question is below 3, you may be lower in self-perceived communication competence. A score near 3 is average, and a score above 3 suggests that you perceive yourself higher in communication competence.

References

1. Petraglia, J. (2009). The importance of being authentic: Persuasion, narration, and dialogue in health communication and education. *Health Communication, 24,* 176–185. Robertson-Malt, S., & Chapman, Y. (2008). Finding the right direction: The importance of open communication in a governance model of nurse management. *Contemporary Nurse: A Journal for the Australian Nursing Profession, 29,* 60–66.

2. National Center for Educational Statistics. (2021). Table 322.10: Bachelor degrees conferred by postsecondary institutions by field of study. *Digest of educational statistics* [online]. https://nces.ed.gov/programs/digest/d21/tables/dt21_322.10.asp

3. Graduate Management Admission Council. (2022). Corporate Recruiters Survey: 2022 Summary Report. https://www.gmac.com/-/media/files/gmac/research/employment-outlook/2022_gmac_corporate_recruiters_survey_summary_report_final.pdf

4. Schmitt, J. (2014, October 22). Communication studies rise to relevance. Huffington Post. https://www.huffpost.com/entry/communication-studies-ris_b_6025038

5. Griffin, E., & Ledbetter, A. (2023). *A first look at communication theory* (11th ed.). McGraw-Hill.

6. Anderson, L. B., Gardner, E. E., & Wolvin, A. D. (2019). Constructing narratives of success in the introductory communication course: Using written self-assessments to understand students' perceptions of learning. *Communication Teacher, 33*(2), 164–178. https://doi.org/10.1080/17404622.2017.1400674

7. Egeci, I., & Gencoz, T. (2006). Factors associated with relationship satisfaction: Importance of communication skills. *Contemporary Family Therapy: An International Journal, 28,* 383–391.

8. Ireland, J. L., Sanders, M. R., & Markie-Dodds, C. (2003). The impact of parent training on marital functioning: A comparison of two group versions of the triple-p positive parenting program for parents of children with early-onset conduct problems. *Behavioural and Cognitive Psychotherapy, 31,* 127–142.

9. Matthias, M. S., Parpart, A. L., Nyland, K. A., Huffman, M. A., Stubbs, D. L., Sargent, C., & Bair, M. J. (2010). The patient-provider relationship in chronic pain care: Providers' perspectives. *Pain Medicine, 11,* 1688–1697.

10. Manne, S., Badr, H., Zaider, T., Nelson, C., & Kissane, D. (2010). Cancer-related communication, relationship intimacy, and psychological distress among couples coping with localized prostate cancer. *Journal of Cancer Survivorship, 4,* 74–85.

11. Hunt, S. K., Simonds, C. J., & Simonds, B. K. (2009). Uniquely qualified, distinctively competent: Delivering 21st century skills in the basic course. *Basic Communication Course Annual, 21,* 1–29.

12. Metallinos, N. (1992, September–October). *Cognitive factors in the study of visual image recognition standards.* Paper presented to the Annual Conference of the International Visual Literacy Association, Pittsburgh. (ERIC Document Reproduction Service No. ED 352936.)

13. McCombs, M. (2014). *Setting the agenda: Mass media and public opinion* (2nd Ed). John Wiley & Sons, p. 14.

14. Anderson, M., Rainie, L., & Smith, A. (2018, July 11). Public attitudes toward political engagement on social media. Pew Research Center. http://www.pewinternet.org/2018/07/11/public-attitudes-toward-political-engagement-on-social-media/

15. Cobb, J. (2016, March). The matter of black lives: A new kind of movement found its moment. What will its future be? *The New Yorker.* https://www.newyorker.com/magazine/2016/03/14/where-is-black-lives-matter-headed

16. Geher, G. (2018, August 14). The polarization of America: Each year we become more fractured and polarized. *Psychology Today.* https://www.psychologytoday.com/us/blog/darwins-subterranean-world/201808/the-polarization-america

17. Geher, G. (2018, August 14). The polarization of America: Each year we become more fractured and polarized. *Psychology Today.* https://www.psychologytoday.com/us/blog/darwins-subterranean-world/201808/the-polarization-america

18. Kushwaha, A. K., Kar, A. K., Roy, S. K., & Ilavarasan, P. V. (2022). Capricious opinions: A study of polarization of social media groups. *Government Information Quarterly, 39,* np. https://doi-org.proxy.library.ohio.edu/10.1016/j.giq.2022.101709

19. Mora, J. (2022). Improv for Democracy: How to bridge differences and develop the communication and leadership skills our world needs. *Communication Research Trends, 41,* 26–28.

20. Coffelt, T. A., & Smith, F. L. M. (2020). Exemplary and unacceptable workplace communication skills. *Business & Professional Communication Quarterly, 83,* 365–384. https://doi-org.proxy.library.ohio.edu/10.1177/2329490620946425

21. Osmani, M., Hindi, N., & Weerakkody, V. (2020). Incorporating information communication technology skills in accounting education. *International Journal of Information and Communication Technology Education, 16,* 100–110. https://doi-org.proxy.library.ohio.edu/10.4018/IJICTE.2020100107

22. Fasano, A. (2018, June 19). Why communication for engineers is so important. The Engineering Management Institute. https://engineeringmanagementinstitute.org/communication-engineers-important/

23. Iriart, V., Forrester, N. J., Ashman, T., & Kuebbing, S. E. (2022). The plant science blogging project: A curriculum to develop student science communication skills. *Plants, People, Planet, 1.* https://doi-org.proxy.library.ohio.edu/10.1002/ppp3.10287

24. Leal, A., Lawson, K. M., Telg, R. W., Rumble, J. N., Stedman, N. L. P., & Treise, D. (2020). Technically speaking: Technical skills needed for agricultural communication baccalaureate graduates. *Journal of Applied Communications, 104,* 1–19. https://doi.org/10.4148/1051-0834.2339

25. Myers, S. A., Baker, J. P., Barone, H., Kromka, S. M., & Pitts, S. (2018). Using rhetorical/relational goal theory to examine college students' impressions of their instructors. *Communication Research Reports, 35,* 131–140. https://doi.org/10.1080/08824096.2017.1406848

26. Helou, S., El Helou, E., & El Helou, J. (2022). Physician communication skills in telemedicine: The role of eye contact. *Studies in Health Technology and Informatics, 290,* 849–853. https://doi.org/10.3233/SHTI220199

27. American Association of Colleges and Universities. (2008). *Fulfilling the American dream: Liberal education and the future of work.* https://www.aacu.org/sites/default/files/files/LEAP/2018EmployerResearchReport.pdf

28. Scott, A. (2013). What do employers really want. *Marketplace*. http://www.marketplace.org/topics/wealth-poverty/education/what-do-employers-really-want-college-grads

29. Balcar, J., & Dokoupilová, L. (2021). Communication and language skills pay off, but not everybody needs them. *International Journal of the Sociology of Language, 2021*, 59–93. https://doi.org/10.1515/ijsl-2020-0021

30. National Association of Colleges and Employers. (2020). Key attributes employers want to see on student resumes. https://www.naceweb.org/talent-acquisition/candidate-selection/key-attributes-employers-want-to-see-on-students-resumes/

31. Kay, A., Levine, L., & Shapiro, E. (2022). Reducing anxiety through workplace communication during COVID-19: Who, what, when, and how. *International Journal of Business Communication*, 1. https://doi.org/10.1177/23294884221105580

32. Walker, R. C., Cardon, P. W., & Aritz, J. (2018). Enhancing global virtual small group communication skills. *Journal of Intercultural Communication Research, 47*, 421–433. https://doi.org/10.1080/17475759.2018.1475292

33. Tiitinen, S., & Lempiälä, T. (2022). Two Social Functions of Stepwise Transitions When Discussing Ideas in Workplace Meetings. *International Journal of Business Communication*, *59*(3), 355–384. https://doi.org/10.1177/2329488418819132

34. Gewertz, C. (2018, September 25). Strong speaking skills are in high demand in the workplace. *Education Week*. https://www.edweek.org/ew/articles/2018/09/26/speaking-skills-top-employer-wish-lists-but.html

35. U.S. Census Bureau. (2017, September 14). New American Community Survey statistics for income, poverty and health insurance for states and local areas. https://www.census.gov/newsroom/press-releases/2017/acs-single-year.html?CID=CBSM+ACS16

36. Berlo, D. K. (1960). *The process of communication.* Holt, Rinehart and Winston, p. 24.

37. Shotter, J. (2000). Inside dialogical realities: From an abstract-systematic to a participatory-wholistic understanding of communication. *Southern Communication Journal, 65*, 119–132. (p. 119)

38. Mead, G. H. (1967). *Mind, self, and society from the standpoint of a social behaviorist.* Charles W. Morris (ed.). University of Chicago Press.

39. ESPN News. (2022, 7 July). Joe Biden awards Presidential Medal of Freedom to Simone Biles, Megan Raponoe. https://www.espn.com/olympics/story/_/id/34207827/joe-biden-awards-presidential-medal-freedom-simone-biles-megan-rapinoe

40. Biles, S. (2018, February 7). I went from foster care to the Olympics. https://www.cnn.com/2018/02/05/opinions/foster-care-education-olympics-opinion-biles/index.html

41. Czubaroff, J. (2000). Dialogical rhetoric: An application of Martin Buber's philosophy of dialogue. *Quarterly Journal of Speech, 86,* 168–189.

42. Bestvater, S., & Shah, S. (2022, June 30). 5 facts about political tweets shared by U.S. adults. Pew Research Center. https://www.pewresearch.org/fact-tank/2022/06/30/5-facts-about-political-tweets-shared-by-u-s-adults/

43. Mahapatra, S. (2022, May 20). Political polarization-how simple words create violence. Redefy. https://www.redefy.org/stories/political-polarization-how-simple-words-create-violence

44. CareerBuilder. (2018, August 19). More than half of employers have found content on social media that cause them not to hire a candidate, according to recent CareerBuilder survey. PR Newswire [online]. https://www.prnewswire.com/news-releases/more-than-half-of-employers-have-found-content-on-social-media-that-caused-them-not-to-hire-a-candidate-according-to-recent-careerbuilder-survey-300694437.html

45. Frampton, J. R., & Fox, J. (2018). Social media's role in romantic partners' retroactive jealousy: Social comparison, uncertainty, and information seeking. *Social Media + Society.* https://doi.org/10.1177/2056305118800317

46. Cotriss, D. (2022, June 29). Keeping it clean: Social media screenings gain in popularity. Business Daily News. https://www.businessnewsdaily.com/2377-social-media-hiring.html

47. See tweet at https://twitter.com/chadwickboseman/status/1299530165463199747

48. Antonello, V. S., Panzenhagen, A. C., Balanzá-Martínez, V., & Shansis, F. M. (2020). Virtual meetings and social isolation in COVID-19 times: Transposable barriers. *Trends in Psychiatry and Psychotherapy, 42*, 221–222. https://doi.org/10.1590/2237-6089-2020-0065

49. Cambridge Dictionary. (2018, November 29). The people's word of 2018.

50. Find the NCA Credo on Ethics at https://www.natcom.org/sites/default/files/Public_Statement_Credo_for_Ethical_Communication_2017.pdf

Frank Gaglione/Digital Vision/Getty Images

2

perception, self, and communication

When you have read and thought about this chapter, you will be able to

1. describe what perception is.

2. identify factors in the perceptual process.

3. explain some of the reasons why people can perceive things differently.

4. describe how selection, organization, and interpretation affect the way you communicate with others.

5. differentiate among figure and ground, closure, proximity, and similarity in communication examples.

6. identify errors you might make when perceiving others that affect your communication with them.

7. recognize how the choices you make about with whom and how you communicate are influenced by your view of yourself.

8. describe how impression management influences your perception of yourself and others.

This chapter introduces you to the role of perception of self and others in communication. The chapter explains what perception is, the factors involved in making perceptions, why differences in perception occur, how errors in perceptions occur, and how you can check your perceptions. Next we explore our perceptions of others and the role of the self in communication.

Does perception affect how we learn? Recently, Chicago Bears fans became angry when the team's placekicker missed a 43-yard field goal. Many disgruntled fans took to social media to suggest that even they could have made the kick.[1] In response, a local brewery set up a goalpost and challenged the public to make the kick in order to win NFL tickets for the following season. How would you prepare for this challenge? You might think that, after watching professional athletes on television for years, you could perform as well as the pros. Or perhaps you would watch YouTube videos to learn how to kick a field goal. In the end, none of the more than 100 Bears fans who tried were able to make the 43-yard field goal.

Tom Grill/JGI/Blend Images

Interestingly, journalist Shankar Vedantam noted that people believe they can perform tasks just by watching instructional videos on YouTube or otherwise, but in reality there is a significant gap between what we perceive we can do and what we can actually do.[2] By watching videos, we create a misperception about our own abilities because we learn vicariously through the videos with little actual instruction, practice, or feedback.

Our perceptions are influenced by what we see, hear, and experience. In turn, those perceptions influence how we communicate with others. In this chapter you will learn about perception, how it affects your sense of self, and how knowledge of perception can improve your communication skills.

Defining Perception

In this chapter we focus on perception, the self, and communication. Differences in perception affect the way we understand ourselves, situations, stories, events, and others. Consequently, perception affects the way we view ourselves and the way we present ourselves. In turn, perception acts like a filter that influences our experiences, our assessment of others, and our communication with them. The way you sense the world—the way you see, hear, smell, touch, and taste—is subjective, uniquely your own. Nobody else sees the world the way you do, and nobody experiences events exactly as you do.

The uniqueness of human experience is based largely on differences in **perception**—the use of the senses to process information about the external environment. Since our perceptions are unique, communication between and among people offers opportunities and challenges.

Contemporary approaches view perception as an active process. **Active perception** means that your mind selects, organizes, and interprets what you sense. Another way to think about this is to think about the last time you and your friends took pictures with your phones. Perhaps you uploaded your picture to Instagram and changed the hues and colors and one of your friends used the vignette editing tool to draw attention to a particular part of the image. Much like in this example, each person's perceptual lens is different. Perception is subjective because you interpret what you sense; you make it your own, and you add to and subtract from what you see, hear, smell, and touch based on your lived experiences or lack thereof. **Subjective perception** is your uniquely constructed meaning attributed to sensed stimuli.

perception
The use of the senses to process information about the external environment.

active perception
Perception in which your mind selects, organizes, and interprets that which you sense.

subjective perception
Your uniquely constructed meaning attributed to sensed stimuli.

Consider how much your inner state affects your perceptions. If you have a bad headache, the pain probably will affect the way you treat your children, the way you respond to your coworkers, and even the way you see yourself in the mirror. Perhaps your general resting facial expression usually looks happy, but if you have an "off" day and are not smiling as much as usual, people may ask you repeatedly if you are okay. This might be frustrating to manage emotionally, especially if you are feeling fine. In contrast, some people have facial expressions that can be perceived as "grumpy" or "mean" when in fact that is not the case at all. For example, some might say that San Antonio Spurs head coach Gregg Popovich always looks like he is in a bad mood or that music mogul Jay-Z looks unhappy. Both men have expressed during interviews that they sometimes don't like the media attention, so this may account for their facial expressions. Yet this does not mean that they are upset or mean people. For example, do you have friends who are asked regularly, "Are you okay?" just because of how other people perceive their facial expression? How have you reacted when people have misread your facial expressions?

Consider also how complicated communication becomes when you know that people have their own views, uniquely developed and varying according to what is happening both outside and inside the mind. Perception is a factor that increases the complexity of communication.

How do you see the world around you? Perhaps comparing the way your mind works to the way a computer works will help you answer this. Think of your conscious experiences as the images that appear on your laptop or tablet. Think of what you sense with your eyes, nose, tongue, ears, and fingertips as that which is read off information in the cloud. The picture you see on the screen is not the same as the bits of data in the cloud; instead, an image is generated from the bits to create something you can see.

Differences in Perception

Perception is a subjective, an active, and a creative process. Differences in perception may be the result of identity factors, people's past experiences and roles, their present feelings and circumstances, and current social and political events.

IDENTITY FACTORS

You are not identical to anyone else. People differ from each other in terms of biological sex assigned at birth, gender, height, weight, body type, senses, ableness, and ethnicity, to name a few factors that make up an individual's identity. How important these aspects of your identity are to you can influence how you perceive and communicate with others. You may be tall or short, have poor eyesight, or have impaired hearing; you may be particularly sensitive to smells; or your body temperature may be colder than those of the rest of your family. Similarly, age, hair color, height, and attractiveness greatly affect the way you feel about yourself and the way others treat you.

gender identity
How you feel about and express your gender.

Gender identity is another factor that can influence perceptions. Gender identity relates to how you feel about and express your gender. Expressions of gender identity can occur through how we talk, act, and dress, which can challenge societal perceptions that are often tied to gender roles.[3]

TEMPORAL CONDITIONS

Differences in perception also may arise from temporary conditions. A headache, fatigue, or a pulled muscle can cause you to perceive a critical comment when a friendly one is being offered. You may not see a stop sign if you are walking while texting or tweeting. Other physiological needs, such as hunger and thirst, may also affect your perceptive skills.

Once you are aware of all the conditions that can affect your perceptions, you might be amazed that we can communicate with each other at all.

PAST EXPERIENCES AND ROLES

Just as your size, biologically assigned sex, and senses can affect your perceptions, so can your past experiences and the various roles you occupy. The concept that best explains the influence of your past experiences on your perceptions is **perceptual constancy**—the idea that your past experiences lead you to see the world in a way that is difficult to change; your initial perceptions persist. "A perceptual characteristic that affects my communication with others," said a male student, "is that I am very well-mannered. I am an only child, and my parents raised me very strictly to always treat others with respect and put them before yourself. I also attended a Catholic elementary, middle, and high school where the golden rule of 'treat your neighbor as yourself' was always endorsed and upheld."[4] What happened to you in the past influences your current perceptions. A bad experience in a given situation may cause you to avoid that situation in the future. Your experiences affect how you respond to professors, police, and politicians.

Roles also influence perceptions. A **role** is the part you play in various social contexts. Jason observed that being "the boss" was effective at work, but not in his student role. "When I worked as a manager for a retail store, my assertiveness and confidence were viewed in a positive light. Many of my subordinates saw these characteristics [as] typical for a leader in my position. If I treated my fellow classmates with the same level of assertiveness that I did at work, I would come across as 'cocky' or 'full of it,' and my communication would be affected negatively."[5]

Your roles affect your communication: to whom you talk, how you talk to them, what language you use, and how you respond to feedback. A good example of how perceptual constancy and role are related is parents' treatment of their children. Even after some people become adults, their parents treat them as they did when they were growing up. Roles also tend to change with context: in your parents' home you are their child; in your own home you may be a roommate or a mother or father; in the classroom you are a student; and at work you may be a product manager, a server, or a retail associate.

PRESENT FEELINGS AND CIRCUMSTANCES

How you feel at the moment affects your perceptions and alters your communication. Your child kept you up all night, so you are tired and stressed. Your friend's "How are you?" releases a torrent of whiny complaints that are not your usual response. A headache, great news about your mother's health, a brief fight before class—all these life experiences influence with whom and how you communicate.

Now that you have seen a few examples of how feelings and situations can impact perception, how can you apply this information to your communication skills? Imagine you are talking to a classmate about an assignment during class. She looks away from you, looks at her phone, and does not respond to your attempts at conversation, but she does ask an occasional question. You might think that she is acting distant and disinterested. Yet she might be trying to listen to the instructor or trying to take notes on her phone and is uncomfortable talking. Or maybe she has had the experience of helping other classmates with their work with no gratitude on their part. It turns out she is confused about the assignment as well and was hoping to ask the instructor to clarify what

perceptual constancy
The idea that your past experiences lead you to see the world in a way that is difficult to change; your initial perceptions persist.

role
The part you play in various social contexts.

• Differences in perception that are created by cultural differences can be changed and challenged in our interactions with others.

Drazen/Getty Images

is due this week for the project. She also is waiting for a text message from her mom to hear if her sister is going to need eye surgery. As you can see, present circumstances and internal states influence your communication with others.

CURRENT SOCIAL AND POLITICAL EVENTS

Your thoughts and feelings about, and involvement with, various current social and political events can affect how you see yourself and how you view and communicate with others. There are any number of issues and causes that you may be or will become passionate about during your college career. In fact, you'll likely be asked to think about an issue or event for a persuasive speech in this class. Do you care about the environment, social justice issues, mental health issues, or animal rights? For example, how do you feel about animal rights? Should student loans be forgiven? What concerns, if any, do you have about occurrences of blackfishing, the practice of white women using makeup to appear black on social media? (You will learn more about this phenomenon in Chapter 14.) What current events are being talked about through public dialogue (for example, on social media, during classes, or on your favorite podcast) that you care about?

The stance you take on these and other social and political issues cultivates a perception within you and others about what it means to be passionate about that cause. Likewise, your stance influences how you view other people who care about that issue and those who you believe do not. For example, if you believe the government should not fund free preschool education, you will form opinions about your classmates who do, which may impact how you communicate with them during class activities. Ultimately, our perceptions do not exist in isolation from the content we consume.

communicating with agility

Growth Mindset and Change

The human brain is like a muscle; given new challenges, it can become stronger. When you are facing challenges and struggles, adopting a growth mindset improves physical and psychological health and well-being and can help you adapt to setbacks.

To cultivate a growth mindset, try these approaches the next time you face a challenge:

1. See challenges as an opportunity to grow and learn something new.

2. Recall times you have successfully done something new. One of your textbook authors uses the phrase "It's only hard until it's not" to work through difficult situations.

3. Write a letter to a real or an imagined person going through the same struggle. What advice would you give that person? Now take that advice for yourself.

Changing how we think takes repetition and consistency. Over time, fostering a growth mindset will increase your resilience and confidence.

Source: Mayo Clinic. (2021). Change your mind to grow. www.mayoclinic.org/healthy-lifestyle/adult-health/in-depth/change-your-mind-to-grow/art-20342132

The Perceptual Process

Every day we are flooded with an abundance of stimuli from multiple sources. Some of the content we actively seek, create, and curate, while other content simply creates unnecessary noise and frustration. Through all of this, the perceptual process helps us engage in sense making and guides us to focus on some stimuli over others. You engage in three important yet separate activities during perception: selection, organization, and interpretation. You are likely unaware of these processes because they occur quickly and all at once.

SELECTION

People do not perceive all the stimuli in their environment at all times. Through selection, you neglect some stimuli and focus on others. For example, when you commute to school, you are bombarded with sights, sounds, smells, and other sensations. You don't remember every car you saw on the road, nor do you focus on every person you pass on the sidewalk. Instead, you choose to pay attention to some things while ignoring many others. At school you probably scan students passing by so that you can pick out any friends or classmates who deserve a nod, wave, or other greeting. While awake, you are always actively engaged in selecting which stimuli to which you will respond—or not.

You also select the messages to which you attend. You may tune out one of your teachers if your phone vibrates or check your text messages during a break instead of reviewing your class notes. You might not listen to your roommate nagging you about cleaning the kitchen but listen to every word of praise from your boss. You hear and see thousands of ads, social media posts, and news stories, but you choose to view only the ones that you find most interesting.

Four types of selectivity are selective exposure, selective attention, selective perception, and selective retention. In **selective exposure** you expose yourself to information that reinforces, rather than contradicts, your beliefs or opinions.[6] Selective exposure explains why you hide videos on TikTok from someone who has opinions that you don't agree with or want to be exposed to. In other words, conservative Republicans are more likely than liberal Democrats to listen to Fox News and read articles in the *National Review*. Liberal Democrats, by contrast, are more likely to watch MSNBC and listen to NPR. Selective exposure has the value of reinforcing and validating our positions, but it has the downside of protecting our biases that can lead to increased polarization.

In **selective attention**, even when you do expose yourself to information and ideas, you focus on certain cues and ignore others. On the train, you might notice the new outfit your friend is wearing but not the prosthetic leg the person in the next row is wearing. At a buffet table, you might be drawn to familiar foods while avoiding anything unfamiliar. In an elevator, you might notice the conversation between the two other passengers but not the music that's being piped in overhead.

In communication, you do not treat all sounds, words, phrases, and sentences equally. You almost always respond to your name or a command, such as "Watch out!" If there are certain words or phrases that you find offensive, you might respond negatively to television shows or people using those words. In classes you don't like, you drag through the course without learning much at all, whereas in your favorite class you are highly attentive. Selective attention is in full-time operation during your waking hours, and your use of this aspect of perception affects your communication in many ways.

After you expose yourself to a message and pay attention to it, you see that message through your own lens. **Selective perception** is the tendency to see, hear, and believe only what you want to see, hear, and believe.[7] Suppose you are watching your favorite football team and your favorite player gets called out of bounds while diving for the end-zone pylon, rendering a reversal of a called touchdown. Despite the numerous rounds of instant replays, you insist to your roommate that the player was in bounds and the touchdown call should be upheld.

We see another example of selective perception in the way teachers observe signs of confusion or frustration from students. A study exploring how different types of teachers respond to the unique needs of people who are English language learners (ELLs) found that some are more adept than others at perceiving nonverbal signals of confusion from ELL students.[8] Teachers who tend to use more interaction and dialogue in their classrooms are quick to observe nonverbal behaviors signaling a lack of understanding; in contrast, teachers who rely more on lecture tend to miss such signals. These findings illustrate how selective perception, perhaps driven by past experiences and roles, can cause some teachers to selectively perceive and react to such nonverbal signs while others do not. Although these findings point to the need for all teachers to be more observant of

selective exposure
The tendency to expose yourself to information that reinforces, rather than contradicts, your beliefs or opinions.

selective attention
The tendency, when you expose yourself to information and ideas, to focus on certain cues and ignore others.

selective perception
The tendency to see, hear, and believe only what you want to see, hear, and believe.

students' nonverbal behaviors, they may also suggest that ELL students can be more active in telling teachers when they have difficulty understanding specific terms or ideas.

Finally, you selectively remember some things while selectively forgetting others. **Selective retention** is the tendency to better remember the things that reinforce your beliefs than those that oppose them.[9] Even a loving parent or parental figure may have put you in "time out" now and then, but your dominant impression of that person as positive gets reinforced by your selectively remembering happy family holidays, vacations, and graduations. Often any negative events are suppressed, unless they were unusually traumatic.

How does selective retention function in your everyday communication? At a local coffee shop you unexpectedly run into a former classmate who disagreed with you about government spending. You immediately remember the person as someone you perceived to be assertive and who dominated the discussion. Do you greet your former classmate or head in the other direction without a word? If you do speak, what do you say? Your selective retention of previous encounters greatly influences your choice.

You remember traumatic events and experiences that you found threatening. You remember when someone was unfairly critical of you, when someone of importance praised your work, or when a family member commented favorably about your Instagram post about donating to a charitable cause. You size up people every day. Based on your memories of your experiences with them—your selective retention—you treat them with respect, talk with them, or avoid them. Such is the power of your selective retention. Next you will learn how organization functions in perceptions and affects communication.

selective retention
The tendency to better remember the things that reinforce your beliefs than those that oppose them.

• Perception is affected by our choice of which messages to attend to and which to ignore.

Pixland/Jupiterimages/Getty Images

organization
The grouping of stimuli into meaningful units or wholes.

figure
The focal point of your attention.

ground
The background against which your focused attention occurs.

ORGANIZATION

The abundance of stimuli that we encounter every day can be overwhelming. For this reason, your brain helps process information in ways that organize what your senses tell you about your surroundings. **Organization** in perception is the grouping of stimuli into meaningful units or wholes. This process typically occurs through four organizational methods: figure and ground, closure, proximity, and similarity.

Figure and Ground

One organizational method helps you distinguish between figure and ground. **Figure** is the focal point of your attention, and **ground** is the background against which your focused attention occurs. When looking at Figure 2.1, what do you see first? Some people might perceive a vase or a candlestick, whereas others perceive twins facing each other. People who see a vase identify the center of the drawing as the figure and the area on the right and left as the ground (background). Conversely, people who see twins facing each other identify the center as the ground and the area on the right and left as the figure.

How do figure and ground work in communication encounters? In your verbal and nonverbal exchanges, you perform a similar feat of focusing on some parts (figure) and distancing yourself from others (ground). When you hear your name in a noisy room, your name becomes figure and the remaining noise becomes ground; with Facebook or Reddit comments about a political topic, you may focus on the ideas you agree with as the figure, and the opinions you don't agree with become the ground.

Here's another example. During a job performance review, your manager may talk about your areas in need of improvement and your strengths, but the so-called areas in

Figure 2.1

An example of figure and ground: a vase or twins?

need of improvement might make you so angry that you don't even remember the strengths. The messages about needed improvements are figure, and the ones about strengths are ground. What gets lost when we focus only on the figure or the ground? In what ways could attending to one or the other more fully give you additional information or allow you to see things from another person's point of view?

Closure

Another way of organizing stimuli is through **closure**, the tendency to fill in missing information to complete an otherwise incomplete figure or statement.

One example of closure happens with text. Can you read these lines?

I cdnuolt blveiee that I cluod aulacity uesdnatnrd waht I was rdanieg. The phaonmneal pweor of the hmuan mnid! It deson't matter in what oredr the ltteers in a wrod are; the olny iprmoatnt tihng is that the frist and lsat ltteer be in the rghit pclae.[10]

You can read these words in spite of the spelling because of your mind's ability to achieve closure. Closure is the reason you can make sense of the incorrectly worded text message your friend sends you when the auto-correct feature changes the words without asking for approval.

Closure functions in your communication interactions with others. For example, your uncle retweets an article in support of stricter border-control policies. You therefore believe he is likely against pathways to citizenship for children of undocumented immigrants. Or, a public speaker begins a speech by saying, "I've had many blessings in my life," and you conclude that the person is religious. In both cases, closure may cause you to misperceive aspects of the people to whom you are listening and respond based on those faulty assumptions. In some cases, however, closure can be helpful. For example, seeing a pothole when you are driving helps you conclude that your car might become damaged if you drive through it. On the first day of class, you might see people make eye contact with you and smile, leading to the perception that they want to talk with you. In that instance, correct or not, closure might lead you to new friendships.

Proximity

You also organize stimuli on the basis of their proximity. According to the principle of **proximity**, people or objects that are close to each other in time or space are seen as

closure
The tendency to fill in missing information in order to complete an otherwise incomplete figure or statement.

proximity
The principle that objects physically close to each other will be perceived as a unit or group.

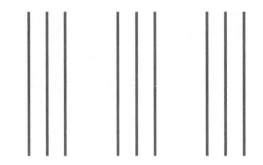

Figure 2.2

An example of proximity: three groups of lines or nine separate lines?

similarity
The principle that elements are grouped together because they share attributes, such as size, color, or shape.

intergroup perspective
The theory that emphasizes the ways in which people in a social interaction identify and categorize themselves or others in terms of group membership and how these categorizations shape perceptions and interactions with others.

meaningfully related. This principle is at work in Figure 2.2. You are most likely to perceive three groups of three lines, rather than nine separate lines.

Proximity works verbally and nonverbally in communication. A nonverbal example is thinking that the two people arriving at a party or event at the same time are dating. A verbal example is if your boss announces that, due to an economic downturn, she is forced to lay off 25 employees. Fifteen minutes later, she calls you into her office. The proximity of the messages leads you to believe that you will be laid off.

Similarity

Similarity is probably the simplest means of organizing stimuli. On the basis of the principle of **similarity**, elements are grouped together because they resemble each other in size, color, shape, or other attributes. In Figure 2.3, you probably perceive circles and squares, rather than a group of geometric shapes, because of the principle of similarity. The saying "Birds of a feather flock together" can hold true as well for human groups, who are often organized by their ethnicity, religion, politics, or interests.

The **intergroup perspective** is one theory that guides research on how people identify and categorize themselves or others in terms of their social group membership, such as race and ethnicity, and how those categories shape perceptions and the ways people

Figure 2.3

An example of similarity: squares and circles or a group of geometric shapes?

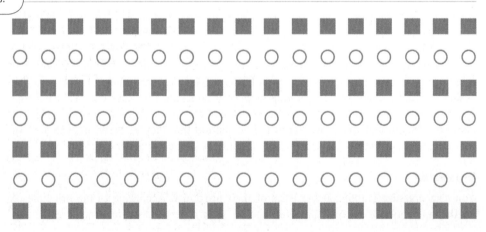

interact with others.[11] Typically, members of an **in-group**—a group that people belong to that gives them a source of pride, self-esteem, and sense of belonging to a social world—engage in activities and hold attitudes that promote a positive image for the in-group compared to the **out-group**, the group marginalized by the dominant culture. This theoretical lens also suggests that people want to view their own social groups positively and tend to favor those in their in-group.[12]

How does similarity work in our relationships and our interactions? Generally, we seek intimate partners, friends, and work colleagues based on similarity. Because our perceptions are egocentric, we choose to interact with people who are similar, in some dimension, to ourselves. In other words, our friends tend to represent some part of ourselves.[13] We tend to reject, or are certainly less interested in interacting with, people who are highly different from the way we see ourselves. The Netflix show *Stranger Things* illustrates the concept nicely: Mike, Dustin, Lucas, and Will initially bond over their shared interest in fantasy gaming through Dungeons and Dragons. In other words, they perceive each other to be in the same common in-group of players, and being part of this group is important to their identities.

INTERPRETATION

The third activity you engage in during perception is interpretation, the assignment of meaning to stimuli. **Interpretive perception**, then, is a blend of internal states and external stimuli. When interpreting stimuli, people frequently rely on the context in which the stimuli are perceived, or they compare the stimuli to other stimuli. Sometimes context helps, but other times it can create confusion in interpretation.

You can become so accustomed to seeing people, places, and situations in a certain way that your senses do not pick up on the obvious. Perhaps this is why we have a false sense of security when we walk and text. We think we won't stumble because we know the path in front of us so well. In a similar way, people who read the following sentence will overlook the problem with it:

The cop saw the man standing on the the street corner.

We achieve closure on the sentence and interpret its meaning without being conscious of the details, so we overlook the repeated *the*. Context provides cues for how an action, an object, or a situation is to be interpreted or perceived. Not seeing the double *the* in the sentence would be no problem for a reader trying to comprehend meaning, but an editor's credibility would be in question if such an error were missed often.

How does interpretation work in our interactions with others? Imagine that you are working in a group in one of your classes. One member of the group always comes prepared and seems to dominate the group interaction and to dictate the direction the project is taking. Another member of the group frequently misses agreed-upon group meeting times, arrives late when he does come, and is never prepared. How do you interpret the behavior of these two people?

Suppose you are more like the first group member than the second. On the one hand, you might feel that the first person is challenging your leadership in the group. On the other hand, you consider the enormous contributions she makes by bringing a great deal of research and planning each time. You dismiss the second person as lazy and unmotivated and as a poor student. You are worried that he will bring down the group grade.

Now suppose you are more like the second group member than the first. You miss meetings, arrive late, and do virtually nothing to prepare. You might interpret the first person's behavior as showing off, but, at the same time, you are glad she is going to lead the group to a good grade. You see the second person as laid-back and fun. In fact, you decide you would like to hang out with him. Thus, our own behavior can lead us to very different interpretations.

in-group
A group that people belong to that gives them a source of pride, self-esteem, and sense of belonging to a social world.

out-group
A group of people excluded from another group with higher status; a group marginalized by the dominant culture.

interpretive perception
Perception that involves a blend of internal states and external stimuli.

Errors in Our Perceptions

Once we understand the active nature of perception and recognize that people hold unique perceptions as a consequence, we can see that we might make errors when we perceive other people. Although many types of errors exist, we discuss only two of the most common errors here: stereotyping and relying on first impressions. Detailed discussions of the many types of errors are beyond the scope of this release of *Human Communication,* but you may discuss them in class.

STEREOTYPING

stereotyping
Making a hasty generalization about a group based on a judgment about an individual from that group.

Stereotyping occurs when we offer a hasty generalization about a group based on a judgment about an individual from that group. How does stereotyping work? First, we categorize other people into groups based on a variety of criteria—age, assigned sex, gender, race, sexual identity, occupation, nation of origin, region of the country, or physical abilities. Initially, this type of categorization is a natural process that helps people interpret their surroundings. Yet stereotyping becomes an issue when we refuse to let people move from these perceived categories. Next, we infer that everyone within that group has the same characteristics. For instance, we might conclude that all lesbians are masculine, that all visually impaired people want help crossing the street, or that all older adults don't know how to use social media. The trouble with stereotyping is that we practically insist that our stereotypes are correct through selective attention (we see what we want to see) and selective retention (we selectively sift through our past for memories that reinforce our stereotypes when they may not be accurate or true). Our expectations and interpretations of the behavior of others are then guided by these perceptions. When we observe people from other groups, we exaggerate or overestimate how frequently they engage in the behaviors that are stereotypically associated with them. We also ignore or underestimate how frequently they engage in the behaviors that are not stereotypically associated with that group.

Unfortunately, our stereotypes of people from different groups are often negative.[14] Working dads may have negative views of dads who stay at home with their children. If you are able-bodied, you might not think someone in a wheelchair can play sports. Researchers have found that these negative stereotypes created different communication patterns when white and Black individuals, for example, interacted. They suggest that "macrolevel interpretations between interracial speakers may be problematic."[15]

Our explanations for the expected and unexpected behaviors of people are frequently in error because we assume situational reasons for unexpected outcomes and personal reasons for expected outcomes. Stereotypes can also be attributed to age differences. For example, older generations may believe that millennials are lazy and entitled and have no interest in societal welfare or change. This can be unfortunate because reports show that millennials are changing the world in meaningful ways and that their actions can have an impact. In fact, the 2017 Millennial Impact Report found that 66% of millennials believe that voting would lead to meaningful change and 29% say that civil rights and racial discrimination are key social issues for them, followed by employment and healthcare reform.[16]

Finally, we often work to differentiate ourselves from people and groups we stereotype. Differentiation occurs when we positively evaluate our own groups and negatively evaluate other groups. For example, those with a particular religious orientation might negatively evaluate other religions, including worshipers of those religions, while favorably evaluating their own group of religious followers. Such differentiation could occur in many ways; one group could assert that it follows religious doctrine more closely, or that the rituals used in its religious ceremony are more appropriate. In another example, college degree holders may assume that their degree affords them greater status and wealth potential than non–degree holders. The point is that, through stereotypes, we construct perceptions that result in even greater assumed differences between groups and people.

Stereotypes can lead to prejudices. **Prejudice** refers to an unfavorable predisposition about an individual because of that person's membership in a stereotyped group. Throughout history and around the world, people have held negative stereotypes, and they have been prejudiced against others. However, such perceptual problems can stand in the way of fruitful communication among people who are different from each other.

Prejudice interferes with our accurate perceptions of others, and it can lead to discrimination. For example, women might not be hired for particular jobs because of prejudice against them. People might be disallowed housing because of their religious beliefs. People might fear others because of their racial or ethnic background. The color of people's skin, the texture of their hair, the shape and size of their body, and their clothing are sometimes used to identify an out-group.

FIRST IMPRESSIONS

When you meet someone for the first time, you seek to form a **first impression**—an initial opinion about people upon meeting them. Frequently, first impressions are based on other people's appearance and may form in as little as three seconds.[17] The nonverbal cues they offer are particularly powerful. We notice clothing, height and weight, physical attractiveness, and interaction skills. From these nonverbal cues we make judgments about others. Research suggests that our brains process a great amount of verbal and nonverbal cues when we meet someone, or simply look at the person's photo on Instagram, and we make fairly accurate first impressions based on this limited information. This means that the pictures you post (and even what you choose not to post) on TikTok convey a first impression of you to others who are viewing your social media sites for the first time. Now you have to ask yourself, is this the impression you want others to have of you? See Chapter 9 to learn about personal branding and how to create the "brand" you want for yourself in your in-person and mediated interactions with others.

As we form our first impressions of others, we also compare the new person with ourselves. This can be especially true in business settings. For example, if others appear to be of a professional or social level comparable to our own, we may admire them and cultivate them as valuable contacts.

Our first impressions are powerful, and sometimes they lead to errors in our assessment of others. Often these initial impressions are based on perceptions of attractiveness and trustworthiness. Imagine a businessperson who has traveled all day and arrives late for a meeting. Her flight was delayed, her luggage was lost en route, and she arrives in jeans and a T-shirt. New business acquaintances might dismiss her simply on the grounds of her appearance. First impressions can be affected by specific situations or circumstances that make our initial assessment inaccurate. Just the same, we tend to cling to these impressions in future interactions. Rather than altering our opinion, we filter out new information that disputes our original appraisal.

A study on how facts don't change first impressions found that even when people were told the sexual orientation of someone, and it contradicted what they initially thought, the participants still identified whether the person was gay or straight based on their first impressions of how the person looked. Even though snap judgments are natural cognitive responses, they can lead to stereotyping, which we discussed earlier in the chapter.[18]

Our perceptions of others rest on a subjective, an active, and a creative perceptual process. Our perceptions of others are unique, and we perceive individuals in multiple ways through multiple interactions. We can more fairly appraise others and their behavior by understanding common attribution and perceptual errors and the extent to which we are engaged in them.

One way to reduce these perceptual errors is through **perception checking**, a process of describing, interpreting, and verifying that helps you understand others and their

prejudice
An unfavorable predisposition about an individual because of that person's membership in a stereotyped group.

first impression
An initial opinion about people upon meeting them.

perception checking
A process of describing, interpreting, and verifying that helps us understand another person and his or her message more accurately.

• First impressions are
quick, powerful, and
sometimes inaccurate.

Laurence Mouton/Getty Images

buildIng behavIors

Check Your Perceptions

Learning to check your perceptions is one of the most effective ways that you can reduce the chance that misperceptions will negatively affect your communication with others. You can practice perception checking in nearly every conversation. One way of doing this is to interject into the conversation your perception of the other person's feelings. For example, if your coworker is telling you about an uncomfortable interaction with a customer, you might perceive that your coworker was frustrated. If you relay that perception and ask if it was correct, you have just engaged in perception checking. By taking your perceptions into the open in dialogue with the other person, you not only have the opportunity to correct misperceptions, but you also demonstrate that you are an active, empathetic listener (a concept you will learn more about in Chapter 5).

messages more accurately. Perception checking has four steps. *First,* you describe to the other person the behavior—including the verbal and nonverbal cues—that you observed. *Second,* you describe how that behavior is making you feel. *Third,* you suggest plausible interpretations. *Fourth,* you seek verification through asking questions or observing for clarification, explanation, or amplification. (See Chapter 3 for more on the process of perception checking.)

Perception checking may be even more important in our business interactions. Suppose a coworker interrupts you several times during a meeting. You begin by describing the behavior: "I've noticed in our last two meetings that you have been interrupting me when I am sharing my ideas." You then share your feelings: "This behavior is making me frustrated." You then suggest alternative interpretations: "Perhaps you disagree with me" (first interpretation). "Maybe you are really excited about this project and can't wait to share your ideas" (second interpretation). Finally, you ask if your interpretations are correct or allow your coworker the opportunity to offer a different reasoning: "Can you tell me what you intended?"

In perception checking, you must suggest interpretations that do not cause the other person to be defensive. In the first instance, imagine that you offered as one explanation "Maybe you are just a rude person." The other person is most likely to become defensive. In the second instance, you could have offered, "Maybe you never learned that it's rude to interrupt people." Most likely, embarrassment and a loss of face would follow.

Another example occurred in Falls Church, Virginia, at a medical clinic where patients from Central America did not keep their appointments. The healthcare workers had to do some follow-up to learn about the cultural differences. They needed to describe the behavior of keeping appointments, suggest an interpretation, but then allow the patients to explain the practice. Perception checks were also necessary when physicians learned that breast self-exam programs for Muslim women needed to be conducted before regular hours so that no men were on the property. Women from other countries report being surprised by the directness and invasiveness of male physicians' questions and sometimes do not answer these questions truthfully or fully.[19] The healthcare workers must continue to do perception checks to ensure that the women are receiving the best medical care possible.

Who Are You?

Discussing perception naturally leads us to look at self-perception. How you perceive yourself plays a central role in communication, regardless of whether the communication is face-to-face, on social media, or in a text message. An early step in considering yourself a communicator is to think about who you are.

HOW YOU BECAME WHO YOU ARE

What you know about yourself includes your past, present, and future. Your family is one of the most influential factors in your life, and because of this your family helped shaped how you think, believe, and behave.

The **personal identity** that you have developed influences your perceptions of others.[20] If you see yourself as a shy person who keeps to yourself or likes to spend time with just a few close friends, then you may perceive others who are more outgoing as attention seekers. Your self-perception will have a profound effect on your communication with others. Importantly, your self-perceptions are not static.

Personal identities can be changed, and people can improve their behavior as a result. For example, some teens who came from low-income backgrounds and struggled academically were taught strategies that allowed them to develop a "new academic possible self." These students then achieved higher grades, scored higher on standardized tests, and showed greater academic initiative. At the same time, their levels of depression, absenteeism, and in-school misbehavior declined.[21] Also, students who perceive that their parents or parental figures are involved in their school experience are more satisfied with school, believe in their abilities, and perform significantly better on national exams such as the ACT.[22]

How can personal identity research be applied to communication? When a speaker creates a message that highlights shared values with listeners, then the listeners perceive a social group identity match and are more likely to be persuaded by the message. Other factors may interfere with this cause–effect relationship, however. For example, if the shared values are unexpected because of someone's political party membership or other social group affiliations, the message may be rejected and the persuasive attempt may fail.

Your awareness of who you are develops in your communication with yourself—that is, your intrapersonal communication. In this way, intrapersonal communication includes self-perceptions, memories, feelings, attitudes, options, and mood. Intrapersonal communication can be viewed as talking to ourselves; it is also synonymous with thinking. Intrapersonal communication appears to be the most common context of communication, the foundation for the other contexts.

Your awareness of who you are also develops in your communication with others. Once you mastered language, **symbolic interactionism**—the process of development of the self through the messages and feedback received from others[23]—shaped you in ways that made you what you are today. You may have been rewarded for athletic skill or overlooked for speaking too little in class. The result is the person you see in the mirror today.

To explore who you are, you may be assigned a speech of self-introduction. This speech may be the first one you deliver in class. Since you know more about yourself than does anyone else in the classroom, you may feel less anxiety about this assignment. Of course, you will want to provide some basic information about yourself—your name, where

personal identity
Perception of what makes an individual unique with regard to various personality characteristics, interests, and values.

symbolic interactionism
The process in which the self develops through the messages and feedback received from others.

sizing things up

What Messages Shaped You?

Most of the memorable messages college students receive about education come from their parents, and those messages help students make decisions during difficult or transitional times. Take a minute to write down the most memorable message that you received from a parent or parental figure telling you about college. This can be a message about going to college, succeeding in college, or any other circumstance surrounding college. Now take a look at this message. What is its main point? What does this message mean to you, personally?

The exercise you just engaged in was the same approach used in a research study by one of your textbook authors and her colleagues. We asked 419 college students the same question and found that parental messages about college are both meaningful and significant to college students. Overall, parents' messages about college are about working (and playing) hard, the necessity of attending college, and encouragement and support.

Does your message fit into one of these themes? If so, which one? How have you used this message, if at all, so far in your college experience? The lesson you can learn from this exercise is that others throughout our lives communicate with us about how we are supposed to think and behave. We are shaped by and act in ways that reflect the many messages we receive from parents, teachers, friends, and others.

Source: Kranstuber, H., Carr, K., & Hosek, A. M. "If you can dream it, you can achieve it." Parent memorable messages as indicators of college student success. *Communication Education*, 61(1): 44–66. https://digitalcommons.unl.edu/cgi/viewcontent.cgi?referer=https://www.google.co.in/&httpsredir=1&article=1019&context=commstuddiss

you are from, and your current major in college—but do so in a way that showcases your personal identity.

Instead of beginning your speech of introduction with basic information, consider providing some information that is provocative and that will gain the attention of your audience. For example, one student began, "How many people do you know who fly an airplane and have also jumped out of one?" Another speaker stated, "I've been in 40 of the 50 states." A third noted, "I have two children and am going back to school to advance my career possibilities." These three students found some aspect about themselves to be unique. In one case, the student was adventuresome and a risk taker; the second student had enjoyed a great deal of travel with his family; and the third realized she wanted to go back to school.

The speech of self-introduction will allow you to draw on the information in this chapter, and it will give you a relatively stress-free way to begin finding your voice in this class.

LEARNING MORE ABOUT YOURSELF

Perhaps you now understand why the ancients said, "Know thyself." They, like people today, believed that self-awareness is a discovery worth making. Accurate self-awareness helps you be ready to make sound choices now and in the future. If you dislike chemistry, you might not enjoy a career as a physician or pharmacist. If you like to write and are good at it, you might have a future as a writer or social media content creator. If you are skillful at athletics, perhaps you can take advantage of that talent with scholarships, varsity sports, and even professional sports. What you have learned about yourself in the past, and what you learn about yourself now, will affect your future.

Right now, as you go about your everyday activities, you should be aware of what kind of person you are and who you want to be in the future. In her memoir *Untamed* author and activist Glennon Doyle talks about this as "trusting your knowing." What she means is that we should trust that we know ourselves and listen to our inner voices.[24] Are you shy, timid, and unassertive? Are you active, vigorous, and energetic? Do you welcome change, adventure, and risk? Do you see yourself as capable, unstoppable, and hard-driving? In his book *Let Your Life Speak,* education activist Parker Palmer encourages readers to think deeply about the answers to the questions "What am I?" and "What is my nature?" as a way to find their inner voice and determine the gifts they have been given to share with the world.[25] Answering these and many other questions is the key to finding your authentic selfhood. As Michelle Obama notes in her memoir *Becoming*, "Your story is what you have, what you will always have. It is something to own."[26]

Joseph O'Connor was a high school junior when he spent two weeks in the Sierra Nevada mountain range of eastern California—a challenge that changed his level of self-awareness. Rain poured, hail pelted, and the beauty of dawn at 13,000 feet entranced him. In an article about his new self-awareness, O'Connor wrote:

> The wonder of all I'd experienced made me think seriously about what comes next. "Life after high school," I said to myself. "Uh-oh." What had I been doing the last three years? I was so caught up in defying the advice of my parents and teachers to study and play by the rules that I hadn't considered the effects my actions would have on me.[27]

O'Connor's experience changed his self-awareness, and he went from being a D student to one who made the honor roll.

You don't have to go to the moun-

communicating creatively

Messages to Your Younger Self

As a way to celebrate International Women's Day, YouTube encouraged people to empower young women with the #DearMe campaign. The #DearMe campaign asks digital creators around the world to upload "video letters" to their younger selves that provide the advice and encouragement they wish they had heard when they were younger. The campaign encouraged people to use the hashtag #DearMe on social media to share their messages. Although the initial focus was on young girls, these video letters apply to all who wish to tell their younger selves or others a supportive, clarifying, and/or realistic message. A quick search of the videos yields an array of messages, perspectives, and identities. In this section, you have been learning about how your self-perceptions and others' perceptions of you have, in part, formed who you are. Perhaps you can take the time to create a video message or write a letter to your younger self. What would your letter say? What part does perception play in your message to your younger self?

Source: Brouwer, B. (2015). YouTube launches #DearMe campaign for International Women's Day. Tubefilter. www.tubefilter.com/2015/03/03/youtube-dearme-campaign-international-womens-day/

tains to come to a new awareness of yourself. If you want to learn more about yourself, you can take several steps to achieve that goal. If you want to learn more about your physical self, you can start a new workout program that pushes your physical strength in new ways. You can also talk to your relatives about people in your family. What health ailments do your parents and grandparents face? Are these problems inherited? Knowing your family health history can help doctors diagnose your illnesses, assess your risk level for various diseases, and identify risk-reducing strategies. How can knowing this information make you think differently about how you communicate or behave and the kinds of experiences you seek out or avoid? For example, if a close family member died of lung cancer due to years of smoking, would you avoid smoking cigarettes and people who smoke cigarettes? Would you advocate for antismoking initiatives on your campus?

Identity centers on college campuses are a useful place to learn about your and others identities. Identity centers focus their mission on a specific identity or on social groups, such as a Multicultural Center Veteran Resource Center, an LGBTQI Center, a Black Student Center, a Women's Center, or a Religious Center. Each of these organizations would offer programing dedicated to a specific group. Take a look on your university or college website and see what identity centers are on your campus. Then decide which centers you might like to visit.

If you want to learn more about your personality and how others perceive you, you can talk with your significant other, partner, friends, coworkers, bosses, and even your children if you are a parent. In what ways is your personality similar to and different from the personalities of your family members? For example, you may learn best by doing things hands-on just like your grandfather or lack patience like your mother. Consider other features of your life that will suggest how you are perceived. Do people seek you out to build a friendship? Do others ask you to participate in social events? Do friends ask you for advice?

If you want to know what type of employee you are, you can ask your supervisor, coworkers, and customers. Consider the type of environment that you thrive in and ones that you don't enjoy. Do you like to work alone or with others? What kinds of jobs have you held? Have you been given increasing amounts of responsibility in those jobs, or have you frequently lost jobs? Do you need motivation from others, or do you work to complete a task without reminders from others? Do others seek you out to partner with them on work or school projects?

You may have heard of a number of personality tests such as the Myer-Briggs Type Indicator or the Enneagram, or perhaps you have completed the DiSC assessment for your job. Although there is debate in scholarly communities over the merits of these tests, many employers use them to learn about their employees' strengths and how they work with others. These tests are another tool you can use to learn more about yourself. In her book *The Four Tendencies,* Gretchen Rubin highlights four personality types and describes how to harness the potential of each type and how to manage relationships with others of the same or different types. The four tendencies are upholders, questioners, obligers, and rebels. Each tendency is linked to specific ways for addressing inner (things we want to do) and outer expectations (things other people want us to do). *Upholders* tend to meet inner and outer expectations rather easily. They value rules and plans and are self-motivated. These are your friends who make sure they work out every day before they can meet you for lunch or group members who have completed class project tasks in advance of the deadline. *Questioners* tend to meet their inner expectations but have a harder time meeting outer expectations. If you are a questioner, you need to see the reason behind anything you do and you need to believe the reason in order to be sufficiently motivated to do a task. For some of you, this may make various tasks in your classes or jobs seem like "busy work" if you do not understand or agree with the rationale behind the task. Yet, you can easily spend hours working on a puzzle or training for a marathon because it is a goal you have set for yourself. *Obligers*, the most common tendency, typically meet other people's expectations but struggle to meet their own. Obligers do best when they have accountability for getting their tasks done, and they enjoy working in teams. *Rebels* resist both inner and outer expectations. The option to be free from constraints and to do work that makes them feel challenged in a way that maintains their independence works best for people with this tendency.[28] Which tendency best represents you? How does this impact your school work or your personal interests? What strategies could you employ to more easily meet inner and outer expectations in light of your tendency? Do not box yourself in to your tendency type. Use it instead to understand yourself and to improve your behavior and relationships.

• New experiences may lead to increased self-knowledge.

Matthias Engelien/Alamy Stock Photo

mental health
Our emotional, psychological, and social well-being that affects how we think, feel, and act.

MENTAL HEALTH AND WELL-BEING

Mental health includes your psychological, emotional, and social well-being.[29] According to the World Health Organization, "Mental health is a state of mental well-being that enables people to cope with the stresses of life, realize their abilities, learn well and work well, and contribute to their community."[30] In the last 10 years, symptoms of mental disorders have nearly doubled among college students,[31] and students from ethnic and racial minority groups are less likely than white students to seek out support and treatment.[32] Your mental health can influence your perceptions of yourself and others and shapes how you build relationships with others. As such, it is important to take care of your mental health as you learn more about yourself and begin new relationships. A few ways you can do this are to take care of your body through diet and exercise, seek help from university and community mental health resources, spend time with others and avoid isolating yourself, and take breaks and rest.[33]

How You Present Yourself

In this chapter we have shown the relationship among perception, self-perception, and communication. Communication and perception influence each other. Communication is largely responsible for our self-perceptions. Communication can also be used to change the perceptions that others have of us. We attempt to influence others' perceptions of ourselves through self-presentation, or **impression management**, the sharing of personal details in order to present an idealized self.

In our daily interactions, whether they be face-to-face or online, we present ourselves to people, both consciously and unconsciously. Generally, our self-presentation is consistent with an ideal self-image, allows us to enact an appropriate role, influences others' views of us, permits us to define the situation in our terms, and/or influences the progress of an interaction.

Erving Goffman first described the process of self-presentation.[34] Goffman adopted the symbolic interactionist perspective mentioned earlier. He described everyday interactions through a dramaturgical, or theater arts, viewpoint. His theory embraces individual identity, group relationships, the context (the situation), and the interactive meaning of information. Individuals are viewed as "actors," and interaction is seen as a "performance" shaped by the context and constructed to provide others with "impressions" consistent with the desired goals of the actor. Through impression management, people try to present an idealized version of themselves to reach desired ends.

Your understanding of verbal and nonverbal communication will be enhanced by your understanding of identity and impression management. Three types of communication are used to manage impressions: manner, appearance, and setting. Manner includes both verbal and nonverbal codes. Your manner might be seen as assertive, aloof, serious, immature, friendly, or gracious. Your appearance might suggest a role you are playing (administrative assistant), a value you hold (concern for the environment), or your personality (easygoing). The setting includes your immediate environment (the space in which you communicate) as well as other public displays of who you are (the kind of home in which you live and the type of automobile you drive). Each of these factors can influence how you see yourself and how others see you.

Whether you realize it or not, you engage in impression management in your face-to-face interactions and in your mediated interactions. Think about your use of social media

engaging diversity

Differences in Memory

The dominant culture in the United States places the self in the spotlight, whereas most Asian cultures, such as the Chinese, emphasize the group over the individual. Notice that people in the United States write their given (first) name followed by the family name, whereas the Chinese start with the family name followed by their given name. For the Chinese, the group (family) comes before the self. These differences in emphasis extend even to the way people remember events.

Research by Qi Wang and her associates shows that American adults and children ages 4 to 6 recall their personal memories differently than do indigenous Chinese. Since our self-concept is dependent on our self-awareness, these cultural differences are important. "Americans often report lengthy, specific, emotionally elaborate memories that focus on the self as a central character," says Wang. "Chinese tend to give brief accounts of general routine events that center on collective activities and are often emotionally neutral. These individual-focused vs. group-oriented styles characterize the mainstream values in American and Chinese cultures, respectively."

Source: Han, J. J., Leichtman, M. D., & Wang, Q. (1998, July). Autobiographical memory in Korean, Chinese, and American children. *Developmental Psychology, 34*(4):701–713. www.ncbi.nlm.nih.gov/pubmed/9681262

impression management
Sharing personal details in order to present an idealized self.

sizing things up

The Rosenberg Self-Esteem Scale

Below is a list of statements regarding your general feelings about yourself. Read each statement carefully and respond by using the following scale:

1 = Strongly agree
2 = Agree
3 = Disagree
4 = Strongly disagree

1. On the whole, I am satisfied with myself.
2. At times I think that I am no good at all.
3. I feel that I have a number of good qualities.
4. I am able to do things as well as most other people.
5. I feel I do not have much to be proud of.
6. I certainly feel useless at times.
7. I feel that I am a person of worth, at least the equal of others.
8. I wish I could have more respect for myself.
9. All in all, I am inclined to feel that I am a failure.
10. I take a positive attitude toward myself.

This exercise has no right or wrong answers; instead, the answers will tell you something about how you feel about yourself. A guide for interpreting your responses appears at the end of the chapter.

Source: Rosenberg, M. (1965). *Society and the adolescent self-image.* Princeton University Press.

and how you manage your privacy online. Maybe you hide or block your parents or children or let only friends see certain pictures. These are examples of ways you are actively managing the impression of you that can be perceived through the pictures and comments. Research on this topic suggests that when students know their teachers can view their social networking profiles, they are more apt to make sure their spelling is correct and their pictures are appropriate.[35] There are also generational differences in how people manage their online identity and private information. For example, Boyd found that younger people tend to be public by default and private by choice.[36]

In general, some level of management and maintenance is needed to maintain an online presence. This can lead to feeling as though you have to be online constantly, or it can result in a fear of missing out (FOMO) on opportunities to connect with others. Yet,

be ready... for what's next

Online Presentation of Self

Have you ever "Googled" yourself? If you haven't, take a few minutes and do so now. What comes up when you search for yourself online? You will probably find links to any social media accounts you hold. Have you checked to see what types of pictures, comments, and content are available for the general public to see from your social media sites?

How do you feel about the level of access and privacy surrounding your information on these sites? What perception do you think this information conveys about your identity?

Now might be a good time to change some of your privacy settings on social media, delete unwanted comments, remove your name from photos, or ask friends who have tagged you in their social media posts to remove your name as well.

Taking those few simple steps can help you to critically examine and manage your online reputation, which is important because your online reputation can affect your present and future opportunities. Many employers search online for information about prospective employees before they request interviews, and many employers have policies about how employees can present themselves online. At some point in your academic or professional career, you may even need to promote yourself online as part of your job.

This chapter invited you to know and understand the link between perception and communication. You have learned now that everything from how you look to how you think can affect your communication with others—in regard to whether you communicate, with whom you communicate, and how you communicate. As part of your growing communication skills, you have to take seriously how you look, dress, and present yourself to others. You have learned the power of perception in communication.

current research indicates that if you reduce your time online, doing so can enhance your mental and emotional well-being. A recent experimental study led by psychologist Melissa G. Hunt found that depression and loneliness decreased when college students limited their social media usage to 30 minutes per day, and this result was more pronounced for students who reported feeling more depressed.[37] Hunt speculated that, because the students who limited their social media use engaged in more self-monitoring (another aspect of impression management), they were more aware of how various social media apps regulated their lives. As you think about managing impressions and presenting yourself, how would you feel about reducing your social media use to 30 minutes a day? Would you be concerned about others' perceptions of your reduced online presence? What would you do with that extra time? Many mobile devices now have ways to track how much time you spend online and even allow you to set limits on your social media usage. Over the next week, you should choose one day to limit your social media usage to 30 minutes and see how you feel.

Chapter Review & Study Guide

Summary

In this chapter you learned the following:

1. Perception is the use of our senses to process information about our environment or situation.

2. Differences occur in perception for many reasons, including identity factors, temporal conditions, past experiences and roles, our present feelings and circumstances, and current social and political events.

3. Through selection, we neglect some stimuli in our environment and focus on others. Organization in perception is the grouping of stimuli into meaningful units or wholes. Interpretation is the way we assign meaning to stimuli.

4. Some ways in which we organize stimuli are figure and ground, closure, proximity, and similarity. Figure and ground refers to our focusing on some parts of an experience

(figure) and distancing ourselves from others (ground). Closure is the tendency to fill in missing information. Proximity encourages us to perceive objects close in space or time as meaningfully related, and similarity is the basis on which we group elements that resemble each other in size, color, or shape.

5. Perceptual errors that affect communication include stereotyping and reliance on first impressions.

6. The way you see yourself affects how and to whom you communicate, regardless of the medium.

7. Impression management is a way for you to influence how others perceive you, usually as an idealized version of yourself.

Key Terms

Active perception
Closure
Figure
First impression
Gender identity
Ground
Impression management
In-group
Intergroup perspective
Interpretive perception

Mental health
Organization
Out-group
Perception
Perception checking
Perceptual constancy
Personal identity
Prejudice
Proximity
Role

Selective attention
Selective exposure
Selective perception
Selective retention
Similarity
Stereotyping
Subjective perception
Symbolic interactionism

Study Questions

1. Which of the following may be the result of identity factors, past experiences and roles, and present conditions?

   a. selection
   b. similarity
   c. self-serving bias
   d. differences in perception

2. By neglecting some stimuli and focusing on other stimuli, you are engaging in which process of perception?

   a. organization
   b. selection
   c. classification
   d. interpretation

3. _____is an organizational method whereby missing information is filled in to create the appearance of a complete unit, and _____is another organizational technique whereby elements are grouped based on their similarities in size, color, and shape.

   a. Closure; similarity
   b. Proximity; figure and ground
   c. Similarity; proximity
   d. Closure; proximity

4. Organization in perception occurs when stimuli are grouped into meaningful

   a. parts and figures.
   b. figures and ground.
   c. units or wholes.
   d. context and relationships.

5. Perceptual constancy results because of

   a. identity factors.
   b. past experiences and roles.
   c. figure and ground.
   d. people's present feelings and circumstances.

6. The process of developing yourself through the messages and feedback received from others is known as

   a. symbolic interactionism.
   b. personal identity.
   c. perceptual process.
   d. perceptual consistency.

7. Selection occurs in perception in all of the following ways *except*

   a. attention.
   b. exposure.
   c. distraction.
   d. retention.

8. Which of the following is a perceptual error frequently made by people?

   a. believing stereotypes about people who are different from themselves
   b. believing other people are courageous, whereas they, themselves, are cowardly
   c. believing that others are considerably older than themselves
   d. believing that uneducated people are happier than educated people

9. When people seek to present an ideal version of themselves, they are engaging in

   a. impression management.
   b. active perception.
   c. attribution.
   d. selection.

10. First impressions

   a. generally take weeks or more to develop.
   b. are based on people's sense of humor, their personality, and their religion.
   c. are frequently based on other people's appearance.
   d. are generally accurate and therefore are lasting impressions.

Answers:
1. (d); 2. (b); 3. (a); 4. (c); 5. (b); 6. (a); 7. (c); 8. (a); 9. (a); 10. (c)

Critical Thinking

1. Researchers state that people's perceptions are largely learned because what people see, hear, taste, touch, and smell is conditioned by their culture. What parts of your culture are key factors in how you perceive events in day-to-day life?

2. The chapter discusses how people form impressions of who they are and how communication affects self-perceptions. How does this occur through social media?

For instance, why do people follow the Instagram feeds of people they don't know? How are those popular Instagram users communicating a favorable perception of themselves through their posts that make people want to follow their feeds? How do you see yourself? How is this affected by your past, present, and projected future? How have conversations you have had with friends, coworkers, or other people at college altered the way you see yourself?

Sizing Things Up Scoring and Interpretation

The Rosenberg Self-Esteem Scale

Self-esteem is a central component of self-perception. The Rosenberg Self-Esteem Scale is one of the most popular scales designed to measure your general positive or negative self-assessment. After completing and scoring this scale, talk with your teacher about self-esteem and how your communication behaviors are related to this self-perception.

Scoring of the Rosenberg Self-Esteem Scale is very straightforward. Items 2, 5, 6, 8, and 9 should be reverse-coded. This means that if you answered one of those statements with a 4, your score should be reversed to a 1; and if you answered 3, your score should be reversed to a 2, and so on for the rest of the reverse-coded items. Reverse-coding will account for the fact that some questions are positively worded, whereas others are negatively worded. After reverse-coding, add all scores together; values should range from 10 to 40, with higher values indicating more negative assessments of self-esteem.

References

1. Smith, R. (2019, January 12). What was it like trying to kick Cody Parkey's 43-yard field goal? Amateur hour. *Chicago Sun Times.* https://chicago.suntimes.com/sports/cody-parkey-kick-goose-island-challenge-failure/

2. Vedantam, S. (2019, February). There's a gap between perception and reality when it comes to learning. NPR. https://www.npr.org/2019/02/18/695637906/theres-a-gap-between-perception-and-reality-when-it-comes-to-learning

3. Manning, J., Stern, D. M., & Johnson, R. (2017). Sexual and gender identity in the classroom. In M. L. Houser & A. M. Hosek (Eds.), *Handbook of instructional communication: Rhetorical and relational perspectives* (pp. 170–182). Taylor & Francis.

4. Lutz, C. (2011). Brief Paper One in Communication 114, Introduction to Human Communication, North Dakota State University.

5. Bedsaul, J. (2011). Brief Paper One in Communication 114, Introduction to Human Communication, North Dakota State University.

6. Stroud, N. J. (2017). Selective exposure theories. In Kenski, K., & Jamieson, H. (Eds.), *The Oxford handbook of political communication, 1,* 1–20. https://doi.org/10.1093/oxfordhb/9780199793471.013.009_update_001

7. Stroud, N. J. (2017). Selective exposure theories. In Kenski, K., & Jamieson, H. (Eds.), *The Oxford handbook of political communication, 1,* 1–20. https://doi.org/10.1093/oxfordhb/9780199793471.013.009_update_001

8. Curtin, E. (2005). Instructional styles used by regular classroom teachers while teaching recently mainstreamed ESL students: Six urban middle school teachers share their experiences and perceptions. *Multicultural Education, 12*(4): 36–42.

9. Wilson, J., & Wilson, S. (Eds.). (1998). *Mass media/mass culture.* McGraw-Hill.

10. Mentalblog.com. 2004.

11. Harwood, J., Giles, H., & Palomares, N. A. (2005). Intergroup theory and communication processes. In J. Harwood & H. Giles (Eds.), *Intergroup communication: Multiple perspectives* (pp. 1–17). Peter Lang.

12. Tajfel, H., & Turner, J. C. (1986). The social identity theory of intergroup behavior. In S. Worchel & W. Austin (Eds.), *Psychology of intergroup relations* (pp. 7–24). Nelson-Hall.

13. Leary, M. (2002). The self as a source of relational difficulties. *Self and Identity, 1,* 137–142.

14. Hendrix, K. G. (2002). "Did being black introduce bias into your study?" Attempting to mute the race-related research of black scholars. *Howard Journal of Communication, 13,* 153–171.

15. Hughes, P. C., & Baldwin, J. R. (2002). Communication and stereotypical impressions. *Howard Journal of Communication, 13,* 113–128. (p. 113)

16. Achieve. (2018). *2017 Millennial impact report.* http://www.themillennialimpact.com/

17. Gregoire, C. (2014, May). How to make the perfect first impression (according to science). The Third Metric. http://www.huffingtonpost.com/2014/05/30/the-science-and-art-of-fi_n_5399004.html

18. Society for Personality and Social Psychology. (2014, February 14). Even fact will not change first impressions. *Science Daily.* www.sciencedaily.com/releases/2014/02/140214111207.htm

19. Levine, S. (2006, March 20–26). Culturally sensitive medicine: Doctors learn to adapt to immigrant patients' ethnic and religious customs. *Washington Post National Weekly Edition, 23*(22): 31.

20. Seta, C. E., Schmidt, S., & Bookhout, C. M. (2006). Social identity orientation and social role attributions: Explaining behavior through the lens of self. *Self and Identity, 5,* 355–364.

21. Oyserman, D., Bybee, D., & Terry, K. (2006). Possible selves and academic outcomes: How and when possible selves impel action. *Journal of Personality and Social Psychology, 91,* 188–204.

22. Barwegen, L. M., Falciani, N. K., Putnam, J., Reamer, M. B., & Stair, E. E. (2004). Academic achievement of homeschool and public school students and student perception of parent involvement. *School Community Journal, 14,* 39–58.

23. Mead, G. H. (1934). *Mind, self, and society.* University of Chicago Press.

24. Doyle, G. (2020). *Untamed.* Random House.

25. Palmer, P. J. (1999). *Let your life speak: Listening for the voice of vocation.* Wiley.

26. Obama, M. (2018). *Becoming.* Random House.

27. O'Connor, J. (1998). A view from Mount Ritter. *Newsweek, 131*(21): 17.

28. Rubin, G. (2017). *The four tendencies. The indispensable personality profiles that reveal how to make your life better (and other people's lives better, too).* Random House.

29. Centers for Disease Control and Prevention. (2021). About mental health. https://www.cdc.gov/mentalhealth/learn/index.htm

30. World Health Organization. (2022, June 17). Mental health: Strengthening our response. https://www.who.int/news-room/fact-sheets/detail/mental-health-strengthening-our-response

31. Duffy, M. E., Twenge, J. M., & Joiner, T. E. (2019). Trends in mood and anxiety symptoms and suicide-related outcomes among US undergraduates, 2007–2018: Evidence from two national surveys. *Journal of Adolescent Health, 65*(5), 590–598.

32. Lipson, S. K., Kern, A., Eisenberg, D., & Breland-Noble, A. M. (2018). Mental health disparities among college students of color. *Journal of Adolescent Health, 63*(3), 348–356.

33. Betz, A. (2022). How to take care of your mental health in college. *Education Corner.* https://www.educationcorner.com/mental-health-college.html

34. Goffman, E. (1959). *The presentation of self in everyday life.* Doubleday Anchor. Goffman, E. (1974). *Frame analysis: An essay on the organization of experience.* Harper & Row. Goffman, E. (1981). *Forms of talk.* Basil Blackwell.

35. DiVerniero, R., & Hosek, A. M. (2011). Students' perceptions and sense making of instructors' online self-disclosure. *Communication Quarterly, 59,* 428–449.

36. Boyd, D. (2014). *Its complicated: The social lives of networked teens.* Yale University Press.

37. Hunt, M. G., Marx, R., Lipson, C., & Young, J. (2018). No more FOMO: Limiting social media decreases loneliness and depression. *Journal of Social and Clinical Psychology, 37,* 751–768.

3

language and meaning

When you have read and thought about this chapter, you will be able to

1. define language.

2. recall how language works.

3. recognize the characteristics of language.

4. apply language effectively.

This chapter is about the importance of language and how language functions in communication. Language is powerful because it has the power to create, shape, and challenge meaning. Language is complex, and how it is used and interpreted can bring communities together or create division. In this chapter you will learn about the definition of language, its many characteristics, and its complexities. Finally, you will learn how you can use language more effectively in your day-to-day interactions with others.

The U.S. Department of Agriculture defines *food deserts* as "areas where people have limited access to a variety of healthy and affordable food."[1] The report defining that term concluded that food deserts are more likely to be found in areas with higher levels of poverty and in some urban areas with high concentrations of minorities. The term *food deserts* has become an important metaphor that drives public policy to improve public health by fighting obesity and other health problems related to consumption of highly processed and fast foods.

Journalist Barry Yeoman has joined a growing group of scholars and social issue advocates who criticize the term *food desert* and the metaphor it represents.[2] He observes that the term implies a lack of value in communities labeled as food deserts and also ignores many of the underlying causes that contribute to a lack of access to healthy eating options. For example, the word *desert* implies a lack of ability to produce food. In reality, these neighborhoods could have fresh food, but those products are often too expensive for people living in poverty.

The example of food deserts highlights two important points. First, words and phrases are often created to label things. In this case, the term *food desert* was created to define an observable problem facing millions of Americans. Second, those labels can raise awareness about some issues but also conceal others by incorrectly focusing attention. The food desert metaphor, for instance, implies that the inability to access fresh food is a geographic issue when, in fact, it's largely an economic issue. As you consider these points, you should recognize the importance of language—the words we use not only convey meaning but also imply a certain way of thinking about the world around us.

In this chapter you will learn how to be more precise and ethical in the way you use language while communicating.

Thomas Bullock/Alamy Stock Photo

Defining Language

Language is a collection of symbols, letters, or words with arbitrary meanings that are governed by rules and used to communicate. Language consists of words or symbols that represent things without being those things. People originally assigned arbitrary labels to objects in order to communicate ideas; as new objects are made, new words or symbols are created to aid communication. The word *motorcycle* is a symbol for a vehicle that runs on gasoline, but the symbol is not the vehicle itself. Recently, we have begun to use hashtags in this way, as well. Putting the hash sign (#) in front of a word or acronym creates a hashtag that typically symbolizes an idea, a feeling, a product, and even a social movement. When you listen to others' verbal communication or read written words, you **decode**, or assign meaning to, their words to translate them into thoughts of your own. Because language is an imperfect means of transmission, the thoughts expressed by one person never exactly match what is decoded by another. In other words, language is an imperfect process that often requires corrections.

Verbal communication is essential in practically everything we do, from doing well at work to relating to friends and relatives. Both writing and speaking rely on the use of

language
A collection of symbols, letters, or words with arbitrary meanings that are governed by rules and used to communicate.

decode
The process of assigning meaning to others' words in order to translate them into thoughts of your own.

language. Verbal communication represents one of the two major codes of communication; the other is nonverbal communication.

Our definition tells you that language consists of words or symbols, has rules, and is arbitrary, but the definition does not reveal some of the other important characteristics of language. Language also is intertwined with culture, organizes reality, and is abstract. In this section we take a closer look at each of these characteristics.

LANGUAGE HAS RULES

Language has multiple rules. Three sets of rules are relevant to our discussion: semantic rules, syntactic rules, and pragmatic rules. **Semantics** is the study of the way humans use language to evoke meaning in others. Semantics focuses on individual words and their meaning. Semanticists—people who study semantics—are interested in how language and its meaning change over time.

Whereas semantics focuses on the definition of specific words, **syntax** is the way in which words are arranged to form phrases and sentences. For example, in the English language the subject is usually placed before the verb, and the object after the verb. Other languages have different rules of syntax, including reading from right to left. You **encode** by translating your thoughts into words. Syntax changes the meaning of the same set of words. For example, the declarative statement "I am going tomorrow" uses syntax to signal that someone is leaving the next day. If you change the word arrangement to "Am I going tomorrow?" the statement becomes a question and acquires a different meaning.

Pragmatics is the study of language as it is used in a social context, including its effect on the communicators. Messages are variable, depending on the situation. Ambiguous messages, such as "How are you?" "What's new?" and "You're looking good," have different meanings, depending on the context. For example, many people use such phrases as **phatic communication** or small talk—communication that is used to establish a mood of sociability rather than to communicate important information or ideas. Indeed, they would be surprised if someone offered serious or thoughtful answers to such questions or statements. For instance, have you ever asked a coworker, "How's your day going?" and they responded, "This is the worst day ever," and then proceeded to tell you about the argument they had with their partner? More often than not, when we ask people these types of questions, we don't expect an in-depth answer. However, if you are visiting your grandmother who has been ill, your questions about how she is feeling are sincere and designed to elicit information. Pragmatic rules help us interpret meaning in specific contexts.

LANGUAGE AND CULTURE ARE INTERTWINED

Culture may be defined as all of the socially transmitted behavior patterns, beliefs, attitudes, and values of a particular period, class, community, or population. We often think of the culture of a country (Greek culture), institution (the culture of higher education), organization (the TikTok culture), or group of people (the Jewish culture). Culture and language are thus related as the transmission of culture occurs, in part, through language.

The relationship between culture and language is not as simple as it first appears, however. Let us take the example of gender and communication. In previous decades, books and articles were written on the differences between women and men in their communicative practices. As this research developed, *gender* was expanded to refer to a complex social construct rather than simple biological sex assigned at birth. To further illustrate the important complexity of how we talk about gender, there are different aspects to its definition. For example, the term *gender identity* refers to people's perceptions of their own gender, whereas *gender roles* are the culturally created ways that people are expected to behave based on their gender.[3] Some scholars argue that gender is just as important as social class in understanding variations in communication.[4]

semantics
The study of the way humans use language to evoke meaning in others.

syntax
The way in which words are arranged to form phrases and sentences.

encode
The process of translating your thoughts into words.

pragmatics
The study of language as it is used in a social context, including its effect on the communicators.

phatic communication
Communication that is used to establish a mood of sociability rather than to communicate important information or ideas.

culture
The socially transmitted behavior patterns, beliefs, attitudes, and values of a particular period, class, community, or population.

Language and culture are related in a second way. Culture creates a lens through which we perceive the world and create shared meaning. Language thus develops in response to the needs of the culture or to the perceptions of the world. Edward Sapir and Benjamin Lee Whorf were among the first to discuss the relationship between language and perception. The **Sapir-Whorf hypothesis**, as their theory has become known, states that our perception of reality is determined by our thought processes, our thought processes are limited by our language, and therefore language shapes our reality and our behaviors.[5] Language is the principal way that we learn about ourselves, others, and our culture.

The Sapir-Whorf hypothesis has been illustrated in multiple cultures.[6] The Hopi language serves as an early example. The Hopi people do not distinguish between nouns and verbs. In many languages, nouns are given names that suggest that they remain static over time. For example, we assume that words such as *professor, physician, lamp,* and *computer* refer to people or objects that are relatively unchanging. Verbs are action words that suggest change. When we use words such as *heard, rehearsed, spoke,* and *ran,* we assume alterations and movement. The Hopi, by avoiding the distinction between nouns and verbs, thus refer to people and objects in the world as always changing.

In new ways, popular culture and social media regularly direct the creation of abbreviations.[7] For example, OMG and LOL are archaic. As acronyms become commonplace, people just use them in place of the things they are referencing. Therefore, the acronym becomes the thing it's referencing. Let's use the acronym *AMA* ("ask me anything") to illustrate this concept. As a traditional acronym, AMA would look like you posting on Instagram: "AMA!"—that is, "You can ask me anything and I will answer your questions." In this way, the acronym stands as the symbol for the original phrase.

People who speak different languages have different color terms than those who speak English. The color blue is familiar to most English speakers—both in their vocabulary and as a recognized color. English speakers use the word *blue* to refer to shades ranging from cyan to sky to navy to midnight blue. In Vietnamese and in Korean, a single word refers to blue and green. Japanese speakers use the word *ao* to refer to blue, but the color they are referencing is (for English speakers) green. Finally, Russian speakers do not have a single word for the range of colors that English speakers denote as blue; instead, they have one word for light blue and another for dark blue.

The Sapir-Whorf hypothesis, although complex, is not universally accepted by people who study language. For example, critics point out that Inuits may have a large number of words for snow because of their view of snow or because they actually have more varieties of snow in their world. Artists may have more color terms, and printers more words for different fonts, simply because of their work and environment. Thus, the critics note, thought and language may not be intimately related, but experience and language are. They believe our need to describe our environment and the items within it cause us to create language to do so.

Sapir-Whorf hypothesis A theory that our perception of reality is determined by our thought processes, our thought processes are limited by our language, and therefore language shapes our reality and our behaviors.

LANGUAGE ORGANIZES REALITY

Because you cannot account for all the individual things in the world when you speak, you lump them into groups; thus, all four-legged pieces of furniture with seats and backs are called "chairs." Following is an example of how language would help you organize the process of identifying someone in a crowd:

"See that person over there?"

"Which one?"

"The tall one."

"The one with short brown hair?"

"No, the shorter one with shoulder-length hair and glasses."

Language is used to organize the things you notice about a person, which can include height, hair color, and adornment.

You cannot think of your own identity without words because you are symbolically created through language. Your existence emerges through language, yet language is an inadequate means of describing you. You can describe yourself as "a Muslim," an "Italian Roman Catholic," or a "nontraditional student who is also a veteran," but those words say nothing about your height, weight, age, gender, personality, IQ, ambitions, or dreams. Thus, language creates us, without capturing the complexities of our identities. It takes further interaction and additional time, effort, and communication to understand our identities.

LANGUAGE IS ARBITRARY

denotative meaning
The agreed-upon meaning or dictionary meaning of a word.

connotative meaning
An individualized or personalized meaning of a word, which may be emotionally laden.

To understand language, you need to understand how words engender meaning. Words are arbitrary: they have no inherent meanings; they have only the meanings people give them. For instance, in the English language, a person who was diagnosed with cancer and successfully went through treatment is often referred to as a "survivor" or someone who "battled cancer." These terms are arbitrary, yet they evoke strong emotions. Some people see these terms as a source of strength and hope; others believe they reduce the focus on the long-term effects of diagnoses like cancer by assuming that cancer is something that is beaten once and for all.[8]

When many people use a word to represent an object or idea, the word is included in the dictionary. The agreed-upon meaning, or dictionary definition, is called the **denotative meaning**. Including a word in the dictionary, however, neither keeps its meaning from changing nor tells you the **connotative meaning**—an individualized or personalized meaning that may be emotionally laden. Connotative meanings are meanings others have come to hold because of personal or individual experience. For example, the word *love* holds vastly different meanings for people because of their unique experiences with that concept, despite the agreed-upon denotative meaning that can be found in a dictionary.

To understand connotative meaning further, consider the language that relational couples create. In a romantic relationship, partners may have nicknames for each other, special terms for activities in which they participate, and unique ways to communicate private thoughts in public settings. Yet some relationships require language to illustrate their uniqueness or legitimization in ways that are more *discourse dependent,* meaning that they need language to explain them because they are less traditionally understood.[9] For example, two married women who have children may feel the need to "discursively manage" how their children refer to each parent or how others refer to them as parents. Diana Breshears, a family communication scholar, offers a rationale for this necessity in that the identities of less traditionally formed families are challenged and scrutinized more in our society than are the identities of more traditionally formed families, so less traditionally formed families may require more frequent and expansive language to maintain a positive identity.[10]

Language is symbolic. The words we choose are arbitrary and based on an agreed-upon connection between them and the object or idea we are referencing. Language varies based on a variety of features of the communicators, including their relational history. For example, you may call someone "Grandma" who is not biologically related to you, or you may choose to have your children call one of your best friends "Aunt" as a symbolic gesture to represent how close that person is to you and your family. Researchers have termed the people who are outside blood and legal ties but are considered family *voluntary kin.*[11]

Language and its meaning are personal. Each person talks, listens, and thinks in a unique language (and sometimes several), which contains slight variations of its

• Words can have both denotative and connotative meanings.

Ballysmascanlon/Getty Images

agreed-upon meanings and which may change each minute. It is shaped by your culture, country, neighborhood, job, personality, education, family, friends, recreation, gender, experiences, age, and other factors. The uniqueness of each individual's language provides valuable information as people attempt to achieve common, shared meaning. But because language is so personal, it can also present some difficulties in communication.

The meanings of words also vary when someone uses the same words in different contexts and situations. For example, *glasses* might mean "drinking glasses" if you are in a kitchen but most likely means "eyeglasses" if you are at the optometrist's office. Semanticists say that meaning emerges from context. However, in the case of language, context is more than just the situation in which the communication occurs: context includes the communicators' histories, relationships, thoughts, and feelings.

LANGUAGE IS ABSTRACT

Words are abstractions, or simplifications of what they stand for. Words stand for ideas and things, but they are not the same as those ideas and things. People who study meaning say "the word is not the thing." Semanticist S. I. Hayakawa introduced the "ladder of abstraction," which illustrates that words fall somewhere on a continuum from concrete to abstract.[12] Figure 3.1 shows an example of a ladder of abstraction for a dog named Bentley. The words used to describe him become increasingly abstract as you go up the ladder.

A challenge with abstract language is that it can lead to increased polarization. In recent years, this has become more apparent in political discourse in the United States and in other countries. Currently, the discourse surrounding various issues can be highly abstract, yet we often offer and desire either-or, us-them, or with-against solutions in our responses, perhaps in an attempt to appear more concrete in our positions on these issues. For example, in the United States there is considerable conversation about border security, but it is difficult to determine what is desired when people talk about the need for this type of security. Does being in favor of a concrete border wall to stop undocumented immigration mean that you must be against all immigration? Does being against a border wall mean that you must be in support of open borders? It may be difficult to determine your stance on this issue when there is a lack of clarity surrounding what is meant or desired by the term *border security*. Perhaps you have engaged in debates with friends and family members about this issue and realized that you are, in fact, in favor of the same ideal but are using different words to describe the situation. In the next section we discuss ways to enhance clarity when you are speaking.

Figure **3.1**

The ladder of abstraction.

Source: Adapted from Hayakawa, S. I. (1978). *Language in thought and action*. Orlando, FL: Harcourt Brace Jovanovich.

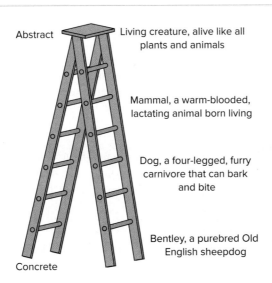

Abstract — Living creature, alive like all plants and animals

Mammal, a warm-blooded, lactating animal born living

Dog, a four-legged, furry carnivore that can bark and bite

Bentley, a purebred Old English sheepdog

Concrete

engaging diversity

Learning New Language Through Song

Software developers are increasingly discovering new ways to make learning another language easier. In doing so, they are opening up new opportunities for intercultural communication. You have likely heard of the language learning programs Babble, Google Translate, or Rosetta Stone, but have you ever thought about singing as a way to learn another language? Now you can download apps like Univoice to listen to and sing songs in another language. Research has shown that this improves your ability to learn a language because you practice pronouncing words and receive instant feedback on your performance. Language instructors believe that tools like this are entertaining and educational and will help with language learning.

Source: PR Newswire Association LLC. "Univoice to unveil new language learning app @ SXSW Founder Louis Black's home." March, 2019. www.prnewswire.com

Language to Avoid When Speaking

When you are verbally communicating, it is important to avoid statements with grammatical errors and the use of slang, clichés, euphemisms, profanity, jargon, regionalisms, and gender-biased, racist, heterosexist, and ageist language. Overall, an important goal for the ways in which you use language should be to use language that is inclusive, rather than exclusive, of others.

GRAMMATICAL ERRORS

Oral communication, in some situations, does not require the same attention to grammar as does written communication. For example, to hear people say, "Can I go with?" and "We're not sure which restaurant we're going to" are common, but neither of these sentences is desirable in written communication. "May I go with you?" and "We're not sure to which restaurant we're going" are correct but sound too formal when spoken in everyday conversation. Although we are often corrected for making grammatical errors in our writing, we are rarely corrected for poor grammar when speaking. On the other hand, some verbal grammatical errors are more obvious than others—for example, "I told him I ain't gonna do it" or "Could you pass them there peanuts?" Communicators who make such errors may find that others form negative opinions about them. Grammatical errors are thus particularly problematic in more formal situations or when another person is assessing your competence. When you are in a classroom, a job interview, or a new relationship, grammatical errors may result in negative perceptions about your credibility as a speaker.

Let's tackle a few of the most common grammatical errors in speaking *and* the correct way to say the same thing.

- Pronoun possession confusion: "Its a beautiful day" should be "It is a beautiful day" or "It's a beautiful day."
- Subject-verb agreement: "Department stores, coffee shops, and salons employs outgoing personnel" should be "Department stores, coffee shops, and salons employ outgoing personnel."
- Then versus than: "If I leave for work now, than I won't be late" should be "If I leave for work now, then I won't be late."

We will look next at words that are a bit too casual for formal presentations but that can slip into your speech if you are not careful, because you might be accustomed to using them every day.

SLANG

slang
Informal, casual language used among equals with words typically unsuitable for more formal contexts.

Slang is informal, casual language used among equals with words typically unsuitable for more formal contexts. In other words, you certainly use slang among friends around campus, but such language may be inappropriate in front of a more formal audience. Consider these examples:

- "You're extra" is slang for "You are being overly dramatic."
- "He was decked in a bar fight" is slang for "He was knocked down hard in a bar fight."

- "My friend clapped back at me on Instagram" is slang for "My friend responded to something negative I said about him on Instagram."
- "The person I met last week slid into my DMs and asked me out" is slang for "The person I met last week direct messaged me on social media and asked me out on a date."[13]

If you want to see hundreds more examples of slang, just type the word *slang* into an online search engine.

CLICHÉS

A **cliché** is an expression that has lost originality and force through overuse. Common clichés include "No pain, no gain," "Beauty is only skin deep," "Another day, another dollar," and "If you love something, set it free." So many clichés exist that avoiding them would be impossible in your day-to-day conversations, and doing so is unnecessary. Clichés can be a shorthand way to express a common thought. But clichés may be unclear to individuals who are unfamiliar with the underlying idea, and they are usually ineffective in expressing ideas in fresh ways.

The following are a few examples of common American clichés. We provide them here not because we want you to use them, but because we want you to think of more original ways to express your ideas:

- all in a day's work
- airing dirty laundry
- the rest is history
- all's fair in love and war
- when it rains, it pours
- an apple a day keeps the doctor away
- at the drop of a hat
- there's an app for that

If you want to see more examples of clichés, just type the word *cliché* into an online search engine.

EUPHEMISMS

Like clichés, euphemisms can confuse people who are unfamiliar with their meanings. A **euphemism** is a socially acceptable synonym used to avoid language that would be offensive in a formal setting. Euphemisms enter the language to "camouflage the naked truth."[14] Most people use euphemisms in their everyday language. Euphemisms frequently substitute for short, abrupt words; the names of physical functions; or the terms for some unpleasant social situations. Although euphemisms are frequently considered more polite than the words for which they are substituted, they distort reality.[15] Below are a few examples from the military, government, business, and sports contexts:

- Military: "Friendly fire" means "killed by your own soldiers" (decidedly unfriendly)
- Government: "undocumented worker" means "illegally in the country" (worker can be deported)
- Business: "preowned" means "used" (and possibly a "junker," a wrecked car)
- Sports: "negative yardage" means "thrown for a loss" (an embarrassing reversal)

Euphemisms are not necessarily to be avoided. Although they can disguise the meaning a person is attempting to convey, they can also substitute for rude or obnoxious commentary. Euphemisms, especially unique euphemisms, can add interest to a conversation. They can also reinforce relational closeness as friends and colleagues regularly use similar euphemisms.

- Slang is frequently used in informal situations.
Fancy/Alamy Stock Photo

cliché
An expression that has lost originality and force through overuse.

euphemism
A more polite, pleasant expression used instead of a socially unacceptable form.

PROFANITY

profanity
A type of swearing that uses indecent words or phrases.

The word *profane* comes from a Latin word meaning "outside the temple." Thus, **profanity**, or verbal obscenities, is a type of swearing that uses indecent words or phrases. Certainly, some people participate in groups in which profanity is common, as it is with the people on *The Real Housewives* TV series. But when you are speaking to people outside your "group"—especially in professional interviews, work teams, or public speaking situations—the use of profanity can offend. Profanity, like slang, may provide a vehicle for establishing group norms, gaining attention, or developing relational closeness in some settings, but it can also make you immediately lose credibility in other situations. Overall, remember that who the speakers are and where they use profanity can alter its effects.[16]

JARGON

jargon
Language particular to a specific profession, work group, or culture and not meant to be understood by outsiders.

Jargon is the language particular to a specific profession, work group, or culture and is not meant to be understood by outsiders. Doctors, for example, often use medical jargon when they talk to each other about diseases, medications, and procedures. Yet when they talk to patients it is often advantageous for doctors to adapt their use of jargon and use language that their patients can understand.

You should consider jargon that you use on the job and how you would translate that jargon to an audience of listeners who were unfamiliar with your work. Very likely, everyone in your class uses some jargon that is unfamiliar to others in the class, but in a communication course the idea is to know how to relate, define, and explain so that your audience learns what you are talking about.

REGIONALISMS

regionalisms
Words and phrases specific to a particular region or part of the country.

Regionalisms are words and phrases specific to a particular region or part of the country. Linguist professor Catherine Davis states that the way we speak is one of the ways that we share with others where we are from and our regional identification.[17] The word *coke* in Texas has the same meaning as *soda* in New York and *pop* in Indiana. When people from different parts of the country try to talk with each other, clarity can break down. Some of us move with frequency from one region of the country to another; others tend to stay in one area. You may believe that you will never leave your home state but then find that you are transferred for a new job. Careful listening, which is almost always a good idea, is especially important when you move to a new region. You can fairly easily identify and learn to use language that is particular to a location. Regionalisms encourage group membership for those who use them.

gender-biased
language
Language that privileges a certain gender over another.

racist language
Language that insults a group because of its race or ethnicity.

• Although medical jargon may obstruct communication with patients, nonverbal cues can provide comfort.

Wavebreak Media Ltd/123RF

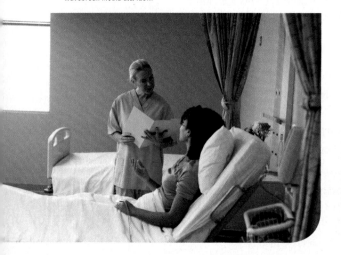

Perhaps the easiest way to illustrate regionalisms is to show the many ways in which people in different areas of the United States refer to those submarine sandwiches that become *hoagies* in Philadelphia, *po' boys* in New Orleans, *grinders* in Boston, *torpedoes* in Los Angeles, *wedgies* in Rhode Island, and *heroes* in New York City.[18] Listen before you order your food or drink when you change locations, because your language can mark you as an outsider.

GENDER-BIASED, RACIST, HETEROSEXIST, AND AGEIST LANGUAGE

Language can communicate prejudice and even silence some members of marginalized groups while privileging other groups.[19] **Gender-biased language**, or gender-specific language, is language that privileges one gender over another; **racist language** is language that insults a group because of its race or ethnicity; **heterosexist language** is language that implies that everyone is heterosexual; and **ageist language** is language that denigrates people for being young or old. Whereas some of the other unique language choices have both positive and negative features, language that is gender-biased, racist, heterosexist, or ageist tends to have only negative consequences. In addition to avoiding these forms of language, you should be mindful about language that privileges able-bodiedness.

Avoid generalizations and stereotypes—beliefs based on previously formed opinions and attitudes—that all members of a group are more or less alike. Your language can unintentionally suggest gender. The language used surrounding gender can recognize or silence the diverse landscape of gender identification. For example, people who identify with a gender or genders different from the one that was assigned to them at birth can fall under the *trans** umbrella, where the asterisk represents all forms of trans identity. Using the term *trans** in spoken (and written) language recognizes the incredibly diverse community and widely varying self-identification.[20]

One example of gender-biased language is the common use of the phrase *hey guys* to greet a group of women or a mixed-gender group. Reporter Joe Pinsker found through interviews that some people believe that the phrase is exclusionary and troubling for trans* and gender-nonconforming individuals.[21] Additionally, many women in male-dominated industries view the term as exclusionary. Some workplaces have begun using technology to resist the use of the phrase. For example, a group of employees who use a shared messaging app during the work day created a customized response that had a bot ask a question such as "Did you mean *you all*?" any time someone typed in "hey guys." Pinsker notes that this example illustrates that organizations are also paying attention to the language used by their members. Linguistics professor John McWhorter indicated to Pinsker that people are beginning to think more deeply about terms they use in everyday language. He acknowledged that, though the meaning of the word *guys* is changing to be considered gender-neutral by many, it still retains a male connotation. To address this concern, some people are opting to use innately gender-neutral terms such as *folks* or *y'all*. In fact, some linguists suggest that "y'all" might eventually become the new plural for "you."[22] Ultimately, using gender-neutral language can promote inclusion.

Racist language seeks to devalue individuals or groups of people based on race or ethnicity. It is important to avoid using racist language as you communicate with others. This is of particular concern given increased instances of hate speech, stereotypic language, and hate crimes reported in the United States.[23] In particular, hate speech is a severe form of negative language that attempts to degrade and dehumanize people, often in ways that are attributed to race.[24] Although hate speech may seem like an extreme example of language use, researchers suggest that hate speech can be viewed on a continuum from subtle and unconscious communication on one end to hate messages and speech on the other end. Viewed in this way, some everyday conversations can

heterosexist language
Language that implies that everyone is heterosexual.

ageist language
Language that denigrates people for being young or old.

communicating with agility

Names and Pronunciation

One way to be adaptable in your communication is to identify and practice new ways of approaching commonly occurring situations. This will ensure that you are prepared to do something a different way than you've done in the past.

For example, it's likely you have been in a situation where you or someone else mispronounced a person's name. How did you and the other person react? Was the error ignored or corrected? If you think you could have reacted differently, what might that have looked like?

Ruchika Tulshyan, founder of the inclusion strategy firm Candour, says that if you are unsure how to pronounce a name, you should simply ask the person. Because names often have cultural significance, she also suggests that this is one way to practice antiracism and allyship. Doing so ensures you are using clear and inclusive language that respects the person's identity.

Source: Wazwaz, N. (2021, April 8). Why pronouncing names correctly is more than common courtesy. *NPR.* www.npr.org/2021/03/12/976385244/why-pronouncing-names-correctly-is-more-than-common-courtesy

include subtle language that may not intend to do harm but can be perceived as racist. As you communicate, avoid using offensive slang related to race; telling racist jokes associated with lifestyle, food, or clothing; and using outdated language to describe groups. It is a best practice to use the terms that are currently acceptable to those groups being discussed.[25]

Similarly, straight people should not decide terms used to reference gay, lesbian, and bisexual people. The visibility of gay, lesbian, and bisexual people has increased in the general cultural, political, and social arenas; yet in many cultures language has masked that reality. At the same time, many people intentionally or unintentionally assume heterosexual orientations in their language choices. If you are not a member of this community, you may not be sensitive to your language that privileges heterosexuality. Rather than assuming someone's sexual orientation, consider using gender-neutral terms such as *partner, companion,* and *significant other* instead of *husband, wife, girlfriend,* and *boyfriend.*

Ageist language is also problematic. Today many people in their 60s, 70s, and even 80s continue to have active lives, many of which include paid labor or service obligations. The workforce, partly because of the economy and partly because of the improved health of older people, is becoming more age-diverse. Ageist language in the workplace negatively affects worker productivity and corporate profitability.[26] In interpersonal communication, ageism is evident in language that infantilizes older people and diminishes their concepts of themselves as vigorous and vital. For example, perhaps you have overheard someone talking slower and louder to an older adult at the grocery store when it clearly wasn't necessary to do so. Communication accommodation theory (CAT) states that this is over-accommodation, or adapting communication beyond what is needed in a given situation.[27] Finally, the use of terms such as *grandma* and *gramps* for older people to whom you are not related signals a bias based on age.[28] Conversely, in the workplace, ageism can occur when organizational practices are biased against younger employees.[29] This can be evident in language such as *kid, girl,* or *boy* or other language that suggests people of a certain, older age are more qualified for leadership roles or opportunities than are those who are younger.

It is important to recognize that the names for different kinds of language are not mutually exclusive; that is, a particular expression can fit in more than one category. Can you see how the brief sentence "How's it going?" can be a cliché and perhaps even a regionalism? Nonetheless, these categories provide a vocabulary you can use to describe the language you hear every day.

building **behaviors**

Test Your Ability to Recognize Weaknesses in Language

To determine how well you understand the uses of language discussed in this section, complete the following quiz. Identify which weakness is displayed in the sentence: clichés, euphemisms, slang, jargon, regionalisms, or gender-biased, racist, heterosexist, or ageist language.

1. This show gives me the feels.
2. These kids today can't lead a team. They can't take their eyes off their screens.
3. She's a cute chick.
4. Don't add insult to injury.
5. The rebel group advocates ethnic cleansing.
6. I'll have a pop with my slice.
7. Who is the reporting authority?
8. That old lady almost ran me over.
9. To a woman: Who's your boyfriend?
10. This patient will need to be intubated.
11. Better late than never.
12. Let me get my tennies and we'll go for a run.
13. I can really burn rubber.
14. I was laid off from work due to right-sizing.

Answers:
1. slang; 2. ageism; 3. gender-biased language; 4. cliché; 5. euphemism; 6. regionalism; 7. jargon; 8. ageism; 9. heterosexist language; 10. jargon; 11. cliché; 12. regionalism; 13. slang; 14. euphemism

Improving Language Skills

You can make specific changes in your language usage that will help you become a more effective communicator. One change you can make is to be descriptive in your language rather than judgmental. Another change is to be concrete in your use of language by using dating and indexing. Finally, you can change your use of language by understanding and practicing the difference between observation and inference.

USE DESCRIPTIVENESS

Descriptiveness is the practice of describing observed behavior or phenomena instead of offering personal reactions or judgments. You can be descriptive in different ways: by checking your perceptions, paraphrasing, using operational definitions, and defining terms.

descriptiveness
The practice of describing observed behavior or phenomena instead of offering personal reactions or judgments.

Check Your Perceptions

One of the most common ways you can be descriptive is through simple perception checks. To communicate effectively with another person, you and the other person need to have a common understanding of an event that has occurred or a common definition of a particular phenomenon. You can check with others to determine whether their perception is the same as yours. Here is a simple process you can follow to check your perceptions about others:

1. Describe the behavior you see and hear.
2. Describe how the behavior is making you feel.
3. Offer two possible explanations for why you think the behavior is occurring.
4. Ask the other person for clarity.

Paraphrase

Paraphrasing can also help you improve your use of descriptive language. **Paraphrasing** is restating another person's message by rephrasing the *content* and *intent* of the message and the feelings of the speaker. Paraphrasing is not simply repeating exactly what you heard. Paraphrasing allows the other person—the original speaker—to make corrections, in case you misinterpreted what was said or the other person's feelings. The original speaker must actively listen to your paraphrase to determine if you understood the content and intent of the message and the feelings behind the message adequately.

paraphrasing
Restating another person's message by rephrasing the content or intent of the message.

It is likely that you have practiced paraphrasing regularly in your everyday life through texting, instant messaging, and tweeting, because these forms force you to paraphrase longer messages into very brief ones. But the important element about paraphrasing in general is not so much being brief as capturing the intended meaning and feelings of the other person's message. Thus, a paraphrase really requires a response about whether it was reasonably accurate. Even a simple statement such as "Do you want to celebrate tonight by going out to eat?" invites a paraphrase such as "Do you mean you want to celebrate by eating tonight at an expensive restaurant?"—to which the original speaker says, "I do want to celebrate, and I do want to go out tonight, but not necessarily to an expensive restaurant." Through statements, paraphrases, and responses to another's paraphrase, the pair increasingly arrive at the intent and content of the original statement about going out to eat tonight.

Use Operational Definitions

Another kind of descriptiveness involves using **operational definitions**—that is, definitions that identify something by revealing how it works, how it is made, or what it consists of. Suppose a professor's syllabus states that students will be allowed an excused absence

operational definition
A definition that identifies something by revealing how it works, how it is made, or what it consists of.

• Define potentially confusing terms to help accurately convey your meaning.

Laurence Mouton/Getty Images

for illness. A student spends a sleepless night studying for an exam in another course, misses class, and claims an excused absence because of illness. The student talks about being too tired to come to class, and the professor explains that illness is surgery, injury, a stomach bug, or a very bad headache. This operational definition of *illness* does not please the student, but it does clarify what the professor means by the term. In another example, a job can be operationally defined by its description. Even abstractions become understandable when they are operationalized. Saying that someone is a "hard worker" does not reveal much, compared with saying that someone turns work in on time, submits products that are exceptionally well written, and serves as a model employee.

Define Your Terms

Confusion can also arise when you use unusual terms or use words in a special way. If you suspect someone might misunderstand your terminology, you must define the term. In such an instance, you need to be careful not to offend the other person; simply offer a definition that clarifies the term. Similarly, you need to ask others for definitions when they use words in new or unusual ways.

Many terms that we see every day are not necessarily well understood. One student gave a presentation on the difference between "GMO" and "non-GMO" foods, terms that many people see on food labels without knowing the difference. By defining the two terms, the student helped the audience to understand labels that are regularly seen but rarely defined.

USE CONCRETE LANGUAGE

concrete language
Words and statements that are specific rather than abstract or vague.

A person who uses **concrete language** uses words and statements that are specific rather than abstract or vague. During a meeting at work in which a coworker is interrupting you, it is vague to say, "You are being rude." In contrast, it would be more advantageous to the conversation and your relationship with your coworker if you say, "You have interrupted me three times when I have begun to talk. I feel as though you do not consider my point of view as important as yours." The concrete statement describes the behavior being observed rather than evaluating the person engaging in the behavior.

Earlier in the chapter, semanticists were briefly mentioned. Count Alfred Korzybski started the field of general semantics with the noble purpose of improving human behavior through the careful use of language.[30] The general semanticists' contribution includes the use of more precise, concrete language to facilitate the transmission and reception of symbols as accurately as possible. Semanticists encourage practices that make language more certain to engender shared meanings. Two such practices are dating and indexing.

Dating

dating
Specifying when you made an observation, since everything changes over time.

frozen evaluation
An assessment of a concept that does not change over time.

Dating is specifying when you made an observation, which is necessary because everything changes over time. Often, you view objects, people, or situations as remaining the same. You form a judgment or view of a person, an idea, or a phenomenon and maintain that view, even though the person, idea, or phenomenon may have changed. Dating is the opposite of **frozen evaluation**, in which you do not allow your assessment to change over time. An example of a frozen evaluation is always seeing certain people as gossips because they once were. When using dating, instead of saying that something is always or universally a certain way, you state *when* you made your judgment and clarify that your perception was based on that experience.

For example, if you took a course with a particular instructor two years ago, any judgment you make about the course and the instructor must be qualified as to time. You may tell someone, "English 101 with Professor Jones is easy," but that judgment may no longer be true. Or suppose you went out with someone a year ago, and now your friend is thinking about going out with that person. You might say that this person is quiet and withdrawn, but that might no longer be accurate: time has passed, the situation is different, and the person you knew may have changed. You can prevent communication problems by saying, "Professor Jones didn't assign a lot of reading for me when I took her class two years ago," or, "Iman seemed quiet and withdrawn when we dated last year, but I haven't really seen Iman since."

Indexing

Indexing is identifying the uniqueness of objects, events, and people. Indexing simply means recognizing the differences among the various members of a group. Stereotyping, assuming that the characteristics of one member of a group apply to all members of a group, is the opposite of indexing. For example, you might stereotype by assuming that, because you have a good communication instructor, all instructors in the department are exceptional, but that might not be the case. Indexing can help you avoid such generalizations. You could say, "I have a great communication instructor. What is yours like?" Or instead of saying, "MacBook computers have a long battery life—I know because I own one," which is a generalization about all MacBook computers based on only one, try saying, "I have a MacBook that has a long battery life. How does your computer do on battery?" And rather than saying, "Firstborn children are more responsible than their younger siblings," try using indexing: "My older sibling is far more responsible than I am. Is the same true of your older sibling?"

communicating creatively

Personality Communicated

Are you an introvert? Or are you more of an extrovert? Or better yet, are you an ambivert? You may think that all the loudest people at a party are extroverts and all the quiet people reading books alone at the coffee shop are introverts. Although some people fall neatly into the ends of the introverted–extroverted personality spectrum, psychologist Robert McCrae suggests that 38% fall somewhere in between. These people are known as *ambiverts*—people who enjoy the solitude and focus of introversion and engage in the outgoing side of extroversion.

Psychologist Dan Pink called the ability to draw on the positives of both the "ambivert advantage." Research has shown that ambiverts are more effective at closing sales than both introverts and extroverts because they use appropriate levels of enthusiasm in their language when attempting to persuade customers and know when to listen and seek input. Think about where you fall on this spectrum and how that reflects the ways you use language to get others to listen to your ideas.

Sources: Gregoire, C. (2014, November 24). Yes, it's possible to be both an introvert and an extravert. *Huffington Post.* www.huffingtonpost.in/2014/11/24/both-introvert-and-extravert-ambivert_n_6177854.html; Grant, A. M. (2013, April 8). Rethinking the extraverted sales ideal: The ambivert advantage. *Psychological Science, 24*(6), 1024–1030. www.ncbi.nlm.nih.gov/pubmed/23567176

indexing
Identifying the uniqueness of objects, events, and people.

DIFFERENTIATE BETWEEN OBSERVATIONS AND INFERENCES

Another way to improve language skills is to discern between observations (descriptions of what is sensed) and inferences (conclusions drawn from observations). For example, during an internship fair, you might make observations about how various interviewers are dressed or how they interact with each other. Perhaps you observe that some wear suits and ties, while others are more casual in jeans and dress shirts. As a result, you might infer that one company would have strict rules, while the other might be more flexible. You might also observe that people working at one booth are laughing and joking around with each other, so you infer that this might be a fun place to start your career. In all, you use the information you have gathered to draw some conclusions about the organization that each internship represents.

sizing things up

Role Category Questionnaire

This chapter taught you how language can be used to create organization and classification. To illustrate this function of language, the role category questionnaire asks you to describe two college instructors, one of whom you consider your favorite and one you consider your least favorite. For both instructors, you should use sentences to describe what makes these people your favorite and least favorite teachers.

When researchers asked students to do this activity, they found that students commented on the age of least favored instructors more than that of favored instructors. Other researchers used 14 million student reviews on RateMyProfessor.com to create an interactive chart that allows users to search for any word and how often it appears by gender and discipline. Overall, words such as *brilliant* and *knowledgeable* are mostly attributed to men and *bossy*, *ugly*, and *helpful* are largely attributed to women. Ultimately, these unconscious biases go beyond students

and teachers to feedback sessions and performance reviews. Benjamin Schmidt, author of the chart, points out that what people write is culture-bound, meaning that it is influenced by one's culture.

Now look at what words, phrases, and labels you used to describe your two instructors. Did you allude to their age, gender, race or ethnicity, physical features, or personality characteristics? If language shapes reality, then what meaning do you attribute to the number of sentences that were inspired by each instructor? This exercise has no right or wrong answers. A guide for interpreting your responses appears at the end of the chapter.

Sources: Edwards, C., & Harwood, J. (2003). Social identity in the classroom: An examination of age identification between students and instructors. *Communication Education, 52*(1), 60–65. Miller, C. C (2015, February 7). Is the professor bossy or brilliant? Much depends on gender. *New York Times.* www.nytimes.com/2015/02/07/upshot/is-the-professor-bossy-or-brilliant-much-depends-on-gender.html#:~:text=Men%20are%20more%20likely%20to,annoying%20or%20as%20playing%20favorites

be ready... for what's next

Is It All About You or Us in the Job Interview?

At this point in the chapter you should feel more confident in your ability to use language more effectively in your everyday life. Yet it's also important that you think about how this ability can promote or hinder your next step in your professional career.

As you are probably well aware, there are more qualified job applicants than there are jobs. One way to set yourself apart from the rest is through the words you use to answer interview questions. Leading business executives offer the following advice for answering two common interview questions:

Interviewer Questions

1. "What has been your biggest professional success so far, and why?"

The interviewer wants to hear *we,* rather than *I,* because *we* highlights that you are a team player.

2. "What has been your biggest failure so far, and why?"[31]

The interviewer wants to hear *I,* rather than *they,* because *I* signals accountability and ownership on your part rather than blaming.

Using pronouns correctly can reveal what kind of employee and team member you are likely to be for the company. Therefore, be mindful of how you respond to these questions.

Source: Fischer, A. (2015, March). These are the two most important words in a job interview. *Fortune.* http://time.com/3728845/job-interview-words/

Chapter Review & Study Guide

Summary

In this chapter you learned the following:

1. Language is a collection of symbols, letters, and words with meanings that are governed by rules and are used to communicate. It is arbitrary, organizes reality, is abstract, and shapes perceptions.

2. People sometimes use language poorly, which can present a barrier to communication. Examples include the following:

   - Grammatical errors
   - Slang
   - Clichés
   - Euphemisms
   - Profanity
   - Jargon
   - Regionalisms
   - Gender-biased, racist, heterosexist, and ageist language

3. You can change and improve your use of language by

   - being more descriptive.
   - being more concrete.
   - differentiating between observations and inferences.

Key Terms

Ageist language
Cliché
Concrete language
Connotative meaning
Culture
Dating
Decode
Denotative meaning
Descriptiveness
Encode

Euphemism
Frozen evaluation
Gender-biased language
Heterosexist language
Indexing
Jargon
Language
Operational definition
Paraphrasing
Phatic communication

Pragmatics
Profanity
Racist language
Regionalisms
Sapir-Whorf hypothesis
Semantics
Slang
Syntax

Study Questions

1. Which of the following is *not* a characteristic of language?

   a. It proves reality.
   b. It organizes reality.
   c. It can be arbitrary.
   d. It can be concrete.

2. Because messages can vary depending on the situation, to examine the context of the communication is important. This concept is called

   a. syntax.
   b. pragmatics.
   c. semantics.
   d. encoding.

3. Which statement reflects the relationship between language and culture?

   a. Language does not progress in response to the needs of the culture, but culture does progress in response to language.
   b. Language is a minor way that we learn about our culture.
   c. Culture creates a lens through which we perceive the world and create shared meaning in our language.
   d. Language and culture are not related.

4. When doctors communicate with technical language, they are using

   a. profanity.
   b. euphemisms.
   c. clichés.
   d. jargon.

5. One way to improve language skills is to restate the content of the other person's message, a process called

   a. defining your terms.
   b. paraphrasing.
   c. using concrete language.
   d. indexing.

6. A word's dictionary definition is its _____ meaning, and an individualized or personalized definition is its _____ meaning.

   a. denotative; connotative
   b. denotative; abstract
   c. connotative; denotative
   d. concrete; connotative

7. Communication may be hindered in all the following cases *except* when we use

   a. improper grammar.
   b. descriptive language.
   c. clichés.
   d. gender-biased language.

8. Dating is important because

   a. people tend to view situations as remaining the same over time.
   b. ideas change little or not at all over time.
   c. people's attitudes remain the same.
   d. people can clarify a perception based on a particular experience in a specific context.

9. Which of the following terms refers to indecent or offensive language?

   a. profanity   c. clichés
   b. jargon   d. regionalisms

10. When you talk about observed behavior instead of offering personal reactions, you are

    a. drawing inferences.
    b. being concrete.
    c. using descriptiveness.
    d. being judgmental.

Answers:

1. (a); 2. (b); 3. (c); 4. (d); 5. (b); 6. (a); 7. (b); 8. (d); 9. (a); 10. (c)

Critical Thinking

1. In some cultures there are many words to describe one thing (for example, snow), but can we talk about something if we have no words to describe it?

2. The Sapir-Whorf hypothesis says that our language shapes our reality. One fact about language is that we use more abstract language to describe groups that are dissimilar to us and more concrete language to describe groups that are similar to us. Why do you think this occurs? Does this practice enhance or reduce the use of stereotypes in our language?

3. In what ways, if any, does the use of anonymous posting on social media contribute to the negative and positive use of language?

4. Does the practice of frequently using abbreviations and acronyms reduce or enhance group identification? Does this practice reduce or enhance relationship development and intergenerational communication?

Sizing Things Up Scoring and Interpretation

Role Category Questionnaire

One way that language might influence how you perceive the world around you is through implicit categories and hierarchies found in language systems. For instance, you might comment that a dog is "cute" and "friendly." Those terms indicate that you place the dog into certain categories and perhaps even rank the dog into some sort of hierarchy. The role category questionnaire (RCQ) provides one mechanism through which you can identify such hierarchies in how you use language.

The traditional method of scoring the RCQ involves circling and then counting each separate construct used to identify the "liked" person and the "disliked" person. A construct is any adjective or other description that you use to describe the people you analyze. All constructs should be counted, even duplicates, although you should not count descriptions of physical appearance. The total value represents a differentiation score; higher scores represent higher levels of cognitive complexity.

To further explore the hierarchical nature of language, think about the following questions:

1. Are the numbers of constructs you identified for "liked" and "disliked" people generally the same or different for both people? Why?

2. In comparing your scores with others in your class, or even friends you ask to complete the RCQ, did gender affect the number of constructs? Are there differences between you and students with other characteristics, such as those who are older, are younger, or have different ethnic backgrounds?

3. Do differentiation scores differ depending on whether the person being described is male or female?

You may develop other ways of analyzing results. For instance, you may observe that there are clusters (that is, hierarchies) of constructs that people use to describe others.

References

1. Dutko, P., Ver Ploeg, M., & Farrigan, T. (2012). Characteristics and influential factors of Food Deserts. United States Department of Agriculture. https://www.ers.usda.gov/webdocs/publications/45014/30940_err140.pdf#page=5

2. Yeoman, B. (2018, September 14). The hidden resilience of "food desert" neighborhoods. Civil Eats. https://civileats.com/2018/09/14/the-hidden-resilience-of-food-desert-neighborhoods/

3. Manning, J., Stern, D., & Johnson, R. (2017). Introduction to social identity in the instructional context. In M. L. Houser & A. M. Hosek (Eds.), *Handbook of instructional communication: Rhetorical and relational perspectives* (pp. 170–182). Taylor & Francis.

4. Schilling-Estes, N. (2002). American English social dialect variation and gender. *Journal of English Linguistics, 30,* 122–137.

5. Whorf, B. L. (1956). Science and linguistics. In J. B. Carroll (Ed.), *Language, thought and reality* (pp. 207–219). MIT Press.

6. Samovar, L. A., & Porter, R. E. (2000). *Intercultural communication: A reader* (9th ed.). Wadsworth. Whorf, Science and linguistics.

7. Walsh, H. (2014, July). 33 cool abbreviations you should know (JIC you didn't already). *Huffington Post.* http://www.huffingtonpost.com/2014/07/24/dictionary-of-modern acronyms_n_5614544.html

8. Ellingson, L. (2017). Realistically ever after: Disrupting the dominant narratives of long-term cancer survivorship. *Management Communication Quarterly, 3,* 321–327.

9. Galvin, K. M. (2006). Diversity's impact on defining the family: Discourse-dependence and identity. In L. H. Turner & R. West (Eds.), *The family communication sourcebook* (pp. 3–19). Sage.

10. Breshears, D. (2010). Coming out with our children: Turning points facilitating lesbian parent discourse with their children about family identity. *Communication Reports, 23*(2), 79–90.

11. Braithwaite, D. O., Bach B. W., Baxter, L. A., DiVerniero, R., Hammonds, J., Hosek, A. M., Willer, E., & Wolf, B. (2010). Constructing family: A typology of voluntary kin. *Journal of Social and Personal Relationships, 27,* 388–407.

12. Hayakawa, S. I. (1978). *Language in thought and action.* Harcourt Brace Jovanovich.

13. urbandictionary.com. (2018).

14. Rothwell, J. D. (1982). *Telling it like it isn't: Language misuse and malpractice/what we can do about it.* Prentice-Hall, 93.

15. Euphamisms. (2015, July 20). http://literarydevices.net/euphemism/

16. Rothwell, J. D. (1971). Verbal obscenity: Time for second thoughts. *Western Speech, 35,* 231–242.

17. Jarenwattananon, P. (2018, March). Y'all heart? An argument for the great southern pronoun. *NPR.* https://www.npr.org/2019/03/09/701701825/yall-heard-an-argument-for-the-great-southern-pronoun?utm_source=facebook.com&utm_medium=social&utm_campaign=npr&utm_term=nprnews&utm_content=20190401&fbclid=IwAR3BV2uqpZxziKOzqC42mubpByLjEOmb2hCqDlt2M0y_RkApDPJ6Q1QXF60

18. Nordquist, R. (2011). Regionalisms. http://grammar.about.com/od/rslg/regionalismterm.htm

19. Hecht, M. L. (Ed.). (1998). *Communicating prejudice.* Sage. Taylor, A., & Hardman, M. J. (Eds.). (1998). *Hearing muted voices.* Hampton Press.

20. Trans* Guide. (2015). http://www.ohio.edu/lgbt/resources/transgender.cfm

21. Pinsker, J. (2018, August 23). The problem with "hey guys." *The Atlantic.* https://www.theatlantic.com/family/archive/2018/08/guys-gender-neutral/568231/

22. Jarenwattananon, P. (2018, March). Y'all heart? An argument for the great Southern pronoun. *NPR.* https://www.npr.org/2019/03/09/701701825/yall-heard-an-argument-for-the-great-southern-pronoun?utm_source=facebook.com&utm_medium=social&utm_campaign=npr&utm_term=nprnews&utm_content=20190401&fbclid=IwAR3BV2uqpZxziKOzqC42mubpByLjEOmb2hCqDlt2M0y_RkApDPJ6Q1QXF60

23. Nir, S. M. (2016, December 8). Finding hate crimes on the rise, leaders condemn vicious acts. *New York Times.* http://www.nytimes.com/2016/12/05/nyregion/hate-crimes-are-on-the-rise-in-new-york-city.html

24. Haas, J. (2012). Hate speech and stereotypic talk. In H. Giles (Ed.), *The handbook of intergroup communication* (pp. 128–140). Routledge.

25. University of Queensland-Australia. (n.d.). Use of outdated terminology. http://www.uq.edu.au/about/use-of-outdated-terminology

26. When words get old: Ageist language. (2008, September 9). *NewsBlaze.* http://newsblaze.com/story/2008090913190200009.wi/topstory.html

27. Giles, H., Coupland, N., & Coupland, J. (1991). Accommodation theory: Communication, context, and consequence. In H. Giles, J. Coupland, & N. Coupland (Eds.), *Contexts of accommodation: Developments in applied sociolinguistics* (pp. 1–68). Cambridge University Press.

28. Nuessel, F., & Stewart, A. V. (1999). Research summary: Patronizing names and forms of address used with older adults. *Names, 47,* 401–409.

29. McNamara, T. K., & Williamson, J. B. (2012). Is age discrimination ever acceptable. *Public Policy & Aging Report, 22*(3), 9–13.

30. Korzybski, A. (1994). *Science and sanity.* Institute of General Semantics.

31. Fortune Media IP Limited.

Prostock-studio/Shutterstock

nonverbal communication

When you have read and thought about this chapter, you will be able to

1. define nonverbal communication.

2. analyze how verbal and nonverbal codes are related.

3. describe types of nonverbal codes.

4. explain two sources of ambiguity in meaning for nonverbal codes.

5. apply strategies for improving your nonverbal communication.

This chapter focuses on the role of nonverbal codes in communication. The chapter first looks at the problems that can occur in interpreting nonverbal codes. Next, some of the major nonverbal codes are identified and defined, including bodily movement and facial expression, bodily appearance, space, time, touching, and vocal cues. The chapter concludes with a discussion of some solutions to the problems you might encounter in interpreting nonverbal codes.

Steve Stine is a successful entrepreneur in Fargo, North Dakota. In the early 1990s, Steve started giving guitar lessons and eventually grew his business to the point of having over 110 students each week. Around 2011, Steve realized that, as a business person, practicing musician, and father, he simply did not have enough time in the day to grow his business more with in-person lessons. Therefore, Steve took his business online and now formally teaches guitar to thousands of students at any given time through his digital company GuitarZoom.com. In addition to his formal lessons, Steve maintains a vibrant social media presence where his free lessons reach millions of guitar students; he recently surpassed more than 20 million views on YouTube and more than 500,000 subscribers to GuitarZoom.com.

Steve does not look like a typical business person or music teacher. He has long hair and tattoos and typically wears some sort of rock-and-roll t-shirt. As Steve described himself during a personal interview with one of your authors, "I look basically the same as I did in high school. I've always had long hair. I've always been that rock guy. I grew up in the '80s, and all of those bands were my idols."

Steve explained how his appearance evolved from his various experiences and passions by stating, "I'm a family man. I love to play on stage and I love to teach, and I think my outer appearance is who I ended up being—its remnants of who I was and who I think I still am." He went on to discuss the relationship between his physical appearance and the multiple roles he enacts as a business person, father, and teacher: "I have never fit that norm. . . . I'm very recognizable because of the way I look. My kids wouldn't want me to get a haircut anyway. . . . The exterior of me comes off as this rock and roll guy. I wouldn't say that person doesn't exist. . . . I've never wanted to change with the norm, because I'm not even sure what that is. I have just always been me, in and out." When asked if his physical appearance had a relationship to his business success, he responded, "If I wear [my] glasses on video, everyone comments on how weird that looks. If I put my hair in a ponytail, people freak out and ask if I cut it. So, [my appearance] has become part of the norm. . . . I wouldn't change because it would sell more [lessons]."[1]

Nonverbal communication is an important part of the messages we use. Steve's story illustrates how aspects of nonverbal communication, such as clothing, hairstyle, and ornamentation such as tattoos, are important elements of how we define ourselves and communicate who we are to others. In this chapter you will learn about the broad range of nonverbal communication options available to you as a communicator.

Steve Stine. Clothing, hair, and ornamentation such as tattoos are some of the many ways we communicate nonverbally.

Photo courtesy of Steve Stine

nonverbal communication
The process of using messages other than words to create meaning with others.

communicating creatively

Nonverbal Creativity During the COVID-19 Pandemic

Think for a moment about how nonverbal communication was affected by the pandemic. In the initial stages of the pandemic, we were physically isolated from one another, which meant that something as meaningful as a comforting hug from a friend or family member was not always possible. As the pandemic progressed, face masks were common, which hampered our ability to read facial expressions. Much of our communication took place through remote online technologies, which presented their own challenges for nonverbal communication. Nonverbal communication scholar Valarie Manusov argued that COVID-19 has had such an effect on nonverbal communication that we need new understandings of how nonverbal communication plays a role in our behaviors.

Consider some of the creative ways that you adapted your nonverbal behaviors to the pandemic. Did you create a special background for remote video calls? Did you take time to send someone a handwritten letter because you could not physically be with them? Did you use a certain mask to help fill in the lower part of your face, or was solid black or white your approach? As the pandemic abated, did you resume the practice of shaking hands? The pandemic was a contextual factor that dramatically impacted our communication; however, it also resulted in creative ways to compensate, some of which will likely remain with us for decades.

The COVID-19 pandemic forced us to be creative in how we use common nonverbal symbols.

Cat Box/Shutterstock

Source: Manusov, V. (2022). Love in the time of COVID-19: What we can learn about non-verbal behaviour from living with a pandemic. In R. J. Sternberg & A. Kostić (Eds.), *Nonverbal communication in close relationships: What words don't tell us* (pp. 251–275). Palgrave Macmillan/Springer Nature. doi: 10.1007/978-3-030-94492-6_10

Defining Nonverbal Communication

This chapter focuses on nonverbal communication and the relationship between nonverbal and verbal communication. The chapter should help you make sense of the most frequently seen nonverbal codes, as well as provide you with some suggestions for improving your nonverbal communication. Let us begin with a definition of nonverbal communication and a brief discussion of its significance.

Nonverbal communication is the process of using messages other than words to create meaning with others. Nonverbal communication can include behaviors that you see, such as facial expressions and gestures; things that you hear, such as vocal volume or the speed of talking; and even nonword vocalizations, such as "ahh" and "umm." You know the importance of nonverbal communication in your own life. Each day you use facial expressions, a light touch or handshake, or even an emoji or animated GIF to express meaning using something other than words. Although it is difficult to estimate precisely how much communication is verbal or nonverbal, researchers estimate that between 60% and 90% of our daily communication behaviors are conducted nonverbally.[2] In fact, scholars argue that nonverbal communication cues show critical aspects of our personality that are perceived by others as we engage in any type of face-to-face communication.[3] Also, recent research shows that nonverbal communication is one of the most important communication behaviors related to successful interpersonal relationships,[4] strong rapport with customers,[5] effective leadership,[6] and successful outcomes in many other types of situations.

Would you estimate that up to 90% of your own communication is nonverbal? Some have started to question the accuracy of that estimate. David Novak, a communication researcher and consultant, warns that attempting to specify percentages associated with particular communication codes, such as verbal and nonverbal communication, is misleading.[7] Because he adopts a meaning-centered definition of communication, similar to the one you learned about in Chapter 1, Novak argues that the process of communication prevents simple distinctions between verbal and nonverbal symbols. When you say "hello" to another person, that verbal symbol combines with nonverbal cues to create meaning through the communication process. The verbal and nonverbal symbols create meaning together, not separately, which makes any attempt at specifying a percentage of communication associated with any particular type of symbol unproductive. Novak concludes that the most productive way to understand nonverbal communication is to consider how it works in combination with other symbols, like words, to create meaning.

How Verbal and Nonverbal Communication Are Related

Both verbal and nonverbal communication are essential for effective interactions with others. How are the two related? Researchers have studied the roles of verbal and nonverbal communication to determine which was more important in a persuasive message. Results showed that the content (verbal portion of the speech) was more important in determining the effect of the speech. However, emphasis and gestures added to some aspects of the presentation and caused the speech to be viewed as lively and powerful.[8] In other words, both the verbal and the nonverbal elements of the speech were considered important for different reasons.

Verbal and nonverbal communication behaviors work together in the communication process to create meaning. That connectedness between verbal and nonverbal communication behaviors can be described in six ways: to repeat, to emphasize, to complement, to contradict, to substitute, and to regulate. Let us consider each of these briefly.

Repeating occurs when the same message is sent verbally and nonverbally. For example, you say that you are "excited" while also displaying a big smile and using animated hand gestures. Or you point to a paper when saying to your instructor, "I need to turn this assignment in early because I will be away during our next class meeting." Pointing at the paper nonverbally repeats the words *this assignment.*

Emphasizing is the use of nonverbal cues to strengthen your message. Hugging a friend and telling him that you really care about him is a stronger statement than using either words or bodily movement alone.

Complementing is different from repeating in that it goes beyond duplicating the message in two channels. With complementing, the verbal and nonverbal codes add meaning to each other and expand the meaning of either message alone. For example, during an intense conversation you might hold up your palm to signal "stop" while you are making a point, signaling to the other person to avoid interrupting you. The verbal and nonverbal messages are independent but add meaning to each other for the listener.

Contradicting occurs when your verbal and nonverbal messages conflict. Often this occurs accidentally. If you have ever been angry at a teacher or parent, you may have stated verbally that you were fine—but your bodily movements, facial expression, and use of space may have exposed your actual feelings. Contradiction occurs intentionally in humor and sarcasm. Your words provide one message, but your nonverbal delivery tells how you really feel.

Substituting occurs when nonverbal codes are used instead of verbal codes. You roll your eyes, stick out your tongue, gesture thumbs down, or shrug. In most cases your intended message is fairly clear.

Regulating occurs when nonverbal codes are used to monitor and control interactions with others. For example, you look away when someone else is trying to talk and you are

repeating
Sending the same message both verbally and nonverbally.

emphasizing
The use of nonverbal cues to strengthen verbal messages.

complementing
Using nonverbal and verbal codes to add meaning to each other and to expand the meaning of either message alone.

contradicting
Sending verbal and nonverbal messages that conflict.

substituting
Using nonverbal codes instead of verbal codes.

regulating
Using nonverbal codes to monitor and control interactions with others.

not finished with your thought. You walk away from someone who has hurt your feelings or made you angry. You nod your head and encourage another person to continue talking.

As we communicate, we naturally allow our verbal and nonverbal communication to interact using these techniques. However, they are not perfectly distinct categories. The raised-palm "stop" signal used while talking is both a complementary message and a regulating message. A tone of voice to suggest sarcasm is both complementing and contradicting. So, while you should understand how these relationships between verbal and nonverbal messages work, you should not assume that they represent perfectly distinct categories of behavior.

To better understand the relationship between verbal and nonverbal communication, consider how people use **American Sign Language (ASL)** to communicate mainly with people who are deaf or hard of hearing. As explained by the U.S. Department of Health and Human Services, ASL is a complete language system that uses hand signs coupled with discrete facial expressions and body postures to convey meaning.[9] Although precise census data do not exist, researchers generally estimate that more than 500,000 people use ASL in the United States.[10] Individuals use many of the same types of nonverbal behaviors in ASL that we discuss in this chapter. However, because the language system has discrete meanings associated with particular hand signals, facial expressions, and body movements, ASL is different from the nonverbal communication behaviors we discuss. Nonverbal communication has many potential symbols and meanings, whereas ASL has much greater clarity on those issues for those who have learned the language. Stated simply, the multiple potential meanings interpreted from nonverbal communication make it distinct from ASL, which has nonverbal language rules that are more similar to verbal communication.

With this understanding of how nonverbal and verbal communication are related, we now turn to specific types of nonverbal behaviors, or what we call "codes."

Nonverbal Codes

American Sign Language (ASL)
A complete language system that uses hand signs coupled with discrete facial expressions and body postures to convey meaning.

nonverbal codes
Messages consisting of symbols that are not words, including nonword vocalizations.

Nonverbal codes are messages consisting of symbols that are not words, including nonword vocalizations. Bodily movement and facial expression, physical attractiveness, the use of space, the use of time, touch, vocal cues, and clothing and artifacts are all nonverbal codes. Let us consider these systematic arrangements of symbols that have been given arbitrary meaning and are used in communication.

BODILY MOVEMENT AND FACIAL EXPRESSION

kinesics
The study of bodily movements, including posture, gestures, and facial expressions.

The study of bodily movements, including posture, gestures, and facial expressions, is called **kinesics**, a word derived from the Greek word *kinesis,* meaning "movement." Some popular books purport to teach you how to "read" nonverbal communication so that you will know, for example, who is sexually aroused, who is just kidding, and whom you should avoid. Nonverbal communication, however, is more complicated than that. Interpreting the meaning of nonverbal communication is partly a matter of assessing the other person's unique behavior and considering the context. You don't just "read" another person's body language; instead, you observe, analyze, and interpret before you decide the probable meaning.

Assessing another person's unique behavior means that you need to know how that person usually acts. A quiet person might be unflappable even in an emergency situation. A person who never smiles might not be unhappy, and someone who acts happy might not actually be happy. You need to know how the person expresses emotions before you can interpret what that person's nonverbal communication means.

To look more deeply into interpreting nonverbal communication, let us consider the work of some experts on the subject: Albert Mehrabian, Paul Ekman, and Wallace Friesen.

Mehrabian studied nonverbal communication by considering its connection to how we display liking, status, and responsiveness.[11]

- *Liking* is expressed by forward leaning, a direct body orientation (such as standing face-to-face), close proximity, increased touching, relaxed posture, open arms and body, positive facial expression, and direct eye contact. Liking is essential in communication. For example, people who work for supervisors who engage in these kinds of behaviors tend to have higher self-reported satisfaction than do people who work for managers who do not use these behaviors.[12]

- *Status,* especially high status, is communicated nonverbally by large gestures, relaxed posture, and infrequent eye contact. During a conversation, an individual with high status might feel more comfortable using forceful gestures than would someone in a low-status role.

- *Responsiveness* is exhibited by movement toward the other person, spontaneous gestures, shifts in posture and position, and facial expressiveness. In other words, the face and body provide positive feedback to the other person.

Ekman categorized movement on the basis of its functions, origins, and meanings.[13] The categories include emblems, illustrators, affect displays, regulators, and adaptors.

- **Emblems** are nonverbal movements that substitute for words and phrases. Examples of emblems are a beckoning first finger to mean "come here," an open hand held up to mean "stop," and a forefinger and thumb forming a circle to mean "OK." Be wary of emblems; they may mean something else in another culture.

  emblems
  Nonverbal movements that substitute for words and phrases.

- **Illustrators** are nonverbal movements that accompany or reinforce verbal messages. Examples of illustrators are nodding your head when you say yes, shaking your head when you say no, stroking your stomach when you say you are hungry, and shaking your fist in the air when you say, "Get out of here!" These nonverbal cues tend to be more universal than many in the other four categories of movement.

  illustrators
  Nonverbal movements that accompany or reinforce verbal messages.

- **Affect displays** are nonverbal movements of the face and body used to show emotion. Watch people's behavior when their favorite team wins a game, listen to the door slam when an angry person leaves the room, and watch men make threatening moves when they are very upset with each other but don't really want to fistfight.

  affect displays
  Nonverbal movements of the face and body used to show emotion.

- **Regulators** are nonverbal movements that control the flow or pace of communication. Examples of regulators are starting to move away when you want the conversation to stop, gazing at the floor or looking away when you are not interested, and yawning and glancing at your watch when you are bored. Turn taking in conversations is generally managed with gestures, gaze, and touch. However, turn-taking regulators vary from one culture to another.[14]

  regulators
  Nonverbal movements that control the flow or pace of communication.

- **Adaptors** are nonverbal movements that usually involve the unintended touching of our bodies or manipulations of a body artifact that serves some physical or psychological need. Some people habitually play with their hair, others adjust their glasses, and some even constantly rub or scratch their hands. We often use these adaptors without knowledge, but they could signal deep thought, anxiety, or distraction to observers.

  adaptors
  Nonverbal movements that usually involve the unintended touching or manipulating of our bodies or artifacts to fulfill some physical or psychological need.

Finally, Ekman and Friesen determined that people's facial expressions provide information to others about how they feel.[15] Consider the smile. Findings are overwhelming that a person who smiles is rated more positively than a person who uses a neutral facial expression. Indeed, you are more likely to be offered a job if you smile.[16]

Perhaps a more provocative finding is that people pay more attention to faces that are angry or threatening and less attention to neutral facial expressions. When adults were presented with multiple faces, including some that appeared threatening, they were more likely to attend to the angry faces than they were to others. Even children have this bias.[17] This response to threatening stimuli may have evolved as a protective means to help people avoid danger.

What is the effect of showing disagreement with a negative facial expression and head shaking, compared to using a neutral facial expression? In a study investigating opponents who stood behind a political speaker and displayed neutral facial expression, occasional negative facial expression, constant negative expression, or both negative and positive expression, surprising results were found. When either negative or negative and positive expressions were used, respondents viewed the speaker as less credible, less appropriate, and less skillful in debate than those with neutral expressions.[18] In other words, some positive facial expressions did not lessen the negative response toward the speaker.

Facial expressions are important in conveying information to others and in learning what others are feeling. Bodily movement and orientation add to that information by suggesting how intense the feeling might be. When you are able to observe and interpret both facial expression and bodily movement, you gain a fuller understanding of the other person's message.

The connection between facial expression and body movement is commonly observed through head nodding. Take a moment to observe others in conversation and pay particular attention to head movements. Nodding the head up and down often acts as an illustrator to accompany verbal agreement. This type of illustrator is so innate that its importance even carries over into virtual environments. Researchers in the United Kingdom programed avatars in a virtual world to closely follow realistic head nodding behaviors observed in humans, such as having the head nods happen in response to what the other person is saying.[19] When study participants engaged in virtual interactions with those avatars, they reported significantly more trust and liking of those characters than they did for avatars that had more random and preprogrammed head movements. Head movements and facial expressions are important cues that help establish shared meaning with others.

communicating with agility

Showing Cooperation by Synchronizing Facial Expressions

Think of situations where you are trying to work something out with another person. Perhaps it is deciding on a place for dinner, negotiating a price with a merchant, or trying to get agreement from your supervisor on how to complete a task. What behaviors might help you signal a cooperative outcome? Recent research reported in the journal *Emotion* found that when two participants began to synchronize, or mirror, their nonverbal behaviors, cooperative outcomes were more likely. This was even true when participants were not allowed to talk. In fact, when not allowed to talk, participants increased their nonverbal behaviors and were far more likely to synchronize their nonverbal expressions. With this knowledge, you can be more agile as a communicator by carefully monitoring another's nonverbal behaviors and synchronizing yours with theirs when appropriate. In situations where you agree with what the other person is saying, you can attempt to mirror their nonverbal expressiveness to implicitly signal cooperation.

Facial expressions show us what others are feeling.

MStudioImages/Getty Images

Source: Zhao, F., Wood, A., Mutlu, B., & Niedenthal, P. (2022). Faces synchronize when communication through spoken language is prevented. *Emotion*. doi: 10.1037/ emo0000799

PHYSICAL ATTRACTIVENESS

Physical attractiveness is the perceived desirability of another person's outward physical appearance. How people perceive physical attractiveness remains subjective—it is in the eye of the beholder. However, scholars and researchers point to evolutionary psychology to explain general features of attractiveness.[20] For instance, males who have a rugged, athletic look may be perceived as stronger and more formidable, which could be linked to historic indications of someone who would be good at protecting a family or tribe. In fact, one study found that perceptions of physical strength, tallness, and leanness accounted for approximately 80% of raters' perceptions of physical attractiveness.[21] For females, similar historic patterns have been observed, where female body types that appear more fit may be perceived as desirable because, historically, that could signal greater chances of survivability. In essence, evolutionary perspectives on physical attractiveness assert that fitness in both males and females is desirable and, thus, is perceived as more attractive.

If historic perceptions of attractiveness guide the impressions of others, what communicative value could attractiveness have? In contrast to the evolutionary psychology scholars, other researchers who generally adopt a social construction perspective suggest that attractiveness is dictated not by evolution but, rather, by the social norms of a culture and situation. For instance, marketing researchers Haiyang Yang and Leonard Lee argued that our perceptions of beauty change regularly based on our impressions of what others think is attractive—they are socially constructed.[22] Such group-based norms could explain why certain hair styles or clothing choices can cause a person to be perceived as more attractive to those who share similar norms and preferences than to others— they are consistent with group norms. By implication, we do use artifacts and other aspects of our appearance as signals to others about our adherence to culturally created norms, and those behaviors can affect how others perceive our attractiveness.

This culturally based understanding of beauty has profound implications. In her 1991 book *The Beauty Myth,* feminist scholar Naomi Wolf criticized the ways in which beauty standards have been used as a tool to control how women dress and how they style their makeup and hair, as well as the standards by which beauty has been evaluated.[23] In essence, Wolf sought to challenge the culturally accepted norms of beauty. In 2018, applied ethicist Heather Widdows published a follow-up to Wolf's book titled *Perfect Me: Beauty as an Ethical Ideal* in which she argued that in today's digital culture, beauty standards have been heightened to an ethical ideal by which people judge themselves as good or bad, successful or unsuccessful.[24] Importantly, both Wolf and Widdows observed that many beauty standards are created by commercialized notions of what constitutes

building behaviors

DON'T FORGET THE

Partly because of the COVID-19 pandemic, nearly everyone has dramatically increased their online communication activity with apps like Microsoft Teams and Slack. Because chat messages are replacing some of the communication that formerly took place in person or over a phone, we naturally adapt our communication behaviors. For instance, the pandemic caused many people to drastically improve their emoji game.

Researchers exploring the use of emojis in the workplace found that the amount of emoji use by employees could accurately predict the likelihood that an employee would quit. Not surprisingly, employees who used more emojis in their workplace chats were far less likely to resign in comparison to employees who used few emojis. Although the researchers observed this relationship, their study could not definitely conclude why this observed relationship existed.

One possibility is that if you are more engaged by work, you are more likely to be engaged online and use more emojis. Think about how your use of emojis could play a role in your workplace satisfaction. If you frequently use emojis, how do you think your peers or even supervisors could react to you? By using emojis, you may create a perception of likability that causes others to engage with you more, which may improve your own engagement. Of course, too much of a good thing can appear frantic, so don't overdo it!

emoji: Yayayoyo/Shutterstock

Source: Lu, X., Ai, W., Chen, Z., Cao, Y., & Mei, Q. (2022). Emojis predict dropouts of remote workers: An empirical study of emoji usage on GitHub. *PLoS ONE, 17.* doi: 10.1371/journal.pone.0261262

physical attractiveness
The perceived desirability of another person's outward physical appearance.

beauty. Clothing, makeup, and other accessories and cosmetic procedures to enhance beauty are all enormous businesses. Others make money by convincing people to look a certain way, such as the fitness industry that promotes specific body norms achieved through memberships in gyms and fitness centers. In fact, some observers have argued that the privileged nature of beauty—meaning that beauty is expensive—has led to a normalization of dissatisfaction with our own bodies.[25]

Because contemporary research shows that perceptions of physical attractiveness change according to cultural norms, scholars have attempted to explore how easily those norms change. In an experiment designed to mimic a dating site, researchers asked participants to quickly rate the attractiveness of other people based on their pictures.[26] What they found was that any particular face was more likely to be rated as attractive if the previous face was also attractive; in contrast, a face was more likely to be rated as unattractive if the previous face was also rated as unattractive. This research indicates that physical attractiveness is, in general, an initial impression that we form and one that is highly influenced by the situation and context.

As a nonverbal code, physical attractiveness is rarely something that we directly control while we are communicating. However, the ways in which people perceive physical attractiveness is something that could influence communication, along with many other variables such as messages, effective listening, and the context. Although physical attractiveness may impact initial impressions, our perceptions of others are more complex and varied. In other words, as we get to know someone, our initial impressions of physical attractiveness have less of an impact as we learn more about the other person. Research reported in the *Journal of Personal Relationships* shows that when individuals have good personalities, others are more likely to view them as desirable friends and romantic partners and rate their physical attractiveness as higher than those with bad personalities.[27] Other recent studies have also shown that bias in favor of attractive job candidates can be counteracted by supposedly less attractive candidates who establish a more powerful nonverbal posture by being expressive, attentive, and confident.[28]

We can be optimistic that beauty standards are becoming more inclusive and diverse. One indication is that *People* magazine, known for its "Most Beautiful" issues, expanded the number of people included in the feature and renamed the issue "The Beautiful Issue." Editor Jess Cagle wrote in a preview of the issue, "[It] will feature beautiful women (and a few men) of all shapes, sizes and colors, and it will celebrate the most beautiful qualities of all: strength, humanity and artistry."[29] This change is important, and the hope is that such trends continue to the point that virtues are emphasized over commercially developed standards for how people look. As communicators, we have the ability to be part of such change. When we communicate with others, we can make choices about what we emphasize with respect to attractiveness. If we choose to focus on virtues other than commercialized norms of physical attractiveness, our small steps can be part of a larger societal change.

• Physical attractiveness is an important nonverbal attribute, but the media may distort realistic views of physical attractiveness.

Antonio de Moraes Barros Filho/WireImage/Getty Images

SPACE

Anthropologist Edward T. Hall introduced the concept of **proxemics**—the study of the human use of space and distance—in his 1966 book *The Hidden Dimension.*[30] Across scholarly writing on this topic, two concepts considered essential to the study of the use of space are territoriality and personal space.

proxemics
The study of the human use of space and distance.

- *Territoriality* refers to the need to establish and maintain certain spaces as your own. In a shared residence hall room, items on a common desk area mark territory. For example, you might place your notebook, pens, and tablet charger on the right side of the desk and your roommate might place books, a cell phone, and a laptop on the left side. While the desk is shared, you are each claiming part of the area. On a cafeteria table the placement of the plate, glass, napkin, and eating utensils marks the territory. In a neighborhood it might be fences, hedges, trees, or rocks that mark the territory. All are nonverbal indicators that signal ownership.

- *Personal space* is the personal "bubble" that moves around with you. It is the distance you maintain between yourself and others, the amount of space you claim as your own. Large people usually claim more space because of their size, and men often take more space than women. For example, in a lecture hall, observe who claims the armrests as part of their personal bubbles.

Hall was the first to define the four distances people regularly use while they communicate.[31] His categories have been helpful in understanding the communicative behavior that might occur when two people are a particular distance from each other. From the closest contact and least personal space to the greatest distance, Hall's categories are intimate distance, personal distance, social distance, and public distance.

- *Intimate distance* is a radius of 18 inches or less around a person, and it is used by people who are relationally close. Used more often in private than in public, this intimate distance is employed to show affection, to give comfort, and to protect. When we are attracted to others, we tend to try to stand or sit closer to them because being in intimate space zones has the potential to create positive perceptions, feelings of satisfaction, and closeness.[32]

- *Personal distance* ranges from 18 inches to 4 feet, and it is the distance used by most Americans for conversation and other nonintimate exchanges.

- *Social distance* ranges from 4 to 12 feet, and it is used most often to carry out business in the workplace, especially in formal, less personal situations. The higher the status people possess, the greater the distance they tend to place between themselves and others.

- *Public distance* exceeds 12 feet and is used most often in public speaking in such settings as places of worship, courtrooms, and convention halls. Professors often stand at this distance while lecturing.

Distance, then, is a nonverbal means of communicating everything from the size of your personal bubble to your relationship with the person to whom you are speaking or listening. A great deal of research has been done on proxemics. Generally speaking, people's sex, size, and similarity seem to be among the important determiners of how they use personal space and perceive the use of personal space by others.

Gender also affects the amount of space people are given and the space in which they choose to communicate.[33] Those who orient more toward masculinity tend to take up and control more space, whereas those who do not orient that way tend to take up and control less space. Even children learn to use space for safety and protection. Because gender orientations are often associated with biological sexes (men tend to be masculine and women tend to be feminine), you can easily see these characteristics play out if you observe others. Men tend to keep distance from other men when talking whereas women tend to stand closer, especially when talking with other women. When children are talking to parents, they tend to stand very close.

Your relationship to other people is related to your use of space. You stand closer to friends and farther from people you dislike. You stand farther from strangers, authority figures, high-status people, physically challenged people, and people from racial groups different from your own. You stand closer to people you perceive as similar or unthreatening, and that closeness communicates trust.

The physical setting also can alter the use of space. People tend to stand closer together in large rooms and farther apart in small rooms.[34] In addition, physical obstacles and furniture arrangements can affect the use of personal space. We even use space when online. By friending, following, or connecting with people on social media, you invite them into your virtual space through your personal profile. Connecting online is similar to taking a step closer to someone in a face-to-face situation. Some apps even use location tagging to help us know when we are in proximity to contacts and friends.

The cultural background of the people communicating also must be considered in the evaluation of personal space. Hall was among the first to recognize the importance of cultural background when he was training American service personnel for service overseas. In 1963, he wrote:

> Americans overseas were confronted with a variety of difficulties because of cultural differences in the handling of space. People stood "too close" during conversations, and when the Americans backed away to a comfortable conversational distance, this was taken to mean that Americans were cold, aloof, withdrawn, and disinterested in the people of the country. USA housewives muttered about "waste-space" in houses in the Middle East. In England, Americans who were used to neighborliness were hurt when they discovered that their neighbors were no more accessible or friendly than other people, and in Latin America, exsuburbanites, accustomed to unfenced yards, found that the high walls there made them feel "shut out." Even in Germany, where so many of my countrymen felt at home, radically different patterns in the use of space led to unexpected tensions.[35]

Cultural background can result in great differences in the use of space and in people's interpretation of such use. As our world continues to shrink, more people will be working in multinational corporations, regularly traveling to different countries, and interacting with others from a variety of backgrounds. Sensitivity to space use in different cultures and quick, appropriate responses to those variations are imperative.

TIME

chronemics
Also called temporal communication; the way people organize and use time and the messages that are created because of their organization and use of that time.

Temporal communication, or **chronemics**, is the way that people organize and use time and the messages that are created because of their organization and use of that time. Time can be examined on a macro level. How do you perceive the past, future, and present? Some people value the past and collect photographs and souvenirs to remind themselves of times gone by. They emphasize how things have been. Others live in the future and are always chasing dreams or planning future events. They may be more eager when planning a vacation or party than they are when the event arrives. Still others live in the present and savor the current time. They try to live each day to its fullest and neither lament the past nor show concern for the future.

One distinction that has been drawn that helps us understand how individuals view and use time differently is the contrast between monochronic and polychronic people. *Monochronic* people view time as very serious and they complete one task at a time. Often their jobs are more important to them than anything else—perhaps even including their families. Monochronic people view privacy as important. They tend to work independently, and they rarely borrow or lend money or other items. They may appear to be secluded or even isolated. Although we cannot generalize to all people, we may view particular countries as generally monochronic. They include the United States, Canada, Germany, and Switzerland. In contrast, *polychronic* people work on several tasks at a time. Time is important, but it is not revered. Interpersonal relationships are more important to them than their work. Polychronic individuals tend to be highly engaged with others. Again, without generalizing to all people, countries such as Egypt, Saudi Arabia, Mexico, and the Philippines tend to be polychronic.

building behaviors

Time Flies

We become better communicators as we are able to distinguish between others' varying behaviors. In the next week, observe at least three of your friends. Describe how each of them uses time differently. Do they tend to be more monochronic or polychronic? What cues did you use to make this assessment? How can you be more effective in your communication with them if they are monochronic? If they are polychronic? Consider adaptations that you can make when you communicate with people who are strongly monochronic or polychronic.

Your orientation toward time can affect how you relate with others. If you are a monochronic person who works or regularly communicates with a polychronic person, you both might feel frustrated with how the other person uses time.[36] However, when you communicate with others who follow your norms for time, you may have more positive perceptions of them. A group of communication researchers were interested in how students in the United States, a monochronic culture, perceived the issue of time, or chronemics, as it relates to email interactions with their teachers. In their study they found that when teachers responded more quickly to emails, students tended to perceive those teachers as more socially attractive, more competent, more caring, and of higher character.[37]

TOUCH

Tactile communication is the use of touch in communication. Because touch always involves invasion of another person's personal space, it commands attention. It can be welcome, as when a crying child is held by a parent, or unwelcome, as in sexual harassment. Our need for and appreciation of tactile communication start early in life.[38] Psychologist William Schutz observed:

> The unconscious parental feelings communicated through touch or lack of touch can lead to feelings of confusion and conflict in a child. Sometimes a "modern" parent will say all the right things but not want to touch the child very much. The child's confusion comes from the inconsistency of levels: if they really approve of me so much like they say they do, why don't they touch me?[39]

Researchers have found that the need for touch is both biologically and socially part of what it means to be human.[40] Because touch is an important signal of intimacy and affection, it fulfills our psychological and social needs for affection while calming us. A hug can be powerful and calming in the right circumstances.

For adults, touch is a powerful means of communication. Touch is usually perceived as positive, pleasurable, and reinforcing. The association of touch with the warmth and caring that began in infancy carries over into adulthood. People who are comfortable with

tactile communication
The use of touch in communication.

touch are more likely to be satisfied with their past and current lives. They are self-confident, assertive, socially acceptable, and active in confronting problems. Think about how you use nonverbal communication. Are you comfortable touching and being touched? Do you frequently hug others or shake hands with others?

Touch is part of many important rituals. In business settings, a handshake can signal commitment or agreement. At the conclusion of athletic games, players and coaches from opposing teams shake hands, bump fists, or even sometimes hug to reestablish camaraderie after competition.[41] In the Christian religious practice of baptism, there can range from as little as a touch on the head during the ceremony to as much as a total immersion in water. Rituals of touch permeate many aspects of our lives to such an extent that they become second nature.

Touch is also an important aspect of healing and caregiving. Physician Bernie Siegel wrote the following in his book on mind–body communication:

> I'd like to see some teaching time devoted to the healing power of touch—a subject that only 12 of 169 medical schools in the English-speaking world deal with at all . . . despite the fact that touch is one of the most basic forms of communication between people. . . . We need to teach medical students how to touch people.[42]

Siegel's appeal did not go unheard. A number of medical schools are now training their students to decode patients' nonverbal cues and to provide nonverbal communication, including touch, to their patients.[43] However, the results of the training are mixed; though students' awareness of nonverbal communication increases, their actual performance does not.[44]

Touch is typically perceived differently depending on gender. Although there are always individual differences in preferences and communication style, psychology researchers Matthew Hertenstein and Dacher Keltner observed the following:[45]

- Males tend to initiate touch more often than females.
- Women are more likely than men to perceive touch from an opposite-gender stranger as unpleasant.
- When women perceive touch as sexual from a male stranger, they are less likely to perceive the touch as friendly.
- When men are touched by a female stranger and perceive it as sexual, they tend to perceive the touch as friendly.

Whereas gender influences the social norms surrounding how touch is perceived, the communication setting is also important. For example, in business settings the concern of being accused of sexual harassment has eliminated a great deal of touch except for handshaking. When touch is used in such settings, the general nonverbal principle is that the higher-status individual gets to initiate touch, but touch is not reciprocal: the president might pat you on the back for a job well done, but in our society you don't pat back. We even see the importance of touch in online communication settings. Take a look at your Instagram feed and you will see how often pictures of people touching are posted. Indeed, new communication tools provide opportunities for hundreds or even thousands of people to witness our use of touch with others.[46]

Further, culture determines the frequency and kind of nonverbal communication. People from different countries handle nonverbal communication differently—even something as simple as touch.[47] Sidney Jourard, a respected humanistic psychologist, determined the rates of touch per hour among adults from various cultures. In a coffee shop, adults in San Juan, Puerto Rico, touched 180 times per hour, whereas those in Paris, France,

touched about 110 times per hour, followed by those in Gainesville, Florida, who touched about twice per hour, and those in London, England, who touched only once per hour.

Touch sends such a powerful message that it has to be handled with responsibility. Touch may be welcomed by some in work or clinical settings, but it is equally likely that touch is undesirable or annoying. Certainly, touch can be misunderstood in such settings, and perhaps even abused as a communication behavior.[48] When the right to touch is abused, it can result in a breach of trust, anxiety, and hostility.

VOCAL CUES

Nonverbal communication includes some sounds, as long as they are not words. We call them **paralinguistic features**—the nonword sounds and nonword characteristics of language. The prefix *para* means "alongside" or "parallel to," so *paralinguistic* means "alongside the words or language."

The paralinguistic feature examined here is **vocal cues**—all of the oral aspects of sound except words themselves. Vocal cues include the following:

- **Pitch:** the highness or lowness of your voice
- **Rate:** how rapidly or slowly you speak
- **Inflection:** the variety or changes in pitch
- **Volume:** the loudness or softness of your voice
- **Quality:** the unique resonance of your voice, such as huskiness, nasality, raspiness, or whininess
- **Nonword sounds:** "mmh," "huh," "ahh," and the like, as well as pauses or the absence of sound used for effect in speaking
- **Pronunciation:** whether or not you say a word correctly
- **Articulation:** whether or not your mouth, tongue, and teeth coordinate to make a word understandable to others (for example, without producing a lisp)

paralinguistic features
The nonword sounds and nonword characteristics of language, such as pitch, volume, rate, and quality.

vocal cues
All of the oral aspects of sound except words themselves.

pitch
The highness or lowness of the voice.

rate
The pace of your speech.

inflection
The variety or changes in pitch.

volume
The loudness or softness of the voice.

quality
The unique resonance of the voice, such as huskiness, nasality, raspiness, or whininess.

nonword sounds
Sounds like "mmh," "huh," and "ahh," as well as the pauses or the absence of sounds used for effect.

pronunciation
Saying a word correctly or incorrectly.

articulation
Coordinating one's mouth, tongue, and teeth to make words understandable to others.

enunciation
Combining pronuncia-
tion and articulation to
produce a word with
clarity and distinction.

silence
The lack of sound.

- **Enunciation:** whether or not you combine pronunciation and articulation to produce a word with clarity and distinction so that it can be understood (a person who mumbles has an enunciation problem)

- **Silence:** the lack of sound

These vocal cues are important because they are linked in our mind with a speaker's physical characteristics, emotional state, personality characteristics, gender characteristics, and even credibility. For example, when you talk to strangers on the telephone, you form an impression of how they might look and how their personality might be described. In addition, vocal cues, alone, have a persuasive effect for people when they are as young as 12 months.[49]

According to Kramer, vocal cues frequently convey information about the speaker's characteristics, such as age, height, appearance, and body type.[50] For example, people often associate a high-pitched voice with someone who is female, younger, and/or smaller. You may visualize someone who uses a loud voice as being big or someone who speaks quickly as being nervous. People who tend to speak slowly and deliberately may be perceived as being high-status individuals or as having high credibility.

A number of studies have related emotional states to specific vocal cues. Joy and hate appear to be the most accurately communicated emotions, whereas shame and love are among the most difficult to communicate accurately.[51] Joy and hate appear to be conveyed by fewer vocal cues, and this makes them less difficult to interpret than emotions such as shame and love, which are conveyed by complex sets of vocal cues. "Active" feelings, such as joy and hate, are associated with a loud voice, a high pitch, and a rapid rate. Conversely, "passive" feelings, which include affection and sadness, are communicated with a soft voice, a low pitch, and a relatively slow rate.

Personality characteristics also have been related to vocal cues. Dominance, social adjustment, and sociability have been clearly correlated with specific vocal cues.[52] Irony, by contrast, cannot be determined on the basis of vocal cues alone.[53]

Although the personality characteristics attributed to individuals displaying particular vocal cues have not been shown to accurately portray the person, as determined by standardized personality tests, our impressions affect our interactions. In other words, although you may perceive loud-voiced, high-pitched, fast-speaking individuals as dominant, they might not be measured as dominant by a personality inventory. Nonetheless, in your interactions with such people, you may become increasingly submissive because of your perception that they are dominant. In addition, these people may begin to become more dominant because they are treated as though they have this personality characteristic.

Vocal cues can help a public speaker establish credibility with an audience and can clarify the message. Pitch and inflection can be used to make the speech sound aesthetically pleasing, to accomplish subtle changes in meaning, and to tell an audience whether you are asking a question or making a statement, being sincere or sarcastic, or being doubtful or assertive. A rapid speaking rate may indicate you are confident about speaking in public or you are nervously attempting to conclude your speech. Variations in volume can be used to add emphasis or to create suspense. Enunciation is especially important in public speaking because of the increased size of the audience and the fewer opportunities for direct feedback. Pauses can be used in a public speech to create dramatic effect and to arouse audience interest. Vocalized pauses—"ah," "uh-huh," "um," and so on—are not desirable in public speaking and may distract the audience.

Silence is a complex behavior steeped in contradictions. During interpersonal conversations, public speeches, and group discussions, silence can be used strategically to your advantage. Intentionally being silent can create a dramatic pause to build drama or punctuate a point.[54] When presenting or discussing difficult information, silence can allow listeners time to process and give meaning to your statements. At the same time, silence may signal the dark side of communication. People in power, in dominant cultures, or in positions of authority may silence others. In fact, the act of silencing others is a powerful political tool that is used to oppress the poor, women, and social movements attempting to challenge political institutions.[55]

CLOTHING AND ARTIFACTS

Objectics, or object language, is the study of the human use of clothing and artifacts as nonverbal codes. **Artifacts** are ornaments or adornments you display that hold communicative potential, including jewelry, hairstyles, cosmetics, automobiles, canes, watches, shoes, portfolios, hats, glasses, tattoos, body piercings, and even the fillings in teeth. Your clothing and other adornments communicate your age, gender, status, role, socioeconomic class, group memberships, and personality. Dresses are seldom worn by men, low-cut gowns are not the choice of shy women, bright colors are avoided by reticent people, and the most recent Paris fashions are seldom seen in the small towns of America.

These cues also indicate the time in history, the time of day, the climate, and one's culture.[56] Clothing and artifacts provide physical and psychological protection, and they can be used to spur sexual attraction and to indicate self-concept. Your clothing and artifacts clarify the sort of person you believe you are. They permit personal expression, and they satisfy your need for creative self-expression.[57]

Many studies have established a relationship between people's clothing and artifacts and their characteristics. Conforming to current styles is correlated with a person's desire to be accepted and liked.[58] In addition, many people feel that clothing is important in forming first impressions.[59]

Perhaps of more importance are the studies that consider the relationship between a person's clothing and an observer's perception of that person. In an early study, clothing was shown to affect others' impressions of status and personality traits.[60] People also seem to base their acceptance of others on their clothing and artifacts. In another early study, women who were asked to describe the most popular women they knew cited clothing as the most important characteristic.[61] Although fashion has undoubtedly changed over time, this relationship between clothing and status has not. A recent study found that women continue to choose clothing based on how they think others will perceive those choices as representative of a place in a social hierarchy.[62]

How people use clothing and artifacts is highly dependent on culture. The dress of Muslim women, which tends to be modest and consist of loose and fairly heavy materials, is distinctive. Some Muslim women cover their entire bodies, including the face and hands, whereas others wear a simple hijab on their heads, with long sleeves and long skirts. Others modify this look with head scarves and Western-style clothing. Distinctive clothing is also present in some Asian cultures. Some Hindu Indian women wear dhotis and saris, at least for formal occasions. Although the skirts are long, frequently the middle area of the body can be glimpsed in these outfits. In America, women of the Mennonite and Amish cultures tend to wear plain clothing that stands in stark contrast to the popular apparel of the dominant culture. Both across cultures and within cultures, clothing norms can differ dramatically.

Body modifications are also a type of artifact. They include tattoos and piercings, which have been popular in recent years. Although they can be removed, the procedures may be both costly and time-intensive. What do tattoos signal to others? Some people might choose to adorn themselves with tattoos and piercings because they believe such artifacts add to their overall attractiveness. However, research suggests potential negative perceptions associated with tattoos and other body art. A group of European sociologists and psychologists exploring perceptions of tattoos on both males and females concluded that body art could

objectics
Also called object language; the study of the human use of clothing and artifacts as nonverbal codes.

artifacts
Ornaments or adornments you display that hold communicative potential.

• What do you conclude about this person based on the clothing and artifacts?

Medioimages/Photodisc/ Getty Images

signal affiliation with a subculture that emphasizes nonconformist behaviors such as sensation seeking and promiscuity.[63]

Historically, uses of clothing and other artifacts have been powerful tools for protest. In the recent history of American culture, women began to wear denim jeans as a sign of independence. More recently, fashion journalist Whitney Bauck explained how the fashion industry has increasingly made political statements through both actions and fashion trends.[64] For instance, major publishers in the fashion industry took stands against the sexual abuse of models and human rights violations against workers. Additionally, supporters of the #MeToo movement wore t-shirts with the movement hashtag to promote the empowerment of women who had been subjected to sexual harassment and assault. Uses of clothing and other artifacts have the potential to create powerful messages, but they can also create polarization. How would you feel if you encountered a person wearing a shirt or button using profanity to describe a political figure or one that read #BlackLivesMatter, #AllLivesMatter, or #BlueLivesMatter? Chances are, you would appreciate some more than others based on your personal convictions, and others may make you angry. Thus, how we use clothing and artifacts can be simple expressions of aesthetics or more complex messages about opinions on sensitive social and political issues.

The Ambiguity of Nonverbal Codes

Just as people have difficulty interpreting verbal symbols, they also struggle to interpret nonverbal codes. The ambiguity of nonverbal communication occurs for two reasons: people use the same code to communicate a variety of meanings, and they use a variety of codes to communicate the same meaning.

ONE CODE COMMUNICATES A VARIETY OF MEANINGS

The ambiguity of nonverbal codes occurs in part because one code may communicate several different meanings. For example, the nonverbal code of raising your right hand may mean that you are taking an oath, you are demonstrating for a cause, you are indicating to an instructor that you would like to answer a question, a physician is examining your right side, or you want a taxi to stop for you. Also consider how you may stand close to someone because of a feeling of affection, because the room is crowded, or because you have difficulty hearing. In these examples, the context, or situation, provides important information for how to interpret each code.

Recently, researchers interested in artificial intelligence (AI) have attempted to precisely decode the multiplicity of meanings associated with nonverbal communication.[65] Despite some successes, such as the ability for AI systems—and potentially even phone apps—to accurately read emotions through facial expressions, the task is daunting. When humans form a facial expression, they use an estimated 10,000 possible combinations of facial muscle movements. Like AI systems, humans naturally process such facial movements as codes that signal meaning. (Humans are currently more efficient than computers.) However, the complexity of so many simultaneous signals means that accurate perception and interpretation of such signals can be challenging, even for the best communicators.

A VARIETY OF CODES COMMUNICATE THE SAME MEANING

Nonverbal communication is not a science; any number of codes may be used to communicate the same meaning. One example is the many nonverbal ways by which adults communicate love or affection. You may sit or stand more closely to someone you love. You might speak more softly, use a certain vocal intonation, or alter how quickly you speak when you communicate with someone with whom you are affectionate. Or perhaps you choose to dress differently when you are going to be in the company of someone you love.

Cultural differences are especially relevant when we consider that multiple cues may be used to express a similar message. How do you show respect to a speaker in a public speaking situation? In some cultures listeners show respect when they avert their eyes; in other cultures listeners show respect and attention by looking directly at the speaker. You may believe that showing your emotions is an important first step in resolving conflict, whereas a classmate may feel that emotional responses interfere with conflict resolution. Although you may have a strong understanding of which codes carry certain meanings in your own culture, those meanings may change completely when interacting with someone from a different culture.

Improving Nonverbal Communication

Skills in being able to effectively interpret and respond to nonverbal cues vary greatly among individuals. You can improve your understanding of nonverbal communication, though, by being sensitive to context, audience, and feedback.

The *context* includes the physical setting, the occasion, and the situation. In conversation, your vocal cues are rarely a problem unless you have distracting speaking habits such as speaking too quickly and using filler words, or you have a speech disorder such as a stutter or a pronounced lisp. Paralinguistic features loom large in importance in small-group communication. For instance, you may need to adapt for distance by talking louder to be heard by people who are sitting far apart. Paralinguistic features are perhaps most important in public speaking because you have to adjust volume and rate, you have to enunciate more clearly, and you have to introduce more vocal variety to keep the audience's attention. The strategic use of pauses and silence is also more apparent in public speaking than it is in an interpersonal context in conversations or small-group discussion. In addition to your vocal cues, the context could affect other nonverbal communication. For example, intercultural contexts could determine the types of bodily movements that are considered appropriate. For instance, in Thailand there is a very specific nonverbal gesture, which looks similar to the "praying" gesture in America, that accompanies greetings and goodbyes.

This nonverbal symbol in Thailand is often used as a way of saying hello, whereas people in Western cultures often think of this as a nonverbal symbol for praying.
GIACOMO MORINI/Shutterstock

The occasion and physical setting also affect the potential meaning of a nonverbal cue. For example, when would it be appropriate for you to wear a cap over unwashed, uncombed hair, and when would doing so be interpreted as inappropriate? The distance at which you communicate may be different based on the setting and the occasion: you may stand farther away from people in formal situations when space allows but closer to family members or to strangers in an elevator.

The *audience* makes a difference in your nonverbal communication, so you have to adapt. When speaking to children, you must use a simple vocabulary and careful enunciation, articulation, and pronunciation. If you are speaking to an audience that includes people who are deaf or hard of hearing, you may need to speak louder or ask a sign-language interpreter to assist. Generally, children and older people in both interpersonal and public-speaking situations appreciate slower speech. Also, adaptation to an audience may determine your choice of clothing, hairstyle, and jewelry. For instance, a job interview will most likely require business attire to signal professionalism and credibility.

Your attention to giving *feedback* can be very important in helping others interpret your nonverbal cues that might otherwise distract your listeners. While you are giving a speech, your listeners' own descriptive feedback—giving quizzical looks, staring, or nodding off—can signal you to talk louder, introduce variety, restate your points, or clarify your message. You can even use nonverbal communication to give your audience feedback. Suppose that you ask the audience a question during the beginning remarks in your presentation, and no one offers an answer. Some speakers might raise their own hand to signal that they are actually seeking a response.

If your conversational partner or audience does not provide you with feedback, what can you do? Practice asking questions and checking on the perceptions of others with whom you communicate. Silence has many meanings, and you sometimes must take great effort to interpret the lack of feedback in a communicative setting. You can also consider your past experience with particular individuals or a similar audience. Do they ever provide feedback? Under what circumstances are they expressive? How can you become more accurate in your interpretation of their feedback?

Although this chapter only introduces you to nonverbal communication, you know that your success in college and in the workplace is dependent on your sensitivity to nonverbal cues and your ability to alter familiar nonverbal cues, given the context and the situation. The following are some suggestions you can use to begin analyzing and improving your own nonverbal communication behaviors:

1. Establish eye contact and demonstrate interest through bodily movement and the use of space and artifacts. A growing concern in our culture is the amount of

sizing things up

Berkeley Nonverbal Expressiveness Questionnaire

In this chapter you learned that nonverbal communication is used to express meaning generally and emotion in particular. Each statement below describes ways in which you express your emotions through nonverbal communication. Respond to each statement using the following scale. A guide for interpreting your responses appears at the end of the chapter.

1 = Strongly disagree
2
3
4 = Neutral
5
6
7 = Strongly agree

1. Whenever I feel positive emotions, people can easily see exactly what I am feeling.
2. I sometimes cry during sad movies.
3. People often do not know what I am feeling.
4. I laugh out loud when someone tells me a joke that I think is funny.
5. It is difficult for me to hide my fear.
6. When I'm happy, my feelings show.
7. My body reacts very strongly to emotional situations.
8. I've learned it is better to suppress my anger than to show it.
9. No matter how nervous or upset I am, I tend to keep a calm exterior.
10. I am an emotionally expressive person.
11. I have strong emotions.
12. I am sometimes unable to hide my feelings, even though I would like to.
13. Whenever I feel negative emotions, people can easily see exactly what I am feeling.
14. There have been times when I have not been able to stop crying even though I tried to stop.
15. I experience my emotions very strongly.
16. What I'm feeling is written all over my face.

Source: Gross, J. J., & John, O. P. (1997). Revealing feelings: Facets of emotional expressivity in self-reports, peer ratings, and behavior. *Journal of Personality and Social Psychology, 72*, 438.

time that people spend with their smart devices, which are artifacts. How much time do you spend on Instagram, Snapchat, and YouTube? Do you plan on "media-free" time while in class, while studying, and while at work? In a recent study, professors attempted to curtail the use of text messaging in class by using positive facial expressions, standing closer to the students, using a relaxed stance, and speaking in an animated manner, but these behaviors did not discourage the use of handheld devices.[66] Consider what you might do to show interest during all communication situations and to avoid being distracted by your phone or unintentionally signaling disinterest through other nonverbal behaviors.

2. Recognize that others may use time differently than you do. In general, it is important to be on time, especially in monochronic cultures such as the United States. You should also think about how your behaviors cause time-stress for others. Waiting until the last minute to ask a critical question, such as how to do an assignment or complete a job task, can cause stress on those on whom you depend.

3. Manage your time to maximize success. Whether you are budgeting time for school activities or attempting to balance your time between work and family, you must make choices that promote success in personal and professional areas. How you choose to budget your time signals to others what you deem as important and also influences how you are able to accomplish important tasks.

engaging diversity

Understanding Differences in Nonverbal Communication

A variety of characteristics can be used to identify distinctions among cultures—many of which include nonverbal differences in how we use gestures, space, touch, and even time. If you come from a country other than the United States, the amount of nonverbal adaptation you will need to undertake depends on how similar your culture is to U.S. culture. Although many nonverbal characteristics will likely be similar—the use of facial expression to convey emotion, for instance—there are also likely to be several differences. Understanding those differences can help you avoid misperceiving others and being misperceived. Key considerations include the following:

- *Americans tend to expect consistent uses of space.* In normal conversations, U.S. speakers tend to stay in Hall's personal distance zone. Standing closer can violate expectations and cause discomfort and unease; standing farther apart can be perceived as unfriendly. Unless you are very close to another person, touching is generally considered a violation of space rather than a signal of warmth, particularly among adults.

- *A greater emphasis is placed on verbal messages.* Although most communication is still done nonverbally during interactions, U.S. speakers tend to be verbally explicit in terms of describing feelings, opinions, and thoughts. A nonnative speaker may need to be more explicit and should not assume that such explicitness is rude—such directness is simply a cultural characteristic.

- *Uses of emblems in the United States are often for less formal messages.* Commonly used emblems range from obscene gestures to specific emblems representing athletic teams. Unlike emblems in other cultures, very few U.S. emblems signify status or respect.

- *Eye contact is expected.* In nearly every communication situation, consistent eye contact is viewed positively as a signal of confidence, warmth, and attentiveness. Even in situations in which there are strong power differences, such as the communication between a supervisor and an employee, eye contact is desirable; a lack of consistent eye contact can cause you to be viewed as untrustworthy or noncredible.

- *For vocal characteristics, bigger tends to be better.* Listeners tend to react positively to speakers who have strong volume, good vocal variety, and forceful projection and articulation.

As a general principle, U.S. speakers tend to be expressive with most nonverbal behaviors, though such expressiveness is typically not found with respect to space and touch. You will notice many other cultural characteristics of U.S. nonverbal behavior as you gain more experience observing native speakers. You may integrate some of those differences into your own communication repertoire; others you may dismiss. Being observant and asking native speakers about their use of various nonverbal behaviors, as well as their expectations for how others use those behaviors, will help nonnative speakers develop their own skills more quickly.

4. Manage your time in your interactions with others. Allow others to share their experiences, and be willing to exchange talk time. Do you tend to interrupt or overlap your statements with others' while they are talking? Try your best to allow others a full hearing.

5. Be aware of professional norms that guide nonverbal communication behaviors. Touching, using intimate physical space, requiring time alone after hours, and engaging in other such behaviors are generally inappropriate.

6. Dress appropriately for the situation. Many students have relaxed standards for classroom attire, as permitted by their schools. However, when you transition out of the student role and into the employee role, even if that is as a student-worker on your campus, you will likely need to wear business casual clothing.

7. Avoid using overly dramatic nonverbal behaviors to intentionally or unintentionally signal disagreement. Most people appreciate hearing about differences in opinions, but they do not value sneers or being mocked.

be ready... for what's next

Learning to Say It Like It Is

As you progress through your college and professional career, you will have opportunities to take on greater levels of responsibility. For example, you will work in teams with individuals who are perhaps older and have more experience. Learning to sound confident in those situations could affect how people perceive you. Being confident is communicated through your nonverbal behaviors. One of the best ways to improve perceptions of your confidence is by training yourself to monitor your posture, use of vocal variety, and eye contact. Those who have upright posture, use vocal variety, and maintain eye contact are perceived as more competent and confident. Also, recall that if you synchronize your nonverbal communication with others, they are far more likely to perceive you as cooperative. As you continue to build your skills as a communicator, being intentional about monitoring your own nonverbal communication is critical for success.

Chapter Review & Study Guide

Summary

In this chapter you learned the following:

1. Nonverbal communication is defined as the process of using messages other than words to create meaning with others.

2. Verbal and nonverbal codes work in conjunction with each other in six ways: to repeat, to emphasize, to complement, to contradict, to substitute, and to regulate.

3. Nonverbal codes consist of nonword symbols.

   - Bodily movements and facial expression include posture, gestures, and other bodily movements and facial expressions, known as kinesics.

   - Physical attraction is a perception based on social norms but is also influenced by nonphysical attributes such as personality.

- Proxemics is the study of the human use of space and distance.

- Temporal communication, or chronemics, is the way people organize and use time and the messages that are created because of their organization and use of that time.

- Tactile communication is the use of touch in communication.

- Paralinguistic features include the nonword sounds and nonword characteristics of language, such as pitch, volume, rate, and quality.

- Objectics, or object language, is the study of the human use of clothing and artifacts as nonverbal codes.

4. Ambiguity in the meaning of nonverbal codes may arise for two reasons.

    • One nonverbal code can communicate a variety of meanings depending on situation, participants, and accompanying verbal messages.

    • A variety of nonverbal codes can communicate the same meanings depending on similar situational factors.

5. You can solve some of the difficulties in interpreting nonverbal codes if you

    • consider all the variables in each communication context.

    • adapt your nonverbal communication to the audience with which you are communicating.

    • consider all the available verbal and nonverbal codes.

    • use descriptive feedback to minimize misunderstandings.

Key Terms

Adaptors	Illustrators	Proxemics
Affect displays	Inflection	Quality
American Sign Language (ASL)	Kinesics	Rate
Articulation	Nonverbal codes	Regulating
Artifacts	Nonverbal communication	Regulators
Chronemics	Nonword sounds	Repeating
Complementing	Objectics	Silence
Contradicting	Paralinguistic features	Substituting
Emblems	Physical attractiveness	Tactile communication
Emphasizing	Pitch	Vocal cues
Enunciation	Pronunciation	Volume

Study Questions

1. What is included in nonverbal communication?

    a. only vocalized cues
    b. only nonvocalized cues
    c. nonword vocalizations as well as nonvocalized cues
    d. vocalized words

2. Nonverbal codes work together with vocalized words to

    a. generalize and broaden.
    b. analyze and synthesize.
    c. confuse and distinguish.
    d. contradict and substitute.

3. One of the difficulties of interpreting nonverbal codes is

    a. one code may communicate several different meanings.
    b. no two nonverbal codes communicate the same meaning.
    c. each nonverbal cue has only one perceived meaning.
    d. observers can easily distinguish meaning from specific nonverbal cues.

4. Bodily movement, facial expression, the use of time, and vocal cues, among other actions, are examples of

    a. kinesics.
    b. complementation.
    c. nonverbal codes.
    d. adaptors.

5. What type of bodily movement is most likely to be used to fulfill a personal psychological need?

    a. emblem
    b. adaptor
    c. illustrator
    d. regulators

6. Pointing to your wrist while asking for the time is an example of a(n)

    a. adaptor.
    b. illustrator.
    c. regulator.
    d. emblem.

7. Which of the following statements would most closely align with the social construction perspective on physical attractiveness?

    a. Physical strength, tallness, and leanness account for 80% of perceptions of physical attractiveness.
    b. Perceptions of physical attractiveness are driven by evolution.
    c. Perceptions of physical attractiveness are unlikely to change over time.
    d. Perceptions of physical attractiveness are driven by social norms.

8. Which of the following statements accurately describes the role of nonverbal communication using the perspective that communication is the creation of shared meaning?

   a. Up to 90% of our communication is nonverbal.
   b. Verbal and nonverbal symbols work together to create meaning.
   c. Verbal symbols carry greater importance than nonverbal symbols.
   d. Only facial expressions create meaning when communicating.

9. In relation to gender and touch, which of the following is true?

   a. Women tend to initiate touch more often than men do.
   b. Women are more likely to perceive sexual touch from a male stranger as friendly.
   c. Males tend to initiate touch more often than do women.
   d. Men are more likely to perceive sexual touch from a female stranger as unfriendly.

10. To effectively signal cooperation, you should

   a. use only vocal cues during the conversation.
   b. avoid the use of touch with the other person.
   c. remain quiet when the other person is talking.
   d. synchronize nonverbal behaviors with the other person.

Answers:
1. (c); 2. (d); 3. (a); 4. (c); 5. (b); 6. (b); 7. (d); 8. (b); 9. (c); 10. (d)

Critical Thinking

1. Much of our discussion of nonverbal communication is based on an assumption that people are physically present. Because more of our school, work, and even family life is being conducted remotely, how can you adapt your nonverbal communication behaviors to signal things like liking, status, and responsiveness in online settings?

2. You have learned that ambiguity can be present when one is trying to interpret the meaning associated with nonverbal codes. Analyze one of your own communication situations in which you had trouble decoding someone's intended meaning because of their use of nonverbal communication. Can you determine if they used a nonverbal code that had multiple possible meanings? Did they use a code that for them had meaning but was unfamiliar to you?

Sizing Things Up Scoring and Interpretation

Berkeley Nonverbal Expressiveness Questionnaire

Simple observation suggests that some people are just more nonverbally expressive than others. Whereas one person may remain stiff and deadpan, another may appear to be landing planes based on the nature of how he or she naturally gestures. The Berkeley Nonverbal Expressiveness Questionnaire assesses the extent to which a person "leaks" implicit meanings (especially emotional) through nonverbal behaviors. Although this scale is typically used to assess expressiveness, you will notice that expressivity is enacted, based on these statements, through nonverbal cues.

The expressivity scale taps three dimensions of nonverbal/emotional expressivity. To achieve a score for each dimension, simply average the values for each item after reverse-coding the items below with the "(R)" next to the item number; higher values indicate higher levels for that dimension. To reverse-code items indicated below, take your original responses and make a 1 become a 7, a 2 become a 6, or a 3 become a 5. If you answered initially with a 7, 6, or 5, do the opposite. After

reverse-coding your answers, average all results related to each of the three dimensions.

- *Negative expressivity.* The extent to which others observe you feeling negative emotions, such as nervousness, fear, and anger. The following items are included in this dimension: 3(R), 5, 8(R), 9(R), 13, and 16.
- *Positive expressivity.* The extent to which others can observe you experiencing positive emotions, such as happiness and joy. The following items should be averaged for this dimension: 1, 4, 6, and 10.
- *Impulse strength.* The extent to which you can control, diminish, or manage your emotional expression. Items for this dimension are 2, 7, 11, 12, 14, and 15.

You can also average the results of all questions to obtain an overall expressiveness value. Higher overall scores indicate, regardless of positive or negative emotions, how expressive you are.

References

1. Steve Stine, entrepreneur in Fargo, North Dakota.

2. Eastman, B. (2015, February 12). How much of communication is really nonverbal? The Nonverbal Group Blog. http://www.nonverbalgroup.com/2011/08/how-much-of-communication-is-really-nonverbal/

3. Hall, J. A., Horgan, T. G., & Murphy, N. A. (2019). Nonverbal communication. *Annual Review of Psychology, 70,* 271–294. https://doi.org/10.1146/annurev-psych-010418-103145

4. Sternberg, R. J. (2022). Non-verbal communication in relationships as a link between affect and social intelligence. In R. J. Sternberg & A. Kostić (Eds.), *Nonverbal communication in close relationships: What words don't tell us* (pp. 363–372). Palgrave Macmillan/Springer Nature. https://doi.org/10.1007/978-3-030-94492-6_14

5. d'Abreu, I. M., Troccoli, I. R., & Sauerbronn, J. F. R. (2021). Rapport building during retail encounters with embarrassed clients. *Journal of Personal Selling & Sales Management, 41,* 330–350. https://doi.org/10.1080/08853134.2021.1925127

6. Franceško, M., & Nedeljković, J. (2022). The role of nonverbal communication in leadership skills. In R. J. Sternberg & A. Kostić (Eds.), *Nonverbal communication in close relationships: What words don't tell us* (pp. 51–74). Palgrave Macmillan/Springer Nature. https://doi.org/10.1007/978-3-030-94492-6_3

7. Novak, D. R. (2020, March 17). Killing the myth that 93% of communication is nonverbal. https://davidrnovak.com/writing/article/2020/03/killing-the-myth-that-93-of-communication-is-nonverbal

8. Nikolaus, J., Roessing, T., & Petersen, T. (2011). The effects of verbal and nonverbal elements in persuasive communication: Findings from two multi-method experiments. *Communications: The European Journal of Communication Research, 36,* 245–271.

9. National Institute on Deafness and Other Communication Disorders. (2018, December 5). *American Sign Language.* U.S. Department of Health & Human Services. https://www.nidcd.nih.gov/health/american-sign-language

10. Mitchell, R. E., Young, T. A., Bacheleda, B., & Karchmer, M. A. (2006). How many people use ASL in the United States? Why estimates need updating. *Sign Language Studies, 6,* 306–335.

11. Mehrabian, A. (1971). *Silent messages.* Wadsworth.

12. Teven, J. J. (2010). The effects of supervisor nonverbal immediacy and power use on employees' ratings of credibility and affect for the supervisor. *Human Communication, 13,* 69–85.

13. Ekman, P. (1997). Should we call it expression or communication? *Innovations in Social Science Research, 10,* 333–344. Ekman, P. (1999). Basic emotions. In T. Dalgleish & T. Power (Eds.), *The handbook of cognition and emotion* (pp. 45–60). Wiley. Ekman, P. (1999). Facial expressions. In T. Dalgleish & T. Power (Eds.), *The handbook of cognition and emotion* (pp. 301–320). Wiley.

14. Yang, P. (2011). Nonverbal aspects of turn taking in Mandarin. *Language and Discourse, 2,* 99–130.

15. Ekman, P., & Friesen, W. V. (1967). Head and body cues in the judgment of emotion: A reformulation. *Perceptual and Motor Skills, 24,* 711–724.

16. Ruben, M. A., Hall, J., & Mast, M. (2015). Smiling in a job interview: When less is more. *Journal of Social Psychology, 155,* 107–126. https://doi.org/10.1080/00224545.2014.972312

17. Siegal, M. (2013). *Knowing children: Experiments in conversation and cognition.* Psychology Press. https://doi.org/10.4324/978023776063

18. Seiter, J. S., Weger, H., Jensen, A., & Kinzer, H. J. (2010). The role of background behavior in televised debates: Does displaying nonverbal agreement and/or disagreement benefit either debater? *Journal of Social Psychology, 150,* 278–300.

19. Aburumman, N., Gillies, M., Ward, J. A., & Hamilton, A. F. de C. (2022). Nonverbal communication in virtual reality: Nodding as a social signal in virtual interactions. *International Journal of Human-Computer Studies, 164,* 1–9. https://doi.org/10.1016/j.ijhcs.2022.102819

20. Sell, A., Likazsweski, A. W., & Townsley, M. (2017). Cues of upper body strength account for most of the variance in men's body attractiveness. *Proceeding of the Royal Society, 284.* https://doi.org/10.1098/rspb.2017.1819

21. Wang, G., Djafarian, K., Egedigwe, C. A., El Hamdouchi, A., Ojiambo, R., Ramuth, H., . . . Speakman, J. R. (2015). The relationship of female physical attractiveness to body fatness. *PeerJ, 3,* e1155. https://doi.org/10.7717/peerj.1155

22. Yang, H., & Lee, L. (2014). Instantaneously hotter: The dynamic revision of beauty assessment standards. In J. Cotte & S. Wood (Eds.), *Advances in consumer research* (pp. 744–745). Association for Consumer Research.

23. Wolf, N. (2002/1991). *The beauty myth.* Harper Perennial.

24. Widdows, H. (2018). *Perfect me: Beauty as an ethical ideal.* Princeton University Press.

25. Garber, M. (2018, April 22). When beauty is a troll. *The Atlantic.* https://www.theatlantic.com/entertainment/archive/2018/04/when-beauty-is-a-troll/558467/

26. Taubert, J., Van der Burg, E., & Alais, D. (2016). Love at second sight: Sequential dependence of facial attractiveness in an on-line dating paradigm. *Scientific Reports, 6,* 1–5. https://doi.org/10.1038/srep22740

27. Lewandowski, G. W., Aron, A., & Gee, J. (2007). Personality goes a long way: The malleability of opposite sex physical attractiveness. *Journal of Personal Relationships, 14,* 571–585. https://doi.org/1350-4126/07

28. Tu, M., Gilbert, E. K., & Bono, J. E. (2022). Is beauty more than skin deep? Attractiveness, power, and nonverbal presence in evaluations of hirability. *Personnel Psychology, 75,* 119–146. https://doi.org/10.1111/peps.12469

29. Cagle, J. (2018, April 17). Editor's note: PEOPLE renames the World's Most Beautiful Issue—and guess who is on the cover. *People.*

30. Hall, E. T. (1966). *The hidden dimension.* Doubleday.

31. Hall, *The hidden dimension.*

32. Argyle, M. (2013). *Bodily communication.* Routledge.

33. Bailey, A., & Kelly, S. (2015). Picture power: Gender versus body language in perceived status. *Journal of Nonverbal Behavior, 39,* 317–337. https://doi.org/10.1007/s10919-015-0212-x

34. Sommer, R. (1962). The distance for comfortable conversation: A further study. *Sociometry, 25,* 111–116.

35. Hall, E. T. (1963). Proxemics: The study of man's spatial relations and boundaries. In I. Galdston (Ed.), *Man's image in medicine and anthropology* (pp. 422–445). International Universities Press.

36. Gleisner, J. (2018, November 27). Time matters—the chronemics of nonverbal communication. Silent Communication. https://www.silentcommunication.org/single-post/2016/03/01/Time-matters-the-chronemics-of-nonverbal-communication

37. Tatum, N. T., Martin, J. C., & Kemper, B. (2018). Chronemics in instructor–student e-mail communication: An experimental examination of student evaluations of instructor response speeds. *Communication Research Reports, 35*(1), 33–41. https://doi.org/10.1080/08824096.2017.1361396

38. Cecchini, M., Baroni, E., Di Vito, C., & Lai, C. (2011). Smiling in newborns during communicative wake and active sleep. *Infant Behavior & Development, 34,* 417–423.

39. Schutz, W. C. (1971). *Here comes everybody.* Harper & Row. p. 16.

40. Remland, M. S., & Jones, T. S. (2022). The functions and consequences of interpersonal touch in close relationships. In R. J. Sternberg & A. Kostić (Eds.), *Nonverbal communication in close relationships: What words don't tell us* (pp. 307–339). Palgrave Macmillan/Springer Nature. https://doi.org/10.1007/978-3-030-94492-6_12

41. Hamilton, S. (2017). Rituals of intimate legal touch: Regulating end-of-game handshake in pandemic culture. *The Senses and Society, 12,* 53–68. https://doi.org/10.1080/17458927.2017.1268821

42. Siegel, B. S. (1990). *Peace, love and healing: Bodymind communication and the path to self-healing: An exploration.* Harper Perennial, p. 134.

43. Piza, F., Piza, P., & Schwartzstein, R. M. (2018). The power of nonverbal communication in medical education. *Medical Teacher,* 1–2. https://doi.org/10.1080/0142159X.2018.1454590

44. Ishikawa, H., Hashimoto, H., Kinoshita, M., & Yano, E. (2010). Can nonverbal skills be taught? *Medical Teacher, 32,* 860–863.

45. Hertenstein, M. J., & Keltner, D. (2011). Gender and the communication of emotion via touch. *Sex Roles, 64,* 70–80. https://doi.org/10.1007/s11199-010-9842-yc

46. Immergut, M., & Kosut, M. (2014). Visualizing charisma: Representations of the charismatic touch. *Visual Studies, 29,* 272–284.

47. Jourard, S. M. (1968). *Disclosing man to himself.* Van Nostrand.

48. Franks, T. M. (2017). Breaching ethics for the sake of a "good" interview. *Journal of Applied Communication Research, 45,* 352–357. https://doi.org/10.1080/00909882.2017.1320570

49. Vaish, A., & Striano, T. (2004). Is visual reference necessary? Contributions of facial versus vocal cues in 12-month-olds' social referencing behavior. *Developmental Science, 7,* 261–269.

50. Kramer, E. (1963). The judgment of personal characteristics and emotions from nonverbal properties of speech. *Psychological Bulletin, 60,* 408–420.

51. Laukka, P., Juslin, P. N., & Bresin, R. (2005). A dimensional approach to vocal expression of emotion. *Cognition and Emotion, 19,* 633–653. Planalp, S. (1996). Varieties of cues to emotion in naturally occurring situations. *Cognition and Emotion, 10,* 137–154.

52. Bateson, G., Jackson, D. D., Haley, J., & Weakland, J. H. (1956). Toward a theory of schizophrenia. *Behavioral Science, 1,* 251–264.

53. Voyer, D., Thibodeau, S.-H., & Delong, B. (2016). Context, contrast, and tone of voice in auditory sarcasm perception. *Journal of Psycholinguistic Research, 45,* 29–53. https://doi.org/10.1007/s10936-014-9323-5

54. Genard, G. (2013, August 25). Public speaking tips: Silence is one of your most powerful tools. Speak for Success. http://www.genardmethod.com/blog-detail/view/25/public-speaking-tips-silence-is-one-of-your-most-powerful-tools#.VN9PZOJwXlk

55. Resende, V. de M., & Silva, R. B. (2016). Critical discourse analysis: Voice, silence and memory—one case about public sphere. *Critical Discourse Studies, 13,* 397–410. https://doi.org/10.1080/17405904.2015.1113191

56. Frith, K. T., Hong, C., & Ping Shaw, K. T. (2004). Race and beauty: A comparison of Asian and Western models in women's magazine advertisements. *Sex Roles, 50*(1/2), 53–61.

57. Boswell, R. (2006). Say what you like: Dress, identity, and heritage in Zanzibar. *International Journal of Heritage Studies, 12,* 440–457.

58. Bashir, N. Y., & Rule, N. O. (2014). Shopping under the Influence: Nonverbal appearance-based communicator cues affect consumer judgments. *Psychology & Marketing, 31,* 539–548. https://doi.org/10.1002/mar.20715

59. Bahns, A., Crandall, C., Gillath, O., & Wilmer, J. (2016). Nonverbal communication of similarity via the torso: It's in the bag. *Journal of Nonverbal Behavior, 40,* 151–170. https://doi.org/10.1007/s10919-016-0227-y

60. Douty, H. I. (1963). Influence of clothing on perception of persons. *Journal of Home Economics, 55,* 197–202.

61. Williams, M. C., & Eicher, J. B. (1966). Teenagers' appearance and social acceptance. *Journal of Home Economics, 58,* 457–461.

62. McNeill, L. S. (2018). Fashion and women's self-concept: A typology for self-fashioning using clothing. *Journal of Fashion Marketing & Management, 22,* 82–98. https://doi.org/10.1108/JFMM-09-2016-0077

63. Wohlrab, S., Fink, B., Kappeler, P. M., & Brewer, G. (2009). Differences in personality attributions toward tattooed and nontattooed virtual human characters. *Journal of Individual Differences, 30*(1), 1–5.

64. Bauck, W. (2018, December 4). 7 ways fashion joined the political conversation in 2017. *Fashionista.* https://fashionista.com/2017/12/fashion-politics-protests-statements-issues-2017

65. Couch, C. (2018, May 16). Can AI learn to understand emotions? *NOVA.* https://www.pbs.org/wgbh/nova/article/affective-computing/

66. Wei, F.-Y. F., & Wang, Y. K. (2010). Students' silent messages: Can teacher verbal and nonverbal immediacy moderate student use of text messaging in class? *Communication Education, 59,* 475–496.

5

RGtimeline/Alamy Stock Photo

listening and critical thinking

When you have read and thought about this chapter, you will be able to

1. discuss three reasons why listening is important in our lives.

2. describe how the process of listening differs from hearing.

3. analyze how noise, perceptions, and your own characteristics can influence the listening process.

4. apply critical thinking, nonverbal, and verbal strategies to become a better listener.

5. apply strategies for effective listening to specific situations, including the workplace, the classroom, and mediated environments.

6. apply ethical listening behaviors.

Listening is our most frequently used but least studied communication skill. In this chapter you will learn about the listening process, some factors that can inhibit effective listening, different types of listening, and strategies for becoming a more effective listener. Our hope is that you will learn that listening, like any other communication behavior, is a skill that must be developed through forethought and practice.

Our listening skills begin to develop when we are young children as our family members and friends read aloud or simply recount stories. Through stories, we learn to recognize and remember details, identify patterns and plots, and pick up on certain emotional cues. As we transition into adulthood, we must continue to refine these listening skills.

Since 2003, the StoryCorps project of National Public Radio (NPR) has collected more than 500,000 stories about people's lives. By visiting storycorps.org, you can access thousands of stories that represent the widest array of human emotions, including those experienced during the COVID-19 pandemic. In his book *Listening Is an Act of Love,* Dave Isay, a founder of StoryCorps, commented, "If we take time to listen, we'll find wisdom, wonder, and poetry in the lives and stories of the people all around us."[1] As you listen to stories on the website, take note of how you recognize the emotions behind the story. What did the speakers say or do to help you better understand their explicit and implicit meanings? If you were in a room with the narrators as they told their stories, how would you react? By continuing to practice listening to stories, you not only will find personal fulfillment but also will continue to develop and refine your listening skills.

G-Stock Studio/Shutterstock

As you will learn, listening is one of the most frequent communication behaviors you will practice. In this chapter you will learn ways to identify your strengths and areas for improvement as a listener in all types of contexts.

The Importance of Listening in Our Lives

Listening is one of our most common communication activities. The International Listening Association examined how much time individuals spend reading, writing, speaking, and listening. Those studies found that people spend the greatest amount of their time listening (an average of 44%), followed by speaking (25%), reading (13%), and writing (11%).[2] Even when you consider online communication, we still spend a great deal of time listening. Figure 5.1 shows the results of a recent study of the communication activities in which college students engage: 63% of their time was spent listening to various types of information, with the largest amount of time devoted to listening to others in face-to-face situations. The rest of their time spent in communication activities was dedicated to speaking, reading, and writing. Continued use of digital and social media will likely expand the proportion of our time listening. According to the Pew Research Center, more than 95% of people ages 13 to 17 access YouTube multiple times each day, which is time spent listening to and watching others.[3] Given how important listening is to our work as communicators, learning to listen well is critical.

As you can imagine from the amount of time we spend listening to others, listening helps us accomplish important things. Listening helps us build and maintain relationships and can even help us determine whether the person we are talking to is being deceitful. How do we learn to be better listeners in our interpersonal relationships? A study reported by Andrew Ledbetter and Paul Schrodt found that listening skills and behaviors are influenced by family communication patterns we experience early in life. As they noted, "When families create an environment where family members are encouraged to openly discuss

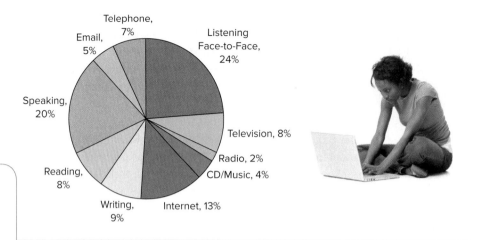

Figure 5.1

Proportions of time spent by college students in communication activities.

Source: Janusik, L., Fullenkamp, L., & Partese, L. (2015). Listening facts. International Listening Association.

(photo): Mike Kemp/Rubberball/ Getty Images

social media listening
The active monitoring of and response to messages on social media platforms by businesses or other types of organizations.

hearing
The act of receiving sound.

listening
The active process of receiving, constructing meaning from, and responding to spoken and/ or nonverbal messages. It involves the ability to retain information, as well as to react empathically and/or appreciatively to spoken and/or nonverbal messages.

active listening
Involved listening with a purpose.

empathic listening
Listening with a purpose and attempting to understand another person's perspective.

critical listening
Listening that challenges the speaker's message by evaluating its accuracy, meaningfulness, and utility.

a variety of topics, children may be more likely to learn how to process complex and ambiguous information without anxiety."[4]

Listening is also recognized as an essential skill for business success.[5] When reflecting on their business successes, executives such as Bill Marriott note that their most important lesson was to create cultures in which managers listen to employees for ideas on how to do things more effectively and efficiently. As a result, better decisions are made.[6] Organizational cultures that emphasize listening can create positive communication between members of the organization and increase employee engagement.[7] In addition to promoting internal cultures of listening, the rapid growth of social media has forced organizations of all types to place a greater emphasis on **social media listening**, which occurs when an organization actively monitors and responds to messages on any type of social media platform.[8] By actively listening to social media messages, organizations are able to track what consumers are saying about their products or services and then use that information to make improvements. Many organizations use sophisticated social media listening/command centers through which they can actively engage and respond to customers on social media to build brand awareness, respond quickly to problems, and generate brand excitement. Both internally and externally, listening is one of the key elements of effective business strategy.

Defining Listening

John Dewey, a twentieth-century educational and social philosopher, observed in his book *The Public and Its Problems* that true democracy happens when we take time to listen to the people around us—our friends and family, our neighbors, and the people in our community.[9] Dewey's observation seems intuitive, though how often have you "faked" listening? Your friend may tell you about something that happened at work, but you only "half listened"; or you listened to neighbors talk about a community event but quickly forgot what they said. In fact, good listening is hard and takes sustained effort. Learning to be an effective listener starts with understanding what the listening process involves and then progresses to trying to improve how you enact that process.

The first step in learning about listening is to understand the distinction between hearing and listening. **Hearing** is simply the act of receiving sound. Although much of this chapter is devoted to listening rather than hearing, there are important things to learn about the physical act of hearing. First, your listening behaviors now will influence your hearing later in life.[10] In fact, many audiologists warn that young adults and even children should be careful when listening to music using headphones or earbuds. When using lower-quality earbuds that do not block external noise, people have a tendency to increase the volume to levels that can cause long-term damage to their hearing. Even without hearing loss stemming from loud noise, some people have other physical problems with their hearing. Tinnitus is a condition that results in a constant "ringing" in the ears. The American Tinnitus Association estimates that over 50 million Americans experience tinnitus to some degree—the condition can be caused by many factors, including allergies and certain types of benign tumors.[11] Thus, we should not assume that everyone can hear equally well, even those in your group of friends.

Hearing is not the same as listening. **Listening**, as defined by the International Listening Association, is "the active process of receiving, constructing meaning from, and responding to spoken and/or nonverbal messages. It involves the ability to retain information, as well as to react empathically and/or appreciatively to spoken and/or nonverbal messages."[12] **Active listening** is "involved listening with a purpose."[13] Active listening includes (1) listening carefully by using all available senses, (2) paraphrasing what we hear both mentally and verbally, (3) checking our understanding to ensure accuracy, and (4) providing feedback. Feedback consists of verbal and nonverbal responses to the speaker and the speaker's message. Those who communicate through sign language can listen according to the definition just provided, though many of them may not be able to hear.

Active listening can occur in different forms, including empathic listening and critical listening:

• Listening for enjoyment is an easy way to relax.

Ken Wramton/Taxi/Getty Images

listening for enjoyment
Listening that occurs in situations involving relaxing, fun, or emotionally stimulating information.

- **Empathic listening** is attempting to understand the perspective of another person. You engage in empathic listening by maintaining awareness, being mindful in the moment, reducing distractions, and responding with empathy to the person with whom you are talking.[14]

- In **critical listening** you challenge the speaker's message by evaluating its accuracy, meaningfulness, and utility. Critical listening and critical thinking go hand in hand: you cannot listen critically if you do not think critically. Skills in critical listening are especially important because we are constantly bombarded with commercials, telemarketing calls, and other persuasive messages.

Not all listening is active listening. **Listening for enjoyment** occurs in situations that are relaxing, fun, or emotionally stimulating. Whether listening to a favorite band or just playing YouTube videos, we often use sound to create an escape from other activities or even to provide simple background noise while we perform other tasks. Besides aiding relaxation, listening to enjoyable music has even been found to reduce pain in hospital patients.[15]

communicating creatively

Podcasts and Critical Thinking

As presented here, you may assume that listening for enjoyment and critical listening are two separate behaviors. While this is true in some situations, you can practice critical listening skills even while listening for enjoyment. More than 41% of U.S. citizens over the age of 12 report listening to podcasts in the past month. While podcasts are a substantial source of enjoyment for many, the long-form audio narratives found in many podcasts also provide meaningful opportunities for critical thinking. For example, the S-Town podcasts from the producers of Serial and This American Life documents a story of murder and mystery in a small town in Alabama. By listening to that long-form audio narrative, listeners engage in critical thinking as they follow plots, characters, and events, all while enjoying a compelling story.

Source: Richter, F. (2021, June 17). The steady rise of podcasts. *Statista.* www.statista.com/chart/10713/podcast-listeners-in-the-united-states/

The Process of Listening

The process of listening is summarized in Figure 5.2. As the illustration shows, we receive stimuli (such as music, words, or sounds) in the ear, where the smallest bones in the body translate the vibrations into sensations registered by the brain. For those who are deaf or hard of hearing, the stimuli received might be the visible behaviors of another person. In both instances, the brain focuses attention on the stimuli and gives them meaning using working memory, which is a part of your short-term memory. Your brain might, for example, recognize the first few bars of a favorite song, the voice of a favorite artist, or the sound of a police siren. On hearing these sounds, you immediately know what they mean. Your interpreted message is then stored in schema that reside in your long-term memory for immediate use or future recall.[16]

As we discuss later in this chapter, people create many barriers, or obstacles, to effective listening. Not all barriers, however, are the fault of lazy, ineffective, or unethical listeners. Because listening is human behavior, natural barriers present themselves at various stages. In the following sections, these natural barriers are explained for each major step in the listening process: attention, working memory, short-term memory, and long-term memory. In fact, if you recall from Chapter 2, you already learned about some of these barriers related to attention and assigning meaning to stimuli. In this chapter we will be discussing similar concepts, perhaps with more specificity.

selective attention
The tendency, when you expose yourself to information and ideas, to focus on certain cues and ignore others.

automatic attention
The instinctive focus we give to stimuli signaling a change in our surroundings, stimuli that we deem important, or stimuli that we perceive to signal danger.

ATTENTION

Anyone who has been a student has heard the command "Pay attention!" What exactly are teachers expecting when they say this? Paying attention means controlling your selective and automatic attention.[17] **Selective attention** is the sustained focus we give to things that are important. Your favorite music, a conversation with your friend, statements made by your date over dinner, and your professor at the front of the class are things that draw your selective attention. Selective attention is a form of selective perception (see Chapter 2). In contrast, **automatic attention** is the instinctive focus we give to important things we experience in our surroundings. A siren, a loud noise, your name

Figure 5.2

The listening process.

(photo): Cavan Images/Alamy Stock Photo

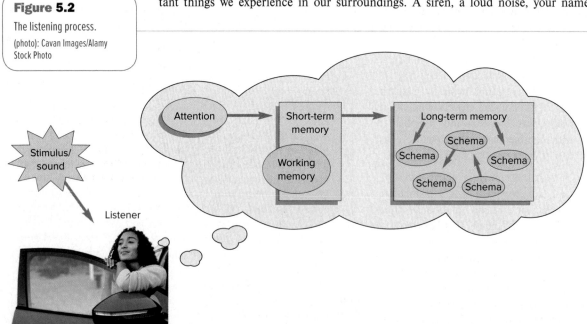

shouted from across the room, or a new person walking into the room can capture your automatic attention. In any listening situation, we must manage our selective attention to keep it from being overwhelmed by our automatic attention. In essence, by saying "Pay attention," your teacher is asking you to ignore your automatic attention and focus your selective attention. However, you should not assume that selective attention means paying attention to only one thing. In fact, we learn to quickly scan our surroundings and assess the importance of several items of interest as they relate to one another.[18] Think about what happens when you drive. As you scan the road in front of you, you must also take care to use your peripheral vision to see activity on the side of the road, such as children playing. You must also listen for important sounds such as horns or emergency sirens. Driving is a complex activity that requires scanning and analyzing hundreds of potential cues; having a conversation is just as complex because the cues are more subtle.

Our ability to quickly scan social media is a valuable and transferable skill. Being able to scan, read, and react to situations, both virtual and face-to-face, is useful in a variety of personal and professional situations. Be warned, however, that excessive reliance on this use of selective attention can cause problems. A recent study found that when students text or use social media during class, their performance on quizzes and tests can drop by as much as one-and-a-half letter grades.[19] Allowing your selective attention to scan too much of your environment can overwhelm your ability to make meaning of specific, and perhaps important, stimuli.

WORKING MEMORY

Once we have paid selective attention to relevant sounds and stimuli, our brain must initially process and make sense of those stimuli. **Working memory** is the part of our short-term memory that interprets and assigns meaning to things we hear. Our working memory looks for shortcuts when processing information. When you hear people speak, your working memory quickly recognizes patterns of sounds that represent words, phrases, and ideas. Using your prior knowledge, which is stored in long-term memory, your working memory assigns meaning to what you are hearing and allows you to respond. Thus, when you hear a family member say, "A storm is coming," your working memory allows you to assign meaning to that sentence and plan your travel or other actions in anticipation of what that sentence means. The patterns we recognize and respond to with working memory resources are critical for effective and efficient communication with others.

working memory
The part of our short-term memory that interprets and assigns meaning to stimuli we pay attention to.

Working memory uses patterns of words or other symbols stored in long-term memory to apply these shortcuts for assigning meaning. Not surprisingly, research has found that when children have difficulty with language development, they have less efficient working memory.[20] That is, when children do not learn language skills and develop strong vocabularies, their working memory must work harder to decipher new information. Of course, the opposite is also true. Helping children develop strong language skills early in life will likely help them become better listeners later.

SHORT-TERM MEMORY

Once interpreted in working memory, information is sent to the short-term or long-term memory. **Short-term memory** is a temporary storage place for information. We all use short-term memory to retain thoughts needed for immediate use. You might think of short-term memory as being similar to a Post-it note. You will use the information on the note for a quick reference but will soon discard it or decide to write it down in a more secure location.

short-term memory
A temporary storage place for information.

We constantly use short-term memory, but it is the least efficient of our memory resources. Classic studies in the field of psychology have documented that short-term memory

• Being startled can break your concentration and cause you to forget what is in short-term memory.

PhotoTalk/Getty Images

is limited in both the quantity of information stored and the length of time information is retained.[21] In terms of quantity, short-term memory is limited to five to nine "bits" of information. A bit of information is any organized unit of information, including sounds, letters, words, sentences, or something less concrete, such as ideas, depending on the ability of working memory to recognize patterns. For instance, experts in a particular area can recognize patterns easily and therefore can organize large amounts of information into a single bit. Non-experts have more difficulty in recognizing patterns and must therefore use more bits to organize the same amount of information. You experienced this as you learned language. When you began reading, you processed each letter individually, so each letter was a bit of information. As you became better at reading, you naturally started to process words, then phrases, and then entire paragraphs or even pages of text as a bit of information within your short-term memory.

If your short-term memory becomes overloaded (for average people, more than nine bits of information), you begin to forget. Short-term memory is also limited to about 20 seconds in duration unless some strategy, such as rehearsal, is used. If you quickly scan and rehearse a definition from your textbook in preparation for a quiz, you will likely remember it. However, if something breaks your concentration and you stop rehearsing the definition, the words will likely be lost. Unfortunately, many listeners rely too much on short-term memory during the listening process. Researchers in the field of communication have found that individuals recall only 50% of a message immediately after listening to it and only 25% after a short delay.[22] Relying on our short-term memory is not a substitute for trying to encode information into long-term memory.

LONG-TERM MEMORY

long-term memory
Our permanent storage place for information, including but not limited to past experiences; language; values; knowledge; images of people; memories of sights, sounds, and smells; and even fantasies.

schemas
Organizational "filing systems" for thoughts held in long-term memory.

Information processed in working memory can also be stored in long-term memory for later recall. Similarly, information temporarily stored in short-term memory can be deemed important and subsequently stored in long-term memory. If short-term memory is the Post-it note in the listening process, long-term memory is the supercomputer. **Long-term memory** is our permanent storage place for information, including past experiences; language; values; knowledge; images of people; memories of sights, sounds, and smells; and even fantasies. Unlike short-term memory, long-term memory has no known limitations in the quantity or duration of stored information.

Explanations of how long-term memory works are only speculative; however, researchers hypothesize that our thoughts are organized according to **schemas**, which are organizational "filing systems" for thoughts held in long-term memory. We might think of schemas as an interconnected web of information. Our ability to remember information in long-term memory is dependent on finding connections to the correct schema containing the particular memory, thought, idea, or image we are trying to recall.

In theory, people with normally functioning brains never lose information stored in long-term memory. How is it, then, that we often forget things we listened to? When we try to access information in long-term memory, we access schemas holding needed information through the use of stimulus cues, which can be words, images, or even smells and tastes. If the cue we receive does not give us enough information to access the corresponding schema, we may be unable to recall the information. Consider, for example, a situation in which you see a person who looks familiar. In this case you recognize the person (a visual cue); however, that stimulus does not provide you with enough information to recall who the person is. If you hear the person's voice or are reminded of a previous encounter with the person, you may then have enough information to activate the correct schema and recall specific details about that person.

Long-term memory plays a key role in the listening process. As we receive sounds, our working memory looks for patterns based on schemas contained in our long-term memory. Thus, our ability to use language, to recognize concepts, and to interpret meaning is based on the schemas we accumulate over a lifetime. If we encounter new information that does not relate to a preexisting schema, our working memory instructs our long-term memory to create a new schema to hold the information.

Barriers to Listening

Although you might agree that listening is important, you may not be properly prepared for effective listening. A 2013 study by a doctoral student at the University of Phoenix found a very strong correlation between listening skills and workplace productivity.[23] Thus, it is not surprising that research conducted during the COVID-19 pandemic found that effective and empathetic listening is one of the most important factors in promoting workplace productivity.[24] Unfortunately, other research has shown that 88% of the employers surveyed indicated that finding individuals with good listening skills is difficult or at least somewhat challenging.[25] In this section we explain several barriers that can challenge our listening effectiveness, including noise, perceptions of others, and yourself. For explanations and examples of these types of barriers, see Table 5.1.

The barriers listed in Table 5.1 are common, but as our cultural listening habits change, these barriers evolve and new ones are added. A conference sponsored by the International Commission on Biological Effects of Noise noted that the proliferation of noise created by humans—everything from cars and airplanes to smartphones and video games—is starting to cause fatal accidents for adults and poorer achievement in children because of the sheer number of audible distractions.[26] Likewise, Lenore Skenazy, writing in *Advertising Age,* complained that smartphones and other personal communication devices might be diminishing ongoing practice with face-to-face communication skills, such as listening.[27] Other studies show that listening to loud, fast music significantly diminishes our ability to comprehend things we read or hear.[28] In sum, these barriers point to one conclusion: our listening practices are more complicated because more and more things draw our attention.

Modern technology, including smartphones, laptops, smartwatches, and tablets, can pose challenges for good listening. If you are in a large class, you have probably even seen people carry on telephone conversations using earbuds to try to conceal their behaviors. When we multitask by trying to listen to someone while texting, posting a picture, or just browsing on the internet, we are likely diminishing our ability to function well as a listener. Recall that short-term memory is limited. When we multitask, we place greater strain on our working memory and short-term memory, which can impede all other aspects of our ability to process information. For instance, assume you are listening to a training podcast for your job and you decide to answer a text from your partner. Each time you stop listening to the podcast to read or answer a text, you lose mental momentum on your listening and have to restart. In fact, our own research on this topic shows that in classroom situations, students record 62% less information in their notes when they multitask by texting or posting on social media during the lesson.[29]

The current polarized social and political climate observed across the globe has started to create poor listening habits. Writing for the Huffington Post, psychologist Chloe Carmichael noted that sociopolitical discord has created "group polarization . . . [where] people who have different views become reactionary and disagree with one another in a knee jerk response."[30] As she explains, one way to counteract such polarization is to practice good listening.

Individuals can have authentic disagreement on particular issues. However, for any two (or more) people, there are also many points of agreement. Your friend may disagree with you on your views about immigration but agree that the immigration system needs revision. You may lean blue while your parents lean red, but you may agree that all politicians should

Table 5.1 Barriers to Listening

Type of Barrier	Explanation and Example
NOISE	
Physical distractions	All the stimuli in the environment that keep you from focusing on the message. Example: loud music playing at a party
Mental distractions	The wandering of the mind when it is supposed to be focusing on something. Example: thinking about a lunch date while listening to a teacher
Multitasking	Trying to do two or more tasks simultaneously. Example: reading an article while carrying on a conversation with family
Factual distractions	Focusing so intently on details that you miss the main point. Example: listening to all the details of a conversation but forgetting the main idea
Semantic distractions	Overresponding to an emotion-laden word or concept. Example: not listening when someone claims to be "conservative" or "progressive"
PERCEPTION OF OTHERS	
Status	Devoting attention based on the social standing, rank, or perceived value of another. Example: not listening to a freshman in a group activity
Stereotypes	Treating individuals as if they were the same as others in a given category. Example: making assumptions about how to interpret the words of another based on race or ethnicity
Sights and sounds	Letting appearances or voice qualities affect your listening. Example: assuming that a person with long hair and tattoos will make poor arguments
YOURSELF	
Egocentrism	Excessive self-focus, or seeing yourself as the central concern in every conversation. Example: redirecting group conversations to your own interests
Defensiveness	Acting threatened and feeling as though you must defend what you have said or done. Example: assuming others' comments are veiled criticisms of you
Experiential superiority	Looking down on others as if their life experiences were not as good as yours. Example: not listening to a coworker who is new
Personal bias	Letting your own predispositions, or strongly held beliefs, interfere with your ability to interpret information correctly. Example: assuming that people are generally truthful (or deceitful)
Pseudolistening	Pretending to listen but letting your mind or attention wander to something else. Example: texting while your professor is lecturing

be held to higher standards of ethical and moral responsibility. As you discuss points of authentic disagreement, rather than saying that you will simply agree to disagree, you should listen carefully for points of common ground. In the end, finding common ground provides pathways for moving forward, whether it be in a relationship or political debate. Common ground may not eliminate disagreement on some issues, but it is far less polarizing and represents careful and skillful listening behaviors.

Beyond the negative effects of technology and polarization on listening habits, recent research by communication scholar Elizabeth Parks suggests that there are generational differences in listening.[31] Her study found that individuals born after 1997, commonly referred to as Generation Z, are significantly more likely than previous generations to engage in evaluative listening, which is associated with being critical and argumentative with another. Parks notes that such listening habits may be common among Gen-Z individuals, but it may run contrary to norms of other generations. This research illustrates how personal biases could diminish the effectiveness of listening among people from different generations.

Ways to Become a Better Listener

sizing things up

Barriers to Listening

The following statements describe how you might react to several specific listening situations. Read each statement carefully and indicate how strongly you agree or disagree by using the following scale:

1 = Strongly disagree
2 = Disagree
3 = Neither agree nor disagree
4 = Agree
5 = Strongly agree

When listening to others I often . . .

1. assume that their viewpoint will be similar to those of other people like them.
2. respect others' opinions, even when they have less experience than I have.
3. think about other things while the person is talking.
4. get distracted by their physical appearance.
5. pay close attention but have trouble remembering their main ideas.
6. feel threatened or that the person is attacking me or my beliefs.
7. get put off by terms or phrases used by others.
8. pay less attention to people who are not important.
9. pay less attention if what they are saying does not pertain to me.

There are no right or wrong answers to these statements. A guide for scoring your responses appears at the end of the chapter.

So far in this chapter we have emphasized the importance of listening while also pointing out barriers to effective listening. Faced with this knowledge, you might wonder how any of us can hope to become effective listeners. After all, the potential barriers are many. Fortunately, each of us can take several steps to overcome these barriers to good listening. In this section we explain how you can become a better listener by recognizing differences, listening and thinking critically, using verbal and nonverbal communication effectively, checking your understanding, and taking good notes.

RECOGNIZE DIFFERENCES IN LISTENING

The first step in becoming a better listener is to recognize that we all have different tendencies that can influence how we listen to others. Although these tendencies can be influenced by many different factors, such as our family life and our early language development, even our gender can influence our listening habits. Have you ever had a conversation with people of the opposite gender and thought afterward that they did not listen well? If so, you are not alone. Debra Tannen, a linguistics professor and acclaimed author of the book *You Just Don't Understand: Women and Men in Conversation,* suggests that men and women have very distinct communication styles, which influence everything from how they use vocal inflections to how they listen. For example, Tannen suggests that men tend to be more instrumental or task-oriented when communicating, whereas women tend to be more relationally

oriented.[32] Furthermore, a woman listening to her female friend talk about her relationship problems will likely keep eye contact with the speaker, listen for emotions to which she can relate, and nod to confirm she understands what her friend is saying. In contrast, a man listening to his male friend talk about his relationship problems will likely make less eye contact while listening for key facts to identify a problem he can help solve. While men and women tend to be comfortable with these communication styles among their own genders, communication frustration can sometimes occur when men and women talk to each other. See Table 5.2 for some of the more commonly observed differences relevant to listening. Tannen's explanation of observed gender differences in listening behaviors should not be applied as a stereotype. Some men may enact listening behaviors more typical of women's listening habits, and vice-versa. Though Tannen's work is useful for understanding possible differences in listening behaviors between people, her conclusions may not apply for many people. Consider how Tannen's findings can help you become more aware of your strengths and weaknesses as a listener.

LISTEN AND THINK CRITICALLY

As mentioned earlier in this chapter, critical listening and critical thinking go hand in hand: you cannot listen critically without also thinking critically. We have already noted that critical listening is a

• Men and women tend to enact different behaviors when listening.

Westend61/Getty Images

Table 5.2 Listening Differences Between Men and Women

Characteristics of Listening	Women	Men
Purpose for Listening	Listen to understand the other person's emotions and to find common interests	Listen in order to take action and solve problems
Listening Preferences	Like complex information that requires careful evaluation	Like short, concise, unambiguous, and error-free communication
Listening Awareness	Are highly perceptive to how well the other person understands	Often fail to recognize when others do not understand
Nonverbal Listening Behaviors	Tend to be attentive and to have sustained eye contact with the other person	Tend to be less attentive and to use glances to monitor reactions and eye contact to indicate liking
Interruptive Behaviors	Interrupt less often, with interruptions usually signaling agreement and support	Interrupt more often, with interruptions often used to switch topics

Sources: Tannen, D. (2011). *You just don't understand: Women and men in conversation.* Harper-Collins; Watson, K., Lazarus, C. J., & Todd, T. (1999). First-year medical students' listener preferences: A longitudinal study. *International Journal of Listening, 13*: 1–11; Weisfeld, C. C., & Stack, M. A. (2002). When I look into your eyes. *Psychology, Evolution and Gender, 4*: 125–147.

form of active listening in which you carefully analyze the accuracy, meaningfulness, and utility of a speaker's message. Similarly, **critical thinking** involves analyzing the speaker, the situation, and the speaker's ideas to make critical judgments about the message being presented. Although we discuss critical thinking in terms of its relationship to critical listening, you also use critical thinking when reading, watching television, or analyzing the ingredients of a tasty meal.

One way to think critically is to analyze the communication situation. Are there characteristics of the situation that tip you off that the information will be important? If your supervisor organized a staff meeting, would you pay more attention if she came in with a somber look on her face after a long meeting with the department manager? The communication context will provide cues about the situation and suggest key things to remain aware of while listening.

A second skill in critical listening is to analyze the credibility of the speaker. **Source credibility** is the extent to which you perceive the speaker as competent and trustworthy. If you wanted to know what procedures are required to study in Europe for a semester, who would give you the best information? Would you be more likely to trust your roommate, who heard about foreign exchange programs during freshman orientation; your adviser, who had an exchange student a few years back; or the director of international programs on your campus? If your car ran poorly, would you trust your neighbor's advice or that of an auto mechanic? The choice seems obvious in these situations. When assessing the credibility of a speaker, you should determine the credibility of the person in relation to his or her qualifications, experience, and potential biases or ulterior motives for taking a certain position.

One way of analyzing the credibility of speakers is to determine whether they are reporting something they have seen or experienced personally or something they have heard from someone else. Also important is whether they are providing factual accounts or opinions. The following questions can guide your preliminary analysis of source credibility.

- *Is the person presenting observations or inferences?* Observations are descriptions of things that can be seen, heard, tasted, smelled, or felt. Inferences are conclusions drawn from observations. You might observe that a number of people who are homeless live in your community. Based on that observation, you might infer that your community does not have enough affordable housing.

- *If presenting observations, are they first-person or second-person?* A **first-person observation** is based on something that was personally sensed; a **second-person observation** is a report of what another person observed. First-person observations are typically more accurate because they are direct accounts rather than inferences drawn from others' accounts.

Although a careful analysis of these questions will help you develop initial perceptions about a person's credibility, your analysis should not end there. The speaker's sincerity, trustworthiness, passion, and use of evidence and reasoning are among many factors that you might take into account to refine your assessment of the speaker's credibility.

After you have analyzed the situation and formed initial impressions about the speaker's credibility, a final step in critical thinking is to analyze the arguments the speaker is making. One of the simplest ways of analyzing an argument is to use Stephen Toulmin's concepts of data, claim, and warrant.[33] As shown in Figure 5.3, Toulmin provides a way of diagramming how the components of an argument fit together. A claim is the overall point or conclusion of the argument. Every argument begins with data, which consist of factual or agreed-upon evidence. Based on the evidence, a speaker uses a warrant to develop a logical connection, or bridge, between the agreed-upon data and the claim. If any of these elements are missing, the argument has no foundation.

critical thinking
Analyzing the speaker, the situation, and the speaker's ideas to make critical judgments about the message being presented.

source credibility
The extent to which the speaker is perceived as competent to make certain claims.

first-person observation
An observation based on something that you personally have sensed.

second-person observation
A report of what another person observed.

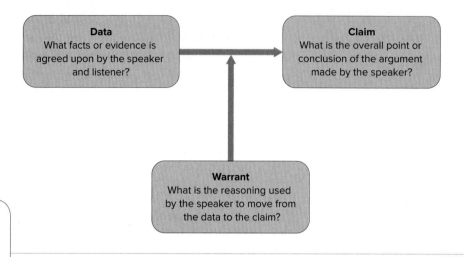

Figure 5.3

Stephen Toulmin's concepts of data, claim, and warrant.

Source: Toulmin, S. E. (1958) *The uses of argument*. Cambridge University Press.

We see examples of Toulmin's argument layout in nearly every persuasive speech. When Apple executives plan events to introduce new product models, or in some instances brand new devices, they typically begin with the data that consumers want technology that is useful and easy-to-use. Then, Tim Cook or other speakers go on to explain how new devices or software updates will accomplish that objective. Through multiple live examples, those presenters develop strong warrants that connect believable assumptions about what consumers want with the conclusion that purchasing Apple's new products will meet those needs. Think about how this strategy was used for the iPhone, iPad, and Apple Watch with great success. Using the questions posed in Figure 5.3, you can analyze nearly any argument to think more critically about what another person is saying.

building **behaviors**

Using TED to Practice Critical Thinking

Critical thinking is one of the most important listening skills you can develop while in college. Being a good critical listener is vital to all aspects of your adult life. You can practice suggestions for critical thinking discussed in this chapter by watching a TED talk on a topic of interest to you (www.TED.com, or use the free mobile TED app). While watching the video, analyze the speaker's credibility and attempt to dissect the arguments presented by the speaker using Toulmin's argument layout.

USE NONVERBAL COMMUNICATION EFFECTIVELY

Although you demonstrate active listening through verbal skills, the majority of your active listening ability is shown through nonverbal communication. The following nonverbal skills are essential to your ability to demonstrate active listening. As you listen to another person, have a friend observe you to determine if you are practicing these skills.

1. *Demonstrate bodily responsiveness.* Use movement and gestures to show your awareness of the speaker's message. Shaking your head in disbelief, conveying the measurements of an object by indicating the size with your hands, and moving toward a person who is quietly disclosing negative information are appropriate bodily responses.

2. *Lean forward.* By leaning toward the speaker, you demonstrate interest in the speaker. A forward lean also suggests responsiveness. In addition, leaning places you in a physical state of readiness to listen to the speaker.

3. *Use direct body orientation.* Do not angle yourself away from the speaker; instead, sit or stand so that you are directly facing the speaker. A parallel body position allows

the greatest possibility for observing and listening to the speaker's verbal and nonverbal messages. When you stand or sit at an angle to the speaker, you may be creating the impression that you are attempting to get away or that you are moving away from the speaker. An angled position also blocks your vision and allows you to be distracted by other stimuli in the environment.

4. *Maintain relaxed but alert posture.* Your posture should not be tense or "proper," but neither should it be so relaxed that you appear to be resting. Slouching suggests unresponsiveness; a tense body position suggests nervousness or discomfort; and a relaxed position accompanied by crossed arms and legs, a backward lean in a chair, and a confident facial expression suggests arrogance. Your posture should suggest to others that you are interested and that you are comfortable talking with them.

• Close proximity, and even touching, can show that you are listening with empathy.

Eric Audras/Onoky/SuperStock

5. *Establish an open body position.* Sit or stand with your body open to the other person. Crossing your arms or legs may be more comfortable, but that posture frequently suggests that you are closed off psychologically as well as physically. To maximize your nonverbal message to the other person that you are "open," you should sit or stand without crossing your arms or legs.

6. *Use positive, responsive facial expressions and head movement.* Your face and head will be the speaker's primary focus. The speaker will be observing you, and your facial expressions and head movement will be the key. You can demonstrate your interest by nodding your head to show interest or agreement. You can use positive and responsive facial expressions, such as smiling and raising your eyebrows.

7. *Establish direct eye contact.* The speaker will be watching your eyes for interest. One of the first signs of a lack of interest is the tendency to be distracted by other stimuli in the environment. For example, an instructor who continually glances out the door of the lecture hall, a roommate who sneaks peeks at the television while you tell a story, and a business executive who regularly looks at the clock during a meeting are all indicating lack of interest. Try to focus on and direct your gaze at the speaker. When you begin to look around the room, you may find any number of other stimuli to distract your attention from the speaker and the message.

8. *Sit or stand close to the speaker.* Establishing close proximity to the speaker has two benefits. First, you put yourself in a position that allows you to hear the other person and that minimizes distracting noises, sights, and other stimuli. Second, you demonstrate your concern or your positive feelings for the speaker. You probably do not stand or sit close to people you do not like or respect or with whom you do not have common experiences. Close physical proximity enables active listening.

engaging diversity

Using Touch as Feedback

We use a variety of nonverbal behaviors to provide feedback and demonstrate that we are listening carefully. Touch is often used to signal that we are listening and to provide feedback. For example, we may use a hug or a simple hand on the shoulder to console someone.

Researchers from multiple fields are developing greater awareness that substantial diversity exists between individuals on how they both practice and perceive empathy. Neuroscientists from Germany found that individuals who are more likely to be empathetic are also more strongly oriented toward touching behaviors. In essence, these individuals are more likely to touch another person when showing empathy and are more likely to perceive touch from another as signaling empathy. Conversely, individuals who dislike being touched may be less likely to engage in empathetic listening behaviors. This research teaches us that diversity in how we perceive the world, such as our perceptions of touch, can substantially impact how we listen to and respond to others.

Source: Schaefer, M., Joch, M., & Rother, N. (2021, February 9). Feeling touched: Empathy is associated with performance in a tactile acuity test. *Frontiers in Human Neuroscience*, doi: 10.3389/fnhum.2021.593425

9. *Be vocally responsive.* Change your pitch, rate, inflection, and volume as you respond to the speaker. Making appropriate changes and choices shows that you are actually listening, in contrast to responding in a standard, patterned manner that suggests you are only appearing to listen. Responding to your roommate or partner's story about an exciting event at work with a dull, monotone "yeah, that's great," accompanied by frequent glances at your phone, would not signal active listening.

10. *Provide supportive utterances.* Sometimes you can demonstrate more concern through nonverbal sounds, such as "mmm," "mmm-hmm," and "uh-huh" than you can by stating, "Yes, I understand." You can easily provide supportive utterances while others are talking or when they pause. You are suggesting to them that you are listening but do not want to interrupt with a verbalization of your own at this particular time. Such sounds encourage the speaker to continue without interruption.

USE VERBAL COMMUNICATION EFFECTIVELY

The notion of the verbal components of listening may seem strange to you. You may reason that, if you are engaged in listening, you cannot also be speaking. Recall though that communication is a process that includes feedback. While listening, you must use both verbal and nonverbal feedback to negotiate meaning with another person. To measure your current competence in this area, consider the skills you regularly practice:

1. *Invite additional comments.* Suggest that the speaker add more details or give additional information. Phrases such as "Go on," "What else?" "How did you feel about that?" and "Did anything else happen?" encourage the speaker to continue to share ideas and information.

2. *Ask questions.* One method of inviting the speaker to continue is to ask direct questions, requesting more in-depth details, definitions, or clarification.

3. *Identify areas of agreement or common experience.* Briefly relate similar past experiences, or briefly explain a similar point of view that you hold. Sharing ideas, attitudes, values, and beliefs is the basis of communication. In addition, such comments demonstrate your understanding.

4. *Vary verbal responses.* Use a variety of responses, such as "Yes," "I see," "Go on," and "Right," instead of relying on one standard, unaltered response, such as "Yes," "Yes," "Yes."

5. *Provide clear verbal responses.* Use specific and concrete words and phrases in your feedback to the speaker. Misunderstandings can occur if you do not provide easily understood responses.

6. *Use descriptive, nonevaluative responses.* It is better to say, "Your statistics are from an organization that is biased against gun control," which is descriptive, than to say, "Your speech was a bunch of lies," which is evaluative. Trivializing or joking about serious disclosures suggests a negative evaluation of the speaker. Similarly, derogatory remarks are seen as offensive. Acting superior to the speaker by stating that you believe you have a more advanced understanding suggests an evaluative tone.

7. *Provide affirmative and affirming statements.* Comments such as "Yes," "I see," "I understand," and "I know" provide affirmation. Offering praise and specific positive statements demonstrates concern.

8. *Avoid complete silence.* The lack of any response suggests that you are not listening to the speaker. The "silent treatment" induced by sleepiness or lack of interest may result in defensiveness or anger on the part of the speaker. Appropriate verbal feedback demonstrates your active listening.

9. *Allow other people the opportunity of a complete hearing.* When you discuss common feelings or experiences, avoid dominating the conversation. Allow others to go into depth and detail, give them the option of changing the topic under discussion, and let them talk without being interrupted.

CHECK YOUR UNDERSTANDING

When we listen to others, we are actually engaging in a specialized form of the perception process (see Chapter 2). Because listening is a specialized form of perceiving, you should engage in perception checking to ensure that your perceptions match what the speaker intends. In the context of listening, rather than calling this perception checking, we might refer to it as checking your understanding. You can check your understanding by practicing these skills:

1. *Ask questions for clarification.* Before testing your understanding of the speaker's message, make sure you have a clear idea of what is being said. Begin by asking questions to gain more information. For specific factual information, you may use closed questions (such as yes or no questions), and for more general information you may ask open-ended questions (questions pertaining to what, when, where, how, and why). Once you have gained sufficient information, you can ask the speaker to check your understanding against what was intended.

2. *Paraphrase the speaker's message.* Using "I statements," attempt to paraphrase what you think the speaker was saying so that the speaker can determine whether your understanding matches what was intended.

3. *Paraphrase the speaker's intent.* Using "I statements," attempt to paraphrase what you interpret as the intent or motivation of the speaker. After hearing your assumptions about the intent, the speaker may talk with you more to refine your understanding.

4. *Identify areas of confusion.* If there are specific aspects of the message that you are still confused about, mention those to the speaker while you are expressing your initial understanding of the message.

5. *Invite clarification and correction.* Asking the speaker to correct your interpretation of the message will invite additional explanation. The ensuing dialogue will help you and the speaker share meaning more effectively.

6. *Go back to the beginning.* As necessary, return to the first step in this process to check your new understanding of the speaker's message and intent. Good listening is a process without clear beginning and ending points, so you should check your understanding at each stage in the process.

TAKE GOOD NOTES

Note-taking is one of the most effective skills you can develop as a listener, particularly as a college student. Several options, or formats, are available to you as a note-taker, including the narrative method, the matrix method, the outline method, the mind-map method, and the Cornell method. You can find additional information about each method by searching online, or your school may have a learning resource center that can provide additional assistance.

• Taking notes is an effective strategy to maintain attention and easily remember information.
fizkes/Shutterstock

• The *narrative method* uses complete sentences and paragraph structure to try to record ideas as close as possible to word-for-word. Many people opt for this approach when using a laptop or tablet. Although this method is useful when exact wording is critical, it is also the most difficult method because people tend to speak faster than we can write. Moreover, these types of notes often lack the organization necessary for efficient review.

- The *matrix method* organizes information into rows and columns, similar to what a spreadsheet looks like. This format is useful when you need to emphasize details within the intersections of multiple categories. Therefore, if you had rows for each of the communication contexts (interpersonal, small group, public speaking, and so on), one column for verbal communication, and a second column for nonverbal communication, the intersecting cells in that matrix would allow you to note an example illustrating nonverbal communication in public speaking, verbal communication in small groups, and any other combination of communication types and contexts.

- The *outline method* uses numbers and letters to indicate main points and subordinate points, respectively. Each set of subordinate points is typically indented under more general or main points. This method requires you to summarize key concepts and points and supporting details. This format of note-taking is effective and a good general-purpose approach. Although more organized than the narrative method, it potentially conceals the types of interrelationships made apparent by the matrix method.

- The *mind-map method* uses a web-like diagram to show how concepts are connected. This visual approach is particularly useful for brainstorming ideas and synthesizing information after a lecture or reading assignment. Using this method during a lecture may be challenging because it may not be immediately apparent how information should visually connect.

- The *Cornell method* uses columns to organize information. For this method you will divide your paper into a wide column on the right and a narrow column on the left. In the wide column, you should record details using an outline format, bullet points, sentences, or key terms. In the smaller column, you should synthesize and identify the main points, make comments to yourself, and note key details such as definitions and answers to known test questions. Like outlining, this is a good general-purpose note-taking approach.

The most effective note-takers use combinations of each method depending on the circumstances. Both the outlining and Cornell methods work well across a variety of situations, though some content might be particularly favorable for a matrix or mind-map format. No single method might be best. Your objective as a learner should be to format notes to fit your study habits and the information you are trying to learn.

We often assume that note-taking is limited to classrooms. However, many people carry small composition books to record notes and reflections from meetings, one-on-one conversations, and other nonclassroom contexts. Many people also take notes digitally using an iPad or similar device equipped with a stylus. Regardless of the technology used, note-taking is a listening skill that is valuable across situations.

Effective Listening in Different Situations

Most listening skills will serve you well in every communication situation. Listening critically, mastering nonverbal cues, and checking your understanding will always aid your comprehension of the message. In this section you will learn about listening skills that are important in some of the most common and important listening situations that you regularly confront.

LISTENING IN THE WORKPLACE

As our nation has shifted from an industrial-based economy to an information-based economy, effective listening has become recognized as an essential skill for workers. Statistics from the U.S. Bureau of Labor Statistics show that by 2031 just over 80% of the workforce in the United States will be employed in service-oriented industries, such as education, healthcare, retail sales, and state and local government.[34] These jobs all have one thing in common—they require employee–customer interaction in which listening skills translate into revenue.

Organizations are increasingly interested in developing effective communication skills for both new and experienced managers. In fact, performance feedback for most managers highlights listening as one of the most important areas for improvement. Research reported in the Public Relations Review suggests that such improvement is necessary.[35] Findings of that study show that in many organizations, managers ineffectively listen to employees' concerns due to limited training on listening skills, an over-reliance on surveys to gather employee feedback, and pseudolistening, one of the barriers mentioned earlier in the chapter. The authors of the study concluded that one of the most important areas of improvement for managers is to engage in ethical listening behaviors that shows concern for others' feelings. They reason that when managers listen with concern for others, they are more likely to use ethical and moral reasoning to make decisions that affect employees.

Even if you are not a manager, being an active listener who seeks to understand others' emotions is a highly effective skill in any organization. The following are some other listening skills that will benefit you in the workplace:

- Be deliberate in paying attention to others who are speaking.
- Use nonverbal feedback to indicate that you are actively listening.
- Refrain from interrupting others when they are talking, even if you are agreeing with them.
- Seek to understand what others are saying before providing a verbal reaction.
- Verbally summarize what you view as the key takeaways and action items that were discussed in a meeting.

LISTENING IN THE CLASSROOM

Take a moment to think about how often, as a student, you find yourself listening to a lecture. If you were to estimate how much of your time is spent listening to lectures, how much would it be? If you said "a lot," you would not be alone. Researchers have estimated that college students spend at least 10 hours per week attending lectures.[36] If you take a typical 15-credit load in a semester, that 10 hours per week translates into about 80% of your time in class being spent listening to lectures.[37] The prominence of listening in students' lives led communication scholars Larry Vinson and Craig Johnson to coin the term **lecture listening**—the ability to listen to, mentally process, and recall lecture information.[38]

lecture listening
The ability to listen to, mentally process, and recall lecture information.

What constitutes effective lecture listening? Although a variety of answers have been offered, educational researcher Michael Gilbert provides the following general suggestions:

1. *Find areas of interest in what you are listening to.* Constantly look for how you can use the information.
2. *Remain open.* Avoid the temptation to focus only on the lecturer's delivery; withhold evaluative judgments until the lecturer has finished. Recognize your emotional triggers, and avoid letting them distract you.
3. *Work at listening.* Capitalize on your mind's ability to think faster than the lecturer can talk. Mentally summarize and review what has been said, mentally organize information, and find connections to what you already know or are currently learning.

4. *Avoid letting distractions distract.* Monitor your attention and recognize when it is waning. If you are becoming distracted, refocus your attention on the lecturer. This is a critical point in today's digital culture. Recent research noted that nonacademic internet use by students during class is common and that such activity is associated with lower grades.[39]

5. *Listen for and note main ideas.* Focus on the central themes of what is being presented, and make notes about those themes. Effective notes outlining the main ideas of a lecture can, in some cases, be more useful than pages of notes containing unorganized details.[40]

As noted earlier, note-taking is an essential listening skill, particularly in the classroom. Research has found that effective note-taking during lectures can increase scores on exams by more than 20%—a difference between receiving a C and receiving an A.[41] Unfortunately, students typically do not record enough notes during a lecture. Research generally shows that less than 40% of the information in a lecture makes it into students' notes. In short, most students are unable to capitalize on the benefits of note-taking simply because their notes are incomplete.

Now that you understand why note-taking is so important, how can you become a more effective note-taker? In your notes your goal should be to record both the outline of the lecture—called organizational points—and the details supporting those points. The most effective way to ensure that you record all of these points is to listen for **lecture cues**—verbal or nonverbal signals that stress points or indicate transitions between ideas during a lecture. Table 5.3 summarizes various types of lecture cues commonly used by teachers. While taking notes, you should listen and watch for these types of cues.

lecture cues
Verbal or nonverbal signals that stress points or indicate transitions between ideas during a lecture.

Table 5.3 Common Lecture Cues Teachers Use

Type of Cue	Example	Main Uses
Written outlines	Points of lecture on transparency or PowerPoint slide	Indicate main and subordinate ideas
Words/phrases	Term written on the whiteboard	Stress important terms and accompanying definitions
Verbal importance cues	"Now, *and this will be on the exam next week,* we will explore . . ."	Stress important concepts deemed essential for recall/understanding
Semantic cues	"Here is an *example [definition, explanation, conclusion, implication,* or *illustration]* of uncertainty reduction theory in action . . ."	Signal common types of details that make up the lecture content
Organizational cues	"The *third thing* I want to discuss today is . . ."	Orally provide indications of main and subordinate points in a lecture
Nonverbal cues	Holding up two fingers when saying, "I will discuss two concepts today . . ."	Can serve any of the functions of nonverbal behaviors discussed in Chapter 4, on nonverbal communication

Research has also examined the importance of lecture cues for students.[42] A group of students were taught about organizational cues and were asked to listen for those cues and take notes during a videotaped lecture. Students in another group were not informed about organizational cues but viewed and took notes during the same lecture. The students who were taught about organizational cues recorded four times the number of organizational points and twice the number of details in their notes. These students were able to capitalize on their note-taking effectiveness; they received the equivalent of an A on a quiz about the lecture. Their counterparts, who were unaware of and did not listen for organizational cues, received the equivalent of a C. This research looked at the effects of teaching students about organizational cues only. Imagine what could have happened if these students had been taught about all types of lecture cues. Fortunately, you are now equipped with this information.

communicating with agility

Listening with Curiosity

Great listening skills are the secret ingredient to being an agile communicator. In classroom situations, in the workplace, or with your family and friends, be intentional in how you listen. If you listen with a mindset of curiosity, you will be far more likely to perceive messages with an open mind, ask questions, and grow your ability to carefully interpret messages from others. In so doing, you will also develop skills in shaping your own messages in response to others. Brian Branagan, an executive coach in Silicon Valley, observed that communication agility is enhanced when we *listen for* rather than *listen to*. When we listen *to*, we are simply hearing words. However, when we listen *for*, we are attempting to understand meaning from another person through their body language, emotions, and other messages. Branagan advises that curious listening, listening *for*, makes it less likely that you will react with emotion and more likely that you will establish clearer understanding with others.

Source: Branagan, B. (2017, October 18). Deep listening: Creating conversational agility. *InfoQ.* www.infoq.com/presentations/deep-listening-conversational-agility/

LISTENING TO MEDIA

Think about how much time you spend watching shows and movies; listening to music; reading magazines, newspapers, or books; sending a snap; chatting online; or just surfing the web. Many of us might avoid that thought because it might frighten us. The Centers for Disease Control and Prevention (CDC) has reported statistics showing that, on a typical day, children who are at least two years old spend over two hours per day watching television.[43] If other forms of media consumption, such as playing video games or using the internet, were factored into these statistics, the number would be much higher. These statistics show that our saturation with mediated messages begins at an early age. Also, the CDC warns that such ubiquitous use of the media might be linked to important health issues, such as childhood obesity.

Given the quantity of mediated communication to which we are exposed each day, we must become critical consumers of such information. Think how much money you would spend if you "bought in" to every commercial you saw, or think how much time it would take for you to read every email you get (including "junk" email). Simply put, good listening behaviors are essential because mediated communication is so prevalent.

One way to be an effective listener in a mediated culture is to have information literacy. **Information literacy** is defined by the American Library Association in the following way: "To be information literate an individual must recognize when information is needed and have the ability to locate, evaluate and use effectively the information needed."[44] According to this definition, information-literate individuals are able to think critically, know when and how to find more information, and know how to evaluate information.

information literacy The ability to recognize when information is needed and to locate, evaluate, and effectively use the information needed.

• Online communication can cause emotional reactions to what other say. When listening on social media or elsewhere online, we benefit by checking our understanding before reacting.

HBRH/Shutterstock

Mediated communication is not limited to advertising and television. In 2022, it was estimated that just over 66% of the world population uses the internet regularly.[45] To put that percentage in perspective, the corresponding 2011 value was 35%.[46] How do people use the internet? As of 2022, average internet users spend roughly 2.5 hours per day on social media.[47] These findings suggest that much of what we listen to and consume comes from online sources. In fact, most college-age students get the majority of their news from online sources rather than more traditional print, broadcast, and cable outlets. Moreover, much of our communication with others flows through digital channels, such as email, text messages, and social media posts.

Online communication requires different approaches to being an effective listener and consumer of communication. The principal problem with online communication—whether you are texting someone or messaging on social media—is that nonverbal communication is difficult. Recall that nonverbal communication provides significant clues about another person's emotions and feelings. Without the ability to see and hear the other person, how can you tell what that person might be thinking? When communicating using digital tools, you may perceive messages in ways not intended. For instance, you may interpret a short message as being angry or abrupt when, in fact, the person was texting while doing something else. When using other tools, such as Instagram or Facebook, remember that our comments and posts are often full of subtexts and hidden meanings. Take care to check your understanding of messages and intentions when consuming personal messages from others.

LISTENING IN A SECOND LANGUAGE

Many of the suggestions provided in this chapter are for both native English speakers and English language learners (ELLs). However, if you are a nonnative speaker, some understanding of how to further develop your listening skills can speed your progress as an effective listener. Research suggests that second-language listening development requires two skills: vocabulary comprehension and metacognitive awareness.[48] Vocabulary comprehension is more than just memorizing lists of terms. Rather, vocabulary is strengthened by recognizing the sounds of words and associating those sounds with their meaning. Being immersed in a new culture will assist you in developing such connections, particularly if you seek out and engage in sustained conversations with others. You can also use television and other media to broaden your listening experiences and assist you in vocabulary development.

In addition to developing your vocabulary, you should try to develop your metacognitive skills. Metacognition is your ability to use "mental strategies" to assist in quickly determining the meaning of words. Learning to decipher words by drawing inferences on their meaning from the context and other words around them is one such strategy. Another example of metacognition is drawing parallels between English vocabulary and your native vocabulary. Through such strategies you will make quicker inferences about what new terms mean and will be able to listen more efficiently.

Of course, if you have difficulty listening because the other person is speaking rapidly or using words you have not heard, you should feel comfortable telling the person. Adaptation to language differences is the responsibility of everyone involved in a communication situation, and you should not take on the entire challenge of trying to make the interaction succeed.

Ways to Be an Ethical Listener

Although effective listening requires you to adapt your verbal, nonverbal, and perception-checking skills to specific situations, such as the workplace, the classroom, and mediated environments, you must also take care to enact ethical listening behaviors. To be an ethical listener, you should practice the following behaviors:

1. *Recognize the sources of your own conversational habits.* Your family, school, and other life experiences have allowed you to develop certain habits, which in some situations could be strengths and in others could represent areas for improvement. Recognizing those habits will allow you to more fully adapt to those with whom you are communicating.

2. *Monitor your communication to recognize when you are engaging in poor listening behaviors.* Perhaps the most important step in becoming an ethical listener is recognizing that you must work hard to be a good listener—a step that begins with an awareness of what you are doing in the situation.

3. *Apply general ethical principles to how you respond.* Planning your responses so that you are respectful to others is an example of how your personal ethics can influence your listening behaviors.

4. *Adapt to others.* Recognize that other people also have unique communication styles and that you might need to adapt your listening behaviors so that you can fully understand what they are trying to say.[49]

be ready... for what's next

Taking Notes with Apps

One of the most important skills that you will develop in college is note-taking. Good notes now may influence your performance on a test or an assignment; good notes after graduation may affect your job performance. Many smartphone, tablet, or laptop apps can be used for note-taking. People often use these apps because they are efficient and provide a secure storage option for important notes.

The recently published book *Digital Distractions in the College Classroom* synthesizes advantages and disadvantages of using digital devices and apps in the classroom. Although taking digital notes can be as effective as taking handwritten notes, using your device to take notes can present a number of distractions, including social media notifications and the temptation to multitask. When using a notetaking app, you should take practical steps to avoid distractions, such as putting your device on airplane mode and silencing notifications. Additionally, many tablets and apps allow you to use digital pencils to take notes by hand. This approach can combine many of the advantages of handwritten notes with digital notes. Using a stylus or digital pencil may help you avoid distractions because it is a more creative and active way of recording information compared to typing.

Source: Flanagan, A. E., & Kim, J. H. Y. (2022). Digital distractions in the college classroom. *IGI Global*.

Chapter Review & Study Guide

Summary

In this chapter you learned the following:

1. Listening is an important skill because it is one of our most common communication activities, it helps us build and maintain relationships, and it is essential for success in most professional situations.

2. Listening is an active process that differs from the physical act of hearing.

   - Hearing is the physical act of receiving a sound. We hear all of the noises around us. Listening is the active process of receiving, paying attention to, assigning meaning to, and responding to sounds. Listening is an active process, whereas hearing is reflexive.

   - Listening is a process that involves attention, working memory, short-term memory, and long-term memory.

   - Listening is generally divided into active, empathic, critical, and enjoyment listening. Active listening, which is listening with a purpose, includes both empathic and critical listening. Empathic listening occurs when you are attempting to understand another person. Critical listening requires evaluating a speaker's message for accuracy, meaningfulness, and usefulness. We also listen to things, such as music, for enjoyment purposes.

3. A variety of barriers prevent many of us from being effective listeners.

   - One barrier is noise, which includes both physical and internal distractions. Physical distractions are any audible noises in the communication environment. Internal distractions can include mental, factual, or semantic distractions.

   - Perceptions of others can include giving attention based on status, interacting with others based on stereotypes, or letting others' appearances distract you.

   - You can become your own barrier to listening when you let egocentrism, defensiveness, experiential superiority, personal biases, or pseudolistening impair your ability to listen effectively.

4. Developing skills in critical thinking, nonverbal and verbal communication, and note-taking will help you become a more effective listener.

   - Critical thinking involves the careful analysis of both the communication situation and the speaker's message. To analyze the message, you should evaluate the arguments and supporting material presented by the speaker and whether or not the speaker is credible.

   - Being nonverbally responsive, using positive facial expressions, making direct eye contact, and providing positive vocal utterances are effective nonverbal strategies.

   - Asking questions, inviting additional comments, using descriptive responses, and providing affirming statements are all examples of effective verbal strategies.

   - Good note-takers typically combine elements of the narrative, outline, matrix, mind-map, and Cornell note-taking methods.

5. Effective listening in the workplace, classroom, and mediated environment requires you to adapt the nonverbal, verbal, and critical thinking skills you learned in this chapter.

6. Ethical listening means that you should recognize and monitor your own communication style, apply general ethical principles to your responses, and adapt your communication style to others.

Key Terms

Active listening
Automatic attention
Critical listening
Critical thinking
Empathic listening
First-person observation
Hearing

Information literacy
Lecture cues
Lecture listening
Listening
Listening for enjoyment
Long-term memory
Schemas

Second-person observation
Selective attention
Short-term memory
Social media listening
Source credibility
Working memory

Study Questions

1. Hearing is a _____ process, and listening is a _____ process.
   a. mental; physical
   b. physical; mental
   c. mental; psychological
   d. physical; physical

2. Which of the following is true of social media listening?
   a. It allows organizations to build brand excitement.
   b. It is declining in effectiveness for organizations.
   c. It hampers an organization's crisis response.
   d. It slows an organization's response to problems.

3. After you have paid attention to a stimulus, you then process the material in a part of your short-term memory called
   a. working memory.
   b. selective attention.
   c. long-term memory.
   d. schema.
4. When you are listening and attempting to understand another person's worldview, what type of listening are you utilizing?
   a. active
   b. critical
   c. empathic
   d. for enjoyment
5. If you are thinking about what happened last weekend at college while listening to your mother on the phone, you are exhibiting what type of barrier to listening?
   a. stereotypes
   b. personal bias
   c. egocentrism
   d. mental distraction
6. What percent of U.S. citizens over the age of 12 report listening to a podcast in the past week?
   a. 22%
   b. 37%
   c. 41%
   d. 54%

7. Which of the following is true of critical thinking?
   a. It focuses solely on the details instead of the main point.
   b. It ignores the context in which communication is occurring.
   c. It is important when making judgments about the message being presented.
   d. It is only associated with listening.
8. Asking questions to clarify information, paraphrasing messages, and identifying confusing areas are examples of
   a. barriers to listening.
   b. listening for enjoyment.
   c. techniques for checking your understanding of a message.
   d. information literacy.
9. Suggestions for lecture listening include
   a. focusing on the lecturer's delivery and avoiding summarizing and reviewing the information.
   b. letting your attention stray in order to think creatively, listening for details, and ignoring lecture cues.
   c. avoiding taking notes so that you can focus on the lecture and the message delivery.
   d. finding areas of interest to you, avoiding distractions, and listening for main ideas.
10. According to the Public Relations Review, which of the following contributes to poor listening in organizations?
    a. poor training of lower-level employees
    b. over-reliance on surveys
    c. listening with concern
    d. a lack of pseudolistening

Answers:
1. (b); 2. (a); 3. (a); 4. (c); 5. (d); 6. (c); 7. (c); 8. (c); 9. (d); 10. (b)

Critical Thinking

1. Identify and explain barriers to listening that you have experienced in your own communication with others. Were you able to overcome the barriers, and if so, how?

2. Take a moment to reflect on a podcast or streaming channel that you regularly listen to. What are some ways in which you engage in active listening while consuming that media?

Sizing Things Up Scoring and Interpretation

Barriers to Listening

Multiple barriers to effective listening confront us on a daily basis. Table 5.1 lists several of the most common barriers. The Barriers to Listening scale created to accompany this chapter helps you determine the type of barrier that may pose the greatest difficulty for you in most situations. You will note that the nine items on the scale closely align with barriers listed in the table.

The Barriers to Listening scale can be assessed question by question to determine which barrier or group of barriers is most challenging for you. You can also average all questions to obtain an overall value indicating the extent to which the barriers listed in the table potentially impede effective listening. If you want to orient responses so that higher values always represent better listening behaviors, reverse-code responses for the following statements: 1, 3, 4, 5, 6, 7, 8, and 9. To do this, an initial response of 1 should be converted to a 5 and a response of 2 should become a 4; do the opposite if your initial response was a 4 or 5.

References

1. Isay, D. (2007). *Listening is an act of love: A celebration of American life from the StoryCorps projects.* Penguin, p. 1.

2. Janusik, L., Fullenkamp, L., & Partese, L. (2015, February 17). Listening facts. International Listening Association. http://d1025403.site.myhosting.com/files.listen.org/Facts.htm

3. Pew Research. (2022, August 8). Teens, social media, and technology 2022. https://www.pewresearch.org/internet/2022/08/10/teens-social-media-and-technology-2022/

4. Ledbetter, A., & Schrodt, P. (2008). Family communication patterns and cognitive processing: Conversation and conformity orientations as predictors of informational reception apprehension. *Communication Studies, 59,* 388–401. (p. 397)

5. Abrams, R. & Groysberg, B. (2021, December 21). How to become a better listener. *Harvard Business Review.* https://hbr.org/2021/12/how-to-become-a-better-listener

6. Mackay, H. (2015, February 9). Listening can be a tough art to master. *Albany Times Union.* http://www.timesunion.com/tuplus-business/article/Listening-can-be-a-tough-art-to-master-6071840.php

7. Jonsdottir, I. J., & Kristinsson, K. (2020). Supervisors' active-empathetic listening as an important antecedent of work engagement. *International Journal of Environmental Research and Public Health, 17,* np. https://doi.org/10:3390/ijerph17217976

8. Muhammad, Z. (2022, June 1). Social media listening is an incredible marketing resource, but are brands taking advantage of it? *Digital Information World.* https://www.digitalinformationworld.com/2022/06/social-media-listening-is-incredible.html

9. Dewey, J. (1947). *The public and its problems.* Swallow Press.

10. Tamesue, T., Tetsuro, S., & Itoh, K. (2009). Prediction method for listening score and psychological impression taking into account hearing loss due to factors such as aging. *Applied Acoustics, 70,* 426–431.

11. American Tinnitus Association (2018). *Understanding the facts* [Webpage]. https://www.ata.org/understanding-facts

12. An ILA definition of listening. (1995). *Listening Post, 53,* 1.

13. Barker, L. L. (1971). *Listening behavior.* Prentice-Hall.

14. Cuny, K. (2012). Unconditional positive regard, empathetic listening, and the impact of digital text driven communication. *International Journal of Listening, 26,* 79–82. https://doi.org/10.1080/10904018.2012.677691

15. Vitelli, R. (2016, May 23). Can listening to music help control pain? *Psychology Today.* https://www.psychology-today.com/us/blog/media-spotlight/201603/can-listening-music-help-control-pain

16. Maftoon, P., & Fakhri Alamdari, E. (2020). Exploring the effect of metacognitive strategy instruction on metacognitive awareness and listening performance through a process-based approach. *International Journal of Listening, 34,* 1–20. https://doi.org/10.1080/10904018.2016.1250632

17. García-Monge, A., Rodríguez-Navarro, H., Bores-García, D., & González-Calvo, G. (2022). Comparison of children's inhibitory control, attention and working memory in three different throwing games: EEG exploratory study. *Retos: Nuevas Perspectivas de Educación Física, Deporte y Recreación, 45,* 502–513.

18. Davidson, K. (2011). *Now you see it: How the brain science of attention will transform the way we live, work, and learn.* Viking.

19. Kuznekoff, J. H., & Titsworth, S. (2013). The impact of mobile phone usage on student learning. *Communication Education, 62,* 233–252.

20. Briscoe, J., & Rankin, P. M. (2009). Exploration of a "double jeopardy" hypothesis within working memory profiles for children with specific language impairment. *International Journal of Language & Communication Disorders, 44,* 236–250.

21. Miller, G. A. (1994). The magical number seven, plus or minus two: Some limits on our capacity for processing information. *Psychology Review, 101,* 343–352.

22. Gilbert, M. B. (1988). Listening in school: I know you can hear me—but are you listening? *Journal of the International Listening Association, 2,* 121–132.

23. Patrick, S. Y. (2013). Perception of workplace active listening skills in relationship to workplace productivity. *Dissertation Abstracts International Section A: Humanities and Social Sciences.*

24. Teirlinck, W. (2021). Learn lessons from COVID. *HR Future, 3,* 30–31.

25. Graduate Management Admission Council. (2014). Graduate recruiters survey. https://www.gmac.com/market-intelligence-and-research/research-library/employment-outlook/2014-corporate-recruiters.aspx

26. Stansfield, S. (2008, December 16). Noise as a public health problem. *ASHA Leader,* 5–6.

27. Skenazy, L. (2009, February 9). Smartphone apps great for marketing, bad for social skills. *Advertising Age,* np.

28. Thompson, W. F., Schellenberg, E. G., & Letnic, A. K. (2011, May 20). Fast and loud background music disrupts reading comprehension. *Psychology of Music.* https://doi.org/10.1177/0305735611400173

29. Kuznekoff, J. H., & Titsworth, S. (2013). The impact of mobile phone usage on student learning. *Communication Education, 62,* 233–252.

30. Carmichael, C. (2017, November 8). Political polarization is a psychology problem and there are some easy ways to address it. *Huffington Post.* https://www.huffingtonpost.com/entry/political-polarization-is-a-psychology-problem_us_5a01dd9ee4b07eb5118255e5

31. Parks, E. S. (2022). Listening across the ages: Measuring generational listening differences with the LCI-R. *International Journal of Listening, 36,* 20–30. https://doi.org/10.1080/10904018.2020.1748503

32. Tannen, D. (2001). *You just don't understand: Women and men in conversation.* HarperCollins.

33. Toulmin, S. E. (1958). *The uses of argument.* Cambridge University Press.

34. U. S. Bureau of Labor Statistics. (2022, September 8). Table 2.1 Employment by major industry sector. https://www.bls.gov/emp/tables/employment-by-major-industry-sector.htm

35. Neill, M. S., & Bowen, S. A. (2021). Employee perceptions of ethical listening in U.S. organizations. *Public Relations Review, 47,* np. https://doi.org/10.1016/j.pubrev.2021.102123

36. Anderson, T. H., & Armbruster, B. B. (1986). *The value of taking notes* (Reading Education Report No. 374). University of Illinois at Urbana-Champaign, Center for the Study of Reading.

37. Armbruster, B. B. (2000). Taking notes from lectures. In R. Flippo & D. Caverly (Eds.), *Handbook of college reading and study strategy research* (pp. 175–199). Lawrence Erlbaum.

38. Vinson, L., & Johnson, C. (1990). The relationship between the use of hesitations and/or hedges and lecture listening: The role of perceived importance and a mediating variable. *Journal of the International Listening Association, 4,* 116–127.

39. Ravizza, S. M., Ultvlugt, M. G., & Fenn, K. M. (2016, February 28). Logged in and zoned out. *Psychological Sciences.* https://doi.org/10.1177/0956797616677314

40. Gilbert, Listening in school.

41. Titsworth, B. S., & Kiewra, K. (1998, April). *By the numbers: The effects of organizational lecture cues on notetaking and achievement.* Paper presented at the American Educational Research Association Convention, San Diego.

42. Titsworth, B. S., & Kiewra, K. (1998, April). *By the numbers: The effects of organizational lecture cues on notetaking and achievement.* Paper presented at the American Educational Research Association Convention, San Diego.

43. Centers for Disease Control and Prevention. (2010, July 16). Television and video viewing time among children aged 2 years—Oregon, 2006–2007. *Morbidity and Mortality Weekly Report, 59,* 837–841.

44. American Library Association. (2001). Report of the Presidential Committee on Information Literacy.

45. Key Internet statistics to know in 2022 (including mobile). (2022, September 9). Broadband Search. https://www.broadbandsearch.net/blog/internet-statistics

46. International Telecommunications Union. (2011). *The world in 2011: ICT facts and figures.* http://www.itu.int/ITU-D/ict/facts/2011/index.html

47. Georgiev, D. (2022, September 5). How much time do people spend on social media in 2022? Techjury. https://techjury.net/blog/time-spent-on-social-media/#gref

48. Vandergrift, L. (2006). Second language listening: Listening ability or language proficiency? *Modern Language Journal, 90,* 6–18.

49. Rehling, L. (2004). Improving teamwork through awareness of conversational styles. *Business Communication Quarterly, 67,* 475–482.

6

interpersonal communication

When you have read and thought about this chapter, you will be able to

1. define interpersonal communication.

2. define interpersonal relationships.

3. explain the importance of interpersonal relationships.

4. describe how self-disclosure affects relationships.

5. describe friendships and how they have changed.

6. explain the importance of cross-cultural relationships.

7. explain the three stages in interpersonal relationships.

8. explain a motive for initiating, maintaining, and terminating relationships.

9. name three essential interpersonal communication behaviors.

10. describe how bargaining and behavioral flexibility can be used to improve interpersonal communication skills.

Interpersonal relationships can be immensely rewarding, but they take effort to build and maintain. This chapter highlights some of the foundational elements of interpersonal relationships and interpersonal communication. You will learn why people start, maintain, and end relationships. You will also study essential skills such as self-disclosing, using affectionate and supportive communication, influencing others, and developing a unique relationship.

The Showtime series *Billions* is making history and generating conversation about gender identity with the groundbreaking character Taylor Mason, the first openly gender nonbinary character on television. Like Taylor, Asia Kate Dillon, the actor who plays Taylor, identifies as gender nonbinary and uses the singular pronouns *they*, *their*, and *them*. In the show, Taylor is a smart hedge-fund intern who must navigate disclosing their preferred pronouns as they meet coworkers at the firm.[1]

This representation of nonbinary gender identity on television is noteworthy as it reflects the lived experiences of people in society, and likely on your college campus. Increasing numbers of students desire the use of gender-inclusive pronouns when referring to themselves.[2] What this means is that you may be in classes with people who do not prefer to be addressed using the gendered pronouns *he* and *she*, but may want to be referred to by gender-neutral pronouns such as *they* or *ve*.[3]

Given an increased focus on pronouns, you might question or be intrigued by this framing of language and wonder how it can affect your interpersonal relationships. As we meet new

Theo Wargo/Getty Images

people, we can't always know what their pronouns are by looking at them. Asking for a person's preferred pronouns is one easy way to show respect for others' gender identities. When people are referred to by the wrong pronoun, it can make them feel devalued, alienated, or unimportant.[4] Self-disclosing your own pronouns as you meet people may make others feel more comfortable doing the same. This is just one example of the complex dynamics at work as we use interpersonal communication to form and maintain relationships.

The Nature of Communication in Interpersonal Relationships

Today our definitions of interpersonal relationships are more complex and variable, in part due to social networking and online dating apps. Even the COVID-19 pandemic altered our capacity for relationships in new ways. For example, we became more adept at virtual interactions to maintain relationship with family and friends, such as by co-viewing television shows or having a weekly game-night on Zoom. Additionally, many people balanced virtual work meetings at home and made decisions about sharing their living spaces by having their camera on or off. People may count dozens, or even hundreds, of others as their "friends." One advantage of these new relationships is the ease with which they can be begun or ended. The disadvantage is that they may be short lived, lack depth and connection, or be unfulfilling. Scholars are fascinated by these new developments in relationships. They see them as raising some important issues about the definitions of interpersonal relationships and interpersonal communication. For what reasons do people form their online relationships? How do people interact when a friendship is exclusively online rather than in face-to-face settings? How do online support groups help people develop relationships to help each other manage grief and loss? These questions are part of the fabric of our society today.

In this section you will discover what interpersonal communication is, what constitutes interpersonal relationships, the importance of interpersonal relationships, what "dark side" challenges we face in interpersonal relationships, and how we develop relationships using self-disclosure.

DEFINING INTERPERSONAL COMMUNICATION

Interpersonal communication is defined by the context, or the situation. In other words, interpersonal communication is the process of using messages to generate meaning between at least two people in a situation that allows mutual opportunities for both speaking and listening. Defined in this manner, interpersonal communication includes our interactions with strangers, with salespeople, and with waitstaff, as well as with our close friends, our lovers, and our family members. This definition is very broad.

We can also think of interpersonal communication as communication that occurs within interpersonal relationships.[5] This idea suggests that interpersonal communication can be limited to those situations in which we have knowledge of the personal characteristics, qualities, or behaviors of the other person. Researchers Gerald R. Miller and Mark Steinberg assert that, when we make guesses about the outcomes of conversations based on sociological or cultural information, we are communicating in a noninterpersonal way. When we make predictions based on more discriminating information about the other specific person, we are communicating interpersonally. When we communicate with others on the basis of general social interaction rules, such as engaging in turn taking, making pleasantries, and discussing nonpersonal matters, we are engaging in impersonal, or nonpersonal, communication. For instance, when you engage in small talk with the barista at your favorite coffee shop, this can be viewed as a form of impersonal communication. When we communicate with others based on some knowledge of their uniqueness as individuals and a shared relational history, we are communicating interpersonally.

None of our interpersonal relationships are quite like any of our other interpersonal relationships. A friendship you might have had in high school is not the same as your new friendships in college. Your relationship with one of your parents or parental figures is uniquely different from your relationship with the other. Likewise, if you have multiple siblings, your relationship with each of them will be different. Even if you have several intimate relationships with people, you will find that none of them is quite like the others. Nonetheless, we have accumulated a great deal of knowledge about how to communicate more successfully in our interpersonal relationships. This chapter will explore that knowledge by first defining what interpersonal relationships are and why we form them. Then you will learn about the skills needed to develop and maintain relationships.

DEFINING INTERPERSONAL RELATIONSHIPS

On the simplest level, relationships are associations or connections. Interpersonal relationships, however, are far more complex. **Interpersonal relationships** may be defined as associations between at least two people who are interdependent, who use some consistent patterns of interaction, and who have interacted for an extended period of time. Consider the various elements of this definition in more detail:

interpersonal relationships
Associations between at least two people who are interdependent, who use some consistent patterns of interaction, and who have interacted for an extended period of time.

- *Interpersonal relationships include two or more people.* Often, interpersonal relationships consist of just two people—for example, a dating couple, a single parent and a child, a married couple, two close friends, or two coworkers. Interpersonal relationships can also include more than two people—for example, a family unit, a group of friends, or a social group.

- *Interpersonal relationships involve people who are interdependent. Interdependence* refers to people's being mutually dependent on each other and having an impact on each other. When individuals are independent of each other, we typically do not define the resulting association as an interpersonal relationship. Friendship easily illustrates this concept. Your best friend, for example, may be dependent on you for acceptance and guidance, whereas you might require support and admiration. If you did not care about your best friend's well-being or needs, then you would not offer guidance and, therefore, you would not truly have an interpersonal relationship.

- *Individuals in interpersonal relationships use some consistent patterns of interaction.* These patterns may include behaviors generally understood across a variety of situations, as well as behaviors unique to the relationship. For example, your partner may always greet you with a kiss. This kiss is generally understood as a sign of warmth and affection. At the same time, you may have unique nicknames for your partner that are not understood outside the relationship.

- Successful interpersonal relationships are based on effective communication.

Kristy-Anne Glubish/Design Pics

- *Individuals in interpersonal relationships generally have interacted for some time.* When you nod and smile at someone as you leave the classroom, or when you place an order at a fast-food restaurant, you do not have an interpersonal relationship. Although you use interpersonal communication to accomplish these activities, one-time interactions do not constitute interpersonal relationships. That said, these interactions could be the beginnings of an interpersonal relationship, should the other elements we've discussed occur. We should note, however, that interpersonal relationships might last for varying lengths of time—some are relatively short but others continue for a lifetime.

THE IMPORTANCE OF INTERPERSONAL RELATIONSHIPS

According to psychologist William Schutz, we have three basic interpersonal needs that are satisfied through interaction with others:

- the need for inclusion, or becoming involved with others;
- the need for affection, or holding fond or tender feelings toward another person; and
- the need for control, or having the ability to influence others, our environment, and ourselves.[6]

Although we may be able to fulfill some of our physical, safety, and security needs through interactions with relative strangers, we can fulfill the needs for inclusion, affection, and control only through our interpersonal relationships.

The interdependent nature of interpersonal relationships suggests that people mutually satisfy their needs in this type of association. Interdependence suggests that one person is dependent on another to have some need fulfilled and that the other person (or persons) is dependent on the first to have the same or other needs fulfilled. For example, a child who is dependent on a parent may satisfy that parent's needs for inclusion and belonging. The parent, in turn, may supply the child's need for affection by spending time with, hugging, or listening to the child.

Complementary relationships—those in which each person supplies something the other person or persons lack—provide good examples of the manner in which we have our needs fulfilled in interpersonal relationships. An example is a friendship between an introverted individual and an extroverted one. The introvert may teach the extroverted friend

complementary relationships
Relationships in which each person supplies something the other person or persons lack.

to be more self-reflective or to listen to others more carefully, whereas the extrovert might encourage the introverted friend to be more outspoken or assertive.

Our needs may also be fulfilled in **symmetrical relationships**—those in which the participants mirror each other or are highly similar. A relationship between two intelligent individuals may reflect their need for intellectual stimulation. Additionally, two coworkers who individually know that they meet goals more easily when they are held accountable may decide to form a running group to hold each other accountable to meeting their exercise goals.

Conflict is inevitable and normal in interpersonal relationships; in fact, conflict can be constructive and creative. Conflict can be healthy when it is used to resolve differences and to "clear the air." However, it can also be dysfunctional. You might have grown up in a family in which sequences of conflict were ever present, and the only way you know how to have a conversation is by yelling to get your point across. Or you might have had parents who never discussed differences, and the only way you know to manage conflict is to walk away or not talk about what bothers you.

Conflict is dysfunctional when you avoid talking about problems or become withdrawn. Conflict is also dysfunctional when you take any criticism or suggestion as a personal attack.

symmetrical relationships
Relationships in which participants mirror each other or are highly similar.

• Interpersonal relationships fulfill basic needs.

Fuse/Getty Images

Do you fight fairly, or do you attack the other person rather than raising the issue that is at stake? If you feel out of control when you are engaged in an argument with a family member, you may experience conflict as dysfunctional. Finally, conflict can be dysfunctional when you store up many complaints about a person and then attack that person with all of them.

If you have experienced conflict as dysfunctional, you can begin to experience it more positively when you follow some straightforward guidelines. First, you need to remain calm. You should also express your feelings in words rather than in actions such as breaking objects, driving recklessly, or consuming too much alcohol. Try to be specific about what is bothering you. Rather than bringing up multiple grievances of the past, try to deal with only one issue at a time. Consider your language and avoid words such as *never* and *always* when describing the problem. Do not exaggerate or invent additional problems that are not central to the discussion. Finally, you may find that it is important to establish some ground rules that both you and your partner adopt.

sizing things up

Interpersonal Motives

We enter into interpersonal relationships for a variety of reasons. Below you will read several statements that describe possible reasons for joining interpersonal relationships. Indicate how likely you are to enter into an interpersonal relationship for each reason using the following scale:

1 = Never
2 = Unlikely
3 = Likely
4 = Frequently

I enter into interpersonal relationships . . .

1. so that I can have influence over others.
2. so that I can share emotions with others.
3. to feel part of a group.
4. to be involved in things with other people.
5. to gain affection from others.
6. to bring control to my life.
7. so that I can have more influence over my surroundings.
8. because I need to know that people like me.
9. because I want to be included in different activities.

A guide for interpreting your responses appears at the end of this chapter.

THE DARK SIDE OF INTERPERSONAL RELATIONSHIPS

Conflict is only one aspect of interpersonal relationships that seems to represent a "dark side" to these most personal affiliations. Although your interpersonal relationships are generally pleasurable and positive, you might also have experienced painful and negative interactions. Communication scholars Brian Spitzberg and William Cupach have provided the most comprehensive treatment of the dark side of relationships.[7] What are some of the qualities of negative relationships? Obsession that includes intense feelings and jealousy can create negative outcomes. Similarly, misunderstanding, gossip, conflict, and codependency can lead to harmful results. Relational abuse, which includes sexual, physical, and emotional abuse, as well as economic distress, is truly harmful to individuals and destroys relationships. In addition, some of the qualities we associate with healthy relationships—self-disclosure, affectionate communication, mutual influence, and the development of a unique relationship—can all become extreme and therefore unhealthy. Effective communication, as you have been learning, is challenging, and interpersonal communication may be the most challenging context of all. This chapter focuses primarily on positive interpersonal relationships and how to improve them.

SELF-DISCLOSURE IN THE DEVELOPMENT OF INTERPERSONAL RELATIONSHIPS

One change that occurs as relationships become deeper and closer is an increasing intentional revealing of personal information. **Self-disclosure** is the process of making intentional revelations about yourself that others would be unlikely to know and that generally constitute private, sensitive, or confidential information. Researchers W. Babnett Pearce and Stewart M. Sharp distinguish among self-disclosure, confession, and revelation.[8] They

self-disclosure
The process of making intentional revelations about yourself that others would be unlikely to know and that generally constitute private, sensitive, or confidential information.

define self-disclosure as voluntary, confession as forced or coerced information, and revelation as unintentional or inadvertent communication.

Psychologist Sidney M. Jourard suggests that self-disclosure makes us "transparent" to others, that disclosure helps others to see us as a distinctive human being.[9] Self-disclosure goes beyond self-description. More specifically, your close relationship with your grandparent, your sexual history, your deepest fears, your proudest moments, and your problems with drugs or alcohol would be considered self-disclosure by most definitions. Self-disclosure is not always negative, but it is generally private information.

Sandra Petronio's communication privacy management (CPM) theory provides a useful framework for helping people think about the rules they create regarding when they will and will not share private information and how they manage privacy boundaries once they have shared private information.[10] Have you ever told someone something in confidence and then said, "Now don't tell anyone else about that"? According to CPM, this is an example of how people intentionally make rules surrounding who has access to their private information. Privacy rules are created to control the permeability of the boundary.[11]

The Importance of Self-Disclosure

Self-disclosure is important for three reasons. First, it allows us to develop a greater understanding of ourselves. Consider the Johari window depicted in Figure 6.1. Joseph Luft and Harrington Ingham created this diagram to depict four kinds of information about a person. The open area (I) includes information that is known to you and to other people, such as your approximate height and weight, and information you freely disclose, such as your hometown, major, or age. The blind area (II) consists of information known to others but unknown to you, such as your personality characteristics that others perceive but you do not recognize or acknowledge. For example, others may think you are stubborn, whereas you think you are fairly flexible. The hidden area (III) includes information that you know about yourself but others do not. Any information that is hidden and that you do not self-disclose lies here. Finally, the unknown area (IV) comprises information that is unknown to you *and* to others. For instance, perhaps neither you nor others know that you have an untapped talent for woodcarving.

The quadrants of the Johari window can expand or contract in size. The quadrants can also have different shapes with different family members, friends, or acquaintances. For example, you might have a very large open area when you are considering the relationship between you and your closest friend. By contrast, the hidden area may be very large when you consider the relationship between you and your employer. As the size of one of the quadrants changes, so do the sizes of all the others.

Figure 6.1

Johari window.

Source: Luft, J. (1984). *Group processes: An introduction to group dynamics.* Mayfield Publishing Company. Copyright 1984, 1970, and 1969 by Joseph Luft. McGraw Hill.

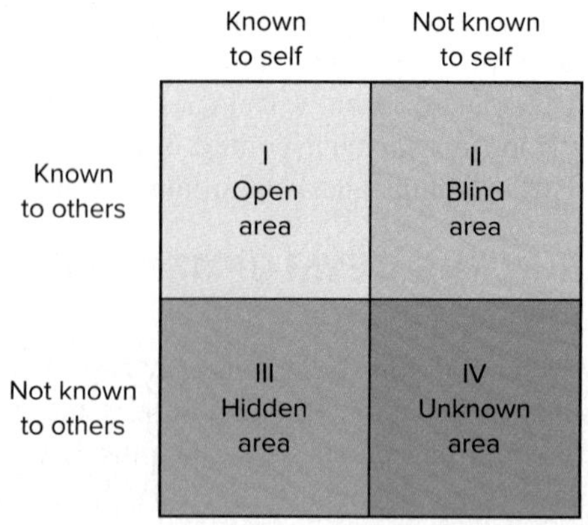

Interpersonal Communication

Second, self-disclosure allows us to develop a more positive attitude about ourselves and others, as well as more meaningful relationships. Most of us have experienced a problem or faced a difficult situation, and we know that sharing our fears or telling others about our anguish provides comfort. For example, imagine that you vandalized property in high school and were caught. You might feel very guilty for having done the wrong thing, for having to pay a large fine, and for damaging someone else's property. If you can find the courage to talk about your feelings to a friend, you might find that you are not alone, that almost everyone gets into trouble at one time or another. Similarly, if you have recently experienced the loss of a family member, you may find that talking about your feelings and sharing your grief will lead to positive growth for you. Hastings found that self-disclosure is a powerful form of communication in grieving and in healing a fractured identity.[12] In addition, self-disclosing on social media provides a possible place for grieving, support, and coping after the loss of a loved one.[13]

Third, self-disclosure is one way relationships grow in depth and meaning. Partners in romantic relationships, for example, can use self-disclosure to intensify a relationship.[14] When you self-disclose more to others, they will most likely disclose more to you. Without the opportunity for self-disclosure and active listening, relationships can be based on superficiality, which can lead to relational termination.

At the same time, self-disclosure can be used inappropriately. Have you ever sat on an airplane next to a stranger who revealed highly personal information to you? Have you ever dated someone who insisted on sharing private information too early in the relationship? In the next section we will consider some of the findings about self-disclosure that may provide guidelines for your self-disclosing behavior.

The Factors Affecting Appropriate Self-Disclosure

Self-disclosure typically unfolds over the lifespan of a relationship. There are many factors that influence the ways in which self-disclosure typically happens as a relationship develops. The following are six principles that guide appropriate self-disclosure.

Disclosure generally increases as relational intimacy increases. We do not provide our life story to people we have just met. Instead, in the developing relationship, we gradually reveal an increasing amount of information. We might begin with positive information that is not highly intimate and then begin to share more personal information as we learn to trust the other person. In this way our disclosure tends to be incremental, to increase over time.

Disclosure tends to be reciprocal. When people offer us information about themselves, we tend to return the behavior in kind. In fact, when people reciprocate self-disclosure, we tend to view them positively; when they do not, we tend to view them as incompetent. Reciprocal disclosure generally does not occur in families. Although parents have an expectation of self-disclosure from their children and adolescents, they do not perceive a need to reciprocate. A variety of factors affect adolescents' disclosures to their parents. Adolescents do not generally feel the need to disclose to their parents, and they are even more reluctant to disclose if their behavior is not sanctioned by their parents.[15] Grandparents may become the target of self-disclosures, since they are sometimes seen as more empathic and positive.[16]

Negative disclosure is directly related to the intimacy of the relationship; however, positive disclosure does not necessarily increase as the relationship becomes more intimate. What does this mean? As we become closer to another person, we are more likely to reveal negative information about ourselves. Positive information, by contrast, flows through conversations from the earliest developmental stages throughout the lifetime of the relationship. Hence, negative information increases over time, but positive disclosure does not necessarily increase.

building **behaviors**

Guidelines for Self-Disclosure

Try the following strategies for appropriate self-disclosure in interpersonal relationships:

1. Gradually increase disclosure as your relationship develops.
2. Reveal information to others as they reveal information to you.
3. Do not disclose negative information until your relationship is established.
4. Do not disclose information that will cause you personal harm.
5. Be sensitive to cultural differences in your self-disclosure.
6. Be aware of nondominant cultural differences in self-disclosure.
7. Be willing to self-disclose in interpersonal relationships.

Consider how, if at all, these guidelines change or remain the same when self-disclosing in online or other digitally mediated contexts.

Disclosure may be avoided for a variety of reasons. Self-disclosure does not flow freely on all topics. You may avoid self-disclosure for reasons of self-protection, relationship protection, partner unresponsiveness, and social appropriateness.[17] At the same time, topics that are taboo or difficult to talk about under some conditions may be appropriate later, when conditions change.[18] For example, parents typically engage in more communication about sex and sexual health as their children age into late adolescence and early adulthood.[19]

Disclosure varies across cultures. Self-disclosure is not uniformly valued or disvalued around the world. For example, one research study found that American college students disclosed significantly more than Japanese college students regardless of whether the relationship was a same- or cross-sex friendship or an intimate relationship.[20]

In online settings, Americans tend to use verbal disclosure more than East Asians, and Koreans tend to share more photos to disclose aspects of themselves than Americans.[21] Cultural norms can influence the ways in which we self-disclose in our relationships.

Relational satisfaction and disclosure are curvilinearly related. Satisfaction is lowest with no disclosure and with excessive disclosure; it is highest when self-disclosure is provided at moderate levels. Consider your own personal relationships. Does this conclusion appear to be accurate?

Friendship

Friendship contributes to our well-being. People who have harmonious sibling relationships and same-gender friends report the highest levels of well-being.[22] Whereas we celebrate romantic relationships, we do not similarly honor friendships. Bill Rawlins, a communication scholar who studies friendship, notes that we ought to have a "friendship day" because our friendships are at least as important as our romantic relationships.[23]

THE VALUE OF FRIENDSHIPS

What does friendship mean? Friendships can be based on shared activities or on the level of information we exchange with others. Young adolescents report that their friendships are based on shared activities, whereas for emerging adults they are based on self-disclosure.[24] The communication of private information appears to gain in importance as people mature. Most people identify both family and nonfamily members as friends.

Friendships also change over time. As people age, family members become more salient as friends.[25] For many older men, their only friend is their spouse,[26] although the same is not true for older women. In fact, research suggests that maintaining small, emotionally meaningful relationships helps with well-being as we age.[27] Do friendships actually improve over time? Although we cannot be sure, we do know that people *perceive* that they do.[28] Perhaps people come to better understand the importance of friendship as they mature.

The quality of friendships is affected by psychological predispositions, such as attachment styles. People who are securely attached to others have lower levels of conflict with their friends and are able to rise above problems in their friendships. People who are avoidant, or not attached, experience higher levels of conflict and lower levels of companionship.[29]

Rawlins provides a six-stage model of how friendships develop.[30] The first stage, role-limited interaction, includes an encounter in which individuals are polite and careful with their disclosures. Second, friendly relations occur when the two people determine that they have mutual interests or other common ground. Third, moving toward friendship allows them to introduce a personal topic or to set up times to get together. Fourth, in nascent friendship they think of themselves as friends and begin to establish their own private ways of interacting. Fifth, the friends feel established in each other's lives, in what is termed a stabilized friendship. Finally, friendships may move to a waning stage, when the relationship diminishes. Not all friendships reach this sixth stage.

Friendships are maintained differently, depending on the intent of the relational partners. Rawlins notes that issues of romantic attraction must be negotiated early in a relationship.[31] Researchers Laura Guerrero and Alana M. Chavez studied friendships in which both people wanted the relationship to become romantic (mutual romance), friendships in which neither person wanted the friendship to become romantic (platonic), and friendships in which one person desired romance but felt that the other did not (desiring or rejecting romance).[32] People in the mutual-romance situation generally reported the most relationship maintenance behavior. Those in the platonic or the rejecting-romance situation had fewer routine contacts and activities, were more likely to talk about other romantic situations, and were less flirtatious. People in the desiring-romance and mutual-romance situations reported the most relationship talk. Clearly, friendships are dynamic and may lead to romantic relationships.

Partners behave differently in their communication with friends and romantic partners. For example, the scope of the "chilling effect," or the suppression of grievances, depends on whether you see the other person as a friend or a romantic partner. One study used binge drinking as the topic to determine whether friends or romantic partners would confront the other person. The researchers found that college students would not talk with their friends about their excessive drinking but they would do so with their romantic partners. In other words, the chilling effect on this topic affected only friendships.[33]

Friendships are not necessarily defined the same way in all cultures. People in collectivist cultures tend to have more intimate but fewer friendships. As people have more contact with other cultures, however, these patterns are showing signs of change. For example, Indonesian people, traditionally from a collectivist culture, now display extensive social contacts.[34]

Over the last several decades, relational development has been enhanced through technology. Researchers highlight both the benefits and challenges of forming, maintaining, and ending relationships using mediated communication. In this way, the influence of technology on our friendships is undeniable.

FRIENDSHIPS AND NEW TECHNOLOGY

Social networking sites, such as TikTok, Facebook, Instagram, Twitch, Snapchat, Discord, Bumble BFF, and LinkedIn, make new kinds of friendships possible by allowing people to communicate with each other online.

TikTok launched in 2016 and became the most downloaded app in the world in 2022, with more than 1 billion active users. According to Emily Dreyfuss, a researcher at Harvard's Shorenstein Center for Media, Politics and Public Policy, TikTok creates and reinforces culture.[35]

Facebook claims that more than 1.97 billion people log in daily.[36] Although we might believe Facebook is distinctly American, 90% of daily users are from outside the United States, and the largest population of users is from India with over 320 million users. Finally, the average Facebook user has 338 Facebook friends.[37]

• Social networking apps provide opportunities for new kinds of interpersonal relationships.

StratfordProductions/
Shutterstock

Twitter (now X) was created in March 2006 and boasted 192 million active users in 2022.[38] "Tweets," or posts, are limited to 280 characters, and the amount of retweets and likes a post has increases its influence. The use of Twitter (X) multiplies when prominent events occur. For example, a tweet from actor Chadwick Boseman's account announcing his death and commemorating his life is one of the most popular on the platform to date, with more than 7.7 million likes and more than 2 million retweets.[39] In another instance, former president Barack Obama's 2017 tweet in response to violence in Charlottesville, Virginia, reached 1.7 million retweets, the highest of that year.[40]

More recently, the app Sit with Us was created by high school student and antibullying activist Natalie Hampton to create a safe space for other high school students to make friends and find classmates with similar interests to sit with at lunch. Students create a profile and sign a pledge that says they'll participate in "open lunches," which are an invitation for other kids to join their lunch table. In this way, the app is creating connections, facilitating friendships, and potentially reducing loneliness and bullying.[41]

Why do people choose to have online friends? Although extraversion and openness to new experiences have some predictive power in identifying people who are likely to use social networking, no clear personality factors distinguish social networkers from others.[42] Perhaps people are motivated to form online friendships because they have a sense of safety and security—they do not need to meet the other person in a face-to-face setting. Others might perceive that online friendships are more exciting than day-to-day relationships. Finally, some people might be attracted to social networking sites because they can create a more idealized self—someone who is more attractive and has a different personality than they actually have.

Although people may have dozens of online friends, they rarely have large numbers of friends with benefits. Friends with benefits (FWB) are those who are not romantically involved but who have agreed to have a sexual relationship. Researchers indicate that for an FWB arrangement to work, both parties must know each other, understand what they mean to each other, and understand the feelings that the emotional and sexual relationship has for both of them. To maintain this type of relationship in a healthy way, both friends must communicate what is expected, consent to the relationship, and discuss how aspects of their relationship change as it evolves.[43]

How do FWB relationships typically conclude? A recent study found that about 36% of the couples stopped having sex but remained friends, 28% stayed friends and remained sexually involved, 26% claimed that they were no longer either friends or lovers, and about 10% of the couples had a relationship that became completely romantic.[44]

Researchers suggest that not labeling a new situation or relationship can allow people to get to know each other and remove some of the pressure; yet developing a friendship before engaging in a sexual relationship creates a foundation to build upon should the relationship progress to an intimate stage.[45]

CROSS-CULTURAL RELATIONSHIPS

Because our culture is increasingly diverse, the likelihood that you will be part of a cross-cultural friendship, or even a romantic relationship, is far greater now than ever before. In many respects, cross-cultural relationships work like any other type of relationship: we enter into them for many of the same reasons, the processes of self-disclosure work the same, and we even initiate and maintain them using many of the same skills.

One difference is that we may feel more tentative in initiating a dialogue with a person from another culture. Perhaps we are afraid of language barriers or of accidentally saying something wrong. In other situations, such as when two people are assigned to a residence hall room as roommates, the relationship may be forced upon them. In either case, one approach to establishing a relationship is to view it as a cooperative learning opportunity in which both participants work together to achieve a mutually shared understanding while learning about each other's culture.[46] In approaching the relationship in this way, try to do the following:

- *Have meaningful personal interaction.* If you feel uncomfortable in the initial stages of interaction, you may be tempted to stick to very safe topics of conversation. Try to talk about some more personal and meaningful topics as well. For instance, what are the similarities and differences between your families? What religions do you practice? What are your hometowns like? What work experiences have you had? By talking about more personal topics like these, you will begin to learn about each other and start the self-disclosure cycle.

- *Maintain equal status.* Research shows that, when one person assumes a role of "leader" or "teacher," the relationship will have more trouble developing. Both members of the relationship should recognize that each has something unique to offer in terms of knowledge, creativity, openness, listening, and so on. Remembering to keep the new relationship focused on interpersonal closeness rather than task concerns can help prevent a perception of inequality in the early stages of the relationship.

- *Find ways to build interdependence.* Any relationship will be stronger if both individuals bring something to it. If each can find ways to help the other, interdependence will form, and the bond of the relationship will grow stronger.

- *Respect individual differences.* People from different cultures are like anyone else. Some are shy, whereas others are outgoing. Some are very cerebral, and others are very practical. Some like romantic comedies, whereas others like action shows. Such differences and even disagreements over them do not mean you cannot make a cross-cultural relationship work; it may simply mean that you don't like certain personality characteristics. Just as with friends from your own culture, you occasionally have to overlook minor disagreements in light of the many areas of agreement.

The Stages in Interpersonal Relationships

Communication and relationship development are symbiotic; that is, communication affects the growth of relationships, and the growth of relationships affects communicative behavior.[47] Although many types of relationships progress through these stages, we will focus on more intimate relationships and how those typically develop.

DEVELOPING RELATIONSHIPS

Relational development does not occur overnight. College students demonstrate a general pattern for the developing intimate and romantic relationship. When college students first meet, they exchange names, majors, and hometowns. They might begin using social media and text each other from time to time. This early investigative stage lasts a fairly short time and allows the people to determine whether they have anything in common.

relational development The initial stage in a relationship that moves a couple from meeting to mating.

If both people find they are compatible, they may begin to spend more time together and go to parties, movies, dinners, and other social events together. They meet each other's friends and eventually engage in intimacy. Because intimacy is an emotional step in a relationship, couples may assess the cost as well as the benefits of becoming intimate with someone to whom they are not committed.[48] As a result of differences in opinion about the desirability of intimacy or the meaningfulness of it, the first fight might ensue shortly after intimacy has occurred. Also, partners are sometimes not equally astute at understanding the nonverbal and verbal cues that lead to intimacy, and one may be confused while the other is keenly aware of the likelihood of engaging in a sexual relationship.[49] Assuming the fight has cleared the air and not ended the relationship, they may meet each other's family. At this point, the two may decide not to date other people. Statuses on social media may also reflect an increase in visibility of the couple's exclusivity. They are no longer interested in dating others. They develop mutual concerns, shared jokes, and a common history.

About this time they express their affection verbally, as one or both disclose, "I love you." Additional shared experiences, such as working on projects or traveling together, might occur next. The two develop rituals to manage both work and play. They might have a common language that allows them to communicate with each other without strangers understanding.

Commitment is often the final formal stage of relational development. Couples begin to spend increasing amounts of time at each other's apartment or room, and one member might suggest moving in together. A proposal of marriage or solidifying the commitment in a way that is meaningful for the couple may follow or precede this suggestion. The couple may determine whether they can care for another by getting a pet or may decide to share finances. Some couples remain at this point for years or forever, whereas others engage in formal ceremonies to legally, spiritually, or otherwise commit to each other. At this stage, couples may or may not decide to have children.

MAINTAINING RELATIONSHIPS

relational maintenance
The stage in a relationship after a couple has bonded and in which they engage in the process of keeping the relationship together.

Once individuals have bonded in a relationship, they enter a stage of **relational maintenance** in which they begin establishing strategies for keeping the relationship together. Communication scholar William Wilmot suggests that relationships stabilize when the partners reach a basic level of agreement about what they want from the relationship.[50] This can occur at any level of intimacy, and even "stabilized" relationships have internal movement.

The relational maintenance stage is not like a plateau. Instead, people become more intimate or closer at some periods and more distant and less close at other times, usually describing a jagged rather than a straight line. Maintained relationships are in motion, and healthy relationships are always changing. A relationship that is static is probably dead or dying.

dialectic
The tension that exists between two conflicting or interacting forces, elements, or ideas.

contradictions
In dialectic theory, the idea that each person in a relationship might have two opposing desires for maintaining the relationship.

Relational communication expert Leslie Baxter and her colleagues, as well as other researchers, have developed and demonstrated the importance of dialectic theory in interpersonal relationships.[51] **Dialectic** refers to the tension that exists between two conflicting or interacting forces, elements, or ideas. When dialectic theory is applied to interpersonal relationships, we acknowledge that relationships often incorporate contradictions or contrasts within them and that relationships are always in process. By **contradictions**, we mean that each person might have two opposing desires for maintaining the relationship—you want to be with your partner, but you also have a need for independent space. *Process* means that relationships are always changing. Thus, relational maintenance cannot be depicted as a flat line but, rather, as one that has peaks and valleys.

What are some of the primary dialectics that Baxter identifies? Three emerged in the early work. The dialectic of *integration/separation* suggests the tension between wanting to be separate entities and wanting to be integrated with another person. The dialectic of *stability/change* suggests the tension between wanting events, conversations, and behavior to be the same and desiring change. The dialectic of *expression/privacy* suggests the tension between wanting to self-disclose and be completely open and wanting to be private and closed. Table 6.1 summarizes Baxter's primary dialectics.

Table 6.1   Baxter's Dialectic Tensions

Dialectical Tension	Example
Integration/Separation	"Let's move in together."/"When we get married, I would like us to keep separate bank accounts."
Stability/Change	"I'm glad we've never moved."/"I'm feeling restless. I think it is time to plan a vacation!"
Expression/Privacy	"I did absolutely the dumbest thing last night. Let me tell you."/"I would rather not explain how I spent the weekend."

The use of media has multiple effects on relationships and may play a greater role than we suspect. For example, people who consume a great deal of television and frequently play video games use fewer relational maintenance strategies than those who are modest or moderate media users. In one study, this difference was particularly strong for those who showed high dependence on video games, perhaps due to the competition games provide for relational development and maintenance time.[52]

At the same time, college students regularly use texting and social media to connect with others who are in both long-distance and geographically close relationships with them. For example, one research study found that couples in long-distance romantic relationships (LDRR) use more relational maintenance behaviors through social networking sites than couples in geographically close romantic relationships (GCRR).[53]

With family and friends, students tend to use self-disclosure (directly discussing the nature of their relationship), positive comments (being cheerful and upbeat), and discussions of social networks (attempting to involve them in a variety of activities) in their messages. When interacting with romantic partners, they also use assurances that include stressing commitment and love.[54]

One research study suggested that social media can influence relationships in three ways.[55] First, they increase the amount of information we have about our partners. For example, while using Instagram we can scroll through our partner's postings and mutual friends' feeds to see our partner's activities. Second, social media provide acceptable ways for couples to monitor their partners without committing severe violations of trust. Third, information that is important to the couple is on display for the public. For example, images of a shared trip and comments about the meaningfulness of the experience may create strong positive feelings within the relationship, especially if friends comment on the posts. In contrast, seeing your partner with an arm around someone else at a party that you did not attend may be viewed as threatening because your mutual friends and acquaintances can see the post. In this way, social media itself is neither positive nor negative for relationships, but the impact of how it is used within a given relationship depends on the quality of the relationship and what behaviors the partners are engaging in on the sites.[56]

WHEN RELATIONSHIPS DETERIORATE

Although all relationships go through a period of development, and many go through the maintenance stage, some deteriorate. **Relational deterioration** may occur because of the pressures of external events, because of differences that develop within the couple, or because of relationships with other people. Couples may first observe that they are spending increasing amounts of time away from each other and they prefer this time of separation.

relational deterioration
The stage in a relationship in which the prior bond disintegrates.

• Relational deterioration is marked by differentiating behavior.

Radius Images/Getty Images

The couple may begin to physically, emotionally, and communicatively pull away from each other. Perhaps they do not attend public events together. They might decide to sleep in separate rooms or separate beds. They no longer appear to be a couple to each other or to others.

The parties may begin to look for others with whom to share their thoughts and feelings. They might find spending time with each other to be boring, stifling, and awkward. If they have children, they might attend the children's events but arrive and leave in separate vehicles. They might arrange events so that they do not have to be alone together.

Next, the couple avoids spending any time at all together. One person may move out. One person might reschedule activities in order to be gone when the other awakens or to come home sufficiently late that the other partner is already sleeping. Communication may actually increase at this point, but it is marked with anger and negative intent.

Finally, the couple may decide to end the relationship. If the couple is legally committed, they will take legal action to end their relationship. They might engage in outright hostility and dissociation. They might divide their common property, returning jewelry and other sentimental gifts to the partner and shedding any symbols of their relationship. Common friends are now divided between the two.

Not all relationships go through these stages, particularly deterioration or termination. People experience movement as they reconnect after periods of little intimacy. They may question their relationship but not move to dissolve it. Sometimes couples move back to the dating stage as they renew their love, perhaps after any children have left home or after retirement.

Communication skills can also alter the trajectory of a relationship. In relationships that are dysfunctional or deteriorating, communication can help heal or remedy problems. In new relationships it can stimulate relational development and growth. Communication skills thus allow us to subscribe to realistic hope in our relationships.

Finally, individuals do not move through each of these stages with everyone they meet. Research has shown that people base decisions to develop relationships on such factors as physical attractiveness, personal charisma, and communication behaviors.[57] In general, we are more likely to attempt to develop relationships with people who are attractive, emotionally expressive, extroverted, and spontaneous. In the next section we will consider some of the theories that suggest why we select some people with whom to relate and why we neglect, or even reject, other people.

Motivations for Initiating, Maintaining, and Terminating Relationships

Most relationships go through definable stages of development, maintenance, and deterioration.

MOTIVATIONS FOR INITIATING RELATIONSHIPS

How do you determine which people you will select to be your friends or intimate partners? Why do you cultivate relationships with them? How does communication figure into the equation?

First, **proximity**—the location, distance, or range between persons and things—is obvious but important. Although online relationships are commonplace, you are unlikely to have very close relationships with people from places you have never been. You are most likely to find others where you spend most of your time. For this reason a roommate or coworker can easily become a friend. People who attend the same religious services, belong to the same social clubs, or live in the same neighborhood are most likely to become friends. People who share a major, a dormitory, a cafeteria, or a car pool are also likely candidates. To underline the power of proximity, consider that changes in location (high school to college and college to job) often change relationship patterns.

Second, from all the people we see, we select the ones we find high in **attractiveness**, which includes physical attractiveness, how desirable a person is to work with, and how much "social value" the person has for others.[58] Attractiveness is not universal, however; it varies from culture to culture and person to person. Because of perceptual differences, you will not be looking for the same person as everyone else.

Responsiveness describes the reason we tend to select our friends and loved ones from people who demonstrate positive interest in us. Few people are more attractive than those who actively listen to us, think our jokes are funny, find our vulnerabilities endearing, and see our faults as amusing. In short, we practically never select our friends from among those who dislike us.

Similarity, the idea that our friends and loved ones are usually people who like or dislike the same things we do is another feature of attractiveness. Whatever we consider most important is the similarity we seek, so some friends or people in loving relationships are bound by their interests, others by their ideology, and still others by their mutual likes and dislikes. Thousands of people find their friends in the same circle where they work: administrative staff with administrative staff, managers with managers, and bosses with bosses. Similarity is a powerful source of attraction.

Complementarity is the idea that we sometimes bond with people whose strengths are our weaknesses. Whereas you may be slightly shy, your friend may be assertive. In situations that call for assertiveness, your friend may play that role for you. A math-loving

proximity
The location, distance, or range between persons and things.

attractiveness
A concept that includes physical attractiveness, how desirable a person is to work with, and how much "social value" the person has for others.

responsiveness
The idea that we tend to select our friends and loved ones from people who demonstrate positive interest in us.

similarity
The idea that our friends and loved ones are usually people who like or dislike the same things we do.

complementarity
The idea that we sometimes bond with people whose strengths are our weaknesses.

• We select friends from among people who are responsive to us.
Don Hammond/Design Pics

communicating
creatively

Using Art to Cope with and Share Difficult Experiences

Often there is excitement when developing new interpersonal relationships and gratitude that comes with maintaining them. It's relatively easy to be there for the fun times, but what about the tough times? It can be difficult to know what to do or say when someone we care about experiences something difficult, especially if you have not had a similar experience. These experiences can range from short-term setbacks, such as a poor grade, to life-altering events, such as the death of a loved one.

Art is one way to help people express grief and trauma and can create ways for people to have conversations about difficult issues. In particular, when people have experienced trauma, researchers have found that art and storytelling can be ways of understanding, coping, healing, and community building. For example, the Scraps of the Heart Project (SOTHP) engages in this important work surrounding the specific experience of baby loss. Founded by Dr. Erin K. Willer, a communication studies associate professor at the University of Denver, the SOTHP is a collective of parents, students, artists, health care providers, and researchers working together to empower families and educate others about baby loss through stories and creative arts. The SOTHP has been able to offer workshops, including scrapbooking, assemblage art, and jewelry making, to grieving parents and their families. Dr. Willer also employs service learning in her classes through which students have worked with the SOTHP to create a children's book, *Help Me Remember: A Storybook for Children and Families Coping with the Death of a Baby,* and a line of grieving cards to support families experiencing baby loss. In 2017, parent and student art works were featured in an exhibit at the University of Denver's Museum of Anthropology. In this way, the SOTHP is giving voice to those experiencing baby loss and creating space for dialogue about this traumatic experience through art.

• The Scraps of the Heart Project, Creative HeARTs Workshop. Participants decorated pumpkins during a fall workshop to honor their babies lost to miscarriage, stillbirth, and neonatal death.

Erin K. Willer

Source: The scraps of the heart project (n.d.). www.scrapsoftheheartproject.com/

engineer may find friendship with a people-loving communication major who takes care of the engineer's social life while the engineer helps their friend with math courses. Complementarity seems to occur in fiscal matters, too. Those who spend more than they should tend to marry those who spend less than is ideal. However, these marriages tend to result in a great deal of conflict over fiscal matters, and the couples report diminished marital happiness.[59]

MOTIVATIONS FOR MAINTAINING RELATIONSHIPS

After you have gotten to know someone, why do you continue to maintain the relationship? You may begin to relate to dozens of people, but you do not continue friendships or romantic relationships with everyone with whom you start a relationship. Have you found it easier or harder to build and maintain relationships since the COVID-19 pandemic? Let us consider some of the motivators that encourage continuing a relationship.

Although we initially develop a relationship on the basis of such factors as attractiveness and personal charisma, we maintain relationships for different reasons. Maintained relationships invite certain levels of predictability, or certainty.[60] Indeed, we attempt to create strategies that will provide us with additional personal information about our relational partners.[61] We also are less concerned with partners' expressive traits (such as being extroverted and spontaneous) and more concerned with their ability to focus on us through empathic, caring, and concerned involvement.[62] Indeed, as relationships are maintained, partners not only become more empathic, but they also begin to mirror each other's behavior.

Gender and Cultural Differences

Motivations for maintaining relationships are not simple. Research findings on maintenance behaviors and gender are mixed. Recent research suggests that the level of femininity and masculinity impacts communication more so than biological sex differences. For instance, one study reported that feminine individuals used more maintenance behaviors as part of their everyday communication to support the relationship, while masculine individuals focused on solving specific problems to maintain the relationship.[63]

People of different ethnicities may express different needs in their interpersonal relationships. For example, one study reported that people from Western countries tend to value fairness in their relationships and communicate in ways to maintain a sense of equity. In the same study, researchers found that Japanese people reported using fewer maintenance strategies than Chinese people.[64]

Satisfying Relationships

Couples can achieve satisfying and long-term relationships. Maintaining positive, satisfying relationships is not easy, but the people who are the most satisfied with their relationships are probably those who have worked hardest at maintaining them. Married partners are most satisfied when they feel highly committed to and interdependent with each other.[65] Researchers found that people in long-term and satisfying relationships are more likely to use joint rather than individual identity pronouns ("we" and "us" rather than "I" or "me").[66] However, recent research suggests that focusing on phones instead of interacting with the person who is next to you decreases relational satisfaction and causes relational conflict.[67]

MOTIVATIONS FOR TERMINATING RELATIONSHIPS

Although our goal may be to maintain satisfying relationships, this outcome is not always possible. Relationships do not last. About 44% of all marriages end in divorce,[68] and in second and third marriages the failure rate is even higher.[69] Why do interpersonal relationships end? What factors encourage people to seek the conclusion, rather than the continuation, of a relationship? We consider a few of those factors here.

Hurtful messages and events are things partners say and do that create emotional pain or upset. Hurtful verbal messages fall into 10 categories of behavior: accusation, evaluation, directive, advise, express desire, inform, question, threat, joke, and lie.[70] Among the most common are accusations (implying or stating fault or offense), evaluation (describing value, worth, or quality), and inform (disclosing feelings that involve the partner). Hurtful events fall into 14 categories: infidelity, jealousy, conflict, deception, temporary termination, other relational uncertainty, lack of emotional support, hurtful behaviors, betraying trust, not standing up for the other partner, distance/moving away, lack of equity, secret keeping, and "other."[71] The most common are infidelity, jealousy, conflict, and deception.

Hurtful messages and events occur in most relationships, even satisfying relationships. They do not always end in disruption of the relationship, but they can if they become a pattern or are so intense that one partner cannot forget them. When people feel hurt by an event that damages a relationship or when the hurtful message highlights a character flaw in the receiver, the receiver of the message tends to withdraw from the person who committed the hurtful act.[72] Vangelisti and Crumley determined that people respond in one of three ways: active verbal responses (for example, attacking the other, defending oneself, or asking for an explanation), acquiescent responses (for example, apologizing or crying), and invulnerable responses (for example, laughing or ignoring the message).[73] People who felt extremely hurt were more likely to use acquiescing responses. Those who felt less hurt used invulnerability more than did those who felt extremely hurt.

hurtful messages and events
Things partners say and do that create emotional pain or upset.

deceptive communication
The practice of deliberately making somebody believe things that are not true.

aggressiveness
The assertion of one's rights at the expense of others and caring about one's own needs but no one else's.

argumentativeness
The quality or state of being argumentative; synonymous with contentiousness or combativeness.

defensiveness
The response that occurs when a person feels attacked.

Deceptive communication—the practice of deliberately making somebody believe things that are untrue—can also lead to relational dissatisfaction and termination. All relational partners probably engage in some level of deception from time to time. The "little white lie," the nonrevelation of the "whole truth," and the omission of some details are commonplace. However, deliberate and regular deception can lead to the destruction of trust and the end of the relationship.

People may tell familiar lies (stories that are manufactured and that they tell again and again) or unfamiliar lies (untruths that are constructed on the spot). They vary the length of their pauses, their eye gaze, and the amount of smiling and laughing in which they engage, depending on whether they are telling familiar or unfamiliar lies. Most observers, however, cannot detect these alterations.[74] In short, we do not seem to be able to accurately identify deceptive behaviors.

Aggressiveness occurs when people stand up for their rights at the expense of others and care about their own needs but no one else's. Aggressiveness might help you get your way a few times, but ultimately others will avoid you and let their resentment show. In general, when partners express verbal aggression toward each other, it threatens couples' sense of safety and stability in the relationship.[75] Aggressiveness is not the same as argumentativeness. **Argumentativeness**, defined as the quality or state of being argumentative, is synonymous with being contentious or combative. People who are argumentative are not verbally aggressive.[76] Indeed, argumentative people may value argument as a normal social communicative activity. Argumentation varies across the life span.[77]

Defensiveness occurs when a person feels attacked. Jack Gibb suggests that trust is essential to healthy relationships.[78] However, trust must be established between individuals and not be based on their roles, positions, or status. In other words, people should come to relationships without all the trappings of the roles they play. Reducing defensiveness is essential to building trust.

Gibb distinguished between behaviors that encourage defensiveness and those that reduce defensiveness. He identified evaluation, control, neutrality, superiority, certainty, and strategy as promoting defensive behaviors in others:

- *Evaluation* occurs when an individual makes a judgment about another person or that person's behavior.

- *Control* suggests that the speaker does not allow the second person to join in the discussion of how a problem should be solved.

- *Neutrality* means that the originator of the message does not show concern for the second person.

- *Superiority* occurs when the first person treats the second as a person of lower status.

- *Certainty* denotes a lack of openness to alternative ideas.

- *Strategy* refers to the employment of manipulative and premeditative behavior.

Gibb then categorized the following behaviors as reducing defensiveness: description, problem orientation, empathy, equality, provisionalism, and spontaneity. These behaviors show the following characteristics:

building **behaviors**

Reducing Defensiveness

Rewrite the following statements in a way that would decrease defensiveness. Use the categories generated by Gibb. For example, you could replace evaluation with description.

1. "What's wrong with you, anyway?"
2. "Who's responsible for the mess in our room?"
3. "I don't really care what you do."
4. "We're not leaving here until I say we're leaving."
5. "We don't need to meet. I know how to solve the problem."
6. "I don't need your help."

Table 6.2 Jack Gibb's Contribution to Reducing Defensiveness

Behaviors That Create Defensiveness	Behaviors That Reduce Defensiveness
Evaluation	Description
Control	Problem orientation
Neutrality	Empathy
Superiority	Equality
Certainty	Provisionalism
Strategy	Spontaneity

- People who use *description* report their observations rather than offering evaluative comments.
- People with a *problem orientation* do not act as though they have the solution but are eager to discuss multiple ideas.
- *Empathy* implies concern for others, as shown through careful listening for both the content and the intent of the other's message.
- *Equality* means that the communicator demonstrates feeling neither superior nor inferior to the second person.
- *Provisionalism* suggests that the communicator does not communicate certainty or a total conviction but is open to other ideas.
- *Spontaneity* implies naturalness and a lack of premeditation.

Gibb suggests that people replace those behaviors that create defensiveness with those that reduce it. Table 6.2 depicts the paired concepts. For example, rather than telling coworkers they are late for a meeting and you do not appreciate waiting, you might note the time they arrived and inquire empathically about their circumstances. Rather than being indifferent toward others and nonverbally suggesting you are superior, inquire about them and express your multiple similarities.

Essential Interpersonal Communication Behaviors

In interpersonal interactions, you need to be aware of many aspects of communication such as your perception of yourself and others, your self-concept, the verbal and nonverbal cues you send to and receive from others, and the ways in which you listen to others. In an interpersonal relationship you also show affection and support, influence others, and develop the unique nature of the relationship. In this section we consider three interpersonal communication areas: affectionate communication; influence, which includes compliance-gaining and interpersonal dominance; and the development of the distinctive relationship.

USING AFFECTIONATE AND SUPPORTIVE COMMUNICATION

Affection, the holding of fond or tender feelings toward another person, is essential in interpersonal relationships. You express your affectionate feelings for others in a variety of ways, often nonverbally as you touch, hug, kiss, or caress the person. You also use

engaging diversity

Close Intercultural Relationships and Creativity

Counselors, mentors, employers, and family members have likely told you about the importance of having intercultural experiences such as studying abroad or learning another language. Recently, Jackson Lu, an organization studies researcher at MIT, found that having a close friendship or romantic relationship with someone from a different culture boosts your creativity. In this study, researchers had participants complete a series of tasks to measure creativity, workplace innovation, and entrepreneurship. The results from this study revealed two interesting findings. First, participants who dated someone from a different culture performed better on problem-solving tasks. Second, non-U.S. participants who stayed in regular contact with U.S. friends after returning to their home country scored higher on innovation and entrepreneurship tasks. Interestingly, the length, not the number, of intercultural friendships a person had predicted the levels of creativity. From these findings the researchers argued that deeply learning about a friend's culture over time has the potential to increase gains in creativity. Lu suggested that intercultural friendships require people to acknowledge differences, and this pushes people to think differently about how to solve problems.

Think about your current relationships. Do any of them involve people from different cultures? If so, how much time have you spent deeply learning about that person's culture? If you do not have any close intercultural friendships, how might you go about learning more about the cultures of the people you already interact with—perhaps people in your classes? Doing so will not only benefit your intercultural awareness but, as Lu's research shows, it can also make you more creative.

Source: Lu, J. G., Hafenbrack, A. C., Eastwick, P. W., Wang, D. J., Maddux, W. W., & Galinsky, A. D. (2017). "Going out" of the box: Close intercultural friendships and romantic relationships spark creativity, workplace innovation, and entrepreneurship. *Journal of Applied Psychology, 102,* 1091–1108.

verbal statements of affection, such as "I care about you," "I really like being with you," or "I love you." Affectionate communication has been linked to improved mental health and wellness,[79] and people who give and receive affection tend to have reduced stress.[80] In fact, according to communication scholar Dr. Kory Floyd, "Among the most consequential forms of relational communication for health and wellness is the tendency to express and receive affection."[81]

Affectionate communication can be risk-laden, and a number of variables affect its appropriateness, such as your own and the other person's gender, the kind of relationship you have, and the context of the interaction.[82] Telling others that you love them may hold significantly different meanings, depending on any of these factors.

Although the expression of affection is generally positive, if the receiver of the message does not reciprocate, the sender may be embarrassed, also known as "losing face." Researchers have shown that expressions of liking do not always result in positive relational outcomes.[83] Interestingly, recent research using Affection Exchange Theory (AET) indicates that people vary in terms of how affectionate they are and that some of this is determined by inherited rather than learned behaviors.[84]

Supportive communication is also important in interpersonal communication. Support includes giving advice, expressing concern, and offering assistance and can vary as a result of the receiver's age[85] and the support provider's goals.[86] In times of distress, comforting messages, such as suggesting a diversion, offering assistance, and expressing optimism, encourage people to feel less upset. At the same time, the recipients of such messages may also feel demeaned. The distressed person is most likely to feel less upset when the comforting message is offered by a close friend rather than an acquaintance.[87] Comfort, then, is viewed as more positive in close interpersonal relationships as opposed to more distant ones.

INFLUENCING OTHERS

compliance-gaining
Attempts made by a source of messages to influence a target "to perform some desired behavior that the target otherwise might not perform."

Influence is the power to affect other people's thinking or actions. It has been studied widely in the context of interpersonal communication. One body of research has focused on compliance-gaining and compliance-resisting. **Compliance-gaining** is a person's attempts to influence a target "to perform some desired behavior that the target otherwise might not perform."[88] It occurs frequently in interpersonal communication. We ask a friend for advice, we ask a parent for financial assistance, or we encourage a relational partner to feel more committed. Compliance-gaining is even at work in the classroom. When students feel connected to each other, they are more likely to get teachers to comply with their requests, such as extending due dates.[89]

Compliance-resisting occurs when targets of influence messages refuse to comply with requests. People who are more sensitive to others and who are more adaptive are more likely to engage in further attempts to influence.[90] Indeed, they may address some anticipated obstacles in their original request, and they may adapt later attempts by offering counterarguments. One research study found several strategies to resist compliance attempts that included withdrawal, exit, voice, sabotage, and engaging decision makers.[91]

Although we often attempt to assert influence in our interpersonal relationships, it is important to remember that you may disagree with the opinions of your friends, partners, coworkers, and family members. For example, you and your sibling may differ on your views on military spending or police officers wearing body cameras. Debate is a healthy part of dialogue and democracy, yet you should remain civil, listen, and be respectful of others' opinions.

compliance-resisting
The refusal of targets of influence messages to comply with requests.

DEVELOPING A UNIQUE RELATIONSHIP

Interpersonal relationships are defined by their uniqueness. Researchers have found that couples who created **personal idioms**—or unique forms of expression and language understood only by them—expressed high relational satisfaction.[92]

In a similar way, through playful interaction and the creation of **rituals**—formalized patterns of actions or words followed regularly—couples create a shared culture. Rituals may become so routine that we do not realize they are part of the fabric of a relationship. However, if a relational partner does not enact them, uneasiness often follows. For example, can you recall a time when your partner failed to call you, say "I love you," or enact another regular behavior? Although the importance of the ritual might never have been verbalized, you probably felt hurt or neglected.

personal idioms
Unique forms of expression and language understood only by individual couples.

rituals
Formalized patterns of actions or words followed regularly.

Researchers suggest that the following rituals are important characteristics of long-term interpersonal relationships:

- *Couple-time rituals*—for example, exercising together or having dinner together every Saturday night
- *Idiosyncratic/symbolic rituals*—for example, calling each other by a special name or celebrating the anniversary of their first date
- *Daily routines and tasks*—for example, if living together, one partner always preparing the evening meal and the other always cleaning up afterward
- *Intimacy rituals*—for example, giving each other a massage or, when apart, talking on the telephone before going to bed
- *Communication rituals*—for example, saying "I love you" before going to sleep
- *Patterns, habits, and mannerisms*—for example, meeting one partner's need to be complimented when going out for a fancy evening and meeting the other's need to be reassured before family events
- *Spiritual rituals*—for example, attending services together or doing yoga together in the evening[93]

• Couple-time rituals help maintain long-term interpersonal relationships.
Szefei/123RF

The Possibilities for Improvement

Can you improve your communication in interpersonal relationships? Most individuals feel it's possible. Are such changes easy? Generally, they are not. You should not expect that an introductory course in communication will solve all your relational problems. Self-help books that promise instant success will probably result only in disillusionment. Courses on assertiveness training, relaxation techniques, and marital satisfaction provide only part of the answer. Improving relationships is a lifelong process that nobody perfects but that many people can pursue for their own benefit.

BARGAINING

bargaining
The process in which two or more parties attempt to reach an agreement on what each should give and receive in a transaction between them.

Often we engage in bargaining in our interpersonal relationships. **Bargaining** occurs when two or more parties attempt to reach an agreement on what each should give and receive in a transaction between them. Bargains may be explicit and formal, such as the kinds of agreements you reach with others to share tasks, to attend a particular event, or to behave in a specified way. Bargains may also be implicit and informal. For example, it might be an unwritten rule between you and your roommates that you cook dinner in exchange for them washing the dishes. You may not even be aware of some of the unstated agreements you have with others with whom you communicate.

An early study on interpersonal bargaining identified three essential features of a bargaining situation:

1. All parties perceive the possibility of reaching an agreement in which each party would be better off, or no worse off, than if no agreement were reached.

2. All parties perceive more than one such agreement that could be reached.

3. Each party perceives the others as having conflicting preferences or opposed interests.[94]

What are some examples of bargaining situations? You may want to go out with friends when your spouse would prefer a quiet evening at home. One person could use the word *forever* to mean a few days or weeks, whereas another assumes the word refers to a much longer period of time. In each of these instances, the disagreement can be resolved through bargaining.

John W. Thibaut and Harold H. Kelley underlined the importance of bargaining in interpersonal communication:

> Whatever the gratifications achieved in dyads, however lofty or fine the motives satisfied may be, the relationship may be viewed as a trading or bargaining one. The basic assumption running throughout our analysis is that every individual voluntarily enters and stays in any relationship only as long as it is adequately satisfactory in terms of rewards and costs.[95]

MAINTAINING BEHAVIORAL FLEXIBILITY

behavioral flexibility
The ability to alter behavior to adapt to new situations and to relate in new ways when necessary.

In addition to applying your understanding of communication concepts, skills, and settings, you can enhance your interactions by using **behavioral flexibility**—the ability to alter behavior to adapt to new situations and to relate in new ways when necessary. Behavioral flexibility allows you to relax when you are with friends or to be your formal self while interviewing for a job. The key to behavioral flexibility may be self-monitoring, always being conscious of the effect of your words on the specific audience in a particular context.

Behavioral flexibility is especially important in interpersonal communication because relationships between people are in constant flux. For example, the family structure has gone through sharp changes in recent years, the United States has an increasingly older population, and changes in the labor force also require new skills and ways of interacting with others. People travel more often and move more frequently. Millions of people live together before getting married or choose not to get married. Many couples are childless by choice and others struggle with infertility.

What kinds of changes can you expect in your own life that will affect your relationships with others? You may change your job 10 or more times and move your place of residence even more frequently. You may marry at least once and have one child or more. You will experience loss of family members through death and the dissolution of relationships. When your life appears to be most stable and calm, unexpected changes will occur.

A flexible person is confident about sharing messages with others, understands the messages others provide, self-discloses when appropriate, and at the same time demonstrates good listening skills. Flexibility lets us show concern for a child who needs assistance, be assertive on the job, yield when another person needs to exercise control, and be independent when called upon to stand alone. A flexible person is not dogmatic or narrow-minded. In short, flexibility means drawing on a large repertoire of communication behaviors as appropriate to the situation.

Changes are not always negative. In fact, many are positive. For instance, when you graduate from college, the changes that occur are generally perceived as positive. When you enter into new relationships, you generally feel better about your life. However, even positive change can be stressful because stress is the body's normal way of responding to change.[96] Author and psychologist Stephanie A. Sarkis suggests that writing down the positive outcomes that resulted from a transition can help you focus on how your circumstances have improved.

communicating with agility

Pivoting Modes of Communication

In recent years, in large part due to the pandemic, we have been asked to be flexible with the ways in which we build and maintain relationships with our family, friends, and coworkers. For example, meetings that traditionally would occur in person can now have standing virtual options, and families can host virtual game nights to maintain a sense of connection despite being far apart. Social interactions play an important role in maintaining our health and well-being. Virtual communication options have been shown to increase our number of interactions, which can reduce loneliness, especially for people with limited mobility or people in secluded areas.[97] In what ways has the pandemic or recent events in your own life motivated you to change modalities of communication to maintain your relationships? What have been the benefits? What have been the drawbacks?

be ready... for what's next

Establishing New Relationships

Life transitions typically provide opportunities for new interpersonal relationships. At college, you have the opportunity to meet people in your classes, on campus, and (if applicable) in your residence hall and dining hall. Each time you start a new term, you will have opportunities for new relationships. Similarly, when you start a new job, you have coworkers to meet. Some life changes involve moving to a completely new community, which opens many opportunities for new relationships. How can you best be ready for establishing new relationships as you confront these life changes? The end of many COVID-19 pandemic restrictions forced us all to rethink what interacting with people in person feels like, as well as our own comfort level with that. How has the pandemic given you new ideas on forming relationships?

As you learned in this chapter, new relationships are built through communication. The following suggestions provide you with strategies for establishing and building new relationships as you go through life changes both big and small.

- *Get comfortable with small talk.* Especially for introverts, small talk can be uncomfortable. However, a few simple tactics can help you engage others in casual conversation in ways that could spark interest in further developing a friendship. Psychologist Marty Nemko explained that some of the simplest ways of starting conversations are most effective.[98] Something as simple as saying, "Hi, I'm Scott and I'm in the College of Communication," invites other people to join the conversation. Asking questions about their areas of interest, hometowns, and hobbies are not mundane; all of those lines of conversation help you in finding areas of common interest.

- *Manage your self-disclosure.* When entering a new group of potential acquaintances, you should recognize that some self-disclosure will be necessary to establish connections, bonds, and trust. In writing about workplace transitions, communication scholars Chad McBride and Karla Bergen noted that individuals should manage personal and professional boundaries by knowing when to share some personal information but to avoid escalating relationships past friendship development to approach romantic or intimate disclosures.[99] In short, you should disclose, but you should also place some limits on how much disclosure you provide.

- *Make eye contact.* When other people notice that you are giving them direct eye contact, they are far more likely to give you attention and become involved in the conversation.[100] When talking with new acquaintances at work, in your neighborhood, or elsewhere, be comfortable looking them directly in the eyes when striking up conversation.

- *Be an active listener.* Active listening will help you in many ways. Active listeners naturally maintain eye contact and also find ways to keep the conversation flowing by connecting their own perspective to the messages they hear from others. Also, when other people perceive that you are a good listener, they will be more likely to want to talk to you again. Good listening is a foundation for any relationship, but it is particularly important in new relationships.

Chapter Review & Study Guide

Summary

In this chapter, you learned the following:

1. Interpersonal communication is the process of using messages to generate meaning between at least two people in a situation that allows mutual opportunities for both speaking and listening.

2. Interpersonal relationships provide one context in which people communicate with each other. Interpersonal relationships are associations between at least two people who are interdependent, who use some consistent patterns of interaction, and who have interacted for a period of time. Interpersonal relationships are established for a variety of reasons.

3. Interpersonal relationships are important because they allow us to fulfill our needs for inclusion, affection, and control. Most interpersonal relationships are positive, but they

also may have a dark side, which could include obsessions, jealousy, misunderstanding, gossip, conflict, codependency, and abuse.

4. Self-disclosure is fundamental to relationships.

5. Friendships are important, but they have changed over time largely due to social media.

6. Cross-cultural relationships are increasingly common.

7. Most relationships go through definable stages of development, maintenance, and deterioration.

8. Interpersonal communication includes affectionate and supportive communication, influence behaviors, and behaviors that allow people to develop unique relationships.

Key Terms

Aggressiveness
Argumentativeness

Attractiveness
Bargaining

Behavioral flexibility
Complementarity

Complementary relationships	Hurtful messages and events	Responsiveness
Compliance-gaining	Interpersonal relationships	Rituals
Compliance-resisting	Personal idioms	Self-disclosure
Contradictions	Proximity	Similarity
Deceptive communication	Relational deterioration	Symmetrical relationships
Defensiveness	Relational development	
Dialectic	Relational maintenance	

Study Questions

1. Which is *not* an element of an interpersonal relationship?

   a. It includes at least two people.
   b. It involves people who are interdependent.
   c. Its patterns of interaction are inconsistent.
   d. Individuals in an interpersonal relationship have interacted for some time.

2. Interpersonal relationships are important because

   a. they fulfill our needs for inclusion, affection, and control.
   b. physical, safety, and security needs cannot be met elsewhere.
   c. they provide financial stability.
   d. we need to interact with people who have similar interests.

3. An extrovert being friends with an introvert demonstrates which type of relationship?

   a. symmetrical
   b. complementary
   c. negotiated
   d. no relationship

4. Obsession, jealousy, gossip, and mental abuse are examples of

   a. healthy interpersonal communication.
   b. most marital relationships.
   c. possible negative qualities of some interpersonal relationships.
   d. positive problem-solving techniques and skills to develop.

5. Which of the following statements regarding friendship is true?

   a. Friendships remain unchanged over time.
   b. All friendships are maintained identically, regardless of relational partners' intent.
   c. The quality of friendship is affected by other psychological predispositions.
   d. For many older women, their only friend is their husband.

6. If two people in a relationship start to merge their social circles and purchase items together, they are exhibiting actions in the

   a. relational development stage.
   b. relational maintenance stage.
   c. relational deterioration stage.
   d. relational dialectic stage.

7. We may begin a relationship with someone based on how desirable that person is to work with in the classroom. This type of motivation is called

   a. responsiveness.
   b. similarity.
   c. complementarity.
   d. attractiveness.

8. A motivation for terminating a relationship by deliberately making somebody believe untrue things is labeled

   a. deceptive communication.
   b. aggressiveness.
   c. argumentativeness.
   d. defensiveness.

9. Your childhood nickname and the pet name your significant other calls you are examples of

   a. compliance-gaining.
   b. personal idioms.
   c. rituals.
   d. contradictions.

10. When you change your behavior to adapt to new situations, you are demonstrating

    a. bargaining.
    b. affectionate communication.
    c. behavioral flexibility.
    d. dialectic tensions.

Answers:
1. (c); 2. (a); 3. (b); 4. (c); 5. (c); 6. (a); 7. (d); 8. (a); 9. (b); 10. (c)

Critical Thinking

1. Consider a friendship you have or had. Explain that friendship in terms of the interpersonal relationship stages. Give examples that describe each stage.

2. How have you maintained your relationships with various people over time? If you have come close to terminating a relationship, how was it regained? Using terminology from the chapter, what was the reason for the near-termination?

3. How, if at all, has social media influenced your ability to initiate conversations with new people?

4. What are the strengths and weaknesses of the stages of interpersonal relationships? When you use this model to understand how relationships progress, are some relationship forms more or less visible?

Sizing Things Up Scoring and Interpretation

Interpersonal Motives

You might have various motives for entering into interpersonal relationships with others. Although the list of motives could be very specific, you learned about inclusion, affection, and control in this chapter. The interpersonal motives questionnaire created for this chapter helps students assess whether one or more of those motives are more dominant in explaining why they enter into relationships. You responded to three questions for each of the three motives. To calculate scores for each motive, add together responses for the indicated items below. Your scores will range from 3 to 12, with higher numbers indicating stronger orientations toward that particular motive.

- *Inclusion.* This motive suggests that we enter into interpersonal relationships to feel part of a group or to be included with others: items 3, 4, and 9.

- *Affection.* This motive stems from our need to share emotion and support with others: items 2, 5, and 8.
- *Control.* To have more instrumental control over our lives and our surroundings, a motivation to control may cause us to enter into relationships: items 1, 6, and 7.

This scale is not designed to generate an overall score; you should calculate scores for each dimension separately. For a variation on this scale, change the target from multiple relationships to a particular relationship, such as the selection of your roommate, your best friend, and so on. When analyzing response patterns, your motives could be multidimensional with high scores for each dimension, or you could emphasize or deemphasize one or more motives.

References

1. Dowling, A. (2017, February 24). Meet TV's first non-binary gender character: Asia Kate Dillon of Showtime's "Billions." *The Hollywood Reporter* https://www.hollywoodreporter.com/live-feed/meet-tvs-first-binary-gender-character-asia-kate-dillon-showtimes-billions-979523

2. *All Things Considered.* (2015, November 8). More universities move to include gender-neutral pronouns. NPR. https://www.npr.org/2015/11/08/455202525/more-universities-move-to-include-gender-neutral-pronouns

3. Lesbian, Gay, Bisexual, Transgender Resource Center. (n.d.). Gender pronouns. https://uwm.edu/lgbtrc/support/gender-pronouns/

4. Lesbian, Gay, Bisexual, Transgender Resource Center. (n.d.). Gender pronouns. https://uwm.edu/lgbtrc/support/gender-pronouns/

5. Miller, G. R., & Steinberg, M. (1975). *Between people: A new analysis of interpersonal communication.* Science Research Associates.

6. Schutz, W. (1958). *The interpersonal underworld.* Science & Behavior Books.

7. Spitzberg, B. H., & Cupach, W. R. (2007). *The dark side of interpersonal communication* (2nd ed.). Lawrence Erlbaum.

8. Pearce, W. B., & Sharp, S. M. (1973). Self-disclosing communication. *Journal of Communication, 23,* 409–425.

9. Jourard, S. M. (1964). *The transparent self: Self-disclosure and well-being.* Van Nostrand Reinhold.

10. Petronio, S. (2002). *Boundaries of privacy: Dialectics of disclosure.* State University of New York Press.

11. Hosek, A. M., & Thompson, J. (2009). Communication privacy management and college instruction: Exploring the rules and boundaries that frame instructor private disclosures. *Communication Education, 58,* 327–349. https://doi.org/10.1080/03634520902777585

12. Hastings, S. O. (2000). Self-disclosure and identity management by bereaved parents. *Communication Studies, 51,* 352–371.

13. Rossetto, K. R., Lannutti, P. J., & Strauman, E. C. (2015). Death on Facebook: Examining the roles of social media

communication for the bereaved. *Journal of Social and Personal Relationships, 32*(7), 974–994.

14. Tardy, C. H., & Smithson, J. (2018). Self-disclosure: Strategic revelation of information in personal and professional relationships. In *The handbook of communication skills* (pp. 217–258). Routledge.

15. Darling, N., Cumsille, P., Caldwell, L. L., & Dowdy, B. (2006). Predictors of adolescents' disclosure to parents and perceived parental knowledge: Between- and within-person differences. *Journal of Youth and Adolescence, 35*, 659–670. Smetana, J. G., Metzger, A., Gettman, D. C., & Campione-Barr, N. (2006). Disclosure and secrecy in adolescent-parent relationships. *Child Development, 77*, 201–217.

16. Tam, T., Hewstone, M., Harwood, J., Voci, A., & Kenworthy, J. (2006). Intergroup contact and grandparent–grandchild communication: The effects of self-disclosure on implicit and explicit biases against older people. *Group Processes and Intergroup Relations, 9*, 413–429.

17. Afifi, W. A., & Guerrero, L. K. (1998). Some things are better left unsaid II: Topic avoidance in friendships. *Communication Quarterly, 46*, 231–249.

18. Roloff, M. E., & Johnson, D. I. (2001). Reintroducing taboo topics: Antecedents and consequences of putting topics back on the table. *Communication Studies, 52*, 37–50.

19. Jensen, L. A., Arnett, J. J., Feldman, S. S., & Cauffman, E. (2004). The right to do wrong: Lying to parents among adolescents and emerging adults. *Journal of Youth and Adolescence, 33*, 101–112. https://doi.org/10.1023/B:JOYO.0000013422.48100.5a

20. Kito, M. (2005). Self-disclosure in romantic relationships and friendships among American and Japanese college students. *Journal of Social Psychology, 145*, 127–140.

21. Kim, J., & Dindia, K. (2011). Online self-disclosure: A review of research. In K. B. Wright & L. M. Webb (Eds.), *Computer-mediated communication in personal relationships* (pp. 156–180). Peter Lang.

22. Sherman, A. M., Lansford, J. E., & Volling, B. L. (2006). Sibling relationships and best friendships in young adulthood: Warmth, conflict, and well-being. *Personal Relationships, 13*, 151–165.

23. Rawlins, W. (1992). *Friendship matters: Communication, dialectics, and the life course.* Aldine de Gruyter.

24. Radmacher, K., & Azmitia, M. (2006). Are there gendered pathways to intimacy in early adolescents' and emerging adults' friendships? *Journal of Adolescent Research, 21*, 415–448.

25. Pahl, R., & Pevalin, D. J. (2005). Between family and friends: A longitudinal study of friendship choice. *British Journal of Sociology, 56*, 433–450.

26. Rawlins, *Friendship matters.*

27. Carstensen, L. L., Fung, H. H., & Charles, S. T. (2003). Socio-emotional selectivity theory and the regulation of emotion in the second half of life. *Motivation and Emotion, 27*(2), 103–123. https://doi.org/10.1023/A:1024569803230

28. Way, N., & Greene, M. L. (2006). Trajectories of perceived friendship quality during adolescence: The patterns and contextual predictors. *Journal of Research on Adolescence, 16*, 293–320.

29. Saferstein, J. A., Neimeyer, G. J., & Hagans, C. L. (2005). Attachment as a predictor of friendship qualities in college youth. *Social Behavior and Personality, 33*, 767–775.

30. Rawlins, *Friendship matters: Communication, dialectics, and the life course.* Aldine de Gruyter.

31. Rawlins, *Friendship matters: Communication, dialectics, and the life course.* Aldine de Gruyter.

32. Guerrero, L. K., & Chavez, A. M. (2005). Relational maintenance in cross-sex friendships characterized by different types of romantic intent: An exploratory study. *Western Journal of Communication, 69*, 339–358.

33. Neary Dunleavy, K., & Booth-Butterfield, M. (2008). Chilling effects and binge drinking in platonic and romantic relationships. *Human Communication, 11*, 39–51.

34. French, D. C., Bae, A., Pidada, S., & Okhwa, L. (2006). Friendships of Indonesian, South Korean, and U.S. college students. *Personal Relationships, 13*, 69–81.

35. Paul, K. (2022, October 23). From dance videos to global sensation: What you need to know about TikTok's rise. *The Guardian.* https://www.theguardian.com/technology/2022/oct/22/tiktok-history-rise-algorithm-misinformation

36. Meta Investor Relations. (2022, July 27). Q2 2022 Earnings. https://investor.fb.com/investor-events/event-details/2022/Q2-2022-Earnings/default.aspx

37. Branka, A. (2022, September 28). Facebook statistics. *Truelist.* https://truelist.co/blog/facebook-statistics/

38. Campbell, S. (2022, October 3). How many people use Twitter in 2022 (Twitter Statistics). *The Small Business Blog.* https://thesmallbusinessblog.net/twitter-statistics/

39. Del Rosario, A. (2020, August 29). Twitter crowns Chadwick Boseman's last post most liked tweet ever: "A tribute fit for a king." *Deadline.* https://deadline.com/2020/08/chadwick-boseman0-twitter-most-liked-tweet-ever-1203026947/

40. Trimble, N. (2017, December 12). Twitter's 10 most-retweeted tweets of the year. *US News and World Report.* https://www.usnews.com/news/national-news/articles/2017-12-12/twitters-top-10-most-retweeted-tweets-of-2017

41. The Bark Team. (2018, August 17). Sit with us app helps kids find a seat at the lunch table. *Bark.* https://www.bark.us/blog/sit-us-app-helps-kids-find-seat-lunch-table/

42. Ross, C., Orr, E. S., Sisic, M., Arseneault, J. M., Simmering, M. G., & Orr, R. R. (2009). Personality and motivations associated with Facebook use. *Computers in Human Behavior, 25*, 578–586.

43. Lachmann, S. (2015, February 3). What it really means to be "friends with benefits." *Psychology Today*. https://www.psychologytoday.com/us/blog/me-we/201502/what-it-really-means-be-friends-benefits

44. Bisson, M. A., & Levine, T. R. (2009). Negotiating a friends with benefits relationship. *Archives of Sexual Behavior, 38,* 66–73.

45. Lachmann, S. (2015, February 3). What it really means to be "friends with benefits." *Psychology Today*. https://www.psychologytoday.com/us/blog/me-we/201502/what-it-really-means-be-friends-benefits

46. Ronesi, L. M. (2003). Enhancing postsecondary inter-group relations at the university through student-run ESL instruction. *Journal of Language, Identity, and Education, 2,* 191–210.

47. Miller, G. R. (1976). *Explorations in interpersonal communication*. Sage.

48. La France, B. H. (2010). Predicting sexual satisfaction in interpersonal relationships. *Southern Communication Journal, 75,* 195–214.

49. La France, B. H. (2010). What verbal and nonverbal communication cues lead to sex? An analysis of the traditional sexual script. *Communication Quarterly, 58,* 297–318.

50. Wilmot, W. W. (1995). *Relational communication*. McGraw-Hill.

51. Baxter, L. (1993). The social side of personal relationships: A dialectical perspective. In S. Duck (Ed.), *Understanding relationship processes: Vol. 3. Social context and relationships* (pp. 139–165). Sage. Baxter, L., & Montgomery, B. (1996). *Relating: Dialogues and dialects*. Guilford Press. Dindia, K., & Baxter, L. A. (1987). Strategies for maintaining and repairing marital relationships. *Journal of Social and Personal Relationships, 4,* 143–158.

52. Chory, R. M., & Banfield, S. (2009). Media dependence and relational maintenance in interpersonal relationships. *Communication Reports, 22,* 41–53.

53. Billedo, C. J., Kerkhof, P., & Finkenauer, C. (2015). The use of social networking sites for relationship maintenance in long-distance and geographically close romantic relationships. *Cyberpsychology, Behavior, and Social Networking, 18*(3), 152–157.

54. Johnson, A. J., Haigh, M. M., Becker, J. A. H., Craig, E. A., & Wigley, S. (2008). College students' use of relational management strategies in email in long-distance and geographically close relationships. *Journal of Computer-Mediated Communication, 13,* 381–404.

55. Utz, S., & Beukeboom, C. J. (2011). The role of social network sites in romantic relationships: Effects on jealousy and relationship happiness. *Journal of Computer-Mediated Communication, 16,* 511–527.

56. Utz, S., & Beukeboom, C. J. (2011). The role of social network sites in romantic relationships: Effects on jealousy and relationship happiness. *Journal of Computer-Mediated Communication, 16,* 511–527.

57. Friedman, H. S., Riggio, J. R. E., & Casella, D. F. (1988). Nonverbal skill, personal charisma, and initial attraction. *Personality and Social Psychology Bulletin, 14,* 203–211.

58. McCroskey, J. C., & McCain, T. A. (1974). The measurement of interpersonal attraction. *Speech Monographs, 41,* 267–276.

59. Rick, S. I., Small, D. A., & Finkel, E. J. (2011). Fatal (fiscal) attraction: Spendthrifts and tightwads in marriage. *Journal of Marketing Research, 48,* 228–237.

60. Perse, E. M., & Rubin, R. B. (1989). Attribution in social and parasocial relationships. *Communication Research, 16,* 59–77.

61. Berger, C. R., & Kellermann, K. (1989). Personal opacity and social information gathering. *Communication Research, 16,* 314–351.

62. Davis, M. H., & Oathout, H. A. (1987). Maintenance of satisfaction in romantic relationships: Empathy and relational competence. *Journal of Personality and Social Psychology, 53,* 397–498.

63. Aylor, B., & Dainton, M. (2004). Biological sex and psychological gender as predictors of routine and strategic relational maintenance. *Sex Roles, 50,* 689–697.

64. Yum, Y. O., & Canary, D. J. (2009). Cultural differences in equity theory predictions of relational maintenance strategies. *Human Communication Research, 35,* 384–406.

65. Givertz, M., Segrin, C., & Woszidlo, A. (2015). Direct and indirect effects of commitment on interdependence and satisfaction in married couples. *Journal of Family Psychology, 30,* 1–7.

66. Sillars, A., Shellen, W., McIntosh, A., & Pomegranate, M. (1997). Relational characteristics of language: Elaboration and differentiation in marital conversations. *Western Journal of Communication, 61,* 403–422.

67. Roberts, J. A., & David, M. E. (2016). My life has become a major distraction from my cell phone: Partner phubbing and relationship satisfaction among romantic partners. *Computers in Human Behavior, 54,* 134–141. https://doi.org/10.1016/j.chb.2015.07.058

68. World Population Review. (2023). Divorce rates by country. https://worldpopulationreview.com/country-rankings/divorce-rates-by-country

69. Divorce.com. (2023). 48 divorce statistics in the U.S. including divorce rate, race, & marriage length. https://divorce.com/blog/divorce-statistics/

70. Vangelisti, A. L., & Crumley, L. P. (1998). Reactions to messages that hurt: The influence of relational contexts. *Communication Monographs, 65,* 173–196.

71. Malachowski, C. C., & Frisby, B. N. (2015). The aftermath of hurtful events: Cognitive, communicative, and relational outcomes. *Communication Quarterly, 63,* 187–203.

72. Vangelisti, A. L., Young, S. L., Carpenter-Theune, K. E., & Alexander, A. L. (2005). Why does it hurt? The perceived causes of hurt feelings. *Communication Research, 32,* 443–477.

73. Vangelisti & Crumley, Reactions to messages that hurt.

74. di Battista, P. (1997). Deceivers' responses to challenges of their truthfulness: Difference between familiar lies and unfamiliar lies. *Communication Quarterly, 45,* 319–334.

75. Bodenmann, G., Meuwly, N., Bradbury, T. N., Gmelch, S., & Ledermann, T. (2010). Stress, anger, and verbal aggression in intimate relationships: Moderating effects of individual and dyadic coping. *Journal of Social and Personal Relationships, 27,* 408–424.

76. Semic, B. A., & Canary, D. J. (1997). Trait argumentativeness, verbal aggressiveness, and minimally rational argument: An observational analysis of friendship discussions. *Communication Quarterly, 45,* 355–378.

77. Schullery, N. M., & Schullery, S. E. (2003). Relationship of argumentativeness to age and higher education. *Western Journal of Communication, 67,* 207–224.

78. Gibb, J. R. (1991). *Trust: A new vision of human relationships for business, education, family, and personal living* (2nd ed.). Newcastle.

79. Floyd, K., Hess, J. A., Miczo, L. A., Halone, K. K., Mikkelson, A. C., & Tusing, K. J. (2005). Human affection exchange: VIII. Further evidence of the benefits of expressed affection. *Communication Quarterly, 53,* 285–303.

80. Floyd, K., Hesse, C., & Pauley, P. M. (2009, November). Writing affectionate letters reduces stress: Replication and extension. Paper presented at the annual meeting of the National Communication Association, Chicago, IL.

81. Floyd, K., Morman, M. T., Maré, J., & Holmes, E. (2021). How Americans communicate affection: Findings from a representative national sample. *Communication Quarterly, 69*(4), 383–409.

82. Floyd, K. (1997). Affectionate communication in nonromantic relationships: Influences of communicator, relational, and contextual factors. *Western Journal of Communication, 61,* 279–298.

83. Floyd, K., & Burgoon, J. K. (1999). Reacting to nonverbal expressions of liking: A test of interaction adaptation theory. *Communication Monographs, 66,* 219–239.

84. Floyd, K., & Denes, A. (2015). Attachment security and oxytocin receptor gene polymorphism interact to influence affectionate communication. *Communication Quarterly, 63,* 272–285.

85. Caplan, S. E., & Samter, W. (1999). The role of facework in younger and older adults' evaluations of social support messages. *Communication Quarterly, 47,* 245–264.

86. MacGeorge, E. L. (2001). Support providers' interaction goals: The influence of attributions and emotions. *Communication Monographs, 68,* 72–97.

87. Clark, R. A., Pierce, K. F., Hsu, K., Toosley, A., & Williams, L. (1998). The impact of alternative approaches to comforting, closeness of relationship, and gender on multiple measures of effectiveness. *Communication Studies, 49,* 224–239.

88. Wilson, S. R. (1998). Introduction to the special issue on seeking and resisting compliance: The vitality of compliance-gaining research. *Communication Studies, 49,* 273–275.

89. Sidelinger, R. J., Bolen, D. M., Frisby, B. N., & McMullen, A. L. (2012). Instructor compliance to student requests: An examination of student-to-student connectedness as power in the classroom. *Communication Education, 61,* 290–308.

90. Ifert, D. E., & Roloff, M. E. (1997). Overcoming expressed obstacles to compliance: The role of sensitivity to the expressions of others and ability to modify self-presentation. *Communication Quarterly, 45,* 55–67.

91. Carr, J. B., & Brower, R. S. (2000). Principled opportunism: Evidence from the organizational middle. *Public Administration Quarterly, 24,* 109–138.

92. Bruess, C. J. S., & Pearson, J. C. (1993). "Sweet pea" and "pussy cat"? An examination of idiom use and marital satisfaction over the life cycle. *Journal of Social and Personal Relationships, 10,* 609–615.

93. Bruess, C. J. S., & Pearson, J. C. (1997). Interpersonal rituals in marriage and adult friendship. *Communication Monographs, 64,* 25–46.

94. Deusch, M., & Kraus, R. M. (1962). Studies of interpersonal bargaining. *Journal of Conflict Resolution, 6,* 52.

95. Thibaut, J. W., & Kelley, H. H. (1959). *The social psychology of groups* (p. 37). John Wiley.

96. Sarkis, S. A. (2017, January). 10 ways to cope with big changes. *Psychology Today.* https://www.psychologytoday.com/us/blog/here-there-and-everywhere/201701/10-ways-cope-big-changes

97. Sahi, R. S., Schwyck, M. E., Parkinson, C., & Eisenberger, N. I. (2021). Having more virtual interaction partners during COVID-19 physical distancing measures may benefit mental health. *Science Reports, 11,* 1–9. https://doi.org/10.1038/s41598-021-97421-1

98. Nemko, M. (2018, December 15). Small talk for people bad at it. P*sychology Today.* https://www.psychologytoday.com/us/blog/how-to-do-life/201812/small-talk-for-people-bad-at-it

99. McBride, M. C., & Bergen, K. M. (2015). Work spouses: Defining and understanding a "new" relationship. *Communication Studies, 66,* 487–508. https://doi.org/10.1080/10510974.2015.1029640

100. Hietanen, J. K. (2018). Affective eye contact: An integrative review. *Frontiers in Psychology, 9,* 1–15. https://doi.org/10.3389/fpsyg.2018.01587

SilviaJansen/iStockphoto/Getty Images

7

inclusive communication

When you have read and thought about this chapter, you will be able to

1. explain why the study of inclusive communication is important.

2. recall foundational principles of inclusive communication.

3. identify theories that help explain challenges and opportunities related to inclusive communication.

4. identify communication challenges to inclusive communication.

5. practice strategies for improving inclusive communication.

This chapter introduces you to concepts related to inclusive communication. Being an inclusive communicator means attending to the communication situation so that everyone feels included and valued. This chapter stresses the importance of communicating effectively in a diverse and ever-changing world. It reveals that the ways in which we communicate have the power to include and exclude others. When you complete this chapter, you should feel more confident about communicating in inclusive ways with others.

The marriage of Prince Harry and Meghan Markle, the first woman of color to become a member of the royal family, brought hopes for the dissolution of the barriers constructed around race in the British monarchy. However, in 2020, Megan and Harry announced that they would be stepping down from their duties as senior members of the royal family, in part due to a lack of inclusivity and support from the royal family. In their 2022 Netflix documentary, *Megan & Harry*,[1] the couple recounted numerous occasions in which they experienced racism and prejudice from members of the royal family, the media, and British society.

This example illustrates that in encounters with people with diverse identities, whether in a family, at work, or with friends, there is potential for new connections, as well as new challenges that must be overcome. In this chapter you will learn how to better understand and practice inclusive communication, which will benefit you both personally and professionally.

The wedding of Prince Harry and Meghan Markle symbolized a hope for progress but also exposed the problems that can be experienced without inclusive communication.

Chris Jackson/Getty Images

The Importance of Studying Inclusive Communication

According to researchers Jerneja Brce and Damjana Kogovsek, "Communication is central to our ability to learn, work, form and maintain relationships, and to participate in society."[2] **Inclusive communication** focuses on reducing barriers so that everyone is included, feels valued, and has access to the communication situation. Inclusive communication seeks to reduce communication barriers, as well as the subsequent prejudice and exclusion people face from society. We begin this chapter by discussing reasons you should study and improve your skills to be an inclusive communicator.

A focus on inclusive communication improves your ability to communicate effectively with diverse audiences. More people are now exposed to different **social identities**, whether it be through international travel, work, school, friends, or family. The United States continues to grow in its diversity. The Brookings Institution projects that by 2045 the white population will make up less than 50% of the total population; the largest demographic increase of minority groups will be from those who are multiracial, Asian, and Hispanic.[3] We likely also interact with people of different gender and sexual identities, people with different religious backgrounds, people from different generations, and people who come from different parts of the country. In short, it is nearly impossible to go through the day without interacting with people from diverse backgrounds, so inclusive communication is vital.

Another reason to study inclusive communication centers on the way it impacts the messages you say and hear and who gets included or excluded in those messages. As the sender of a message, you can choose language that includes or excludes others. As a result, the receiver of the message will determine how safe, supported, and valued they feel in

inclusive communication
Reducing barriers so that everyone is included, valued, and has access to the communication situation.

social identities
The social groups you believe you belong to, such as gender, race, or religion.

engaging diversity

The Value of Silence

One of the more striking differences among cultures is the value of silence. The dominant European American culture in the United States practically fears silence; people often perceive silence as unintended and even embarrassing. However, many East Asian cultures, such as the Japanese; autonomous cultures in the United States, such as the Amish; and Native American cultures, such as the Western Apache of Arizona, view silence as an important way to know and understand another person through intuition. Here are some sayings that illustrate the idea:

- It is what people say that gets them in trouble. (Japanese)
- A loud voice shows an empty head. (Finnish)
- To be always talking is against nature. (Taoist)
- One who speaks does not know. (Taoist)
- The cat that does not mew catches rats. (Japanese)

Compared with some other cultures in the world, the dominant culture in North America tends to emphasize talking more than listening or being silent. When communicating across cultures, Americans may need to adapt their communication behaviors to have a greater acceptance of silence.

Source: Kim, M. S. (2002). *Non-Western perspectives on human communication: Implications for theory and practice.* Sage. (pp. 135, 137).

the situation. Inclusive communication is a relational construct built on the things we say and do. Laura Dobusch, researcher of gender and diversity, argues that building relationships is a fundamental way people experience inclusion.[4] Therefore, the knowledge and skills from this chapter will help you build more inclusive relationships with friends, family, and acquaintances.

Inclusive communication is also important to your professional career. Diversity and inclusive communication are vital to work environments because people from different cultures and social identities provide unique perspectives that can help the organization meet its goals. For example, greater creativity and innovation occur when employees have different skills, experiences, and knowledge, and employees typically report being happier in diverse workplaces.[5] The knowledge and skills you will gain in this chapter can help you build stronger relationships with coworkers and make your work environment more inclusive.

Building skills, knowledge, and empathy toward inclusive communication is a continual process. A commitment toward inclusive communication requires that you keep learning about diverse viewpoints, listen to and seek out the experiences of others, recognize when you are making progress, and acknowledge when you are struggling to be inclusive in your communication.[6]

Principles of Inclusive Communication

You have just learned that inclusive communication focuses on reducing barriers so that everyone is included, feels valued, and has access to the information they need to be effective in the communication situation. Yet, there are many aspects to inclusive communication. This section will discuss the principles of diversity and equity, cultural identity, and intersectionality.

DIVERSITY AND EQUITY

diversity
Aspects of identity that can include, race, ethnicity, gender identity, economic status, and ability that are brought together in some way.

equity
providing equal opportunities for all people without discriminating on the basis of identity.

In addition to understanding what inclusion is, it is important to understand the ways in which diversity and equity function to build inclusion in our relationships, workplaces, and society. **Diversity** typically focuses on various aspects of identity, such as race, ethnicity, gender, economic status, and ability, that are brought together in some way.[7] On many college campuses, diversity is valued because it brings different perspectives and allows students to learn from others and expand their worldview. **Equity** relates to providing equal opportunities for all people without discriminating on the basis of identity. The Gallup organization suggests that equity in the workplace often includes ensuring all employees experience equal pay for their roles and experience, advancement opportunities, and daily work expectations.[8] For example, policies regarding paid time off, parental leave, and remote work flexibility are often hidden in rules and norms that privilege some groups and disadvantages others, creating an unfair workplace. Contemporary workplaces build in policies, and sometimes governing bodies, to help ensure their practices and policies, not just their words, support diversity and inclusion. A focus on inclusive communication can help you participate in these initiatives throughout your career.

CULTURAL IDENTITY

A **culture** is a unique combination of rituals (such as greeting and parting), religious beliefs, ways of thinking (such as how Earth was created), and ways of behaving (such as avoiding certain types of food) that unify a group of people. Often we perceive cultural differences (see Chapter 2 for more on perception) as emerging from nation states, such as France and the Czech Republic; religious groups, such as Muslims, Hindus, and Christians; ethnic groups, such as the Kurds and the Ibos; or even people united by a cause, such as criminal justice activists or animal rights activists.

Dominant identities in a culture are determined by who has the power and influence in traditional social structures such as politics, religious institutions, schools, and businesses. Communication scholars Mark Orbe and Colin Batten identify dominant identities in the United States as male, European American, heterosexual, without disabilities, youthful, middle/upper class, and/or Christian.[9] Other dominant identities in U.S. culture are the college educated, people in the professions, business owners, homeowners, married couples, and people paid a yearly salary rather than by the hour.

In contrast, **nondominant identities** exist within a larger, dominant culture that differ from the dominant identities in one or more significant characteristics. Nondominant identities are often called *marginalized groups* because they are on the edges of the dominant culture; in other words, they exist on the margins. Who are the marginalized groups? Orbe and Batten point to women, people of color, members of the LGBTQ+ community, and people with disabilities as examples. To these groups we could add others: people living in poverty, who have lost their jobs, who are unemployed or underemployed, or who have lost their homes due to an economic downturn, natural disaster, or pandemic.

Women are considered a nondominant identity in the United States because they are underrepresented in positions of power and authority. In fact, some of the initial studies of nondominant identity focused on how little influence women had, even when they were part of workforce teams. Cheris Kramarae, a women's studies scholar, called women a "muted group" because their ideas were undervalued, underestimated, and sometimes unheard.[10] Although the status of women has improved substantially, more work is clearly needed. As of 2021, 144 (or 27%) of the U.S. House of Representatives and Senate are women, which is a 50% increase from 10 years earlier.[11] The 2022 midterm election also marked the first time an openly lesbian woman, Maura Healey, was elected to a governorship.[12] In business, women now constitute 22.4% of small business owners.[13] In Fortune 500 companies, the number of women CEOs reached its record in 2022 with 44, up from 32 in 2017.[14] Despite recent progress for women, a Pew Research poll found that 4 in 10 Americans believe there are double standards for women seeking to break the glass ceiling in business or politics.[15] In essence, women must do more to prove themselves in comparison to their male peers because of male-dominated power structures within the dominant culture.

Nondominant identity groups often face systemic discrimination that becomes a point of contestation in public policy and the law. For example, on June 15, 2020, the Supreme Court ruled in the case *Bostock v. Clayton County*, which held that Title VII of the Civil Rights Act of 1964 (Title VII) includes employment discrimination against an individual

culture
A unique combination of rituals, religious beliefs, ways of thinking, and ways of behaving that unify a group of people.

dominant identity
A cultural identity that gets its power and influence from traditional social structures like politics, religious institutions, schools, and businesses; in the United States the dominant culture is white, male, heterosexual, married, and employed.

nondominant identity
A group that exists within a larger, dominant culture and differs from the dominant identities in one or more significant characteristics.

• Those who experience food insecurity and use community food pantries are members of a nondominant culture.

a katz/Shutterstock

intersectionality
The ways our social identities intersect and overlap, as well as how those with multiple marginalized identities experience systems of oppression and discrimination in multiple ways.

communicating creatively

Music as a Form of Inclusive Dialogue

Gavin Carfoot, a member of the creative industries faculty at Queensland University in Australia, observed that music can play an important role in helping individuals from different cultures find common ground from which to communicate. As he noted, listening to and developing an appreciation for music from other countries, particularly countries that have rich indigenous music traditions, can help listeners discover new avenues for music enjoyment and cultural understanding. Additionally, Carfoot explains that artists from different cultural backgrounds can create "musical hybridity" that promotes "empathy and obligation" to other cultures. If you are a musician, explore opportunities to make music with people from other cultures. If you are not a musician, explore world music as a way of broadening your inclusive cultural awareness.

Source: Carfoot, G. (2016). Musical discovery, colonialism, and the possibilities of intercultural communication through music. *Popular Communication, 14*, 178–186. doi: 10.1080/15405702.2016.1193184

on the basis of sexual orientation or gender identity.[16] This example highlights how public policy and law indicate how the rights of nondominant identity groups are negotiated within the larger dominant identities in a culture.

For another example of how communication is related to dominant and nondominant identities, consider food insecurity among college students. A recent survey showed that 39% of college students report that they have food insecurity—that is, they often go without food because of several factors, most notably because they cannot afford it.[17] Other surveys suggest that the percentage is much higher, being closer to 50%.[18] As a result, many colleges and universities have created food pantries where students can gain free access to food. Unfortunately, researchers from the University of Florida found that only 38% of students experiencing food insecurity make use of such pantries.[19] In their study, the most often cited reason for not visiting food pantries was the perceived social stigma. Consider how the communication of the dominant culture (food-secure individuals) might create such perceptions among the nondominant, food-insecure students.

INTERSECTIONALITY

Intersectionality, a term credited to critical race theory scholar Kimberlé Williams Crenshaw, refers to the ways in which our social identities intersect and overlap, as well as how those with multiple marginalized identities experience systems of oppression and discrimination in multiple ways.[20] Intersectionality has many popular cultural and scholarly definitions, and it has been used by scholars and activists as a theory, a method, and a framework to examine how diverse identities, contexts, and structures privilege some and not others. For example, Black women in the United States were overlooked for their gender when Black men were granted voting rights and were often excluded for their race from the larger feminist movement, which privileged white women.[21] When considering your own identity, you likely don't think of yourself as only a student. You likely think about many aspects of your identity such as your race, ethnicity, age, gender, sexual orientation, and abilities or disabilities. Some of these identities may be more important to you than others, but they all impact your perceptions of yourself and influence your communication with others. A focus on intersectionality acknowledges that many people hold multiple marginalized social identities, and inclusive communication offers space to invite, listen, and understand our own and others' intersectional identities and experiences.

building behaviors

Understanding Our Own Identity Complexity

In this section you have learned the characteristics of dominant and nondominant identities. Many of us have attributes that simultaneously align us with dominant and nondominant identities. For instance, a person who is a first-generation college student from a primarily Anglo European background who does not practice religion has multiple layers of identity. Some of these identities align closely with the dominant group (being white and a college student), but others align more closely with nondominant groups (being a first-generation college student and not being a member of a religious group).

List at least 10 of your personal attributes and briefly explain how each attribute could align toward dominant or nondominant groups. After analyzing your own characteristics, consider how you would react to the following situations:

- Attending a university with monuments to Confederate generals on the campus
- Using a food assistance program provided by your community or university
- Attending a religious service with members of an immigrant community
- Being offered admission to an exclusive country club
- Participating in a same-sex marriage ceremony

Were there any instances in which you felt conflicted about how you would react? How were your feelings about these situations influenced by your personal characteristics?

Theories Related to Inclusive Communication

There are many theories from the disciplines of psychology, sociology, linguistics, and communication that help us understand identity and how to be inclusive in our communication. Next, we will discuss three of these theories: social identity theory (SIT), communication accommodation theory (CAT), and contact theory.

SOCIAL IDENTITY THEORY

Social identity theory (SIT) explains how individuals form a sense of self and how they categorize themselves and others into social groups. This theory proposes that individuals derive their self-esteem not only from personal characteristics (for example, their personality) but also from the collective status of the groups to which they belong.[22] If you have a strong allegiance to a sports team, a student organization, or a place of worship, those organizations have likely influenced your self-concept at various points in your life. Social identity is therefore a crucial aspect of an individual's overall self-concept.

SIT is particularly useful in understanding how people identify with their cultural heritage. People tend to have a sense of pride and solidarity with people who have similar cultural backgrounds, and this feeling is often strengthened by the perception of common values, traditions, and cultural heritage. Cultural allegiance is also a way of

social identity theory A theoretical framework that explains how individuals form a sense of self and how they categorize themselves and others into social groups.

When older and younger adults interact, it is important to accommodate communication in ways that meet each other's needs.

DigitalVision/The Good Brigade/Getty images

communication accommodation theory A communication theory that explains how people adjust their communication style to match the styles of others.

distinguishing oneself from others. Although such allegiance can be an important part of your identity, it can also lead to misperceptions. For instance, you may assume that people of similar cultural backgrounds as you are more similar and alike than they actually are, and you may incorrectly assume that people from different cultures are more different from you than they actually are.

COMMUNICATION ACCOMMODATION THEORY

Communication accommodation theory (CAT) explains how people adjust their communication style to match the styles of others. The theory suggests that individuals alter their communication to fit in with the norms and expectations of a particular social group, to establish social relationships, and to show respect for the person they are communicating with.[23] Communication accommodation is a dynamic process that involves constant adjustments to the way individuals speak, listen, and use nonverbal cues. CAT can be seen in the way people adjust their speech style when speaking to someone from a different cultural background. For example, if you travel to Thailand, you will quickly observe a greeting ritual that involves a slight bow coupled with hands held together under the chin. As you observe this common greeting ritual, you may begin to do this when greeting others as a sign of respect to members of the culture you are visiting.

sizing things up

Communication Accommodation and Age

CAT explains how we change our communication to decrease (diverge) or increase (converge) perceptions of distance to others based on group membership. One way this can happen is with age group identification. Consider the following scenario and your reactions.

When was the last time you interacted with someone significantly older than you, perhaps in their 70s or 80s? How did you feel during that interaction? Did you approach communication with them or try to avoid it? If you did communicate with them, did you speak louder than usual because you anticipated they might not be able to hear you? Or did you use your normal volume? Did you attempt to help them do something? Did they ask for help or did you assume they needed it?

Your answers to these questions reveal different forms of accommodation:

1. *Accommodation* occurs when both parties communicate in ways that match their needs. This would look like helping an older adult cross the street if they asked you to, and not doing so if you knew they did not have mobility issues.
2. *Overaccommodation* occurs when we misjudge the other person's needs and do too much. This would look like the younger person raising their vocal volume too much in a way that the older adult does not need.
3. *Underaccommodation* occurs when we misjudge the other person's needs and don't do enough. This might look like the younger person not explaining slang terms that they know the older person might not know, or not recognizing that they are speaking too fast to be understood.

Now that you know several types of accommodation, which do you think you engage in most often when you are interacting with older adults? Which ones do you think older adults engage in when talking to you? Think about how you can find a balance among the accommodation strategies the next time you interact with an older adult in your life.

CONTACT THEORY

Contact theory, credited to psychologist Gordon Allport, explores the conditions under which positive attitudes and behaviors can develop between different social groups. The theory suggests that the mere physical presence of people from different social groups in close proximity to one another is not enough to produce positive intergroup outcomes. Instead, several key factors must be present, such as equal status between the groups, a common goal, and the presence of a supportive authority figure. When these conditions are present, individuals from different groups can engage in meaningful interaction and build positive relationships, which can then lead to a reduction in prejudice and an increase in intergroup harmony. An example of contact theory in action can be seen in efforts to better integrate law enforcement officers with members of a community, a strategy typically called community policing.[24] When enacted effectively, community policing promotes a safe community through positive intergroup relations between the public and police officers.

contact theory
A theory that explains the conditions under which positive attitudes and behaviors can develop between different social groups.

Challenges to Inclusive Communication

Inclusive communication is subject to challenges that can impact effective interpersonal communication. For example, how we select, organize, and interpret visual and message cues is even more important among people from different cultures than among friends from the same culture. Attribution and perceptual errors are more likely to occur between people with many differences or intersectional identities. Several additional challenges to inclusive communication and interactions include ethnocentrism, stereotyping, prejudice, unconscious bias, and microaggressions. Becoming aware of these issues can help you avoid them or reduce their effects. Keep in mind that these barriers to inclusivity do not occur in every exchange.

ETHNOCENTRISM

One challenge that occurs during communication between different cultures is that people bring the ideals of their culture to the interaction. **Ethnocentrism** is the belief that your own group or culture is superior to all other groups or cultures. People are ethnocentric if they see and judge the rest of the world only from their own culture's perspective. Some common examples include thinking that everyone should speak English, that people in the United States should not have to learn languages other than English, and that the culture of the United States is better than that of any other country. Each of us operates from an ethnocentric perspective to some degree,[25] but problems arise when we interpret and evaluate other cultures negatively compared with our own. Generally, a lack of interaction with other cultures fosters high levels of ethnocentrism and encourages the notion of cultural superiority. Ethnocentrism makes others feel defensive.

ethnocentrism
The belief that your own group or culture is superior to other groups or cultures.

In ethnocentrism you use your own culture as the measure that others are expected to meet; **cultural relativism** is the belief that another culture should be judged by its own context rather than measured against your culture. Someone who is not Asian who says that the Asian custom of bowing is odd overlooks the long history of bowing to one another as a sign of respect. To communicate effectively with people from different cultures, you need to accept people whose values and norms may be different from your own. An effective communicator avoids ethnocentrism and embraces cultural relativism.

cultural relativism
The belief that another culture should be judged by its own context rather than measured against your culture.

STEREOTYPING

Ethnocentrism is not the only perceptual trap you can fall into that reduces inclusive communication. Equally problematic is the tendency to stereotype people in cultural

• Stereotypes can occur when you encounter cultures with which you have had little contact.

skynesher/E+/Getty Images

stereotype
A generalization about some group of people that oversimplifies their culture.

groups. Communication scholars Everett Rogers and Thomas Steinfatt define a **stereotype** as "a generalization about some group of people that oversimplifies their culture."[26] Stereotypes, large and small, permeate both dominant and nondominant identity groups within a culture, as well as across cultures. In short, stereotypes are omnipresent in the world around us and even permeate our own thinking.

In his contact theory, Allport observed that people are more likely to stereotype individuals and groups with whom they have little contact.[27] Sometimes stereotyping occurs because people have had a negative or positive experience with a person from another culture. In one study, people stereotyped African Americans after only one observation of a negative behavior. In another, simply hearing about an alleged crime was sufficient to stereotype African Americans.[28] Clearly, people are willing to stereotype with very little evidence.

How do people feel about receiving either negative or positive comments that reflect on their social group rather than on them as individuals? According to one study, people generally respond adversely to negative comments that are about them either as an individual or as a member of a social group. They also respond negatively if the comment is positive but reflects a stereotype. Participants in this study reported that even positive stereotypes caused increased anger and a desire to avoid the speaker.[29]

What can people do who feel that another is stereotyping them? A study that tested the effectiveness of confrontation found that it helps. Although confrontations elicited negative emotions and evaluations toward the person doing the confronting, they also resulted in fewer stereotypic comments from the initial speaker. This change in behavior may be due to the negative self-directed affect that the stereotyping speaker felt.[30]

PREJUDICE

prejudice
An unfavorable predisposition about an individual because of that person's membership in a stereotyped group.

Whereas ethnocentrism is thinking your culture is better than others and stereotyping is acting as if all members of a group were alike, **prejudice** is a negative attitude toward a group of people just because they are who they are. Often the groups on the receiving end of prejudice are marginalized groups—people in poverty, people of color, people who speak a language other than English, and members of the LGBTQ+ community. People who are accustomed to being on the receiving end of prejudice can become highly aware of that prejudice. One study compared Black Americans to white Americans in how accurately they could identify nonverbal signals of prejudice during 20-second video clips.[31] The Black participants were more accurate in identifying nonverbal signals of prejudice than were white participants.

Sometimes the group experiencing the prejudice is actually larger than the group exhibiting prejudicial behaviors. For example, many countries, including the United States, show prejudice against women (as evidenced by the wage gap and the glass ceiling that limits career advancement) even though they are a numerical majority. Women experience sexist incidents—demeaning and degrading comments and sexual objectification—much more than men do, and they experience depression, anger, and lower self-esteem because of such incidents.[32] In many other countries, people who are a numerical minority control the fates of and show prejudice toward a group that is larger but has less power.

UNCONSCIOUS BIAS

Unconscious bias describes the ways our unconscious cognitions engage stereotypes and biases that unknowingly impact our behaviors. Unconscious biases arise from several factors. **Confirmation bias** is a form of cognitive bias that addresses the tendency to pay attention to behaviors and ideas that reinforce our existing belief structures. For instance, your friend Pam hasn't texted you back for a week, so you believe she is avoiding you. You hear from your mutual friend that Pam regularly texts back within a few minutes, so you use this as evidence to confirm your belief that Pam is avoiding you, which might not be the case. **Attribution bias** occurs when we positively evaluate behaviors and situations from people in our in-group and judge those in the out-group more harshly, even when they engage in the same behavior as the ingroup. A classic example of this is if you are in a rush for class and cut someone off on the highway, you will likely rationalize that you are a good person running late; however, if someone does this to you, you will likely think they are an impatient and reckless driver. Finally, **affinity bias** is the tendency to build relationships with people who share your interests and background.[33] For example, when students are asked to work in groups of their choice, affinity bias might lead students to work with people with the same major rather than others with different majors.

engaging diversity

Meeting, Greeting, and Eating

As you consider the ideas of cultural relativism, look at this list of nonverbal behaviors from around the world. Each of these behaviors needs to be judged not in comparison with what people do in the United States but in terms of its meaningfulness in another culture.

- U.S. citizens and Europeans shake hands in greeting, whereas an even larger number of Chinese, Taiwanese, and Japanese people bow when meeting.
- In China and other Pacific Rim countries, hosts and guests exchange small, nicely wrapped presents, especially in formal visits.
- Men and women in Russia, Italy, and France give each other a cheek-to-cheek hug and even a kiss on the cheek when greeting.
- Citizens of Pacific Rim countries exchange business cards on meeting by using both hands as if handing off a delicate gift. They look at and even comment on the card.
- Chinese people and other Asians eat with chopsticks, whereas people in many countries influenced by the British customarily eat with the fork in the left hand and the knife in the right hand. North Americans tend to hold the fork in the right hand.
- Muslim men in Malaysia and in some other countries touch their heart after shaking hands as if to say their greeting is "from the heart."
- Many Jews eat kosher food that has been blessed by a rabbi; many Muslims eat halal foods prepared by custom by a butcher who faces east and says the name of Allah while draining the animal's blood. Traditionally, neither Jews nor Muslims eat pork.
- Whereas North Americans are famous for their "fast foods," much of the rest of the world takes time to eat, to savor the food, and to enjoy conversations with others.

unconscious bias
Unconscious cognitions engage stereotypes and biases that unknowingly impact our behaviors.

confirmation bias
When we pay attention to behaviors and ideas that reinforce our existing belief structures.

communicating
with agility

Steps for Managing Unconscious Bias

Identifying unconscious bias in ourselves typically requires a shift in how we normally think about our behaviors and how we talk with others. The following are four ways you can begin to manage unconscious bias in your own life:

1. **Personal awareness**. Conduct a self-examination to identify your beliefs and values that can lead to unconscious bias.

2. **Acknowledgment**. Recognize the ways in which you could have or have engaged in unconscious bias in the past.

3. **Empathy**. Actively listen to people who are different from yourself and seek to understand their views and experiences.

4. **Education**. Increase your knowledge about how unconscious bias impacts your communication. Ask others to challenge you when they notice you are engaging in unconscious biases.

Source: Adapted from Bucknor-Ferron, P., & Zagaja, L. (2016). Five strategies to combat unconscious bias. *Nursing, 46*(11), 61–62.

attribution bias
When we positively evaluate behaviors and situations from people in our in-group and judge those in an out-group more harshly.

affinity bias
Tendency to build relationships with people who share similar interests and backgrounds.

microaggressions
Talk that can send insulting messages that devalue people from marginalized communities.

MICROAGGRESSIONS

In recent years, the general public has become increasingly aware of **microaggressions**, or everyday verbal or nonverbal communication that can insult or devalue people in marginalized communities.[34] Kevin Nadal, a professor of psychology, noted in an episode of Life Kit on National Public Radio that microaggressions are common occurrences and that people may not be aware they are experiencing them or engaging in them.[35] While overtly racist comments are easy to identify, microaggressions are often subtle and nuanced and can be intentional or unintentional. In general, microaggressions can be focused on stereotypes of many aspects of identity such as of age, race, gender, and sexual orientation.

Professor Nadal suggests addressing microaggressions with the following three steps:

1. *Educate yourself.* Watch documentaries and read personal essays, blogs, and research articles to understand the experiences of people in marginalized groups so you can understand how their experiences differ from your own. This ensures that you come to the conversation with information, rather than expecting the people from the marginalized group to be your main source of information.

2. *Set realistic conversation expectations.* As you prepare for the conversation, consider if the discussion will actually help and acknowledge that one conversation typically won't change a person's worldview. If motivation and interest are present, additional conversations could take place.

3. *Be aware of your mental health.* Conversations about microaggressions require emotional labor, especially on the part of those in the marginalized group. Therefore, it is important to balance productive arguments and conversations with time for rest.

Strategies for Improving Inclusive Communication

Effective communication often takes considerable time, energy, and commitment. The strategies presented here will provide you with some ways to improve inclusive communication and avoid additional challenges. Having some strategies in advance will prepare you for new situations with people with diverse identities and will increase your confidence in your ability to communicate effectively with a variety of people.

1. *Conduct a personal self-assessment.* How do your own attitudes toward other identities influence your communication with people from those groups? One of the first steps toward improving your inclusive communication skills is an honest assessment of your own communication style, beliefs, and prejudices.

2. *Practice supportive communication behaviors.* Supportive behaviors, such as empathy, encourage success in intercultural exchanges. Defensive behaviors tend to hamper effectiveness.

3. *Develop sensitivity toward diversity.* One healthy communication perspective holds that you can learn something from all people. Diverse populations provide ample opportunity for learning. Take the time to learn about other cultures before a communication situation, but don't forget that you will also learn about others simply by taking a risk and talking to someone who is different from you. Challenge yourself. You may be surprised by what you learn.

4. *Avoid stereotypes.* Generalizations go only so far; avoid making assumptions about another's social group identity, and get to know individuals for who they are.

5. *Avoid ethnocentrism.* You may know your own culture the best, but that familiarity does not make your culture superior to all others. You will learn more about the strengths and weaknesses of your own culture by learning more about other cultures.

6. *Develop code sensitivity.* **Code sensitivity** refers to the ability to use the verbal and nonverbal language appropriate to the cultural norms of the individual with whom you are communicating. The more you know about another's culture, the better you will be at adapting your communication.

code sensitivity
The ability to use the verbal and nonverbal language appropriate to the cultural norms of the individual with whom you are communicating.

7. *Use and encourage descriptive feedback.* Effective feedback encourages adaptation and is crucial in inclusive communication. Both participants should be willing to accept feedback and exhibit supportive behaviors. Feedback should be immediate, honest, specific, and clear.

8. *Manage conflicting beliefs and practices.* You have your own beliefs that are, in part, manifested from your own culture. There may be moments when your cultural beliefs and values are in conflict with those of another culture. If you develop acquaintances who practice those cultural beliefs, how will you respond? For instance, how will you respond if your roommate practices religious beliefs other than your own? If you decide to take a job in a country that limits the rights of free speech, how will you choose to behave? Thinking about how you will reconcile your own beliefs against the values of another social identity group helps you better plan to avoid or at least manage tensions that could develop.

• Freedom of expression and a diversity of perspectives are fundamental to a civil society.
Pamela Moore/Getty Images

reflexivity
Being self-aware and learning from interactions with the intent of improving future interactions.

Of course, the most effective strategy for improving your inclusive communication competence is practice. Fortunately, the increasing diversity of our own culture means that inclusive communication practice can take place with the people at the corner market, at your place of employment, or even with the student sitting next to you in class. To learn from these many instances, you must learn to be reflexive. **Reflexivity** means being self-aware and learning from interactions with the intent of improving future interactions. That is, you are able to assess the interaction, identify what went well in the conversation and what could have been done better, and then learn from those observations. Through reflexivity you will not only improve your intercultural communication skills but also become a more effective communicator in nearly every situation.

be ready... for what's next

Getting Involved with Other Social Identities

Did you know that spending time with people who are from different social identity groups has a positive effect on your attitudes during your college years? For example, researchers have shown that when college students have a large percentage of friends from different ethnic groups, especially during sophomore and junior years of college, they tend to be less biased in favor of their own ethnic group. Additionally, by the end of their senior year, students tend to feel less anxious when interacting with members of different ethnic groups.[36]

In an effort to develop new friendships with people from different social identity groups, make it a point to ask questions and attend events at your school or in your community. The following is a list of questions to help get the conversation started.

1. What makes people feel like they are part of this group?
2. Are there any rites of passage that are unique to this group?
3. How do people in this social identity group celebrate traditions or rituals?
4. In what ways does this group use language to signify who is a member and who isn't a member?

Chapter Review & Study Guide

Summary

In this chapter you learned the following:

1. The study of inclusive communication is important because we are increasingly interacting with people with different identities.
2. Inclusive communication seeks to reduce communication barriers and subsequent prejudice.
3. Diversity and equity help build relationships among a variety of different people in fair and just ways.
4. A culture is a unique combination of rituals, ways of thinking, and ways of behaving.

- Dominant identities includes those who have power and can influence traditional social structures such as politics, religion, schools, and businesses.
- Nondominant identities exist within the broader culture and differ from the dominant culture in one or more significant characteristics.

5. Social identity theory, communication accommodation theory, and contact theory explain and describe challenges and opportunities toward inclusive communication.

6. Ethnocentrism, stereotyping, prejudice, unconscious bias, and microaggressions present challenges to inclusive communication.
7. You can strive to improve your own communication competence by
   - conducting a personal self-assessment
   - practicing supportive communication behaviors
   - developing sensitivity toward diversity
   - avoiding stereotypes
   - avoiding ethnocentrism
   - developing code sensitivity
   - using descriptive feedback
   - managing conflicting beliefs and practices
   - practicing reflexivity

Key Terms

Affinity bias
Attribution bias
Code sensitivity
Communication accommodation theory
Confirmation bias
Contact theory
Cultural relativism
Culture

Diversity
Dominant culture
Equity
Ethnocentrism
Inclusive communication
Intersectionality
Microaggressions

Nondominant identity
Prejudice
Reflexivity
Social identities
Social identity theory
Stereotype
Unconscious bias

Study Questions

1. Which of the following statements is *not* true?
   a. Inclusive communication improves your ability to communicate with diverse audiences.
   b. Inclusive communication is based on relationships with others.
   c. Diversity is important to work environments.
   d. Building inclusive behaviors is a short-term process.

2. Which statement describes a characteristic of nondominant identities?
   a. People who are part of nondominant identity groups are not part of the dominate culture.
   b. People in nondominant identity groups have the power and authority to make decisions that impact others.
   c. People in nondominant identity groups are underrepresented in positions of power.
   d. People in nondominant identity groups are rarely marginalized.

3. When people with multiple marginalized social identities experience systems of oppression and discrimination in many ways, this refers to
   a. diversity.
   b. intersectionality.
   c. equity.
   d. accommodation.

4. When people bring prejudices of their culture to intercultural interactions, they are being
   a. ethnocentric.
   b. stereotypic.
   c. accommodating.
   d. collectivist.

5. When people stereotype, they
   a. judge another person's culture by its own context.
   b. make a generalization about a group of people that oversimplifies their culture.
   c. believe their own culture is superior to other cultures.
   d. avoid making degrading comments with relation to sexual objectification.

6. When people engage in unconscious bias, they
   a. deliberately promote stereotypes.
   b. engage in accommodation.
   c. desire increased contact.
   d. unknowingly engage in biases.

7. The subtle unintentional or intentional attempts to devalue people from marginalized communities are called
   a. mircoaggressions.
   b. confirmation biases.
   c. prejudice.
   d. stereotypes.

8. When you have a negative attitude about other people just because they are who they are, you are demonstrating
   a. prejudice.
   b. ignorance.
   c. ethnocentrism.
   d. stereotyping.

9. A person changing the way they speak to fit in with the norms and expectations of a particular social group is explained by which theory related to inclusion?
   a. Communication accommodation theory
   b. Contact theory
   c. Social identity theory
   d. Ethnocentric theory

10. If you are trying to improve your inclusive communication, which of the following should you avoid doing?
    a. conducting a personal self-assessment
    b. practicing supportive communication behaviors
    c. resisting changing your own beliefs
    d. challenging stereotypes

Answers:
1. (d); 2. (c); 3. (b); 4. (a); 5. (b); 6. (d); 7. (a); 8. (a); 9. (a); 10. (c)

Critical Thinking

1. In recent years, controversy has erupted surrounding challenges to diversity and inclusion programing in high schools and colleges. How, if at all, do you think diversity initiatives in schools can improve inclusive communication?

2. What are the dominant and nondominant identities where you live? By what means does the dominant culture in your area reinforce its rules for living? How does it communicate its rules to all others?

References

1. Hess, E. (Producer), & Garbus, L., & Sashin, E. (Directors). (2022). *Harry & Meghan* [video file]. Netflix. https://www.netflix.com/

2. Brce, J. N., & Kogovsek, D. (2020). Inclusion, inclusive education and inclusive communication. In B. Saqupi & S. Bercnik (Eds.), *Selected topics in education* (pp. 161–184). Albas.

3. Frey, W. H. (2018, March 14). *The US will become "minority white" in 2045, census projects*. Brookings Institution. https://www.brookings.edu/blog/the-avenue/2018/03/14/the-us-will-become-minority-white-in-2045-census-projects/

4. Dobusch, L. (2021). The inclusivity of inclusion approaches: A relational perspective on inclusion and exclusion in organizations. *Gender, Work & Organization, 28*(1), 379–396.

5. Cole, B. M. (2020, September 15). 8 reasons why diversity and inclusion are essential to business success. *Forbes.* https://www.forbes.com/sites/biancamillercole/2020/09/15/8-reasons-why-diversity-and-inclusion-are-essential-to-business-success/?sh=721beddc1824

6. Cordivano, S. (2019, November 13). Inclusive communication: Three principles. *Medium.* https://medium.com/sarah-cordivano/inclusive-communication-three-principles-cb8dbb6361cd

7. Moody, J. (2020, March 31). Diversity in the college and why it matters. *U.S. News & World Report.* https://www.usnews.com/education/best-colleges/articles/diversity-in-college-and-why-it-matters

8. Pendell, R. (2022, September 26). Workplace equity: The "E" in DEI and why it matters. *Gallup.* https://www.gallup.com/workplace/401573/workplace-equity-dei-why-matters.aspx

9. Orbe, M. P., & Batten, C. J. (2017). Diverse dominant group responses to contemporary co-cultural concerns: U.S. intergroup dynamics in the Trump era. *Journal of Contemporary Rhetoric, 7*, 19–33.

10. Kramarae, C. (1981). *Women and men speaking.* Newbury House.

11. Blazina, C., & Desilver, D. (2021, January 15). A record number of women are serving in the 117 congress. *Pew Research Center.* https://www.pewresearch.org/fact-tank/2021/01/15/a-record-number-of-women-are-serving-in-the-117th-congress/

12. Daniels, C. (2022, November 9). Ten candidates who made history Tuesday night. *The Hill.* https://thehill.com/homenews/house/3726601-ten-candidates-that-made-history-tuesday-night/

13. Guidant Financial. (2022). 2022 women in business trends. https://www.guidantfinancial.com/small-business-trends/women-in-business/

14. Hinchliffe, E. (2022, May 23). The number of women running Fortune 500 companies reaches record high. *Fortune*. https://fortune.com/2022/05/23/female-ceos-fortune-500-2022-women-record-high-karen-lynch-sarah-nash/

15. Women and leadership. (2015, January 14). *Pew Research Center*. http://www.pewsocialtrends.org/2015/01/14/women-and-leadership/

16. U.S. Equal Employment Opportunity Commission. Protections against employment discrimination based on sexual orientation or gender identity. https://www.eeoc.gov/laws/guidance/protections-against-employment-discrimination-based-sexual-orientation-or-gender

17. The Hope Center. (2018, October 15). Basic needs security among students attending Georgia colleges and universities. https://hope4college.com/wp-content/uploads/2018/10/GeorgiaSchools-10.16.2018.html#intersections_of_food_insecurity,_housing_insecurity,_and_homelessness

18. Goldrick-Rab, S., Cady, C., & Coca, V. (2018, September 28). Campus food pantries: Insights from a national survey. The Hope Center. https://hope4college.com/wp-content/uploads/2018/10/2018-CUFBA-Report-web3.pdf

19. El Zein, A., Mathews, A. E., House, L., & Shelnutt, K. P. (2018). Why are hungry college students not seeking help. Predictors of and barriers to using and on-campus food pantry. *Nutrients*, 10, 1–14. https://doi.org/10.3390/nu10091163

20. Syracuse University. (2022, September 21). *FYS 101: Intersectionality*. https://researchguides.library.syr.edu/fys101/intersectionality

21. Coles, S. M. (2020, July 13). Black women often ignored by social justice movements. *American Psychological Association.* https://www.apa.org/news/press/releases/2020/07/black-women-social-justice

22. Nicholls, S. B., & Rice, R. E. (2017). A dual-identity model of responses to deviance in online groups: Integrating social identity theory and expectancy violations theory. *Communication Theory*, 27(3), 243–268. https://doi.org/10.1111/comt.12113

23. Gallois, C., Watson, B. M., & Giles, H. (2018). Intergroup communication: Identities and effective interactions. *Journal of Communication*, 68(2), 309–317. https://doi.org/10.1093/joc/jqx016

24. Twayman, S. (2022, March 31). Community policing: Reimaging public safety for the 21st century. *Third Way*. https://www.thirdway.org/report/community-policing-reimagining-public-safety-for-the-21st-century

25. Chakraborty, R. (2017). A short note on accent-bias, social identity and ethnocentrism. *Advances in Language and Literary Studies, 8*, 57–64. https://doi.org/10.7575/aiac.alls.v.8n.4p.57

26. Rogers, E. M., & Steinfatt, T. M. (1999). *Intercultural communication.* Waveland Press.

27. Allport, G. W. (1954/1958). *The nature of prejudice.* Addison-Wesley; Doubleday.

28. Henderson-King, E., & Nisbett, R. E. (1996). Anti-black prejudice as a function of exposure to the negative behavior of a single black person. *Journal of Personality and Social Psychology, 71*, 654–664.

29. Garcia, A. L., Miller, D. A., Smith, E. R., & Mackie, D. M. (2006). Thanks for the compliment? Emotional reactions to group-level versus individual-level compliments and insults. *Group Processes and Intergroup Relations, 9*, 307–324.

30. Czopp, A. M., Monteith, M. J., & Mark, A. Y. (2006). Standing up for a change: Reducing bias through interpersonal confrontation. *Journal of Personality and Social Psychology, 90*, 784–803.

31. Richeson, J. A., & Nicole Shelton, J. (2005). Brief report: Thin slices of racial bias. *Journal of Nonverbal Behavior*, 29, 75–86. https://doi.org/10.1007/s10919-004-0890-2

32. Suttie, J. (2018, October 4). How women can use their anger for good. *Greater Good Magazine*. https://greatergood.berkeley.edu/article/item/how_women_can_use_their_anger_for_good

33. Nalty, K. (2016). Strategies for confronting unconscious bias. *The Colorado Lawyer*, 45(5), 45–52.

34. Sue, D. W., Capodilupo, C. M., Torino, G. C., Bucceri, J. M., Holder, A., Nadal, K. L., & Esquilin, M. (2007). Racial microaggressions in everyday life: Implications for clinical practice. *American Psychologist*, 62(4), 271–286.

35. Limbong, A. (2020, June 9). Microaggressions are a big deal: How to talk them out and when to walk away. *NPR*. https://www.npr.org/2020/06/08/872371063/microaggressions-are-a-big-deal-how-to-talk-them-out-and-when-to-walk-away

36. Sidanius, J., Levin, S., van Laar, C., & Sears, D. O. (2008). *The diversity challenge: Social identity and intergroup relations on the college campus.* Russell Sage Foundation.

Comstock/SuperStock

small-group communication

When you have read and thought about this chapter, you will be able to

1. explain what characterizes small-group communication.

2. recall the two functions of small groups.

3. explain how culture develops in small groups.

4. compare and contrast task, maintenance, and self-centered roles in groups.

5. describe how effective leadership is accomplished in small groups.

6. apply a process for group problem solving and decision-making.

7. discuss two technology tools that can be used to facilitate small-group communication.

8. apply skills necessary for effective and ethical group communication in face-to-face and virtual settings.

Small groups permeate nearly all facets of our lives. Our families, our jobs, our courses, and our friends are all invigorated and driven by small groups of people. In this chapter, we address several issues related to small-group communication. After discussing generally what small-group communication is, we turn to theories explaining concepts such as leadership, group culture, and small-group decision-making. The chapter concludes by discussing several processes related to small-group effectiveness: cohesiveness, the use of technology, and skills used by ethical group communicators.

Boston Strong.[1] It was a mantra that echoed across a devastated city and nation shortly after the Boston Marathon bombing on April 15, 2013. You may have seen the blue and yellow block-letter shirts or many of its variations, but do you know how the catchphrase started? "Boston Strong" was coined by Nicholas Reynolds, a visual and media arts major, and Chris Dobens, a marketing communication major, from Emerson College in Boston, Massachusetts. Nick and Chris were sitting in dorm rooms, less than a mile from the marathon site, and felt the need to do something to help their local community.

In an interview, Nick stated, "We wanted something everyone could rally behind." These inexpensive shirts provide a way for college students and others to support their community in remembrance of the tragedy because a portion of the proceeds from their sales goes to victims of the marathon bombing through the One Fund. The campaign has raised over $1 million, and people from all over the world post pictures of themselves wearing their Boston Strong T-shirts on the Boston Strong website.[2]

Nick and Chris partnered with Lane Brenner, a communication studies major, to manage the social media presence by creating Twitter (X) hashtags and promoting a Facebook page. Lane shared the following about working in this small group:

> Working with only two other people on such a large undertaking was stressful at times, but had a multitude of benefits. Nick, Chris, and I were easily able to hash out ideas in a casual setting where each of us felt heard and had a chance to contribute. Due to this, we could make decisions quickly and efficiently and implement them without needing to go through any red tape.[3]

What do you think were some of the challenges Nick and Chris faced as they initially created the campaign together? How can decision-making and problem solving occur when multiple voices need to be heard? As you consider these questions, you will begin to recognize many of the issues surrounding group communication.

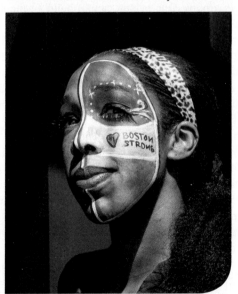

Rick Friedman/Corbis/Getty Images

Has something in your community or on your campus compelled you to act but you were unsure how to do so? Small groups help provide ideas and energy for addressing those types of situations. Nick, Chris, and Lane had only experience, a computer, an idea, and a phrase . . . it was simple and made a lasting difference. It worked because a small group of like-minded college students made it happen.

Groups are all around us; they are inescapable, and as you've read, they can accomplish extraordinary things. In this chapter, you will explore the characteristics of groups, how communication works within groups, the various roles within groups, how leaders use their skills, and how group members can ethically and effectively make decisions and solve problems.

The Importance of Learning About Small Groups

Small groups are the basic building blocks of our society. Families, work teams, support groups, religious circles, and study groups are all examples of the groups on which our society is built. In organizations, the higher up you go, the more time you will spend working in groups. Membership in small groups is both common and important. In fact, most types of jobs increasingly rely on team-based work, and an increasing number require flexible and remote teams. Working in remote teams became increasingly more apparent in the wake of the COVID-19 pandemic and to the present in ways that have changed the landscape of how groups do their work. A 2021 *Future Workforce Report* by Upwork indicated that 40.7 million American workers will be fully remote in the next five years.[4] In a recent study, Yang (2022) and colleagues found that a move to remote work resulted in less communication between different groups and increased communication and closeness within one's own working groups. They also found that connections between coworkers stagnated and people made fewer new connections to other colleagues. We hope that the communication skills in this chapter will help you manage these newer challenges when you are involved in groups and teamwork.[5]

Small groups are important for four reasons. First, working in groups is an aspect of nearly every human activity. William Schutz, a psychologist who studied group interaction, said that humans have needs for inclusion, affection, and control.[6] The need for **inclusion**—the state of being involved with others—suggests that we need to belong to, or be included in, groups with others. As humans, we derive much of our identity, our beliefs about who we are, from the groups to which we belong. Starting with our immediate families, because they are one of the most influential social groups in our lives,[7] and including such important groups as members of a neighborhood place of worship, interest groups such as those concerned with preventing sexual assault on campus, and social groups such as book clubs—all of these help us define who we are. The need for **affection**—the emotion of caring for others and/or being cared for—means that we humans need to love and be loved, to know that we are important to others who value us as unique human beings. Finally, we have a need for **control**—the ability to influence our environment. We are better able to exercise such control if we work together in groups. One person cannot build a school, a bridge, or a new business. We need others to meet our needs.

Second, because group work is the norm in business and industry, knowing how groups function and having the ability to operate effectively in them will be highly valued skills. This is especially true given the rise in remote work and remote teamwork. A recent article in *Forbes* indicates that empathetic listening, agility, communicating through modern means such as pictures and video, emotional intelligence, hybrid and remote teamwork, and public speaking are among skills employers expect of new hires and skills even seasoned employees need to gain through upskilling (gaining or enhancing certain skills and practices).[8]

Third, being an effective group or team member is a skill you can learn about, develop, and master. As helpful as groups can be to any organization, they often fail because group leaders have not thought through exactly what they want the groups to accomplish or because group members have not been trained in how to behave appropriately as part of a team.[9] Group members need training to understand the dynamics of small-group interaction.

Finally, groups can be an important way for Americans to participate in the democratic process and understand how and why we differ on various issues. By talking in groups, we can become more confident in articulating our own beliefs, which, in turn, may lead us to be more vocal about our beliefs in a variety of contexts.[10] For example, during the 2014 election, small groups played a key role in increasing voter turnout. At Illinois State University (ISU), a small group of communication instructors created assignments in their public-speaking classes designed to get students more involved in civic issues. As a result of this effort, students engaged in an annual "issues fair" at which small groups of students presented information

inclusion
The state of being involved with others; a human need.

affection
The emotion of caring for others and/or being cared for.

control
The ability to influence our environment.

about local, state, and national issues by setting up tables and booths on their campus quad. These students helped raise awareness of how political issues were relevant to other college students. Those efforts not only significantly increased student-voter turnout but also persuaded the county board of elections to expand early voting locations to the campus.

ISU then created the Social Media Analytics Command Center (SMACC) that hosted a campus watch party for the 2015 State of the Union (SOTU) address. At this event, students worked in small groups to analyze the social media chatter about the SOTU in real time. The small groups analyzed 1,688 posts that contained the #iSOTU hashtag and they found that the tweets had the following relationships:

- *Cliques*—groups of Twitter (X) handles that frequently mentioned each other or were mentioned together.
- *Degree*—the number of connections to other Twitter (X) handles by means of retweets or mentions.
- *Betweenness*—the extent to which a Twitter (X) handle serves as a connection between other handles in the network. A Twitter (X) handle with a high level of betweenness has influence over what flows and does not flow through the social network.
- *Authority*—the extent to which a Twitter (X) handle is a definitive source of information. A Twitter (X) handle with a large amount of authority is frequently retweeted or mentioned by other Twitter (X) handles or groups of Twitter (X) handles.[11]

This example illustrates how groups can organize and voice opinions through social media.

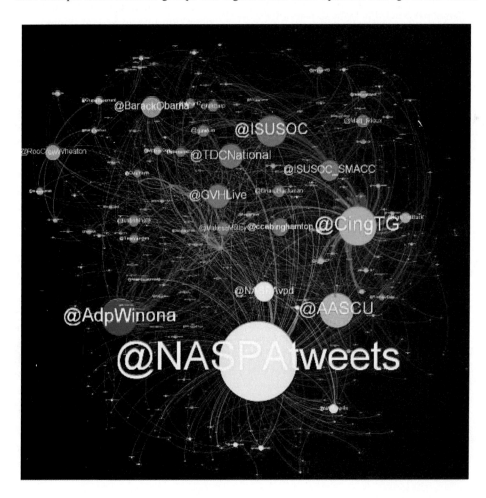

- A social network map of the cliques formed by Twitter (X) accounts that either used or were mentioned in conjunction with the #iSOTU hashtag during President Obama's 2015 State of the Union address.

Social Media Analytics Command Center/Illinois State University

• Being a part of a group gives us feelings of inclusion and affection.

Shutterstock

small-group communication
Interaction among three to nine people working together to achieve an interdependent goal.

engaging diversity

Groups Help Us Maintain Culture

If you travel 10 minutes northeast of Hermann Park in central Houston, you will find yourself in the middle of the greater Third Ward. Houston's Third Ward is distinctive for many reasons: it is the home of Texas Southern University, it is one of the original political subdivisions of Houston, and it is just adjacent to downtown Houston and the world-renowned Texas Medical Center campus. The Third Ward has also been the home for much of Houston's African American community. As an article in the *Houston Business Journal* points out, the Third Ward has been threatened with losing its historic identity because of gentrification, or the influx of higher-income development within lower-income areas. Lower-income residents who can no longer afford the increasing rent or property taxes mainly feel the effects of gentrification because they often become displaced. As a result, the historical roots of the area are ripped apart.

Small groups of residents in Houston's Third Ward are doing their part to combat the negative effects of gentrification. A group of artists created Project Row Houses (www.projectrowhouses.org) in 1993 as a way to build community through art. In 2018, Project Row Houses celebrated 25 years of service. It embraces the philosophy that communities created through art can revitalize inner-city neighborhoods such as the Third Ward. Recently, artist Jackie Sumell was part of a Project Row Houses exhibit called "Round 48: Beyond Social Practice," which raised awareness for incarcerated mothers, who make up 80% of the female prison population. As part of the installation, visitors planted seedlings chosen by the incarcerated mothers and shared pictures of the plants' growth with them through the Flikshop app, which allows messages and images to be printed and mailed as postcards to inmates. In this way, Project Row Houses uses art to highlight the interconnections of urban spaces, cultural issues, and cultural identity.

Sources: Bradford, N. (2007, July 22). Houston's Third Ward battles an identity crisis. *Houston Business Journal.* www.bizjournals.com/houston/stories/2007/07/23/focus1; Project Row Houses. (n.d.). About. https://projectrowhouses.org/about/about-prh; Tommaney, S. (2018, October 9). Project row houses brings night bakery, pics for prison moms and chill house. *Houston Press.* www.houstonpress.com/arts/things-to-do-check-out-round-48-beyond-social-practice-at-project-row-houses-10934179

Defining Small-Group Communication

Small-group communication is the interaction among three to nine people who are working together to achieve an interdependent goal.[12] This definition implies several things:

• Groups must be small enough that members are mutually aware that the group is a collective entity. Groups typically contain between three and nine people but may be larger if members perceive the group as an entity. Research does show that groups of three or four people are more productive than are larger groups of five or more people.[13] So, if given a choice, working with a smaller group may produce better results.

• The substance that creates and holds the group together is the interaction between members.

• Group members are interdependent— they cannot achieve their goals without the help of other group members. If you watch reality TV shows such as *The Amazing Race,* then you have seen examples of how groups of people must work as interdependent units to achieve success.

Based on this definition, *communication* is the essential process within a small group. Communication creates a group, shapes each group in unique ways, and allows the group to function. As with other forms of human communication, small-group communication involves sending verbal and nonverbal signals that are perceived, interpreted, and responded to by other people. Group members pay attention to each other and coordinate their behavior in order to accomplish the group's assignment. In fact, group communication is like any other form of communication; however, the greater number of people makes communication even more challenging.

The Types and Functions of Small Groups

Think for a moment about the different groups to which you belong. You may regularly study with other students from your English class, you may belong to an a cappella singing group on campus or a political group, you may be assigned to participate in a student service-learning group, and you likely have a group of friends with whom you socialize. What are the key differences among these groups? In answering that question, you might think about differences that point to the type of group or the function that the group serves in your life. There are two types of groups:

- **Assigned groups** occur when individuals are appointed to be members of the group. A student union advisory board is an example of an assigned group.
- **Emergent groups** occur when a group of individuals decide to form a cohesive group out of personal need or desire, but they are not appointed to be part of the group. A group of friends who meet at college are an emergent group.

We can also classify groups according to the function they serve:

- **Task-oriented groups** are formed for the purpose of completing tasks, such as solving a problem or making a decision. A group of students studying for an exam are taking part in a task-oriented group.
- **Relationship-oriented groups** are usually long term and exist to meet our needs for inclusion and affection. Your family is an example of a relationship-oriented group.

Classifying groups according to whether they are task oriented, relationship oriented, assigned, or emergent is important because a primary tension felt in groups is balancing the task and the interaction (relational) side of group work. Because people form groups, and because groups can grow and change through communication, lines between these types and functions can easily blur. Members of relationship-oriented groups, such as families, engage in work, make decisions, and must cooperate to complete tasks. Members of task-oriented groups forge strong personal bonds and provide each other with affection and recognition. In fact, some of the best task-oriented groups are those that benefit from strong relational bonds so that members feel appreciated and valued. If positive relationships are established among group members, an assigned group can start to look and feel like an emergent group. As we interact with members of that group, a relationship-oriented social group may emerge. Just as our personal relationships can go through several turning points, our group membership is also constantly in flux.

However, certain group members' identities may affect a group's dynamics, even though they are not directly related to the group's task. It is natural for group members to engage in relationally oriented communication as they get to know each other, and it is possible that they may talk about issues that are not tied to the group task. In doing so, this reveals aspects of group members' identities that are different from those of other members. For example, you may decide to go out for pizza with the group you have been assigned to in your marketing class, and the conversation turns toward politics and the federal budget. You realize quickly that there are significant differences of opinions based

assigned groups
Groups that evolve out of a hierarchy whereby individuals are assigned membership to the group.

emergent groups
Groups resulting from environmental conditions leading to the formation of a cohesive group of individuals.

task-oriented groups
Also called secondary groups; groups formed for the purpose of completing tasks, such as solving problems or making decisions.

relationship-oriented groups
Groups that are usually long term and exist to meet our needs for inclusion and affection.

• A family is an example of a relationship-oriented group.

Hill Street Studios/Crystal Cartier/Blend/Getty Images

on political affiliations in your group, and you wonder if this is going to influence your work together for class. Groups are not immune to current societal events. It is important to listen to and learn from others' opinions and to continue to focus on the group's task while honoring differences of opinions.

Establishing Culture in Small Groups

When small groups are created, they immediately begin developing a unique group culture. Some group cultures are pleasant, empowering, and motivating, whereas others are aggressive, hostile, and demeaning. In this section you will learn how group culture develops as a result of group norms, role structures enacted by group members, group cohesiveness, and diversity.

THE DEVELOPMENT OF GROUP NORMS

norms
Informal rules for group interaction created and sustained through communication.

The first time group members communicate, they begin to establish the **norms**—informal rules for interaction created and sustained through communication—that will eventually guide the members' behaviors. Norms for group behavior tell us implicitly, and sometimes explicitly, how we are to act and behave with others in the group. At first, the full range of human behavior is available to members. For example, they may greet each other formally ("Director," "Doctor," "Professor," and so on), or they may speak informally and use first names. Some group members may shake hands when they first meet, whereas others may hug or bow. The initial pattern of behavior tends to set the tone for subsequent meetings and to establish the general norms that members will follow. The norms of any group tend to mirror the norms of broader cultures in which the group exists. Such norms are also created and altered through communication between group members. As the group interacts, and as leaders exercise authority, the norms of the group can be modified to help the group function more effectively. Of course, sometimes bad norms also develop, which can negatively affect the group's outcomes.

Most norms are not established directly. For example, if Ali comes late to a meeting and no one seems bothered, other members may get the message that coming to meetings on

time is unnecessary. By saying nothing to Ali, the group, without consciously thinking about it or formally "deciding," has begun to establish a norm that members need not be on time.

Norms often develop rapidly, without members consciously realizing what is occurring. For example, repeated behaviors, such as members always sitting in the same seats, show how easily norms can emerge through communication. Groups naturally use feedback to enforce norms. If a group member continually texts during meetings, another group member or a leader might say, "We need to put our devices away and focus," to indicate that a norm has been violated.

Members should pay attention to group norms to ensure that they are appropriate to the group task. When groups are working on a task in the classroom, it is common for members to discuss other topics, such as a band playing at the local club, turning back to the task at hand only when the teacher walks by. Such norms for playfulness, although important for relationship development, may begin to distract the group from assigned tasks. In general, groups needs to balance time for fun and time for work.

THE DEVELOPMENT OF ROLES FOR GROUP MEMBERS

Every group member enacts a unique **role**, which is a consistent pattern of interaction or behavior exhibited over time. In movies, characters enact roles to drive the story; in small groups, members enact roles to drive the interaction of the group. Whereas actors learn their roles from scripts, group members create their roles spontaneously during interactions with others and while drawing on their unique skills and attitudes. Just as an actor plays different roles in different films, individuals enact many diverse roles in the numerous groups to which they belong.

role
The part you play in various social contexts.

The Types of Group Roles

Two major types of group roles are formal and informal. A **formal role** (sometimes called a *positional role*) is an assigned role based on an individual's position or title within a group. You may have a job in which you are assigned to send a GroupMe message

formal role
Also called positional role; an assigned role based on an individual's position or title within a group.

reminding group members about tasks to complete before the next meeting. Your job duty could even state that your role is to keep track of finances or to record agenda items for future meetings. As a result of your formal role, other group members might expect you to behave in certain ways: they might expect you to be organized and have the ability to locate information quickly and without warning. Formal roles bring expectations, and your job is to understand and meet those expectations.

An **informal role** (sometimes called a *behavioral role*) is a role that develops naturally, or spontaneously, within a group. The role of each group member is worked out through interactions with the rest of the group and changes to meet emerging needs of the group. Informal roles strongly reflect members' personality characteristics, habits, and typical ways of interacting within a group. If you are the type of person who likes to talk in front of others, you might take on the role of a facilitator. By contrast, if you are less talkative, you might be a person who takes on behind-the-scene roles, such as conducting research or creating documents for the group. If you are the most competent social media user in your group, you might create a Facebook group for the members or coordinate WhatsApp threads to stay in touch in between meetings. Informal roles allow you to play to your strengths; of course, to develop informal roles you may need to talk to other group members about your preferences and abilities.

informal role
Also called behavioral role; a role that is developed spontaneously within a group.

Behaviors That Define Roles

Roles enacted by group members create a set of behaviors that help the group achieve its objectives. An effective group is like a jigsaw puzzle; each group member performs a slightly different role, but each set of behaviors is coordinated to work with the others so that a complete picture is formed.

One way of understanding the various types of behaviors performed by group members is to classify them as task, maintenance, or self-centered behaviors. **Task functions** are behaviors that are directly relevant to the group's purpose and that affect the group's productivity; their purpose is to focus group members productively on their assignment. **Maintenance functions** are behaviors that focus on the interpersonal relationships among group members; they are aimed at supporting cooperative and harmonious relationships. Both task and maintenance functions are considered essential to effective group communication. By contrast, **self-centered functions** are behaviors that serve the needs of the individual at the expense of the group. The person performing a self-centered behavior implies, "I don't care what the group needs or wants. *I* want . . . ." These group members use self-centered functions to manipulate other members for selfish goals that compete with group goals. Examples of statements that support task, maintenance, and self-centered functions are shown in Table 8.1. The list is not exhaustive, however; many more functions could be added.

task functions
Behaviors that are directly relevant to the group's purpose and that affect the group's productivity.

maintenance functions
Behaviors that focus on the interpersonal relationships among group members.

self-centered functions
Behaviors that serve the needs of the individual at the expense of the group.

Behaviors are the building blocks for roles. These behavioral functions combine to create a member's informal role, which is a comprehensive, general picture of how a particular member typically acts in a group. An example of how individual functions combine to create a role is shown in Figure 8.1. As you can see, information-giving and information-seeking behaviors primarily characterize the information specialist role. The storyteller role comprises several behaviors, including dramatizing, relieving tension, supporting, summarizing, and clarifying. Numerous other informal roles can be created through combinations of behaviors.

Emerging Technology and Group Roles

New technology and social media are changing the ways in which groups interact, as well as the amount and frequency of their interactions. Studies show that students who

Table 8.1 Examples of Task, Maintenance, and Self-Centered Statements

TASK FUNCTIONS AND STATEMENTS	
Initiating and Orienting	"Let's make a list of what we still need to do."
Information Giving	"Last year, the club spent $150 on publicity."
Information Seeking	"Omar, how many donations did the Child and Family Advocacy Center report last year?"
Opinion Giving	"I don't think the cost of parking stickers is the worst parking problem students have."
Clarifying	"Martina, are you saying that you couldn't support a proposal that increased student fees?"
Extending	"Another thing that Toby's proposal would let us do is allow us to have a wider outreach."
Evaluating	"One problem I see with Amara's idea is that the budget may not cover it."
Summarizing	"So we've decided that we'll add two sections to the report, and Jim and Aisha will write them."
Coordinating	"If Xixi gets everyone's sources by Monday, then Terrell and I can prepare the references page for Tuesday's meeting."
Consensus Testing	"We seem to be agreed that we prefer the second option."
Recording	"I think we decided at our last meeting. Let me check the minutes."
MAINTENANCE (RELATIONSHIP-ORIENTED) FUNCTIONS AND STATEMENTS	
Establishing Norms	"It doesn't help to talk about other group members when they aren't here. Let's stick to the issues."
Gatekeeping	"Pat, you look like you want to say something about the proposal."
Supporting	"I think Keisha's point is well made, and we should look at it more closely."
Harmonizing	"Jin and Sally, I think there are areas where you are in agreement, and I would like to suggest a compromise that might work for you both."
Tension Relieving	"We're getting tired and cranky. Let's take a 10-minute break."
Dramatizing	"Let me tell you about this one time five years ago when we had something similar happen in this company."
Showing Solidarity	"We've really done great work here!"
SELF-CENTERED FUNCTIONS AND STATEMENTS	
Withdrawing	"Do whatever you want. I don't care."
Blocking	"I don't care if we've already voted. I want to discuss it again!"
Status and Recognition Seeking	"I have a lot more experience fundraising than any of you, and I think we should do it the way I know works."

participate in social media as part of a class feel more connected to their peers than do students who do not participate in social media. Using social media creates a more collaborative and engaging learning environment for people to discuss ideas.[14] Research shows that collaborating with classmates on a given topic through social media can help

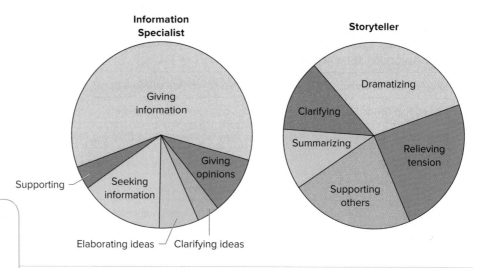

Figure 8.1

Behavioral functions combine to create roles.

Galanes, G. J., and J. K. Brilhart. *Communicating in Groups: Applications and Skills.* Brown & Benchmark, 1993. Copyright © 1993. Times Mirror Higher Education Group, Inc. All rights reserved. Reprinted by permission.

groups develop a stronger sense of community.[15] With increased accessibility to news and media, everyone can now be an information giver and an information seeker. As a result, we may have to rethink how group roles are derived and assigned. For example, perhaps it may be a disadvantage or no longer necessary for only one person to be tasked with being an information giver.

GROUP COHESIVENESS

group climate
The emotional tone or atmosphere members create within the group.

Another important element that helps shape a group's culture is the **group climate**, which is the emotional tone or atmosphere that members create within the group. For example, you have probably attended a group meeting where the tension silenced everyone. That atmosphere of tension describes the group's climate. Three factors that contribute heavily to group climate are trust, cohesiveness, and supportiveness:

- *Trust* means that members believe they can rely on each other. Two types of trust relevant to group work are task trust and interpersonal trust. Task trust develops when you have confidence that others will get their jobs done in support of the group's goals. Interpersonal trust emerges when you perceive that others are working in support of the group rather than trying to achieve personal gain or to accomplish hidden agendas.

- *Supportiveness* refers to an atmosphere of openness in which members care about each other and create cohesiveness. Examples of both supportive and defensive statements are found in Table 8.2.

- *Cohesiveness* is the attachment members feel toward each other and the group. Highly cohesive groups are more open, handle disagreement more effectively, and typically perform better than less cohesive groups.[16]

groupthink
An unintended outcome of cohesion in which the desire for cohesion and agreement takes precedence over critical analysis and discussion.

Although cohesiveness is generally desirable for groups, dangers arise from too much cohesion. **Groupthink** occurs when the desire for cohesion and agreement takes precedence over critical analysis and discussion. According to sociologists, groupthink can destroy effective decision making. Several historical decision-making blunders have been attributed to groupthink, including the escalation of the Vietnam conflict, the space shuttle *Challenger* disaster, and potentially the *Columbia* shuttle disaster over Texas.[17] Although

---

Table 8.2 Examples of Defensive and Supportive Statements

Behavior	Description	Sample Statement
DEFENSIVE BEHAVIORS AND STATEMENTS		
Evaluation	Judging another person	"That's a completely ridiculous idea."
Control	Dominating or insisting on your own way	"I've decided what we need to do."
Manipulation	Trying to verbally push compliance	"Don't you think you should try it my way?"
Neutrality	Not caring about how others feel	"It doesn't matter to me what you decide."
Superiority	Pulling rank, maximizing status differences	"As group leader, I think we should . . ."
Certainty	Being a "know-it-all"	"You guys are completely off base. I know exactly how to handle this."
SUPPORTIVE BEHAVIORS AND STATEMENTS		
Description	Describing your own feelings without making those of others wrong	"I prefer the first option because . . ."
Problem Orientation	Searching for the best solution without predetermining what that should be	"We want to produce the best results, and that may mean some extra time from all of us."
Spontaneity	Reacting honestly and openly	"Wow, that sounds like a great idea!"
Empathy	Showing you care about the other members	"Jan, originally you were skeptical. How comfortable will you be if the group favors that option?"
Equality	Minimizing status differences by treating members as equals	"I don't have all the answers. What do the rest of you think?"
Provisionalism	Expressing opinions tentatively and being open to others' suggestions	"Maybe we should try a different approach . . ."

groupthink may be difficult to detect when you are in a group, researchers have identified the following observable signs of groupthink:

- An illusion of invulnerability by the group
- An unquestioned belief in the morality of the group
- Collective efforts by group members to rationalize faulty decisions
- Stereotypic views of enemy leaders as evil, weak, or ineffective
- Self-censorship of alternative viewpoints
- A shared illusion that all group members think the same thing
- Direct pressure on group members expressing divergent opinions
- The emergence of "mind guards" to screen the group from information contradictory to the prevailing opinion

Research psychologist Irving Janis's original description of groupthink suggests that these characteristics lead to groupthink, and consequently result in bad decisions, recent studies suggest that Janis's groupthink characteristics actually occur after the group has already made a poor decision.[18] Once groups make decisions, group members try to create and reinforce a consensus in support of the decision, even in the face of evidence that the decision is a poor one. The desire for consensus then leads to all of the groupthink characteristics identified by Janis.

Groupthink is possible in nearly every group. To prevent groupthink from occurring, groups should

- seek all pertinent information,
- carefully assess the credibility of information relevant to the decision at hand,
- assign members to present counterarguments, and
- maintain a commitment to finding the best possible outcome as supported by the available evidence.

In addition to groupthink, aspects of group members' identities can also influence group interactions. According to professor of psychology Thomas G. Plante, research and theory in social psychology shows that small groups are at risk of having polarizing views disrupt healthy dialogue, just as they do on social media and in other types of discussions.[19] In a *Psychology Today* article, Plante noted that several social forces, including politics, race, gender, and socioeconomic level, can create polarization in groups.[20] For example, if a small group were tasked with brainstorming ways to reduce poverty and its effects in a community, group members' socioeconomic statuses, as well as other characteristics, have the potential to create conflict surrounding the topic. Such conflict can occur among group members, which Plante calls "in-group" conflict, or between members of the group and others, which he calls "out-group" conflict. How can you challenge instances of polarization and conflict if they arise in your group? The common in-group identity model suggests that you can find what your group members have in common and then make that feature one of the most important aspects of your group, rather than focusing on all the ways you are different.[21] An "us versus them" mentality usually does not lead to good outcomes, and you would be better served by thinking and behaving in

• Group members must make counterviewpoints known to help the group avoid groupthink.

ColorBlind Images/Blend Images LLC

ways that promote compassion and respect. Importantly, having this mindset and acting in these ways can promote people with diverse viewpoints to get along.

DIVERSITY AND GROUP CULTURE

Although we typically think of culture as belonging to very large groups of people, small groups also develop cultures. **Group culture** is the socially negotiated system of rules that guide group behavior. Group culture differs from national and ethnic cultures in that group cultures are relatively unstable and short-term phenomena. Group cultures are constantly in flux, and they disappear when the group dissolves. National and ethnic cultures change slowly and are relatively persistent. If you compare two groups from your own life, you can easily understand the concept of group culture. Your group of friends has implicit rules for behavior—inside jokes, slang, norms for touching, and shared objectives. Your group likely has a culture different from that of an assigned group of students you work with in one of your classes. Classroom groups are typically more formal, less cohesive, and more task oriented. The two groups reflect different cultures that have emerged.

The culture of a group can be influenced by many things. The norms and behaviors of group members can influence culture; so, too, can the diversity among group members.

Within-group diversity is the presence of observable and implicit differences among group members. We observe within-group diversity when group members differ based on visible characteristics. For example, we can visually distinguish between some aspects of able-bodied and non-able-bodied group members. Group diversity can be implicit when members of a group have differing values, attitudes, political beliefs, and perspectives—personal characteristics that cannot be seen. Table 8.3 shows common examples of observable and implicit within-group diversity.

Differences between group members can have an impact on how they interact with one another and how effectively the group functions. To illustrate the effects of group diversity on group members' behaviors, here are several research findings on differences between how self-identified men and women may interact in groups:

- In online discussion groups and other forms of digitally mediated communication, women tend to use more exclamation points as markers of friendliness—thus emphasizing the relational aspects of group communication.[22]
- Although men are typically more influential in standard communication contexts, this difference diminishes in groups, especially when more than one woman is present. In such situations, the influence of women is roughly equal to that of men.[23]
- Research has observed no differences in perceived leadership ability regardless of whether the group is primarily task or relationship oriented; earlier research had shown that women were better leaders in relationship-oriented groups.[24]

group culture
The socially negotiated system of rules that guide group behavior.

within-group diversity
The presence of observable and implicit differences among group members.

Table 8.3 Observable and Implicit Within-Group Diversity

Differences	Definition	Example
Observable	Within-group diversity based on physical characteristics that can be seen	Visible aspects of able and non-able-bodiedness, perceived gender, height, eye color
Implicit	Within-group diversity based on individuals' worldviews, perspectives, and other personality characteristics	Religious orientation, educational background, political affiliation

In addition to gender differences, cultural differences can also influence group dynamics. For instance, it is likely that work groups and even classroom groups will have at least one member who is an English language learner (ELL). You might assume that group members who speak English with different levels of proficiency can diminish the cohesiveness of the group. That assumption would be incorrect, however. Research shows that having various primary languages represented in a group does not impede group cohesiveness as long as members continue to have frequent interactions.[25]

In such situations, all group members should make sure that ELL members are fully included. Strategies for helping nonnative speakers feel included are (1) providing written information in advance of discussions, (2) asking someone in the group to take notes that can be copied and distributed to all group members, (3) viewing difference as a group strength, and (4) matching tasks to members' abilities. Particularly with the last suggestion, finding out the strengths of all group members is important. ELL group members often do not speak as frequently as native English speakers, but this does not mean they do not have highly developed skills in other areas, such as computers, artwork, record keeping, and so on.

If you are a nonnative speaker who is part of a group with mostly native speakers, you can enhance your assertive communication in the group. You should ask questions to clarify the group's activities or points made during discussion. You should also let group members know about skills you have that could be useful to the group. Finally, try to recognize that in most situations, group discussions are as much about relationship building as task accomplishment. Taking time to get to know other members of your group will not only help all of you build confidence in each other but can also lead to meaningful friendships outside class or the workplace.

The Role of Leadership in Small Groups

For most groups to work effectively, some structure is necessary. Noted group communication scholar Gloria Galanes observed that group leaders must attend to four issues: (1) identifying the task of the group, (2) creating cohesiveness among the group members, (3) monitoring and adapting the behaviors of the group members as needed to accomplish tasks, and (4) keeping the group focused on the task at hand.[26]

DEFINING LEADERSHIP

leadership
A process of using communication to influence the behaviors and attitudes of others to meet group goals.

Michael Z. Hackman and Craig E. Johnson define **leadership** as a process of using communication to influence the behaviors and attitudes of others to meet group goals.[27] A leader is a person who influences the behavior and attitudes of others through communication. In small groups, there are two types of leaders: *designated* and *emergent*. A **designated leader** is someone who has been appointed or elected to a leadership position, such as a chair, team leader, coordinator, or facilitator. An **emergent leader** is someone who becomes an informal leader by exerting influence toward the achievement of a group's goal but does not hold the formal position or role of leader. Groups benefit from having a designated leader because designated leaders add stability and organization to the group's activities. An emergent leader can be any group member who helps the group meet its goals. Groups work best when all members contribute skills and leadership behaviors on behalf of the group.

designated leader
Someone who has been appointed or elected to a leadership position.

emergent leader
Someone who becomes an informal leader by exerting influence toward achievement of a group's goal but does not hold the formal position or role of leader.

power
Interpersonal influence that forms the basis for group leadership.

How do leaders, designated or emergent, gain their ability to influence others? Group leaders use **power**, or interpersonal influence that forms the basis for group leadership, to guide actions of the group and behaviors of group members. As explained by William W. Wilmot and Joyce L. Hocker, power is tied to the types of roles that people have in a group.[28] As they note, power flows from specific roles in a group, such as when a designated leader has authority to influence group members' behaviors. Power is also a group dynamic that influences interpersonal connections between group members. They identify three ways in which power exists within a group:

- *Distributive power* occurs when the leader exerts influence over others.
- *Integrative power* highlights interdependence with another person or persons to achieve mutually agreed-upon goals.
- *Designated power* reflects the importance of relationships between people. Marriages, families, and groups often hold such power for us.

Whereas Wilmot and Hocker describe the connections between power and group roles, a classic study by John P. French and Bertram Raven describes different *tactics* through which group members enact power:

- *Reward power* is the ability to give followers what they want and need. This type of power is most likely used by leaders who can offer rewards, but it can also be enacted by emergent leaders who negotiate the possible outcomes for the group that will benefit members.
- *Punishment power* is the ability to withhold from followers what they want and need. An extreme form of punishment power is *coercion,* in which compliance is forced through hostile acts. Both designated and emergent leaders can attempt to use punishment.
- *Referent power* is power based on others' admiration and respect. Charisma is an extreme form of referent power that inspires strong loyalty and devotion from others. Referent power may be used by any group member who, because of reputation or credentials, commands respect and admiration from others.
- *Expert power* is power that arises when the other members value a person's knowledge or expertise. Group members who have specific skills or particular areas of knowledge can use expert power.
- *Legitimate power* is power given to a person because of a title, position, or role. It is most likely used by a designated leader.[29]

Understanding how to use power to influence small groups is not easy. Galanes describes the process of leadership as a balancing act, where leaders must learn to manage various tensions, identified in Table 8.4. Group leaders must understand how to use power in ways that balance several of these tensions in an effort to push the group to achieve its goals while building and maintaining a positive culture.

Table 8.4 Tensions Present for Group Leaders

Tension	Description
Leader centered vs. group centered	Does the leader maintain complete control over the group, or are aspects of group control given to members of the group?
Listening vs. talking	Does the group leader spend more time talking (to set an agenda for group action) or listening (to build trust and cohesiveness)?
Task vs. nontask emphasis	Does the group focus primarily on task-related behaviors or primarily on nontask behaviors? One focus could get the job done quicker; the other could build cohesiveness.
Process vs. outcome focus	Does the group focus only on outcomes, or does it also focus on getting tasks done "the right way"?

Source: Based on Galanes, G. (2009). Dialectical tensions of small group leadership. *Communication Studies, 60,* 409–425.

WAYS OF ENACTING LEADERSHIP

Since Aristotle's time, people have been interested in what makes a good leader. Is leadership a skill you are born with? Can you learn to be a leader? In this section you will learn about three ways of thinking about effective leadership: leadership as style, leadership as communication competence, and leadership as planning. Although they are presented as separate perspectives, effective leaders learn to embrace key elements from each simultaneously.

Leadership Styles

democratic leaders
Leaders who encourage members to participate in group decisions.

laissez-faire leaders
Leaders who take almost no initiative in structuring a group discussion.

autocratic leaders
Leaders who maintain strict control over their group.

Style approaches to studying leadership focus on the patterns of behavior that leaders exhibit in groups. Considerable research has examined three major styles of designated leader: democratic, laissez-faire, and autocratic. **Democratic leaders** encourage members to participate in group decisions, even major ones: "What suggestions do you have for solving our problem?" **Laissez-faire leaders** take almost no initiative in structuring a group discussion; they are nonleaders whose typical response is "I don't care; whatever you want to do is fine with me." **Autocratic leaders** maintain strict control over their group, including making assignments and giving orders: "Here's how we'll solve the problem. First, you will . . . ." Autocratic leaders ask fewer questions but answer more than democratic leaders; they make more attempts to coerce and fewer attempts to get others to participate.[30]

Groups vary in the amount of structure and control their members want and need, but research findings about style have been consistent.[31] Most people in the United States prefer democratic groups and are more satisfied in democratically, rather than autocratically, led groups.

The style approaches imply that a single leadership style works for all situations in a group. However, most scholars believe that the style should match the needs of the specific situation. For example, if you are in a group working on a class project and the deadline is tomorrow, a democratic leadership style might be ineffective because it takes longer to make decisions.

Communication Competencies and Leadership

• Democratic groups allow group members to take part in decision-making.

Syda Productions/Shutterstock

Communication scholars who adopt the communicative competencies approach have tried to focus on the communicative behaviors of leaders as they exercise interpersonal influence to accomplish group goals. They ask such questions as "What do effective leaders do?" The communication competency model of group leadership, developed by J. Kevin Barge and Randy Y. Hirokawa,[32] is one of the most comprehensive models to address this question. This model assumes that leaders help a group achieve its goals through communication skills (competencies). Two competencies include the task and interpersonal, or relationship, distinctions discussed earlier. Leaders must be flexible to draw from a personal repertoire of such competencies. Some of the most important leader competencies are described briefly here:

• Effective leaders are able to clearly and appropriately communicate ideas to the group without dominating the conversation.

• Effective leaders communicate a clear grasp of the task facing the group.

• Effective leaders are skilled at facilitating discussion.

- Effective leaders encourage open dialogue and do not force their own ideas on the group.
- Effective leaders place group needs over personal concerns.
- Effective leaders display respect for others during interaction.
- Effective leaders share in the successes and failures of the group.

Leadership and Planning

In addition to exhibiting an appropriate style and being a competent communicator, effective leaders must learn to plan. Although planning cannot prevent all problems from occurring, some upfront work can increase the likelihood of successful outcomes. Here are some tips for planning effective meetings.

1. *Know the task at hand.* Later in the chapter you will learn about the group problem-solving model. Effective leaders should understand the problem facing the group and take care to communicate that task to group members.

2. *Know the people.* As you will learn, individual group members have different skills, motivations, frames of reference, and knowledge bases. Understanding how to draw on group members' strengths and manage interpersonal dynamics is a key role of the group leader.

3. *Collect information.* The group leader should attempt to become knowledgeable on all issues facing the group. If you are knowledgeable, you will know when discussions are off track.

4. *Distribute leadership.* In certain situations, leadership should be distributed among all group members. The designated leader may need to delegate responsibility, especially when smaller tasks need to be assigned to individual group members. Distributed leadership, whereby all members share in leadership responsibilities, can result in highly productive group outcomes.[33]

5. *Organize the discussion.* Although some types of group discussions may not need much organization—a short class discussion assigned by your teacher, for instance—most discussions need more structure. The group leader should plan an agenda for the discussion. The agenda should be adapted to the task at hand; however, a general template for the agenda is provided in Figure 8.2. As you can see, the typical agenda requires group members to agree on minutes from the past meeting to clear up any confusion or disagreement, make announcements, hear reports, consider new business, and reconsider old business as necessary.

sizing things up

Leadership Power in Groups

When we enact leadership in small groups, we use a variety of methods to create and enact power that is used to influence others. Below are several statements to help you assess which types of power you typically use during your small-group interactions. Respond to each statement using the following scale:

0 = Never
1 = Rarely
2 = Occasionally
3 = Often
4 = Very often

During group interactions, I generally attempt to influence others' opinions by

1. showing benefits for agreeing with my viewpoint.
2. threatening to not work as hard if they do not agree with me.
3. being open and friendly with everyone in the group.
4. showing that I have a lot of knowledge or information about the topic.
5. telling them that my assigned or volunteered role should allow my opinion to carry weight.
6. offering to help them with their tasks if they follow my way of thinking.
7. using subtle threats if they do not agree with me.
8. demonstrating that I am honest and trustworthy.
9. explaining how my background and experiences give me a uniquely qualified perspective.
10. pointing out that I was told to lead the discussion, project, or task.

This exercise has no right or wrong answers. A guide for interpreting your responses appears at the end of the chapter.

GROUP AGENDA

DATE

I. *Approval of minutes from previous meeting(s).* The group facilitator should determine if there are any changes to the minutes and have group members vote to approve the minutes.

II. *Announcements.* Members of the group should make announcements relevant to the group but not necessarily tied to group business. For example, a group member might read a thank-you note from a person the group helped or might provide personal announcements that may be of interest to group members. Such announcements should be brief.

III. *Reports.* Individuals assigned to collect information or carry out tasks should report on their progress. If a report results in an action item—that is, something the group should discuss and vote on—the report should be included under new business. Reports in this segment of the meeting should be informative, but they do not necessarily require action at this time.

IV. *New business.* Items in this part of the agenda can include important discussions and/ or action items. Discussions may or may not result in a vote, but action items should be voted on by the group.

V. *Old business.* Occasionally, action items and discussion from previous meetings may not be complete. In such cases those items should be listed under old business and approached in the same way as new business, with appropriate discussion and voting as necessary.

Figure 8.2

Standard group agenda template.

Problem Solving and Decision-Making

A primary task facing many groups is solving problems: student clubs need to raise money, church groups need to plan activities, and social groups must find fun things to do. Group members must be both creative and critical to arrive at the best solutions to these problems. Groups are usually (but not always) better problem solvers than individuals because several people can provide more information than one person. Group members can bring greater resources to bear on a problem, can collectively have a broader perspective, and can more easily spot flaws in each other's reasoning. However, trade-offs occur. Group problem solving takes longer, and sometimes personality, procedural, or social problems make working as a team difficult for members. Group problem solving is usually more effective when the process is systematic and organized because a group that does not have an overall plan for decision-making is more likely to make a poor decision.[34] In this section you will learn techniques for making group problem-solving efforts more systematic and organized, as well as other work you can accomplish in groups.

communicating with agility

Agile Leadership

Leadership requires self-reflection and adaptability. Organizational consultants Bill Joiner and Stephen Jones believe leaders must grow through the following three stages to develop and use new skills to meet objectives in any situation:

- *Expert leaders* are highly focused on task accomplishment, problem solving, and tactical completion of objectives.

- *Achiever leaders* are effective in coordinating interdependent people and strategic resources to accomplish outcomes.

- *Catalyst leaders* are highly visionary and develop a culture that focuses on positive change and adaptability to meet objectives.

Rather than progressing through each step, leaders build on their skills to become more collaborative, adaptable, and effective.

Source: Agile Leadership Journey. (2023). *What is leadership agility?* www.agileleadershipjourney.com/leadership-journey/leadership-agility

EFFECTIVE GROUP PROBLEM SOLVING

When groups succeed, it is in part because they have followed a coordinated process for analyzing and discussing the problem and its solutions. Effective problem solving is systematic and follows a procedure. Typically, the problem-solving process includes determining the discussion question, identifying the criteria, identifying potential solutions, and evaluating potential solutions.

Determining the Discussion Question

Problem-solving groups typically handle three basic types of discussion questions. Questions of *fact* deal with whether something is true or can be verified. Questions of *value* ask whether something is good or bad, better or worse. Cultural and individual values and beliefs are central to questions of value. Questions of *policy* ask what action should be taken. The key word *should* is either stated or implied in questions of policy. Examples of each type of question are presented in Figure 8.3.

Regardless of the type of discussion question guiding a problem-solving group, the leader must state the question appropriately. Remember, a key task of effective leaders is to help focus the group on what is being discussed. First, the language and terminology should be concrete rather than abstract. If ambiguous terms such as *effective, good,* or *fair* are used, providing examples helps each group member have as close to the same meaning as possible. Second, a well-stated discussion question helps group members know when the solution has been achieved. For

Figure 8.3

Examples of questions of fact, value, and policy.

(top): Brand X Pictures/Getty Images; (middle): Comstock/Getty Images; (bottom): Siede Preis/ Getty Images

FACT

How has the divorce rate changed in the past 15 years?

How many first-generation students are currently enrolled in college?

What percentage of college students graduate in four years?

How often, on average, does a person speak each day?

What occupations earn the highest annual incomes?

VALUE

Why should people seek higher education?

How should Americans treat international students?

Does our legal system provide "justice for all"?

How should young people be educated about HIV?

What is the value of standardized tests for college admission?

POLICY

What courses should students be required to take?

Should the state's drunk-driving laws be changed?

What are the arguments for and against mandatory retirement?

Should the United States intervene in foreign disputes for humanitarian reasons?

What advantages should government provide for businesses willing to develop in high-risk areas of a city?

PROBLEM QUESTIONS

How can we reduce complaints about parking on campus?

What can we do to increase attendance at our club's activities?

How can we make Ginny Avenue safer to cross?

SOLUTION QUESTIONS

How can we increase the number of parking spaces in the campus lots?

How can we improve publicity for our club's activities?

How can we get the city council to reduce the speed limit on Ginny Avenue?

Figure 8.4

Problem questions versus solution questions.

PNC/Photodisc/Getty Images

example, a task force charged with "completing a report by May 15 on why membership has dropped from 100 to 50 members" knows exactly what to do by what deadline. Finally, a group should start its problem solving with a problem question rather than a solution question. Problem questions focus on what is wrong and imply that many solutions are possible for resolving the problem. Problem questions do not bias a group toward one particular solution. Solution questions, by contrast, slant the group's discussion toward one particular option. They may inadvertently cause a group to ignore creative or unusual options because they blind members to some alternatives. Examples of problem and solution questions appear in Figure 8.4.

Identifying Criteria

criteria
The standards by which a group must judge potential solutions.

Criteria are the standards by which a group must judge potential solutions. For example, a solution's likely effectiveness ("Will it work?"), acceptability ("Will people vote for our proposal?"), and cost ("Does this option keep us within the budget?") are common criteria. Group members should discuss and agree on criteria before adopting a solution. Because criteria are based on the values of group members, two members, each using rational tools of decision-making, can arrive at different conclusions. The more similar group members are in age, gender, ethnicity, background, attitudes, values, and beliefs, the more easily they can agree on criteria.

Two kinds of criteria are common. Absolute criteria are those that *must* be met; the group has no leeway. Important criteria are those that *should* be met, but the group has some flexibility. Group members should give the highest priority to criteria that must be met. Ideas that do not meet absolute criteria should be rejected, and the rest should be ranked on how well they meet important criteria. Examples of absolute and important criteria are presented in Figure 8.5.

Figure 8.5

Absolute criteria versus important criteria for a new student union.

wavebreakmedia/Shutterstock

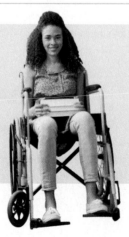

ABSOLUTE CRITERIA

(*Must* be met)

- Must not cost more than $2 million
- Must be wheelchair-accessible
- Must include flexible space that can be arranged in different ways

IMPORTANT CRITERIA

(*Should* be met)

- Should be centrally located
- Should have stage space for concerts
- Should be attractive to all campus constituencies, including traditional and nontraditional students, faculty, and staff

Identifying Potential Solutions

One of the most important jobs a leader has is to encourage group creativity. One technique that can promote innovation and creative thought among groups is brainstorming.[35] Brainstorming is most effective when group members are free to identify multiple ideas, they are asked to defer any judgment (positive or negative) until all ideas have been identified, and the ideas are succinct. Critical evaluation kills creativity, so the main rule of brainstorming is "no evaluation," at least during the brainstorming process. Evaluation of the ideas takes place *after* the group has exhausted its options.

As a leader, you must carefully guide the brainstorming phase of group discussions. You should start with a specified time period in which brainstorming will occur. Before starting dialogue, providing group members with a few minutes to consider the question before responding can help them start individual brainstorming. As ideas are presented to the group, they should be recorded and displayed for all to see; doing so can generate additional ideas. The initial time period for brainstorming can be modified based on the discussion. If ideas start to become repetitive, you may need to stop sooner; if ideas are still unique and interesting, you may need to slightly extend the time. In research this is called "looking for saturation." When all the new ideas have been tapped out (saturated), that is a good time to stop.

Evaluating Potential Solutions

After group members have adequately brainstormed potential solutions, the final task is to evaluate the ideas. At this stage in the discussion, the criteria the group has identified are used to judge the efficacy of each idea generated through brainstorming. Before proceeding to this step, it may be useful to determine whether various ideas can be organized together in some way. Solutions failing to meet absolute criteria are eliminated quickly. Once the nonviable alternatives are eliminated, group members must evaluate each alternative based on the remaining important criteria. Eventually, the group must determine which alternative best meets the set of important criteria they identified.

OTHER WORK TO ACCOMPLISH IN GROUPS

Although this section has highlighted the role of problem solving in small groups, other important types of work are also accomplished in group settings. In fact, groups serve multiple functions, sometimes simultaneously. In addition to helping us perform task functions, such as solving problems, groups also allow us to do the following:

1. *Make decisions.* Many groups exist to make decisions that are unrelated to specific problems. For example, student groups on your campus make daily decisions, such as planning events, launching community outreach projects, and maintaining facilities. These decisions do not necessarily solve problems; rather, they sustain the day-to-day functions of the groups.

2. *Effect change.* Some groups want to influence society but do not have the power to make decisions. You might belong to a community association or the student government organization on your campus. Those groups attempt to influence change even though they may not have the power to make final decisions on that change.

3. *Negotiate conflict.* Groups are often created to resolve conflict. In Los Angeles, small groups were used to bring Latino American and Armenian American high school students together to resolve racial tensions. In fact, the National Communication Association in partnership with the Southern Poverty Law Center has used this strategy across the nation to promote intercultural understanding and to help resolve racial conflict.

4. *Foster creativity.* Groups help us achieve a level of creativity not possible when working alone. The idea that "two heads are better than one" is magnified in groups. People working together to identify creative ideas will likely be more successful than one person working alone.

5. *Maintain ties between stakeholders.* A final function for small groups is to bring together stakeholders. **Stakeholders** are groups of people who have an interest in the actions of an organization. For example, most schools have parent-teacher organizations. The principal of a school might bring together selected teachers and parents to discuss issues facing the school so that open lines of communication between the stakeholders (parents, teachers, and administrators) can be maintained. Various organizations, including businesses, government agencies, and nonprofit organizations, use groups to establish and maintain communication among multiple groups of stakeholders.

stakeholders
Groups of people who have an interest in the actions of an organization.

As you can see, groups exist for many reasons. Although the heart of group activity may indeed be problem solving, not all groups exist solely for that purpose.

Technology and Group Communication Processes

Throughout this course you have learned how technology affects various forms of human communication, and group communication is no different. Groups of all types use technology to find and analyze information, to facilitate interaction among group members, and even to aid in the decision-making process.

Technology has advanced such that many tools have become available to help support the work of groups by allowing people to create, collaborate, and share information online. Consider how the following resources can help groups work more efficiently:

- *Facebook.* Besides helping group members stay connected as friends, Facebook allows you to create a group page for any group to which you belong. On the group page you can post information, links to other resources, agendas, and other information that may help group members stay prepared. You can also create events to alert group members to upcoming meetings.

- *Dropbox.* Dropbox is a free file-sharing service that allows you to create shared folders so that group members can all store, have access to, and edit group documents.

- *Evernote.* This free resource can be used for **content curation**, the collection and storage of information from across the web. Your group might locate several webpages, videos, and

content curation
The collection and storage of documents and other multimedia from the web, covering a specific topic.

• Computers can be used to facilitate group communication.

Ariel Skelley/Getty Images

other resources and use Evernote to maintain a research file in shared notebooks. Evernote is a powerful note-taking tool, so you can use the service to record and publish notes from meetings, as well as collaborate on notes. The Work Chat feature also allows you to instant-message with people who are working on the project.

- *Google Documents.* Google provides a free version of office programs used for word processing, spreadsheets, and presentations. Files can be created, shared, and edited by all group members.

- *Canva.* This free (for basic use) platform allows users to create professional-looking visual representations on content and data in flyer, brochure, and other formats.

- *Skype/Zoom/Teams.* These resources can be used for online videoconferencing so that group members can meet remotely to share ideas, images, screens, and folders.

- *Trello.* This free project management app provides a visual overview of a project and who is working on each task. The app uses a series of boards and cards that can be broken down by task, similar to Pinterest. In this way, each board has its own project and is filled with the cards, or tasks, that need to be completed. Group members can share boards and collaborate within the platform.

- *Asana.* This is one of many free web- and mobile-based applications that allow teams to plan and manage projects. Each group gets a workspace where members can assign tasks to users and include notes, comments, and attachments, as well as use tags to label and group similar tasks.

- *Todoist.* This free productivity app can be used to create lists of

communicating creatively

Collaborative Coworking

What images and feelings arise in you when you think about working in a cubicle? Like many people, you may think it reflects an outdated way of organizing a workspace and limits coworker interaction. Initially, organizations thought creating open workspaces was the answer, but it turns out that open workspaces promote less productivity, increase the use of sick days, and reduce morale.

Now consider the images and feelings that arise in you when you think about working in a collaborative common area that includes space for meetings and casual gatherings among coworkers or a place you could go to bounce ideas off of others in a shared workspace in your local community. These types of spaces are flourishing in contemporary industries. Many contemporary organizations are turning to a design approach that considers employee work and privacy needs. For example, designers are creating team rooms but also quiet spaces, where people can make personal calls and have one-on-one meetings, that encourage some degree of privacy. Frank Chalupa, president and cofounder of Amata Office Solutions, indicates that

> a circular or rectangular layout is one way to achieve this, as it avoids dead-end hallways that workers might not pass through if their offices are located elsewhere. It's also important to scatter amenities throughout a workplace so employees aren't walking by the same offices or workstations each day.

Villa Bonne Nouvelle ("House of Good News"), or VBN, in Paris, France, uses a *corpoworking* approach, a cousin to coworking, where half of its workforce is represented by in-house employees and the other half by freelancers. Together the teams are set up in temporary stations so that programmers and engineers learn how to work with and from people external to the main company. VBN noted that, overall, teams worked better and more efficiently and reported greater satisfaction and engagement, as well as increases in depression upon returning to the traditional office space.

Additionally, coworking spaces are popping up in many local communities to provide space for freelancers, start-ups, and small businesses. These spaces offer a relaxed, productive environment to workers who would typically work at home or in another space. For example, organizers in Champaign-Urbana, Illinois, spent time conducting focus groups within the community to determine what kind of coworking space was needed. The result was *Lodgic*, a workspace that offers drop-in childcare, a market cafe, and a restaurant. The workspace offers 24-hour work zones, internet, direct-to-desk food and drink, bike storage, showers, locker rooms, a print center, technology support, meeting rooms, quiet spaces, and private drop-in offices.

When you think about the type of physical environment that you want to work in, what does it look like? What types of communication and collaboration opportunities do you want with your coworkers? You may want to begin implementing some of these workspace plans into task-oriented groups to which you belong. This will help you get a sense of how you work and communicate best in groups and teams.

Source: Chalupa, F. (2015). Coworking 2.0: Collaboration meets privacy in the workplace. *Huffpost,* Verizon Media.

building behaviors

Harnessing Technology for Your Group

Digital tools to support the work of a group are a valuable resource that can help you with any group to which you belong. Go to Trello.com and explore the various ways in which you can create boards and cards to support the management of a team project you are part of for one of your classes or student organizations. Create a board for each project and then create a card for each of the major tasks for each project. You can add due dates to the cards, create checklists for tasks, and upload documents and weblinks to each card, among many other features. You can add members of your group to the boards, communicate about the project in the chat feature, and even connect and sync your boards to your online calendar to complete tasks on time.

tasks and subtasks for projects so users can easily keep track of tasks and deadlines.

- *Slack.* Slack is a free collaborative communication application that makes office communication organized and searchable using different channels for projects, departments, and stakeholders. Team members can use a chat feature and share documents, GIFs, and videos.
- *GroupMe.* This is a free group texting application that works like a private chat room for your small group.
- *Toggl.* This is a free time-tracking program that allows team members to track how much time they are spending on projects and associated tasks.
- *Texting.* Although you are probably well versed in using text messaging for social interactions, many students find it easy to use text messages for quick reminders and general announcements. For example, if a room change occurs a half hour before a meeting, one group member can text the entire group with the update.
- *Google Jamboards.* This is a free visual collaboration and communication tool through Google that allows multiple users to visually collaborate and storyboard ideas using a sticky-note format.

These resources show just some of the options available online that can be used to facilitate the work of groups. Of course, how you use the web for group work is limited only by your imagination. A variety of services and social media sites can be readily adapted to support the work of your group.

Regardless of which resources a group uses, it is important that group members create rules surrounding how they will and will not share private information created as a result of these tools. For example, if the group determines that individual group members cannot use the research summaries created for the current project for other courses, then the group members must be accountable and uphold this rule. Similarly, group members may decide that they will not share with nongroup members any private information generated during group chats.

Of course, not all group technology automatically improves group communication. As communication researcher Paul Turman points out, groups communicating entirely through technology may find that group norms and basic structures for how the group operates are more difficult to create in computer-mediated environments.[36] He cautions that computer-mediated groups must take more time to explicitly talk about how the group will function and about various norms for communication among group members.

How to Communicate in Small Groups

Each member of a group must take personal responsibility to help support the functions of the group. How can you best do that? The ability to speak fluently and with polish is not essential, but the ability to speak clearly, ethically, and honestly is. Other members of the group will understand your views more easily if you follow this advice:

1. *Relate your statements to preceding remarks.* Public speakers do not always have the opportunity to respond to remarks by others, but small-group members do. Your

statement should not appear irrelevant. Clarify the relevance of your remark to the topic under discussion by linking your remark to the preceding remark:

- Briefly note the previous speaker's point that you want to address—for example, "I want to piggyback on Bill's comment by noting that we can meet our goal by . . ."

- State your point clearly and concisely.

- Summarize how your point adds to the comments made by others—for example, "I agree with Bill. We need to fund-raise, but we can't get so caught up in raising money that we forget about our goal of volunteering."

2. *Use conventional word arrangements.* When you speak, use clear, common language so that people can understand you. Consider this comment: "I unequivocally recognize the meaningful contribution made by my colleague." Although the language might impress some, a simple "I agree" would work just as well. Here are some ways to improve your verbal clarity while in group discussions:

- After connecting your idea to the discussion or previous speaker, state your point and then provide one piece of supporting information or additional explanation.

- Explain to group members how you perceive the importance of what you are saying. Not all comments are critical; some are just ideas. Letting others know how important you think something is may influence how they react and respond.

- When done, ask if anyone needs you to clarify your point.

3. *Speak concisely.* The point here is simple: don't be long-winded. The main advantage of small groups is their ability to approach a problem interactively. If you monopolize the discussion, that advantage may be diminished or lost completely. To learn to speak concisely, try the following:

- Write down your idea before speaking. Those who are wordy during group discussions often spend much of their time trying to figure out what they want to say.

sizing things up

Adapted Competent Group Communication Evaluation Form

Think about a problem-solving-type group you are currently involved in. For each of the eight competencies listed below, indicate how you believe you are performing the behavior using the following scale:

1 = Unsatisfactorily
2 = Satisfactorily
3 = Excellently

Group Task Competencies (1–5)

1. *Defines and analyzes the problem*—appropriately defines and analyzes the problem that confronts the group.
2. *Identifies criteria*—appropriately participates in the establishment of the group goal and identifies criteria for assessing the quality of the group outcome.
3. *Generates solutions*—appropriately generates solutions or alternatives.
4. *Evaluates solutions*—appropriately evaluates the solutions or alternatives identified by group members.
5. *Maintains task focus*—appropriately helps the group stay on the task, issue, or agenda item the group is discussing.

Group Relationship Competencies (6–8)

6. *Manages conflict*—appropriately manages disagreements and conflict.
7. *Manages climate*—appropriately provides supportive comments to other group members.
8. *Manages interaction*—helps manage interaction and appropriately invites others to participate.

A guide for interpreting your responses appears at the end of the chapter.

Source: Beebe, S. A., Barge, J. K., & McCormick, C. (1995). *The competent group communicator: Assessing essential competencies of small group problem solving.* Presented at the annual meeting of the Speech Communication Association, San Antonio, TX.

- Try to talk for no more than one minute at a time. Of course, this time limit is arbitrary, but one minute should be enough time to get an idea out for consideration, and you can always answer questions to clarify as needed.

4. *State one point at a time.* Sometimes this rule is violated appropriately, such as when a group member is presenting a report to the group. However, during give-and-take discussion, stating only one idea promotes efficiency and responsiveness. To ensure this practice, try the following strategies:

- As a group, appoint a process observer to be in charge of keeping the group discussion moving along and preventing any member from bringing up more than one idea at a time. After using the process observer a few times, these behaviors become second nature.

- If you have several ideas that vary in importance, provide some of the less important points to group members in written form for later reflection. Save discussion time for the most important ideas.

Being an Ethical Group Member

The unique nature of small groups requires attention to special ethical concerns regarding the treatment of speech, people, and information. First, as noted in the National Communication Association Credo of Ethics, the field of communication strongly supports the value of free speech. Many secondary groups are formed because several heads perform better than one, but that advantage will not be realized if group members are unwilling or afraid to speak freely in the group. An important ethical principle for small groups is that group members should be willing to share their unique perspectives. However, they should also refrain from saying or doing things that prevent others from speaking freely. Members who are trustworthy and supportive are behaving ethically.

Second, group members must be honest and truthful. In a small group they should not intentionally deceive one another or use biased information to persuade other members to adopt their point of view.

Third, group members must be thorough and unbiased when they evaluate information. Groups are used to make any number of decisions, both large and small. Such decisions will be only as good as the information on which they are based and the reasoning the members use to assess the information. Group members must consider *all* relevant information in an open-minded, verified, and unbiased way by using the best critical-thinking skills they can; otherwise, tragedies can result.

Fourth, group members must behave with integrity. That is, they must be willing to place the good of the group ahead of their own goals, interests, and desires. Some individuals cannot be team players because they are unable or unwilling to merge their personal agendas with those of the group. If you make a commitment to join a group, you should be the kind of team member who will benefit rather than harm the group. If you cannot in good conscience give a group your support, you should leave the group rather than pretend to support the group.

group conflict
An expressed struggle between two or more members of a group.

Finally, group members must learn to manage **group conflict**, which is an expressed struggle between two or more members of a group.[37] Although some conflict can actually help groups make better decisions because ideas are debated and tested more vigorously, too much conflict may result in decreased group cohesiveness and can cause the group to cease functioning. To manage conflict, group members must be ethical in the way they approach disagreement and be willing to listen to and compromise with others. Ethical disagreement happens when you express your disagreement openly, disagree with ideas rather than people, base your disagreement on evidence and reasoning, and react to disagreement positively rather than defensively.[38]

be ready... for what's next

Resolving Group Conflicts

The hope is that you engage in meaningful group work like Lane, Chris, and Nick did with the Boston Strong campaign. Yet it's inevitable that you will also find yourself engaged in difficult group experiences. Difficult group experiences occur because of the task at hand or relationships among the group members.

Perhaps you are currently experiencing problems with a group project. Maybe group members are missing meetings or regularly coming late to meetings. What are you and the other members doing as a group about these problematic behaviors, if anything? What would you do if your group's final presentation occurred and one of your group members failed to show up?

One option would be to talk to your instructor about the situation. The instructor may determine that it is up to the group to decide what to do about missing the group member's grade. How does the group handle this situation? Does the group member get the same grade as the rest of the group for the project? Does the group determine that a reduction in grade is warranted for the absence?

If you experience these situations as part of class projects, they are actually important opportunities for you to build the behaviors you've read about in this chapter. For example, though it may be uncomfortable to tell a group member that the rest of the group is frustrated with the habitual lateness, it is far better to deal with it early on rather than let the behavior continue.

If you find yourself in situations like this, talk to your group members about the problem and perhaps seek the advice of your instructor. It is likely that your instructor will want you and the other members to try to work these problems out as a group. This is a good thing because it will ultimately provide you with real examples of how you've handled conflict in groups that you can talk about during future job interviews. Remember, one of the top skills employers want college graduates to have is team-building skills, and having experiences to highlight how you have managed conflict—rather than avoided it—provides evidence of your ability to work effectively in groups and teams.

Chapter Review & Study Guide

Summary

In this chapter, you learned the following:

1. Small-group communication is the interaction among three to nine people working together to achieve an interdependent goal. Small groups can be classified as task related, relationship related, assigned, or emergent. Many groups can blur boundaries among these types of groups.

   - Task groups are formed to accomplish something, such as solving a problem.

   - Relationship groups are formed to meet our needs for inclusion and affection.

   - Assigned groups occur because individuals are appointed to the group by someone else.

   - Emergent groups occur naturally as individuals meet and decide to become interdependent.

2. Groups form unique cultures as members interact with one another:

   - From the first time group members talk, they start to develop norms for how the group will interact. As those norms develop, individual group members begin to take on certain roles in the group.

   - Strong group cultures can lead to greater cohesiveness, which can more strongly tie group members together. Groups must take care that cohesiveness does not lead to groupthink.

   - Group members must also work to avoid and reduce experiences of polarization.

   - Diversity among group members can influence, both positively and negatively, the culture of a group.

3. Leadership is the process of using communication to influence the behaviors and attitudes of people to meet group goals. Various theories discuss how leadership affects small-group communication:

   - The most effective leaders are able to adapt their leadership skills to the needs of the group. All members of the group can share leadership responsibilities.

   - Leaders must learn to manage various tensions within a group, such as the tension between task and relational goals.

4. Group decision making has four steps:

   - Determine the discussion question.
   - Identify the criteria for potential solutions.
   - Identify potential solutions.
   - Evaluate potential solutions.

5. Small-group communication can utilize technology to help facilitate communication and decision-making:

   - Group decision support systems use special software to facilitate brainstorming and decision-making. Group members are able to anonymously present ideas to other members and are able to anonymously rate and vote for specific alternatives.

   - A variety of free web services and tools can be used to facilitate group communication and group work.

6. To effectively communicate in small groups, you must use clear language and make concise comments that are related to the comments of other group members. You should try to keep your comments limited to one issue at a time.

7. Ethical behaviors in group contexts include allowing others to speak without fear, being honest and truthful, carefully evaluating alternatives, acting with integrity, and managing conflict ethically.

Key Terms

Affection	Formal role	Norms
Assigned groups	Group climate	Power
Autocratic leaders	Group conflict	Relationship-oriented groups
Content curation	Group culture	Role
Control	Groupthink	Self-centered functions
Criteria	Inclusion	Small-group communication
Democratic leaders	Informal role	Stakeholders
Designated leader	Laissez-faire leaders	Task functions
Emergent groups	Leadership	Task-oriented groups
Emergent leader	Maintenance functions	Within-group diversity

Study Questions

1. "Groups meet needs," "Groups are everywhere," and "Working effectively in groups requires training" are statements that explain

   a. types of small groups.
   b. reasons for studying small-group communication.
   c. ways of interacting in small groups.
   d. methods of studying small-group communication.

2. What is true of small groups?

   a. They are comprised of three to nine people.
   b. Members are interdependent.
   c. Group members work toward a common goal.
   d. All of the above are correct.

3. A group that meets via Skype to discuss integrated urban housing developments for cities near Los Angeles is an example of a

   a. relationship-oriented group.
   b. task-oriented group.
   c. cluster-oriented group.
   d. meeting-oriented group.

4. A process of using communication to influence the behaviors and attitudes of others to meet group goals and to benefit the group is

   a. groupthink.
   b. inclusion.
   c. leadership.
   d. role.

5. According to French and Raven, referent power is

   a. power based on others' admiration and respect.
   b. the ability to give followers what they want and need.
   c. power that arises when other members value a person's knowledge or expertise.
   d. the ability to withhold from followers what they want and need.

6. Informal rules for group interaction, the emotional tone created within a group, and group member roles are comprised in

   a. leadership skills.
   b. brainstorming techniques.
   c. maintenance functions.
   d. a group's culture.

7. Determining a discussion question, identifying the criteria, identifying potential solutions, and evaluating potential solutions are steps in

   a. group conflict.
   b. group diversity.
   c. group problem solving.
   d. groupthink.

8. Which of the following statements is true?

   a. Groups exist solely for problem solving.
   b. Effective leaders do not adapt their leadership skills to the needs of the group.
   c. Technology can be utilized to help facilitate communication within small groups.
   d. Groupthink is a helpful and effective method of decision-making.

9. When communicating with other group members, you should

   a. use technical language to appear more credible.
   b. state numerous points at a time.
   c. be long-winded.
   d. relate your remarks to previous statements.

10. To manage group conflict ethically, members must

   a. be willing to listen to and compromise with others.
   b. base their disagreements on feeling and intuition.
   c. disagree with people rather than ideas.
   d. defend their ideas and refuse to listen to others' ideas.

Answers:

1. (b); 2. (d); 3. (b); 4. (c); 5. (a); 6. (d); 7. (c); 8. (c); 9. (d); 10. (a)

Critical Thinking

1. Think of the groups to which you belong. Do they mesh with the text's definition of a small group? What are the groups' functions? What type of leader does each group have? What group norms are you expected to abide by?

2. What are the benefits of and drawbacks to group processes when groups attempt to implement technology resources such as Evernote, Asana, and Google Documents to aid in their workflow? Have you experienced any of these benefits or drawbacks personally?

Sizing Things Up Scoring and Interpretation

Leadership Power in Groups

The Leadership Power in Groups scale assesses your use of French and Raven's categories of power. You can assess your use of power along these dimensions by averaging together (add your responses together and then divide by 2) your responses to the following statements:

- Reward Power: Statements 1 and 6
- Punishment Power: Statements 2 and 7
- Referent Power: Statements 3 and 8
- Expert Power: Statements 4 and 9
- Legitimate Power: Statements 5 and 10

Adapted Competent Group Communicator Evaluation

The Competent Group Communicator evaluation assesses your level of competence surrounding eight group task and relational activities. Competencies 1–5 focus on group tasks, and higher overall scores in this section equal higher competency with group tasks. Competencies 6–8 focus on relational behaviors in groups, and higher overall scores in this section equal higher competency with relational aspects within a group setting. A total score can be calculated by adding together the scores on competencies 1–8. Higher scores suggest higher overall group communication skills.

Averages for your responses to any particular category of power that are above 3 suggest that you rely on that type of power frequently. Averages of 2 or below indicate that you use that type of power infrequently, if at all. Your results may show that you rely on several types of power frequently, that you typically focus on only one, or that you generally rely on none. Any of these outcomes can help you better understand your leadership approach in group situations.

References

1. Emerson College. (n.d.). Students coin "Boston Strong," raise $800k. http://www.emerson.edu/news-events/emerson-college-today/students-coin-boston-strong-raise-800k#.VKihwVaaT3o

2. Boston Strong. (n.d.). Charity T-shirts. http://www.staystrongbostonstrong.org

3. Brenner, L. (2015). Personal communication.

4. Ozimek, A. (n.d.). Future workforce report 2021: How remote work is changing business forever. *Upwork*. https://www.upwork.com/research/future-workforce-report

5. Yang, L., Holtz, D., Jaffe, S., Suri, S., Sinha, S., Weston, J., Connor J., Shah., N., Sherman, K., Hecht, B., & Teevan, J. (2022). The effects of remote work on collaboration among information workers. *Nature Human Behaviour, 6*(1), 43–54. https://doi.org/10.1038/s41562-021-01196-4

6. Schutz, W. C. (1958). *FIRO: A three-dimensional theory of interpersonal behavior*. Rinehart.

7. Braithwaite, D. O., Bach, B. W., Baxter, L. A., DiVerniero, R., Hammonds, J., Hosek, A. M., . . . , & Wolf, B. (2010). Constructing family: A typology of voluntary kin. *Journal of Social and Personal Relationships, 27,* 388–407.

8. Forbes Panel. (2022, April 11). 15 skills employers seek in 2022 (and ways to gain them midcareer). *Forbes*. https://www.forbes.com/sites/forbescoachescouncil/2022/08/11/15-skills-employers-seek-in-2022-and-ways-to-gain-them-midcareer/?sh=26e099e0481a

9. Vengel, A. (2006). Lead your team to victory: The do's and don'ts of effective group influence. *Contract Management, 46,* 69–70.

10. Zorn, T. E., Roper, J., Broadfoot, K., & Weaver, C. K. (2006). Focus groups as sites of influential interaction: Building communicative self-efficacy and effecting attitudinal change in discussing controversial topics. *Journal of Applied Communication Research, 34,* 115–140.

11. Carpenter, N. J., & Soti, P. (2015). *#iSOTU social media analysis report*. Unpublished report, Social Media Analytics Command Center, School of Communication, Illinois State University.

12. Galanes, G. J., & Adams, K. H. (2009). *Effective group discussion*. McGraw-Hill.

13. Whelan, S. A. (2009). Group size, group development, and group productivity. *Small Group Research, 40,* 247–262.

14. Jackson, C. (2011). Your students love social media . . . and so can you. *Teaching Tolerance, 39,* 38–41. http://www.tolerance.org/magazine/number-39-spring-2011/your-students-love-social-media-and-so-can-you

15. Top, E. (2012). Blogging as a social medium in undergraduate courses: Sense of community best predictor of perceived learning. *Internet and Higher Education, 15,* 24–28. https://doi.org/10.1016/j.ihe-duc.2011.02.001

16. Barker, D. B. (1991, February). The behavioral analysis of interpersonal intimacy in group development. *Small Group Research, 22,* 76–91; Kelly, L., & Duran, R. L. (1985). Interaction and performance in small groups: A descriptive report. *International Journal of Small Group Research, 1,* 182–192.

17. Ferraris, C. (2004). Investigating NASA's intergroup decision-making: Groupthink and intergroup social dynamics. International Communication Association Convention, May 2004.

18. Henningsen, D. D., Henningsen, M. L., Eden, J., & Cruz, M. G. (2006). Examining the symptoms of groupthink and retrospective sense making. *Small Group Research, 37,* 36–64.

19. Plante, T. G. (2004). *Do the right thing: Living ethically in an unethical world*. New Harbinger.

20. Plante, T. G. (2017, September 5). Polarization of groups never ends well. *Psychology Today*. https://www.psychologytoday.com/us/blog/do-the-right-thing/201709/polarization-groups-never-ends-well

21. Gaertner, S. L., & Dovidio, J. F. (2014). *Reducing intergroup bias: The common ingroup identity model*. Routledge.

22. Waseleski, C. (2006). Gender and the use of exclamation points in computer-mediated communication: An analysis of exclamation points posted to two electronic discussion lists. *Journal of Computer Mediated Communication, 11,* 1012–1024.

23. Carli, L. L. (2001). Gender and social influence. *Journal of Social Issues, 57,* 725–742.

24. Won, H. L. (2006). Links between personalities and leadership perception in problem-solving groups. *Social Science Journal, 43,* 659–672.

25. Lauring, J., & Selmer, J. (2010). Multicultural organizations: Common language and group cohesiveness. *International Journal of Cross Cultural Management, 10,* 267–284.

26. Galanes, G. (2003). In their own words: An exploratory study of bona fide group leaders. *Small Group Research, 34,* 741–770.

27. Hackman, M. Z., & Johnson, C. E. (2013). *Leadership: A communication perspective* (4th ed.). Waveland Press.

28. Wilmot, W. W., & Hocker, J. L. (2007). *Interpersonal conflict* (7th ed.). McGraw-Hill.

29. French, J. R. P., & Raven, B. (1981). The bases of social power. In D. Cartwright & A. Zander (Eds.), *Group dynamics: Research and theory* (3rd ed.). McGraw-Hill.

30. Foels, R., Driskell, J. E., Mullen, B., & Salas, E. (2000). The effects of democratic leadership on group member satisfaction. *Small Group Research, 31,* 676–702.

31. Brown, M. E., & Trevino, L. K. (2006). Socialized charismatic leadership, values congruence, and deviance in work groups. *Journal of Applied Psychology, 91,* 954–962.

32. Barge, J. K., & Hirokawa, R. Y. (1989). Toward a communication competency model of group leadership. *Small Group Behavior, 20,* 167–189.

33. Barge, J. K., & Hirokawa, R. Y. (1989). Toward a communication competency model of group leadership. *Small Group Behavior, 20,* 167–189.

34. Gouran, D. S., & Hirokawa, R. Y. (1986). Counteractive functions of communication in effective group decision-making. In R. Y. Hirokawa & M. S. Poole (Eds.), *Communication and group decision-making.* Sage.

35. Blomstrom, S., Boster, F. J., Levine, K. J., Butler, E. M., & Levine, S. L. (2008). The effect of training on brain-storming. *Journal of the Communication, Speech, & Theatre Association of North Dakota, 21,* 41–50.

36. Turman, P. (2005). Norm development, decision-making, and structuration in CMC group interaction. *Communication Teacher, 19,* 121–125.

37. Galanes, G. J., & Adams, K. H. (2009). *Effective group discussion.* McGraw-Hill; Wilmot, W. W., & Hocker, J. L. (2007). *Interpersonal conflict* (7th ed.). McGraw-Hill.

38. Galanes, G. J., & Adams, K. H. (2009). *Effective group discussion.* McGraw-Hill.

Shutterstock

workplace communication

When you have read and thought about this chapter, you will be able to

1. describe the structures of workplace communication as they are created within diverse types of organizations.

2. analyze communication strategies involved in each stage of organizational assimilation.

3. apply communication behaviors that will demonstrate communication competence in the workplace.

4. recognize ethical workplace communication behaviors.

The very fabric of our social, cultural, and economic worlds is intertwined with various organizations, including schools, clubs, places of worship, and the workplace. Our ability to communicate effectively and ethically within these various organizations determines, in large part, our opportunities for personal, social, and economic advancement. In this chapter you will learn about various skills related to workplace communication.

Entering the spring semester of his third year in college, Sedric Granger has already cultivated a number of experiences as a member of organizations. He is an active member of a student organization, has served as a sports reporter for a local NPR affiliate, has worked with ESPN-3 as a reporter and playcaller, has done on-field and on-court announcing at collegiate athletic events, and has interned for a local developmental-league baseball team. As Sedric participated in each organization, he needed to manage his communication behaviors to be successful.

Sedric Granger, a college student, used workplace communication to facilitate his involvement with multiple organizations.

Courtesy of Sedric Granger

Sedric explained in an interview with one of the authors that his primary strategy has been to cultivate personal networks to learn new positions and roles. He explained, "When entering into a new space, it is crucial to find experienced individuals to learn from. One key fact that I learned was that everyone in the organization has been in my position at one point and is looking to share their knowledge." Sedric's story teaches an important lesson about how to communicate in an organization. When you become connected to a new organization, effective communication with others will be critical to a successful transition into your new role, which is the focus of this chapter.

Defining Workplace Communication

Each of us belongs to several different **organizations**, which are social collectives, or groups of people, in which activities are coordinated to achieve both individual and collective goals. As a student, you belong to many organizations. A recent survey by the National Center for Educational Statistics found that as many as 40% of part-time college students and 10% of full-time college students work at least 20 hours per week.[1] As students work, they are members of their university and their place of employment and must balance the demands of both organizations. You may belong to a place of worship, student clubs, and community service organizations. And of course, we are all connected to local, state, and national government organizations. To contribute meaningfully to these organizations, you must have some understanding of how communication functions in these settings, as well as an understanding of the skills that are most salient to organizational contexts.

We define **organizational communication** as the ways in which groups of people both maintain structure and order through their symbolic interactions and allow individual actors the freedom to accomplish their goals. From this definition you should be aware of the following points. First, we use verbal and nonverbal communication to create structure. Through organizational communication, hierarchy is established among people. For instance, there are supervisors and subordinates, with formal or informal rules

organizations
Social collectives, or groups of people, in which activities are coordinated to achieve both individual and collective goals.

organizational communication
The ways in which groups of people both maintain structure and order through their symbolic interactions and allow individual actors the freedom to accomplish their goals.

economic orientation
Organizations that manufacture products and/or offer services for consumers.

political orientation
Organizations that generate and distribute power and control within society.

integration orientation
Organizations that help mediate and resolve discord among members of society.

pattern-maintenance orientation
Organizations that promote cultural and educational regularity and development within society.

about how they communicate with each other. Second, we use communication to create order. How we discuss problems, how we arrive at decisions, and how we celebrate successes are all organizational processes that are created in and through organizational communication. Third, we use organizational communication to accomplish personal goals. Through the structure and order found in most organizations, we have an ability to use communication to demonstrate our creativity, ability, and potential so that we are better able to accomplish personal goals in support of the organization. Consequently, communication simultaneously creates structure and freedom as we enact our roles within the organization. In this section you will learn about organizational communication as it flows through communications networks in various types of organizations.

TYPES OF ORGANIZATIONS

Sociologist Talcott Parsons classified organizations into four primary types: economic, political, integration, and pattern maintenance.[2] Although some organizations might overlap these categories, we usually can classify organizations according to their primary functions in society. For instance, a labor union has a primarily political function as it represents members' interests to management, local and state governments, and other unions. At the same time, unions obviously have an interest in promoting economic vitality. Although they span more than one organization type, unions have a primary function that allows clear classification.

Organizations with an **economic orientation** tend to manufacture products and/or offer services for consumers. Small businesses, which according to the U.S. Small Business Administration account for 99.9% of all U.S. employer firms and employ about half of all private-sector employees, are examples of organizations with an economic orientation.[3] Of course, large corporations, banks, and media organizations also have economic orientations.

Organizations with a **political orientation** generate and distribute power and control within society. Elected local, state, and federal officials and police and military forces are political organizations. Of course, there are Democrats and Republicans in the United States who form organizations with political orientations, but as of May 2018 there were 209 other political parties operating within various states.[4] Political organizations must adhere to rules established in formal documents, such as the U.S. Constitution, while they attempt to influence the ideology of the electorate.

Organizations with an **integration orientation** help mediate and resolve discord among members of society. Our court system, public interest groups, and conflict management centers are all examples of integration-oriented organizations. One unique characteristic of communication within integrative organizations is the necessity for impartiality. A judge, for example, must not be biased against defendants, and public interest groups must demonstrate that their objective benefits all of society, not just a few individuals.

• Schools are pattern-maintenance organizations because they teach people how to effectively participate in society.

Andersen Ross/Blend Images/Getty Images

Organizations with a **pattern-maintenance orientation** promote cultural and educational regularity and development within society. Organizations that teach individuals how to participate effectively in society, including families, schools, and religious groups, promote pattern maintenance. Communication within organizations focused on pattern maintenance emphasizes social support. Your family or your religious group, for instance, provides you with personal and spiritual support, and schools support individuals by helping them learn.

COMMUNICATION NETWORKS

Competent workplace communicators understand that the workplace comprises multiple communication networks. **Communication networks** are patterns of relationships through which information flows in an organization. Organizational communication scholar Cynthia Stohl describes communication networks as capturing "the tapestry of *relationships*—the complex web of *affiliations* among individuals and organizations as they are woven through the collaborative threads of communication."[5] Communication networks can take many forms, depending on the complexity of the organization. However, we typically classify these networks as formal or informal in nature.

Formal communication consists of messages that follow prescribed channels of communication throughout the organization. The most common way of depicting formal communication networks is with organizational charts such as the one in Figure 9.1. Organizational charts provide clear guidelines as to who is responsible for a given task and which employees are responsible for others' performance. When communication occurs in formal networks, information typically flows in three ways:

- **Downward communication** occurs whenever superiors initiate messages to subordinates. Ideally, downward communication should include such things as job instructions, job rationale, policy and procedures, performance feedback, and motivational appeals.
- **Upward communication** occurs when messages flow from subordinates to superiors. For instance, if you have regular meetings with your supervisor, you should be prepared with updates on projects, explanations of difficulties that you encounter, and progress toward your personal objectives for growth as a member of the organization.[6]
- **Horizontal communication** flows between people who are at the same level of the organizational hierarchy. It influences organizational success by allowing members to coordinate tasks, solve problems, share information, and resolve conflict.

communicating with agility

Hybrid Organizations

Many of the significant issues facing society are complex and require organizations to be agile in how they enact traditional characteristics of organizations. Take for instance the apparel company Patagonia. As an international retail company, Patagonia has an obvious economic imperative. However, the company's website also references environmental activism, fair trade, and ethical work practices. Patagonia's emphasis on these values, which is generally referred to as a social enterprise orientation, means that it simultaneously achieves economic, integration, and pattern maintenance objectives. The hybrid nature of Patagonia and many other organizations requires agility both for the organization and its members. For instance, Yvon Chouinard, founder of Patagonia, emphasized that the mission of Patagonia is to "use business to inspire and implement solutions to the environmental crisis." As you participate in organizations, you may find similar hybrid orientations. In that case, you will need to remain agile in how you discuss multiple, and sometimes competing, goals of the organization.

Source: Chouinard, Y. (2013, May 6). *Introducing Patagonia Works, a new kind of company.* Patagonia Works. www.patagoniaworks.com/press/2014/5/5/patagonia-launches-20-million-change-and-patagonia-works-a-holding-company-for-the-environment

---

communication networks
Patterns of relationships through which information flows in an organization.

formal communication
Messages that follow prescribed channels of communication throughout the organization.

downward communication
Messages flowing from superiors to subordinates.

upward communication
Messages flowing from subordinates to superiors.

horizontal communication
Messages between members of an organization who have equal power.

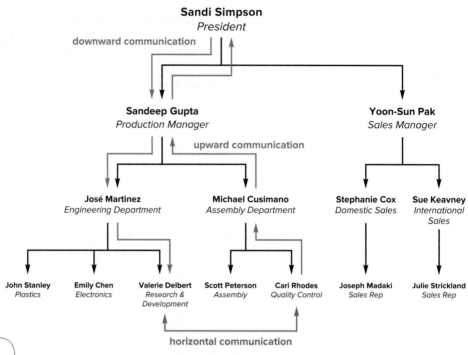

Figure 9.1

Formal communication flow.

informal communication
Interactions that do not follow the formal upward and downward structures of the organization but emerge out of less formal interactions among organizational members.

organizational communities
Groups of similar businesses or clubs that have common interests and become networked together to provide mutual support and resources.

boundary spanner
An individual who shares information between groups and establishes a strategic vision for collaboration.

Informal communication consists of interactions that do not follow the formal upward and downward structures of the organization but emerge out of less formal interactions among organizational members.[7] For example, coworkers who work from home might use private email accounts, WhatsApp, or other noncompany mechanisms to have informal discussions about other employees, their boss, or other issues about their jobs.[8] These informal networks, sometimes referred to as "grapevine communication," are typically very accurate, with 80% to 90% of the information being correct.[9] An understanding of formal and informal networks within organizations is critical as you join and try to fit in at a new organization.

Communication networks can also extend beyond organizations. **Organizational communities** are established when *several organizations—similar businesses, clubs, or community service organizations—have overlapping interests and become networked together to provide mutual support and resources.*[10] For example, a group of organic farms in your area might act together to make connections with local restaurants and grocery stores to sell their goods. If the farmers and the restaurants form networks to coordinate menus with seasonal local foods, those networks can evolve as the organizational community grows. Social media helps facilitate organizational communities. When one organization follows another, information can be shared. For organizational communities to thrive, key individuals must step forward to be boundary spanners. A **boundary spanner** not only shares information between groups but also provides strategic vision for how the groups can actively work together and form a community.

Communication and Organizational Assimilation

Because you belong to multiple organizations of varying types, you regularly go through the process of assimilating into organizations. **Organizational assimilation** is the process by which you engage in formal and informal communication with others to learn your work roles, become accustomed to standard practices, and enact core values of the organization. In many organizations, the term "onboarding" is used to identify the formal aspects of organizational assimilation.

Throughout our lives, we join and leave multiple organizations. For instance, Pew Research revealed that one in five workers are very or somewhat likely to change jobs in the next six months.[11] As we spend time in specific organizations, our roles may change either because the organization changes or we get promoted. Consequently, organizational assimilation will be required throughout your life and is an important communication process to understand.

Communication researchers who study organizational assimilation break the process down into three elements:[12]

- **Anticipatory socialization** is the communicative process through which one intentionally and unintentionally learns about occupational choices and sets career expectations. Examples could include career day events in school, discussion with family and friends about careers, and learning about career fields through media sources.

- **Organizational encounter** occurs after formally entering an organization and involves formal training, mentorship, and experiences to become familiar with a role within an organization. Some elements of organizational encounters may begin as you become familiar with a specific organization. For instance, during an informational interview or employment interview, you may learn specific characteristics of the roles performed by employees, as well as elements of the organization's culture. The majority of the encounter step takes place after you formally join an organization and begin onboarding and other training.

- **Metamorphosis** is the process of moving beyond the entry phase, gaining skills and confidence in a role, embracing the values of the organization, and beginning to (re)define a role in the organization. As people settle into their roles and work to become more self-reliant, they begin to enter into metamorphosis, which can last for months or even years before the role changes and they potentially re-enter the other phases.

For each aspect of organizational assimilation, the communication strategies outlined in this section will be important to your success as you navigate your role in a job, student organization, community group, or other organizations to which you belong.

ANTICIPATORY SOCIALIZATION

From your youngest days of childhood you have received messages from the media, family members, teachers, and friends that have already influenced which vocations and careers you find most appealing. Careers are specific professions in which you are trained to earn income, whereas vocations are more general activities that are fulfilling and important to you. Our careers often connect to our vocational preference, but our vocational preference may also go beyond our specific job. For example, you may develop a preference for a vocation that involves working with your hands in a creative way and follow that preference to do volunteer work in your community. Specific careers that may use that vocational preference could be an artist, landscape designer, interior decorator, and many others. Although your preferences for vocations and careers may change over time, informal messages are critical as you begin to make choices about potential college majors, jobs, and future ambitions related to your developing vocational and career preferences.

Anticipatory socialization occurs well before you seek employment or membership with a particular organization. Figure 9.2 summarizes the process of anticipatory socialization. Depicted as an inverted funnel, anticipatory socialization begins with learning about

organizational assimilation
Using formal and informal communication with others to learn work roles, become accustomed to standard practices, and enact core values of the organization.

anticipatory socialization
The communicative process through which one intentionally and unintentionally learns about occupational choices and sets career expectations.

organizational encounter
The formal training, mentorship, and experiences that help someone become familiar with their role within an organization.

metamorphosis
The process of moving beyond the entry phase, gaining skills and confidence in a role, embracing the values of the organization, and beginning to (re)define a role in an organization.

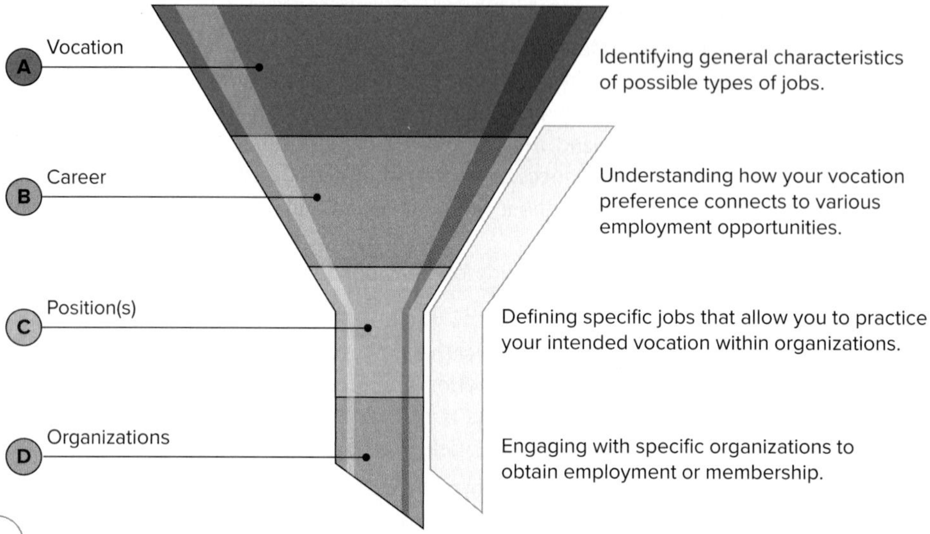

A　Vocation — Identifying general characteristics of possible types of jobs.

B　Career — Understanding how your vocation preference connects to various employment opportunities.

C　Position(s) — Defining specific jobs that allow you to practice your intended vocation within organizations.

D　Organizations — Engaging with specific organizations to obtain employment or membership.

Figure 9.2

Anticipatory Socialization

broad vocations and fields in which you may have interests. Do you like to work with your hands? Are you artistic? Do you enjoy working with technology? Are you an effective writer? Answers to these questions, which are part of your self-perception, can help you identify potential vocations or general characteristics of possible job fields. For instance, if you have interest in art and technology, you may determine that communication design is a field in which you may want to work.

As you learn more about potential vocations, you will begin to identify specific jobs that bring all of your interests together. Using the previous example, if you have an interest in a vocation that involves working with your hands in a creative way, you may learn through conversations, social media, and other sources that there are many types of careers that involve those characteristics. As your vocational interests and career exploration become more refined, you may focus your career interests further and decide to pursue positions in organizations that allow you to do landscape design or something similar.

Although anticipatory socialization may begin during childhood and last for several years as you accumulate new knowledge and experiences, many of your interests will become more focused as you progress through high school and college. This general time frame is not a hard rule, however. As you continue learning and having new experiences, you may have defining moments that cause you to pursue entirely new vocations or careers. The following strategies can be used to clarify potential employment opportunities that match your preferred vocation: conduct a self-inventory, create a personal network, and use technology effectively.

Conducting a Self-Inventory

What do you really know about yourself? When was the last time you took inventory of your assets and liabilities as a potential employee? Could you express these qualities intelligently? Analyzing answers to these questions will allow you to discover the attributes and values that define your personal brand.

Companies and other organizations conduct SWOT (strengths, weaknesses, opportunities, threats) analyses to better understand the current and future strategic opportunities for the organization. SWOT analyses are not just for organizations; individuals can also use them to assess potential vocations, careers, and interests.[13] A personal SWOT analysis would consider the following:

- *Strengths*, or the skills or characteristics that will make you distinctive. You should consider the experiences you have had, the skills you have developed, and the gifts that characterize you as an individual.

- *Weaknesses*, or the areas in which you have small or substantial opportunities for improvement and characteristics that might disadvantage you in the job market. You should consider areas in which you lack training or experience, bad work habits that others have observed, and even ways in which your social media presence could create negative impressions of you.

- *Opportunities*, or external forces that could benefit you if you are able to act decisively and take advantage. For instance, what are the areas in which your local economy is projected to grow? Are there areas in your field where new technologies are transforming the workplace, particularly technologies with which you have some experience?

- *Threats.* External factors that could negatively impact you as you enter the job market. For example, is your preferred industry expanding or contracting in your local economy? Will technology disrupt your field so much that there will be fewer jobs?

As you can see, the personal SWOT analysis is a way for you to assess your own strengths and weaknesses in relation to a variety of jobs within one or more sectors. Using your personal inventory, you may find ways to best align your strengths with particular types of jobs that will suit you very well. Additionally, you will be able to use your SWOT analysis to articulate your own assets to others, as well as to try to rectify apparent weaknesses. Throughout your education you have already began to cultivate a personal brand. The SWOT analysis will allow you to highlight characteristics of that brand and align them with potential careers.

Creating a Personal Network

Many people assume that the key to landing a good job is having a good résumé. Though partly true, this conventional wisdom is also incomplete: the key to finding a great job is connecting with others, and that requires having a great personal network. A **personal network** is an intricate web of contacts and relationships designed to benefit the participants—including identifying leads and giving referrals.[14] People in your network, including family, friends, people you have met at social functions, and people with whom you have worked and studied, can assist you in learning about different types of jobs that align with your personal inventory and can also help you identify leads with specific organizations.

    Because many college students have not yet had significant work experience, developing a personal network is critical to post-college employment. Here are strategies you can use to develop your network:

- *Create an inventory of your network.* Using your phone, email, and social media contacts, inventory the people in your social network who could assist you in your job search.

personal network
A web of contacts and relationships that can help you gain job leads and can provide job referrals.

communicating creatively

Podcasting Your Personal Brand

In addition to using a self-inventory to better understand your personal brand, you should actively create and manage your brand. Author and professional speaker Seth Price observed the power of podcasting by noting, "There are few things more personal than the sound of the human voice." As a result of mobile technology and readily available distribution platforms, anyone can create podcasts both to build audiences and to exhibit their personal brand for public consumption. What topics are you passionate about? In what areas do you have specialized knowledge? Developing a podcast or other forms of digital content is an easy way for you to demonstrate your knowledge, skills, and personality to others. Moreover, making a podcast is easy and can likely be accomplished with equipment you already have, such as a smartphone, tablet, or laptop. The work you put into your blog can show that you are actively engaged in your profession while also demonstrating that you have valuable digital skills.

Source: Price, S. (2018, March 20). How to easily start podcasting and build a powerful personal brand. www .sethprice.net/podcasting-for-personal-branding/

• Volunteering is a great way to make connections and expand your personal network.

Ariel Skelley/Blend Images/The Agency Collection/Getty Images

Talk with those who have significant work experience to make them aware that you are in the job market.

• *Cultivate your social media network.* LinkedIn and other social media platforms are ready-made potential networks. Analyze your social media networks for key individuals who could be helpful. Take time to carefully develop your profile and add people to your network over time. You should start building and expanding your network as soon as possible because platforms such as LinkedIn are identified as primary recruiting tools for businesses and other organizations.

• *Contact the career services office on your campus.* Most campuses offer several job fairs throughout the academic year or provide other networking opportunities. Taking advantage of these face-to-face meeting opportunities can be a productive use of your time.

• *Join student chapters of professional organizations on your campus.* For instance, students studying communication often join clubs such as the National Communication Association, the Association for Women in Communication, the Public Relations Society of America, and the Society for Professional Journalists. Campus chapters of these organizations provide useful networking opportunities for members.

• *Consider an internship.* Internships can lead to valuable networking opportunities because they provide you with practical experience while also allowing you to meet people who can serve as future employment references. Some internships even turn into full-time jobs. Most colleges and universities offer options for students to earn course credit for internships—you should talk with your academic adviser about such options on your campus.

• *Volunteer.* Simply taking the time to volunteer in your community can open many doors. Besides giving you the satisfaction that comes from helping others, your hard work and dedication will be noticed by others. Volunteering for a community organization will allow you to get to know many different types of people in your community, thus expanding your network.

• *Practice good interpersonal skills.* When interacting with people who could become part of your network, be a good interpersonal communicator. Being polite, listening well, and finding ways to help others can be pivotal in people remembering you later. A strong network consists of people with whom you have a mutually enriching relationship, not just a group of people of whom you ask favors.

engaging diversity

Being Bilingual Helps the Job Search

As a result of globalization, organizations increasingly function in a multilingual world. Even small businesses routinely work in a global market. As a result, language skills can benefit you significantly as you seek employment. For public service jobs, Arabic, Mandarin, Farsi, and Urdu are in high demand.

Source: Vye, A. (2022, April 22). The best languages to learn for government jobs. *Chron.* https://work.chron.com/languages-learn-government-jobs-23554.html

Using Technology Effectively

Once you have defined your personal brand and created your network, you can embark on the exciting, and sometimes frustrating, journey of matching your skills with potential jobs. Your personal network may reveal several options; however, you should also use your personal SWOT analysis to identify possibilities that you had not previously considered.

There are online tools that can match your current skills with potential careers. You can conduct basic web searches, such as "matching skills with careers," to reveal many of these tools. Here are a few examples to get you started:

- The U.S. Department of Labor has created a mobile app called CareerInfo where you can explore various careers. This app integrates data from multiple statistical resources to help you discover job outlooks and salary ranges in various sectors of the economy.

- The website myskillsmyfuture.org allows you to enter current or previous job titles to explore other options that have related skillsets. For instance, if you have worked as a server at a restaurant your customer-service orientation coupled with additional training could allow you to work effectively in a healthcare environment.

- The website Jobscan has a career change tool where you can upload your resume and have it analyzed for careers connected to transferable skills you already have.

ORGANIZATIONAL ENTRY

As you narrow your interests and begin to identify potential job options, you will start to make contact with specific organizations. You will need to prepare written and electronic materials, such as a résumé and cover letters, to prepare yourself for job applications. When preparing such documents you should consult colleagues, mentors, your campus's career services center, and online resources to determine best practices in your field.

Your written credentials will rarely be sufficient to obtain employment. As you engage specific organizations, you will rely on verbal and nonverbal communication to succeed in your job interviews. The following approaches can help you develop strategies for effective communication as you progress through the organizational entry phase.

Preparing for an Interview

Your initial step in preparing for a job interview is to carefully research the organization. Although you may not have much time for this step, knowing about the organization and the position for which you applied is critical to successfully answering questions during the interview. Your research efforts can be focused around three general goals:

- *Understand the job.* A **job description** defines the position in terms of its responsibilities and scope. Although the format can vary, job descriptions may include information on job duties and responsibilities; the knowledge and skills necessary to accomplish those duties; working conditions; relationships with coworkers, supervisors, and external stakeholders; and the extent of supervision required. You will likely find the formal job description online, either on the company website or on a job search database. Besides providing you with information about the company's expectations, the job description serves as the legal basis on which the job interview is conducted, including the focus of interview questions. If you have sufficient time, you can use your professional and social networks to solicit others' perspectives on the type of job for which you applied.

- *Understand the organization.* Job applicants and interviewees lose all credibility when they cannot demonstrate even superficial knowledge of the organization to which they are applying. Besides using obvious sources of information, such as the organization's website and social media accounts, check your library for specialized resources, such as the LexisNexis Company Insight database or the BusinessWeek Company Insight Center, to find information about the company's finances, executive officers, and other pertinent facts. Of course, small businesses

job description
The responsibilities and scope of a position within a company.

- Study the job description carefully so that you can learn the exact skills needed to succeed.
Peopleimages/Getty Images

may not be indexed in such databases, but a local library or chamber of commerce may have information about these organizations.

- *Understand the field.* To present yourself as a mature candidate for any job, you will want to illustrate knowledge of your chosen field by demonstrating awareness of new trends, market forces, and other matters. Keep current on all aspects of your field because employers will view you more positively if you are conversant on these issues. Professional trade magazines are a resource for this type of research.

Remember that the primary purpose of an interview is to analyze the knowledge and skills of a particular applicant in relationship to the required and desired skills in the job description. Taking time to learn about these issues will allow you to advocate for a close fit between your qualifications and those specified by the employer.

Answering Questions Effectively

Answering questions effectively is critical for interviewees. Research has shown that various strategies are associated with successfully answering questions.[15] Four key guidelines emerge from that body of research: (1) offer relevant answers, (2) substantiate your claims with evidence, (3) provide accurate answers, and (4) be positive.

Your answers should be relevant to the question asked and to the job description. As an interviewee, you should never evade questions; rather, you should respond to them thoroughly and directly. In discussing your skills and abilities, try to relate them to the specific position for which you are interviewing. Whenever possible, specify how and why you think you are well suited to the job. By so doing, you demonstrate your knowledge of the position and illustrate the transferability of your knowledge and skills to the job at hand.

Whatever claims you make about your experience, always provide support. Some interviewees give terse, underdeveloped responses, forcing the interviewer to probe endlessly. Presenting claims without evidence can sound self-serving. If you offer evidence for your assertions, the objective facts and supporting examples will confirm your strengths. Take care to avoid talking for too long when responding. After you have provided a direct answer and presented an example or other form of evidence, summarize your point and wait for a response or the next question. A long, rambling answer can be just as negative as an underdeveloped one.

All employers are searching for honest employees, so always provide accurate information. If an employer finds out you have misrepresented yourself during the interview by exaggerating or lying, everything you do and say will become suspect. Successful interviews feature candid conversation. If

building behaviors

Practicing Interview Questions

Practice answering these typical job interview questions with a partner.

1. Why would you like to work for us?
2. What do you know about our products and services?
3. Have you worked remotely, and if so, how did you structure your work environment to be productive?
4. What do you think your previous supervisors would cite as your strengths? Weaknesses?
5. Describe a typical strategy that you would use in a customer service call.
6. What criteria do you use when assigning work to others?
7. How do you follow up on work assigned to others?
8. Which aspect of your education has prepared you most for this position?
9. Which course did you enjoy most in college?
10. If you had your education to do over again, what would you do differently, and why?
11. Why did you choose the major that you chose?
12. What do you think is the greatest challenge facing this field today?
13. Which area of this field do you think will expand the most in the next few years?

Table 9.1 Answering Questions Effectively

Question	Ineffective Answer	Effective Answer
"Describe your best attribute as an employee."	"I'm really organized."	"I take time to ensure that materials and documents are put away before leaving my desk. This promotes security and allows me to stay organized."
"Have you ever coded HTML?"	"I think that I had to do something with HTML when working on my online portfolio."	"I have not actually coded HTML, but I am comfortable working on webpages that use plain text content management systems like you find on social media sites."
"Have you experienced conflict in the workplace?"	"Yes! One of my previous bosses was always mad at everyone, and it was always horrible to go to work!"	"I did experience conflict with a coworker, but I was able to resolve the problem amicably by communicating less by email and more through face-to-face interactions where we could clarify our perceptions more effectively."

you are asked a question you cannot answer, simply say so and do not act embarrassed. An interviewer will have more respect for an interviewee who admits to ignorance than for one who tries to fake an answer.

Being accurate does not mean confessing to every self-doubt or shortcoming. In fact, be as positive as possible during interviews, because in a sense you are "selling" yourself to the employer. To volunteer some limitations or claim personal responsibility for past events is fine, especially in the context of challenges you have met or problems you have encountered. However, avoid being overly critical of others and yourself. You can highlight your strengths and downplay your weaknesses, but always be honest.

Table 9.1 provides examples illustrating these suggestions. Notice how the effective answers demonstrate honesty while presenting the best case possible for the interviewee.

Asking Questions Effectively

Any potential employer will likely recognize that you have questions about the job and organizational environment. After answering the interviewer's questions, you should be prepared to ask questions. This gives you the insight you need to decide if you want this particular job, shows your interest in the job, and demonstrates communication skills.

Recognize that your questions make indirect statements about your priorities, ambitions, and level of commitment. Consequently, avoid questions that focus on financial issues such as salary, vacation time, and benefits. Instead, devise questions that elicit information about the company and job that you were unable to obtain through your research. Arrange questions so that the most important ones come first, because you may not get a chance to ask all of your prepared questions. Although your questions will need to be tailored to the organization, here are general types of questions relevant in most interview situations:

- "Do you assign mentors to help new employees fit in with the culture of the company while learning their new job roles?"
- "What is the average length of time that an employee works for the company?"
- "What percentage of entry-level employees stay with the company and get promoted?"
- "How would you describe the culture of the company?"

Preparing for Illegal Questions

Legally, employers must approach the hiring process with reference to the laws that govern employment. These laws, known as equal employment opportunity (EEO) laws, ensure that individuals are selected for employment without bias. Although a variety of laws can exist at the state level, the pertinent federal statutes are as follows:

- *Title VII of the Civil Rights Act of 1964* prevents employment discrimination based on race, color, sex, religion, or national origin.

- *The Equal Pay Act of 1963* aims to end the practice of unequal pay for men and women for equal work.

- *The Pregnancy Discrimination Act of 1978* makes it illegal to discriminate, either through hiring or promotion, based on pregnancy or related medical issues.

- *The Age Discrimination in Employment Act of 1967* makes it illegal for employers to refuse to hire applicants who are 40 years of age or older because of age alone.

- *The Americans with Disabilities Act of 1990* prevents discrimination against qualified applicants because of a disability and requires employers to make reasonable accommodations for them to apply for and perform work.[16]

To comply with these laws, employers should (1) describe the qualities and skills needed for the position they hope to fill, (2) construct questions that relate to those attributes, and (3) ask the same questions of all candidates for the position. These questions are known as bona fide occupational qualification (BFOQ) questions. BFOQ questions should be about skills, training, education, work experience, physical attributes (such as the ability to lift a certain weight or similar types of physical activity required for a job), and personality traits. With rare exceptions, questions should not be about age, gender, race, religion, physical appearance, disabilities, ethnic group, or citizenship.

Even with carefully planned BFOQ questions, employers will occasionally pose questions to interviewees that are intentionally or unintentionally illegal. For example, interviewers might ask, "Are you married?" or "How old are your children?" when, in fact, they should really ask, "Is there anything that would prevent you from being able to travel frequently?" Often, illegal questions are unintentionally asked by untrained interviewers who are trying to be polite. In any circumstance you must carefully consider how to respond to illegal questions, using one or more of these strategies:

- *Weigh the severity of the violation against your desire for the job.* If you really want the job and the violation was minor, you may opt to provide a short answer or tactfully try to rephrase the question to avoid being forced to provide irrelevant information.

- *Ask for clarification.* If you suspect that the illegal question is actually attempting to reference a BFOQ for the job, you can clarify what skills, knowledge, or attitudes the interviewer is attempting to assess.

- *Be assertive.* You can tell the interviewer that the question is not related to the attributes specified in the job description or that the question, as phrased, asks for information you do not have to provide. A less aggressive option is to politely decline to answer the question as phrased.

- *Report the violation.* If the interviewer continues to ask illegal questions or is otherwise offensive, you might consider reporting the violation to that person's superior or to the federal Equal Employment Opportunity Commission (www.eeoc.gov) or a similar state agency.

Transitioning to Employee

After the employment interview, you may receive a job offer. Making a final decision about accepting a job involves careful consideration of multiple pieces of information. Here are tips for conducting negotiations with your potential employer and making a final decision:

1. *Wait for the appropriate time.* The interview is not the ideal place to discuss salary expectations and other points of negotiation. In the interview you have little bargaining power. Once the company makes an offer, you are in demand and have a better chance of negotiating various items.

2. *Know what you want in advance.* Once you have been offered the job, you should be prepared to begin the negotiation process. Conduct research to determine common salary ranges for your type of position. Online salary databases, such as www.salary.com, provide national and regional salary profiles for different types of jobs. Depending on the type of position, you may also be able to negotiate moving expenses, the start date, continuing education funding, and other types of benefits.

3. *Understand the implications of taking the job.* If the job requires moving, you may want to investigate the living expenses of the new community. Try using an online cost-of-living calculator to compare where you live now with the place you will live if you accept the job.

4. *Get it in writing.* Be aware that a job offer and your acceptance of it are legally binding documents. Take care to ensure that all negotiated items are included in the offer letter, and do not write an acceptance letter until you have a correct offer letter in hand.

5. *Be tactful in your response.* Regardless of whether you are accepting or declining the job offer, your official response should be professional. If you accept the position, your acceptance letter should thank the interviewer and formally state that you are accepting the position as described in the offer letter. If you decline the offer, you should state your reasons for not accepting the offer, explicitly decline the offer, and end on a pleasant note.

After you have accepted a job, you will likely begin a formal onboarding process that may last for several days or several months, depending on the nature of the position. As a new employee, you should develop communication strategies that will facilitate a smoother transition into your new role. During your training, your initial objectives are to learn technical skills such as software systems and other tools that you will use to complete your job tasks while at the same time beginning to understand the culture of the company. Learning both hard skills, such as software tools or work processes, and soft skills, such as how to appropriately contribute to the work culture, is more easily achieved if you adopt one or more of the following communication orientations:[17]

1. *Be ethical in how you communicate.* When learning new information from supervisors and coworkers, be honest about your strengths, weaknesses, and areas for growth. Adopting a "fake it" approach will not only delay your growth but can also lead to negative perceptions of you by others.

2. *Be humble.* Recognize that others are supporting you as you learn aspects of your position and be genuine in how you show appreciation. As a new employee, arrogance can lead to errors and can cause others to be less helpful.

3. *Be assertive.* As you gain confidence in your role, find ways to demonstrate leadership, proactive work, and independent thought. As you begin to act assertively, use communication with others to verify that your planned actions will be productive and effective.

4. *Be proactive.* As you transition through training and become a co-worker, continually look for opportunities to improve both technical skills and soft skills. Observing others, seeking mentorship, asking for informal feedback, and taking steps to be a proactive self-learner are all traits that will allow you grow more quickly and become an invaluable asset to your organization.

METAMORPHOSIS

After entering an organization and transitioning through training, employees gradually enter a state of organizational assimilation known as metamorphosis. In this stage, your role as a member of the organization continues to grow and shift as you learn new skills, achieve greater levels of experience, pursue new opportunities for growth, and begin to take on new leadership roles. Your communication during the metamorphosis stage involves behaviors focused on maintaining stability with your role in the organization while also growing in your ability to have positive impact and expand your opportunities. Communication scholars Michael Kramer and Vernon Miller highlight five areas of competence that can help you settle into an organization and strive for continued success:[18]

1. *Use socialization tactics.* Although organizations have formal tactics, such as training, to promote socialization into metamorphosis, there are also individual strategies that are effective. Identifying a role model, someone who understands the organization and the job requirements, and using that person as a guide can help new members of an organization learn their role(s) and begin to innovate on how to perform their tasks more effectively.

2. *Address unmet expectations.* New members of an organization often experience differences between their expectations and actual experiences surrounding a position or an organization. These differences may relate to compensation, required time commitment, bureaucratic rules, and even dress codes. New employees must either negotiate unmet expectations with others or reconcile internally how positive aspects of the position are more important.

3. *Interpret messages.* Throughout a new employee's socialization process, coworkers may tell stories that provide important messages about people, values, rituals, and other aspects of the organization's culture. Actively listening to these messages and using such information to guide behaviors will help new members fit into an organization.

4. *Seek information.* New members of an organization should actively seek out information that will help them succeed. Key strategies include asking direct and indirect questions, asking third parties, and observation. For example, if you were seeking information on an organization's personal time off expectations, you could ask your supervisor a direct question about policies. You could also ask a peer an indirect question about how an absence you observed was handled by their supervisor; the answer might provide you with guidance for your own circumstances. Alternatively, you might ask someone who use to work at the company what their experiences were; a knowledgeable third party might provide details that organization insiders would be reluctant to communicate.

5. *Learn the organizational culture.* As newcomers learn more about an organization's culture and move from outsiders to insiders, they transition fully into metamorphosis. Culture can be present across an organization but might also be unique within specific departments or units. For example, large companies may be bureaucratic, but individual departments may have vibrant and

supportive cultures. Learning about organizational culture requires some of the tactics previously mentioned, such as interpreting messages and seeking information; however, Kramer and Miller note that new employees must use those tactics purposefully to quickly identify key values and norms within an organization.

These competencies are best thought of as guiding strategies to become an effective member of an organization over time. To enact these strategies, you must employ a wide variety of communication skills.

Before turning to those specific communication skills, here are some final points to consider about organizational assimilation. First, these stages are not perfectly linear. Throughout your time with an organization your role(s) will shift, you will learn to do new things, and you will hopefully find ways to expand your opportunities. Second, the rate of change in all industries means that the number of times that you will cycle through each of the organizational assimilation stages will also rapidly increase. Just one example of such change is the increasing recognition that remote work will be part of many careers. In fact, a recent post-pandemic survey found that 97 percent of the workers surveyed would like to work remotely for at least part of their work time.[19] Think about how remote work would impact your communication with others as you perform your work in an organization.

Communication Skills Needed on the Job

Previous sections of this chapter provided you with general information about organizations and taught you about the organizational assimilation process. This section emphasizes skills relevant to your role as an employee or organizational member, particularly those that will be critical during the metamorphosis stage.

WORKPLACE COMMUNICATION COMPETENCE

Before turning to specific communication skills, we begin by discussing the general nature of communication competence in the workplace. Communication competence is the extent to which you are able to be effective at a broad range of verbal and nonverbal communication skills in particular settings. A study by Joann Keyton and colleagues reviewed literature on workplace communication and synthesized over 300 communication behaviors into the four general categories listed in Table 9.2. According to their research, competent workplace communicators effectively share information by asking and answering questions, providing feedback, and engaging in discussions with others. They engage in relationship maintenance by appropriately using humor, engaging in small talk with others, and creating positive relationships. To engage in organizing behaviors, competent communicators are clear on how they schedule tasks and actions and manage others, while also being very effective listeners. Finally, competent communicators avoid complaining and continual displays of frustration.[20]

SPECIFIC WORKPLACE COMMUNICATION SKILLS

Whereas the previous discussion of communication competence provides a broad strategy for improving your workplace communication skills, this section highlights seven specific behaviors that will help you improve your workplace communication in a variety of settings: immediacy, supportiveness, strategic ambiguity, interaction management, cross-cultural skills, conflict management, and customer service.

Table 9.2 Workplace Communication Competence Categories

Category	Definition	Representative Behaviors
Information sharing	Effectively sending and receiving job-related content to and from others	Giving and receiving feedback, asking others for opinions, asking and answering questions, showing respect, engaging in discussion
Relationship maintenance	Creating and continuing positive workplace connections with others	Creating relationships, engaging in small talk, using humor appropriately
Avoiding negative emotion	Reducing continual outward displays of negativity surrounding your job or the organization	Avoiding displays of frustration and anger, reducing complaints about your job or coworkers
Organizing	Using communication to promote coherent work flow	Discussing schedules, making decisions, resolving problems, planning, managing others effectively

Source: Adapted from Keyton, J., Caputo, J. M., Fore, E. A., Fu, R., Leibowitz, S. A., Liu, T., Polasik, S. S., Gosh, P., & Wu, C. (2013). Investigating verbal workplace communication behaviors. *Journal of Business Communication, 50*, 152–169.

Immediacy

immediacy
Communication behaviors intended to create perceptions of psychological closeness with others.

When people engage in communication behaviors intended to create perceptions of psychological closeness with others, they are enacting **immediacy.** Immediacy can be both verbal and nonverbal. Smiling, reducing physical distance, and using animated gestures and facial expressions are all examples of nonverbal immediacy behaviors, whereas calling people by their first names, using "we" language, and telling stories are examples of verbal immediacy behaviors. Using immediacy has been shown to have positive effects in the workplace. For instance, it can improve the relationship between supervisors and subordinates[21] and encourage people to engage in higher levels of self-disclosure.[22] In sales situations, higher levels of self-disclosure can be helpful because they create more rapport between the salesperson and the customer and allow the salesperson to learn valuable information that gives a product or service more value for that customer.

• Professional touch, such as a handshake, can help establish immediacy between people.

Michael Zhang/123RF

Supportiveness

People engage in **supportive communication** when they listen with empathy, acknowledge the feelings of others, and engage in dialogue to help others maintain a sense of personal control. Supportive communication is an important skill in any context, including workplace settings. In fact, recent research suggests that supportive supervisor communication is one of the most important factors influencing employees' job satisfaction.[23]

To enhance your supportive communication skills, consider the following strategies adapted from communication professors Terrance Albrecht and Betsy Bach's discussion of supportive communication:

- *Listen without judging.* Being judgmental while listening to a coworker's explanation of a problem can cause you to lose your focus on what is really being said.
- *Validate feelings.* Even if you disagree with something your coworkers say, validating their perceptions and feelings is an important step in building a trusting relationship.
- *Provide both informational and relational messages.* Supportive communication involves both helping and healing messages. Providing a metaphorical "shoulder to cry on" is equally as important as providing suggestions and advice.
- *Be confidential.* When coworkers share feelings and personal reflections with you, maintaining their trust and confidence is essential. Telling others or gossiping about the issue will destroy your credibility as a trustworthy coworker.[24]

supportive communication
Listening with empathy, acknowledging others' feelings, and engaging in dialogue to help others maintain a sense of personal control.

Strategic Ambiguity

When learning to be competent communicators, we often assume that being competent always means being clear. Communication scholar Eric Eisenberg disagrees with this assumption and points out that clarity is essential for competent communication only when clear communication is the objective of the communicator.[25] Professional and workplace communication often features the use of **strategic ambiguity**—the purposeful use of symbols to allow multiple interpretations of messages. You have probably witnessed instances of strategic ambiguity on your college campus. At the beginning of each year, various student organizations undertake recruitment drives to gain new members. When presenting their organization, whether a student club or a Greek organization, members are often strategically ambiguous about some aspect of it. After all, recruiting would be difficult if we knew there were really only a few members or there was significant political infighting in the club. When you enter the workforce, you will encounter new examples of strategic ambiguity. During orientation, for example, you might learn about your new company's mission statement. Such mission statements are often strategically ambiguous so that all stakeholders (employees, managers, owners, and so on) can find relevant meaning in them. Competent communicators not only must be skillful in recognizing the use of strategic ambiguity but also must be able to use it themselves when necessary.

strategic ambiguity
The purposeful use of symbols to allow multiple interpretations of messages.

Interaction Management

Workplace communication is somewhat different from other types of communication situations because conversations tend to flow between the technical jargon associated with the workplace and other topics brought up to relieve stress and pass time. Thus, computer technicians might talk about megabytes and megapixels one minute and speculate about next week's episode of *This Is Us* the next. Competent workplace communicators engage in **interaction management** to establish a smooth pattern of interaction that allows a clear flow between topics and ideas. Using pauses, changing pitch, carefully listening to the topics being discussed, and responding appropriately are skills related to interaction management.

interaction management
Establishing a smooth pattern of interaction that allows a clear flow between topics and ideas.

Being an effective communicator with coworkers and clients requires carefully observing how they prefer to talk. Recognizing that one coworker always talks about technical matters related to the job, whereas another always likes to chit-chat about family, is important; adapting your conversational style to the different styles of these individuals will help you fit in more easily. If you aspire to managerial positions in your company, the ability to communicate well with various individuals is critical.

Cross-Cultural Skills

The changing nature of the U.S. workplace makes it increasingly a cross-cultural setting. If you take a job where the predominant language spoken is not your natural or primary language, you will need to develop cross-cultural skills to aid your transition. Because you have both a new language and a new set of technical terms to learn in your workplace, questions are the most effective strategy for avoiding misunderstanding. Ask questions as needed to clarify instructions or expectations, and pay careful attention to your coworkers. By observing them and asking questions as necessary, you can learn important vocabulary and skills for interacting with customers or clients. Finally, keeping a journal of your daily activities is a good idea. The first few days and weeks may seem overwhelming, but you will learn a great deal. Keeping a journal can help you retain vocabulary, directions, and other important pieces of information more easily.

You will also need to consider ways that you should adapt your communication behaviors if you are in a work setting where a fellow employee is not a native speaker. You can help ease your coworker's transition through some relatively easy steps. First, provide important directions, policies, and procedures in writing. Second-language speakers often find written information easier to process because the pace of spoken language can be challenging. Second, take time to explain. You can help your coworker learn vocabulary and interaction skills more quickly if you take a few moments to explain how and why you communicate the way you do. Finally, be patient. Becoming impatient and frustrated will introduce new problems and make the situation worse for everyone. Patience makes the transition easier and will likely prevent problems from recurring.

Recall from Chapter 7 that there are multiple other behaviors, values, and perspectives through which cultural differences could emerge in the workplace. How do you provide and respond to constructive criticism? What does silence mean during a meeting or discussion? What values should guide your interactions with customers or clients? Answers to these and many other questions could vary from one culture to another.[26] In addition to language, you should be prepared to analyze your cultural setting and adapt your own behaviors as necessary to be a valued and productive member of the organization.

Conflict Management Skills

Communicating in organizations is not an easy task. In fact, a pervasive part of organizational life is conflict—both destructive and productive. Destructive conflict can destroy work relationships, whereas productive conflict can create a needed impetus for organizational change and development. Workplace conflict can occur because of mundane issues, such as one person playing a radio too loudly, or serious issues, such as office politics pitting one faction of employees against another. Indeed, conflict management skills are not just desirable but necessary for effective workplace communication.

People often view conflict negatively because they associate it with anger. However, conflict occurs anytime two or more people have goals they perceive to be incompatible. When one employee wants to work late to finish a joint project and another wants to go home to be with family, conflict can occur. In short, workplace conflict is a fact of life—the rule rather than the exception.

You can use a variety of techniques to manage conflict productively. Wilmot and Hocker suggest several approaches:

- *Avoidance.* With the avoidance style, you deny the existence of conflict. Although avoidance can provide you with time to think through a situation, continued avoidance allows conflict to simmer and flare up with more intensity.
- *Competition.* With the competition style, you view conflict as a battle and advance your own interests over those of others. Although the competition style can be necessary

when quick decisions must be made or when you are strongly committed to a position, it can be highly detrimental to your relationships with your coworkers.

- *Compromise.* With a compromise style, you are willing to negotiate away some of your position as long as the other party in the conflict is willing to do the same. Compromise can be an effective strategy because it is a win–win proposition for both parties, but when used too often, it can become a sophisticated form of conflict avoidance.

- *Accommodation.* With the accommodation style, you set aside your views and accept those of others. Accommodation can maintain harmony in relationships, but it is problematic in many situations, because tacit acceptance of others' views can stifle creative dialogue and decision-making.

- *Collaboration.* A collaborative style relies on thoughtful negotiation and reasoned compromise whereby both parties agree that the negotiated outcome is the best possible alternative under the circumstances. Although collaboration takes more time and effort to enact, it typically results in the best possible outcome for all parties.[27]

Customer Service Skills

We often hear that we now live in a "service economy," in which U.S. companies increasingly make money by providing services rather than goods. In this kind of business environment, one of the most important forms of external communication occurs in providing service to organizational customers. Business professors Mary Jo Bitner, Bernhard Booms, and Mary Tetreault define the **customer service encounter** as "the moment of interaction between the customer and the firm."[28] During this moment the organizational representative provides professional assistance in exchange for the customer's money or attention.

Customer service means different things to different people. For some it means being friendly, shaking hands warmly, and initiating pleasant conversations with clients. For others, customer service means processing customers efficiently and quickly. Still others view it as listening intently to identify individual needs and providing sufficient information and support to meet those needs. All these perspectives are legitimate; however, the *customer* is the ultimate judge of whether customer service interactions are satisfying.

sizing things up

Conflict in the Workplace

Workplace contexts create potential for conflict because they force us to accomplish important task outcomes while managing relationships with others. The way we manage conflict can influence how effective we are as organizational communicators. Below you will find several statements; for each one, indicate how well the statement describes you by using the following scale:

1 = Does not describe me at all
2 = Does not describe me very well
3 = Describes me somewhat
4 = Describes me well
5 = Describes me very well

1. When working on problems, I try to win arguments to support my opinion.
2. When communicating at work, I generally let others have their way.
3. If I sense a conflict brewing, I would rather find a way to leave.
4. When in a conflict with a coworker, I work to find common ground to resolve the conflict.
5. When I disagree with someone, I am willing to give up some of my own position as long as others are willing to do the same.
6. I am quick to give up on my opinion when I sense conflict coming.
7. I am generally willing to meet others halfway to resolve conflict.
8. When in a conflict, my interests are most important.
9. I generally avoid conflict in the workplace.
10. When involved in a conflict, talking things through is the best way to find a solution.
11. I generally resolve conflict by compromising with the other person.
12. I often try to find ways to delay having to face a conflict situation.
13. When in a conflict, having dialogue can often resolve the situation.
14. I tend to give up on my views to resolve conflicts with others.
15. When in a conflict, I approach the other person ready for battle.

There are no right or wrong answers to these questions. A guide for interpreting your responses appears at the end of this chapter.

customer service encounter
The moment of interaction between the customer and the firm.

Table 9.3 Compliance-Gaining Strategies Used by Customer Service Representatives

Strategy	Example
Promise: Promising a reward for compliance	"If you purchase this car, I'll give you tickets to a football game."
Threat: Threatening to punish for noncompliance	"If you don't buy the car before the end of the week, I cannot guarantee the 1% interest rate."
Pre-giving: Rewarding the customer before requesting compliance	"I will give you $50 just for test-driving this new car."
Moral appeal: Implying that it is immoral not to comply	"Since you have small children, you should be looking at our crossover utility model with more safety features."
Liking: Being friendly and helpful to get the customer in a good frame of mind to ensure compliance	"Good afternoon. Thank you for taking time to come into our store today. How can I help you?"

Source: Adapted from Ford, W. Z. (1998). *Communicating with customers: Service approaches, ethics, and impact.* Hampton Press.

emotional labor
Jobs in which employees are expected to display certain feelings in order to satisfy organizational role expectations.

• Restaurant and retail jobs are among the types of jobs where emotional labor is commonly experienced by workers.

JohnnyGreig/Getty Images

Regardless of how employees understand the concept of customer service, most providers have the goal of influencing their customers' behaviors. An extensive body of research covers communication techniques for gaining compliance. In her book *Communicating with Customers: Service Approaches, Ethics, and Impact,* communication professor Wendy Ford reviews compliance-gaining strategies used by customer service representatives, which are summarized in Table 9.3.

A wide range of occupations require interactions between employees and clients or customers. In many of these, the provision of service often involves some degree of emotional content.[29] Nurses interact with dying patients in a hospice, ministers counsel troubled parishioners, and social workers help physically abused women. Emotional communication also characterizes other, less obvious occupations. Flight attendants must appear happy and attentive during flights,[30] and volunteer coaches must hide frustration when coaching young athletes who do not follow direction.[31]

Arlie Hochschild was the first scholar to deal with this phenomenon, in her book *The Managed Heart.*[32] She uses the term **emotional labor** to refer to jobs in which employees are expected to display certain feelings in order to satisfy organizational role expectations. Research has indicated that, although emotional labor may be fiscally rewarding for the organization and the client, it can be dangerous for the service provider and can lead to negative consequences, such as burnout, job dissatisfaction, and high turnover.[33]

Ethical Dimensions in the Workplace

Whether you are a new member of an organization or have been in a particular role for many years, ethical communication is critical to your success. This section discusses three communication topics that highlight the role of ethics in organizations: aggressive communication, dishonesty, and sexual harassment.

AGGRESSIVE COMMUNICATION

Verbal aggressiveness is communication that attacks the self-concepts of other people in order to inflict psychological pain.[34] It is on the rise in organizational settings, though sometimes unrecognized by management. A recent summary of literature on workplace aggression identified the following types:

- *Abusive supervision* occurs when a supervisor engages in sustained behaviors via hostile verbal and nonverbal messages but does not rise to the level of physical aggression.
- *Bullying* occurs when one person is subjected to ridicule, offensive statements, teasing, social isolation, or other abuse by one or more individuals over an extended period of time.
- *Incivility* is frequent rude behavior that may or may not have the intent of being harmful. Uncivil people may or may not know they are being rude.
- *Social undermining* is action meant to socially isolate another person from a larger group. Whereas incivility can occur unwittingly, social undermining is intentional and often planned.[35]

The psychological pain produced by verbal aggression and other aggressive behaviors includes embarrassment, feelings of inadequacy, humiliation, hopelessness, despair, and depression. If you feel you are the victim of workplace aggression, consult a human resource manager, a union representative, or a trusted manager for advice.

DISHONESTY

Political figures and other prominent individuals are constantly scrutinized for the honesty and accuracy of their statements. When you speak to others, whether for personal or professional reasons, they rely on you to be honest. One might assume that for communication to work effectively, all parties must both enact and assume honesty. Is it appropriate for you to misrepresent information to your supervisor to make your performance appear better? Is it ethical to integrate key words into your résumé so that electronic search engines will highlight them, even if you do not truly possess the requisite skills for that job? Nicole Amare and Alan Manning, scholars who specialize in business and professional communication, observe that individuals at all levels of organizations have a personal responsibility to act with integrity and to be honest.[36] Even deciding with whom you should be honest is important. For example, if you know a fellow employee is underperforming, should you confront your peer first or go straight to your supervisor?

Honesty is at the heart of personal ethics and must begin with open communication and trust. The fears that drive people to dishonest behaviors at work can often be countered by establishing open communication with coworkers.

SEXUAL HARASSMENT

Sexual harassment includes a set of behaviors that constitute workplace aggression. Unfortunately, instances of sexual harassment litter the news, and sexual harassment has been a problem in the workplace for decades.

sexual harassment
Unwelcome, unsolicited, repeated behavior of a sexual nature.

What is sexual harassment? The Equal Employment Opportunity Commission (EEOC) defines **sexual harassment** as

> unwelcome sexual advances, requests for sexual favors, and other verbal or physical conduct of a sexual nature if (1) submission to the conduct is made a condition of employment, (2) submission to or rejection of the conduct is made the basis for an employment decision, or (3) the conduct seriously affects an employee's work performance or creates an intimidating, hostile, or offensive working environment.[37]

Simply put, sexual harassment is unwelcome, unsolicited, repeated behavior of a sexual nature.

quid pro quo sexual harassment
A situation in which an employee is offered a reward or is threatened with punishment based on his or her participation in a sexual activity.

hostile work environment sexual harassment
Conditions in the workplace that are sexually offensive, intimidating, or hostile and that affect an individual's ability to perform his or her job.

The EEOC definition outlines two different, although sometimes overlapping, types of sexual harassment. The first type, **quid pro quo sexual harassment**, occurs when an employee is offered a reward or is threatened with punishment based on participation in a sexual activity. For example, a supervisor might tell an employee, "I'll give you Friday off if you meet me at my place tonight." The second type is **hostile work environment sexual harassment**, or conditions in the workplace that are sexually offensive, intimidating, or hostile and that affect an individual's ability to perform a job. For example, if two males talk explicitly about the physical features of a female colleague in her presence, sexual harassment has occurred.

Most instances of sexual harassment are neither exposed nor reported. Instead, the victim usually avoids the situation by taking time off, transferring to another area, or changing jobs. The perpetrator is usually someone in the organization with authority and status—with power over the victim—and the victim feels exposure or confrontation will backfire. Notably, cultural shifts are taking place across industries to combat the silencing of victims. Starting in the Hollywood entertainment industry, the #TimesUp movement began with over 300 Hollywood executives, agents, actors, writers, directors, and producers who wanted to expose systemic sexual exploitation in the workplace.[38] Their efforts resulted in several high-profile condemnations of serial sexual predators in the industry and led to similar criticisms of systemic sexual exploitation in other industries such as journalism, science, and higher education.

Although many people often think of the most serious offenses as constituting sexual harassment (for example, offering career benefits in exchange for sex), the EEOC's definition indicates that a wide range of communication behaviors can constitute sexual harassment. Although harassment is often judged by its effects on the victim, not on the intentions of the harasser, a person need not suffer severe psychological or work outcomes to be a victim. The courts use the "reasonable person rule" to determine whether a reasonable person would find the behavior in question offensive. One limitation of this rule, however, is evidence that men and women view messages that have sexual overtones differently.[39] In particular, unsolicited sexualized messages sent from men to women are more likely to be perceived as harassment than are similar messages sent by women to men.

Increasingly, organizations are developing "duty to report" policies concerning sexual harassment, domestic violence, child abuse, and other such crimes. The "duty to report" concept was legally created to ensure that health professionals, educators, and others who work with children would report potential instances of child abuse to authorities.[40] Similar obligations extend to cases of sexual harassment. Although no federal law requires victims or witnesses to report cases of sexual harassment, courts have found that once supervisors are made aware of such harassment, they must take steps to end the behaviors. Many colleges and universities have developed specific policies that require faculty, staff, and others to report cases of sexual harassment to the institution's **Title IX officer**, the person designated to promote antidiscrimination compliance on campus.

Sexual harassment is a serious and pervasive problem in modern organizational life because of the effects it has on victims and the entire organization. Addressing sexual harassment is a communication challenge facing organizations as they attempt to communicate law, rules, and norms to employees.

Title IX officer
The person designated by a college or university (or similar type of organization) to promote compliance with the U.S. Department of Education Title IX requirements, including the investigation of alleged sexual discrimination.

be ready... for what's next

Structuring Your Communication Time

Following the COVID-19 pandemic, opportunities (if not expectations) for remote work have accelerated. As a result, it is increasingly important for remote workers to learn how to structure their work time as they navigate their organizational roles.

When working remotely, you have more agency to determine how you allocate time for various tasks. Although personal preference plays a major role, Jeff Haden, a nationally respected writer on topics related to organizational culture, explained that simple preferences may not be optimal. Citing studies from neuropsychology, Haden suggests that individuals tend to be better at making tough decisions earlier in the day and doing more mundane tasks later in the day.[41] Haden's suggestions have implications for how you can develop, plan, and implement your personal communication strategies each day.

- *Use the morning for strategy.* Whether you are planning for a meeting with your supervisor or simply thinking through how you will engage with customers throughout the day, taking time to plan your messages and key points is important. Use the morning to make important decisions about what you want to say, how you want to present your message, and how you will overcome potential roadblocks.

- *Plan your tactics.* Once you have developed a strategy for important communication opportunities throughout your day, take time to plan how to best accomplish your objectives. If you need to prepare materials such as visual resources, allot time for that work immediately after your strategy planning.

- *Plan to accomplish more routine tasks as your day wraps up.* For instance, if you have a job that involves email or chat interactions, save those for later in the day.

Chapter Review & Study Guide

Summary

In this chapter, you learned the following:

1. Workplace communication takes place within the context of an organization.

   - Organizations are generally classified as having one of four primary functions in society: economic production, political participation, integration, and pattern maintenance. Some organizations follow a hybrid model where they attempt to achieve outcomes related to more than one function.

   - Communication within organizations follows networks. These networks provide for formal communication flow, including upward communication, downward communication, and horizontal communication. Networks also allow informal, or "grapevine," communication.

2. Organizational assimilation is the formal and informal communication activities that help employees learn work roles,

become accustomed to standard practices, and enact core values of an organization.

- Anticipatory socialization is the process through which people intentionally and unintentionally learn about occupational possibilities and develop career expectations. Conducting a self-inventory, establishing a personal network, and using technology effectively are important communication strategies in this stage.

- Organizational encounter occurs after employees enter an organization and receive formal and informal training to succeed. During the encounter stage, preparing for a job interview, answering and asking questions effectively, and preparing for illegal questions are important communication strategies.

- Metamorphosis occurs when employees gain confidence in their organizational role, embrace the values of an organization, and begin to (re)define their roles. Communication strategies important during metamorphosis are socialization tactics, addressing unmet expectations, interpreting messages, information seeking, and learning the organization's culture.

3. During the metamorphosis stage, workplace communication competence involves using verbal and nonverbal communication effectively in a variety of organizational settings.

- Specific behaviors that contribute to your communication competence include immediacy, supportive communication, strategic ambiguity, interaction management, cross-cultural skills, conflict management, and customer service skills.

- Cross-cultural understanding requires that you act with sensitivity toward those who are different, including those who do not speak your language well.

- Conflict management approaches include avoidance, competition, compromise, accommodation, and collaboration. Each approach may have utility in specific situations; however, the collaborative approach works best in most situations.

- Customer service interaction skills include using compliance-gaining strategies with customers while engaging in emotional labor.

4. Unethical workplace communication includes aggressive communication, dishonesty, and sexual harassment.

- Workplace aggression occurs when individuals intentionally or unintentionally use verbal or nonverbal aggressive behaviors toward others.

- Dishonesty occurs when someone misrepresents, lies, or acts without integrity in how they communicate with others.

- Sexual harassment is the abuse of power involving either quid pro quo harassment or a hostile work environment.

Key Terms

Anticipatory socialization
Boundary spanner
Communication networks
Customer service encounter
Downward communication
Economic orientation
Emotional labor
Formal communication
Horizontal communication
Hostile work environment sexual harassment
Immediacy
Informal communication
Integration orientation
Interaction management
Job description
Metamorphosis
Organizational assimilation
Organizational communication
Organizational communities
Organizational encounter
Organizations
Pattern-maintenance orientation
Personal network
Political orientation
Quid pro quo sexual harassment
Sexual harassment
Strategic ambiguity
Supportive communication
Title IX officer
Upward communication

Study Questions

1. An organization with this orientation generates and distributes power and control within society.

   a. economic
   b. political
   c. pattern maintenance
   d. integration

2. Information flows in an organization through patterns of relationships known as

   a. communication networks.
   b. organizational communication.
   c. objective statements.
   d. pattern maintenance.

3. When information is transferred formally from workers to their boss, which type of communication takes place?

   a. horizontal
   b. societal
   c. political
   d. upward

4. During which stage of organizational assimilation should one use a job description to prepare for an interview?

   a. organizational encounter
   b. anticipatory socialization
   c. onboarding
   d. metamorphosis

5. Which workplace communication competence category includes behaviors surrounding giving and receiving feedback?

   a. organizing
   b. avoiding negative emotion
   c. relationship maintenance
   d. information sharing

6. During which stage of organizational assimilation should you be prepared to react to change and (re)define your work roles?

   a. organizational encounter
   b. anticipatory socialization
   c. onboarding
   d. metamorphosis

7. Which technique of conflict management is used to maintain relationship harmony but stifles creative dialogue and decision making?

   a. compromise
   b. accommodation
   c. avoidance
   d. collaboration

8. Customer service representatives are using which of the following compliance-gaining strategies when implying that it would be wrong not to comply?

   a. promises
   b. pre-giving
   c. threats
   d. moral appeals

9. Which type of aggressive workplace communication involves attempts to isolate a person from a larger group?

   a. abusive supervision
   b. bullying
   c. incivility
   d. social undermining

10. If your boss says, "You can leave work early on Fridays if you go on a date with me," this is a type of sexual harassment called

    a. quid pro quo sexual harassment.
    b. hostile work environment sexual harassment.
    c. emotional labor.
    d. nothing; it is not sexual harassment.

Answers:
1. (b); 2. (a); 3. (d); 4. (a); 5. (d); 6. (d); 7. (b); 8. (d); 9. (d); 10. (a)

Critical Thinking

1. Pick one organization that you have belonged to for some time. For example, you may select a workplace, a student organization, or your school. Reflect on the topic of metamorphosis and explain how you reacted to changes in the organizational environment and/or changes to your role in the organization. How did communication influence your reaction to those changes?

2. Think about some of your past jobs. In the workplace, did people display immediacy, supportiveness, strategic ambiguity, or interaction management? What did they do to demonstrate these behaviors? What conflict management skills did your supervisors use? Were they successful?

Sizing Things Up Scoring and Interpretation

Conflict in the Workplace

People have different natural orientations toward how conflict should be resolved. Although most people adapt to their circumstances to select approaches to conflict resolution, predispositions might make some options more likely than others. The Conflict in the Workplace scale assesses your predispositions toward five approaches for managing conflict.

You should average the responses to determine scores for each one of the five dimensions:

- *Avoidance:* attempting to deny the existence of conflict; items 3, 9, and 12
- *Competition:* viewing conflict as a battle; items 1, 8, and 15
- *Compromise:* being willing to negotiate away some things if others will as well; items 5, 7, and 11

- *Accommodation:* setting aside your views and accepting the views of another; items 2, 6, and 14
- *Collaboration:* using dialogue to reach a mutually beneficial solution; items 4, 10, and 13

As worded, this scale can be used to assess a general predisposition toward conflict resolution. You can adapt the scale by

tying it to various scenarios of conflict to determine whether approaches toward conflict resolution differ from situation to situation or because of the source of conflict, and so on. For example, you could complete the scale once when thinking about conflict with your roommate and again when thinking about conflict with your parents or another family member.

References

1. National Center for Education Statistics. (2022). College student employment. *Condition of Education.* U.S. Department of Education, Institute of Education Sciences. https://nces.ed.gov/programs/coe/indicator/ssa

2. Parsons, T. (1963). *Structure and process in modern societies.* Free Press.

3. Small Business Administration. (2018, August). Frequently asked questions. https://www.sba.gov/sites/default/files/advocacy/Frequently-Asked-Questions-Small-Business-2018.pdf

4. Ballotpedia. (2023, 6 January). List of political parties in the United States. http://ballotpedia.org/List_of_political_parties_in_the_United_States

5. Stohl, C. (1995). *Organizational communication: Connectedness in action.* Sage. (p. 18)

6. Drader, A. (2022, October 28). *Be a great leader, master the one-on-one* [Blog]. Growth Partners Consulting. https://www.growthpartnersconsulting.com/post/be-a-great-leader-master-the-one-on-one

7. Susskind, A. M., Schwartz, D. F., Richards, W. D., & Johnson, J. D., (2005). Evolution and diffusion of the Michigan State University tradition of organizational communication network research. *Communication Studies, 56,* 397–418.

8. Fay, M. J., & Kline, S. L. (2011). Coworker relationships and informal communication in high-intensity telecommuting. *Journal of Applied Communication Research, 39,* 144–163.

9. Caudron, S. (1998). They hear it through the grapevine. *Workforce, 77,* 25–27.

10. Monge, P., Heiss, B., & Margolin, D. (2008). Communication network evolution in organizational communities. *Communication Theory, 18,* 449–477.

11. Kokchhar, R., Parker, K., & R. Igielnik (2022, July 28). *Majority of U.S. workers changing jobs are seeing real wage gains.* Pew Research Center. https://www.pewresearch.org/social-trends/2022/07/28/majority-of-u-s-workers-changing-jobs-are-seeing-real-wage-gains/

12. Gupta, P., Prashar, A., Giannakis, M., Dudot, V., & Dwivedi, Y. (2022). How organizational socialization occurring in virtual setting unique: A longitudinal study of socialization. *Technological Forecasting & Social Change, 185.* https://doi.org/10.1016/j.techfore.2022.122097

13. Quast, L. (2013, April 15). How to conduct a personal SWOT analysis. *Forbes* [Online]. https://www.forbes.com/sites/lisaquast/2013/04/15/how-to-conduct-a-personal-s-w-o-t-analysis/#75b1c24328d8

14. Boase, J. (2008). Personal networks and the personal communication system. *Information, Communication & Society, 11,* 490–508.

15. Tey, C., Ang, S., & Van Dyne, L. (2006). Personality, biographical characteristics, and job interview success: A longitudinal study of the mediating effects of interviewing self-efficacy and the moderating effects of internal locus of causality. *Journal of Applied Psychology, 91,* 446–454.

16. Lawsuit free hiring: The 5 laws you need to know & 4 steps you need to take. (2010, January). *HR Specialist: Employment Law, 40,* 4.

17. YEC Council. (2020, August 7). Eight essential skills to look for in new hires. *Forbes.* https://www.forbes.com/sites/theyec/2020/08/07/eight-essential-skills-to-look-for-in-new-hires/?sh=392b2d6b3fa9

18. Kramer, M. W., & Miller, V. D. (2014). *Socialization and assimilation: Theories, processes, and outcomes.* In L. L. Putnam & D. K. Mumby (Eds.), *The Sage handbook of organizational communication: Advances in theory, research, and methods* (3rd Ed.). Sage.

19. *2022 state of remote work.* (2022). Buffer. https://buffer.com/state-of-remote-work/2022

20. Keyton, J., Caputo, J. M., Fore, E. A., Fu, R., Leibowitz, S. A., Liu, T., . . . & Wu, C. (2013). Investigating verbal workplace communication behaviors. *Journal of Business Communication, 50,* 152–169.

21. Teven, J. J., McCroskey, J. C., & Richmond, V. P. (2006). Communication correlates of perceived Machiavellianism of supervisors: Communication orientations and outcomes. *Communication Quarterly, 54,* 127–142.

22. Lee, D. & LaRose, R. (2011). The impact of personalized social cues of immediacy on consumers' information disclosure: A social cognitive approach. *CyberPsychology, Behavior, & Social Networking, 14,* 337–343.

23. Alegre, I., Mas-Machuca, M., & Berbegal-Mirabent, J. (2016). Antecedents of employee job satisfaction: Do they matter? *Journal of Business Research, 69*, 1390–1395. https://doi.org/10.1016/j.busres.2015.10.113

24. Albrecht, T. L., & Bach, B. W. (1997). *Communication in complex organizations: A relational approach.* Harcourt Brace.

25. Eisenberg, E. M. (1984). Ambiguity as strategy in organizational communication. *Communication Monographs, 51*, 227–242.

26. Clark, D. (2014, June 19). How to succeed in a cross-cultural workplace. *Forbes.* https://www.forbes.com/sites/dorieclark/2014/06/19/how-to-succeed-in-a-cross-cultural-workplace/#59a72fa5c972

27. Wilmot, W. W., & Hocker, J. L. (2005). *Interpersonal conflict* (7th ed.). McGraw-Hill.

28. Bitner, M. J., Booms, B. H., & Tetreault, M. S. (1990). The service encounter: Diagnosing favorable and unfavorable incidents. *Journal of Marketing, 54*, 71–84. (p. 71)

29. Chi, N.-W., & Chen, P.-C. (2019). Relationship matters: How relational factors moderate the effects of emotional labor on long-term customer outcomes. *Journal of Business Research, 95*, 277–291. https://doi.org/10.1016/j.jbusres.2018.08.019

30. Arcy, J. (2016). Emotion work: Considering gender in digital labor. *Feminist Media Studies, 16*(2), 365–368. https://doi.org/10.1080/14680777.2016.1138609

31. Hayton, J. W. (2017). "They need to learn to take It on the chin": Exploring the Emotional Labour of student volunteers in a sports-based outreach project in the North East of England. *Sociology of Sport Journal, 34*, 136–147. https://doi.org/10.1123/ssj.2016-0098

32. Hochschild, A. (1983). *The managed heart: Commercialization of human feeling.* University of California Press.

33. Tracy, S. (2005). Locking up emotion: Moving beyond dissonance for understanding emotional labor discomfort. *Communication Monographs, 72*, 261–283.

34. Infante, D., Riddle, B., Horvath, G., & Tumlin, S. (1992). Verbal aggressiveness: Messages and reasons. *Communication Quarterly, 40*, 116–126.

35. Herschovis, M. S. (2011). "Incivility, social undermining, bullying . . oh my!": A call to reconcile constructs within workplace aggression research. *Journal of Organizational Behavior, 32*, 499–519.

36. Amare, N., & Manning, A. (2009). Writing for the robot: How employer search tools have influenced résumé rhetoric and ethics. *Business Communication Quarterly, 72*, 35–60. https://doi.org/10.1177/1080569908330383

37. Equal Employment Opportunity Commission. (n.d.). *Sexual Harassment.* http://www.eeoc.gov/laws/types/sexual_harassment.cfm

38. Garber, M. (2018, January 2). *Is this the next step for the #MeToo movement?* The Atlantic [Online]. https://www.theatlantic.com/entertainment/archive/2018/01/beyond-metoo-can-times-up-effect-real-change/549482/

39. Matthews, S. J., Giuliano, T. A., Thomas, K. H., Straup, M. L., & Martinez, M. A. (2018). Not cool, dude: Perceptions of solicited vs. unsolicited sext messages from men and women. *Computers in Human Behavior, 88*, 1–4. https://doi.org/10.1016/j.chb.2018.06.014

40. Resnik, D. B., & Randall, D. C. (2018). Reporting suspected abuse or neglect in research involving children. *Journal of Medical Ethics, 44*, 555–559. https://doi.org/10.1136/medethics-2017-104452

41. Haden, J. (2022, November 11). *New neuroscience reveals the best way to structure your day.* Inc. https://www.inc.com/jeff-haden/new-neuroscience-reveals-best-way-to-structure-your-workday.html

Edhar Yuralaits/123RF

topic selection and audience analysis

How do you choose what to speak about? Many public speakers get stuck on this first step in creating a speech and spend way too much time trying to decide on a topic. They have too many choices and cannot settle on just one. So this chapter will help you to more quickly determine what topics are important to you and to your audience, how to more rapidly narrow the focus so that you do not waste time by exploring too many avenues, and how to accurately analyze the audience to make sure they will care about what you have to say. Your ability to effectively inform or persuade an audience rests on your skill in selecting an appropriate topic and in adapting that topic to the particular audience. Once you have mastered these skills for your classroom audience, you can apply them at work and in the community.

As an undergraduate student, Maddie Sloat transformed her passion for social issues in her community into *The Period Project*, an initiative dedicated to providing period hygiene products to local women in poverty. As a public advocate for this cause, Sloat stated in an interview, "I think because women are supposed to be lady-like, and we're supposed to keep things to ourselves, we've created this taboo around menstruation, because it's turned into this shameful, personal issue. Really, it's not. It's something that affects half of the global population."[1]

Maddie Sloat, founder of The Period Project, purchases $500 worth of products for a local shelter.

Aliviah Chaplin

Suppose you shared Sloat's conviction and wanted to advocate for better access to women's hygiene products as part of a class presentation. To prepare your presentation, you would need to start by asking yourself how much you know about this issue in your community. For instance, are there luxury taxes on hygiene products in your state that could make access difficult for women living in poverty? Next, you would have to determine how passionate you are about the topic. Finally, you would need to analyze your audience's perceptions and level of knowledge about the topic, and then adapt your message accordingly. As Sloat noted, there is a taboo surrounding this topic, so how will you confront that challenge when presenting your ideas?

How you select and focus your topic is critical to the success of your presentation. In this chapter you will learn some quick and effective ways to arrive at a topic without wasting time and effort. You will also learn how to size up your audience so that you successfully inform and persuade them.

How to Select a Topic Appropriate for You and Your Audience

Finding a topic that is right for you and for your audience can be a challenge. Some speakers spend far too little time finding a suitable topic and end up speaking on something that audience members cannot connect with. Others spend too long searching for topics, get forced into making a last-minute decision, and sacrifice valuable preparation time. Although you should devote adequate attention to thoughtful topic selection, this step should require only a small amount of your speech preparation time. This section explores some strategies for making an efficient and effective choice, beginning with two ways to quickly generate a list of ideas.

USE BRAINSTORMING

Brainstorming consists of thinking of as many topics as you can in a limited time so that you can select one that will be appropriate for you and your audience. Individual brainstorming (brainstorming by yourself as opposed to in a group) can be an effective way to find a topic for your public speech, reports, and term papers. Selecting a topic from a list of many that you've generated through brainstorming can be much easier than trying to think of just one perfect idea. Research shows that the quality of brainstorming increases as people brainstorm more topics.[2] Furthermore, the most effective results of brainstorming tend to appear later in the brainstorming process. The researchers reason that as people brainstorm, they continually refine their ideas to make them more concrete and effective.

You'll find individual brainstorming to be relatively quick and easy. First, give yourself a limited time—say, five minutes—and without trying to think of titles or even complete thoughts, write down as many potential topics that interest you as you can. When your time is up, you should have a rough list of possible ideas or topics for your speech. Repeat this step if you want an even larger list.

Second, select the *three* items from your list that are the most appealing to you as topics for your speech. Third, from those three topics choose the *one* you think would be most appealing to both you and your audience. An alternative strategy, which we look at next, is to target your own interests as possible topics.

SURVEY YOUR INTERESTS

Public speaking starts with the self—with what you know, have experienced, or are willing to learn. Self-analysis can help you uncover the areas in which you are qualified to speak.

To survey your interests, consider the following:

- What do you like best and least at work; about family life; about your community; and about our government, politics, and policies?
- What causes take up your time and energy: your religion, your political party, and your position on important current issues?
- What particular issues bother you personally that you want to bring to the attention of others: discrimination, environmental concerns, and health care?
- What topics are the focus of podcasts, YouTube videos, TED Talks, or blogs that you view?

How do you select from among the topics that emerge through your brainstorming or a survey of your interests? After identifying potential topics from your personal interests, you must then assess your knowledge and commitment to the topic. The ideal topic for your presentation is one about which you are highly knowledgeable and for which you have great passion. Topics for which you are have great passion but less knowledge are also effective provided that you have adequate time to conduct additional research.

ASSESS YOUR KNOWLEDGE OF THE TOPIC

Once you have established that your topic is interesting to you and to your audience, you need to determine what you and your audience know about the subject. You are in the best position if you know more about the topic than the audience does. You can identify what you already know and what you still need to know about your topic by making several lists. The first list should describe all the information you can recall about the topic. The second list should identify information you still want to learn about the topic. A third list should identify what you think your audience already knows or needs to know about the topic. This will be helpful as you begin your research.

For example, let's say a family member was recently diagnosed with type 2 diabetes and, as a result, you have become interested in the issue. As you consider presenting an informative speech about type 2 diabetes, you would first make a list of all the things you already know about this illness. Next, you would make a list of all the information you need to learn more about related to type 2 diabetes. For instance, perhaps you do not know what parts of the body are affected by the illness or how it is different from type 1 diabetes. This list will help you begin gathering ideas for future research. Finally, it would be useful to think about what aspects of this illness your audience might already know and where they might be confused or need additional clarification. Later in this chapter you will learn several ways to analyze your audience so that you know how best to adapt your presentation to their needs.

EVALUATE YOUR COMMITMENT TO THE TOPIC

Even a topic about which you're well informed is not a good choice for a presentation unless you feel some commitment to it. **Commitment** is a measure of how much time and effort you put into a cause. For example, you know many children are waiting to be adopted, you deeply want more people to be concerned about heart disease and cancer because your relatives died from these diseases, or you want less government interference in our personal lives. You spend time and effort on what you care about, so those causes can guide you to select an ideal topic for you and your audience.

commitment
A measure of how much time and effort you put into a cause; your passion and concern about the topic.

Be aware, however, that commitment to a topic may not be enough to overcome poor preparation. A study exploring whether commitment to a topic is related to speech performance found it was not; the strongest predictor of speech performance is the work put into preparation.[3] Although you may need to be committed to a topic to put in adequate preparation for a speech, commitment may not be enough to help you deliver an effective presentation.

CONSIDER THE RELEVANCE OF THE TOPIC

You will want to consider the relevance of the topic to your audience. Some topics have endured for decades, if not centuries:

- How much should government be allowed to intervene in our lives?
- Should the United States use military force to promote democracy?
- What can and should we do for people who are living in poverty and marginalized in our society?
- What is the best balance between government regulation and the protection of citizens?
- Should concern for the environment limit our exploration for oil?

Even very young people have probably heard plenty about many long-standing issues, although more mature audiences, including returning college students, are likely to have more sophisticated ideas about them. Younger audiences may have less hardened positions, however. What all this means is that groups of different ages can be treated differently. You will also want to treat mature topics in new ways, not just rehash what the audience has heard repeatedly in the past. The effective presenter takes into account both the age of the issue and the age of the audience and skillfully adapts the topic to the particular audience for maximum effect.

building behaviors

Using the Internet to Increase Your Knowledge of the Topic

You can find information about any topic by using Google or another search engine and appropriate key words. To find specific information and some unique sources for your topic, take a close look at podcasts. You can find them by doing an internet search for "podcast directory." Select a particular category—for instance, "environment"—and you will usually find hundreds of podcasts that reveal specific information about topics such as "living green." Take care to evaluate the information you hear on podcasts—some podcasts are based more on research or have expert guests and therefore are more reliable than others. As always, remember to disclose in your speech where you found your information.

Here are some suggestions that can keep you on track to success because violating these three suggestions has resulted in poor evaluations for students who ignore them:

- Stick to vital topics; do not select a trivial topic. You might find TikTok videos on making sandwiches fascinating, but the topic is neither vital nor necessarily of interest to a general audience.
- Beware of overused topics—unless you have a novel approach. Gun control and puppy mills are important topics, but unless you have something new to offer, it is likely your audience has heard about these topics.
- Do not demonstrate with visual resources that are banned on campus, such as firearms, illegal drugs, and alcohol.

sizing things up

Evaluating Topics

Brainstorming and eventually selecting an effective speech topic begins with a thorough self-assessment of your own interests and knowledge. Below you will find several topics followed by pairs of opposing adjectives arranged on a scale, or continuum. Check the space on the continuum that best represents your opinion of each topic's appropriateness as a subject for you to speak about. The space closest to "interesting," for example, represents "extremely interesting," and the space in the middle of each pair stands for "neutral." This exercise has no right or wrong answers, but if your teacher approves, you can compare your answers with those of others in your class. You might learn something about your captive audience's attitudes in the process. For additional information, refer to the guide for interpreting your responses that appears at the end of this chapter.

1. Politics
Interesting (5) (4) (3) (2) (1) Uninteresting
Good   (5) (4) (3) (2) (1) Bad
Confident   (5) (4) (3) (2) (1) Not Confident
Relevant   (5) (4) (3) (2) (1) Irrelevant

2. The Environment
Interesting (5) (4) (3) (2) (1) Uninteresting
Good   (5) (4) (3) (2) (1) Bad
Confident   (5) (4) (3) (2) (1) Not Confident
Relevant   (5) (4) (3) (2) (1) Irrelevant

3. The Economy
Interesting (5) (4) (3) (2) (1) Uninteresting
Good   (5) (4) (3) (2) (1) Bad
Confident   (5) (4) (3) (2) (1) Not Confident
Relevant   (5) (4) (3) (2) (1) Irrelevant

4. Education
Interesting (5) (4) (3) (2) (1) Uninteresting
Good   (5) (4) (3) (2) (1) Bad

Confident   (5) (4) (3) (2) (1) Not Confident
Relevant   (5) (4) (3) (2) (1) Irrelevant

5. Health
Interesting (5) (4) (3) (2) (1) Uninteresting
Good   (5) (4) (3) (2) (1) Bad
Confident   (5) (4) (3) (2) (1) Not Confident
Relevant   (5) (4) (3) (2) (1) Irrelevant

6. Technology
Interesting (5) (4) (3) (2) (1) Uninteresting
Good   (5) (4) (3) (2) (1) Bad
Confident   (5) (4) (3) (2) (1) Not Confident
Relevant   (5) (4) (3) (2) (1) Irrelevant

7. Diversity
Interesting (5) (4) (3) (2) (1) Uninteresting
Good   (5) (4) (3) (2) (1) Bad
Confident   (5) (4) (3) (2) (1) Not Confident
Relevant   (5) (4) (3) (2) (1) Irrelevant

8. Religion
Interesting (5) (4) (3) (2) (1) Uninteresting
Good   (5) (4) (3) (2) (1) Bad
Confident   (5) (4) (3) (2) (1) Not Confident
Relevant   (5) (4) (3) (2) (1) Irrelevant

9. Interpersonal conflict
Interesting (5) (4) (3) (2) (1) Uninteresting
Good   (5) (4) (3) (2) (1) Bad
Confident   (5) (4) (3) (2) (1) Not Confident
Relevant   (5) (4) (3) (2) (1) Irrelevant

10. Poverty
Interesting (5) (4) (3) (2) (1) Uninteresting
Good   (5) (4) (3) (2) (1) Bad
Confident   (5) (4) (3) (2) (1) Not Confident
Relevant   (5) (4) (3) (2) (1) Irrelevant

Once you have selected a possible topic, evaluate whether it is important to your audience. First, you have the advantage of hearing every speech your classmates deliver, so their topic selections give you a good idea of what they think are important subjects. Second, you are in a college context where important issues arise about student rights to freedom of expression and the costs of tuition, books, food, and lodging; and often guest speakers come on campus to address issues of interest to college students. Third, your college exists in a community where issues occur between town and gown: noise ordinances, parking restrictions, housing and zoning regulations, and overpriced housing. Fourth, you can be among the few who actually know about the larger context to national and international issues that can affect students whether they know it or not. So you can be among the first to warn them of issues such as recessions, employment trends, interest rates, food insecurity, and new legislation or U.S. Supreme Court decisions that will affect them now or in the near future. The importance of a topic, then, can be as close to home as another student's speech or as far away as financial failure in a distant land, as long as you can relate that topic by demonstrating its importance to your audience.

Practice Narrowing Your Topic

Even after thinking about their topic's importance and their own knowledge and commitment, beginning presenters often select a topic that is too large for their time limit. Ending animal cruelty, addressing food insecurity among college students, knowing how to buy a car, and overcoming an addiction may meet the requirements of importance, knowledge, and commitment, but they are too broad. They will produce hundreds of sources, giving you much more information than you can manage. If you take the time to carefully narrow a topic *before* you begin your search for additional information, you can save much time and even more frustration. Speakers can narrow a speech topic by using an approach called *concept mapping*. Figure 10.1 shows one example of concept mapping. Starting with the general topic of college, the speaker is able to visually identify four subtopics: applying to college, types of colleges, programs offered, and financial aid. Each subtopic is broken down further into more specific areas. Visually mapping the topic-narrowing step in this

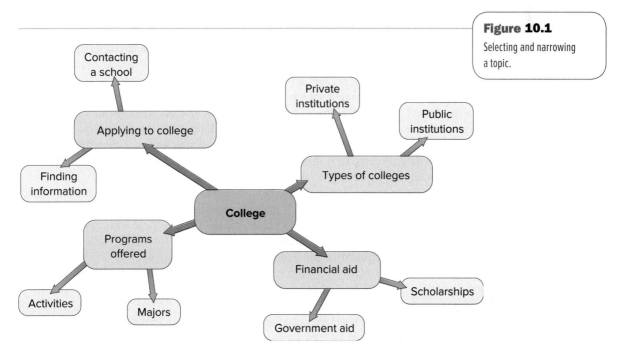

Figure 10.1
Selecting and narrowing a topic.

way can help you see important dimensions of a particular topic as well as connections between several dimensions of the topic.

Another way to narrow a topic is to take a broad and even abstract category, such as music, and list as many smaller topics as you can that are at least loosely related to it:

- The development of country/western music
- The influence of Prince on music and gender roles
- Music therapy
- Elementary music education
- The history of the electric guitar
- Hip-hop artists as role models

Extend your list of more specific and concrete topics until you have a large number from which to choose.

How will you know when your topic is narrow enough? Consider the following: (1) the amount of information available about it, (2) the amount of information you can convey within the time limits for the speech, and (3) whether you can discuss the topic in enough depth to keep audience members interested.

Still another approach is to examine lists of topics that are current and have interest among your audience members, such as foodborne illnesses, food insecurity, student loan forgiveness, or net neutrality. For example, the topic "Name-Image-Likeness (NIL) for Student Athletes" is a national issue that affects students at nearly every university. Recent policy changes at universities, in state legislatures, and in national athletic governing organizations now allow student athletes to earn income from their NIL used in advertisements, public engagements, and other events. Although NIL opportunities benefit student athletes, some argue that NIL essentially transforms college athletics into a pay-for-play experience, especially for the most productive athletes.[4] Presentations on this topic can analyze the benefits and problems associated with NIL as they affect students, universities, and college athletics as a whole.

Analyze Your Audience

audience analysis
The collection and interpretation of audience information obtained by observation, inference, research, or questionnaires.

Audience analysis is the collection and interpretation of audience characteristics through observation, inference, research, and questionnaires. Why should you analyze your audience? Especially, why should you analyze an audience of classmates?

Suppose you are giving a speech arguing that universities should enact tougher policies to protect free speech on college campuses. To give an effective presentation, you should know not only state law (many states have statutes that provide specific mandates for the protection of free speech) but also how most of your audience members feel about free speech on your campus. If they agree with your view, you will probably take a different persuasive approach than if they disagree.

If you plan to inform audience members about the benefits of student athletes benefiting from Name-Image-Likeness (NIL) incentives for playing college sports, you will want to know if anyone in the audience has played college sports. Those who have might have different feelings than nonathletes about being compensated for their athletic skills, which will influence their attitudes about your information.

In both of these examples, you must use audience analysis to learn about your audience members' beliefs and backgrounds; such information will be invaluable as you select and narrow your topic.

Audience analysis for public speaking is similar to target marketing in advertising and public relations. The process can be as simple as surveying a group to determine age, gender, and race or ethnicity or as complicated as polling a group of people to discover their feelings on your topic. The insights you gain about the people to whom you speak will ensure that your speech is as effective as possible.

Next we examine four methods of analyzing an audience. They are based on your observations of the audience, your inferences, your research, and your questions and their answers.

OBSERVATION

Effective public speakers must engage in active observation, using their senses of sight, hearing, smell, and touch to build information about their audience. An effective lawyer observes jurors' verbal and nonverbal behavior and decides which arguments, evidence, and witnesses are influencing them. Activists and fund-raisers have usually spent years watching others and learning which approaches, arguments, and evidence are most likely to be accepted by an audience.

building behaviors

Sizing Up Your Audience

Some people are much better than others at sizing up an audience. Evaluate your own skill at analyzing an audience by inferring audience characteristics. For example, what is the approximate range in age, what cultures are represented, how many individuals wear attire or symbols that indicate their religion, how many wear athletic attire, do any have the names of fraternities or sororities on their clothing, and do any wear uniforms that indicate armed forces or the kind of work they do? Perhaps your instructor will allow you to check the accuracy of your inferences if classmates are willing to reveal some of this information.

You can learn to observe your class. For every speech you give, you might listen to 20 or 25 given by others, each of which gives you a unique opportunity to discover your classmates' responses. Do they respond well to speakers who come on strong or to speakers who talk to them as equals? Do they like speeches about work, leisure, or ambition? Do they respond well to numbers and statistics, stories and examples, or graphs and pictures displayed using PowerPoint? Even though your classroom audience may not have gathered just to hear you, you have an advantage over most public speakers: after all, how many of them have had the opportunity to hear every one of their listeners give a speech? Your classmates' responses to a variety of speakers, topics, and visual resources will give you a rich base of information about this audience, which you can use to your advantage when it is your turn to speak.

INFERENCE

To draw an **inference** is to make a tentative generalization based on some evidence. We infer from a person's wedding band that they are married, and from the children tugging at their sleeve that they are a parent. We infer that the person holding their arm is their spouse. We are basing these inferences on thin data, and they may be incorrect. The more evidence on which an inference is based, the more likely it is to be accurate.

inference
A tentative generalization based on some evidence.

You can base inferences on the observed characteristics of your audience, on demographic information, and on information obtained from questionnaires (discussed later in this section). An **indirect inference** is one we draw by observation. You might, for example, find that most of the students at a particular college hold part-time jobs (an observation). You might further infer that the school is expensive, that financial aid is limited, or that the cost of area housing is high. You might also infer, from your limited information, that most of the students in this school value their education, are exceptionally well motivated, or believe in saving money.

indirect inference
A tentative generalization based on observation.

A **direct inference** is based on deliberately gathered data. You could, for example, ask either orally or in writing how many students in the class have part- or full-time jobs; how many are married, have families, or have grown children; how many plan to become wealthy; whether they were raised in an urban, a suburban, or a rural setting; and how many have

direct inference
A tentative generalization based on deliberately gathered data.

strong religious ties. The answers to these questions provide valuable information about your audience. If you plan to deliver a presentation encouraging your audience to support veterans, your teacher will likely allow you to ask your classroom full of listeners how many of them have friends or relative who are veterans. Their answers to a simple question or two will certainly give you a head start on informing or persuading them.

RESEARCH ON YOUR AUDIENCE

When speaking outside the classroom, you can improve your chances of success by carefully researching your audience. That research can include inside informants, others who belong to the group, and an organization's website. Often the best inside informant is the person who invited you to speak to a group. Because you are a successful athlete, a high school asks you to speak at its annual athletic awards banquet. You will want to know from the person who invited you who is going to be in the audience (athletes only, or their parents and friends as well?), where the presentation is going to occur (in a crowded gym, a hotel banquet room?), how long you are expected to speak, and what they would like you to talk about. Similarly if you are asked to speak to a student club or a nonprofit organization, you need to ask similar questions.

In addition, you will want to research the organization. Girls on the Run, for example, is a nonprofit organization that uses running to encourage girls' fitness and confidence through small running teams.[5] In addition to using running as a form of physical fitness, the girls attend workshops that focus on personal development, teamwork, and relationships. Fortunately, you can find out more about them and other service organizations through online searches because most business, social, and religious groups have websites that detail their purpose. You can adapt your message to a group of nonrunners or male college students by knowing the mission of Girls on the Run.

THE QUESTIONNAIRE

A more formal way to collect data on which you can base inferences is to ask your audience to fill out a **questionnaire** consisting of written questions developed to obtain the demographic characteristics and the attitudes, beliefs, and values of your audience.

Finding Demographic Characteristics

An important step in the process of speech preparation is discovering the audience's demographic characteristics. The term *demographics* means "the characteristics of the people." **Demographic analysis** is the collection and interpretation of data about the characteristics of people: name, age, gender, hometown, year in school, race or ethnicity, major subject, religion, and organizational affiliations. By describing the audience in detail, demographic information can reveal to public speakers the extent to which they will have to adapt themselves and their topics to their listeners.

Seasoned public speakers usually rely heavily on demographic information. Politicians send staff ahead to find out how many blue-collar workers, faithful party members, older adults, union members, and hecklers they are likely to encounter. They consult opinion polls, population studies, and reliable persons in the area to discover the nature of a prospective audience. Conducting a demographic analysis of your class can serve a similar purpose—analysis will help you design a speech better adapted to your audience.

The groups to which your audience members belong, for instance, can signal support for or hostility toward your topic. How can you learn about these groups? Stickers you observe on students' computers can signal your audience's attitudes about coffee corporations, sustainability, and political parties. In the classroom, many signs, such as jackets or shirts with slogans, religious symbols and attire, sorority or fraternity letters, or ethnic dress, indicate memberships that may also reflect attitudes about topics.

questionnaire
A set of written questions developed to obtain demographic and attitudinal information.

demographic analysis
The collection and interpretation of data about the characteristics of people.

As one example, Diego wanted to deliver a persuasive speech on student loan forgive-ness, so he asked before class one day how many students in the class obtained loans for their schooling. Most did. He knew from the outset that he had potentially strong support in the audience, but he also knew that he had selected a topic that required persuasion to change the audience's mind about the potential economic effects of forgiving student debt. He started his speech by addressing some issues discussed in the media about loan forgiveness: students are irresponsible, taxpayers should not bail out rich kids, forgiveness is unfair to those who have already paid, and forgiveness will harm the financial system. Diego's approach to audience analysis allowed him to tailor his speech in a way that sup-ported his persuasive call to action: to have audience members combat disinformation about student loan forgiveness. Diego asked just one question of his audience before class; you can do the same or develop a very brief questionnaire. You can gather and summarize demographic information from questions similar to the following:

_____1. I am
    a. a first-year student.
    b. a sophomore.
    c. a junior.
    d. a senior.

_____2. I am
    a. 17–21 years old.
    b. 22–35 years old.
    c. 36–45 years old.
    d. over 45 years old.

_____3. I am
    a. single.
    b. married.
    c. divorced or separated.
    d. widowed.

_____4. I have
    a. no children.
    b. one child.
    c. two children.
    d. more than two children.

The audience members do not have to identify themselves by name to provide this infor-mation. Keeping the questionnaires anonymous encourages honest answers and does not reduce the value of the information.

Finding Attitudes, Beliefs, and Values

You can also use questionnaires to discern audience attitudes, beliefs, and values on an issue before giving the speech. An **attitude** is a predisposition to respond favorably or unfavorably to a person, an object, an idea, or an event. Attitudes are regarded as quite stable and often difficult to change. If your audience shares many attitudes, beliefs, and values, your audience analysis may be easy. However, if they differ you will have to do a more in-depth audience analysis to uncover their viewpoints. For example, a speech about police body cameras may be received differently at a local police department than at a local community relations committee meeting.

Attitudes toward politics, sexual identity, religion, drugs, and even work vary in dif-ferent geographic areas and cultures. Regardless of the purpose of your speech, the atti-tudes of audience members will make a difference in the appropriateness of your topic and the way you present it. For this reason effective public speakers learn as much as possible about audience attitudes before they speak. Some examples of attitudes follow:

attitude
A predisposition to re-spond favorably or unfa-vorably to a person, an object, an idea, or an event.

Anti-government	Pro-business	Pro-conservation
Anti-gun control	Pro-green	Pro-technology
Anti-pollution	Pro-choice	Pro-vaccination
Anti-immigration	Pro-life	Anti-refugee
Pro-animal rights	Anti-tax	Pro-free trade

belief
A conviction; often thought to be more enduring than an attitude and less enduring than a value.

A **belief** is a conviction. Beliefs are usually considered more enduring than attitudes, but our attitudes often spring from our beliefs. Your belief in healthy eating habits may lead to a negative attitude toward overeating and obesity and a positive attitude toward balanced meals and nutrition. Your audience's beliefs make a difference in how they respond to your speech. They may believe in upward mobility through higher education, in higher pay through hard work, or in social welfare. Or they may not believe in any of these ideas. Beliefs are like anchors to which our attitudes are attached. To discover the beliefs of an audience, you need to ask questions and to observe carefully. Some examples of beliefs follow:

value
A deeply rooted belief that governs our attitude about something.

Hard work pays off.

Good people will be rewarded.

Taxes are too high.

Work comes before play.

Anyone can get rich.

Government should be small.

Education pays.

Wickedness will be punished.

Knowing your audience's beliefs about your topic can be a valuable aid in informing and persuading them.

A **value** is a deeply rooted belief that governs our attitude about something. Both beliefs and attitudes can be traced to a value we hold. Learned from childhood through family, religion, school, and many other sources, values are often so much a foundation for the rest of what we believe and know that we do not question them. Sometimes we remain unaware of our primary values until they clash. For example, a person might have an unquestioned belief that people have the right to be and do whatever they wish—basic values of individuality and freedom—until it comes to sexuality.

You can collect information on attitudes, beliefs, and values in at least three ways. One way is through a questionnaire that places audience members in identifiable groups, as the following questions do:

_____ 1. I am

    a. active in organizations.

    b. not active in organizations.

_____ 2. I see myself as

    a. conservative.

    b. liberal.

    c. independent.

_____ 3. I see myself as

    a. strongly religious.

    b. moderately religious.

    c. not religious.

engaging diversity

Dangerous Speech Project

Susan Benesch, a human rights lawyer at Harvard University, founded the Dangerous Speech Project to study dangerous speech and ways to counteract it. More specifically, the project works to identify inflammatory language that can motivate groups to violence. The Dangerous Speech Project contends that incendiary public speech increases steadily before outbreaks of mass violence and is found in many languages, cultures, and religions. Part of the mission of the project is to distinguish "dangerous" speech from other forms of distasteful and offensive language that typically do not give rise to violence.

Benesch uses five contextual elements that form the "dangerous speech guidelines" for identifying dangerous speeches:

1. The speeches take place in social or historical contexts rife with violence—for example, long-standing struggles for scarce resources.

2. The audience has grievances or fears that speakers use to their advantage.

3. The speakers are highly influential and charismatic.

4. The messages of the speeches are clearly understandable as calls to violence.

5. The speakers employ an influential medium—typically radio or television.

A major goal of the Dangerous Speech Project is to find the best ways to prevent violence. To do so, the project works not only to make audiences less motivated to respond with violence but also to diminish the use of dangerous speech in a way that protects freedom of expression.

Source: Dangerous Speech Project. 2022. *What is dangerous speech?* https://dangerousspeech.org/about-dangerous-speech/

Table 10.1 Ranking Values

Rank five of the following values in their order of importance to you. If you can also persuade some of your classmates or the entire class to do this, you will have information that will help you prepare your speech.

_____ Wisdom	_____ Wealth	_____ Fame
_____ World peace	_____ Security	_____ Health
_____ Freedom	_____ Fulfillment	_____ Love
_____ Equality	_____ Education	_____ Faith

How does your ranking compare with those of your classmates? What other values might help you with your speech?

A second method is to ask people to rank values, such as hard work, higher education, high pay, and security, using a scale such as the one in Table 10.1. People's ranking of their values can provide additional information about their attitudes and beliefs.

The third method is to list word concepts that reveal attitudes and then ask respondents to assess their attitudes toward these specific issues, using an attitudinal scale such as the one in Figure 10.2. The reactions to these and similar words or phrases can provide information that will help you approach your audience successfully. For example, if most persons in your audience are neutral to mildly favorable toward taxing tobacco, then your speech advocating higher tobacco taxes could be designed to move their attitudes from mildly favorable to strongly favorable. If the responses are negative, then you may have to work just to move your audience closer to a mildly unfavorable attitude or toward neutrality.

The values your audience members hold and the order in which they rank them can provide important clues about their attitudes and beliefs. A speaker who addresses an audience without knowing its members' values is taking a risk that can be avoided through careful audience analysis. The relationships among attitudes, beliefs, and values are illustrated in Figure 10.3.

Figure 10.2

Sample attitudinal scale. Compile data that indicate the attitudes of your classmates on one of these topics. What does this information tell you about how to approach your audience about this topic?

For each word or phrase, indicate your attitude toward it by determining how strongly you favor or disfavor it.

	Strongly favor	Mildly favor	Neutral	Mildly disfavor	Strongly disfavor
Government bailouts of business	◯	◯	◯	◯	◯
Unions' right to collective bargaining	◯	◯	◯	◯	◯
Student loan forgiveness	◯	◯	◯	◯	◯
Employer-sponsored childcare	◯	◯	◯	◯	◯
Military spending	◯	◯	◯	◯	◯
Recreational marijuana	◯	◯	◯	◯	◯

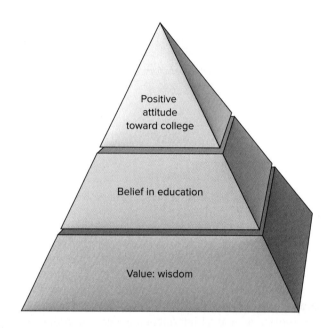

Figure 10.3

Relationships among attitudes, beliefs, and values.

• The public speaker must consider opinions among audience members that reflect different values.

Rena Schild/Shutterstock

Adapt to the Audience

Audience analysis yields information about your listeners that enables you to adapt yourself and your message to that audience. A speech is not imposed on a collection of listeners; a message is negotiated between a speaker and an audience and is designed to inform, entertain, inspire, teach, or persuade that audience. This negotiation is based on your analysis of your audience.

ADAPTING YOURSELF

In public speaking you have to adjust to information about the audience. Just as a college senior preparing for a job interview adapts to an interviewer in dress, manner, and language, a public speaker prepares for an audience by adapting to its expectations. How you look, how you behave, and what you say should be carefully tailored to your audience and the occasion. For most college classrooms, business casual attire is appropriate for speeches.

ADAPTING YOUR LANGUAGE

The language you use in your speech, as well as your gestures, movements, and even facial expressions, should be adapted to your audience. Recall the aspects of language to use and avoid from Chapter 3 as you work on adapting your speech to your audience. Additionally, you should note that audience members may not correctly comprehend what you say. To account for this, adapt your presentation by speaking clearly to emphasize key points, show key phrases or terms on a slide, repeat key ideas for emphasis, and carefully monitor nonverbal feedback from audience members for signs of misunderstanding.

ADAPTING YOUR TOPIC

Public speakers should be permitted to speak on nearly any topic; after all, the First Amendment provides some protection for free speech. However, practical considerations may lead you to avoid certain topics, which will typically be unique to specific situations and contexts. For instance, you would almost certainly never speak about how to create biological weapons or commit financial fraud.

communicating creatively

Delivering a Provocative Speech

To engage your audience, you must deliver a provocative speech. Public speaking coach Anett Grant suggests that speakers can effectively use provocative language and ideas to accomplish the following:

- *Cut through clutter and confusion.* Provocative speakers challenge their audience by stating positions unequivocally and without hesitation. For example, rather than just telling the audience that the state of math education in the United States is cause for concern, provocative speakers ask the audience to take risks to make change happen. This might include a call to action to remove calculus and trigonometry classes from schools and teach students how to use real world data, such as census data or household spending trends.

- *Get audience members' attention.* Provocative speakers use language, emotion, and body language to get attention. Grant explains that these actions are like a siren on an emergency vehicle. When using provocative language or presenting provocative ideas, you are likely to arouse curiosity and focus from your audience.

- *Create solidarity.* Provocative speakers frame clear perspectives on situations that may resonate with audience members. For instance, if you claim that a certain university policy is unfair to students, your classmates may immediately view you as a leader who advocates for their interests.

Although provocative language and ideas have the potential to make you and your speech more dynamic, Grant warns that you can have too much of a good thing. Being bold with your message can improve your speech, but going to the extreme of being overly dramatic or polarizing can diminish your credibility and alienate audience members. Effective speakers consider how to best push their stances while appearing reasonable, knowledgeable, and trustworthy.

Source: Grant, A. (2018, November 3). *4 instances where provocative language can be effective (and when it goes too far).* Fastcompany. www.fastcompany.com/90261716/4-instances-where-provocative-language-can-be-effective-and-when-it-goes-too-far

communicating
with agility

Pandemic Personalities

The social effects of the COVID-19 pandemic will linger for some time. For some, positive effects have included recognizing the importance of personal connections and learning to bake sourdough bread. However, a recent study found that as a result of the pandemic, people generally have a more difficult time expressing sympathy, embracing novel situations, being extroverted, and taking responsibilities toward others into consideration.

How should our common experiences of the pandemic, such as fear, isolation, and uncertainty, shape how we frame messages to others? How can you make your messages agile and effective given this knowledge of the pandemic's effects on our social orientation toward others?

The pandemic affected the well-being of many, which requires adaptation by the speaker.

Iakov Filimonov/123RF

Source: Sutin, A. R., Stephan, Y., Luchetti, M., Aschwanden, D., Lee, J. H., Sesker, A. A., et al. (2022). Differential personality change earlier and later in the coronavirus pandemic in a longitudinal sample of adults in the United States. *PLoS ONE, 17.* https://doi:10.1371/journal.pone.0274542

Of course, the right to speak on nearly any topic does not free you from the consequences of how your messages is received. This is why you have a significant responsibility to adapt the way you approach your subject, given the audience to which you are speaking. Using audience analysis, you must figure out how to best approach your topic to meet your audience's needs and remain ethical in your communication. You may adjust your language, visual resources, supporting evidence, or even the points you make during the presentation. For example, suppose you want to speak in favor of physician-assisted suicide, and your audience analysis indicates that the majority of your listeners are opposed to it. You need not conclude that the topic is inappropriate. You may, however, adapt to the members of your audience by starting with a position closer to theirs. Your initial step might be to make audience members feel less comfortable about their present position so that they are more prepared to hear your views.

ADAPTING YOUR PURPOSE AND GOAL

You should also adapt the purpose of your speech to your audience. Teachers often ask students to state the purpose of a speech—what you want your audience to know, understand, or do. At first you might think your purpose should be to inform your audience about fashion trends in the United States, but you discover through your audience analysis that most of your classmates are concerned about the environment, wage fairness, and cheaply made products. As a result, you adapt your purpose to an informative speech that explains principles and approaches to sustainable fashion, which is a movement that advocates for wage fairness, safe working conditions, and environmental responsibility in the fashion industry and among consumers.[6]

The **immediate purpose** of your speech is what you want listeners to take away with them. An immediate purpose has four essential features. First, it is highly specific. Second, it includes the phrase *should be able to* (or *will be able to*). Third, it uses an action verb, such as *state, identify, report, name, list, describe, explain, show,* or *reveal.* Fourth, it is stated from the viewpoint of the audience. Stated differently, the purpose is based on what you want to accomplish as a speaker, but how you communicate your purpose must be audience centered. Your immediate purpose moves audience members toward a **long-range goal**, or the end purpose you have in mind. Some examples will illustrate the difference. Here are examples for an informative speech:

> *Immediate purpose:* After listening to this speech, the audience should be able to identify three properties of the most advanced televisions available today.

> *Long-range goal:* To increase the number of people who will choose wisely the next time they replace or purchase a television set.

Here are examples for a persuasive speech:

> *Immediate purpose:* After listening to my speech, the audience will be able to describe the low nutritional value of two popular junk foods.

> *Long-range goal:* To dissuade listeners from eating junk food.

In this section on adapting to your audience, you learned that you do not have to change yourself or your position on an issue, but you can present yourself and your arguments in ways that are more likely to result in success. You learned that even the words you choose are strategic; that is, you select your words with care so that they convince and persuade rather than offend. You can shape your topic without giving up your integrity by providing information where needed and by persuading without risking a hostile audience response. Finally, you aim for some immediate effects that are possible in a brief presentation, knowing that you have a long-range goal in mind as well.

New media and cutting-edge technology have already made you an expert of sorts in audience analysis. You may have a TikTok or Instagram profile that attracts people who like you to follow you, just as audience members might attend an event where you are speaking in real life. You can use technology to sharpen your skill in audience analysis by considering how social media sites invite you to present both yourself and your message to an audience. You might be a political junkie on Instagram but a foodie on TikTok, just as in public speaking you are adapting yourself and your message for others.

immediate purpose
A statement of what you intend to accomplish in this particular presentation. Also, a highly specific statement using "should be able to" plus an action verb to reveal the purpose of a presentation from the audience's point of view.

long-range goal
The larger goal or end purpose you have in mind for your presentation.

be ready... for what's next

Difficult Audience Members

Difficult audience members can express distracting behaviors in many ways, such as sleeping, taking too much time with questions and comments, interrupting, and talking to others. When encountering difficult audience members, remember the following:

1. *Don't look for a fight.* You may be tempted to counter aggression with aggression, but escalating a situation could reflect negatively on you.

2. *Be empathetic.* If you can show you understand the audience member, you may be able to deescalate the situation.

3. *Redirect the conversation.* As the speaker, you can control the pace of the conversation and shift to another aspect of your topic if an audience member takes your speech off track.

4. *Don't take it personally.* Some audience members may never agree with you. You do not have to win over every audience member. Your objective should be to have the greatest impact possible with your speech.

Chapter Review & Study Guide

Summary

In this chapter, you learned the following:

1. Selecting a topic appropriate for you and your audience involves a few key strategies.
   - Try brainstorming and surveying your interests.
   - Assess your knowledge of the topic.
   - Evaluate your commitment to the topic.
   - Consider the relevance of your topic to your audience.
   - Determine the topic's importance to you and your audience.

2. Narrowing your topic saves time and energy and increases relevance to your audience.

3. Audience analysis—employing observation, inference, research, and questionnaires—is needed so that you can better adapt your speech to your audience.
   - Observe your audience for demographic and membership cues.
   - Draw direct and indirect inferences about your audience.

   - Research your audience with inside informants and the internet.
   - Use a questionnaire to assess attitudes, beliefs, and values.

4. Adapting yourself, your language, your topic, and your purpose and goal in public speaking enables you to craft a message designed to inform, entertain, inspire, teach, or persuade your audience.
   - Without compromising yourself, you can adapt yourself to an audience.
   - Your language choices must be adapted to the specific audience.
   - Any topic can be adapted to a particular audience.
   - Your purpose depends heavily on what you can accomplish with a particular audience.
   - Your long-range goal also depends on where the audience stands on an issue.

Key Terms

Attitude	Demographic analysis	Long-range goal
Audience analysis	Direct inference	Questionnaire
Belief	Immediate purpose	Value
Brainstorming	Indirect inference	
Commitment	Inference	

Study Questions

1. What is one basic strategy to keep in mind when selecting a topic for a presentation?
   a. Take a lot of time when choosing a topic.
   b. Begin with a subject you already know.
   c. Select a topic you know nothing about.
   d. Choose a topic that does not affect you personally.

2. The most effective results of brainstorming occur
   a. at the beginning of your brainstorming.
   b. during the middle of your brainstorming.
   c. at the end of your brainstorming.
   d. after at least one day has passed.

3. When you investigate the audience's demographics, interests, and concerns, you are
   a. brainstorming.
   b. surveying your interests.
   c. analyzing the audience.
   d. creating a captive audience.

4. Which level of audience analysis includes collecting data about the characteristics of people?
   a. audience type
   b. audience interest in the topic
   c. audience's attitudes, beliefs, and values
   d. demographic analysis

5. A deeply rooted belief that affects how we respond to an idea or a concept is a(n)
   a. attitude.   c. thought.
   b. mood.   d. value.

6. A method of audience analysis that draws tentative generalizations based on some evidence is
   a. observation.   c. a questionnaire.
   b. inference.   d. a survey.

7. If you ask people to rank concepts in order of importance or ask them questions that place individuals into identifiable groups, you are
   a. conducting a questionnaire.
   b. brainstorming.
   c. narrowing.
   d. inferring.

8. Which method of analysis requires using your senses to interpret information about the audience?
   a. involvement   c. judgment
   b. value   d. observation

9. When adapting your language, you should
   a. assume that audience members will understand your terms.
   b. assume that audience members will misinterpret your language.
   c. ignore nonverbal feedback from the audience.
   d. avoid using slides to show key phrases or terms.

10. After observing that many of your audience members are on their mobile devices, your _____ may allow you to conclude that their attention is divided.
   a. survey results
   b. passive senses
   c. projection tendency
   d. indirect inference

Answers:

1. (b); 2. (c); 3. (c); 4. (d); 5. (d); 6. (b); 7. (a); 8. (d); 9. (b); 10. (d)

Critical Thinking

1. Choose a broad topic, then narrow it by creating your own concept map (see Figure 10.1). At what point do the topics become too specific to be discussed in depth? Which are still too broad for a brief presentation? Choose a few that are just right.
2. Because of the pandemic and other world events, audience members may have greater difficulty expressing sympathy, embracing novel situations, and assuming responsibility toward the well-being of others. Recognizing the stress that your audience members may be facing, determine a strategy that you could use to adapt your message to your audience so that it is relevant and resonates with their feelings.

Sizing Things Up Scoring and Interpretation

Evaluating Topics

Personal inventories are typically qualitative in nature; that is, you write down topics about which you are interested or knowledgeable. The scale created for this chapter provides a quantitative way of assessing interest in 10 broad topic areas. Results of this survey can be used in two ways. First, you may select a topic area in which you score very high and use that as a guide for generating speech topics. Second, if you average responses from your classmates, you can use this information as a simple audience-analysis survey.

To score this survey, notice that each topic has a four-item semantic-differential scale. Rather than writing or circling numbers, simply check a space to indicate how strongly a particular adjective represents your views toward the general topic. From left to right on each semantic-differential item, score responses as a 5, 4, 3, 2, or 1 based on which space you checked. Thus, higher values will indicate more positive perceptions toward that topic. Sum scores for the four items under each topic area to achieve a total score between 4 and 20. Values closer to 20 indicate more positive perceptions toward that topic.

References

1. Warren, A. (2016). *The period project*. Ohio University.
2. Danes, J. E., Lindsey-Mullikin, J., & Lertwachara, K. (2020). The sequential order and quality of ideas in electronic brainstorming. *International Journal of Information Management, 53*. https://doi.org/10.1016/j.ijinfomgt.2020.102126
3. Mazer, J., & Titsworth, S. (2008). *Testing a common public speaking claim: An examination of students' ego-involvement with speech topics in the basic communication course*. National Communication Association Convention.
4. Auerbach, N. (2022, March 10). Schools question whether the NCAA can enforce pay-for-play rules in NIL: "Is there going to be accountability?" *The Athletic*. https://theathletic.com/3173521/2022/03/10/schools-question-whether-the-ncaa-can-enforce-pay-for-play-rules-in-nil-is-there-going-to-be-accountability/
5. Girls on the Run. (n.d.). Who we are. https://www.girlsontherun.org/Who-We-Are
6. Catelli, A., & Milligan, E. (2018, August 17). Ready-to-wear and re-wear meet sustainable fashion. *Bloomberg Quick Take*. https://www.bloomberg.com/news/articles/2018-08-17/ready-to-wear-and-re-wear-meet-sustainable-fashion-quicktake

chapter 11

credibility and evidence

When you have read and thought about this chapter, you will be able to

1. explain the importance of source credibility in public presentations.

2. apply the dimensions of credibility to improve how audience members perceive you.

3. develop a research strategy for finding support for your presentation.

4. identify eight types of supporting materials for your ideas.

5. demonstrate the ability to attribute information to sources, both verbally and in writing.

6. recognize ethical principles to follow for credibility and supporting materials.

Effective public presentations are an artfully drafted combination of you, your ideas, and the ideas and opinions of others. How you present yourself, your ideas, and your evidence will determine how much trust the audience places in the points you make. In this chapter, you will learn about source credibility and the ways that you can increase your credibility by using strong evidence.

During the winter of 2022 the world witnessed Russian troops invade Ukraine, and reports of attacks on civilians became commonplace. On March 17, 2022, former California Governor Arnold Schwarzenegger released an impassioned video presentation,[1] which was later published in written form by *The Atlantic*.[2] Schwarzenegger stated that he wanted to inform members of the Russian army about "things going on in the world that have been kept from you, terrible things that you should know about."

Schwarzenegger began by recounting several instances in which he befriended Russian citizens and stressed his deep affection for the Russian people. He then used statistics, examples, and stories to highlight the atrocities being committed by Russia on Ukrainians. He stressed that the Russian government "has lied not only to its citizens, but also to its soldiers."

Schwarzenegger used various tactics to bolster his credibility and supported his points with compelling evidence. The end result was not a cessation of conflict, but his words did become a focal point in the worldwide discourse opposing the invasion of Ukraine.

Arnold ✓
@Schwarzenegger

I love the Russian people. That is why I have to tell you the truth. Please watch and share.

attn:

Некоторым солдатам сказали, что они пойдут воевать с нацистами.
Some of the soldiers were told they were going to fight Nazis.

Arnold Schwarzenegger speaking against the Ukrainian invasion by Russia.
Source: Twitter/Arnold Schwarzenegger

Source Credibility and Its Importance

The most important resource you have for convincing an audience is yourself. Audiences do not want to hear from someone they do not trust or respect. They will not listen to or retain information from someone who has not earned the right to talk about that subject. Finding ways to convince your audience that you are trustworthy and qualified is among the most important objectives for any speaker. In the public speaking classroom you are the source of the message. You need to be concerned about your **source credibility**—the audience's perception of your effectiveness as a speaker. You may feel that you do not have the same credibility as a high public official, a great authority on a topic, or an expert in a narrow field. Nonetheless, you can be a very credible source to your classmates, colleagues,

source credibility
The extent to which the speaker is perceived as competent to make the claims he or she is making.

or friends. Source credibility is not something a speaker possesses, like a suit of clothes. Instead, the audience determines credibility. Credibility is like many other subjective perceptions—just as each person might have a slightly different impression of whether a song is good, each person may also have a slightly different perception of a speaker's credibility.

As you begin thinking about how you can convince audience members of your credibility, consider the following questions you need to specifically address during your presentation:

- What are your motives for speaking on this topic?
- Why are you qualified to speak on this topic?
- What work have you done to ensure that your information is correct?
- In what ways will the audience benefit from your information?
- Why did you choose to present the information in the way that you did?
- What are you *not* telling the audience, and does omitting that information create an unbalanced or biased perspective?

These questions are not a checklist you should run through as you speak. Effective speakers find ways to address these questions more subtly, through the natural course of their presentation. The results add up to the kind of credibility that means audience members are more likely to trust and respect what the speaker has to say.

Credibility is a challenging issue for beginning speakers. Whereas highly experienced speakers typically have a lifetime of experience from which to establish credibility, most college students lack significant expertise on many topics. Fortunately, students can establish credibility through their sincerity and goodwill, resources available to anyone. And credibility is essential. If you have it, the audience will listen and likely remember much of what you say; speakers who lack or fail to establish credibility during their presentation have little chance of having any impact other than boredom.

The audience's perception of a speaker's credibility arises from a combination of factors, including the speaker, the topic, the situation, and the message. Your experiences can qualify you to speak on certain topics. Have you served in the armed forces overseas? You may have earned the right to speak on national defense, the price of being in the

• College students can use their personal experiences to establish credibility. For instance, a soldier who served as a medic could establish strong credibility to speak on medical issues.

Chris Hondros/Getty Images

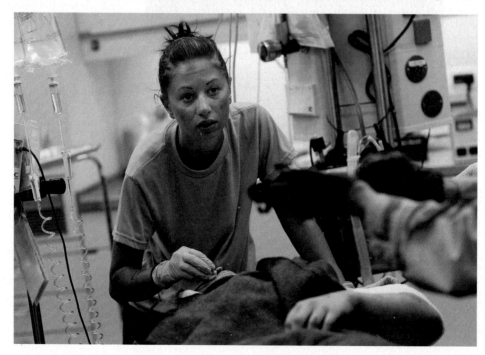

National Guard, and the inside story of war. Did you grow up in another country? You may have earned the right to speak on that country's culture, food, or customs. Your qualifications influence the audience's perceptions about your credibility.

How do you establish your qualifications? Students often state that they have done research on the topic—usually a heavy dose of the first three to five hits on Google. Do you think that makes them credible? Probably not. Rather than relying on research alone, a sincere statement about why you are interested in a particular topic might be convincing for a group of peers in a college classroom. The same approach may not suffice if you are giving the same speech to a group of community activists or business professionals. What it takes to be credible depends on the audience you are addressing, so you'll want to anticipate what each audience will expect.

A final factor influencing your credibility is your message. It should be obvious that a poorly conceived message will lack credibility. Besides relying on research, therefore, you should also focus on relevance. Messages that are connected to the lives of your audience will be perceived as more credible than messages they see as unimportant or disconnected.[3] Stated simply, if audience members perceive the topic as important, they are more likely to perceive you as important and therefore credible.

Dimensions of Credibility

What do audience members perceive that signals speaker credibility? According to research, four of the most important dimensions of credibility are competence, trustworthiness, dynamism, and common ground.

COMPETENCE

The first aspect of credibility is **competence**—the degree to which a speaker is perceived as skilled, qualified, experienced, authoritative, reliable, and informed. A speaker does not have to live up to all these adjectives; any one of them, or a few, might make the speaker credible. A machinist who displays metalwork in a speech about junk sculpture as art is as credible as a biology student explaining the effects of solar radiation on skin. They have different bases for their competence, but both can demonstrate expertise in their areas of specialization.

competence
The degree to which a speaker is perceived as skilled, qualified, experienced, authoritative, reliable, and informed; an aspect of credibility.

There are several things you can do to improve your competence as a speaker. First, you should become familiar enough with your information and speech that you do not have to rely on extensive notes. Constantly referring to notes for every point can lead audience members to perceive that you really do not understand the information. Second, focus on translating ideas. If you are able to take relatively complex ideas and make them understandable for audience members by using metaphors, vivid descriptions, visual aids, and other resources, you will appear more competent. Third, make yourself comfortable with the speaking situation. If you plan to use technology, make sure that you know how to use the computer, the software, and other resources. Finally, audience members will perceive you as more competent if you deliver the speech well (see Chapter 13).

Public speaking coach John Bowe[4] suggests speakers avoid these common mistakes that can diminish credibility:

1. Reading from slides. If you restate what audience members can easily see, you may appear to lack confidence and knowledge.

2. Diverting attention. A statement about using Google in your research process may divert audience members' attention from the information you found.

3. Using filler words. Repeatedly saying phrases like "you know" or "uhh," or "umm" signals lack of confidence. Speakers often use such filler words to buy time as they process what they want to say next. Ample and realistic practice-runs can help you reduce this habit.

4. Using jargon. Terms like "value proposition," "collaboration," and "synergy" do have legitimate uses; however, they are often overused in ways that cloud meaning. Avoid using jargon as shorthand for something meaningful that you want to say.

5. Hedging words. Multiple research studies in education show that when teachers use hedging words or phrases like "perhaps," "possibly," "sort of," and "maybe," students become confused. For example, when speaking about healthy eating, should you say, "Sugar is maybe one of the things that could impact your health," or should you say, "Eating sugar or high-glucose foods can increase your risk for diabetes"? The latter is far more precise and allows you to appear more confident.

TRUSTWORTHINESS

trustworthiness
The degree to which the speaker is perceived as honest, fair, sincere, friendly, honorable, and kind; an aspect of credibility.

dynamism
The extent to which the speaker is perceived as bold, active, energetic, strong, empathic, and assertive; an aspect of credibility.

The second aspect of credibility is **trustworthiness**—the degree to which a speaker is perceived as honest, fair, sincere, friendly, honorable, and kind. We judge people's honesty by their past behaviors and whether we perceive them to have goodwill toward their listeners. A study exploring the perceived credibility of individuals who appear on television asking for citizens to help solve crimes found that perceived trustworthiness influences perceptions of honesty, which potentially determines if a speaker is perceived as credible.[5] So, too, your classmates will judge your trustworthiness based on how you represent your past behaviors and establish goodwill.

Trustworthiness and goodwill are difficult to establish in a short speech. After all, the trust we give to others typically develops after we have known them for some time. During a speech, both what you say and how you say it can affect audience members' perceptions of your trustworthiness. First, you should take care to present fair and balanced information. Using reliable sources and presenting other viewpoints can show audience members that the conclusions you draw are accurate. Talking with a confident tone and maintaining eye contact are also important tools in building trust at the beginning of your speech. A recent research study found that, in general, male speakers with lower-pitched voices were perceived as more trustworthy, whereas for female speakers, this effect was less pronounced.[6]

DYNAMISM

• Speakers like Magic Johnson, an advocate for HIV/AIDS prevention and a former NBA player, gain credibility because of their trustworthiness and dynamism.
Erik Pendzich/Stock Photo

The third aspect of credibility is **dynamism**—the extent to which an audience perceives the speaker as bold, active, energetic, strong, empathic, and assertive. Audiences value behavior described by these adjectives. Perhaps when we consider their opposites—timid, tired, and meek—we can see why dynamism is attractive. People who exude energy and show the passion of their convictions impress others. Watch or listen to Oprah Winfrey on television and note how she looks and sounds. Through her vocal and nonverbal delivery, she captures the essence of dynamism. You can learn to be dynamic. Evidence indicates that the audience's perception of your dynamism will enhance your credibility.

Dynamism is exhibited mainly by voice, movement, facial expressions, and gestures. A person who speaks forcefully and rapidly and with considerable vocal variety; a speaker who moves toward the audience, back behind the lectern, and over to the visual aid; and a speaker who uses facial expressions and gestures to make a point are all exhibiting dynamism.

COMMON GROUND

Common ground occurs when you and your audience share an understanding of the world, either in broad terms or in relationship to specific issues.[7] (See Figure 11.1.) Common ground comes about in two ways. First, you and your audience might share common ground prior to your speech. If you have significant commonality—you are similar in age, you have the same general education level, or you have similar socioeconomic backgrounds—you are likely to have much in common. Common ground is also created through the act of communicating. As you begin to speak, you express a certain way of looking at the world or a particular topic. Do you take a stance on whether there is too much national debt? Do you assume people value health over personal freedom? As you present information, you begin staking claims for particular ways of thinking about issues. In so doing, you will establish greater common ground with some audience members and reduce it with others.

Making a connection with your audience can mean simply establishing a shared trajectory—showing that we are all doing something together. In a speech at an awards ceremony for young aspiring scientists, Mary Sue Coleman, then president of the University of Michigan, established common ground in this way:

> *America has long been recognized as a global leader in science and technology. But we know . . . that our nation is slipping in how we prepare and nurture the talent of tomorrow. Your hard work shows us what is possible. . . . Your ideas and theories are going to lead our country to new cures, solutions and technologies. That is why I am so happy to be here tonight: to congratulate you, encourage you, and provide a little advice about being a scientist in a country that absolutely must place more value on discovery, innovation and the creation of new knowledge.*[8]

Speaking as a scientist, Coleman was able to create common ground with her audience by pointing to a shared objective—to elevate the training of future scientists. Coleman's approach recognized that she and her audience, who were not yet in college, would share a perspective at some future time when the students matured into scientists like her. Her approach established common ground in the present by pointing to where her audience would eventually be. Other approaches to building common ground can include pointing to past shared experiences or present shared circumstances.

building behaviors

Establishing Common Ground with Classmates

Common ground is best established when you can show relationships among yourself, your audience, and the topic, as illustrated in Figure 11.1. Using knowledge of your classmates, list ideas that could establish common ground. For example, if giving a speech on the need for increased state support for education funding, you could point out that you and your classmates share the experience of paying increasingly higher tuition bills.

common ground
The degree to which the speaker's values, beliefs, attitudes, and interests are shared with the audience; an aspect of credibility.

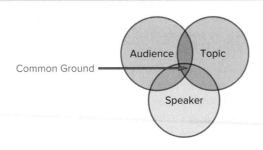

Figure 11.1
Common ground is best established when you can show connections among the topic, your audience, and yourself.

STRATEGIES FOR IMPROVING CREDIBILITY

Credibility is influenced by topics, messages, audiences, and circumstances. You may hold the speaker in high regard before the speech, but during the speech your perception of the speaker may diminish, and then after the speech you may think better of the speaker again because you decide the message has merit. Here are practical approaches for improving your credibility during your presentation:

- Speeches with higher-quality arguments convey more credibility on the speaker.[9] Lower-quality argumentation, such as relying on internet memes, cause listeners to be more skeptical of the message if they are not already in agreement and more polarized if they are in agreement.[10]

sleeper effect
A change of audience opinion caused by the separation of the message content from its source over a period of time.

- Sometimes a **sleeper effect** occurs when audience members' opinions change over time because the source and message get separated in the listeners' minds: a low-credibility speaker's message can gain influence and become persuasive, whereas a high-credibility speaker's message can diminish long after a particular message is delivered and, consequently, lose its persuasiveness.[11] Crafting a clear and persuasive message can help capitalize on the possibility of a positive sleeper effect.

- Self-disclosure can increase credibility because such disclosure can help audience members connect more with you as a person, which potentially increases their perceived connection with you and your message.[12] However, inappropriate self-disclosure can harm credibility because your message can appear overly personal. Use self-disclosure appropriate to the topic, and don't over-rely on it.

- Speakers who appear younger may be perceived as less credible than those who appear older.[13] Dress professionally when speaking to help increase your perceived age.

- Presenting a message that favors one side of an issue often looks like bias to listeners, resulting in lower perceived credibility.[14] Research also shows that for highly partisan and polarizing issues, emotionally laden and intense language can diminish the credibility of your claims.[15]

- People who are perceived to use referent and expert power are seen as more competent, trustworthy, and likable.[16] Build rapport with your audience and stress your personal knowledge of and careful research on the topic (see Chapter 8).

- Speaking with fluency and using gestures can increase perceptions of credibility, including competence, character, and caring.[17] Take care to speak at a moderate pace, enunciate your words, and practice your delivery.

- Your use of evidence, the audience's perception of the topic's importance, and your competence as a speaker interact to influence your credibility. Persuasion scholars John Reinard and Kristeena Myers found that, although the use of any type of evidence increases your credibility, the effects are even greater when the audience perceives the topic to be important and you to be competent.[18]

- When someone else introduces you to your audience, the timing and content of the introduction are important to your credibility. Mike Allen, a communication scholar who specializes in persuasion, found that, if you do not have automatic credibility based on your qualifications, it may be best to delay letting the audience know your qualifications until after you have spoken.[19]

- Research on public health messages during the COVID-19 pandemic found that experts were generally perceived as higher in expertise on the topic but no more or less trustworthy than average citizens.[20] Listeners often recognized expertise but also trusted the experiences of average people. These findings suggest that narratives about average people's experiences on a topic may be particularly useful in garnering trust from an audience.

How to Be Strategic in Finding Information

In addition to your personal credibility, the effectiveness of your presentation will be determined by the credibility of evidence you use to support your points. This section will help you develop strategies for identifying and avoiding fake news and locating highly credible information.

RECOGNIZING DISINFORMATION AND MISINFORMATION

Because of polarized political rhetoric, nearly everyone has heard the term "fake news." Fake news means something different depending on whom you ask because the term has become highly partisan. However, the concept is real. Throughout the web and social media, it is possible to observe outright false or highly misleading stories that are depicted as news. For our purposes, we refer to this as **disinformation**, which is the intentional misrepresentation of facts with the intent of intensifying polarization on issues of concern. In addition to disinformation, you may also encounter **misinformation**, which occurs when a source gets facts wrong or unintentionally mischaracterizes information.

Journalist Claire Wardle developed a way of understanding a range of problematic behaviors that can mislead readers and viewers.[21] Figure 11.2 provides an overview of those behaviors. Misinformation and disinformation can occur across a spectrum from potentially misleading to intentionally deceptive. As a speaker, your objective is to use the highest quality of information possible to support your points. Being able to recognize and avoid using sources that exhibit these characteristics is important in attaining that objective. Of course, you may decide that some sources that fall on this continuum are still important to use. For example, a parody might be an effective way to gain attention at the start of a speech, or a misleading headline or picture might provide a way for you to analyze public misperceptions of a given topic. In such instances, you should explain to your audience the nature of the information as parody or misleading. Because this is a nuanced position to take, it is prudent to ask others, including your teacher, for feedback before your speech. Unless you are making a specific point about false or deceptive content, you should avoid imposter, manipulated, or fabricated content entirely.

When researching, you should be wary of sources that lack verifiable authorship, frequently use emotionally laden language, are highly partisan, or make unverifiable claims or innuendos. The Digital Resource Center at Stony Brook University recommends following the IMVAIN approach to evaluate source credibility:

- Independent: If the source has a self-interest in one side of a topic, it is not independent. Independent sources are more credible.

- Multiple: Having multiple sources that support a point increases the likelihood that the information is accurate.

disinformation
The intentional misrepresentation of facts with the intent of polarizing opinions.

misinformation
Unintentional use of incorrect facts or mischaracterization of facts.

Figure 11.2

Types of Misinformation and Disinformation

Adapted from Wardle, C. (2017, February 16). Fake news. It's complicated. *First Draft*. https://firstdraftnews.org/fake-news-complicated/

Parody	**False Connection**	**Misleading Content**	**False Context**	**Imposter Content**	**Manipulated Content**	**Fabricated Content**
No malicious intent but could mislead	Headlines or visuals are inconsistent with story	Use of partial or misleading evidence to frame a narrative	Accurate information is shared but with misleading context	Real sources are impersonated by another	Accurate information or imagery is intentionally manipulated to deceive	Content is 100% false and intentionally designed to deceive and/or do harm

Potentially Misleading ⟷ Intentionally Deceptive

- Verify: Sources that provide evidence to support their points are better than sources that make assertions without evidence.
- Authoritative/Informed: Sources that have demonstrated expertise on a given topic are better than uninformed sources.
- Named: Sources that explicitly identify their sources are better than those with anonymous sources.[22]

PRINCIPLES FOR EFFECTIVE RESEARCH

Students at all levels generally understand that research is important, though few recognize that research is the foundation for everything else you do in your speech. Table 11.1 analyzes how a good research plan can help nearly every aspect of the speechmaking process, including delivery. This section explains approaches you should embrace and those you should avoid when planning your research strategy.

Refine Your Topic

Poor research strategies often result from poorly worded thesis statements or vague ideas for topics. Take time to think carefully about what your topic is and how others might think of it. After collecting some initial research, perhaps through a carefully planned Internet search, narrow your topic further. Finding ways to reduce the amount of information you need to review and evaluate will speed up your workflow and help you find higher quality sources.

Think of Research as a Process

Experts rarely assume they have all of the answers. In fact, many researchers will claim that at the conclusion of a research project they have more questions than answers. You should embrace the same philosophy when conducting research. Start early, research repeatedly while integrating ideas into your presentation, and then do more research. Waiting until the last minute to start your research, viewing it as just another hoop to jump through for your assignment, locks you into an outcome of ineffective research.

Use a Variety of Sources

Not all sources tell you the same thing. On any given speech topic—global poverty, for example—you can obtain different information from each type of source. Personal experience might tell you how poverty is felt in our own lives, either directly or indirectly;

Table 11.1 Research and the Speech Preparation Process

Preparation Step	Benefit of Research
1. Selecting a topic	Research helps you discover and narrow topics.
2. Organizing ideas	Research helps you identify main and subordinate points.
3. Researching support materials	Research provides facts, examples, definitions, and other forms of support to give substance to your points.
4. Preparing an introduction and a conclusion	Research may reveal interesting examples, stories, or quotations to begin or end the speech.
5. Practicing and delivering the speech	Because your speech is well researched, you will feel more confident and will seem more credible.

magazine and newspaper articles might give general background about regions where poverty is most rampant; scientific journals might provide detailed statistics showing how poverty is linked to disease, famine, and even conflict; and websites might describe groups committed to reducing poverty and its effects.

When devising your research plan, be committed to locating a variety of sources. Using only Google will skew your research to certain types of information while excluding others. Likewise, finding one really good book on poverty and relying only on that resource will limit the details you can integrate into your presentation. Having source variety will help you find better information and various types of evidence to use. The ability to thoroughly research a topic is an important skill that will benefit you in future courses and in your career.

Evaluate Sources Carefully

Merely finding sources does not ensure that you have effectively researched your speech. Regardless of what type of source you have found, apply critical criteria to evaluate its quality. Table 11.2 describes several **heuristics**, or *mental shortcuts,* that people use when evaluating sources. Using these is definitely better than simply selecting the first five sources from a Google search. For instance, a poorly constructed website or sloppy article could be indicative of sloppy work overall, so the aesthetic appeal heuristic could be useful. However, these shortcuts can lead to faulty conclusions about the quality of any given source and should not be used alone.

Although we naturally rely on heuristics when forming first impressions about sources, we should use more robust criteria, such as those in the IMVAIN approach, when evaluating them. In addition to being objective, independent, and verifiable, sources should meet the following criteria before you include them in your presentation:

heuristics
Mental shortcuts used to make decisions—for instance, evaluating sources.

- *Is the supporting material clear?* Does the source present information in a clear and simple manner? Sources that lack clarity could indicate a lack of true understanding on the part of the creator.

Table 11.2 Heuristics Used to Evaluate Research

Heuristic	Description
1. Reputation	Trusting a source because it has a recognizable name or brand (For example, you might trust CNN because it is a large media organization.)
2. Endorsements	Believing information because others say it is believable (For example, you might trust a source because reader comments attached to a story are positive.)
3. Consistency	Trusting one source because it says something similar to what other sources say (For example, you might believe one website because another website says the same thing.)
4. Expectancy violation	Mistrusting a source because it says something contrary to what you thought or contrary to what other sources say
5. Persuasive intent	Mistrusting a source because it makes an obvious attempt to be persuasive
6. Aesthetic appeal	Trusting a source because it is well designed and visually appealing

Source: Items 1–5 are adapted from Metzger, M. J., Flanagan, A. J., & Medders, R. B. (2010). Social and heuristic approaches to credibility evaluation online. *Journal of Communication, 60,* 413–439.

- *Is the supporting material relevant?* Loading your speech with irrelevant sources might make it *seem* well researched; however, critical listeners will see through this tactic. Include only sources that directly address the key points you want to make.

- *Is the supporting material current?* Knowledge changes on a daily basis. What we thought was true about the war on drugs, the internet, health, and the economy a few years ago is now irrelevant. Use older sources sparingly, and attempt to find up-to-date information.

These criteria are not yes or no questions. Sources will meet some criteria well and fail to meet others. Your job as a speaker is to weigh the benefits and drawbacks of each source and determine whether or not to include it in your speech. Indeed, you have an ethical responsibility to carefully evaluate your sources.

LOCATING INFORMATION FOR YOUR PRESENTATION

Although audience members look at several factors to determine your credibility, you have control over only some of them. For instance, you can practice your delivery to avoid mispronunciations, you can work to improve your gestures, and you can take care to create a well-organized speech. In addition, you can improve your own credibility by borrowing on the credibility of others. In this section you will learn how to conduct research and gather supporting material from personal experience, other people, written and visual resources, and the internet. We also discuss how to evaluate those sources and use them effectively in your speeches.

Personal Experience

personal experience
Your own life as a source of information.

The first place you should look for materials for the content of your speech is within yourself. Your **personal experience**—your own life as a source of information—is something about which you can speak with considerable authority. Having a personal connection to your topic that can be explained to your audience will not only add credibility to your presentation, but it will also establish a personal connection with your audience.

However, you should ask yourself some critical questions about your personal experience before you use it in your speech. Some experiences may be too personal or too intimate to share with strangers or even classmates. Others may be interesting but irrelevant to the topic of your speech. You can evaluate your personal experience as evidence, or as data on which proof may be based, by asking yourself the following questions:

1. Was my experience typical?

2. Was my experience so typical that it will bore an audience?

3. Was my experience so atypical that it was a chance occurrence?

4. Was my experience so personal and revealing that the audience may feel uncomfortable?

5. Was my experience one that this audience will appreciate or from which this audience can learn a lesson?

6. Does my experience really constitute proof or evidence of anything?

Also consider the ethics of using your personal experience in a speech. Will your message harm others? Is the experience your own or someone else's? Experience that is not first-hand is probably questionable because information about others' experiences often becomes distorted as the message is passed from one person to another. Unless the experience is your own, you may find yourself passing along a falsehood.

Other People

Speakers often overlook the most obvious sources of information—the people around them. The easiest way to secure information from other people is to ask them in an informational interview.

sizing things up

Research Attitudes Scale

You have a variety of sources in which you can locate evidence and information. Read each statement below and respond using the following scale:

1 = Strongly disagree
2 = Disagree
3 = Neither agree nor disagree
4 = Agree
5 = Strongly agree

1. I feel confident when using the internet to find good information.
2. I like to use journals to find good articles on a topic.
3. I find it easy to locate good books on a given topic.
4. I have confidence in using reference materials to find good research on topics.
5. I find it easy to locate good newspaper or magazine articles on topics.
6. I like to look for good books when researching a topic.
7. I find it easy to locate good journal articles on topics.
8. I like to use good reference materials when researching.
9. The internet is easy to use when looking for good information.
10. I am confident in my abilities to find good newspaper or magazine articles on topics.
11. I am confident in my ability to find good books on a topic.
12. It is easy to use the reference section in the library to find good information.
13. I like to search for good newspaper or magazine articles on topics.
14. I like to use the internet to search for good information.
15. I am confident in my ability to locate good journal articles on a topic.

There are no right or wrong answers to these questions. A guide for interpreting your responses appears at the end of the chapter.

How do you find the right people? Your instructor might have some suggestions about whom to approach. Good and accessible sources of information are professors and administrators who are available on campus. They can be contacted during office hours or by appointment. Government officials, too, have an obligation to be responsive to your questions. Even big business and entire industries have public relations offices that can help you with information. Your objective is to find one or several people who can provide you with the best information in the limited time you have to prepare your speech.

An interview can be an important and impressive source of information for your speech—if you conduct it properly. After you have carefully selected the person or persons you wish to interview, follow these suggestions:

1. *On first contact with your interviewee or the interviewee's assistant, be honest about your purpose.* For example, you might say, "I want to interview Dr. Schwartz for 10 minutes about the plans for student aid for next year so that I can share that information with the 20 students in my public speaking class." Notice that this request tells the person how much time the interview will take.

2. *Prepare specific questions for the interview.* Think ahead about exactly what kind of information you will need to satisfy yourself and your audience. You should conduct at least some research before the interview so that you will be able to ask better questions. Keep your list of questions short enough to fit the time limit you have suggested to the interviewee.

3. *Be respectful toward the person you interview.* Remember that the person you interview is doing you a favor. You do not need to question aggressively like a talk show host. Instead, dress appropriately for the person's status, ask your questions politely, and thank your interviewee for granting you an interview.

4. *Tell the interviewee you are going to take notes so that you can use the information in your speech.* If you are going to record the interview, you need to ask the interviewee's permission. Be prepared to take notes in case the interviewee does not wish to be recorded. Even if you record the interview, it's a good idea to take notes as a backup in case something happens to the recording.

5. *When you quote your interviewees or paraphrase their ideas in your speech, use oral footnotes to indicate where you got the information.* Here's an example: "According to Dr. Fred Schwartz, the director of financial aid, the amount of student financial aid for next year will be slightly less than it was this year."

Sometimes the person you interview will be a good resource for additional information. For example, if you were preparing a speech on the topic of learning disabilities, you might opt to interview the campus coordinator for disability services. Through the course of the interview, that person might be able to suggest others on campus who specialize on the topic, such as professors or health professionals. Of course, even with an expert, you should also use other types of resources so that differing opinions and alternate explanations can be identified.

Written and Visual Resources from the Library

reference librarian
A librarian specifically trained to help you find sources of information.

Modern libraries, such as the ones found at most colleges and universities, are portals to digital information. Rather than helping you find a particular book or article, a **reference librarian**—someone specifically trained to help you locate sources of information—is far more likely to teach you how to use your school's particular library system and one or more of the available electronic databases.

Here are some practical principles of library research that you can adapt to your unique situation:

1. *Start at the center and work your way out.* The reference desk is the practical "center" of your library. To find anything, you will start with a search of some type; the reference desk is there to help you conduct that search, so start by asking for help there. In addition to starting at the center of the library, you should begin by searching at the center of your topic. Following the principle that topics will be narrowed as you conduct research, start by researching the broad and typical

elements of your topic. As you gain more information, you will be able to narrow your search to more specific (and possibly off-center) aspects of your topic.

2. *Understand that not all sources are equal.* Modern libraries offer access to many different types of sources, including books, academic journals, trade magazines, and popular press sources such as magazine and newspaper articles. Each will provide you with different types of information, and each will likely be indexed in a different database. Table 11.3 identifies several different types of sources and suggests how you might use them as evidence. A key principle when conducting good research is that source variety is important—finding and using a variety of sources from this list is wise.

3. *Know your databases.* Some university libraries can provide access to hundreds of electronic databases. With so many options, figuring out which databases to use can seem daunting. Following the principle that you should start at the center, generalized databases such as Academic Search Premier and Lexis-Nexis are excellent places to begin. The library computer catalog will also help you locate books and other

Table 11.3 Types of Sources

Source	Description
Fiction books	Some plots or characters can be used to illustrate points you are making in your speech.
Nonfiction books	Nonfiction books include historical, political, social, and scientific studies. Research reported in books tends to be very detailed but can also be somewhat out of date.
Academic journal articles	Most academic journal articles undergo careful editorial review and blind peer review, which can help ensure high-quality information. Academic articles tend to report the results of very specific studies.
Government documents	The federal government produces publications ranging from compilations of congressional testimony to the results of million-dollar scientific studies. Many university libraries have a separate department for government documents.
Trade journal articles	Trade journals are targeted toward professionals in a particular profession or discipline. Trade journals tend to be practical but based on solid research.
Reference books	Your library reference department will have a number of reference books, including dictionaries, biographies, and atlases. Depending on your speech topic, such sources can be very useful.
Encyclopedias	Encyclopedias are excellent places to start researching topics about which you know absolutely nothing. Encyclopedia entries provide short, easy-to-read explanations but tend to be dated and too general.
Magazine articles	Magazine articles provide timely information and tend to provide more in-depth coverage. The disadvantage of magazine articles is that they are typically written by journalists with little or no expertise on the topics they write about. Although they may quote experts, they still make decisions on what to use and how to present information to the reader.
Newspaper articles	Newspaper articles are among the timeliest sources of print information. Although they are up to date, they are written by journalists who may have little or no expertise on the topics they write about. Similar to magazine articles, the writer chooses what sources to use and how to present that information to readers. In comparison to magazine articles, newspaper articles tend to provide fewer details because they are shorter in length.
Webpages	Webpages are easily accessible and can provide current information on a given topic. Because webpages can be created by anyone, you should take care to verify the actual source of the webpage, confirm that source's credibility, and verify the information presented.

• Google can be a good starting point for research, but relying only on that resource can limit the types of information that you locate. Using multiple search portals is a better strategy.

Google

| +You | Search | Images | Maps | Play | YouTube | News | Gmail | Documents | Calendar | More ▾ |

Google   "Library of Congress" history

Search   About 19,500,000 results (0.34 seconds)

Everything

Images

Maps

Videos

News

Shopping

More

San Francisco, CA

Change location

Show search tools

History - About the Library (**Library of Congress**)
www.loc.gov › About the Library
The **Library of Congress** was established by an act of Congress in 1800 when President John Adams signed a bill providing for the transfer of the seat of ...

Jefferson's Legacy: A Brief **History** of the **Library of Congress** -- TH...
www.loc.gov/loc/legacy/loc.html
The development of the **Library of Congress** cannot be separated from the **history** of the nation it serves. Nor can it be separated from the philosophy and ideals ...

Jefferson's Legacy: A Brief **History** of the **Library of Congress** ...
www.loc.gov/loc/legacy/
Official guide to the development of its role as a national library, with descriptions of its buildings, a timeline of acquisitions and a list of Librarians of Congress.

American Memory from the **Library of Congress** - Home Page
memory.loc.gov/
The home page for the American Memory **Historical** Collections from the **Library of Congress**. American Memory provides free access to **historical** images, maps, ...

Library of Congress - Wikipedia, the free encyclopedia
en.wikipedia.org/wiki/Library_of_Congress
Jump to Modern **history** (1939–Present): Even the **Library of Congress** assisted during the war effort, ranging from the storage of the Declaration of ...

resources in your library. Once you have located initial information, you may wish to consult more specific and specialized databases. For example, if you are preparing a presentation about a medical topic, you may wish to consult MEDLINE. And if you are preparing a persuasive speech, you may wish to consult the Opposing Viewpoints Resource Center to find "pro" and "con" articles on topics ranging from adoption to welfare reform. Remember that the reference librarian is trained to help you select and use the right databases for your topic.

4. *Recognize that good research requires reading, thinking, and doing more research.* Many students assume their research task is over with one Google search or a quick trip to the library. Although the "one trip fits all" approach is appealing, it does not work well. Once you have obtained initial research on your topic, the best thing you can do is to spend time reading those sources, revising your outline, and conducting more research to fill in gaps and find more specific information. Good research takes time, but the end result is outstanding evidence that is sure to impress.

The Internet

The internet has been integrated into nearly every aspect of our lives, appearing on our smartphones, televisions, and even upscale refrigerators. We have access to more information than ever, but not all of it is useful, and filtering through the junk can be overwhelming.

Good web searches start with a plan, and a general strategy is provided here. Depending on the nature of your topic and your specific assignment, you might need to perform additional steps.

1. *Use search engines and other portals.* A **search engine** is a webpage designed to help you search for information; Google is the prime example. Although search engines will locate thousands of sites that contain the word or phrase you are searching for, they also return hundreds of irrelevant websites. An alternative approach is to use a more specialized search engine. For instance, for some topics Google Scholar might be much better than the standard Google search engine. In addition, there are thousands of other types of information portals online. YouTube and TED provide portals for finding video, iTunes is a portal for finding podcasts, and Visually is a portal for interesting information graphics. Using a variety of search engines and other portals can diversify your research and help you find better information.

2. *Refine your search.* Many students assume one search will be sufficient. As you discover more information, try using different combinations of search terms. Sometimes adding a few words or rearranging words can make an important change in what your search engine returns. Also, try using more advanced techniques, such as Boolean operators, to narrow searches. Table 11.4 provides recommendations on how to more effectively narrow your searches. Searching for information is easy; being smart about your searches is more challenging. Your objective should be to narrow the search until you have separated the garbage from the gold.

Table 11.4 Using Boolean Operators to Narrow Your Web Search

Boolean Operator	Description	Example
Exact-match searching	By default, browsers return any webpage containing the word you asked it to search for. For example, if you wanted to search for sites that use only the term *inform,* typing that term into a search engine would return sites with the words *informative, information, informal, informing,* and so forth. To prevent this problem, type your search term enclosed in double quotations marks. You can use the same option to search for exact phrases.	*"inform"; "Country Music Association Awards"*
Combining terms in a search	If you are looking for webpages that use similar terms that could mean the same thing in the context of your research, you can use *or* to combine terms in the search. For instance, if you wanted sites that contained either *race* or *marathon,* you could combine both terms in one search. Alternatively, you could use *and* to identify sites that contain both terms.	*race OR marathon; race AND marathon*
Excluding terms	Sometimes you may want to search for a word or phrase but, because it is used in multiple contexts, you need to exclude some types of pages. Suppose you wanted to search for the word *apple* with the intention of finding out about the fruit, not the company. One way of accomplishing that search is to type in *apple* followed by words you want to exclude, with each preceded by a minus sign.	*Apple – computer – iPhone – iPad*
Using wildcards	Wildcards, or symbols (usually an asterisk) that stand in for an unknown character, can expand your search. For example, suppose you wanted to search for state laws pertaining to voter registration. You could search for each state separately (for example, *state of Alaska voter registration laws*), or you could combine the wildcard with quotation marks to search for all states while keeping your search narrowed to documents containing the exact phrase you are interested in.	*"state of * voter registration laws"*

Source: Adapted from Google. (n.d.). Refine web searches. https://support.google.com/websearch/answer/2466433

3. *Evaluate carefully all sources of information found on the internet,* especially when you use sources outside your university's web domain. Later in the chapter we focus specifically on this issue, but it cannot be stated too many times. The critical skills in research are both locating *and* evaluating sources of information. Perhaps you are picky about your clothes or your food. You should be equally picky about the information you consume and, in this case, serve to others.

Keep in mind that people have different motives for creating webpages. Some websites are intended to be informative, others are intended to persuade, and still others are out to make money. Some are designed to conceal their true motive: a website might look informative but actually tell only part of a story to lure you into making an uninformed decision. One way to understand the motive of websites is to pay attention to the server extension. Figure 11.3 explains the parts of a web address and the characteristics of web addresses with different server extensions. No single type of web address—based on the server extension—is necessarily better than another. However, you can make initial judgments about the credibility of a site by looking at the extension. Remember that ".com" sites are trying to make money, ".gov" sites are maintained by the government and are typically oriented toward public service, and ".edu" sites are associated with colleges and universities.

Although only a start, this information can help you sift through certain types of sites that have the potential to present misleading or even deceptive information.

Figure 11.3

Breaking down web addresses.

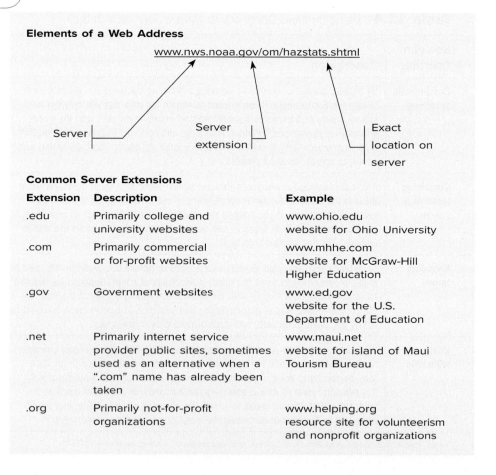

Elements of a Web Address

www.nws.noaa.gov/om/hazstats.shtml

Server | Server extension | Exact location on server

Common Server Extensions

Extension	Description	Example
.edu	Primarily college and university websites	www.ohio.edu website for Ohio University
.com	Primarily commercial or for-profit websites	www.mhhe.com website for McGraw-Hill Higher Education
.gov	Government websites	www.ed.gov website for the U.S. Department of Education
.net	Primarily internet service provider public sites, sometimes used as an alternative when a ".com" name has already been taken	www.maui.net website for island of Maui Tourism Bureau
.org	Primarily not-for-profit organizations	www.helping.org resource site for volunteerism and nonprofit organizations

Types of Supporting Material

Now that you know where to look for information, the next step is pulling key facts, quotations, stories, and other details out of those sources to use in your presentation. Such details are called **supporting material**, which consists of details you can use to substantiate your arguments and to clarify your ideas. In this section you will learn about examples, narratives, surveys, testimony, numbers and statistics, analogies, explanations, and definitions.

EXAMPLES

Examples—specific instances used to illustrate your point—are among the most common supporting materials found in speeches. Sometimes a single example helps convince an audience; other times a relatively large number of examples may be necessary to achieve your purpose. For instance, you could support the argument that a university gives admission priority to out-of-state students by showing the difference between the numbers of in-state and out-of-state students who are accepted in relation to the number of students who applied in each group. Likewise, in a persuasive speech designed to motivate everyone to vote, you could present cases in which a few more votes would have meant a major change in election results.

You should be careful when using examples. Sometimes an example is so unusual that an audience will not accept the story as evidence or proof of anything. For instance, would you find information obtained from Hawaii a good example for illustrating the price of consumable goods? Probably not, because Hawaii is geographically isolated and requires many of its consumable goods to be transported to the islands. A good example must be plausible, typical, and related to the main point of the speech.

Two types of examples are hypothetical and factual: a *hypothetical* example is fictional but realistic, whereas a *factual* example is based on real circumstances. Either type can be brief or extended. Here is an extended hypothetical example:

> Suppose that you were looking for information online about trends in carbon dioxide emissions in the United States for the past 50 years. You locate a *Washington Post* story that appears, from the headline, to contain information of interest to your search. Upon clicking on the story, you are asked to enroll in a digital subscription to the *Washington Post* to access the story. In that instance, you are faced with the same decision as millions of news consumers, whether or not to establish a digital subscription for news.

The following is a brief factual example:

> Apple's launch of a streaming news service is part of a growing worldwide trend, as a 2018 Reuters Institute for the Study of Journalism report stated that the average number of people paying for online news has increased worldwide, with the most significant gains coming in European countries such as Sweden (up 6%).[23]

The brief factual example is *verifiable,* meaning it can be supported by a source that the audience can check. The extended hypothetical example is not verifiable because it provides fictional analyses of potential excuses used by students. Both types of examples are useful to illustrate and clarify ideas.

NARRATIVES

Whereas examples are intended primarily to present factual information, **narratives**—stories to illustrate an important point—focus on telling a human story. Think about the difference between hearing that NFL quarterback Joe Burrow started a foundation (a factual

supporting material
Information you can use to substantiate your arguments and to clarify your position.

examples
Specific instances used to illustrate your point.

narratives
Stories to illustrate an important point.

example) and hearing a story about how the daily food insecurity of his classmates led him to create a foundation to relieve hunger (a narrative).

Narratives are important parts of speeches. In addition to adding interest and capturing attention, narratives can help you accomplish the following in your presentations:

1. Stories can help audience members recognize when something important is missing. For example, a story about wellness among college students could highlight the fact that professional counseling services are difficult to access on many college campuses.[24]

2. Stories can evoke emotions. As you tell a story, you introduce characters and plots that help audience members connect with your topic. For example, research professor Dr. Brené Brown is skilled at using narratives to develop emotions on her podcasts.

3. Stories help us envision new possibilities. Communication scholars Brittany Peterson and Lynn Harter have observed that stories are powerful in helping us understand how to think differently about systemic problems and inequities.[25] For example, a story about how music and art therapy programs in hospitals uplift patients can challenge the dominant narrative that health therapies can only be based in technology.

SURVEYS

surveys
Studies in which a sample of the population is asked a limited number of questions to discover public opinions on issues.

Another source of supporting material commonly used in speeches is **surveys**, studies in which a sample of the population is asked a limited number of questions to discover public opinions on issues. Surveys are commonly reported in full by the organization that conducted the survey, such as Pew Research, and then summarized in other outlets such as online news sites, newspapers, and magazines. Surveys are valuable sources of information. One person's experience with alcohol can have an impact on an audience, but a survey indicating that one-third of all U.S. adults abstain, one-third drink occasionally, and one-third drink regularly provides better support for an argument. You should ask some important questions about the evidence found in surveys:

- *How reliable is the source?* A report in a professional journal of sociology, psychology, or communication is likely to be more thorough and more valid than one conducted by a nonexpert using social media.

- *How broad was the sample used in the survey?* In political and other polls, you have seen mention of a "margin of error." Larger sample sizes reduce the margin of error, which can boost confidence in the accuracy of a poll's results.

- *Who was included in the survey?* Did everyone in the sample have an equal chance of being selected, or were volunteers asked to respond to the questions? If people are randomly selected to be in a survey, the results are less likely to be biased by a particular viewpoint. Using social media or an email survey could bias results in a certain way because certain types of people had greater opportunity to participate than others.

- *How representative was the survey sample?* For example, a survey of *Southern Living*'s readers may not provide data that is typical of the population in your state if you are from a northern state such as Oregon or New Hampshire.

- *Why was the survey conducted?* Was the survey performed for any self-serving purpose—for example, to create clickbait—or did the government conduct the study to help establish policy or legislation?

TESTIMONY

Testimonial evidence consists of written or oral statements of others' experiences used by a speaker to substantiate or clarify a point. One assumption behind testimonial evidence is that you are not alone in your beliefs, ideas, and arguments: other people also support them. Another assumption is that the statements of others should help the audience accept your point of view because those other people may have additional credibility that can transfer to your argument. The three kinds of testimonial evidence you can use in your speeches are lay, expert, and celebrity.

- **Lay testimony** is statements made by an ordinary person that substantiate or support what you say. In a speech, lay testimony might be the words of your relatives, neighbors, or colleagues concerning an issue. Such testimony shows the audience that you and other ordinary people support the idea.

- **Expert testimony** is statements made by someone who has special knowledge or expertise about an issue or idea. In your speech you might quote a mechanic about problems with an automobile, an interior decorator about the aesthetic qualities of fabrics, or a political pundit about an election.

- **Celebrity testimony** is statements made by a public figure who is known to the audience. In your speech you might point out that a famous politician, a syndicated columnist, or a well-known entertainer endorses the position you advocate.

Although testimonial evidence may encourage your audience to adopt your ideas, you need to use such evidence with caution. An idea may have little credence even though many laypeople believe in it, an expert may have a controversial view, and a celebrity usually is paid for endorsing a product.

NUMBERS AND STATISTICS

Numbers and statistics are other types of evidence useful for clarification or substantiation. Because numbers are sometimes easier to understand and digest when they appear in print, public speakers often have to simplify, explain, and translate their meaning in a spoken presentation. For example, instead of saying, "There were 323,462 high school graduates," you should say, "There were more than 300,000 graduates." You can also simplify the number 323,462 by writing it on a visual aid, such as a PowerPoint slide, and making a comparison, such as "Three hundred thousand high school graduates is equivalent to the entire population of Lancaster."

Statistics—numbers that summarize numerical information or compare quantities—are also difficult for audiences to interpret. For example, an audience will have difficulty interpreting a statement such as "Electric vehicle sales increased 47%." Instead, you could round off the figure to "nearly 50%," or you could reveal the actual dollar value of EV automotive sales this year and last year. Whenever you quote an average, a median, or a mode of a set of values, you are using statistics. You can also help the audience interpret the significance with a comparison. For example, you can say, "That is the biggest increase in sales experienced across all types of vehicles in our city this year."

You can greatly increase your effectiveness as a speaker if you illustrate your numbers and statistics by using visual resources, such as pie charts, line graphs, and bar graphs. You should both say and show your

testimonial evidence
Written or oral statements of others' experience used by a speaker to substantiate or clarify a point.

lay testimony
Statements made by an ordinary person that substantiate or support what you say.

expert testimony
Statements made by someone who has special knowledge or expertise about an issue or idea.

celebrity testimony
Statements made by a public figure who is known to the audience.

statistics
Numbers that summarize numerical information or compare quantities.

- Using graphs and tables can help you present statistics and numbers more effectively.
Monty Rakusen/Getty Images

figures. Try using visual imagery—for example, "That amount of money is greater than all the money in all our local banks" or "That many discarded tires would cover our city 6 feet deep in a single year."

ANALOGIES

analogy
A comparison of things in some respects, especially in position or function, that are otherwise dissimilar.

An **analogy** is a comparison of things that are otherwise dissimilar. For instance, in a speech about historic flooding in Nebraska, Governor Pete Ricketts stated, "We want people to know that we've got a very serious situation here in Nebraska, but we're used to that pioneer spirit of getting things done."[26] Ricketts drew an analogy between the current flooding and conditions faced by pioneers during westward expansion. The two situations are not the same, but for purposes of his statement, they imply a similar ethic of perseverance. An analogy provides clarification, but it is not proof because the comparison inevitably breaks down. Analogies can be impactful for framing an idea but must also be accompanied by other forms of evidence to fully substantiate a point.

EXPLANATIONS

explanation
A means of idea development that simplifies or clarifies an idea while arousing audience interest.

Explanations are another important means of clarification and persuasion that you will often find in written and visual sources and in interviews. An **explanation** clarifies what something is or how it works. A good explanation usually simplifies a concept or an idea by explaining the idea from the audience's point of view. If you have ever watched Sanjay Gupta from CNN or other medical correspondents, you've seen them attempt to explain highly technical medical procedures in ways that lay audiences can understand. Explanations are the lifeblood of great journalism; they are also critical for great speeches. Explanations may be thought of as strategies for explaining topics that combine multiple other types of support. So, for instance, an explanation of the COVID-19 virus may contain quotations from experts, statistics, and examples.

definitions
Determinations of meaning through description, simplification, examples, analysis, comparison, explanation, or illustration.

DEFINITIONS

Some of the most contentious arguments in our society center on **definitions**, or determinations of meaning through description, simplification, examples, analysis, comparison, explanation, or illustration.

Definitions in a public speech enlighten the audience by revealing what a term means. Sometimes you can use definitions that appear in standard reference works, such as dictionaries and encyclopedias, but simply trying to explain the word in language the audience will understand is often more effective. For example, suppose you use the term *subcutaneous hematoma* in your speech. *Subcutaneous hematoma* is jargon used by physicians to explain a blotch on your flesh, but you could explain the term in this way: *"Subcutaneous* means 'under the skin,' and *hematoma* means 'swelled with blood,' so the words mean 'blood swelling under the skin,' or what most of us call a 'bruise.'"

communicating with agility

Stories about Numbers

When using statistics in a presentation, it is tempting to show a graph and assume the data speaks for itself. Nothing can be further from the truth for agile communicators. In fact, a key skill in modern organizations is to tell the story behind the numbers. If a sales report shows an increase in sales, why do you think that happened? If data show health disparities among demographic groups, what could explain that?

The organization Gapminder has developed expertise in using statistics to tell stories of inequities in human services. Ola Rosling, president of Gapminder, recently spoke about worldwide sustainability goals at the United Nations Assembly. He discussed progress toward these goals by acting like a sports commentator describing a race. His visual aid even depicted movement of icons, representing specific goals, as they moved toward deadlines analogous to the finish line of a race. His agility in presenting complex information in an engaging narrative is an effective communication strategy in any presentation.

Source: Rosling, O. (2020, September 18). *The SDKs aren't the same old same old.* https://youtu.be/v7WUpgPZzpl

THINK ABOUT THE MIX

When selecting supporting material for your presentation, you should think carefully about the various types of material that you integrate. Each type of supporting material has different argumentative and artistic features, so integrating a variety of types of supporting material can increase the logical and emotional appeal of your speech. In public speaking, there are no rules on the types or mixtures of supporting material. However, here are some principles to follow:

communicating creatively

Identifying Sources Visually

Inexperienced speakers often struggle with citing sources during their presentations. Many forget to cite sources altogether. Those who remember often have difficulty in effectively identifying sources of information for audience members. A creative way to identify sources is to use visual aids (see Chapter 13). For example, when using a quotation from an individual, create a slide showing a picture of the person and use text to briefly describe your source's title or other qualifications. By showing the source visually, you will establish the source's qualifications. In fact, when you use a picture, your audience will likely connect better with the source and perceive the source, and you, as more credible.

- *Balance your supporting material.* Because supporting material differs in presentation and tone, relying on a single type of supporting material can result in perceptions that your presentation is incomplete. For example, using only quotations can diminish your voice, and using only statistics can become overwhelming for audience members.

- *Match your support to the topic.* If your topic is emotionally charged, examples and narratives will assist you in conveying the emotion. If your topic is highly controversial, statistics can impose a greater sense of rationality to perhaps tone down polarized viewpoints.

- *Match supporting material to your purpose.* Use of narratives and examples may increase the vividness of your presentation, which may diminish the impact of statistics. Contrarily, using many statistics can potentially diminish the effect of narratives.[27] Although you should have some variety, you should determine your primary objective and emphasize supporting material that is consistent with that objective.

- *Tie supporting material together.* A detailed statistic may need to be followed by an explanation so that audience members can better understand the information. A survey might be paired with a quotation from an expert to discuss implications from the survey.

In summary, there are many types of supporting material that you can include in any type of presentation. You should consider your objective, your audience, and your message to identify the best possible mix of support to help you achieve your goals as a speaker.

How to Cite Sources of Information

All the work you put into conducting great research will be lost if you do not find ways to explain the sources that you used. When reading or watching the news, how often have you heard reports from anonymous sources? It turns out that the use of anonymous sources decreases both the credibility and the believability of news stories.[28] The same holds true for speeches. If you do not identify your sources and show why they are credible, you can damage your own credibility.

You will provide references for your sources both on your outline and during your presentation. **Bibliographic references** are complete citations that appear in the "references" or "works cited" section of your speech outline (or term paper). Your outline should also contain **internal references**, which are brief notations of which bibliographic reference

bibliographic references Complete citations that appear in the "references" or "works cited" section of your speech outline.

internal references Brief notations indicating a bibliographic reference that contains the details you are using in your speech.

building behaviors

Verbally Citing Sources

Making verbal citations is one of the most important skills you will learn in this course, and it will benefit you for years to come. Start by drafting possible ways to state your sources in written form. For each source you plan to use in your presentation, write down statements similar to those in Table 11.5 that you could use when identifying your sources. You should not read aloud from these drafts during your presentation, but planning the wording ahead of time will help you state the information more effectively. When writing your drafts, take care to emphasize the credentials, expertise, and timeliness of the sources.

verbal citations
Oral explanations of who the source is, how recent the information is, and what the source's qualifications are.

contains the details you are using in that section of your speech. Internal and bibliographic references help readers understand what sources you used to find specific details, such as statistics, quotations, and examples. Ask your instructor whether you should use a particular format for references. See Chapter 12 for more on how you should prepare a bibliography for your outline using common style guidelines.

In addition to citing sources in your outline, you must provide verbal citations during your presentation. **Verbal citations** tell listeners who the source is, how recent the information is, and what the source's qualifications are. The examples in Table 11.5 illustrate how to orally cite different types of sources.

Students often have the most difficulty citing webpages. Remember that the web address is only that—an address. Although you should list it in the references or works cited page of your outline, giving the address during your presentation is seldom necessary unless you want your audience to visit that website. Instead, cite the author or organization that produced the web page.

• The decision to use some web resources, such as *Wikipedia*, is controversial. Ask your instructor before using *Wikipedia* or similar sites as sources in a speech or paper.

Wikipedia

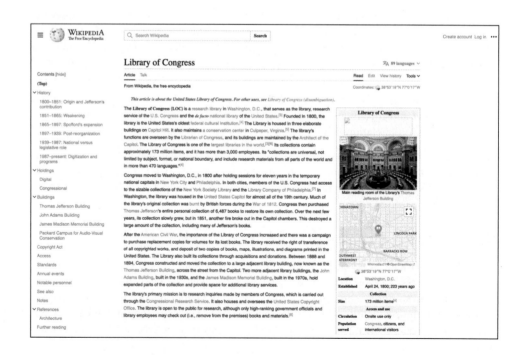

Table 11.5 Examples of Verbal Citations

Type of Source	Example Verbal Citation
News article	"According to an article from the *New York Times* website on November 1, 2022, the RSV virus can lead to more than 3.5 million hospitalizations per year across the globe."
Research study	"Communication researcher Irem Sot reported in a 2022 study that TikTok users perceive that platform as being a safe space where other users listen."
Webpage	"According to a statement on the website of the American Red Cross, which I visited on November 3, 2022, the Red Cross provided more than 1.6 million meals and snacks as part of the Hurricane Ian relief efforts."
Graphic or picture	"As you can see in this graph, displayed on the *FiveThirtyEight* website in August, the number of Americans who refused to get the COVID vaccine remained unchanged for most of the pandemic."

Ethical Principles to Follow for Credibility and Research

As you have learned, credibility is something that is perceived by audience members. Because credibility is based on perceptions, you have an ethical obligation to be honest with your audience. The well-known adage that you can fool all the people some of the time may be accurate, but an ethical communicator avoids fooling anyone.

ETHICS AND SOURCE CREDIBILITY

To determine whether you are behaving ethically, answer the following questions:

- *Are your speech's immediate purpose and long-range goal sound?* Are you providing information or recommending change that would be determined worthy by current standards? Attempting to sell a substandard product or to encourage people to injure others would clearly not be sound; persuading people to accept new, more useful ideas and to be kinder to each other would be sound.

- *Does your end justify your means?* This time-honored notion suggests that communicators can have ethical ends but may use unethical means of bringing the audience to a particular conclusion. You may want listeners to join the armed forces, but should you use scare tactics to achieve your goal?

- *Are you being honest with your audience?* Are you well informed about the subject instead of being a poseur who only pretends to know? Are you using good evidence and reasoning to convince your audience? Are your passions about the subject sincere?

Your credibility does lie in the audience's perception of you, but you also have an ethical obligation to be the sort of person you project yourself to be. In addition, you must consider the influence of your message on the audience. Persuasive speeches, in particular, may lead to far-reaching changes in others' behaviors. Are the changes you are recommending consistent with standard ethical and moral guidelines? Have you thoroughly studied your topic

engaging diversity

Building Credibility Across Cultures

How we define credibility depends on many factors, some of which are determined by our culture. When communicating with audiences from other cultures, what steps should you take to build trust and credibility? The American Management Association[29] identifies eight tips for building credibility by respecting other cultures:

1. Demonstrate cultural competence by understanding your own biases that stem from your culture that could cause you to stereotype individuals from other cultures.

2. Self-regulate your biases by not allowing them to cloud your judgment of others.

3. Take your time to check your perceptions about others before drawing conclusions.

4. Identify ways that you can establish common ground that connects across cultures.

5. Be observant of others' reactions and adapt your communication to them when possible.

6. Show empathy for the perspectives of people from other cultures.

7. Be flexible in how you interact and engage in discussion with others.

8. Demonstrate curiosity for other cultures. This will help you avoid letting biases influence your communication and will show your willingness to learn other cultural traditions and customs.

so that you are convinced of the accuracy of the information you are presenting? Are you presenting the entire picture? Are you using valid and true arguments? In short, are you treating your listeners in the way you wish to be treated when someone else is speaking and you are the listener?

ETHICS AND SUPPORTING MATERIAL

Throughout this release of *Human Communication* we have emphasized various ethical requirements for communication that stem from the NCA Credo on Ethics. And at various points in this chapter, we have pointed out ethical obligations faced by speakers when searching for and using supporting materials. The first point in the National Communication Association Credo on Ethical Communication states that accuracy and honesty are essential for ethical communication.[30] In this final section we summarize the ethical obligations faced by speakers when working with supporting materials, as well as new ethical obligations emerging as a result of material generated by artificial intelligence (AI):

- *Speakers have an ethical obligation to find the best possible sources of information.* The internet and full-text databases certainly provide us with easier research options; however, these tools do not necessarily improve the quality of our research. Nor are the best sources of information always available online or in full-text form. When you speak, your audience depends on you to present the best and most accurate information possible. As a result, many communication instructors emphasize the importance of using *high-quality* sources of information during a presentation. That's why selecting a variety of sources, including professional media outlets, reputable organizations with information on the internet, and possibly even personal interviews, can help improve the overall quality of your presentation.

plagiarism
The intentional use of information from another source without crediting the source.

incremental plagiarism
The intentional or unintentional use of information from one or more sources without fully divulging how much information is directly quoted.

- *Speakers have an ethical obligation to cite their sources of information.* Of course, one reason to cite sources of information is to avoid **plagiarism**, which is the intentional use of information from another source without crediting the source. All universities have specific codes of conduct that identify sanctions levied against those who are caught plagiarizing. Although cases of full plagiarism are rare, students often mistakenly commit **incremental plagiarism**, which is the intentional or unintentional use of information from one or more sources without fully divulging how much information is directly quoted. This includes using large chunks of information from webpages and other sources—many times this information is directly copied and pasted from the website. Failing to clearly identify what is directly quoted, even accidentally, is a form of plagiarism.

- Speakers have an obligation to use new AI tools ethically. One way of using AI is to brainstorm ideas. In that instance, AI functions like a search engine, so you may not need to cite your use of the technology. However, if you use AI to generate more detailed content that eventually becomes part of your presentation, you must verify all facts, reframe the ideas in your own presentation style, and cite how you guided the AI through prompts to generate your content. Confirm the citation formatting with your instructor or the style guide needed for your discipline.

- *Speakers have an ethical obligation to fairly and accurately represent sources.* How often have you heard politicians and other public figures complain that the media take their comments "out of context"? To avoid unfair and inaccurate representations of sources, whether they are newspaper articles, webpages, books, or even interviews, you must ensure that you fully understand the points being made by the source. Remember, for example, that two-sided arguments are often used to present a point. A **two-sided argument** is one in which a source advocating one position presents an argument from the opposite viewpoint and then goes on to refute that viewpoint. To take an excerpt from a source in which the opposing argument is being presented for refutation and to imply that the source was advocating the opposing argument is unethical. As a speaker, you are free to disagree with points made by the sources you consult; however, you may not misrepresent them.

two-sided argument
A source advocating one position presents an argument from the opposite viewpoint and then goes on to refute that argument.

Locating, understanding, and incorporating supporting material is one of the most important tasks you will undertake as a presenter of information and argument. As illustrated by Table 11.1, research affects every step in the process of preparing and delivering a presentation. Taking care to effectively and ethically use your information will make you a better speaker and will garner the respect of your peers and teachers.

be ready... for what's next

How to Be an Expert

As a college student, you are just starting to build a portfolio, or set of credentials, to establish your credibility in a particular area. You should not think of credibility as something that is there or not there. Rather, credibility and expertise are developed over time.[31] Some people are more credible than others. So, if you are in the early stages of building credibility, what should it look like several years, or even decades, later?

In fact, there is a good deal of research exploring the characteristics of experts—those who are at the highest levels of credibility in a particular area. These studies have explored expertise in many different domains, as diverse as chess playing, medicine, and sports. Common to all of these areas are the following characteristics of experts:

- There is a certain quantity of time that is necessary to achieve expertise. Literally thousands of hours of practice or study are necessary to reach expert status.

- The quality of how you spend your time is important. Simply rehearsing something to maintain a skill is not sufficient to reach expert status. You must calibrate practice to continually advance your skill in performing a task, recognizing clues, and drawing conclusions.

- Your practice should allow for instant feedback and for opportunities to repeat newly learned tasks until you do them correctly. Professional athletes have natural skills, but the very best athletes carefully challenge themselves to improve through multiple sources of critique and feedback from others.

- Experts are self-aware. Rather than being satisfied with maintaining a set level of performance, experts always have an understanding of what the next level of proficiency could be. There is always another goal that is established.

Based on these typical characteristics of experts, what can you do to go beyond being credible and develop strong expertise? Your journey down that path has already started, but it is up to you to determine how far and how quickly you want to take that journey.

Chapter Review & Study Guide

Summary

In this chapter, you learned the following:

1. Source credibility is important because it helps audience members understand why you are qualified and trustworthy enough to present on the topic in question.

   - Source credibility is the audience's perception of your qualifications and effectiveness as a speaker. Although you must provide information that establishes your credibility, audience members ultimately decide the degree to which you are credible.

   - Your credibility is determined by a combination of the topic, the situation, and your qualifications. To analyze credibility, you should ask, "Why am I credible to speak on this topic in this situation?"

2. Source credibility is created from the audience's perceptions of four dimensions of credibility:

   - Competence is the speaker's qualifications to speak on a topic.

   - Trustworthiness is the perceived dependability and ethics of the speaker.

   - Dynamism is the extent to which the speaker appears confident and comfortable to the audience. A lack of dynamism can make the speaker appear less competent and less trustworthy.

   - Common ground exists when there is perceived shared understanding between the speaker and the audience. The shared understanding or experience can happen in the past, present, or future.

3. Because your credibility is influenced by the information you use to support your ideas, you must develop a good strategy for identifying and selecting high-quality information that can later be used as supporting material.

   - You should carefully evaluate sources to determine if they contain misinformation or disinformation, either of which could cause you to present misleading information to your audience.

   - To be most effective, you should think of research as a process in which you select a variety of high-quality sources to present information on a carefully focused topic.

   - Your research strategy should consider use of multiple types of sources, including your own personal experience, information from interviews that you conduct with others, various types of library resources, and online resources.

   - You should carefully evaluate all types of sources to determine whether they are clear, verifiable, competent, objective, relevant, and current.

4. There are eight types of supporting material that you can use to support ideas in your speech: examples, narratives, surveys, testimony, numbers and statistics, analogies, explanations, and definitions.

5. When using supporting material from sources that you have found, you must correctly reference those sources, both in writing in your outline and orally during your presentation.

   - Your outline should contain a reference section at the end where complete bibliographic references are provided. You should consult with your teacher about specific requirements for the formatting of those citations.

   - In the text of the outline, you should use internal citations to indicate where information from other sources is integrated.

   - During your speech, you should use verbal citations to tell audience members about your sources.

6. You should follow core ethical principles to establish your credibility and in the use of evidence.

   - You have an obligation to be honest with your audience by using good evidence. Your purpose in speaking should be reasonable and sound, and you should use methods of presenting information that are justified.

   - You have an ethical obligation to find the best possible sources to use in your presentation, to cite those sources during the presentation, and to accurately represent what those sources say.

Key Terms

Analogy	Dynamism	Lay testimony
Bibliographic references	Examples	Misinformation
Celebrity testimony	Expert testimony	Narratives
Common ground	Explanation	Personal experience
Competence	Heuristics	Plagiarism
Definitions	Incremental plagiarism	Reference librarian
Disinformation	Internal references	Search engine

Sleeper effect
Source credibility
Statistics

Supporting material
Surveys
Testimonial evidence

Trustworthiness
Two-sided argument
Verbal citations

Study Questions

1. Which of the following statements regarding source credibility is *not* true?
   a. Source credibility is the audience's perception of the effectiveness of a speaker.
   b. Source credibility depends on the speaker, the subject discussed, the situation, and the audience.
   c. Source credibility is something a speaker possesses.
   d. The audience determines source credibility.

2. Which aspect of source credibility is the degree to which a speaker is perceived as honest, friendly, and honorable?
   a. competence
   b. trustworthiness
   c. dynamism
   d. common ground

3. Which aspect of credibility would be negatively affected if you used jargon or filler words or read from your slides?
   a. competence
   b. trustworthiness
   c. dynamism
   d. common ground

4. Which of the following types of misinformation are most likely to be intentionally deceptive?
   a. manipulated content
   b. parody
   c. misleading content
   d. false connection

5. Which of the following cannot be utilized effectively when gathering evidence for your speeches?
   a. personal experience
   b. library resources
   c. the internet
   d. a friend's speech

6. Which type of source undergoes blind peer review to ensure high-quality information and contains specified studies?
   a. nonfiction books
   b. academic journal articles
   c. government documents
   d. trade journal articles

7. Brief notations in your outline that indicate a reference used in your speech are called _____ references, whereas _____ references are complete citations that appear in the references section of the speech outline.
   a. internal; bibliographic
   b. verbal; internal
   c. bibliographic; external
   d. external; verbal

8. When evaluating sources, you should ensure that the supporting material
   a. contains jargon and technical explanations.
   b. includes relevant and irrelevant information.
   c. contains bias and is subjective.
   d. is verifiable.

9. Which type of supporting material includes written or oral statements of others' experiences?
   a. examples
   b. testimonial evidence
   c. numbers and statistics
   d. definitions

10. To develop expertise, research suggests that your practice should
    a. take as few hours as possible.
    b. involve instant feedback.
    c. maintain basic skills.
    d. avoid repetition.

Answers:
1. (c); 2. (b); 3. (a); 4. (a); 5. (d); 6. (b); 7. (a); 8. (d); 9. (b); 10. (b)

Critical Thinking

1. Using the internet, choose a topic and find two sources that could be used to provide information on the topic. One source should be high in credibility, and the other should be low in credibility. Discuss the differences between the sources, and explain why you selected them to illustrate high and low credibility.

2. Go to the Pew Research Center's website (PewResearch.org) and click on the "Short Reads" tab at the top. Select an article that interests you. Analyze how the author uses statistics and explains the meaning or narrative surrounding the statistics. Create at least one slide showing the statistic and practice how you would explain the statistic to your audience.

Sizing Things Up Scoring and Interpretation
Research Attitudes Scale

Effective speakers use a variety of types of supporting materials and research in their speeches. The scale created for this chapter helps you assess your strengths and weaknesses in using various types of research resources. After completing and scoring the scale, you can use the results as a diagnostic tool to determine strategies for which you may need additional assistance from your teacher or a reference librarian.

The Research Attitudes Scale assesses your comfort and ability in using five different types of research resources: the internet (items 1, 9, and 14), journals (items 2, 7, and 15), books (items 3, 6, and 11), reference materials (items 4, 8, and 12), and popular press sources (items 5, 10, and 13). You should sum the responses to questions for each resource to find specific scores. Scores of 3 to 6 indicate areas needing greater attention or assistance.

References

1. Schwarzenegger, A. (2022, March 17). *Arnold Schwarzenegger tells Putin to "stop this war."* YouTube. https://www.youtube.com/watch?v=fWClXZd9c78

2. Schwazenegger, A. (2020, March 17). I have a message for my Russian friends. *The Atlantic.* https://www.theatlantic.com/ideas/archive/2022/03/schwarzenegger-russia-ukraine-war-message/627100/

3. Heikkilä, H., Kunelius, R., & Ahva, L. (2010, August). From credibility to relevance. *Journalism Practice, 4,* 274–284.

4. Bowe, J. (2022, February 14). *Avoid these 5 types of words and phrases that make you sound 'immature,' says speech expert.* CNBC. https://www.cnbc.com/2022/02/14/avoid-these-words-and-phrases-that-make-you-sound-immature-says-speech-expert.html

5. Baker, A., Porter, S., Brinke, L., & Mundy, C. (2016). Seeing is believing: Observer perceptions of trait trustworthiness predict perceptions of honesty in high-stakes emotional appeals. *Psychology, Crime & Law, 22,* 817–831. https://doi.org/10.1080/1068316X.2016.1190844

6. Kim, M. (2022, July 6). Think leader, thinking deep voice? CEO voice pitch and gender. *Academy of Management Review.* https://doi.org/10.5465/AMBPP.2022.17778

7. Kecskes, I., & Zhang, F. (2009). Activating, seeking, and creating common ground. A socio-cognitive approach. *Pragmatics & Cognition, 17,* 331–355.

8. Coleman, M. S. (2011) "I was a teenage scientist." *Vital Speeches of the Day, 77*(5): 181–184. https://www.vsotd.com/issue/2011-5/i-was-teenage-scientist

9. Hosman, L. A., & Siltanen, S. A. (2011). Hedges, tag questions, message processing, and persuasion. *Journal of Language & Social Psychology, 30,* 341–349.

10. Huntington, H. E. (2020). Partisan cues and internet memes: early evidence for motivated skepticism in audience message processing of spreadable political media. *Atlantic Journal of Communication, 28,* 194–208. https://doi.org/10.1080/15456870.2019.1614589

11. Heinbach, D., Ziegele, M., & Quiring, O. (2018). Sleeper effect from below: Long-term effects of source credibility and user comments on the persuasiveness of news articles. *New Media & Society, 20,* 4765–4786. https://doi.org/10.1177/1461444818784472

12. Hannah, M., & Meluch, A. L. (2022). The Risks and Benefits of Disclosing to Students: College Instructors' Perceptions of their Disclosures in the Classroom. *Texas Speech Communication Journal, 46,* 31–45.

13. Masip, J. (2003). Facial appearance and judgments of credibility: The effects of facial babyishness and age on statement credibility. *Genetic, Social & General Psychology Monographs, 129*(3): 269–311.

14. Fico, F., Richardson, J. D., & Edwards, S. M. (2004). Influence of story and structure on perceived story bias and news organization credibility. *Mass Communication & Society, 7,* 301–318.

15. Carnahan, D., Ulusoy, E., Barry, R., McGraw, J., Virtue, I., & Bergan, D. E. (2022). What should I believe? A conjoint analysis of the influence of message characteristics on belief in, perceived credibility of, and intent to share political posts. *Journal of Communication, 72,* 592–603. https://doi.org/10.1093/joc/jqac023

16. Teven, J. J. (2010). The effects of supervisor nonverbal immediacy and power use on employees' ratings of credibility and affect for the supervisor. *Human Communication, 13,* 69–85.

17. Rodero, E., Larrea, O., Rodríguez-de-Dios, I., & Lucas, I. (2022). The Expressive Balance Effect: Perception and Physiological Responses of Prosody and Gestures. *Journal of Language & Social Psychology, 41,* 659–684. https://doi.org/10.1177/0261927X221078317

18. Reinard, J., & Myers, K. (2005, May). *Comparisons of models of persuasive effects of types of evidence introductions.* Paper presented at the International Communication Association Convention.

19. Allen, M. (2002). Effect of timing of communicator identification and level of source credibility on attitude. *Communication Research Reports, 19,* 46–55.

20. Geiger, N. (2022). Do People Actually "Listen to the Experts"? A Cautionary Note on Assuming Expert Credibility and Persuasiveness on Public Health Policy Advocacy. *Health Communication, 37,* 677–684. https://doi.org/0.1080/10410236.2020.1862449

21. Wardle, C. (2017, February 16). Fake news. It's complicated. *First Draft.* https://firstdraftnews.org/fake-news-complicated/

22. Digital Resource Center (2022, November 3). Introducing IMVAIN. Stonybrook University. https://digitalresource.center/content/introducing-imvain

23. Newman, N. (2019, March 25). *Overview and key finding of the 2018 report.* Reuters Institute for the Study of Journalism. http://www.digitalnewsreport.org/survey/2018/overview-key-findings-2018/

24. Choy, E. (2022, October 30). 3 Business storytelliing strategies that will help you explain complex ideas. *Forbes.* https://www.forbes.com/sites/estherchoy/2022/10/30/3-business-storytelling-strategies-that-will-help-you-explain-complex-ideas/?sh=33b89a3a103c

25. Peterson, B. L. & Harter, L. M. (2022). *Brave spacemaking: The poetics & politics of storytelling.* Kendall Hunt.

26. Savage, S. (2019, March 20). *Nebraska governor: Worst flooding damage in our state's history.* FOX Business. https://www.foxbusiness.com/features/nebraska-governor-worst-flooding-damage-in-our-states-history

27. Han, B. & Fink, E. L. (2012). How do statistical and narrative evidence affect persuasion? The role of evidentiary features. *Argumentation and Advocacy, 49,* 39–58.

28. Sternadori, M. M., & Thorson, E. (2009). Anonymous sources harm credibility of all stories. *Newspaper Research Journal, 30,* 54–66.

29. American Management Association. (2022, January 27). 8 keys to communicating across cultures with credibility. https://www.amanet.org/articles/8-keys-to-communicating-across-cultures-with-credibility/

30. National Communication Association. (2019, April 2). Credo on ethical communication. https://www.natcom.org/sites/default/files/Public_Statement_Credo_for_Ethical_Communication_2017.pdf

31. Rasmussen, L. (2021, September 13). *What is expertise and how can you develop it?* Global Cognition. https://www.globalcognition.org/what-is-expertise/

Hero Images/Getty Images

organizing presentations

When you have read and thought about this chapter, you will be able to

1. create an effective introduction that captures the interest of your audience in your topic, the purpose of the speech, and the development of the talk.

2. outline a presentation.

3. describe the most frequently used patterns of organization in public presentations.

4. use transitions and signposts that link ideas and indicate direction to the audience.

5. create an effective conclusion.

6. compile a list of references to accompany your complete outline.

In this chapter you will learn how to organize your presentation. In addition to learning about principles of outlines and three types of outlines for speeches, you will examine the three main parts of a speech: introduction, body, and conclusion. You will also learn the functions of each part and how to effectively organize the content. Understanding the parts of a speech, the functions of each part, and ways to organize the entire message is essential to becoming a successful presenter.

Gentrification is a phenomenon in which low-income urban areas experience an influx of wealthier individuals who repair or rebuild homes, which attracts new businesses. As a result of these "improvements," housing prices typically rise, which displaces many of the original residents who can no longer afford to live there.

Bree Jones, a former investment banker with Morgan Stanley, founded the nonprofit organization Parity, which is devoted to promoting equitable housing and combatting the negative effects of gentrification. Jones spoke on the topic of gentrification during a TED Talk in September 2022, which you can find by searching for her name on the TED website.

Bree Jones used a problem-solution pattern for her TED Talk on gentrification.

Tribune Content Agency LLC/Alamy Stock Photo

Jones began her presentation by asking audience members to picture a scenario in which they found a home they loved but were unable to purchase it because the cost to repair it would exceed the home's market value, one of the conditions that leads to gentrification. After using this technique to gain attention, Jones described the process of gentrification, as well as its negative effects. Finally, she outlined the approaches used by her organization to create quality affordable housing in historically Black neighborhoods. Jones used a problem-solution organizational pattern, which is one of the most commonly used patterns for a persuasive speech.

Principles of Outlining

Once you have thoroughly researched your topic, the primary planning strategy for your speech involves creating an outline. An **outline** is a written plan that uses symbols, margins, and content to reveal the order, importance, and substance of your speech. An outline shows the sequence of your arguments or main points; indicates their relative importance; and states the content of your arguments, main points, and subpoints. The outline is a simplified summary of your speech. The outline differs from a manuscript, which is an exact, word-for-word text of what you will say.

Why should you learn how to outline? Here are three good reasons:

- Outlining is a skill that can be used to develop written compositions, to write notes in class, and to compose speeches.
- Outlining reinforces important skills, such as determining what is most important, what arguments and evidence will work best with this audience, and roughly how much time and effort will go into each part of your presentation.
- Outlining encourages you to speak conversationally, because you do not have every word in front of you.

outline
A written plan that uses symbols, margins, and content to reveal the order, importance, and substance of a presentation.

• Creating an outline will help you structure your speech in the most effective way possible.

Ingram Publishing

parallel form
The consistent use of complete sentences, clauses, phrases, or words in an outline.

You will find that learning how to outline can provide you with a useful tool in your classes and at work. Outlining is versatile and easy to learn as long as you keep six principles in mind:

- *Principle 1: Link your outline to your immediate purpose and long-range goal.* All the items of information in your outline should be directly related to your immediate purpose and long-range goal. The immediate purpose is what you expect to achieve *immediately following your presentation.* You might want the audience to be able to distinguish between a row house and a townhouse, to watch a particular documentary through an online service, or to talk with others about a social issue. All these purposes can be achieved shortly after the audience hears about the idea. The long-range goal is what you expect to achieve by your message *in the days, months, or years ahead.* You may be talking about a candidate two months before the election, but you want your audience to vote a certain way at that future date. You may want to push people to be more tolerant toward persons of your race, gender, sexual orientation, or religion, but tolerance is more likely to develop over time than instantly—so your goal is long range.

- *Principle 2: Use parallel form.* **Parallel form** relies on the consistent use of complete sentences, clauses, phrases, or words, but not a mixture of these. Writing professors Diana Hacker and Nicole Sommers, in their text on writing, explain, "Readers expect items in a series to appear in parallel grammatical form."[1] So do listeners. Most teachers prefer an outline consisting entirely of complete sentences because such an outline reveals the speaker's message more completely. The sample outline in this section is composed entirely of complete sentences; the form is parallel because no dependent clauses, phrases, or single words appear by themselves in any of the points or subpoints.

- *Principle 3: Each outline part is a single idea.* That is, the outline should consist of single units of information, usually in the form of complete sentences that express a single idea:

I. Government regulation of handguns should be implemented to reduce the number of murders in this country.

  A. Half the murders in the United States are committed by criminals using handguns.

  B. Half the handgun deaths in the United States are caused by relatives, friends, or acquaintances of the victim.

- *Principle 4: Your outline symbols signal importance.* In the portion of a sample outline that follows, the **main points**, or most important points, are indicated by Roman numerals, such as I, II, III, IV, and V. The number of main points in a 5- to 10-minute message, or even a longer presentation, should be limited to the number you can reasonably cover, explain, or prove in the time permitted. Most five-minute messages have two or three main points. Even hour-long presentations must have a limited number of main points because most audiences are unable to remember more than seven main points.

main points
The most important points in a presentation; indicated by Roman numerals in an outline.

subpoints
The points in a presentation that support the main points; indicated by capital letters in an outline.

     Subpoints provide specific information related to each main point and are indicated by capital letters, such as A, B, C, D, and E. Ordinarily, two subpoints under a main point are regarded as the minimum if any subpoints are to be presented. Like main points, subpoints should be limited in number; otherwise, the audience may lose sight of your main points. A good guideline is to present two or three of your best pieces of supporting material in support of each main point. Subpoints may be divided further into sub-subpoints, which are typically very specific details, such as statistics or examples, and are indicated by standard numbers, such as 1, 2, and 3. At this level of the outline, it is sometimes not possible, due to time constraints, to always include two details (or sub-subpoints) under each letter. In such cases the best approach is to include the detail (or sub-subpoint) within the text of the subpoint. For example, if you have a subpoint, designated by a letter, and have time to include only one example to develop the subpoint, you should combine that example into the text of the lettered subpoint rather than having only one sub-subpoint underneath.

- *Principle 5: Your outline margins signal importance.* The margins of your outline are coordinated with the symbols assigned to the outline items, so the main points all have the same left margin, the subpoints all have a slightly larger left margin, and sub-subpoints have a still larger one. The larger the margin on the left, the less important the item is to your purpose. Microsoft Word and other word processing programs have built-in outlining features that can help you organize numbering, lettering, and margin indentation. As you practice your speech, such indentation will help you see where you are more easily.

- *Principle 6: Your outline is an organized summary of the message you will deliver.* To simplify, the outline should be less than every word you will speak but should include all important points and supporting materials. Some instructors say an outline should be about one-third the length of the actual presentation, if the message were in manuscript form. However, you should ask what your instructor expects, because some instructors like to see a very complete outline, whereas others prefer a brief outline. Nonetheless, even a complete outline is not a manuscript but a summary of the talk you intend to deliver, a plan that includes the important arguments or information you intend to present.

The following partial outline shows how the principles of outlining are applied. In the sections that follow, you will learn how to use these principles to construct a speech outline containing an introduction, a body, a conclusion, and references.

Sample Partial Outline Illustrating the Principles of Outlining

Take Time for Breakfast!

Immediate purpose: After listening to this speech, audience members should be able to commit to taking 10 minutes each morning to eat breakfast because of the many benefits.

Body

I. Students who eat breakfast perform better in school.

A. Research studies have reported that people who eat breakfast have more energy throughout the day and, consequently, greater levels of concentration.

B. Improved concentration aids in several aspects of school performance, including the ability to take notes, retain information that you have read or heard, and solve complex problems.

CONTINUED

Principle 1: Main points link to the immediate purpose.

Principle 2: Main points use parallel wording to help listeners follow the structure of the speech.

Principle 3: Each item in the outline is a single idea.

Principle 4: The outline uses Roman numerals, capital letters, and numbers to indicate main points, subpoints, and details.

II. Students who eat breakfast are healthier than those who don't.

    A. Eating breakfast jump-starts your metabolism for the day.

       1. A healthy metabolism can help you regulate blood sugar, avoid overeating, and have energy for activity.

       2. WebMD reports that eating breakfast is a critical component of maintaining a healthy weight.

    B. Eating breakfast provides you with nutrients that can boost your immune system and help protect you from communicable diseases like the common cold or even the flu.

Types of Outlines

When preparing your speech, you will begin by creating a rough draft outline. You will then turn the rough draft outline into a sentence outline, which serves as the primary outline showing the substance of the ideas you cover. After finalizing the sentence outline, you will create a keyword outline, which will serve as your speaking notes. This section describes and provides an example of each type of outline.

THE ROUGH DRAFT

To begin the process of creating your outline you should (1) select a topic that is appropriate for you, your audience, your immediate purpose, and the situation; (2) find arguments, examples, illustrations, quotations, stories, and other supporting materials from your experiences, from written and visual resources, and from other people; and (3) narrow your topic so that you can select the best materials from a large supply of available evidence (see Chapters 10 and 11).

rough draft
The preliminary organization of the outline of a presentation.

Once you have gathered materials consistent with your immediate purpose, you can begin by developing a **rough draft** of your outline—a preliminary organization of the outline. The most efficient way to develop a rough draft is to choose a limited number of main points important for your immediate purpose and your audience.

Next, you should see what materials you have from your experiences, from written and visual resources, and from other people to support these main ideas, including facts, statistics, testimony, and examples. What arguments, illustrations, and supporting materials will be most likely to have an impact on the audience? Sometimes speakers get so involved in a topic that they select mainly those items that interest them. In public speaking you should select the items likely to have the maximum impact on the audience, not on you.

Composing an outline for a speech is a process. Even professional speechwriters may need to make significant changes to their first draft. Some of the questions you need to consider as you revise your rough draft follow:

- Are your main points consistent with your immediate purpose?
- Do your subpoints and sub-subpoints relate to your main points?
- Are the items in your outline the best possible ones for the audience, the topic, you, the immediate purpose, and the occasion?
- Does your outline follow the principles of outlining?

Even after you have rewritten your rough draft, you would be wise to have another person—perhaps a classmate—examine your outline and provide an opinion about its content, organization, and integration of evidence.

A rough draft of a speech does not necessarily follow parallel form, nor is it as complete as the sentence outline, which often develops out of the rough draft. Mostly, the rough draft provides an initial blueprint for how ideas will fit together in your speech. Your rough draft outline will evolve as you conduct additional research, identify new ideas to discuss, and refine how those ideas are organized. When you are ready to finalize your outline, you have several options. However, the sentence outline is preferred by many communication instructors.

The following rough draft outline on autonomous vehicles shows what a rough draft might look like, though you should recognize that a rough draft will change and evolve as you research and further refine your speech.

Sample Rough Draft Outline
The Promise of Autonomous Vehicles

Immediate purpose: After listening to my speech, the audience should be able to explain how increasing use of autonomous vehicles potentially improves transportation safety.

  Mention my major in information technology.

I. Defining what autonomous vehicles are

   A. Sensors to monitor vehicle and surroundings

   B. Uses artificial intelligence to navigate, control vehicle, and avoid crashes

II. Autonomous vehicles will grow in use.

   A. PR Newswire article—industry will top $800 billion by 2035

   B. Will account for 8% of urban miles driven in U.S. by 2025

III. Autonomous vehicles can increase safety.

   A. Driver error and distractions are a major source of accidents.

   B. From 2017 to 2018 the number of times a human driver had to take control of a Waymo autonomous vehicle dropped by 50%, indicating the technology is improving.

   C. Autonomous vehicles share information and learn from accidents.

IV. Conclusion

   A. Should consider using autonomous vehicle technology

   B. Don't be afraid of a robot car.

A rough draft may include important ideas not yet fully integrated into your outline.

Rough drafts help you begin forming ideas and organization but may not yet include fully developed points.

Rough drafts are where you can begin integrating evidence as your research progresses.

A rough draft may include a mixture of complete sentences and words or phrases.

Rough drafts are an early plan that you will shape into a fully developed speech outline.

THE SENTENCE OUTLINE

sentence outline
An outline consisting entirely of complete sentences.

The sentence outline does not have all the words that will occur in the delivered speech, but it does provide a complete guide to the content. A **sentence outline** consists entirely of complete sentences. It shows in sentence form your order of presentation; what kinds of arguments, supporting material, and evidence you plan to use; and where you plan to place them. A look at your outline can help you determine strengths and weaknesses. You might note, for instance, that you have insufficient information about one main point or a surplus of information on another.

Because the sentence outline is a complete blueprint for your presentation, you should be able to identify all necessary elements such as the introduction, main points, and conclusion. As you will learn in the next sections, each of these presentation sections has elements, and those elements should be visible in your sentence outline. For example, where are you trying to gain and maintain attention? Where are you trying to back up a major argument with supporting materials such as statistics, testimony, or examples? Where will you provide oral source citations for evidence that you present? Your sentence outline provides a plan for answering these and other important questions.

The following sample outline shows how the autonomous vehicle outline was transformed into a sentence outline. Each idea is developed as a complete sentence. Notice how the introduction and conclusion contain specific elements and how the body of the speech develops main ideas. You will learn about these elements in detail later in this chapter.

Sentence outlines should include all elements of the speech, including an introduction, a body with main points, and a conclusion.

Sample Sentence Outline

The Promise of Autonomous Vehicles

Immediate purpose: After listening to my speech, the audience should be able to explain how increasing use of autonomous vehicles potentially improves transportation safety.

Introduction

I. *Attention getter*: Imagine you called Lyft or Uber for a ride home and the car that showed up did not have a driver but drove itself. Would you get in?

II. *Listener relevance*: Autonomous vehicle technology is rapidly expanding and will soon be commonly used as a means of public and private transportation across the country.

III. *Speaker credibility*: As an Information Technology major, I will specialize in designing data networks necessary for autonomous vehicles to function correctly and, consequently, have already begun research on this technology.

IV. *Thesis*: Use of autonomous vehicles has the potential to increase transportation safety.

V. *Preview*: The two points I will discuss are the expansion of autonomous vehicle technology and the potential ways that they can improve safety.

Body

I. Autonomous vehicle use is rapidly expanding.

   A. Autonomous vehicles are self-driving cars, trucks, and other forms of public transportation.

      1. Autonomous vehicles use sensors and artificial intelligence software to navigate trips, control the vehicle, and avoid crashes.

      2. In the consumer market, Tesla vehicles are equipped with basic self-driving technology, and other manufacturers are implementing similar technology, such as lane monitoring and adaptive cruise control.

      3. The largest company testing vehicles is Waymo, which logged 1.2 million miles in 2018 (Madrigal, 2019).

   B. Autonomous vehicle technology is projected to grow.

      1. Sales of autonomous vehicles is projected to top $800 billion by 2035 (PR Newswire, 2018).

      2. Industry analysts project that autonomous vehicles will account for 8% of all urban miles driven in the U.S. by 2025 [show graph].

II. Autonomous vehicles have the potential to increase transportation safety.

   A. In traditional vehicles, the most prominent safety feature is the driver, a human being who can be easily distracted.

      1. Statistics show that over 90% of car crashes are the result of driver error (Hancock, 2018).

      2. Texting and driving are common causes of crashes [show picture].

      3. Driver impairment, such as from alcohol, is a cause of crashes.

CONTINUED

The outline is not an exact manuscript of your speech, but the points in the outline provide a complete summary of the ideas you cover.

Internal citations are used to indicate where sources are integrated into the outline.

Sentence outlines should indicate where you use visual aids in your speech.

B. From 2017 to 2018, the number of times a human driver had to take control of a Waymo autonomous vehicle dropped by 50%, indicating that the technology is improving rapidly (Madrigal, 2019).

C. Fleets of autonomous vehicles share information to learn from accidents, making it more likely that similar accidents will be avoided by all vehicles with access to that information (Turck, 2018).

Conclusion

I. *Brakelight function*: Autonomous vehicles are expanding and have the potential to increase safety.

II. *Summary*: Today, you have learned about the development of autonomous vehicle technology and specific reasons why they might protect travelers from accidents, particularly those resulting from driver error.

III. *Specific audience action*: I hope that my speech causes you to think about autonomous technology that might already be available to you and to consider using fully autonomous vehicles when they become available to consumers here, or in cities that you visit.

IV. *Clincher*: You should not be afraid of using a robot car to get home, as it might just save your life!

References

Hancock, P. (2018, February 3). Are autonomous cars really safer than human drivers? *Scientific American*. https://www.scientificamerican.com/article/are-autonomous-cars-really-safer-than-human-drivers/

Madrigal, A. (2019, February 14). Waymo's robots drove more miles than everyone else combined. *The Atlantic*. https://www.theatlantic.com/technology/archive/2019/02/the-latest-self-driving-car-statistics-from-california/582763/

PR Newswire. (2018, July 11). $7 trillion annual market projected for autonomous autos by 2050. https://www.prnewswire.com/news-releases/-7-trillion-annual-market-projected-for-autonomous-autos-by-2050-877929258.html

Turck, M. (2018, July 9). How much safer should self-driving cars be? Try 0%. *Forbes*. https://www.forbes.com/sites/mitchturck/2018/07/09/how-much-safer-should-self-driving-cars-be-try-0/#368975a31a84

Each section of the outline starts renumbering with the roman numeral "I."

The sentence outline includes a reference list.

THE KEYWORD OUTLINE

Using a manuscript for your entire speech may invite you to become too dependent on the manuscript. Too much attention to notes reduces your eye contact and minimizes your attention to audience responses. Nonetheless, you can become very proficient at reading from a manuscript on which you have highlighted the important words, phrases, and quotations. A sentence outline may be superior to a manuscript in that it forces you to extemporize, to maintain eye contact, and to respond to audience feedback. Keywords and phrases can also be underlined or highlighted on a sentence outline. An alternative method is simply to use a **keyword outline**, an outline consisting of important words or phrases to remind you of the content of the speech.

A keyword outline shrinks the ideas in a speech considerably more than does a sentence outline. It ordinarily consists of important words and phrases, but it can also include statistics or quotations that are long or difficult to remember. The example below is a keyword outline resulting from the previous, sentence outline.

keyword outline
An outline consisting of important words or phrases to remind you of the content of the presentation.

Sample Keyword Outline

The Promise of Autonomous Vehicles

Introduction
  I. Imagine self-driving car shows up to take you home
 II. Autonomous vehicles will be common
III. My IT major is preparing me to work in this field
 IV. Autonomous vehicles can increase safety
  V. Autonomous vehicles: more common and can improve safety

Body
 I. Autonomous vehicles increasing
   A. Definition and types
     1. Use sensors and artificial intelligence
     2. Tesla has basic autonomous technology
     3. Waymo logged 1.2 million miles (Madrigal 2019–*The Atlantic*)
   B. Autonomous vehicle tech will grow
     1. PR Newswire–$800 billion by 2035
     2. 8% of urban miles driven by 2025 [Graph]

CONTINUED

The keyword outline identifies all elements of the presentation, including the introduction, body with main points, and conclusion.

Keyword outlines include minimal information to help you remember what you intend to say.

Keyword outlines can include specific items, such as source citations, to help you remember to say them during your presentation.

II. Autonomous vehicles will increase safety

   A. Problem of human drivers

      1. Hancock in *Scientific American* 2018—90% of car crashes from driver error

      2. Texting [Picture]

      3. Impairment from alcohol

   B. Madrigal article—50% drop in people taking control of Waymo cars in 2017-2018

   C. Turck 2018 *Forbes*—Vehicles share and learn from information

Conclusion

   I. Autonomous vehicle tech expanding and can increase safety

  II. Learned about development and benefits

 III. Consider using when available

 IV. Don't be afraid of robot cars

> Keyword outlines can include reminders for visual aids.

The Introduction

introduction
The first part of your presentation, in which you fulfill the five functions of an introduction.

The **introduction**, the first part of your presentation, lets audiences assess you as a speaker. During your first few sentences, and certainly in the first few minutes of your speech, audience members decide whether to listen to you. They also decide whether your topic is important enough to hear. In those crucial early minutes, you can capture your listeners' attention and keep their focus, or you can lose their attention—perhaps for the remainder of the presentation.

The five functions of an introduction are to gain the audience's attention, to arouse interest, to state the purpose and thesis of your speech, to establish your credibility, and to briefly forecast for listeners the organization of your speech and the way you will develop your ideas. You do not need to fulfill the functions in this order. Gaining audience attention often comes at the beginning, but maintaining attention is an important function throughout the speech. Forecasting the speech's organization often comes toward the end of an introduction, but it does not have to be last. Let us systematically explore the five functions and some examples of each.

GAINING AND MAINTAINING AUDIENCE ATTENTION

The first function of an introduction is to gain and maintain attention by involving your audience in your topic. Here are some suggestions:

- *Bring to the presentation the object or person about which you are going to speak.* For example, a student speaking on health foods brings a tray full of healthy foods and shares them with the audience after the speech; a student speaking on weight lifting brings a friend to demonstrate the movements during the speech.

- *Invite your audience to participate.* Ask questions and invite audience members to raise their hands and answer. Or if you are speaking about the benefits of exercise, you could ask audience members to stand and stretch their back muscles as a way to gain their attention.

- *Let your clothing relate to your presentation.* For example, a nurse talking about the dangers of acute hepatitis wears a nurse's uniform; a construction worker dons a hard hat.

- *Exercise your audience's imagination.* Have the audience members close their eyes and imagine they are poised on a ski slope, standing before a judge on a driving-while-intoxicated charge, or slipping into a cool Minnesota lake on a hot and humid day. For example, Preston Gilderhus, a student in industrial engineering and management, presented a talk on the importance of bees. He began, "Imagine the world without apples, oranges, strawberries, or carrots. None of these foods would exist without bees."

- *Start with sight or sound.* For example, a student who gave a powerful presentation on motorcycle safety showed six slides as he talked about the importance of wearing a helmet while riding. Only one item appeared in color on each slide: a photograph of a crushed or battered helmet that had been worn by someone who lived through a motorcycle accident. He spoke of safety; the battered helmets reinforced the message.

- *Arouse audience curiosity.* Five hundred white people gathered to hear a presentation on diversity. The speaker was a Chinese man dressed in traditional Chinese attire. He started his presentation by saying nothing; he just slowly scanned his audience. The audience, accustomed to speakers who start by speaking, was mystified by his quiet demeanor but was exceedingly attentive. Then the speaker said, "Do you know how it feels to stand in front of a group this large and to see no one who looks like you?"

- *Role-play.* For example, a student invited an audience member to pretend to be a choking victim. The speaker then "saved" the victim by demonstrating the maneuver she was teaching the audience.

- *Show a very short video.* A football player speaking on violence in that sport showed a short video of punt returns. He pointed out which players were deliberately trying to maim their opponents with face guards—as they have been taught to do.

- *Present a brief quotation or have the audience read something you have provided.* One enterprising student handed every class member an official-looking letter right before his speech. Each letter was a mock personalized court summons for a moving violation detected by a police-owned spy camera at a busy intersection.

- *State striking facts or statistics.* Emily Knilans, a first-year human development and family science student, began her speech on the importance of drinking water by saying, "The human brain weighs about 3 pounds, about 2.4 of those pounds are water, and water contributes to all mental functions."

- *Self-disclose.* Tell audience members something about yourself—related to the topic—that they would not otherwise know: "I am addicted to checking my phone for messages"; "I was an Eagle scout"; "I am adopted."

- *Tell a story, or narration.* ZamZam, a student from Somalia, began her presentation by telling the audience about her family's escape from refugee camps and their migration to the United States when she was 5 years old.

These suggestions for gaining and maintaining audience attention certainly are not the only possibilities available to you, but they have all been used successfully by other students. Your introduction should not simply imitate what you read in this section; instead, think of ideas of your own that will work best for you and your audience.

• Using an audience member to illustrate a specific physical activity can help you gain attention for a speech about health and well-being.

annastills/123RF

Here are three cautions about gaining and maintaining attention: First, no matter what method you use, avoid being overly dramatic. In one case, a student who pretended to cut himself and sprayed fake blood all over the front of the room got his teacher and his audience so upset that they could not listen to his presentation.

Second, always make sure your attention-getting strategy is related to your topic. Some speakers think every public speech must start with a joke, but this is a big mistake if you are not good at telling jokes or your audience is not interested in hearing them. Topically relevant jokes may be acceptable, but they are still just one of hundreds of ways a speaker can gain attention. Another overused device is writing something such as "S-E-X" on a whiteboard and then announcing your speech has nothing to do with sex—you just wanted to gain the audience's attention. Your attention-getting strategy here has nothing to do with the topic.

Finally, be wary of guests, animals, or other distracting objects because these can be so distracting that audience members will stop listening to what you are saying. They can all be effective to gain audience attention, but they must not take center stage while you and your message become background noise.

AROUSING AUDIENCE INTEREST

The second function of an introduction is to arouse audience interest in the subject matter. The best way to do so is to clearly show how the topic is related to the audience. A highly skilled speaker can adapt almost any topic to a given audience. Do you want to talk about a technical topic such as 5G broadband? Nearly everyone uses a mobile device to access information for entertainment, to read the news, and to connect with others. What will 5G broadband allow us to do that is currently not possible? Will we be able to have conversations with hologram images of friends and family? How will videos and movies change to take advantage of such capability? If you can arouse the audience's interest in personally relevant topics, you will find it easier to encourage them to listen

to your speech about some of the technical details associated with the technology. Similarly, speeches about your life as a parent of four, as a camp counselor, or as the manager of a business can be linked to audience interests. The following example from a student speech on drinking and driving relates the topic to the audience:

> Do you know what the leading cause of death is for people who attend this college? As some may have guessed, the leading cause of death among students at this college is car accidents. Not just ordinary car accidents, but accidents in which the driver has been drinking.

The speaker related her topic to the audience by specifying a problem that affects their local community of students. In so doing, she signaled that the focus of her speech will be personally relevant to each audience member.

STATING THE IMMEDIATE PURPOSE AND THESIS

The third function of an introduction is to state the immediate purpose and thesis of your speech. Recall from Chapter 10 that each speech will have an immediate purpose and a long-range goal. On your outline, you will explicitly state your immediate purpose because that statement is necessary as a planning tool. When you present your speech, however, you will typically say a thesis statement during your introduction, which is a complete, declarative sentence stating what your speech will accomplish with the audience. Consider the following immediate purpose and how it was turned into a thesis statement for the presentation:

- *Immediate purpose:* "After hearing this speech, the audience should be able to mix three common household products to make their own antiseptic and reduce germs in their home."

- *Thesis statement:* "You can use readily available household products to make your own antiseptic to kill germs in your house."

sizing things up

Clarity Behaviors Inventory

The first step in understanding how to sound organized when presenting information is to learn how others do this. As college students, you have the opportunity to watch teachers present information nearly every day. Below are 12 statements describing things a teacher might do. Select a teacher from another class, and think of that teacher when responding to the statements. Or consider another student who has already presented in your class. Use the following scale to respond:

1 = Strongly disagree
2 = Disagree
3 = Neither agree nor disagree
4 = Agree
5 = Strongly agree

1. The speaker verbally stresses important issues presented in the presentation.
2. Written examples of topics covered in the presentation are provided in the form of handouts or visual materials (PowerPoint, dry-erase board, or chalkboard).
3. The organization of the talk is given to me in written form, either on paper or as part of a visual aid, such as on a presentation slide or whiteboard.
4. The speaker tells us what definitions, explanations, or conclusions are important to make note of.
5. The speaker explains how we are supposed to see relationships between topics covered in the presentation.
6. The speaker provides us with written descriptions of the most important things in the presentation.
7. The speaker explains when something being presented is important for us to know.
8. The speaker provides us with written or visual definitions, explanations, or conclusions of topics covered in the presentation.
9. The speaker verbally identifies examples that illustrate concepts we are supposed to learn from the talk.
10. Written explanations of how ideas in the presentation fit together are presented on the whiteboard, on the overhead, on PowerPoint, or in handouts.
11. The speaker explains when an important definition of a concept is being provided.

This exercise can measure both oral and written clarity. A guide for interpreting your responses appears at the end of the chapter.

Source: Adapted from Titsworth, S., Novak, D., Hunt, S., & Meyer, K. (2004, May). The effects of teacher clarity on affective and cognitive learning: A causal model of clear teaching behaviors. International Communication Association, New Orleans, LA. Used by permission of the author.

Why both? An immediate purpose is needed to guide planning so that your main points, evidence, and analysis all work toward a clear outcome that you have in mind. Your thesis statement is how you translate your desired outcomes into a clear statement to your audience of what you will accomplish in your speech. Both are related, but one focuses on your planning and the other on how you express that intention to your audience.

ESTABLISHING YOUR CREDIBILITY

The fourth function of an introduction is to describe any special qualifications you have to enhance your credibility. You can talk about your experience, your research, the experts you interviewed, and your own education and training in the subject. Although you should be wary about self-praise, you need not be reserved in stating why you can speak about the topic with authority. Here is an example of establishing credibility through self-disclosure:

> You can probably tell from my fingernails that my day job is repairing automobiles, a job I have held at the same dealership for over 12 years. I have repaired thousands of cars. That is why I want to tell you today why you and your insurance company have to pay such high prices for repair.

For more information about establishing source credibility, see Chapter 11.

FORECASTING DEVELOPMENT AND ORGANIZATION

The fifth function of an introduction is to forecast the organization and development of the presentation. The forecast provides a preview of the main points you plan to cover. Audience members feel more comfortable when they know what to expect. You can help by revealing your plan for the speech. Are you going to discuss a problem and its solution? Are you going to make three main arguments with supporting materials? Let your audience know what you plan to do early in your speech.

Sample Introduction Outline

For-Profit College Closures

Immediate purpose: After listening to this speech, audience members will be able to explain how for-profit college closures can negatively affect the academic success of students.

Introduction

   I. *Attention getter*: What would you do if your college announced it is closing its doors and all of your hard work and investment was for nothing?

  II. *Listener relevance*: On December 5, 2018, 19,000 college students like you and me found their degrees in jeopardy when the for-profit college organization Education Corporation of America announced it would be closing 70 campuses.

 III. *Speaker credibility*: As a college student, I know just how much time, money, and energy we put into our degrees, and the idea of losing it all due to an institutional decision is absolutely terrifying.

  IV. *Thesis*: For-profit college closures are an all too common reality that is negatively affecting thousands of lives.

   V. *Preview*: In this presentation, I will address what for-profit education is, why the campuses close, and how you can get involved and help college students affected by for-profit college closures.

A question arouses the audience's imagination.

The speaker creates relevance for an audience of college students.

The speaker establishes credibility by noting personal status as a college student.

The thesis statement makes a clear, definitive point that will be developed in the presentation.

Main points are clearly identified for the audience.

building behaviors

Crafting an Effective Introduction: Things to Avoid

Here are some tips for strengthening your introduction by avoiding some common mistakes. Once you've drafted your introduction, check it against this list.

- Do not start talking until you are up in front and settled. Starting your speech on the way up to the lectern is bad form.
- Do not say negative things about you or your abilities, such as "I'm not used to public speaking," "I've never done this before," or "I couldn't be more nervous than I am right now." You are supposed to build your credibility in the introduction, not give an audience more doubts about your ability.
- Do not let your nonverbal unease overcome your message. Crossing your legs, refusing to look at the audience, jingling the change in your pocket, repeatedly pushing your hair off your face—all of these signal to the audience your lack of confidence. So act confident even if you are not.
- Do not say negative things about your message, such as "I didn't have much time to prepare this speech," "I couldn't find much information on my topic," or "I really don't know much about this issue." Do the best you can to convey your message, but do not tell the audience to disregard your message.

The Body

Most speakers begin composing their presentations with the body rather than the introduction because they need to know the content of the presentation in order to write an effective introduction.

body
The largest part of a presentation, which contains the arguments, evidence, and main content.

The **body** of a presentation is the largest portion of the presentation in which you place your arguments and ideas, which contain supporting materials such as examples, narratives, survey results, testimonies, statistics, analogies, explanations, and definitions. Since you usually do not have time to state in a presentation everything you know about a subject, you need to decide what information to include in the body and what to exclude. Because not all the material you will use may be of equal importance, you need to decide placement—first, last, or in the middle. Generally, the most important information should be placed first or last. Audiences remember information in these positions more easily than they recall information in the middle of the body. Selecting, prioritizing, and organizing are three skills that you will use in developing the body of your speech.

Just as the introduction of a speech has certain functions to fulfill, so does the body. These are its main functions:

- Increase what an audience knows about a topic (informative presentation).
- Change an audience's attitudes or actions about a topic (persuasive presentation).
- Present a limited number of arguments, stories, and ideas.
- Provide support for your arguments and ideas.
- Indicate the sources of your information, arguments, and supporting materials.

You already know something about organization. Every sentence you utter is organized. The words are arranged according to rules of syntax for the English language. Even when you are in conversation, you organize your speech. The first statement you make is often more general than what follows. For instance, you might say, "I don't like that candidate for Congress," after which you might say why you aren't a fan. You probably don't start by stating specific facts, such as voting records, positions on health care, or personal issues that have been reported on the gossip pages. Likewise, when we compose a speech, we tend to limit what we say, prioritize our points, and back them as necessary with support—all organized according to principles we have either subconsciously learned (such as the rules of syntax) or consciously studied (such as the rules of organization).

ORGANIZATIONAL PATTERNS

organizational patterns
Arrangements of the contents of a presentation.

You can outline the body of a presentation using a number of **organizational patterns**, arrangements of the contents of the message. Exactly which pattern of organization is most appropriate for your presentation depends in part on your purpose and on the nature of your material. For instance, if your purpose is to present a solution to a problem, your purpose lends itself well to the problem/solution organizational pattern. If your material focuses on events that occurred over time, then it might be most easily outlined within a time-sequence pattern.

In this section we will examine four organizational patterns, prototypes from which a skilled presenter can construct many others: time-sequence pattern, cause/effect pattern, problem/solution pattern, and topical-sequence pattern. Keep in mind that a number of organizational patterns may appear in the same message; for example, an overall problem/solution organization may have within it a time-sequence pattern that explains the history of the problem.

The Time-Sequence Pattern

The **time-sequence pattern** is a method of organization in which the presenter explains events in chronological order. Most frequently seen in informative presentations, this pattern can serve in presentations that consider the past, present, and future of an idea, an issue, a plan, or a project. It is most useful for such topics as the following:

Steps in Gaining Approval for Vaccines

Developing a Video Game

The Process of Creating a Data Visualization

Obtaining TSA Pre-Check Authorization

Any topic that requires attention to events, incidents, or steps that take place over time is appropriate for this pattern of organization. Following is a section of a brief sentence outline of a speech organized in a time-sequence pattern.

time-sequence pattern
A method of organization in which the presenter explains events in chronological order.

Sample Partial Time-Sequence Pattern Outline

Seat Belts and Public Transportation Safety

Immediate purpose: After listening to this speech, audience members will be able to describe the history of seat belt use in public transportation, how seat belts are used today, and what is likely to happen with seat belts in the future.

The immediate purpose forecasts the chronological organization.

Body

I. The history of seat belts shows how they evolved into a highly effective safety feature.

   A. Seat belts were initially introduced to U.S. consumers in the 1960s with two anchor points—one on each side of the waist—or what we might simply call a lap belt.

   B. Design advancements improved the safety effectiveness of seat belts.

      1. Swedish engineer Nils Bohlin created a seat belt that also included a shoulder anchor that was easier to use, protective, and affordable.

      2. Bohlin and Volvo introduced the modern seat belt in 1959 (Lamelson-MIT Program).

II. Today's seat belts, despite improving safety, are inconsistently required.

   A. The *Smithsonian Magazine* estimates that this single invention has saved the lives of millions.

Terms such as history help make the time-sequence organizational pattern apparent to listeners.

CONTINUED

B. All cars produced after the late 1960s must have seat belts for safety.

C. There is no requirement for seat belts in some of the most commonly used public transportation options.

    1. The *New York Times* reported in May 2018 that not all buses are legally required to have seat belts.

    2. MacKechnie (2018) noted that many municipal buses lack seat belts and other safety features to protect passengers.

III. In the future, seat belts may become more standard in public transportation.

A. Parent and professional advocates with the American Academy of Pediatrics are fighting for all school buses to be equipped with seat belts.

B. Furthermore, the National Conference of State Legislatures articulated on December 21, 2018, that eight states currently require their buses to have seat belts, whereas the remaining 42 states do not.

C. The addition of seat belts would increase the cost of making and purchasing buses (MacKechnie, 2018).

> When discussing the current state of a topic, recency of sources is important.

> Because this speech is more informative in nature, no specific action step is called for by the speaker.

cause/effect pattern
A method of organization in which the presenter first explains the reasons for an event, a problem, or an issue and then discusses its consequences or results.

communicating creatively

Online Brainstorming

As you engage in topic selection and organization for your presentation, you may find it useful to use online brainstorming tools. A general internet search for "online brainstorming" will yield numerous sites that you can use to storyboard and visually map your ideas. Some programs use visual elements such as sticky notes and word clouds. Others contain forums that allow you to collaborate with other students and your teacher by posting your thoughts on a common topic. You can also brainstorm outside class at your convenience, testing ideas with others in a safe environment. Take advantage of online programs that allow you to work individually to map out your thoughts or collaborate with others to share ideas and receive valuable feedback.

The Cause/Effect Pattern

When using a **cause/effect pattern**, the presenter first explains the reasons for an event, a problem, or an issue and then discusses its consequences or results. The presentation may be cause–effect, effect–cause, or even cause–effect–effect. A presentation on inflation that uses the cause/effect pattern might review the causes of inflation, such as low productivity, and then review the effects of inflation, such as high unemployment and interest rates. The cause/effect pattern is often used in informative presentations that seek to explain an issue. This pattern differs from the problem/solution pattern in that the cause/effect pattern does not necessarily reveal what to do about a problem; instead, the organization allows for full explanation of an issue.

The cause/effect pattern of organization is common in fields as varied as medicine (tobacco causes cancer), economics (when a recession ends, corporate profits rise, the economy improves, and inflation increases), and education (people with a college education nearly double their annual earnings). The main points in the following partial outline illustrate the cause/effect pattern.

Sample Partial Cause/Effect Pattern Outline

The Failing of America's Infrastructure

Immediate purpose: After hearing this speech, audience members should be able to describe the causes and effects of deteriorating national infrastructure.

Body

I. Two factors contribute to our infrastructure's precarious state: age and funding.

   A. Our existing infrastructure is old, and we haven't been updating it (Zurich Financial, 2018).

      1. Vehicle travel on U.S. highways has increased 387% since 1956, and most of the interstate highway system is over 50 years old.

      2. In 2014, a 90-year-old water main in Los Angeles ruptured and resulted in millions of dollars in damage.

   B. We haven't fixed infrastructural problems because the federal and state governments haven't offered enough financial support.

      1. The American Society of Civil Engineers estimates that more than $1.5 trillion dollars is needed to upgrade current infrastructure in the U.S.

      2. The Congressional Budget Office noted that, in 2016, state spending on infrastructure was $342 billion and federal spending was $98 billion.

II. As a result of our aging and underfunded infrastructure, we find ourselves coping with dangerous effects on our health and on our safety.

   A. Professor of architecture Dr. Kordyn Smith explained to *Scientific American* that, when water lines become damaged, pathogens can enter the pipes and put everyone drinking that water at risk.

   B. The American Society of Civil Engineers report card explained that while 56,007 bridges in the U.S. are "structurally deficient," we're still using them. In fact, Americans make 188 million trips over these dangerous bridges every single day.

The word contribute is a signal that causes are being explained. The main point also previews the two primary causes.

Brief factual examples are used to illustrate the aging infrastructure problem.

The term *result* is a signal that effects are being discussed.

A source with qualifications is identified to explain one of the effects.

The Problem/Solution Pattern

problem/solution pattern
A method of organization in which the presenter describes an issue and proposes a resolution to that problem.

The third pattern of organization, used most often in persuasive presentations, is the **problem/solution pattern**, in which the presenter describes an issue and proposes a resolution. A message based on this pattern can be divided into two distinct parts, with an optional third part in which the presenter meets any anticipated objections to the proposed solution.

The problem/solution pattern can contain other patterns. For example, you might discuss the problem in time-sequence order, and you might discuss the solution using a topical-sequence pattern. Some examples of problem/solution topics follow:

Reducing Fat in Your Diet	Improving Indoor Air Quality
Boosting Your Immune System	Eliminating Nuclear Waste

Each example implies both a problem and a solution.

The problem/solution pattern of organization requires careful audience analysis because you have to decide how much time and effort to spend on each portion of the speech. Is the audience already familiar with the problem? If so, you might be able to discuss the problem briefly, with a few reminders to the audience of the problem's seriousness or importance. However, in most cases you will want to discuss the problem in enough detail so that the audience understands the *need for change*. Then, after explaining the problem, you should provide specific steps to take to resolve the problem. The following partial outline uses a problem/solution pattern to develop the topic of voting rights.

This problem/solution speech is persuasive in nature. An example manuscript of this speech is provided in Chapter 15.

The first point in this speech establishes the problem being addressed.

Sample Partial Problem/Solution Pattern Outline

Protecting Voting Rights

Immediate purpose: After listening to this speech, audience members should be able to take actions to advocate in favor of strengthening voting rights in the United States.

Body

I. Newly established voter fraud laws are unnecessary and create problems for citizens wanting to vote.

    A. Many of the new voting laws require an official photo ID, which can pose problems for people.

        1. Not everyone has a driver's license because not everyone can afford to own, insure, and maintain a vehicle.

        2. Furthermore, as the *Washington Post* of May 23, 2016, reported, elderly Americans struggle to get identification cards because many do not have the birth certificates required by the DMV.

B. These laws silence minority voices.

    1. Native Americans living on reservations may not have street addresses required for official IDs (NPR, October 13, 2018).

    2. The American Bar Association noted that the voter ID laws privilege white Americans and the middle class.

    3. As civil rights attorney Deuel Ross told *Wired* (January 4, 2018), "Whether it's intended to harm 600,000 African American and Latino voters or 2 million, our concern is people are passing these laws with the intent to discriminate or the effect of discriminating" (para. 18).

C. Voter ID laws are not justified based on available evidence.

    1. Voter identification laws claim that they want to prevent fraud, but as *PBS News Hour* (2018) notes, the presidential commission tasked with exploring the problem discovered a problem didn't exist.

    2. If voter fraud isn't a widespread issue, then why do we continue to pass laws to fix it?

    3. These laws are unnecessary, diminish people's individual liberties, and should be repealed by strong legislation protecting the rights of all citizens to vote.

II. There are solutions that you and I can take to support the voting rights of all Americans.

A. First, you can reach out to organizations fighting to get these laws repealed, such as the American Civil Liberties Union. Contact Robert Hoffman at rhoffman@aclu.org to show your support and get involved.

B. Second, you can reach out to the grassroots program Spread the Vote, which is helping targeted Americans get the identification cards they need to vote. Volunteer! Donate! Get involved with groups that are making a difference every day.

C. Third, you can visit Congress.gov to find senators and representatives from our state or your home state. Contact their offices by email or other means and let them know that you support legislation to protect the rights of citizens to vote without unnecessary barriers.

Margin notes:

A quotation with statistics builds a specific argument.

The first point ends with analysis arguing that there is a need for change resulting from the problem.

The second main point signals a transition to solutions.

Each subordinate point is listed in order to highlight specific solution steps.

engaging diversity

Cultural Preferences in Speech Organization

The dominant culture in North America embraces linear organizational patterns that have a distinct beginning, a middle, and an end; that tend to state early and boldly who the speaker is and what the main point is; and that are detailed in structure with main points, subpoints, and even sub-subpoints. Do not assume that all cultures are the same. For example, when presenting a persuasive message, people from Western cultures, such as the United States, typically make direct points about perceived problems and solutions they think will be productive. In some other cultures, including indigenous American cultures, nonlinear thinking is often used. Rather than stating explicitly what solutions would be ideal for specific problems, a nonlinear thinker might tell stories that provide abstract analogies to both problems and solutions. Ankit Sharma, a digital business advisor, suggests that nonlinear thinking will become increasingly important as big data, artificial intelligence, and digital communication technology continue to evolve. Consequently, developing ways to express ideas in nonlinear messages may help you adapt to diverse cultures and build important skills for the new digital economy.

Source: Sharma, A. (2022, May 17). How 'non-linear' thinking and 'creativity' can increase our probability of success. LinkedIn. www.linkedin.com/pulse/how-non-linear-thinking-creativity-can-increase-our-success-sharma?trk=articles_directory

The Topical-Sequence Pattern

The **topical-sequence pattern**, used in both informative and persuasive presentations, emphasizes the major reasons the audience should accept a point of view by addressing the advantages, disadvantages, qualities, and types of a person, place, or thing. This pattern can be used to explain to audience members why you want them to adopt a certain point of view. It is appropriate when you have three to five points to make, such as three reasons people should buy used cars, four of the main benefits of studying communication, or five characteristics of a good football player. The topical-sequence pattern of organization is among the most versatile. The topical-sequence pattern can be seen in the main points in the following partial outline.

topical-sequence pattern
A method of organization that emphasizes the major reasons an audience should accept a point of view by addressing the advantages, disadvantages, qualities, and types of a person, place, or thing.

> The first point discusses definitions and examples of blackfishing.

> Brief examples are used as supporting material.

Sample Partial Topical-Sequence Pattern Outline

Blackfishing on Social Media

Immediate purpose: After listening to my speech, audience members will be able to explain what blackfishing is and why this social media behavior is inappropriate.

Body

I. Blackfishing is a social media phenomenon where white individuals change their appearance to look like they are Black.

   A. BBC News of December 5, 2018, defines blackfishing as "a term used for someone accused of pretending to be Black or mixed-race on social media" (para. 2).

   B. The women currently accused—Emma Hallberg, Aga "Alicja" Brzostowska, and Jaiden Gumbayan—claim they aren't trying to be a different race but, rather, appreciate the culture and its style.

C. Black social media influencers who strive to embrace their heritage argue that white women copy their style—and profit from it—without knowing the criticisms Black women have experienced for their natural bodies.

D. As one of the criticized women, Jaiden notes there's a "fine line between appreciation and appropriation."

II. Blackfishing has been compared to blackface minstrelsy to explain why it is insulting to African Americans.

A. As early as the 1820s, white men would cover their faces in charcoal paste and parody the dances of Black culture, creating caricatures of the Black experience for entertainment purposes and belittling the historical hardships faced by Black people in America.

B. It's not surprising that social media users began drawing parallels between blackface minstrelsy and blackfishing, arguing that some white people on social media changed their appearance to appear Black to try to gain greater numbers of followers and heightened notoriety.

III. The act of blackfishing has several serious implications.

A. Blackfishing may reflect a lack of understanding about how race issues are experienced in social media environments, which can potentially result in other types of insensitive behaviors.

B. Social media influencers who appropriate African American culture are commodifying a culture without respecting past pain stemming from blackface minstrelsy.

C. As social influencers seek product endorsements, blackfishing users could literally be taking money away from actual Black influencers who would otherwise obtain the endorsement deal.

D. Finally, when celebrities and popular social media figures blackfish, they send the message to their followers that cultural appropriation is acceptable.

> A quotation is used as supporting material.

> Elements of a topical outline can mimic other organizational patterns. In the second point, the speech develops a cause-effect pattern to discuss the problems associated with blackfishing.

> The final main point in the body synthesizes arguments in the presentation by discussing larger social implications.

TRANSITIONS AND SIGNPOSTS

So far, we have examined the strategies you can use to generate and organize your main points. Next, we will look more closely at how you will communicate that organization to the audience with transitions and signposts.

building behaviors

Tips for Using Note Cards

A keyword outline fits easily on 3- by 5-inch or 4- by 6-inch note cards or on 8½- by 11-inch paper. If you choose note cards, the following suggestions may be useful:

- Write instructions to yourself on your note cards. For instance, if you are supposed to write the title of your speech and your name on the whiteboard before your presentation begins, then you can write that instruction on the top of your first card.

- Write on one side of the cards only. It is better to use more cards with your keyword outline on one side only than to write front and back, which is more likely to result in confusion.

- Number your note cards on the top so that you can keep them in order. If you drop them, you can quickly reassemble them.

- Write out items that might be difficult to remember. Extended quotations, difficult names, unfamiliar terms, and statistics are items you may want to include on your note cards to reduce the chances of error.

- Practice delivering your presentation at least two times using your note cards. Effective delivery may be difficult to achieve if you have to fumble with unfamiliar cards.

- Write clearly and legibly.

If your instructor allows you to use your smartphone or tablet to create a speaking outline, you should still include instructions to yourself, write out items that may be difficult to remember, and practice using your outline.

A **transition** is a bridge between sections of a message that helps a presenter verbally move from one idea to another. Transitions also relax the audience momentarily. A typical transition is a brief flashback and brief forecast that tell your audience when you are moving from one main point to another.

The most important transitions are between the introduction and the body, between the main points in the body, and between the body and the conclusion. Other transitions can appear between elements of the introduction, elements of the conclusion, or specific subpoints in the body of the speech. Transitions always explain the relationship between one idea and another. Transitions are the mortar between the building blocks of the speech. Without them, cracks appear and the structure is less solid. Table 12.1 provides examples of transitions.

Signposts are ways in which a presenter signals to an audience where the presentation is going. Signposts, as the name implies, are like road signs that tell a driver there is a curve, bump, or rough road ahead; they are a warning, a sign that the presenter is making a move. Whereas transitions are often a sentence or two, signposts can be as brief as a few words. Transitions review, state a relationship, and forecast; signposts merely point.

You'll want to avoid using signposts that are too blatant, such as "This is my

transition
A bridge between sections of a presentation that helps the presenter move smoothly from one idea to another.

signposts
Ways in which a presenter signals to an audience where the presentation is going.

Table 12.1 Examples of Transitions

Transition Type	Example Statement
Transition from one main point to another	"Now that we have seen why computers are coming down in cost, let us look next at why software is so expensive."
Transition from a main point to a visual aid	"I have explained that higher education is becoming more and more expensive. This bar graph will show exactly how expensive it has become over the past five years."
Transition that includes an internal summary and a preview	"You have heard that suntanning ages the skin, and I have shown you pictures of a Buddhist monk and a nighttime bartender who hardly ever exposed themselves to direct sunlight. Now I want to show you a picture of a 35-year-old woman who spent most of her life working in direct sunlight."

introduction," "Here is my third main point," or "This is my conclusion." More experienced presenters choose more subtle but equally clear means of signposting, such as "Let me begin by showing you . . . ," "A third reason for avoiding the sun is . . . ," or "The best inference you can draw from what I have told you is . . . ." Following are examples of common transitions and signposts used in speeches:

- "First, I will explain . . ."
- "Another reason for . . ."
- "The key point in this graph is . . ."
- "The conclusion you should draw is . . ."

Transitions and signposts help presenters map a message for the audience. Transitions explain the relationships in the message by reflecting backward and forward. Signposts point more briefly to what the presenter is going to do at the moment. Both transitions and signposts help bind the message into a unified whole.

The Conclusion

Like the introduction, the **conclusion** fulfills specific functions. These four functions need not occur in the order shown here, but they are all normally fulfilled in the last minutes of a presentation:

conclusion
The part that finishes the presentation by fulfilling the four functions of an ending.

- Forewarn the audience that you are about to finish your speech.
- Remind the audience of your thesis statement and the main points of your presentation.
- Specify what the audience should think or do in response to your speech.
- End the speech in a manner that makes audience members want to think and do as you recommend.

Let us examine these functions of a conclusion in greater detail.

The first function, the **brakelight function**, warns the audience that the end of the presentation is near. Can you tell when a song is about to end? Do you know when someone in a conversation is about to complete a story? Can you tell in a TV drama when the narrative is drawing to a close? The answer to these questions is usually yes because you receive verbal and nonverbal signals that songs, stories, and dramas are about to end.

brakelight function
A forewarning to the audience that the end of the presentation is near.

How do you use the brakelight function in a presentation? One student signaled the end of her speech by stating that her time was up: "Five minutes is hardly time to consider all the complications of this issue." Another speaker giving a presentation on the evolution of masculinity began his conclusion by stating, "Thus, men have the potential for much greater role flexibility than our society encourages." The word *thus,* like *therefore,* signals the conclusion of a logical argument and indicates that the argument is drawing to a close.

You can fulfill the second function of a conclusion—reminding the audience of your thesis or the main points in your message—by restating the main points, summarizing them briefly, or selecting the most important point for special treatment. A student ended her persuasive speech on legalizing drug purchases from Canada by briefly summarizing her message:

> We have discussed the rising cost of prescription drugs, the problem with Medicare, myth and reality concerning importation of prescription drugs, and solutions that can be implemented to solve this issue.

• An effective way to conclude a speech is with an inspirational statement.

lightpoet/Shutterstock

The third function of a conclusion is to specify what you expect audience members to do as a result of your presentation. Do you want the audience to simply remember a few of your important points? Then tell them one last time the points you think are worth remembering. Do you want the audience to write down the argument they found most convincing, sign a petition, or talk to their friends? If so, state what you would regard as an appropriate response to your presentation. One student's presentation on unions concluded with the slogan "Buy the union label," specifying what she expected of the audience.

The fourth function of a conclusion is to provide a "clincher," a memorable statement that encourages listeners to think and do as you recommend. There are many options for selecting a clincher:

- Conclude with a rhetorical question: "Knowing what you know now, will you feel safe riding with a driver who has had a few drinks?"

- Conclude with an interesting statement: "When you are making the choice between bottled and tap, just remember that there is no such thing as 'new' water; the water we drink today is the same water the dinosaurs drank, so whatever you choose, you'll be choosing well."

- Conclude with a quotation: "As John F. Kennedy said, 'Forgive your enemies, but never forget their names.'"[2]

- Conclude with a literary passage: "We conclude with the words of Ralph Waldo Emerson, who wrote, 'It is one light which beams out of a thousand stars; it is one soul which animates all men.'"[3]

- Conclude with a demonstration or an action: a tennis player demonstrates proper form for serving the ball.

One caution about conclusions is that when ending a presentation, as in initiating one, you should avoid being overly dramatic. Do not behave in a way that will offend members of your audience, create high tension, or frighten listeners. A better idea is to conclude your presentation with an inspirational statement, words that make audience members glad they spent the time and energy listening to you. One student delivered a single line at the end of his talk on using seat belts: "It is not who is right in a traffic accident that really counts," he said. "It is who is left." That conclusion was clever and memorable, it provided a brief summary, and it was an intelligent and safe way to end a presentation.

The following example outline of a conclusion illustrates how all elements of the conclusion are integrated into the outline format. Take note that the Roman numerals for main points in the conclusion restart with Roman numeral I.

building **behaviors**

Crafting an Effective Conclusion: Things to Avoid

Once you've drafted your conclusion, check it against this list of things to avoid in a speech conclusion:

- Do not end abruptly with no forewarning.
- Remind the audience of your main points, but do not provide a detailed replay of everything you did in the speech.
- Do not say negative things about your own presentation, such as "Well, I guess that didn't go so well," "I probably should have done more research," or "I sure messed up that assignment."
- Do not let your own nonverbal communication signal a poor presentation by letting your voice trail off at the end, by dropping your arms and looking defeated, or by walking off to your seat as you finish.

Sample Conclusion Outline

DNA Testing

I. *Brakelight function*: The potential issues surrounding DNA-testing companies are concerning, but I hope that you find comfort in the fact that you can protect your genetic information.

II. *Summary*: Today, we discussed what DNA-testing companies are, how they use your genetic data, and how you can ensure that your data stays safe.

III. *Specific audience action*: I hope that this information will inspire you to take precautionary action and research DNA-testing companies before sending off your saliva sample.

IV. *Clincher*: At the end of the day, is finding out your ancestry this way worth giving up your genetic information? Is it worth giving up what makes you *you*?

> Labeling each part of the conclusion in your sentence outline can help ensure that each element is included.

> Your conclusion should make your recommended action-step(s) clear to your audience.

The References

When you have completed your sentence outline, you may be asked to provide a list of **references**, or the sources you used in your presentation. The main idea behind a reference list is to inform others of what sources you used for your speech and to enable them to check those sources for themselves. Each entry in your references should be written according to a uniform style. Several accepted style manuals can answer your questions about the correct format. The *Publication Manual of the American Psychological Association* (APA), the *MLA Handbook,* and the *Chicago Manual of Style* are among the more common. Since some teachers prefer MLA and others prefer APA, you should ask your instructor's preference. You can learn more about APA style at www.apastyle.org and more about MLA style at www.mla.org/style. Because it is so efficient to find examples of the two styles on the internet, we do not provide a comprehensive set of examples here.

An example of an APA-style reference list for a presentation on voting rights is provided below. When learning to use any style guide, pay particular attention to formatting details such as indentation, use of capitalization and punctuation, use of text enhancements such as italics, and the order in which information is presented. For instance, the following references are listed alphabetically by the author's last name or the name of the organization; all lines after the first line of each citation are indented; in the title of an article or book, the first letter of the title and the first letter of the subtitle are capitalized, whereas others are typically not unless they are proper nouns; and the title of journal articles and the volume number are italicized. Style manuals such as APA are updated regularly, so make sure you are using the most current edition of any style manual.

references
A list of sources used in a presentation.

References

AARP. (2012, August 30). *Can we still vote?* https://www.aarp.org/politics-society/government-elections/info-01-2012/voter-id-laws-impact-older-americans.html

American Bar Association. (2018, December 12). *Chapter 10: Voter ID as a form of voter suppression.* https://www.americanbar.org/publications/state_local_law_news/2015-16/spring/chapter_10_voter_id_a_form_voter_suppression/

communicating
with agility

Being Agile with Artificial Intelligence

Artificial intelligence (AI) tools can assist with the creation of outlines and other documents. Here are some ways you could use AI during the outlining process:

- Direct ChatGPT to brainstorm specific issues or arguments related to your speech topic.
- Use the Grammarly AI tool to check spelling and grammar and to create source citations in a specific style.
- Use Beautiful.ai to create visual resources that can help you express your ideas effectively.

Opportunities to use AI to aid speechmaking will continue to increase. AI should not substitute for your own efforts. Agile communicators will work to understand these tools and employ them ethically to increase the effectiveness of their presentations.

American Civil Liberties Union. (n.d.). *Fighting voter suppression.* https://www.aclu.org/issues/voting-rights/fighting-voter-suppression

Brennan Center for Justice. (2012, October 15). *Voter ID.* https://www.brennancenter.org/analysis/voter-id

Domonoske, C. (2018, October 13). *Many native IDs won't be accepted at North Dakota polling places.* NPR. https://www.npr.org/2018/10/13/657125819/many-native-ids-wont-be-accepted-at-north-dakota-polling-places

Horwitz, S. (2016, May 23). Getting a photo ID so you can vote is easy. Unless you're poor, Black, Latino or elderly. *Washington Post.* https://www.washingtonpost.com/politics/courts_law/getting-a-photo-id-so-you-can-vote-is-easy-unless-youre-poor-black-latino-or-elderly/2016/05/23/8d5474ec-20f0-11e6-8690-f14ca9de2972_story.html

Jaffe, I. (2018, September 7). *For older voters, getting the right ID can be especially tough.* NPR. https://www.npr.org/2018/09/07/644648955/for-older-voters-getting-the-right-id-can-be-especially-tough

Lapowsky, I. (2018, January 4). *A dead-simple algorithm reveals the true toll of voter ID laws.* Wired. https://www.wired.com/story/voter-id-law-algorithm/

Library of Congress. (n.d.). *15th Amendment to the U.S. Constitution.* https://www.loc.gov/rr/program/bib/ourdocs/15thamendment.html

Rock the Vote. (n.d.). *Get ready to vote.* https://www.rockthevote.org/voting-information/

Span, P. (2017, November 24). Older voters stymied by tighter ID requirements. *New York Times.* https://www.nytimes.com/2017/11/24/health/voting-eligibility-elderly.html

Spread the Vote. (n.d.). *Volunteer.* https://www.spreadthevote.org/volunteer/

Villeneuve, M. (2018, August 3). *Report: Trump commission did not find widespread voter fraud.* PBS. https://www.pbs.org/newshour/politics/report-trump-commission-did-not-find-widespread-voter-fraud

be ready... for what's next

Organizing Ideas with Mind Maps

As you are working on your rough draft outline, you can use free mind mapping apps and websites to help you envision different groupings of information that will become potential main points. Using the material you discovered in this chapter, what possible organizational patterns exist for your informative or persuasive speech topic? One free online tool you can use is Mindmap Maker (https://app.mindmapmaker.org). Using that or a similar type of tool, create a mind map of your speech. As you play with ideas, arrange and rearrange as necessary to find various possible organizational approaches. Through that process, you will be able to see how the various details in your presentation fit together into a cohesive whole. Moreover, you might even be able to use your mind map as a visual resource during your presentation.

Digital mind mapping tools are powerful ways for you to merge vast amounts of information into your own voice. Learning to use mind maps is a tangible skill that can be useful to you in other courses and throughout your career.

Chapter Review & Study Guide

Summary

In this chapter, you learned the following:

1. An effective outline for a presentation follows six principles:
   - It relates the information presented to the immediate purpose and long-range goal.
   - It is an organized summary of the message you will deliver.
   - It expresses ideas in single units of information.
   - It indicates the importance of items with rank-ordered symbols.
   - Its margins indicate the importance of each entry visually.
   - It states entries in parallel form (such as complete sentences).

2. During the speech preparation process you will typically prepare three outlines:
   - The rough draft outline identifies your topic and immediate purpose and begins to identify main points and details that will be in the speech.
   - The sentence outline will be the fully developed outline of ideas and is written using complete sentences. The sentence outline will typically identify where sources are used in the outline.
   - The keyword outline is condensed from your full sentence outline and is used for the actual presentation.

3. An effective introduction fulfills five functions, which can occur in any order:
   - It gains and maintains audience attention.
   - It arouses audience interest in the topic.
   - It states the immediate purpose and thesis of the presentation.
   - It establishes the presenter's credibility.
   - It forecasts the organization and development of the presentation.

4. The most frequently used patterns of organization in public presentations are the
   - time-sequence pattern, with items presented chronologically over time.
   - cause/effect pattern, which posits a cause that results in some effect.
   - problem/solution pattern, which poses a problem followed by a suggested solution.
   - topical-sequence pattern, with items listed as a limited number of qualities or characteristics.

5. Transitions and signposts link ideas and indicate direction to the audience.
   - Transitions are used to move from one idea to another, such as when you move between main points in the body of the speech.
   - Signposts signal important details, such as when you draw attention to a conclusion that should be drawn from a graph or chart.

6. An effective conclusion fulfills certain functions:
   - It forewarns listeners that the presentation is about to end.
   - It reminds the audience of the central idea and main points of your presentation.
   - It specifies what you expect from the audience as a result of the presentation.
   - It ends the presentation in a manner that encourages the audience to think and act as you recommend.

7. Often a list of references, or sources, accompanies the sentence outline.

Key Terms

Body	Organizational patterns	Signposts
Brakelight function	Outline	Subpoints
Cause/effect pattern	Parallel form	Time-sequence pattern
Conclusion	Problem/solution pattern	Topical-sequence pattern
Introduction	References	Transition
Keyword outline	Rough draft	
Main points	Sentence outline	

Study Questions

1. Which function of the introduction shows how the topic is related to the audience?

   a. gaining and maintaining audience attention
   b. arousing audience interest
   c. stating the purpose and thesis
   d. establishing speaker qualifications

2. Stating your purpose in the introduction

   a. is necessary because informative speeches do not invite learning, and this is your only opportunity to explain.
   b. is unnecessary because the audience will learn of the purpose in the body of the speech.
   c. is not appropriate because you will lose an element of surprise in the body of the speech.
   d. is important because audience members are more likely to learn and understand if your expectations are clear.

3. Which of the following is a primary function of the body of a speech?

   a. changing the audience's attitudes or actions for an informative speech
   b. supporting your arguments through assertions and personal opinions
   c. gaining the audience members' attention
   d. presenting a limited number of arguments, stories, and ideas

4. Which of the following statements is *not* true with regard to outlining?

   a. It uses symbols, margins, and content to reveal the order, importance, and substance of a presentation.
   b. All items of information in your outline do not need to be directly related to the speech's purpose and long-range goal.
   c. It encourages a conversational speaking tone because not every word is in front of you.
   d. Items should appear in parallel form.

5. Which type of outline consists mostly of important words or phrases but not complex information?

   a. main point
   b. sentence
   c. keyword
   d. cause/effect pattern

6. If you were giving a speech about the parking problem at your university with possible means to resolve it, which organizational pattern would be best?

   a. time-sequence
   b. cause/effect
   c. problem/solution
   d. topical-sequence

7. When a speaker explains a progression of events in chronological order, which organizational pattern is most likely being used?

   a. time-sequence
   b. cause/effect
   c. problem/solution
   d. topical-sequence

8. Which of the following helps speakers move from one idea to another by reviewing, stating a relationship, and forecasting?

   a. transitions
   b. signposts
   c. subpoints
   d. goals

9. Reminding the audience of the speech's central idea and main points, specifying what is expected of audience members, and ending soundly are functions of the

   a. introduction.
   b. transitions.
   c. brakelight.
   d. conclusion.

10. A reference list is

    a. a list of the sources that you might have considered to use in your presentation.
    b. ideas that you do not want to forget as you are preparing your presentation.
    c. a list of sources organized as books, articles, interviews, and other sources.
    d. a list of sources that you actually used in your presentation.

Answers:
1. (b); 2. (d); 3. (d); 4. (b); 5. (c); 6. (c); 7. (a); 8. (a); 9. (d); 10. (d)

Critical Thinking

1. Using the suggestions from the text for developing an introduction, how would you gain the audience's attention for an informative speech on the topic of college debt? Why did you choose these methods?

2. Pick a topic for a speech that interests you and brainstorm how you could use each of the organizational patterns described in this chapter. Analyze which pattern would be most effective for your topic, your immediate purpose, and your audience.

Sizing Things Up Scoring and Interpretation

Clarity Behaviors Inventory

This chapter helps you learn how to organize presentations. A significant body of literature in communication and education addresses the issue of "clarity" in academic settings. Although nearly all of this research approaches clarity from the perspective of the teacher—how to present clear lessons to students—this research is directly translatable to other types of speaking situations. The Clarity Behaviors Inventory (CBI) was developed by one of this textbook's authors and his colleagues to assess students' perceptions of teachers' clarity. You can use this survey to analyze the clarity of one of your other teachers. You should *not* identify the teacher you are rating. As you compare your teacher's score with those from your classmates, discuss some of the things those teachers do that likely results in differences in scores. How can you learn from this to influence how you deliver your speeches?

The CBI is used to assess teachers' clarity in both written and oral form. Calculate scores for both dimensions of clarity by averaging responses to the following items:

- *Written clarity:* items 2, 3, 6, 8, and 10
- *Verbal clarity:* items 1, 4, 5, 7, 9, and 11

In both cases, higher values indicate higher levels of clarity. You can also average all items on the survey to obtain an overall assessment of clarity. An average score of 1 or 2 indicates low clarity, and an average of 4 or 5 indicates high clarity.

References

1. Hacker, D., & Sommers, N. (2011). *A writer's reference* (7th ed.). Bedford Books of St. Martin's Press, 63.

2. O'Brien, D. (2005). *How to develop a brilliant memory week by week: 52 proven ways to enhance your memory skills.* Duncan Baird Publishers.

3. Emerson, R., & Porte, J. (1983). *Essays & lectures.* Literary Classics of the U.S.

Syda Productions/Shutterstock

delivery and visual resources

chapter 13

When you have read and thought about this chapter, you will be able to

1. explain four methods of delivery.

2. explain each of the vocal and nonverbal aspects of delivery.

3. describe methods for managing your communication apprehension.

4. recognize when you should use visual resources in your speech.

5. apply design principles to make visuals for presentations.

Many presentations with valuable content never reach the listener because of poor delivery skills. This chapter explores the delivery of your presentation and the various visual aids you may use. You will discover four modes of delivery and the various vocal and bodily aspects of delivery, as well as approaches to reduce your anxiety about speaking in front of an audience. Attention in a public presentation is supposed to be on you, not on your visuals, but you will learn in this chapter that you can use Internet resources, such as YouTube videos, Google images, and PowerPoint slides, to make your presentation attractive to the eye and the ear.

On February 24, 2019, Lady Gaga was awarded an Oscar for Best Original Song for her and Bradley Cooper's heartfelt duet "Shallow" in the film *A Star is Born.* Gaga's acceptance speech is an example of a highly effective delivery.[1] First, her delivery was authentic. When watching the speech, the audience could hear the emotional cadence of her delivery—it was rapid but included emotional breaks in her voice. Second, Gaga used very natural gestures. She not only used her arms but also used the trophy as part of her physical presentation. The audience could feel her pride as they witnessed her holding the Oscar so tightly. Third, Gaga's eye contact was appropriately directed toward people in the audience to whom she was giving thanks, such as Bradley Cooper, and later toward the camera when she stated to viewers, "What it's about is not giving up. If you have a dream, fight for it."

Gaga's speech was effective in its delivery because of the authentic way she delivered it. She captured the audience's attention, brought additional emphasis to what she was saying, and established an emotional connection with her audience.

Though few speaking situations will approach the emotions involved in receiving an award such as an Oscar, all speaking situations benefit from effective delivery.

Lady Gaga used authentic delivery during her 2019 Oscar acceptance speech.

Valerie Macon/AFP/Getty Images

Defining Delivery

Delivery is the presentation of a speech using your voice and body to communicate your message. People have contradictory ideas about the importance of speech delivery. Some people think that it's not what you say but how you say it that really counts. According to others, what you say is more important than how you say it. Actually, what you say *and* how you say it are both important.

A solid message chosen to accomplish specific goals with your audience, coupled with a delivery style demonstrating energy and passion, should be your objective for every speech.[2] Just as you cannot ignore the need to prepare your speech well in advance, you also cannot ignore the need to practice your delivery. Delivery is like other learned behaviors, such as playing basketball, sewing, or cooking: a lack of practice will show. In this section you will learn about the methods of delivering a presentation; the next section will teach you the building blocks of effective delivery.

In most public speaking situations there are four general methods of delivery: extemporaneous, impromptu, manuscript, and memorized. These methods vary in the amount of preparation required and in their degree of spontaneity. Although they are all possible choices, students of public speaking are least likely to use the manuscript and memorized methods. They may be asked to try the impromptu method at times, but most speech assignments require the extemporaneous method.

delivery
The presentation of a speech using your voice and body to communicate your message.

- During her acceptance speech for the GLADD award, Beyoncé used extemporaneous delivery to present an impassioned speech about her work as an advocate.

Everett Collection/Shutterstock

extemporaneous method
A carefully prepared and researched presentation delivered in a conversational style.

impromptu method
Delivery of a presentation without notes, plans, or formal preparation; characterized by spontaneity and conversational language.

manuscript method
Delivery of a presentation from a script of the entire speech.

THE EXTEMPORANEOUS METHOD

A presentation delivered in the **extemporaneous method** is carefully prepared and practiced, but the presenter delivers the message conversationally without heavy dependence on notes. This method places equal importance on the message and the audience, with the speaker focused not on notes but on the ideas being expressed. Considerable eye contact, freedom of movement and gesture, the language and voice of conversation, and the use of an outline or key words to keep the speaker from reading or paying undue attention to the written script characterize this method.

The word *extemporaneous* literally means "on the spur of the moment" in Latin; however, as practiced in the classroom, this method of delivery only *appears* to be spontaneous. In fact, the processes of planning your speech and creating your outline require you to invest considerable effort before you actually deliver your presentation.

You have seen this method of delivery in the classroom; in some professors' lectures; sometimes in the pulpit; often in political and legal addresses; and usually in speeches by athletes, businesspeople, and community leaders who are experienced speakers. In each of these cases the speaker typically has planned several talking points but avoids reading those points to the audience, favoring instead a more natural appearance. Learning to use the extemporaneous method effectively is critical to your success as a speaker because it is the most common approach used both in the classroom and in professional situations outside the classroom.[3]

THE IMPROMPTU METHOD

In the **impromptu method** you deliver a presentation without notes, plans, or formal preparation and with spontaneity and conversational language. The word *impromptu* has Latin and French roots and means "in readiness."

You use the impromptu method when you answer a question in class, when you introduce yourself in a meeting, and when you give people directions on the street. At a celebration or an informal gathering you may be asked to say a few remarks to welcome people or to express thanks. When executives or other visitors tour your workplace, you may be asked to talk about what you do. All these situations require your impromptu speaking skills, because you have no time to prepare but must still provide clear and relevant comments.

Ordinarily, this method of delivery does not allow for practice and planning beforehand. The impromptu method encourages you to "think on your feet" without research, preparation, or practice. Although you cannot practice your actual speech, you can (and should) practice speaking on various topics without specific preparation.

THE MANUSCRIPT METHOD

As the name implies, in the **manuscript method** you deliver your presentation from a script of the entire speech. The advantage is that you know exactly what to say. The disadvantages are that the written message invites you to pay more attention to the script than to the audience, discourages eye contact, and prevents response to audience feedback.

Professors, clergy, and politicians—especially those who are likely to be quoted—sometimes use this method of delivery, but students are rarely asked to, except when reading an essay, a poem, or a short story to the class. Reading from a manuscript, whether it is prepared as a word-for-word script or a set of presentation slides, is difficult to do well. For most public speaking situations, you should use the extemporaneous method rather than the manuscript method.

THE MEMORIZED METHOD

A presentation delivered in the **memorized method** is committed to memory. This method requires considerable practice and allows ample eye contact, movement, and gestures. However, it also discourages the speaker from responding to feedback, from adapting to the audience during the speech, and from choosing words that might be appropriate at the moment. In other words, memorization removes spontaneity and increases the danger of forgetting. You have experienced this method if you ever acted in a play and memorized your part. Politicians, athletes, and businesspeople who repeatedly speak to the same kind of audience about the same subjects often end up memorizing their speeches. Even professors, when they teach a class for the third time in a week, may memorize the lesson for the day.

Like the manuscript method, the memorization method is extremely difficult to pull off well. If you practice your speech several times, you will begin to memorize certain parts through repetition. However, your goal should be extreme familiarity rather than absolute memorization. Such familiarity will give you confidence but will help you avoid potential problems associated with rigid memorization.

THE REMOTE METHOD

The **remote delivery method** has the same characteristics as other delivery methods but is delivered through a digitally mediated channel, such as Microsoft Teams, Google Hangouts, or Zoom. As a result of the COVID-19 pandemic, remote speaking has become common. Prior to the pandemic, as many as 80% of business presentations had some remote component, such as including audience members from another location, and that trend has continued as organizations increasingly allow some degree of remote work.[4]

Because of the technology involved, additional care is necessary to use this method effectively. For minimal expense, you can purchase a better microphone, camera, and light than what is found inside a laptop. You will likely use notes when presenting remotely, and they can be displayed on your computer screen so you can look ahead rather than down at a piece of paper. Thoughtful speakers will use chat or discussion features to keep their audience engaged and turn what would have been rhetorical questions into opportunities for

memorized method
Delivery of a presentation that has been committed to memory.

remote delivery method
Delivering a presentation through digitally mediated technology.

sizing things up

Engaging Delivery Assessment

One way to learn about your delivery is to think carefully about how others deliver presentations. As a college student you get to observe presentations nearly every day when you watch teachers lecture. Below you will find statements describing how your teacher uses various delivery techniques. Select the teacher from the class *immediately before* your communication class and, with that teacher in mind, answer the following questions using this scale:

0 = Never
1 = Rarely
2 = Occasionally
3 = Often
4 = Very often

The teacher I observed . . .

1. has natural variation in pitch—it is not monotone or overly varied.
2. speaks at a pace that is easy to follow—not too fast or too slow.
3. speaks at a volume that is easy to hear.
4. does not have many vocalized pauses such as "uhh" and "umm."
5. uses movement of the hands and body to be dynamic and emphasize points.
6. uses facial expressions to convey emotion.
7. makes eye contact to establish perceptions of closeness.
8. articulates words clearly so that they are easy to understand.
9. has a delivery style that is smooth rather than choppy.

This exercise has no right or wrong answers. A guide for interpreting your responses appears at the end of the chapter.

commentary.[5] Make sure to sit an appropriate distance from your camera so your head and shoulders are in the frame. If your setup allows, consider delivering your presentation while standing. When standing, you have more effective breathing and are able to gesture and move more naturally, which will allow you to better display emotion and enthusiasm.

Behaviors That Influence Delivery

Effective delivery is a learned behavior. Accomplished musicians must practice daily to achieve success; the same is required for excellent delivery. Fortunately, we all get chances to practice every day. Our conversations with others teach us everything we need to know to be great deliverers of speeches. Think for a moment about how you behave when you talk with others. You naturally use gestures; you naturally vary your vocal pitch, volume, and inflections; and you naturally maintain eye contact. You work hard at improving your verbal and nonverbal delivery skills, starting as an infant and continuing throughout your life. So why is it that some people struggle as public speakers?

Giving presentations is different from casual conversation. You become the center of attention; hundreds of eyes may be focusing just on you. That fact alone can cause us to forget what we have learned over the course of our lifetime. We look for safety blankets in the form of lecterns to hold onto and notes to read, and we fall back on rapid delivery to get the whole thing done. These problems are not limited to the classroom. John Takash, president of the Chicago-based Victory Consulting Firm, identified five common delivery problems in business presentations: (1) using nonwords, (2) failing to pause and let audience members think, (3) failing to maintain eye contact, (4) speaking with a lack of confidence and volume, and (5) standing on one spot.[6] All these are problems with verbal and nonverbal delivery. The key to effective delivery is training yourself not to wrap yourself in safety blankets, and you achieve that through practice.

Before learning about ways to practice effectively, let's first discuss vocal and nonverbal aspects of delivery.

VOCAL ASPECTS OF DELIVERY

Just as different musicians can make the same notes sound quite different, public speakers can say the same words in different ways to get various reactions from the audience. The way you say words creates emotion. The seven vocal aspects of presentation are pitch, rate, pauses, volume, enunciation, fluency, and vocal variety. As we'll see next, your objective with these aspects of vocal delivery should be to naturally vary your voice and not talk in a monotone.[7] Using vocal variance will help you sound more passionate and convincing during your presentation.

Pitch

pitch
The highness or lowness of the voice.

Pitch is the highness or lowness of a speaker's voice—the voice's upward and downward movement, the melody produced by the voice. Pitch is what makes the difference between the "ohhh" you utter when you earn a poor grade in a class and the "ohhh" you utter when you are surprised by a friend's news. The pitch of your voice can make you sound either lively or listless. As a speaker, you learn to avoid the two extremes: the lack of change in pitch that results in a monotone and repeated changes in pitch that result in a singsong delivery. The best public speakers use the full range of their normal pitch.

One technique for learning to strategically use pitch is to think about how you use bold, italics, and different-style fonts when you write. There are certain words in a written document that you may want to *emphasize*. When speaking, you may want to do the same thing. When talking about the national debt, for instance, you may want to emphasize the "T" in "trillion" to highlight the unimaginable scope of the issue. Obviously your voice does not have buttons like a word processor to make that happen. When emphasizing the word vocally, you might naturally raise your pitch an octave or so to make it stand out—the vocal equivalent of bold and italics.

Rate

How fast should you speak when delivering a public presentation? Instructors often caution students to "slow down" because talking fast is a sign of anxiety or nervousness. At the same time, talking too slowly can bore the listener because we think much faster than people typically talk. What is the best way for you to deliver your speech?

Rate is the speed of delivery, or how fast you say your words. The normal rate for U.S. speakers is between 125 and 190 words per minute, but many variations occur. You need to remember that your rate of delivery depends on you—how fast you normally speak—and on the situation—few people talk fast at a funeral. Rate also depends on the audience and the subject matter. Audience members unfamiliar with the topic material may have a hard time following rapid delivery—the situation and topic may necessitate a slower approach.

Your rate of delivery can be used strategically to build drama during your presentation. Think about a great action sequence in a movie. Typically, the background music has a more upbeat tempo to emphasize the action. So, too, in a speech, your rate of delivery can be used to build excitement. Talking slowly at a pep rally may curb spirit, but fast delivery can get fans pumped up. Varying your rate of delivery can help you set certain moods as your speech develops.

rate
The pace of your speech.

Pauses

A third vocal characteristic of speech delivery is the **pause**—an absence of vocal sound used for dramatic effect, transition, or emphasis. Presentations are often a steady stream of words without silences, yet pauses can be used for dramatic effect and to get an audience to consider content. The speaker may begin a speech with rhetorical questions: "Have you had a cigarette today? Have you had two or three? Ten or eleven? Do you know what your habit is costing you in a year? A decade? A lifetime?" After each rhetorical question a pause allows audience members to answer the question mentally.

Pauses invite the audience to think, which is a silent but important form of engagement. When using pauses, make sure they are long enough to have this desired effect but not so long that they become uncomfortable. Use your instincts while speaking and remember that the pause will feel longer to you as the speaker than it does to the audience.

By contrast, **vocalized pauses** are breaks in fluency that negatively affect an audience's perception of the speaker's competence and dynamism. The "ahhhs" and "mmhhs" of the beginning speaker are disturbing and distracting. Unfortunately, even some experienced speakers have the habit of filling silences with vocalized pauses.

pause
The absence of vocal sound used for dramatic effect, transition, or emphasis.

vocalized pauses
Breaks in fluency that negatively affect an audience's perception of the speaker's competence and dynamism.

Volume

Volume is the relative loudness of your voice. Variations in volume can convey emotion, importance, suspense, and changes in meaning. When speaking more loudly we also tend to speak more quickly and at a higher pitch; when speaking more softly we tend to be lower

building behaviors

Diagnosing Problems with Vocalized Pauses

After creating your outline and visual materials, you should practice your speech out loud. Once you have practiced several times and feel comfortable with the material, record your speech using your cell phone, your computer, or some other device. When playing back the recording, note the total time and make a tally mark each time you say any type of vocalized pause. How many did you have? Did you notice a pattern that might explain why you inserted them? Were they in places where you were transitioning between ideas? Places where you were unsure of the material? Once you identify possible causes, how can you try to work those vocalizations out of your delivery?

and slower. Thus, changes in volume often happen in conjunction with changes in tone and rate of delivery. You can use a stage whisper in front of an audience, just as you would whisper a secret to a friend. You can speak loudly and strongly on important points, letting your voice carry your conviction. Volume can also change with the situation. For example, a pep rally may be filled with loud, virtually shouted speeches teeming with enthusiasm, whereas a eulogy may be delivered at a lower, respectful volume. An orchestra never plays so quietly that patrons cannot hear, but the musicians vary their volume. Similarly, a presenter who considers the voice an instrument learns how to speak softly, loudly, and in between to convey meaning.

Enunciation

enunciation
Combining pronunciation and articulation to produce a word with clarity and distinction.

Enunciation, the fifth vocal aspect of speech delivery, is the pronunciation and articulation of sounds and words. In everyday conversation we are informal, and our friends know how we talk. In speeches, however, you need to think more carefully about how you enunciate the syllables of words. In a large room, better enunciation may be necessary in order for people in the back to fully understand you. You can also overenunciate words to give them emphasis, the verbal equivalent of typing "I am R-E-A-L-L-Y happy!" Enunciation is especially important for words that have similar sounds. How are its two components, pronunciation and articulation, different?

pronunciation
Saying a word correctly or incorrectly.

Pronunciation is the act of correctly saying *words*. The difference between saying "Washington" and "Worshintun" is pronunciation. Sometimes people use alternate pronunciations of words, if not outright mispronunciations, because of dialects that they grew up with. However, in other instances, speakers mispronounce words because they are simply unfamiliar with the terms. If speakers have little established credibility, such mispronunciations resulting from lack of familiarity can doom their chances of building it. The best way to avoid pronunciation errors is to look up unfamiliar words. Most online dictionaries have options for hearing how a word is correctly pronounced via a small audio file.

articulation
Coordinating one's mouth, tongue, and teeth to make words understandable to others.

Articulation—the accurate production of *sounds*—is the second part of enunciation. If you order "dry toast" (without butter) and get "rye toast" or ask for a "missing statement" and get a "mission statement," you are experiencing the results of poor or careless articulation. Among the common articulation problems are the dropping of final consonants and "-ing" sounds ("goin'," "comin'," and "leavin'"), the substitution of "fer" for "for," and the substitution of "ta" for "to." An important objective in public presentations, as in all communication, is to articulate accurately.

Fluency

fluency
The smoothness of delivery, the flow of words, and the absence of vocalized pauses.

The sixth vocal characteristic of delivery is **fluency**—the smoothness of the delivery, the flow of the words, and the absence of vocalized pauses. This quality is often more notable by its absence: a fluent speaker will present an effortless flow of words that moves along at a natural pace, which listeners may take for granted as they focus on the message. A nonfluent speaker will present a speech that sounds choppy and disjointed, and these errors draw attention to themselves.

To achieve fluency, public speakers must be confident about the content of their speeches. If they know what they are going to say and have practiced the words over and over, they will reduce disruptive repetition and vocalized pauses. Speakers must pace, build, and time the various parts of the speech so that they unite in a coherent and fluent whole. If you misjudge your time and then try to rush through the ending of your speech, your fluency can suffer.

Vocal Variety

vocal variety
Vocal quality, intonation patterns, inflections of pitch, and syllabic duration.

The seventh vocal aspect of speech delivery—one that summarizes many of the others—is **vocal variety**. This term refers to voice quality, intonation patterns, inflections of pitch, and how you draw out spoken sounds and syllables. In public speeches, vocal variety is encouraged because studies show that variety improves effectiveness. One of the founders of the National Communication Association, Charles Woolbert, found in a very early study of public reading that audiences retain more information when there are large variations in rate, force, pitch, and voice quality.[8] Woolbert's research is relevant even today. Having variety in your voice is consistently identified as one of the most important speaking skills, though achieving it can be challenging for inexperienced speakers.

Daniel Bullock and Raúl Sánchez, two professional communication trainers, have explained that vocal variety is how you use your voice to convey the same type of emphasis you would use when typing bold, italics, question marks, and exclamation points.[9] For example, when stating, "I have *two* points to make," you may naturally emphasize the number to help your audience understand your organization. When stating, "I *disagree* with that argument," you may speak more loudly and slowly when saying "disagree" to make your stance more forceful. In any speaking situation, your vocal variety is a powerful tool to focus your audience members' attention, highlight key points, and improve your presence as a speaker.

NONVERBAL ASPECTS OF DELIVERY

The importance of delivery has been recognized for thousands of years. In *Rhetorica ad Herennium,* the great Roman orator Cicero observed, "Delivery is the graceful regulation of voice, countenance, and gesture."[10] Whereas the previous section talked in detail about the voice, this section focuses on how to use your body to effectively convey meaning. The nonverbal aspects of presentation are gestures, facial expressions, eye contact, and movement.

Gestures

Gestures are movements of the head, arms, and hands that illustrate, emphasize, or signal ideas in a speech. People rarely worry about gestures in conversation, but when they give a speech in front of an audience, arms and hands seem to be bothersome. The most common mistake inexperienced speakers make is holding onto a lectern, a laptop or tablet, or notes. Some teachers ban the use of these items to help students overcome the tendency to rely on them.

gestures
Movements of the head, arms, and hands to illustrate, emphasize, or signal ideas in a presentation.

Gestures during a speech are effective at captivating attention, even in a streamed and online format. Vanessa Edwards, founder of the communication website *Science of People,* studied the 10 most viewed TED talks of all time and the 10 least viewed talks.[11] She found that the most-viewed TED speakers used, on average, 465 hand gestures during their 18-minute talks, whereas the least viewed speakers used an average of only 272.

Gestures also help you as a speaker to stay focused on your message. Your gestures amount to what education professor Todd Finley[12] calls "embodied cognition," meaning that your body and mind work together to release mental strain through your gestures, creating a calming effect. Overuse of gestures can become distracting to your audience. As a speaker, you should use gestures to release stress, but practice controlling them so they appear natural.

What can you do to help yourself gesture naturally when delivering your presentation? The answer is to connect your feelings to your behavior. When speakers really care about a topic, you can see their passion in the way they deliver their message: they are more animated, their face shows a range of emotion, their voice is strong, and their eyes connect with yours. Students speaking on a variety of topics ranging from environmental awareness to business ethics have demonstrated that passion and conviction translate into effective delivery. In addition to focusing on finding a topic about which you are passionate, you should also concentrate on your message. Being self-conscious about your delivery, or trying to focus too much on "perfect" delivery, can actually backfire and cause your delivery to seem unnatural. Some students trained in competitive speaking exhibit unnatural delivery behaviors that cause audience members to become so focused on delivery that they lose the message of the speech. Focusing on your message and your conviction is more important than trying to sound like the next master orator.

Facial Expressions

facial expressions
Any nonverbal cues expressed by the speaker's face.

Though gestures are powerful, your face is the most expressive part of your body. **Facial expressions** consist of the nonverbal cues expressed by the speaker's face. Eyebrows rise and fall; eyes twinkle, glare, and cry; lips pout or smile; cheeks can dimple; and a chin can jut out in anger or drop in surprise. Some people's faces are a barometer of their feelings; others' faces seem to maintain the same appearance whether they are happy or sad or in pain. Because you do not ordinarily see your own face when you are speaking, you may not be fully aware of how you appear when you give a speech. In general, speakers are trying to maintain a warm and positive relationship with the audience, and they signal that intent by smiling as they would in conversation with someone they liked. However, the topic, the speaker's intent, the situation, and the audience all help determine the appropriate facial expressions in a public speech. You can discover the appropriateness of your facial expressions by having friends, relatives, or classmates tell you how you look when practicing your speech. You can also observe how your instructors use facial expressions to communicate. Although you can observe your facial expressions by practicing in front of a mirror, many people find this technique distracting. A better strategy might be to record your speech using a computer or phone and then watch the video to observe how you use facial expressions during your speech.

Eye Contact

eye contact
The extent to which a speaker looks directly at the audience.

Eye contact refers to the extent to which the speaker looks directly at the audience. Staring down the audience is too much of a good thing, but staring at your notes is poor delivery.

bodily movement
What the speaker does with his or her entire body during a presentation.

Lack of eye contact is one of the most common problems speakers have when making presentations.[13] It can suggest that you lack knowledge, are unsure of your position, or are even being deceitful. Appropriate eye contact, by contrast, creates connections with the audience.

building behaviors

Moving Eye Contact Around

Experienced speakers learn how to spread their eye contact around to multiple audience members. One technique for learning to do this is to divide the audience into different sections—think of the sections as analogous to rooms in a house or countries on a map. Your objective early in the speech should be to visit each location with your eyes. Some locations may seem more pleasing because people in that "room" or "country" might give you better nonverbal responses. Perhaps that's a place you can visit more often as the speech progresses. Using this approach will help you build rapport with your audience. Even when you are visiting other sections with your eyes, audience members will notice that you are trying to connect with the entire room and will react more positively to you and your ideas.

How can you learn to maintain eye contact with your audience? One way is to know your speech so well that you have to glance only occasionally at your notes. A speaker who does not know the speech well is manuscript-bound. Delivering an extemporaneous speech from key words or an outline is a way of encouraging yourself to keep an eye on the audience. One of the purposes of extemporaneous delivery is to enable you to adapt to your audience. That adaptation is not possible unless you are continually observing the audience's behavior to see whether your listeners appear to understand your message.

Movement

A fourth physical aspect of delivery is **bodily movement**—what speakers do with their entire body during a presentation. Sometimes the situation limits movement. The presence of a fixed microphone, a lectern, a pulpit, or any other physical feature of the environment may limit your activity. The length of the speech can also make a difference. If your speech is short, movement may be less important. For a speech lasting longer than a few minutes, movement can help keep audience members more engaged.

Good movement is appropriate and purposeful. The "caged lion" who paces back and forth to work off anxiety is moving in a way that distracts; a speaker who stands in one spot creates boredom. You should move for a reason, such as walking a few steps when delivering a transition, thereby literally helping your audience "follow you" to the next idea. Some speakers move toward the audience when expressing points they regard as more important.

communicating with agility

Adapting to Remote

Both during the pandemic and after, remote presentations are increasingly common throughout the public and private sector. You and your classmates may even be taking this class in a remote or online format. When delivering remote presentations, all of the recommendations in this chapter apply. However, to increase your effectiveness as you transition to a remote or online presentation, you should give extra attention to how you use visual resources.

Most remote connection applications like Zoom or Microsoft Teams allow you to display computer content like PowerPoint slides. When you are displaying remotely, the text and images will be relatively small for the audience as compared to an in-person presentation where the image is displayed on a large screen. Keep visual resources simple and large to make them easier to read in remote presentation settings.

Because eye contact is vital, you should always strive to face the audience, even when moving. Speakers who read from slides typically turn their back on the audience. Instead, position your body, particularly your face, in ways that allow you to establish a rapport with your audience.

You can learn through practice and observation. Watch your professors, teaching assistants, and fellow students when they deliver their speeches to determine what works for them. (They may provide positive or negative examples.) Then determine what works best for you when you practice your speech. You can use the form in Figure 13.1 to evaluate your own and others' nonverbal delivery.

Figure 13.1

Evaluation Form for Nonverbal Aspects of Delivery

Use this form to evaluate your own and others' vocal and nonverbal delivery, using this scale: 1 = excellent, 2 = good, 3 = average, 4 = fair, 5 = weak.

VOCAL ASPECTS OF DELIVERY—THE VOICE

_____ Pitch: upward and downward inflections

_____ Rate: speed of delivery

_____ Pause: appropriate use of silence

_____ Volume: loudness of the voice

_____ Enunciation: articulation and pronunciation

_____ Fluency: smoothness of delivery

_____ Vocal variety: overall effect of all of the above

BODILY ASPECTS OF DELIVERY

_____ Gestures: use of arms and hands

_____ Facial expression: use of the face

_____ Eye contact: use of eyes

_____ Movement: use of legs and feet

DELIVERY TIPS FOR NONNATIVE SPEAKERS

If you are a student who speaks English as a second language, you may be particularly concerned about your delivery. After all, you must simultaneously remember what you want to say and select and correctly pronounce the appropriate words. Here are some suggestions for how to work on delivery issues that may be of unique concern to you:

- *Recognize that you are not alone.* For most speakers the actual delivery of the speech is what causes the most anxiety. Even native speakers worry that they will forget what they intend to say or that they will say something incorrectly. If you have anxiety about delivery, your classmates will certainly empathize with you.

- *Give yourself time.* Most of the other suggestions on this list require that you devote some extra time to improving your delivery. This means you may need to begin working on your speeches much earlier than many of your classmates.

- *Check pronunciation.* On several online pronunciation dictionaries, you can look up words and hear them pronounced. For new and unfamiliar words or for words with many syllables, such resources can help you determine and practice correct pronunciation.

- *Talk with your instructor about reasonable goals.* If you are still working on several pronunciation or grammar issues, you can use your public speaking class as an opportunity to improve. With your instructor's help, identify a short list of items that you can work on over the course of the term. Your practice efforts will be more focused, and your instructor will have a clearer idea of what to concentrate on when giving feedback. If you do not set such objectives beforehand, both you and your instructor may have difficulty concentrating on specific and attainable areas for improvement.

- *Understand that eye contact is important.* Especially if you come from a culture that does not emphasize eye contact, you should recognize that U.S. audiences tend to weight this nonverbal delivery characteristic very heavily. To improve your eye contact, first get more comfortable maintaining eye contact during conversation. As this skill improves during one-on-one interactions, you can then work on better eye contact during speeches.

- *Practice using audio and video recordings.* By listening to and watching yourself, you will be better able to isolate specific ways to improve your delivery. While observing a recording, make a list of two to four things you could do to improve your delivery, and then practice the speech again while focusing on those items.

engaging diversity

Communication Apprehension with Diverse Audiences

When presenting to audience members from a culture other than your own, you may experience heightened anxiety. Such apprehension could stem from your worries that your audience may not be able to understand you or that you may accidentally say or do something inappropriate. Managing anxiety stemming from diverse audiences may require specific strategies. For instance, saying that you and your audience members are from different cultures that may involve unique customs, signals of respect, and communication approaches may allow both you and the audience members some freedom to approach the situation with less anxiety. Accepting that unintentional mistakes may be made and that such instances can be learning opportunities is a sign of openness and respect. Additionally, more experiences speaking with diverse audiences will give you opportunities to develop your own techniques for becoming comfortable speaking while also helping your audience be comfortable with you.

Source: Bernstein, R. S., Bulger, M., Salipante, P., & Weisinger, J. Y. (2020). From Diversity to inclusion to equity: A theory of generative interactions. *Journal of Business Ethics, 167*(3), 395–410. https://doi.org/10.1007/s10551-019-04180-1

Ways to Reduce Your Fear of Presenting

Anxiety is a natural part of speaking. Beginning public speakers often feel fear before and during their early presentations. Even experienced speakers are sometimes apprehensive when they face a new audience or a new situation. How, then, do we reduce and control any fear of presenting?

The person who has studied this subject the most, James McCroskey, refers to the fear of presenting as **communication apprehension**, which is defined as "an individual's level of fear or anxiety associated with either real or anticipated communication with another person or persons."[14] This definition implies a couple of points to note. First, apprehension can stem from any type of communication. Just as some people fear public speaking, others have significant apprehension during interpersonal conversations. Second, apprehension can stem from anticipated interactions with others. In fact, much of the anxiety associated with public speaking stems from *anticipation* rather than from the act of speaking itself.

Communication apprehension is connected to all aspects of our communication with others. Research shows that people who have higher levels of communication apprehension tend to view themselves as lower in communication competence.[15] Research also shows that communication apprehension tends to diminish over time as individuals become more experienced with making presentations.[16]

In the context of public speaking, apprehension has a more specific name: *public speaking anxiety*. High levels of public speaking anxiety not only can result in shaking knees, dry mouth, and other physical symptoms but also can create a self-fulfilling prophecy. People who are high in public speaking anxiety often spend less time preparing, which creates a series of cascading problems with the speech—everything that can go wrong will go wrong.[17]

Fear of presenting is similar to other fears in life: You cannot overcome it unless you want to. Fortunately, you can reduce fear in many ways, including the following:

- The **skills approach** reduces fear by systematically improving your presenting skills. In other words, by taking a course in public speaking you can learn, through the coaching of your teacher and your fellow students, to reduce your anxiety. You will find that repeatedly exposing yourself to something you find threatening—such as standing in front of an audience to give a speech—reduces your fear over time.

- Remember that much of our public speaking anxiety occurs in anticipation of the actual speech. We often begin framing negative thoughts about what can happen, and those thoughts build negative momentum, which dramatically increases our anxiety.[18] The **positive-thinking approach** reframes those negative thoughts as positive ones. Table 13.1 provides examples. Reframing your perceptions of speaking to include a growth mindset, which is the perspective that you can learn from mistakes and improve a skill, will help you redefine your anxiety as a source of energy and motivation to prepare, practice, and deliver an effective message.[19]

- The **visualization approach** invites you to picture yourself succeeding, as the positive-thinking approach does, but with the addition of imagery.[20] See yourself striding to the front of the room with confidence; see yourself speaking loudly enough for all to hear without a sign of fear; and see yourself moving through the speech with an attentive audience eagerly receiving your message. Athletes often use visualization along with practice to perform better on the field or court. Visualizing the act of shooting a free throw can help improve technique and consistency. The same principle can be effective as you prepare for your speech.

- The **self-managed approach** means that you reduce your fear of presenting with self-diagnosis and a variety of therapies. In other words, you attempt to uncover your fear, then decide what approach might reduce them. Communication scholar Karen Dwyer points out that many therapies can reduce your fears, but no single therapy works for all people.[21] You might decide that group therapy with a psychologist at the health service center would work best

communication apprehension
An individual's level of fear or anxiety associated with either real or anticipated communication with another person or persons.

skills approach
Reducing fear by systematically improving presenting skills.

positive-thinking approach
Using positive thoughts to bolster speaker confidence.

visualization approach
Picturing yourself succeeding.

self-managed approach
Reducing the fear of presenting with self-diagnosis and a variety of therapies.

- Communication apprehension is common for inexperienced speakers. Such anxiety tends to diminish as you gain more experience.
Andresr/Getty Images

Table 13.1 Negative Thoughts Reframed in Positive Ways

Negative Thinking	Positive Thinking
I'm afraid of public speaking.	I see public speaking as a personal challenge.
I don't want to go up front.	I have the courage to go up front.
I don't want to see all those eyes.	I appreciate the attention I get.
I'm afraid my voice won't work.	I plan to speak with confidence.
They will see I'm afraid.	I'll act confident until I feel confident.
Things will go wrong.	I'll work hard to be prepared and do my best.

relaxation approach
Combining deep relaxation with fear-inducing thoughts.

Figure 13.2

Calming normal communication apprehension.

Source: Gamble, Teri Kwal, and Gamble, Michael, (2012). Communication works (11th ed.). McGraw-Hill. © 2012 The McGraw-Hill Companies, Inc.

Raymond Patrick/The Image Bank/Getty Images

for you. Or you might decide that taking a public speaking course will be enough to help you overcome your fear of presenting.

- The **relaxation approach** trains you to associate public speaking with positive thoughts.[22] Although you can do this by yourself, another person, such as a facilitator, usually provides the relaxation commands. The facilitator asks you to relax (actually lying down helps) and to think of a situation in which you are totally unstressed. The facilitator links your relaxed state to a word, such as *calm.* After repeating this process, you start relaxing whenever you hear the word (you have been conditioned). The facilitator then walks you through whatever frightens you ("You are now walking to the front of the room") and says "calm" at the first signs of fright. This approach takes time, but the procedure does work for most people with high anxiety about presenting. See Figure 13.2 for a formula for this relaxation technique.

To practice relaxation techniques, do the following:

1. Sit in a comfortable chair or lie down in a comfortable place. As much as possible, rid the area of distracting noises. If possible, play relaxing music or the sounds of nature.

2. Begin with your face and neck, and tense the muscles. Then relax them. Tense again and hold the tensed position for 10 seconds. Relax again.

3. Tense your hands by clenching your fists. Relax. Tense again and hold for 10 seconds. Relax.

4. Tense your arms above your hands and to your shoulders. Relax. Tense again and hold for 10 seconds. Relax.

5. Tense your chest and stomach. Relax. Tense again and hold for 10 seconds. Relax.

6. Tense your feet by pulling the toes under. Relax. Tense again and hold for 10 seconds. Relax.

7. Tense your legs above the feet and up to the hips. Relax. Tense again and hold for 10 seconds. Relax.

8. Tense your entire body and hold for 10 seconds. Relax and breathe slowly.

9. Repeat the word *calm* to yourself. This will help you relate the word to the relaxed feeling you are now experiencing. In the future, when you feel anxious, the word *calm* should help you arrest the apprehension you experience.

When to Use Visual Resources

Do you learn best when you read something, when you watch something, or when you do something? Certainly, some skills are best learned by doing. Reading about how to insert streaming video into a PowerPoint presentation or watching another person perform the task is no substitute for trying to perform the task yourself. However, not everything lends itself to doing. You cannot "do" economics in the same way you can change a tire. Because so much of public speaking deals with issues and topics that cannot be performed, you must know the most effective methods of communicating in a public presentation. Often this means showing audience members visual representations of what you are speaking about.

Visual resources are any items that can be seen by an audience for the purpose of reinforcing a message, including the way you dress, words on a dry-erase board, and items you bring in for a demonstration. Setting up a computer to display images or slides is another use of visual resources. A student who wears scrubs when talking about careers in the medical field, one who provides a handout with an outline of the speech for the class, and yet another who brings in chemistry equipment are all using visual resources. As you can see, the options are many and diverse, and some work better than others. A handout could distract audience members, whereas chemistry equipment could bring a speech to life. Learning to use visuals effectively is a key skill for speakers.

A classic study, still cited as a definitive justification for using visual aids, shows that using visual supplements for your presentation dramatically improves the chances that audience members will remember what you say.[23] Figure 13.3 shows the benefits of visual aids. More recent research has considered whether PowerPoint slides have the same benefits as those discovered in the earlier study. When hearing lectures with slides and without slides, students tend to remember spoken information better when slides are not present, but they remember visual images such as graphs and pictures more easily when these are shown rather than described.[24] The implication is that you need to use visuals when visual imagery is important; hide them when what you are saying is most important.

A list of various types of visual resources and their advantages and disadvantages is shown in Table 13.2. Remember that most instructors have rules governing the use of visual resources. Few instructors allow live animals, and university policies usually forbid bringing to campus firearms, illegal substances or materials, and anything

• Using a model to visually illustrate your descriptions can add interest and clarity to your presentation.

Morsa Images/Stone/Getty Images

visual resources
Any items that can be seen by an audience for the purpose of reinforcing a message.

> ## Figure **13.3**
>
> Immediate and delayed retention of spoken and viewed information.
>
> Source: Data from Zayas-Boya, E. P. (1977–1978). Instructional media in the total language picture. *International Journal of Instructional Media*, 5, 145–150.

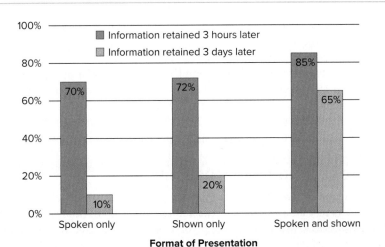

Format of Presentation

Table 13.2 Advantages and Disadvantages of Some Typical Visual Aids

Type	Advantages	Disadvantages
Dry-erase board	• Easy to use • Allows impromptu reactions from the audience	• Requires turning your back to the audience • Can be difficult to read
Poster displays	• Allow you to plan ahead for content and style • Can demonstrate creativity	• Can look unprofessional if not done well • Can cost money if professionally produced
Handouts	• Provide a takeaway for audience members • Can provide notes to help audience members with details	• Can create distractions • Can leave a mess if listeners don't take handouts with them
Models	• Provide greater realism • Can demonstrate greater detail for explanation	• Can be expensive to obtain • Can be difficult to transport, depending on size
People	• Can add realism • Can increase audience members' attention	• Can be unpredictable • Can make time management more difficult, particularly if there is a lack of planning and practice
Computers	• Allow preplanning for content and design • Can present diverse information	• Can be difficult to prepare if you don't have expertise • Requires that speaker be able to react to glitches

potentially dangerous to others. A good rule of thumb to follow is to *always* tell your teacher in advance what you plan to use as a visual resource. Prevent problems before they become problems. Remember, too, that you must practice with any visual aid you opt to use.

Principles for Using Visual Resources

Visual resources lose their effectiveness if they are not integrated effectively into your presentation. In this section you will learn tips for presenting visual information and for creating visual resources.

TIPS FOR PRESENTING VISUAL INFORMATION

When using visual aids, be prepared to handle them effectively. If you use a computer to display PowerPoint or a YouTube video, what will you do if the computer crashes? How should you best prepare visual aids so that they look professional and are not too cluttered? In addition to following the tips in Figure 13.4, plan to carefully analyze your approach to using visual aids. If you are relying on technology, have a backup in case the technology fails. Strive for professionalism—homemade posters are often sloppy and lack the professionalism expected by audiences. Finally, if others cannot look at your visual aid and in a few seconds be able to explain what they see, you may have included too much information. Your visual points should be clear and concise, just like your verbal points.

TIPS FOR CREATING VISUAL RESOURCES

slide-deck visuals
A collection of slides, usually created with a computer program, that are displayed during a presentation.

Apple's Keynote and Microsoft's PowerPoint remain the staple visual aids for most public speakers. There is very little difference between these two options. Both employ an approach referred to as **slide-deck visuals**, which help you create, arrange, and display various slides. Following basic visual design principles can dramatically increase the artistic appeal of your

- *Do not talk to your visual resources.* Keep your eyes on your audience.
- *Display visual resources only when you are using them.* Before or after they are discussed, they usually become a needless distraction to the audience. For instance, when presenting a slide, you can typically push "B" on the keyboard or a button on most remotes and clickers to display a black screen. Pressing "B" or the clicker button again will bring back your slide presentation.
- *Make sure everyone in the room can see your visual resources.* Check the visibility of your visual resources when you rehearse before your speech. If the classroom is 25 feet deep, have a friend or family member determine if the visual resources can be read from 25 feet away. Above all, make sure you are not standing in front of your visual resources.
- *Leave visual resources in front of the audience long enough for complete assimilation.* Few things are more irritating to an audience than to have half-read visual resources whipped away by a speaker.
- *Use a pointer or your arm closest to your visual aid for pointing to specific points of interest.* The pointer keeps you from masking the visual, and using your closest arm helps you to avoid closing off your body from the audience. In the image shown, the speaker is pointing to a drawing with her closest arm, which allows her to remain visible to the audience.

Figure 13.4

Tips for using visual resources.

Monty Rakusen/Getty Images

slides and help you make your points more effectively.[25] The remainder of this section discusses strategies for using these types of programs effectively.

Use Images, Not Words

The most common mistake speakers make when designing slides is to approach it as a writing assignment rather than a visual creativity assignment; therefore, they create slides filled with words, not pictures or images. Visual aids should be visual, and few word-based slides are visually appealing. You should look for ways to decrease your reliance on words and increase your use of graphics. Figure 13.5 shows two options for creating a slide that shows the average cost of college tuition. Notice how the slide with bullet points appears crowded, is hard to read, and contains much less information. The chart, by contrast, contains more information and is much clearer. When using text, make sure it is consistent in font and style.

Use Tables and Charts

Tables and charts are among the most effective ways to represent certain types of information, or data. Each type of visual resource is best for representing specific types of information.

Tables use text and often numbers to efficiently summarize, compare, and contrast information for your audience. Because the rows and columns in tables intersect to identify specific information, tables allow for comparison of information. For instance, if you wanted to compare statistics showing peoples' perceptions about technology over time, a table could be an efficient way to organize such information. As Figure 13.6 shows, you can compare responses to survey questions, presented in rows, where they intersect with the three columns representing years in which the survey was conducted. As you can see, negative perceptions about technology have generally increased over time.

Bar charts visually represent numeric values associated with different categories. The bars in such a chart can represent several different types of values, such as a simple count

Figure 13.5

Using images rather than words can increase the clarity of your visual resources.

Source: Courtesy of Scott Titsworth

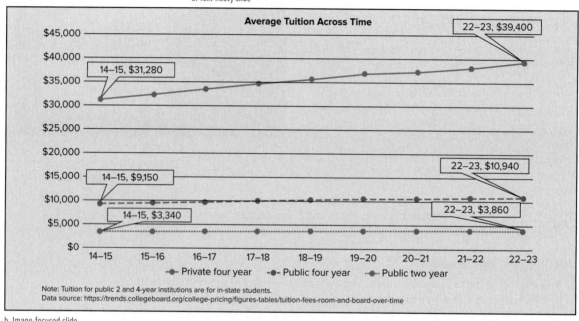

Average Tuition Across Time

- For 4-year, private nonprofit universities the average tuition in 2014–2015 was $31,280 and in 2022–2023 it was $39,400.
- For 4-year, public universities the average in-state tuition in 2014–2015 was $9,150 and in 2022–2023 it was $10,940.
- For 2-year, public colleges the average in-state tuition in 2014–2015 was $3,340 and in 2022–2023 it was $3,860.
- This information came from https://trends.collegeboard.org/college-pricing/figures-tables/tuition-fees-room-and-board-over-time

a. Text-heavy slide

Note: Tuition for public 2 and 4-year institutions are for in-state students.
Data source: https://trends.collegeboard.org/college-pricing/figures-tables/tuition-fees-room-and-board-over-time

b. Image-focused slide

Figure 13.6

Tables organize words and numbers.

Source: Courtesy of Scott Titsworth

Has communication technology made the world a better or worse place?

Answer	2000	2010	2018
Better Place	66%	57%	48%
Neither Better nor Worse	27%	35%	31%
Worse Place	7%	9%	21%

Note: Data represent Internet users 16 years of age and older.
Data source: Cole, J.I., Berens, B., Suman, M., Schramm, P., Zhou, L. (2018). *The 2018 digital future report: Surveying the digital future*. The University of Southern California. www.digitalcenter.org/wp-content/uploads/2018/12/2018-Digital-Future-Report.pdf

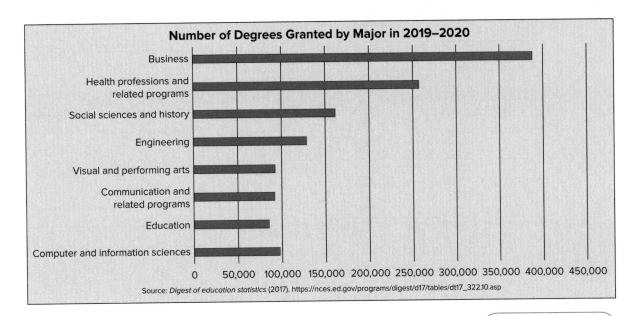

Figure 13.7

Bar charts show differences in values.

Source: Courtesy of Scott Titsworth

or sum of items in a category, an average, or a percentage. If depicting the number of students at your university by major, each bar would represent the number of students in each of the majors offered.

When information is displayed *horizontally*, the result is called a *bar chart*. Charts can also display bars *vertically* and in such cases are called *column charts*. In general, column charts are better used when the data set is lengthy, and bar charts are better when data labels are long. Figure 13.7 shows a bar chart illustrating values for the top-10 college majors, as indicated by the number of degrees granted during the 2019–2020 academic year. The bar chart is preferable in this circumstance because the names of the majors are too long to display in vertical columns.

Line charts use points connected by lines to show changes in value over time for one or more categories. Line charts plot a horizontal *x*-axis against a vertical *y*-axis. Because line charts are particularly useful for plotting values across time, the *x*-axis often represents a time series, such as months, years, or financial quarters. In Figure 13.8, the *x*-axis shows academic years beginning with 2014–2015 and continuing through 2019–2020. The *y*-axis shows the number of degrees granted, which range from 0 to 400,000. Each line in the chart represents the number of graduates from a particular major, as indicated in the legend at the bottom. The markers, shown as dots in the lines, indicate the number of majors of a particular type for each academic year. For instance, in the 2016–2017 academic year, the number of graduating business majors was 381,109, and in the 2019–2020 academic year, that number rose to 387,851. During the same time period, the number of health sciences graduates rose from 236,931 to 257,282. With only those values to review, you may lack sufficient information to draw much of a conclusion. However, if you examine all lines on the chart, you might easily conclude that the number of health sciences majors is growing at a much more rapid rate than the other majors, including business.

Pie charts are used to illustrate percentages of a whole. A pie chart is drawn as a circle with different colored segments representing each piece of the whole. The relative size of each segment represents its specific percentage of the entire circle. Suppose you wanted to visually represent the numbers of men and women in the U.S. Congress. Figure 13.9 shows a pie chart that illustrates the relative percentage difference among the seats.

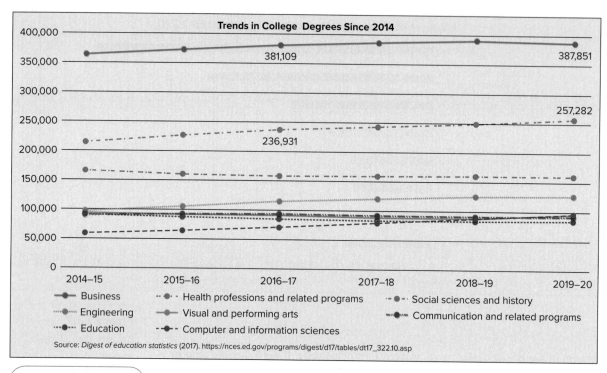

Source: *Digest of education statistics* (2017). https://nces.ed.gov/programs/digest/d17/tables/dt17_322.10.asp

Figure 13.8
Line charts show trends over time.

Source: Courtesy of Scott Titsworth

Minimize Rather Than Maximize Details

People have a natural tendency to include too much information in their visual aids. Notice the difference between the slides in Figure 13.10. The top slide is an effective chart, but if you wanted to make the point that many asylum recipients in the United States are from Asia, the bottom slide has more impact.

Capitalize on What's Available

Figure 13.9
Pie charts show percentages of a whole.

Source: Courtesy of Scott Titsworth

Keynote and PowerPoint are more robust when you use them to display a variety of multimedia. For instance, using the free website keepvid.to, you can create a

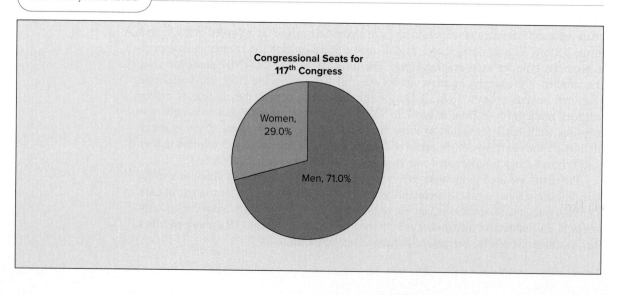

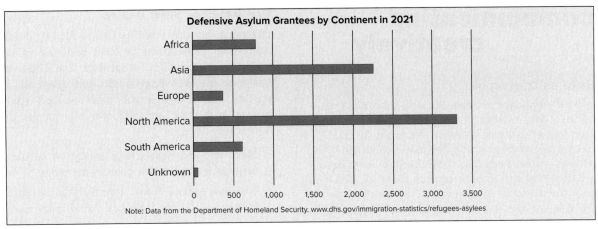

a. Slide with multiple details

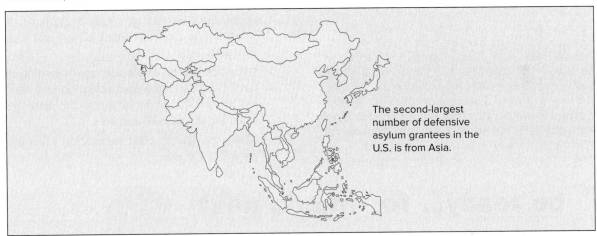

b. Slide emphasizing one detail for impact

> **Figure 13.10**
>
> Minimizing details can increase the impact of your visual resources.
>
> Source: Courtesy of Scott Titsworth

downloadable file of a YouTube video and embed the movie into your Keynote or PowerPoint file to play a short clip. You can even trim the clip to play exactly the portion you want. Likewise, you can embed MP3 music files or other audio files and have them automatically play when you advance to a new slide. These are only a few of the multimedia options available. Although you should try to utilize these options if they are appropriate for your message, audience, and situation, remember that you need to practice with them. The visual interest they add also increases the complexity of your presentation, which means that more can go wrong.

Alternatives to PowerPoint are available and commonly used. For example, Visme (www.visme.co/) offers a user-friendly but advanced platform for creating infographics and visually appealing presentations. Adobe Spark, Google Slides, and other applications are also viable alternatives to PowerPoint, but all still rely on the fundamental approach of showing one slide after another; they simply offer alternative ways of creating those slides.

Whatever approach you decide to use, remember that your primary purpose is to deliver an effective message. The visual resources you employ can be critical in helping or hindering your audience's interest and understanding. The better your visuals are, the more time they will likely take to create, and the more practice you will need. An excellent way to see how visuals enhance messages is to watch any TED (www.ted.com) presentation. Those speakers use a variety of visual resources and emphasize many of the principles discussed here. You can also search online for "infographics" to find clever examples of how details, including statistics and historical facts, can be displayed visually.

communicating creatively

Build an Infographic

Information graphics, or infographics, are visual representations of data, information, and knowledge. You regularly see infographics online, in newspapers, or even on the evening news when weather information is presented. Infographics are effective visual aids because, when done well, they take large amounts of information and make it easy to understand—usually in a visually appealing way. The style and approach you use to make an infographic can be very creative, as long as the content remains clear for the listener.

Several free tools are available online to assist you in making infographics, such as Infogram, Piktochart, and Venngage. You can find many more just by searching for "free infographic tools" online. Infographics offer a creative way to add visual interest to your presentation. Because effective infographics should make information clear to your audience, your role as the speaker is to boil down what's important to learn from the infographic. Rather than talking about each detail, narrate the big picture for the audience.

Use Inclusive Slide Design

Designing slides so that they can be read by those with visual impairments or color blindness is an important responsibility for speakers. The following tips from the Web Accessibility Initiative[26] are a starting point, though you may also ask your instructor if there are resources on campus to further assist you.

- Make text and visuals large enough to be seen easily from the furthest point in the room.
- Use easy-to-read fonts, especially those with thicker and bolder typefaces. Avoid fancy fonts that mimic handwriting.
- Use sufficient color contrast. If your room is bright, use dark text on a light background. If your room is dark, use a dark background with light text.
- Using red and green together can pose difficulties for those with red-green colorblindness. Also, red text on darker backgrounds can cause eye strain for all audience members.
- Always provide a verbal explanation when displaying visual aids.

be ready... for what's next

Augmented and Virtual Reality for Presentations

Rapid advancement in augmented and virtual reality (AR/VR) has provided meaningful opportunities for presenters to use this technology as part of the presentation process. Although few communication courses make use of such technology, integration of AR/VR into public speaking training and practice is likely to increase in the following ways.

- *AR/VR for Training.* Companies are already developing virtual speech training programs that use immersive 360º video to simulate speaking in front of large audiences so presenters can practice their speeches and feel more comfortable in front of audiences. Initial evidence exploring the effectiveness of virtual practice sessions is mixed. Students recognize the utility of such practice opportunities[27] but also tend to report even higher levels of apprehension as they prepare and deliver their practice speeches.[28] As training protocols continue to advance, these negative experiences with AR/VR may diminish.

- *Speaking in the metaverse.* In addition to creating simulated virtual environments for speaking practice, the metaverse offers a completely virtual environment where public speaking and advocacy are becoming common. The metaverse is an immersive digital world that was born out of video gaming. By using avatars, participants in the metaverse engage in social events like concerts and make purchases with digital currency. Higher education institutions are already creating metaverse versions of classes,[29] and in 2022 the president of France delivered a speech about technology that was streamed to the metaverse for participants to watch.[30] Because virtual environments like the metaverse are connected to our physical environments, opportunities for advocacy and public speaking will continue to increase.

AR/VR, including the metaverse, is not yet commonly used by presenters. However, digital technology progresses rapidly in how it affects everyday practices, so this technology could soon offer new and interactive approaches for presenters.

Chapter Review & Study Guide

Summary

In this chapter, you learned the following:

1. Delivery is how you use your voice and body to communicate your message to the audience. There are four general methods of delivering a presentation:

   - the extemporaneous method, in which the speech is carefully prepared but appears relatively spontaneous and conversational.
   - the impromptu method, which actually is spontaneous and without specific preparation.
   - the manuscript method, whereby the presenter uses a script throughout delivery.
   - the memorized method, which employs a script committed to memory.
   - the remote method uses characteristics of any other method but is delivered through digitally mediated technology such as Microsoft Teams, Google Hangouts, or Zoom.

2. There are various vocal and bodily behaviors you can use to improve your delivery.

   - Vocal aspects of delivery include pitch, rate, pauses, volume, enunciation, fluency, and vocal variety.
   - Nonverbal aspects of delivery include gestures, facial expression, eye contact, and movement.

3. Most speakers experience nervousness before giving a speech. There are five general approaches to managing your communication apprehension related to speaking:

   - The skills approach requires taking steps to improve your competence as a speaker. By improving your skills, you will gain more confidence.
   - Positive thinking can reframe fears into steps you'll use to improve your speaking.
   - The visualization technique lets you mentally picture yourself doing well during a speech.
   - The relaxation technique, usually enacted by a trained facilitator, trains you to associate public speaking with relaxing thoughts.
   - Self-management occurs when you focus on what your actual fears are and develop techniques for addressing specific fears rather than the general condition.

4. Using visual resources in your presentation can increase interest in your speech and help the audience retain more of what you say. Three days after your speech, audience members typically remember only about 10% of what you said if your speech does not include visuals; if you include visuals they typically remember about 65%.

5. Many speakers create unappealing slides because they do not follow general principles of design when creating PowerPoint or Keynote slide decks. These design principles can help you make clearer and more appealing slides:

   - Use images, not words.
   - Use tables, charts, and graphs to represent data and other information.
   - Minimize details so that your slides do not become cluttered.
   - Use multimedia resources to add interactivity, but practice with your materials several times to predict and avoid problems.

Key Terms

Articulation
Bodily movement
Communication apprehension
Delivery
Enunciation
Extemporaneous method
Eye contact
Facial expressions
Fluency

Gestures
Impromptu method
Manuscript method
Memorized method
Pause
Pitch
Positive-thinking approach
Pronunciation
Rate

Relaxation approach
Remote delivery method
Self-managed approach
Skills approach
Slide-deck visuals
Visual resources
Visualization approach
Vocal variety
Vocalized pauses

Study Questions

1. Which method of delivery encourages you to improvise and speak without previous research or preparation?

   a. extemporaneous
   b. impromptu
   c. manuscript
   d. memorized

2. Using Zoom to deliver a presentation would be characteristic of which delivery method?

   a. remote method
   b. impromptu method
   c. extemporaneous method
   d. memorized method

3. _____ is the highness or lowness of a speaker's voice, and _____ is the smoothness of delivery and flow of words.

   a. Volume; rate
   b. Pitch; fluency
   c. Rate; vocal variety
   d. Pitch; enunciation

4. Gestures are movements of the head, arms, and hands

   a. used to improve source credibility.
   b. that appear rehearsed and out of rhythm.
   c. used to illustrate, emphasize, or signal ideas.
   d. that convey a relationship with the audience.

5. The verbal communication behavior that allows you to convey emphasis is called

   a. articulation.
   b. enunciation.
   c. vocal variety.
   d. pitch.

6. If you are nervous or anxious about giving your presentation, you may be experiencing

   a. gestures.
   b. communication apprehension.
   c. cognitive modification.
   d. audience adaptation.

7. Why are visual resources used?

   a. Speakers do not need to prepare as much because they can just read their PowerPoints.
   b. They are appropriate for all types of speeches.
   c. People tend to learn and retain more when they both see and listen.
   d. They are fun to watch.

8. If you were charting a single-year's worth of values showing the number of majors in a given year, and the names of the majors were somewhat long, what type of chart should you use?

   a. line chart
   b. pie chart
   c. bar chart
   d. column chart

9. To display changes in data over time, it is best to use a

   a. pie chart.
   b. bar chart.
   c. table.
   d. line graph.

10. Which type of visual resource is best to efficiently summarize, compare, and contrast information for audience members?

   a. pie chart
   b. table
   c. line chart
   d. bar chart

Answers:
1. (b); 2. (a); 3. (b); 4. (c); 5. (c); 6. (b); 7. (c); 8. (c); 9. (d); 10. (b)

Critical Thinking

1. Assume that you are giving a presentation in a virtual environment like the metaverse. What would you want your avatar and digital speaking location to look like to maximize the effectiveness of your message?

2. Select a section in this chapter and create an infographic that could be used to teach others how to improve their delivery, manage communication apprehension, or use visual aids. As you create the infographic, you will use critical thinking and creativity to identify the most important points, then convey them in an artistic way.

Sizing Things Up Scoring and Interpretation

Engaging Delivery Assessment

Add each of your responses together for a grand total that could range from 0 to 36. Generally speaking, scores below 18 suggest that delivery could be improved, scores between 18 and 26 suggest average effectiveness, and scores of 27 or higher suggest very good to excellent delivery. After determining the score for your teacher in the class before your communication class, does this general assessment ring true to you? In other words, if your teacher is in the "average" range, do you think that fits with your general impression? The reason for this question is that some scholars argue that delivery is more than the simple sum of the parts. In other words, there could be instances where your general impression of a person's delivery carries more weight than several specific delivery behaviors added together.

References

1. Bailey, A. (2019, February 25). Here's Lady Gaga's moving Best Original Song speech from the Oscars. *Elle*. https://www.elle.com/culture/celebrities/a25740522/lady-gaga-oscars-2019-acceptance-speech-transcript/

2. Elliott, J. (2022, July 25). *How to improve your public speaking (and build your business)*. United States Chamber of Commerce. https://www.uschamber.com/co/grow/thrive/public-speaking-improvement-tips

3. Dwyer, S. (2001). Selling an idea: Extemporaneous speaking in sales education. *Journal of Personal Selling & Sales Management, 21*, 313–321.

4. De Haff, B. (2018, January 19). *80 percent of presentations at work are delivered remotely—here is how to get it right.* Inc. https://www.inc.com/brian-de-haaff/80-percent-of-presentations-at-work-are-delivered-remotely-here-is-how-to-get-it-right.html

5. Lee, M. (2021, March 24). *Ask the expert: Top tips for virtual presentation success.* Prezi Blog. https://blog.prezi.com/ask-the-expert-top-tips-for-virtual-presentation-success

6. Takash, J. (2011, September). Five tips to help you deliver a more effective speech. *Smart Business Chicago.* http://www.sbnonline.com/article/joe-takash-five-tips-to-help-you-deliver-a-more-effective-speech/

7. Roark, R. M. (2006). Frequency and voice: Perspectives in the time domain. *Journal of Voice, 20,* 325–354.

8. Woolbert, C. (1920). The effects of various modes of public reading. *Journal of Applied Psychology, 4,* 162–185.

9. Bullock, D. & Sánchez, R. (2022, April 13). Don't underestimate the power of your voice. *Harvard Business Review.* https://hbr.org/2022/04/dont-underestimate-the-power-of-your-voice

10. Cicero, M. T., & Caplan, H. (1981). *Ad C. Herennium: De ratione dicendi (Rhetorica ad Herennium).* Harvard University Press.

11. Van Edwards, V. (2022, November 9). *60 hand gestures you should be using and their meaning.* Science of People. https://www.scienceofpeople.com/hand-gestures/

12. Finley, T. (2022, October 13). *Tips for using hand gestures to support learning.* George Lucas Educational Foundation. https://www.edutopia.org/article/tips-using-hand-gestures-support-learning

13. LeFebvre, L., LeFebvre, L. E., & Allen, M. (2021). Exploring eye contact in virtual environments: The compositor mirror tool, areas of interest, and public speaking competency. *Communication Studies, 72*(6), 1053–1072. https://doi-org.proxy.library.ohio.edu/10.1080/105109 74.2021.2011353

14. McCroskey, J. C. (1997). Oral communication apprehension: A summary of recent theory and research. *Human Communication Research, 4,* 78–96. (p. 78)

15. Teven, J. J., Richmond, V. P., McCroskey, J. C., & McCroskey, L. L. (2010). Updating relationships between communication traits and communication competence. *Communication Research Reports, 27,* 263–270.

16. Marcel, M. (2022). Communication apprehension across the career span. *International Journal of Business Communication, 59*(4), 506–530. https://doi.org/10.1177/2329488419856803

17. Bodie, G. D. (2010). A racing heart, rattling knees, and ruminative thoughts: Defining, explaining, and treating public speaking anxiety. *Communication Education, 59,* 70–105.

18. Vassilopoulos, S. H. (2005). Anticipatory processing plays a role in maintaining social anxiety. *Anxiety, Stress & Coping, 18,* 321–332.

19. Nordin, K., & Broeckelman-Post, M. A. (2019). Can I get better? Exploring mindset theory in the introductory communication course. *Communication Education, 68*(1), 44–60. https://doi.org/10.1080/03634523.2018.1538522

20. Ayres, J. (2005). Performance visualization and behavioral disruption: A clarification. *Communication Reports, 18,* 55–63.

21. Dwyer, K. K. (2000). The multidimensional model: Teaching students to self-manage high communication apprehension by self-selecting treatments. *Communication Education, 49,* 72–81.

22. Friedrich, G., & Goss, B. (1984). Systematic desensitization. In J. A. Daly & J. C. McCroskey (Eds.), *Avoiding communication: Shyness, reticence, and communication apprehension* (pp. 173–188). Sage.

23. Zayas-Boya, E. P. (1977–1978). Instructional media in the total language picture. *International Journal of Instructional Media, 5,* 145–150.

24. Savoy, A., Proctor, R. W., Salvendy, G. (2009, May). Information retention from PowerPoint and traditional lectures. *Computers & Education, 52*(4): 858–867.

25. Duarte, N. (2010). *Resonate: Present visual stories that transform audiences.* Wiley. Reynolds, G. (2009). *Presentation Zen: Simple ideas on presentation design and delivery.* New Riders.

26. W3C Web Accessibility Initiative. (n.d.). *How to make your presentations accessible to all.* https://www.w3.org/WAI/teach-advocate/accessible-presentations/

27. Vallade, J. I., Kaufmann, R., Frisby, B. N., & Martin, J. C. (2021). Technology acceptance model: Investigating students' intentions toward adoption of immersive 360° videos for public speaking rehearsals. *Communication Education, 70*(2), 127–145. https://doi.org/10.1080/03634523.2020.1791351

28. Davis, A., Linvill, D. L., Hodges, L. F., Da Costa, A. F., & Lee, A. (2020). Virtual reality versus face-to-face practice: A study into situational apprehension and performance. *Communication Education, 69*(1), 70–84. https://doi.org/10.1080/03634523.2019.1684535

29. Stewart, N. K. (2022). Virtual reality, metaverse platforms, and the future of higher education. *Media Development, 3,* 10–15.

30. Hunter, M. (2022, October 10). *Emmanuel Macron makes metaverse history.* FullyCrypto. https://fullycrypto.com/emmanuel-macron-makes-metaverse-history

14

informative presentations

When you have read and thought about this chapter, you will be able to

1. identify the goal and immediate behavioral purpose for an informative presentation.

2. recall strategies for creating information interest.

3. recall principles for selecting informative content.

4. explain the two forms of information overload.

5. apply skills for informative speaking.

The goal of informative presentations is to enhance an audience's knowledge and understanding of a topic. In this chapter you will learn how to choose topics for an informative speech and how to develop behavioral purposes for them. The chapter discusses techniques that will help you effectively present an informational speech to an audience. Effective informative speakers demonstrate certain skills that contribute to their effectiveness, so this chapter covers the skills of defining, describing, explaining, narrating, and demonstrating. Finally, the chapter includes a full script example of an informative presentation.

nformative presentations have various purposes for teaching audience members about people, particular events, facts, ideas, or even ways of thinking. One of those purposes is to help audience members learn new information. This was the purpose for Stevie Nicks when she was honored as the first woman of only 23 artists to be inducted twice into the Rock and Roll Hall of Fame. Much of Nicks's presentation discussed her journey as an artist, how she navigated a solo career while remaining in the band Fleetwood Mac, and the significance of being the only female artist to be inducted twice into the hall of fame. She also shared advice that a friend gave her about navigating her first solo album and maintaining her presence in the band: "You can do both, and you can have both. You just have to do it with love." This statement speaks to universal feelings that many people have about balancing multiple goals. Throughout the speech, Nicks recounted the kind of sound and influences she wanted for her solo album and how various artists she met along the way, including Tom Petty, shaped her career.

Dimitrios Kambouris/The Rock and Roll Hall of Fame/Getty Images

Nicks's description of how she navigated the beginning of her solo career, coupled with an explanation of the kind of sound she wanted for her album, helped audience members better understand the journey of one of the most successful female rock and roll artists. Although you may not be ready for induction into the Rock and Roll Hall of Fame, you have important stories to tell, and your audience can benefit from hearing your perspective. This is what informative speaking can help you accomplish.

Source: Spanos, B., Wang, A. X., & Exposito, S. (2019, March 30). Read Stevie Nicks's riotous rock hall induction speech. *Rolling Stone*. www.rollingstone.com/music/music-news/stevie-nicks-rock-and-roll-hall-of-fame-2019-814259/

Preparing an Informative Presentation

To prepare an informative speech, ask yourself the following:

- Why deliver the speech? That is, what is your goal for informative speaking?
- What kinds of topics best lend themselves to informative speaking?
- What are the immediate behavioral purposes of informative speaking, and how can you determine whether you have fulfilled them?

IDENTIFYING YOUR GOAL

Informative speakers have multiple goals, such as to increase what the audience knows about the topic, explain information that will be useful, clarify complex issues, demonstrate something useful, illustrate how things are related in space, or arouse interest in topics that might initially seem boring or uninteresting but that really are important.

To increase what the audience knows about a topic is one kind of informative speaking that is very much like what you experience in higher education every day, because it is like most teaching. Your professors are trying to increase what you know. Some examples of topics for such a presentation follow:

What can we learn from cave drawings?
What is chronic fatigue syndrome?
What are the possibilities of geothermal power?
What creates wind energy?

Speeches on these topics help audience members increase knowledge about particular, and sometimes unique, issues.

To help your audience learn information that will be useful to them is another common goal of informative presentations. You take courses that provide useful information, such as on food and nutrition, exercise physiology, wellness, and intercultural communication. In this kind of informative speaking you can also imitate or adapt strategies that you have seen in the classroom, in your workplace, in workshops, or in seminars in which you have participated. Some examples of topics for such a presentation follow:

How can you stay fit using a minimalist workout?
How can you take easy steps to avoid the flu?
How can you make your home energy efficient?
What are traditional greeting customs in Bolivia?

These topics, and many others like them, increase what the audience knows and provide a path for those who wish to take it. Unlike the persuasive presentation that presses the audience to act, the informative speech provides useful information the listener can choose to use or not. Think of the difference between commercial and public broadcasting. Commercial stations carry advertisements that end with an action step suggesting or often insisting on a purchase, but public broadcasters are allowed only to name a sponsor without pushing for an action. Similarly, informative presentations give you information on which you *could* act, but the primary purpose is to tell you about tools, not to insist that you use them.

To clarify complex issues is another goal of informative presentations. Many complex issues emerge every day: increased violence in parts of the world, economic systems that sharply divide the rich and the poor, patient and provider well-being, cases of widespread food insecurity, abuse of children and the elderly, and personal privacy on the internet. We hear about these issues, but most of us do not fully understand their causes or effects. An informative speech can tackle such complex issues and clarify them. Here are some questions this type of presentation might answer:

What is the historic relationship between Israel and the Palestinians?
What happens when your bank account is hacked?
What factors contribute to burnout among nurses?
How do you create a strong and unique password to protect your online information?

These topics and many more are available through the news as it unfolds daily, weekly, and monthly. When selecting this type of topic, think about issues, situations, and events that leave people confused or concerned and explain to your listeners what the issue can mean to them.

To demonstrate something useful is another possible goal of an informative presentation. Listeners remember better if they not only hear what you say but also do it. That's why a demonstration presentation often has more impact on an audience than one that relies on words and images only. Some possible topics for a demonstration presentation follow:

> How can you use the Heimlich maneuver to save a life?
> What is the correct way to lift weights?
> What are the basic computer coding skills everyone should have?
> What is the process of investing in a Roth IRA?

These and other topics lend themselves nicely to showing an audience how something looks or works. In some cases—such as the Heimlich maneuver—you can even have audience members participate to show that they understand your message.

To illustrate how things are related in space is an additional type of informative presentation. Much of what engineers, architects, electricians, and fashion designers do is demonstrate how to relate items in space. Here are some examples of this type of informative presentation:

• The informative speaker must arouse the interest of the audience and show the significance of the topic.
Marco Iacobucci EPP/ Shutterstock

> How can you take a photograph that blurs out the background?
> What are the sources of international computer hacking?
> What are the major tourist spots in the Caribbean?
> What is the geography of the brain?

Finding your way around a foreign city, showing the locations of the best-rated restaurants on Yelp.com, and locating the main features of a national park all require that you inform your listeners about spatial relationships.

Finally, *to arouse interest in topics that might at first seem uninteresting or boring* is a legitimate goal of an informative presentation. Teachers often try to arouse your interest in subjects that you might find uninteresting or boring; when they are effective, they use strategies you can also employ. Some examples of topics that might at first appear uninteresting but can be lively, given the right treatment, follow:

> What are the lessons learned from Shakespeare?
> How do fuel cells work?
> What surprising species can you find in your backyard?
> What are the most common phobias?

IDENTIFYING YOUR IMMEDIATE BEHAVIORAL PURPOSE

Two important questions for the informative speaker are these:

• What do you want your audience to know or do as a result of your presentation?

• How will you know whether you are successful?

Students learn better if they know exactly what the instructor expects them to learn. Similarly, an audience learns more from an informative presentation if the speaker states exactly what they are expected to know or do. The results of your informative presentation will remain unknown, however, unless you make them behavioral; that is, your presentation should result in change you can observe. An instructor discovers whether students learned from a lecture by giving a quiz or having the students answer questions in class. In the same way, the informative speaker seeks to discover whether a message was effectively communicated by seeking overt feedback from the audience. This overt feedback is about the **immediate behavioral purposes** of your presentation—the actions you expect from an audience during and immediately after a presentation.

The most common immediate behavioral purposes in an informative presentation encourage listeners to do the following:

- *Define words, objects, or concepts.* For example, after hearing a presentation, audience members can define the term *foreclosure,* tell what anthropologists mean by an *artifact,* or provide a meaningful definition for the concept of *eminent domain.* A statement of purpose for a presentation to define looks like this: "My purpose is to have my listeners tell me upon asking that the law allows government to acquire private or commercial property as long as the government pays market rates in a concept called 'eminent domain.'"

- *Describe objects, persons, or issues.* For example, after hearing a presentation listeners can describe sedimentary rock formations or describe in a way we can all understand the pros and cons of single-payer healthcare. A statement of purpose for a presentation to describe looks like this: "My purpose is to have my listeners correctly explain back to me the main arguments for and against a single-payer healthcare system."

- *Distinguish between different things.* For example, after hearing a presentation the audience should be able to distinguish between fossil fuel and electric cars or the difference between a gluten-free diet and the keto diet. A statement of purpose for a presentation to distinguish between different things looks like this: "My purpose is to have my audience show me that they can tell the difference in performance between a fossil fuel vehicle and an electric car."

- *Compare and/or contrast items.* For example, after hearing a presentation the audience should be able to contrast a real diamond with a cubic zirconia, faux fur with actual animal fur, and whether Netflix or Hulu is the better streaming subscription. A statement of purpose for a presentation to compare and/or contrast looks like this: "My purpose is to have members of the audience be able to accurately tell a friend about the major differences between real and fake fur."

In each of these immediate behavioral purposes of an informative speech, the audience can be asked to prove they know and understand the speaker's purpose by stating, writing, or demonstrating what they have learned.

Presenting Information Effectively

Audience analysis can help you determine how much audience members already know and how much you will have to tell them. Then you have to decide how to generate information interest, demonstrate information relevance, reveal extrinsic motivation, design informative content, avoid information overload, and organize content in your presentation.

CREATING INFORMATION INTEREST

An informative presentation is more effective if the presenter can generate audience interest in the information. In earlier chapters you read about the need to gain interest during the introduction to the speech, but that interest shouldn't stop there. During an informative speech, you want to maintain interest throughout the body and even in the conclusion of the speech. In this way, interest is like a thread that weaves throughout the presentation. Arousal of interest during the speech is related to how much the audience will comprehend. You could use the following **rhetorical questions**—questions asked for effect, with no answer expected—to introduce an informative speech and to arouse audience interest later on in the speech: "Are you aware of the number of abused children in your hometown?" "Can you identify five warning signs of colon cancer?" Depending on the audience, these rhetorical questions could arouse interest.

rhetorical questions
Questions asked for effect, with no answer expected.

Another method is to arouse the audience's curiosity. For example, you might state, "I have discovered a way to add 10 years to my life," "The adoption of the following plan will ensure more joy in your life," or "I know the foundation for achieving relational success." Giving out a brief quiz on your topic early in the speech arouses audience interest in finding the answers. Wearing a piece of clothing that relates to your topic can make people wonder why you are wearing it and pay more attention as a result. And an object you created will likely inspire the audience to wonder how you made it. Asking rhetorical questions and arousing curiosity are just a few of the many ways the presenter can generate and maintain interest in a topic.

DEMONSTRATING INFORMATION RELEVANCE

A second way to make an informative presentation effective is to demonstrate **information relevance**—the importance, novelty, and usefulness of the information to the audience. When selecting a topic for an informative presentation, carefully consider the relevance of the topic to the particular audience. Skin cancer from sun exposure might be a better topic in the summer when students are sunbathing than in the winter when they spend more time inside. Whereas a presentation on taxes could be dull, a speech on how current tax laws cost audience members more than they cost the rich might be more relevant, and a speech on three ways to reduce personal taxes might be even more relevant. In contrast, a speech on raising racehorses, writing a textbook, or living on a pension might be informative but not relevant because of the financial status, occupation, or age of the listeners. Thus, you should exercise some care in selecting a topic that interests your audience.

information relevance
The importance, novelty, and usefulness of the information to the audience.

extrinsic motivation
A method of making information relevant by providing the audience with reasons beyond the presentation itself for listening to the content of the presentation.

REVEALING EXTRINSIC MOTIVATION

A third way to present information effectively is to create **extrinsic motivation**—reasons beyond the presentation itself for listening to its content—for the audience. An audience is more likely to listen to and comprehend a presentation if reasons exist outside the speech itself for concentrating on the content.[1] A teacher who tells students to listen carefully because they will be tested on the information during an exam is using extrinsic motivation. A speaker can use extrinsic motivation at the beginning of a presentation by telling an audience, "Attention to this speech will alert you to ways you can increase energy and creativity," or "After hearing this speech, you will never purchase a poor-quality used computer again."

Extrinsic motivation is related to the concept of information relevance. The audience member who would ordinarily lack interest in the topic of music might find that topic

engaging diversity

Culture and Relevance

Culture can influence the way information is understood and valued. For example, most students from Western cultures, such as the United States, the United Kingdom, Australia, and Canada, want to understand how information is useful to them personally. For example, while listening to a speech, they will consider the information valuable if it can help them in some way. However, students from Confucius cultures, such as mainland China, Taiwan, Korea, Japan, and Singapore, consider how information can benefit their family, community, or other groups they belong to before considering how it can affect them personally. Of course, these are generalizations, and particular individuals from any particular culture may have different preferences. Speakers must use careful audience analysis to the best of their ability to understand cultural influences so that their message is seen as useful and meaningful to as many audience members as possible.

Source: Kang, H., & Chang, B. (2016). Examining culture's impact on learning behaviors of international students from Confucius culture studying in Western online learning context. *Journal of International Studies, 6,* 779–797.

building behaviors

Relating the Topic to the Audience

Either by yourself or with a partner, think or talk about your answer to each of the following:

- What can you do in your presentation to generate information interest, to make your audience desire more?
- What can you do to make sure the audience knows the importance and usefulness of your topic?
- What reasons beyond the presentation itself (extrinsic motivation) does the audience have for listening to you?

relevant when it is linked to learning about the ways music can reduce stress. The audience member's interest in finding ways to reduce stress is an extrinsic motivation for listening carefully to the presentation.

Speakers typically mention external reasons for listening *before* the message they want the audience to remember. A statement such as "You will need this background material for the report due at the end of this week" provides extrinsic motivation for the managers who hear it from their employer. Similarly, in an informative presentation, you may be able to command more attention, comprehension, and action from audience members if they know some reasons outside the presentation itself for attending to your message.

DESIGNING INFORMATIVE CONTENT

informative content
The main points and subpoints, illustrations, and examples used to clarify and inform.

A fourth way to effectively present information to an audience is to select **informative content**—the main points and subpoints, illustrations, and examples you use to clarify and inform. The following principles can guide you in selecting your speech content:

- *Audiences tend to remember and comprehend generalizations and main ideas better than details and specific facts.* The usual advice to speakers—to limit content to a relatively small number of main points and generalizations, say two to five—is well founded. Audiences are unlikely to remember a larger number of main points.

communicating with agility

Pivoting to enhance audience engagement

The following situation will likely happen to you at some point in your life. You have prepared what you think is an engaging presentation; however, after a few minutes of your talk, you realize many audience members seem disengaged. As a presenter, it is important to have a host of strategies to re-engage the audience. Here are a few strategies you can try:

- Have the audience journal responses to a question or their reactions to what you've said so far.
- Ask audience members to turn to the person next to them and share a time that they experienced something related to your topic.
- Walk around during your presentation and interact directly with audience members.
- Engage technology during your presentation, such as by asking the audience to access links or QR codes to surveys and polls on your topic. Allow the audience to see the responses and discuss the results.

- *Relatively simple words and concrete ideas are significantly easier to retain than are more complex materials.* Long or unusual words may dazzle an audience into thinking you are intellectually gifted or verbally skilled, but they may also reduce audience understanding of the content. Keep the ideas and the words used to express those ideas at an appropriate level.

- *Humor can make a dull presentation more interesting to an audience, but humor does not seem to increase information retention.* The use of humor also improves the audience's perception of the character of the speaker and can increase a speaker's authoritativeness when a presentation is dull.

- *Early remarks about how the presentation will meet the audience's needs can create anticipation and increase the chances that the audience will listen and understand.* Whatever topic you select, you should tell audience members early in your presentation how the topic is related to them. Unless you relate the topic to their needs, they may choose not to listen.

- *Calling for overt audience response, or actual behavior, increases comprehension more than repetition does.* As an informative presenter, you can ask for overt responses from audience members by having them perform the task being demonstrated. For example, after showing the audience a Tik-Tok video with a new dance move, you could have members pair up and practice the dance moves they are comfortable doing. You could also have the audience stand, raise hands, or write out responses to indicate affirmative understanding of your statements. For example, you can say, "List three ways to reduce stress during midterms that were discussed during my presentation." Having an audience go through an overt motion provides feedback for you and can be rewarding and reinforcing for both you and your listeners.

- Having the audience practice what you preach greatly increases their comprehension.

Fotostorm/E+/Getty Images

AVOIDING INFORMATION OVERLOAD

A fifth strategy for effectively presenting content, especially during an informative presentation, is to avoid **information overload**—providing much more information than the audience can absorb in terms of quantity and complexity.

Information overload comes in two forms. One is *quantity:* the speaker tells audience members more than they want to know about a subject, even if they were interested in it. This can decrease interest and understanding, even if the audience was initially excited about the topic.

The second form of information overload is *complexity:* the speaker uses language or ideas that are beyond the capacity of the audience to understand. An engineer or a mathematician who uses detailed formulas or a philosopher who shares highly abstract ideas may leave the audience feeling frustrated and more confused than before the speech.

The solution to information overload is to speak on a limited number of main points, use the most useful supporting materials, and keep the language of the message at a level the audience can understand.

information overload
Providing much more information than the audience can absorb in terms of amount and complexity.

ORGANIZING CONTENT

Finally, in order for a presentation to be effective, the content of the presentation needs to be organized. The following recommendations offer guidance on how to organize your presentation:

1. Tell an audience what you are going to tell them (forecast), tell them, and tell them what you told them.

2. Use transitions and signposts to increase understanding.

3. Tell your audience which points are most important.

4. Repeat important points for better understanding.

Table 14.1 An Informative Presentation Checklist

_____	1.	Does your audience have some generalizations to remember from your details and specific facts?
_____	2.	Have you used simple words and concrete ideas to help your audience remember?
_____	3.	Can you comfortably use humor in your presentation, if it is appropriate to do so?
_____	4.	Have you told your listeners early in your presentation how your message will meet their needs?
_____	5.	Have you determined ways to actively engage the audience in your presentation?
_____	6.	Have you avoided information overload?
_____	7.	Have you used transitions, highlighted the most important points, and included some repetition in your presentation?

sizing things up

Using Language Effectively

Much of our communication with others, particularly informative speaking, uses language to express meaning. Not surprisingly, one source of miscommunication is the use of language that others do not understand. Take a moment to assess your use of various approaches to improving the clarity of your language. The following statements are things you might do to help others understand you more clearly. Read each question carefully and respond using the following scale:

1 = I never do that.
2 = I sometimes do that.
3 = I regularly do that.
4 = I frequently do that.

1. Use descriptive statements to check your perception.
2. Restate another person's message by repeating what you thought the person meant.
3. Describe exactly how you think something works, how it happens, or what it consists of.
4. Explain the meaning of important words you use.
5. Specify the time when you made the observation.
6. Identify the uniqueness of objects, events, or people you encounter so that others can categorize or contextualize them.
7. Use words others do not understand.
8. Talk in abstract terms.
9. Base your messages only on your own perceptions.
10. Make statements that do not provide the situation or timing of your observation.
11. Talk about people, places, and things from a general viewpoint, rather than precisely.
12. Go with your instinct about what you think the other person means.

A guide for interpreting your responses appears at the end of the chapter.

Audiences can more easily grasp information when they are invited to anticipate and to review the organization and content of your speech. That is why the body of your presentation is bracketed by a preview of what you are going to say and a summary, or review, of what you said.

When you have completed this section on how to effectively present your material, check your presentation against the checklist in Table 14.1.

Skills for Informative Speaking

Highly effective informative speakers demonstrate certain skills that contribute to their speaking effectiveness. One of these skills is *defining;* much of what an informative speaker does is reveal to an audience what certain terms, words, and concepts mean. Another is *describing;* the informative speaker often tells an audience what something looks, sounds, feels, and even smells like. A third skill is *explaining,* or trying to say what something is in words the audience can understand. A fourth skill is *narrating*—an oral interpretation of a story, an event, or a description. A fifth skill is *demonstrating,* or showing an audience how to do something. In this section you will learn ways to improve each of these skills.

DEFINING

Far from being dull, definitions often give shape to the issues we debate in our society. For example, what is a family? Is it defined by legal ties, biological ties, or the roles people fulfill in your life? Are the characteristics of Generation Z different from those of millennials? What constitutes a plant-based diet?

We can define by using comparison and contrast, synonyms and antonyms, and even operational definitions. A **comparison** shows the similarity between something well known and something less known. A student explained that tying a scarf (unfamiliar to most) is similar to tying your shoelace (familiar to all). A **contrast** clarifies by showing differences: "He was taller than you, had longer hair, and had sharper features."

A **synonym** defines by using a word similar in meaning to the one you are trying to define. A student speaking about depression used synonyms to help the listeners understand: "A depressed person feels demoralized, purposeless, isolated, and distanced from others." An **antonym** defines an idea by opposition. A student defined "a good used car" by what it is not: "Not full of dents, not having high mileage, not worn on the seats, not using lots of oil, and not involved in a serious accident."

An **operational definition** defines by explaining a process. An operational definition of a cake is the sequence of actions depicted in a recipe. An operational definition of concrete is the formula-driven sequence of ingredients correctly added over the correct time period.

DESCRIBING

To deliver a more powerful message, speakers are better off being concrete than abstract, specific instead of general, and accurate instead of ambiguous (see Chapter 3). Effective descriptions also have other qualities such as **imagery**, a figure of speech that arouses the senses and stimulates your synapses to see, hear, and feel what the words are saying.

Look first at this description of Reggie Watts, who started his career as a singer with bands but ended up being a stand-up comedian. Here is how one writer characterized him:

> He arrives on stage with enormous amber rings dripping like tree sap from his fingers, his Afro a Miracle-Gro spider plant. Sometimes he's painted a pinkie nail pink. He might be wearing a ridiculous sweater.[2]

That's how he looks. Here is how he sounds:

> Then he lays down a track. He starts with the sound of a kick drum, from deep in his throat, recorded into a loop sampler—a small machine often used by guitarists to layer melodies. He adds a snare with a few controlled exhales. A couple of high notes with his tongue against his teeth. And then he starts to sing, in French or gibberish German. Morphing imperceptibly into a cockney slang, he seems to be talking about something from a human-resources manual or a dating disaster . . . .[3]

Do these words help you picture in your mind what Reggie Watts looks and sounds like? In two sentences the words tell you that he wears large amber rings, wears his hair in an uncontrolled Afro, colors his pinkie nail pink, and does not care much about his clothing. The actual imagery occurs with words such as "enormous amber rings dripping like tree sap" and "his Afro a Miracle-Gro spider plant." Words can paint pictures in the mind that appeal to the senses.

Another figure of speech appears in the description of Watts's voice. **Metaphor** likens one thing to another by treating it as if it were that thing. The paragraph on how Watts sounds is metaphorical in that the writer describes his voice as if it were an entire band: "sound of a kick drum," "recorded into a loop sampler," "he adds a snare"—all done with voice and throat. You can perform similar magic with your own words if you recognize the potential of speaking with imagery and metaphor.

comparison
Shows the similarity between something well known and something less known.

contrast
Clarifies by showing differences.

synonym
Defines by using a word similar in meaning to the one you are trying to define.

antonym
Defines an idea by opposition.

operational definition
A definition that identifies something by revealing how it works, how it is made, or what it consists of.

imagery
The use of words that appeal to the senses and create pictures in the mind.

metaphor
A figure of speech that likens one thing to another by treating it as if it were that thing.

• Singer-turned-comedian Reggie Watts.
©Noah Kalina

building behaviors

Practicing Explanations

Think of something you have explained to others many times at work or at home—for example, a job skill, a hobby, a course project, or a favorite TV show, film, website, or app. Does your explanation get increasingly efficient with practice? The answer is probably yes. To help prepare for your informative speech, practice some of the explanations from your presentation on others before you address an audience so that they will be easy to understand.

explanation
A means of idea development that simplifies or clarifies an idea while arousing audience interest.

narrating
The oral presentation and interpretation of a story, a description, or an event; includes dramatic reading of prose or poetry.

demonstrating
Showing the audience what you are explaining.

communicating creatively

The Moth: True Stories Told Live

Often during an informative speech, information is shared about other people's lives, or narratives are used as a tool to share facts and evidence. At some point, you will likely have an opportunity to bring people together to listen to your story. How would you tell a story about your life that maintains audience interest? For inspiration, you could turn to The Moth, an organization that produces a series of live shows in which storytellers explore, usually in unique ways, their own truthful and authentic narratives. The Moth was founded in 1997 in New York City by novelist George Dawes Green, who wanted to bring people together over mesmerizing stories. Each show has a theme, and the presenters have no notes to aid in their delivery. In this way, audiences can connect with the storytellers and learn about different experiences they may never have personally encountered. You can learn more about the unique storytelling approach by listening to The Moth Podcast or by tuning in to The Moth Radio Hour played on more than 480 radio stations.

Source: The Moth. *About*. https://themoth.org/about

EXPLAINING

A third skill for the informative presenter is explaining an idea in words the audience can understand. An **explanation** simplifies or clarifies an idea while arousing audience interest.

An important step in explaining is analyzing, deconstructing, or dissecting something to enhance audience understanding. Unless you become skilled at dissecting a concept, your explanation may leave audience members more confused than they were before your presentation. Determine what you can do to make the concept more palatable to the audience. For example, if you were to try to explain to someone the purpose of Pinterest, you might say that it is a website and an app where you can "pin" images that link to websites to multiple online boards, just like you would pin magazine articles or pictures to a corkboard.

NARRATING

A fourth skill for informative speakers is **narrating**—the oral presentation and interpretation of a story, a description, or an event. In a presentation, narration includes the dramatic reading of lines from a play or a poem, the voice-over on a series of slides, and the reading of a quotation or a selection from a newspaper, blog, or magazine.

The person who uses narration in a presentation moves just a little closer to oral interpretation of literature, or even acting, because the narration is highlighted by being more dramatic than the surrounding words. Sections of your presentation that require this kind of special reading also require special practice. If you want a few lines of poetry in your presentation to have the desired impact, you will need to rehearse them.

DEMONSTRATING

A fifth skill for informative speakers is **demonstrating**—showing the audience what you are explaining. Some topics are communicated best through words; other topics are best communicated by demonstrating. You can talk about self-defense, efficient ways to breathe while swimming laps, and weight lifting. However, nothing enhances understanding better than seeing and trying self-defense moves, practicing different breathing approaches while swimming, or actually lifting some weights while learning about them.

Example Informative Presentation

So far in this chapter, you have learned how to select a topic for your informative presentation; how to determine immediate behavioral purposes and goals for the informative presentation; how to present information to an audience; how to organize the informative presentation; and how to define, describe, explain, narrate, and demonstrate the concepts in your presentation. In this section we will look at the manuscript of an actual informative presentation.

As you might imagine, many informative speeches can be trivial in nature, such as the best Taylor Swift album, how to eat a low-fat diet, or the origin of the coffee bean. These are all interesting topics, but they might not challenge you to stretch your informative speaking skills or provide essential new knowledge to your audience.

It takes skill to frame an emotionally charged or potentially polarizing topic in an informative style. Challenge yourself to take those topics you are passionate about and not save them for a persuasive speech. Rather, see how you can address your goals in a way that provides information to your audience and allows them to draw their own inferences about an issue. Then perhaps later on, you may decide to continue with the same topic for your persuasive speech. In the following example, you will see how a student took the topic of blackfishing and used an artful approach to explain a contemporary and controversial topic in an informative style.

As you look at the informative speech example, notice how the speaker gains and maintains the audience's attention, relates the topic to herself and to the audience, establishes credibility, and forecasts the organization and development of the topic. Notice also how the speaker clarifies the topic with examples high in audience interest; translates the ideas into language the audience can understand; and defines, describes, and explains ideas. The marginal notes will help identify how the speaker fulfilled the important functions of the introduction, body, and conclusion of an informative presentation.

Blackfishing on Social Media

Search for "Emma Hallberg" on Instagram and you'll find a user who appears to be a Black Swedish model. However, she's not actually Black. According to BBC News of December 5, 2018, Emma is one of many white women accused of blackfishing—that is, of pretending to be Black or mixed-race on social media platforms. However, unlike Rachel Dolezal, a white woman and former NAACP president who explicitly identifies as Black, these women are not claiming to be Black. They're adopting the physical appearance and style of Black women while maintaining their identities as white women. In other words, you can think of them as playing Black. I spend a lot of time

Attention-getting device

Personal experience to establish credibility

CONTINUED

on social media, so when I found an article about cultural appropriation (a dominant group adopting characteristics of a minority group) on my favorite sites, I knew I needed to learn more. Cultural identities are incredibly personal, so blackfishing is a sensitive subject in need of further exploration. As you may witness celebrities and social media influencers blackfishing, my goal is that you will understand what blackfishing is, how it compares to blackface, and the importance of the consequent implications.

To understand why this trend is culturally contested, we must recognize what blackfishing is. The previously cited BBC News defines blackfishing as "a term used for someone accused of pretending to be Black or mixed-race on social media." The women currently being accused—Emma Hallberg, Aga "Alicja" Brzostowska, and Jaiden Gumbayan—claim they aren't trying to be a different race but, rather, appreciate the culture and its style. However, Black social media influencers who strive to embrace their heritage argue that white women copy their style—and profit from it—without knowing the criticisms Black women have experienced for their natural bodies. As one Black woman explained, when white women blackfish, Black social media influencers are "pushed to the side." For centuries, women of color have been criticized for their hair, their complexion, their bodies, their clothes, and their dialects. A writer for *Glamour* magazine of November 14, 2018, stated, "White women work so hard to achieve the same looks we were born with—and they're celebrated for them while we're still shunned." One of the criticized women, Jaiden, admits that there's a "fine line between appreciation and appropriation."

If we review the history of blackface minstrelsy, we can see why blackfishing is seen as the appropriation of African American culture. In his book *The Complexity and Progression of Black Representation in Film and Television*, David L. Moody explains that, as early as the 1820s, white men would cover their faces in charcoal paste and imitate the dances of Black culture, creating a parody of the Black experience for entertainment purposes and belittling the historical hardships faced by Black people. In essence, white people would play Black caricatures for fun. With this description in mind, it's not surprising that social media users are drawing parallels between blackface minstrelsy and

Thesis of speech

Relates the topic to the audience and previews the main points

Acknowledges both sides of the controversy for a more balanced speech

Transition between subpoints

Transition between subpoints

blackfishing, arguing that white people are applying dark makeup for their own benefit—to gain greater numbers of followers and heightened notoriety on social media.

The trend of blackfishing has several serious implications. First, blackfishing functions as a case study for broader conversations about race and society. For instance, it might be perceived as a form of color-blindness, the perspective that race does not exist. The *Huffington Post* of January 23, 2014, noted that one social media user claimed that race doesn't matter and that we can transcend our races. Nevertheless, conversations about a post-racial society have the potential to overlook inequalities that minorities have historically experienced. Therefore, informative conversations like this about the historical background of race performances can help us reflect on the significance of race and the need for equality. Second, influencers who appropriate Black culture may not know about the history of blackface. Thus, they may not realize the similarities between their acts and past events. Those criticized for blackfishing haven't endured the same struggles the Black community has faced, so sharing information about the history of blackface can help all of us reflect on the messages we could be sending by appropriating Black culture. Third, as social influencers seek product endorsements, blackfishing users could literally be taking money away from actual Black influencers who would otherwise obtain the endorsement deal. Finally, when popular social media influencers blackfish, they send the message to their followers that this kind of cultural appropriation is socially acceptable. However, both influencers and the platform have the capability of sharing information about the history that makes blackfishing problematic. Informing other social media users why blackfishing isn't just appreciation illustrates how social media allows for educational expression.

> Signposts (numbering) organize points

Today, we have examined what blackfishing is, how it compares to blackface minstrelsy, and the implications that arise. Blackfishing appeared to start out of admiration and a lack of knowledge about historical performances of race. While I'm not advocating that any of us take action on this issue, I hope you now have a better understanding of the act of blackfishing and why it is controversial. In the end, we need to better understand this issue to guide our future behavior.

> Rephrasing and restatement of thesis

> Reiteration of informative goals of the presentation

> Closing

CONTINUED

References

Cole, O. A. (2014, January 23). On the oft-repeated lie that racism on social media isn't "real" racism. *Huffington Post.* https://www.huffingtonpost.com/entry/on-the-oftrepeated-lie-th_b_4575754

Moody, D. L. (2016). *The complexity and progression of Black representation in film and television.* Lexington Books.

Payne, T. (2018, November 14). White influencers appearing Black is the Instagram trend no one asked for. *Glamour.* https://www.glamour.com/story/white-influencers-appearing-black-instagram

Virk, K., & McGregor, N. (2018, December 5). Blackfishing: The women accused of pretending to be Black. *BBC News.* https://www.bbc.com/news/newsbeat-46427180

be ready... for what's next

Understanding Learning Styles

Informative presentations take many forms. In many organizational settings, leaders and managers must give informative presentations to help employees better understand new products, initiatives, and ways of doing things. In these types of speaking situations, you must think more like a teacher and recognize that your audience members will have different preferences for learning. For example, consider these typical learning-style preferences:

- **Visual learners** prefer to learn through pictures, diagrams, and other visual resources that emphasize spatial relationships.
- **Aural learners** prefer to hear information.
- **Verbal learners** prefer to use speech and writing to process information.
- **Kinesthetic learners** prefer to use their body and touch.
- **Logical learners** prefer logic and reasoning.
- **Social learners** prefer to learn in groups through dialogue.
- **Solitary learners** prefer working in isolation through personal reflection.

When preparing your informative messages, an advanced approach is to plan activities and opportunities that emphasize several of these learning preferences. Of course, presentations that teach across these various learning preferences require additional planning and take more time for the actual presentation to be completed. However, the payoff is that audience members may leave with a much stronger understanding of the information you want them to learn.

Chapter Review & Study Guide

Summary

In this chapter, you learned the following:

1. Before you offer an informative presentation, you need to know
   - the goals of informative presentations.
   - the kinds of topics that are most appropriate.
   - the kinds of immediate behavioral purposes that are appropriate for informative presentations and how to determine if you have fulfilled them.

2. The strategies for informing others include
   - generating interest in the audience for the information.
   - achieving information relevance by relating information to the audience.
   - using extrinsic motivation, reasons beyond the presentation itself for understanding the presentation's content.

3. Shaping the informative content requires
   - limiting the number of main points.
   - limiting the number of generalizations.

   - selecting language the audience can understand.
   - using specifics to illustrate an abstract idea.
   - including humor when appropriate.
   - revealing how the information meets audience needs.
   - avoiding information overload.
   - organizing content for greater understanding.

4. The skills for informative presentations include
   - defining meanings for an audience.
   - describing by using specific, concrete language.
   - explaining by clarifying and simplifying complex ideas.
   - narrating by using stories to illustrate your ideas.
   - demonstrating by showing a process or procedure to your audience.

Key Terms

Antonym
Comparison
Contrast
Demonstrating
Explanation
Extrinsic motivation

Imagery
Immediate behavioral purposes
Information overload
Information relevance
Informative content
Metaphor

Narrating
Operational definition
Rhetorical questions
Synonym

Study Questions

1. The goal of informative presentations is to
   a. induce change in the audience.
   b. discourage the audience from taking action.
   c. increase an audience's knowledge or understanding of a topic.
   d. identify a problem and determine a solution.

2. How do you make an informational topic interesting to the audience?
   a. Relate your own experiences with the subject.
   b. Avoid telling stories of your own experiences with the subject.
   c. Maintain the gaps in your listeners' knowledge of your subject.
   d. Arousing interest is not important.

3. Which is *not* an appropriate topic for an informative presentation?
   a. CPR techniques
   b. animals and their positive effects on the elderly
   c. wedding traditions
   d. encouraging people to donate blood

4. If audiences are able to describe information or define words related to your topic during and after a presentation, you have successfully accomplished your
   a. demonstration.
   b. immediate behavioral purposes.
   c. imagery.
   d. information overload.

5. The first step in planning your presentation should be
   a. asking a few people questions after the presentation is complete.
   b. teaching or informing your audience.
   c. determining what objectives you want your audience to meet.
   d. surveying the audience.

6. Asking rhetorical questions and arousing curiosity are two ways a speaker can create
   a. immediate behavioral purposes.
   b. topics for informative speeches.
   c. persuasive messages.
   d. interest in the topic.

7. When you are presenting information to an audience, your topic's importance, novelty, and usefulness constitute a key factor known as
   a. information relevance.
   b. information interest.
   c. informative content.
   d. information overload.

8. Which of the following is *not* a guideline to follow when choosing the content of your presentation?
   a. Use relatively simple words because they are easier to understand.
   b. Tell the audience early in your presentation how the topic is related to them so that they will choose to listen.
   c. Develop as many main ideas and use as many details as possible to make the presentation interesting.
   d. Ask for overt responses from audience members to increase comprehension.

9. When organizing the content of your presentation, you should
   a. keep the topic a mystery until the body of the speech.
   b. use transitions to increase understanding.
   c. let the audience decide which points are the most important.
   d. avoid repeating important points so that the audience isn't bored.

10. _____ simplify or clarify ideas while stimulating audience attention, and _____ shows the audience what you are explaining.
    a. Explanations; demonstrating
    b. Definitions; narrating
    c. Descriptions; demonstrating
    d. Narrations; defining

Answers:
1. (c); 2. (a); 3. (d); 4. (b); 5. (c); 6. (d); 7. (a); 8. (c); 9. (b); 10. (a)

Critical Thinking

1. Assume that you are speaking to a group of potential students who are undecided on their major. Based on your knowledge of your major, how could you create information interest to entice the potential students to desire additional information about it?

2. Using your informative speech topic, identify potential approaches to adapt your speech to each of the various learning-style preferences discussed in this chapter. Based on your class, which of these strategies should you consider including in your presentation? Are there factors related to your speaking assignment or classroom that make some of these strategies more feasible than others?

Sizing Things Up Scoring and Interpretation

Using Language Effectively

Informative speeches require effective language use to help audience members learn new information. The scale created for this chapter emphasizes the importance of language during informative speaking.

The 12-item scale allows you to assess how well you implement the following strategies to improve your language use:

- *Perception checking:* items 1 and 9
- *Paraphrasing:* items 2 and 12
- *Using operational definitions:* items 3 and 8

- *Using definitions:* items 4 and 7
- *Dating:* items 5 and 10
- *Indexing:* items 6 and 11

The second item in each category (items 9, 12, 8, 7, 10, and 11) should be reverse-coded before calculating scores (a score of 1 is now a 4, a 2 is now a 3, and vice versa). Using scores for each language strategy, you can self-assess areas in which your language use could be improved. Scores of 5 or higher suggest areas in which you have strength, whereas scores lower than 5 suggest potential areas for improvement.

References

1. Petrie, C. R., Jr., & Carrel, S. D. (1976). The relationship of motivation, listening, capability, initial information, and verbal organizational ability to lecture comprehension and retention. *Speech Monographs, 43,* 187–194.

2. Tourtelot, N. (2008, December). Lunatic. *Esquire, 150*(6): 167. https://classic.esquire.com/article/2008/12/1/lunatic

3. Tourtelot, N. (2008, December). Lunatic. *Esquire, 150*(6): 167. https://classic.esquire.com/article/2008/12/1/lunatic

EPG_EuroPhotoGraphics/Shutterstock

persuasive presentations

When you have read and thought about this chapter, you will be able to

1. define a persuasive presentation.

2. identify your immediate purpose and long-range goal.

3. recognize if your reason for persuading is adoption or discontinuance.

4. recall the advantages of the classroom setting.

5. compare and contrast proposition of fact, policy, and value.

6. compare and contrast evidence and proof.

7. recall ways to test evidence.

8. explain the three forms of proof.

9. use the Monroe Motivated Sequence to organize your persuasive message.

10. apply ethical considerations to your presentation.

11. identify ways to resist persuasive efforts by others.

Persuasive speaking happens all the time whether you realize it or not. An attempt to get a friend to go to a concert with you, advocating to a teacher about aspects of your project or a grade you earned, introducing a new product, convincing a group to use a new method of fundraising, and attempting to change attitudes about people experiencing homelessness are all variations on making persuasive presentations.

If you won an award, would you use your acceptance speech as an opportunity to advocate for an issue you believe in? Increasingly, social media influencers and celebrities are using their platforms to highlight causes that are important to them. For example, during her acceptance speech for the Golden Globe Award for Best Supporting Actress, Regina King pledged that 50% of her hires would be women for all the projects she produces in the next two years. She went further in her speech and issued a call to action to everyone in a position of power to commit to hiring and supporting women in an effort to reduce the gender gap in their respective industries.[1]

Have you ever felt called to action for a cause or issue that you believed in? How many times have you been the persuasive speaker calling others to action? Have you ever thought about all the different ways persuasion affects you in your everyday life?

The vast majority of jobs require that you persuade other people. An important challenge is to learn how to use this potent force in ways that are not harmful to others. That is why this chapter is dedicated to helping you learn just what persuasion is and how it functions. You will learn the purposes and goals of persuasion, as well as strategies that persuaders use to induce change in other people. Because some people try to change other people in unfair and deceptive ways, the chapter provides ethical guidelines for persuasion. At the end of the chapter, you will understand what persuasion is, how it works, ethical strategies, and ways to resist persuasion.

Regina King at the Golden Globe Awards.

John Shearer/Getty Images

Preparing for a Persuasive Presentation

Most people have an abstract or inaccurate understanding of how persuasion works. For instance, some people think it is the skillful manipulation of words or actions to get people to do something they would not otherwise do. Forcing people to unwillingly think or behave as you wish is not persuasion but **coercion.** Likewise, tricking people or using fraudulent means to gain compliance is not persuasion but **manipulation.** Both coercion and manipulation override a person's ability to make choices based on accurate and trustworthy information and ideas. Thus, neither resembles persuasion. Given the rise in disinformation, it is increasingly important to ground your persuasive arguments in facts and evidence and ethically use emotional appeals to persuade your audience.

You will likely be expected to deliver at least one persuasive presentation in your class and perhaps many in your lifetime. A **persuasive presentation** is a message strategically

coercion
The act of forcing people to think or behave as you wish; not a form of persuasion.

manipulation
The act of tricking people or using fraudulent means to gain compliance not a form of persuasion.

persuasive presentation
A message designed to strategically induce change in an audience.

designed to induce change in the audience in some way consistent with your purpose. Here are some examples of persuasive topics:

New Rules Needed for Drug Testing Among Olympic Athletes

Technology in the Classroom

Prohibiting Fracking

Later Start Times for High School

Revising Immigration Laws in the United States

To begin preparing for your persuasive speech, you must first select a topic. You can generate possible topics by using brainstorming or concept mapping, as described in Chapter 10. Then make sure your topic relates to you (source credibility) and your audience (audience analysis) and is a topic of importance. Finally, you will have to establish your immediate purpose and your long-range goal.

IDENTIFYING YOUR IMMEDIATE PURPOSE

In Chapter 10 you learned you should have an immediate purpose of what you hope to achieve with your speech. Given that a single presentation to a captive audience is unlikely to produce dramatic results, you need to be realistic about anticipated results. You might state, "After listening to my presentation, the audience should be able to write down the social media handles of legislators so that they can communicate with them about lowering our tuition."

IDENTIFYING YOUR LONG-RANGE GOAL

You should also have a long-range goal for your persuasive presentation. You know, for instance, that your single persuasive effort to alert your listeners to steroids and designer drugs used by athletes is not going to produce a lot of action. But you also know that the more your audience hears about this issue from many sources, the more likely something will be done about it. You may be just one drop in a pond, but if enough raindrops fall, the pond itself will change. Your long-range goal could be stated like this: "My long-range goal is to encourage my listeners to learn more about this issue over time so that eventually new methods of support will be in place to help students' mental health at school."

Persuading Effectively

Many factors, on both your part and the part of the audience, can determine whether you are able to effectively persuade your audience. The way you reveal the purpose of your speech, what behaviors you want your audience to adopt or discontinue, the type and source of information you use to support your claims, and where your speech takes place all factor in to how successful you can be as a speaker.

REVEALING THE PURPOSE OF THE PRESENTATION

In an informative presentation you state clearly at the outset what you want to accomplish and tell the audience what you want them to learn. In a persuasive presentation, however, your listeners may reject your intention to change their thinking or behavior unless you prepare the way, so you need to analyze the audience to determine when and how you should reveal your immediate purpose.

If you are not asking for much of a change, you may reveal your purpose in the introduction of the speech. However, if it will require some preparation before your audience is willing to accept your immediate purpose, then you should provide your reasons first and reveal your action step toward the end of the presentation. If you ask your listeners for too much change, you are likely to get a **boomerang effect**—that is, the audience will like you and your message less after the presentation than they did before. To avoid this effect, analyze your audience and decide when you should reveal your purpose. See Chapter 10 for more on how to analyze an audience, including using demographic analysis and surveys.

boomerang effect
The audience likes you and your message less after your presentation than they did before.

IDENTIFYING YOUR REASON FOR PERSUADING

Most persuasive presentations in the classroom have one of two immediate purposes: persuading the audience to do something new or persuading the audience to stop doing something they presently do. These two immediate goals are called adoption and discontinuance.

Adoption means listeners start a new behavior as a result of the persuasive presentation. For example, they start exercising or start eating healthy foods. **Discontinuance** is a persuasive purpose rooted in convincing listeners to stop some current behavior, with the hope that doing so improves their lives or the global community. For example, you could advocate for purchasing less fast fashion clothing made from synthetic materials designed to wear out easily but not decay in landfills. Discontinuance and adoption are challenging persuasive purposes well worth your efforts in a presentation. They can change your listeners' lives in very positive ways.

adoption
Listeners start a new behavior as a result of the persuasive presentation.

discontinuance
A persuasive purpose rooted in convincing listeners to stop some current behavior.

captive audience
A group consisting of people who did not gather to hear about your particular topic.

voluntary audience
A group that came to hear you, in particular, talk about your topic.

ADVANTAGES OF THE CLASSROOM SETTING

After reading that years of public service campaigns have failed to change U.S. consumers' eating, exercise, and smoking habits, you might wonder why anyone should expect you to be successful in a classroom presentation. The key factor is that face-to-face persuasive efforts are more effective than public service campaigns for at least two reasons.

One reason is that face-to-face communication allows you to reach people on a personal level, hear their stories, and share your story related to the topic at hand. A second reason a face-to-face presentation is more effective is that the classroom has a **captive audience** consisting of people who did not, in most cases, gather to hear about your particular topic. In other words, your classmates are not a **voluntary audience** that came to hear you, in particular, talk about your topic. Voluntary audiences listen to a speaker because they already care about the topic and often are in agreement with the speaker. In the classroom, you are going to persuade some people in your audience who never would have gone to a speech about that topic.

communicating
with agility

Emotion and Persuasion

When conversing with others with whom you disagree, you may feel uncomfortable, react hostilely, or avoid the conversation all together. However, Harvard negotiator Dan Shapiro argues that if we focus more on the process of *how* we argue than *what* we argue, we can communicate more effectively. He notes three steps to take in emotionally charged conflicts:

1. **Know your core beliefs and values**. Opposing views can trigger emotional reactions when they threaten our identity. Knowing who you are and what you stand for can help you listen with an open mind.

2. **Listen to the other person**. Understand their views and why they hold those views. Even if you don't agree, let the other person know you hear them and appreciate their perspective.

3. **Find common ground with the other person**. Rather than being in opposition to one another, reframe the conversation so you and the other person are on the same side of an issue, trying to find a solution.

Source: Wetzel, J. (2022, October 26). Harvard negotiator teachers you how to argue in a way that leads to better understanding. *Upworthy*. www.upworthy.com/harvard-negotiator-teaches-you-how-to-argue

• Understanding your audience is a key aspect of persuasive speaking.

Hero Images Inc./Alamy Stock Photo

micro-persuasion
An attempt to change others with as few words or symbols as possible as in a tweet.

communicating
creatively

Narrative Sense-Making, Persuasion, and Well-Being

We often think of storytelling as being used in a speech to capture an audience's attention or illustrate an example. However, storytelling also helps with persuasion because it invites us to make sense of the speaker's ideas.

In her theory of communicated narrative sense-making (CNSM), Dr. Jody Koenig Kellas argues that storytelling has the capacity to help people connect, construct identities, teach lessons, and cope with life's complexities. Through storytelling, people can make sense of difficult experiences, such as health diagnoses. Through interactional storytelling (jointly telling stories with others), we can engage in communicated perspective-taking (CPT), which allows us to see experiences from others' perspectives while attending to and confirming their point of view.

The organization Braver Angels uses interactional storytelling for persuasion by bringing people from different political and social backgrounds together online to reduce divisions in America. Their workshop takes two participants from different backgrounds through a series of guided questions that allow them to share their stories with each other. Participants then engage in CPT by sharing what they learned about the other person's views and identifying areas of commonality. Both parties then identify actions they can take in their everyday lives to bridge differences with others. Often, the participants continue to talk to each other after the workshop. In this way, persuasion can occur through storytelling and perspective-taking rather than formal debate, enabling deeper interpersonal connection and understanding.

Sources: Braver Angels. (2002). *1:1 Conversations across difference*. https://braverangels. org/online/1-1-conversations/; Kellas, J. K. (2021). Communicated narrative sense-making theory: Bridging storytelling, relationships, and well-being. In D. Braithwaite & P. Schrodt (Eds.), *Engaging theories in interpersonal communication: Multiple perspectives* (pp. 117–129). Routledge.

Methods of Persuasion

On a daily basis you use and encounter small forms of persuasion in the form of **micro-persuasion**, or the attempt to change others with as few words or symbols as possible (as in a social media post), but at other times you will have to try to sway a person or an entire audience with a well-developed argument. Either way, to persuade others in school, at home, or at work, you must employ strategies chosen to work best on your listeners. The strategies described in this section will work only if you have correctly determined that your audience will respond positively to them. Here again, audience analysis is the key to effectiveness because only the evidence that an audience accepts becomes proof. Understanding how to test evidence before you present it can help you to present only information that is likely to persuade your audience.

USING ARGUMENT TO PERSUADE: FACT, POLICY, AND VALUE

Listeners who know or like logic respond positively to arguments with evidence that constitutes proof. Lawyers and debaters are well versed in logical argument, and many educated people respond positively to this approach. An **argument** consists of a proposition that asserts some course of action. Ordinarily, the proposition concerns a question of fact, policy, or value. An example of a **proposition of fact**—an assertion that can be proved or disproved to be consistent with reality—is the statement "College students average $30,000 in student loan debt."[2] To demonstrate the accuracy of this fact, you could cite Emma Kerr and Sarah Wood's *US News and World Report* article from September 13, 2022, "See How Average Student Loan Debt Has Changed."

An example of a **proposition of policy**—a proposal to create or retain a rule—is the statement "Student tuition and fees should cover access to group fitness centers at the university gym." In this speech you would show how student fees do not currently pay for group fitness classes and then advocate for a change in the policy perhaps by showing how these classes would increase student health and well-being and campus involvement.

An example of a **proposition of value**—a statement of what we should embrace as important to our culture—is the statement "We must make children's nutrition and healthy eating habits a priority in all schools." In this speech you would provide evidence that school lunch options need improvement and that children need more time to eat lunch to build mindful habits around food. You could also illustrate how these actions can reduce obesity and improve overall health in children, all of which should be a central focus in today's society.

THE DIFFERENCE BETWEEN EVIDENCE AND PROOF

Evidence is the facts that support a claim. As anyone who watches any of the *CSI* spin-offs knows, evidence is what forensic scientists produce to convict felons. They bring out DNA tests, fingerprints, weapons, fiber samples, and bloodstains as evidence that a person committed a specific crime. In argumentation you are more likely to use other kinds of evidence, such as examples, surveys, testimonials, and numbers and statistics (see Chapter 11). The question? Is your evidence proof to your listeners?

Proof is evidence that the receiver believes. In other words, you can listen to evidence without believing it, and if you do not believe it, you are not going to accept the presenter's argument. Suppose a presenter is arguing that you should accept the policy proposition that "the United States should abolish the death penalty." The evidence is that the Bible says, "Thou shalt not kill,"[3] an idea that is elevated in importance because it is a commandment Moses brought down from the mountaintop on a tablet of stone. A person who believes that the Bible is without error and that we should obey every word will accept the commandment as proof. A person who does not accept the

---

argument
A proposition that asserts some course of action.

proposition of fact
An assertion that can be proved or disproved as consistent with reality.

proposition of policy
A proposal of a new rule.

proposition of value
A statement of what we should embrace as important to our culture.

evidence
The facts that support a claim.

proof
Evidence that the receiver believes.

• Collecting evidence: a scene from the television show *CSI*.

Robert Voets/CBS Photo Archive/Getty Images

Bible as an authority or who sees contradictions in it like the various offenses for which individuals can be stoned to death might not accept the commandment as proof. In other words, many things can constitute evidence, but only those items the audience accepts constitute proof.

HOW TO TEST EVIDENCE

tests of evidence
Questions that can be used to assess the validity of evidence.

Your evidence must meet the **tests of evidence**—questions you can use to assess the validity of the evidence in your presentations or in those of others.

1. *Is the evidence consistent with other known facts?* For instance, is the statement accurate that big business and the extremely rich bolster economic inequality by not paying taxes and using their power to influence markets and policy?[4] Many sources specify how wealth in the United States is increasingly concentrated in the hands of a few, while the bulk of the population has gained little and lost much in the past decade. Just Google "wealth top 1%" for a number of links about wealth inequity. This statement is consistent with known facts about income and wealth.

2. *Would another observer draw the same conclusions?* Perhaps we could find two witnesses who agree they saw someone trip and fall, but getting people to interpret facts the same way is a tricky business. Nearly all experts agree that climate change is occurring, but broad disagreements occur about its extent and cause. When other observers agree with your inferences and you can cite them, your persuasive argument is strengthened.

3. *Does the evidence come from unbiased sources?* Professors are more often perceived as unbiased than are politicians and business leaders. But everyone has biases, so you should seek sources of information that are as free of conflicts of interest as possible. Additionally, it is important to determine if the source is using evidence and data to make its argument or if it is relying on emotional appeals in a way that attempts to discredit the facts.

4. *Is the source of the information qualified by education and/or experience to make a statement about the issue?* If you wanted to use education as a source of information about immigration issues and the economy, you could interview your economics professors and cite education and degrees earned for their qualifications. However, if you wanted to share information about how undocumented people feel, the story of José Antonio Vargas, an undocumented Filipino immigrant and Pulitzer Prize-winning journalist, could be more useful to provide a narrative account of someone's experience.[5] Remember that sources can be qualified by education and/or by experience.

5. *If the evidence is based on personal experience, how typical is that experience?* Personal experience that is typical, generalizable, realistic, and relevant can be good evidence. If many people have been treated badly by the nearby bookstore, then your own bad experience there is usable evidence about its quality. If you are one of the very few people who have had a bad experience, then your story is not usable evidence.

6. *If statistics are used as evidence, are they current, applicable, and interpreted so that the audience can understand them?* Let's say you are going to explain tuition increases at your school over the past five years. Admissions, the registrar, and the business office all are reliable sources. You can help your audience understand the percentages of change, average increases, and amounts of increase by comparing your school's figures with those of other schools like yours. Use

statistics carefully. To demonstrate how misleading they can be, a "whopping" 8% tuition increase is only $200 on a tuition bill of $2,500.

7. *If studies and surveys are used, are they authoritative, valid, reliable, objective, and generalizable?* Many studies, surveys, and even online evaluations of products are sponsored by the very companies that benefit from the research. The easiest way to check objectivity is to see who authorized the study. If it was performed by an independent source, such as a university, an independent laboratory, or a professional survey company, such as JD Power or Gallup, it is more likely to be valid and trustworthy.

8. *Are the speaker's inferences appropriate to the data presented?* One instance or even a few does not allow for a generalization. For example, if many employees have been falsely accused of misusing paid time off, then you could support a generalization for that claim.

9. *Is important counterevidence overlooked?* Often, in our haste to make a positive case, we ignore or omit counterevidence. For example, a speech that shares only the negative aspects of allowing students to use mobile devices in the classroom would be overlooking the many benefits. Stating that mobile devices in the classroom reduce student learning would fail to highlight counterevidence that shows how the use of mobile technology can enhance student learning, engagement, and interest. Recognize that most complex issues include some aspects that are worthy of highlighting.

engaging diversity

Norms for Persuasion

How we prepare and react to persuasive messages can vary from one culture to the next. For example, if you are from a high-context culture, you may prefer to be less direct when communicating. If you are from a highly individualistic culture, you may prefer to advance your own opinion without taking other viewpoints into consideration. When preparing your persuasive speech, you will likely need to blend some of the persuasive norms of your culture with the persuasive norms of U.S. culture.

This chapter explains many of those Western norms. If you opt to use norms from your culture, you may need to provide some explanation for what you are doing. Chinese traditions value action over words to persuade. Appeals that include explanations of how you as the speaker did what you are asking others to do is considered essential—it is more effective and builds trust in the speaker.[6] For example, speakers advocating to increase volunteerism at older adult centers would need to share their volunteer work with older adults as a critical part of their persuasive appeals. In Western cultures, doing the work, such as volunteering, prior to attempting to persuade can enhance credibility, but it is not typically seen as an expectation for persuasion. Although you should not abandon the norms for persuasion you are familiar with, your persuasive messages may need additional explanation to be adapted to the expectations of your audience.

Evidence that meets these nine tests has met the requirements of credible, ethical, and trustworthy evidence. It may seem like it will take a substantial amount of time to analyze each piece of evidence you find, but it is worth the effort. Doing so is especially important in increasingly polarizing political climates where challenges to claims and evidence are increasing from all sides and on all mediated platforms. In your arguments, you will be called on to verify your evidence.

Forms of Proof

To persuade an audience you need to know some methods of doing so. In this section you will learn about some methods of persuasion that began in ancient Greece and have been refined for centuries. Aristotle in his *Rhetoric* wrote about three modes of proof: *ethos, pathos,* and *logos*. *Ethos* refers to the reputation, authority, and integrity of the speaker; *pathos* refers to the use of emotional means of persuasion; and *logos* refers to persuasion by using logical argument. In addition to credibility, emotion, and logic, people

ethos
Called "source credibility" today, the reputation, authority, and integrity of the speaker.

pathos
The use of emotional "proofs" in an argument.

logos
The use of logical reasoning in an argument.

are highly influenced by visuals, which makes persuasion through visualization an effective method you can utilize when attempting to persuade an audience.

LOGOS, OR LOGICAL PROOF

First we take a close look at logical proof, including how to form, analyze, and rebut inductive and deductive arguments.

The Structure of Argument

inductive argument
A logical structure that provides enough specific instances for the listener to make an inferential leap to a generalization that summarizes the individual instances.

Inductive argument provides enough specific instances for the listener to make an inferential leap to a generalization that summarizes the individual instances. For example, you might try to demonstrate that "low taxes are bad for our economy." Your specific instances might include the following:

Underfunded schools

Underfunded federal programs

Unrepaired and poorly maintained roads and highways

Underfunded social programs for low-income people

Increased tuition due to decreased government support

This series of individual instances can lead to an "inferential leap" to a generalization that low taxes are bad for our economy.

deductive argument
A logical structure that uses a general proposition applied to a specific instance to draw a conclusion.

syllogism
A logical structure that contains a major premise (a generalization) applied to a particular instance (a minor premise) that leads to a conclusion.

Another logical structure is **deductive argument**, which uses a general proposition applied to a specific instance to draw a conclusion. For example, from the major premise (generalization) "All drunk driving is dangerous," you can move to the minor premise "Joann drives after drinking" to conclude that "Joann is dangerous." This logical structure is called a **syllogism**; it contains a major premise (a generalization) applied to a particular instance (a minor premise) that leads to a conclusion.

Ways to Rebut Arguments

rebuttal
Arguing against someone else's position on an issue.

In class, at home, and in the workplace, others may rebut your arguments. A **rebuttal** is an argument against someone else's position on an issue. If someone in your class gives a presentation with which you profoundly disagree, you may deliver a passionate persuasive presentation opposing that person's position on the issue. There are several ways to rebut arguments.

The weak points in any inductive argument are the clarity of the proposition, the quality of the individual instances, and the place where the inferential leap occurs. In the argument about local taxes, you could argue that it needs to state more clearly to what taxes the proposition refers. Does it refer to all taxes? To city or municipal taxes? To property taxes only? The proposition is unclear. On the quality of the individual instances, does the presenter have any evidence that citizens' services are negatively affected because taxes decrease? Finally, how many instances must you have before you make the inferential leap? For example, how many individual instances are needed to persuade people that cyber crime is on the rise? With inductive arguments, speakers make inferential leaps from one or more instances. To rebut an inductive argument you can always challenge the quality of those instances or make the point that not enough instances were provided to establish support for the proposition.

Likewise, you can always rebut deductive arguments by questioning the major premise, the application of the minor premise, and the meaning of the conclusion. Is all texting while driving dangerous? Perhaps the answer depends on how the states view texting while driving. Some states have a complete ban on texting while driving, others ban teenage and new drivers from texting, and several states have no formal laws governing texting and driving. Although there is no agreement on the type of laws that should govern texting and driving, violations of the law typically include monetary sanctions, criminal misdemeanor charges, or jail time. In this case, depending on the law, it might be difficult to determine how distracted someone was while texting depending on the state where the violation occurred.

The point is that you can critically analyze both inductive and deductive arguments.

ETHOS, OR SOURCE CREDIBILITY

The fact is that you can persuade some listeners because you have earned the right to speak. Popular politicians, entertainers, and community leaders have such credibility. In your own life you have been able to either use your own competence, trustworthiness, and dynamism or share common ground with the audience to gain compliance. Likewise, you have seen others use these techniques as they attempt to persuade you. For example, you are more likely to listen to advice about what classes to take from third-year students in your major over the first-year students. However, even in the classroom some presenters have more source credibility than others. The lesson here is that who and what you are can help you persuade others, but this is not enough to be an ethical speaker. See Chapter 11 for more on source credibility.

PATHOS, OR EMOTIONAL PROOF

You may not be dazzled by a string of statistics that show how many people slide into bankruptcy each year, but you might get tears in your eyes about a local family—very much like yours—that was so consumed by credit card debt that they had to declare publicly that they would never be able to pay their debts.

Although logical and emotional appeals are often seen as diametrically opposed concepts, most of our behavior and beliefs are based on a mixture of emotional and rational factors. A speaker may persuade an audience to accept immediate behavioral purposes for emotional, rather than logical, reasons. A story about one person's bad experience with a local bike shop may inspire many audience members to take their business to another store. The experience may have been a one-in-a-thousand situation or as much the customer's fault as the manager's. Such is the power of our emotions that they can persuade us to defy the law, fight another nation, or ignore the evidence.

The **fear appeal** is one of the most common appeals to emotion. Political ads remind us of impending economic collapse, predict that an opponent will tax us into oblivion, and suggest that only one political party can increase job prospects. Financial gurus use fear to guide investments (bonds are losers, stocks are winners, or vice versa), businesses use fear to invite sales (prices go up this Wednesday), and auto dealers use fear to close a sale (this one is the last of this model at this price). Fear appeals get us to brush our teeth, use deodorant, engage in safer-sex practices, buy certain clothing, and enact the latest approach to a whole-food lifestyle.

fear appeal
Eliciting fear to change behavior.

Clearly, fear appeals work in advertising and in everyday life. As a speaker you can use fear appeals in an ethical manner if you do not exaggerate the threat and if you offer means of avoiding the fear. In other words, a presenter who arouses fear in an audience has an ethical obligation to provide reassurance as well. This sentence illustrates fear appeals and reassurances in a single thesis statement: "Not brushing your teeth can lead to gum disease and tooth loss, so listen to my tips on dental hygiene." A presentation that combines fear with reassurance results in greater shifts of opinion, and the audience holds the presenter in higher regard.[7]

Other examples of emotional appeals are testimonials at funerals about the virtues of the deceased, appeals to loyalty and dedication at retirement ceremonies, appeals to patriotism in times of crisis, and appeals to justice in times of legal strife. Narratives are also

building behaviors

Using Silence

When you think about giving a presentation, the last thing you probably want to think about are moments of silence. To an emerging speaker, the idea of engaging silence as an actual planned part of your delivery might seem bizarre. However, when used well, silence can create dramatic tension, build anticipation, and give your audience time to reflect on your message. Here are a few ways that using silence can help you with your next presentation:

- Silence gives you time to think about what you will say next.

- Silence enhances the value of what you are saying because it gives your audience a chance to process key information.

- Silence reduces the use of filler words such as "like," "you know," and "um" or repeating words such as "actually."

Using silence in these ways also shows that you are in command of the presentation and are confident in your ability to be present in the moment.

Source: Newman, R. (2019, April). This is why silence is an important part of your presentation. *Fast Company*. www.fastcompany.com/90328068/the-importance-of-silence-in-presentation

powerful strategies for introducing emotion because stories often detail the experiences of others and create identification between the audience and those mentioned in the stories.

PERSUASION THROUGH VISUALIZATION

Companies spent $233,000 *per second* for an ad in the 2022 Super Bowl between the Los Angeles Rams and the Cincinnati Bengals. It can be argued companies would not spend that much money if advertising did not work.[8] However, those 30-second spots do not make an argument with evidence, tell an emotional story, or even dazzle viewers with source credibility. Instead, they use **persuasive imagery** to persuade by means of quick, amusing scenes of youthful drinkers having fun, beautiful vehicles speeding down mountain roads without guardrails, and piles of junk food being washed down with gallons of soft drinks. Words are not important here; the emphasis is on beguiling the eye.

You can use imagery in your persuasive presentations with either PowerPoint or more advanced software, such as Prezi, and you can imitate some advertising techniques by studying impressive videos on YouTube. You should check with your teacher about using YouTube video clips in your presentations, because teachers are wary about too much YouTube in a presentation that is supposed to be your work. As long as you do not allow the video to dominate your presentation, you can make it more visual and more exciting for your audience.

persuasive imagery
The advertiser's method of persuading an audience with fast-paced and dazzling visualization of products.

Organizing Your Persuasive Message: The Monroe Motivated Sequence

You already know that you may not want to announce your immediate purpose at the outset of a persuasive message because you may need to build toward acceptance at the end. Here we consider some macro-organizational features: how you build, construct, or design your presentation to achieve your persuasive purpose.

Some organizational patterns are used more often in persuasive presentations: cause/effect, problem/solution, and topical-sequence (see Chapter 12). The topical-sequence pattern is especially useful in arguing the advantages and disadvantages of some course of action.

This next pattern of organization is not another topical sequence. Instead, this pattern is a series of moves designed to persuade. Developed by University of Iowa professor Alan Monroe, the **Monroe Motivated Sequence** has been used successfully for four decades and is popular for having five easy-to-follow steps:

Monroe Motivated Sequence
A problem-solving format that encourages an audience to become concerned about an issue; especially appropriate for a persuasive presentation.

- *Step 1: Attention.* You gain and maintain audience attention, and you determine a way to focus it on the content of your presentation.

- *Step 2: Need.* Once you have the audience's attention, you show audience members how the speech is relevant to them. You arouse a need for the change you **suggest** in your persuasive presentation.

One technique for planning and organizing a persuasive speech is to use Monroe's Motivated Sequence.

Step 1: Gain Attention

Start a speech on distracted driving by showing a picture of a car that was struck from behind due to another driver who was texting while driving.

Step 2: Establish Need

Make distracted driving relevant to your audience by pointing out that they and their friends are at risk from such behaviors.

Step 3: Satisfaction

Point out that awareness and commitment are the two necessary elements to reduce traffic accidents resulting from distracted driving.

Step 4: Visualization

Explain how every person is important in raising awareness and securing commitment not to be distracted while driving. You could have the audience imagine the impact it would have on their community if all audience members put away their phones every time they drove for the next week.

Step 5: Call to Action

Ask each audience member to place a "My Phone's Away—Yours?" window decal on their car to build awareness about not being distracted.

Figure 15.1

Monroe's Motivated Sequence.

Xuanyu Han/Getty Images

- *Step 3: Satisfaction.* Your speech either presents the information the audience needs or suggests a solution to their needs. You satisfy the audience by meeting their needs with your plan.
- *Step 4: Visualization.* You reinforce your idea in the audience's minds by getting the audience to *see* how your information or ideas will help them.
- *Step 5: Action.* Once the audience has visualized your idea, you plead for action. The audience might remember your main points in an informative presentation and state them to others, or the audience may go out and do what you ask in a persuasive presentation.[9]

The Monroe Motivated Sequence is an appropriate organizational pattern for persuasive presentations, especially when the audience is reluctant to change or to accept a proposed action. See an illustration of the sequence in Figure 15.1.

Ethical Considerations

Ethics are a set of principles of right conduct. Many of our standards for ethical behavior are codified into law. We do not slander or libel someone who is an ordinary citizen. We do not start a panic that can endanger the lives of others. And we do not advocate the overthrow of our government.

Many other principles of ethics are not matters of law, but violations of these unwritten rules do have consequences. No law exists against pointing out acne sufferers in the audience during your speech on dermatology or knowingly misleading your audience about the existence of a problem, but audience members may find your methods so distasteful that they reject you and your persuasive message.

Here are some generally accepted ethical standards that govern the preparation and delivery of a persuasive presentation:

- *Accurately cite sources.* When you are preparing and delivering your speech, you should be very careful to gather and state your information accurately. Specifically, you should reveal from whom you received information. Making up quotations, attributing an idea to someone who never made the statement, omitting important qualifiers, quoting out of context, and distorting information are all examples of ethical violations.

- *Respect sources of information.* Show respect for your sources, especially people you interview, by demonstrating their credibility as completely as possible. These people are willing to share information with you, so it behooves you to treat them and their information with respect, in person and in your presentation.

- *Respect your audience.* Persuasion is a process that works most effectively with mutual respect between presenter and receiver. Attempts to trick the audience into believing something, lying, distorting the views of your opposition, and exaggerating claims for your own position are all ethically questionable acts. A presenter should speak truthfully and accurately; the best persuasive presenters can accurately portray the opposing arguments and still win with their own arguments and evidence. Audiences can be hostile toward a person who has tricked them or who has lied, distorted, or exaggerated information simply to meet an immediate behavioral purpose or a long-range goal.

- *Respect your opponents.* Persuasive presentations invite rebuttal. Nearly always, people in or outside your audience think your ideas or positions are wrong. A good rule of thumb is to respect your opponents, not only because they may be right but also because effective persuasive speakers can take the best the opposition has to offer and still convince the audience they should be believed. Do not indulge in name-calling or in bringing up past behaviors that are irrelevant to the issue. You should attack the other person's evidence, sources, or logic—not the person. Few issues about which people persuade are ever settled, and you may find in time that your opponent's position is better in many respects than your own.

You may get the impression from these four ethical guidelines that every persuasive speaker

sizing things up

Need for Cognition

The way we construct and respond to persuasive messages depends, in part, on the way we process information. One of the personality characteristics that govern information processing is our need for cognition, or our tendency to put significant effort into thinking about things such as arguments and ideas. Below are 10 statements that describe how you might like to process information. Read each question carefully and respond using the following scale:

1 = Strongly disagree
2 = Disagree
3 = Neither agree nor disagree
4 = Agree
5 = Strongly agree

1. I prefer complex to simple problems.
2. Thinking is not my idea of fun.
3. I would rather do something that requires little thought than something that is sure to challenge my thinking abilities.
4. I find satisfaction in thinking hard for a long time.
5. I only think as hard as I have to.
6. I try to avoid situations where there is a good chance I will have to think hard about something.
7. I enjoy a task that involves coming up with new solutions to problems.
8. I enjoy thinking abstractly.
9. I prefer a task that is intellectual and difficult to one that does not require much thought.
10. I enjoy solving puzzles.

This exercise has no right or wrong answers; instead, your responses provide insight into your own ways of thinking. A guide for interpreting your responses appears at the end of the chapter.

Source: Perse, E. (1992, Winter). Predicting attention to local television news: Need for cognition and motives for viewing. *Communication Reports, 5,* 40–49. Western States Communication Association.

Below is some final advice on what kinds of arguments are most persuasive and where you should consider placing them for maximum effectiveness:

1. Place your best argument first for a "primacy effect," meaning early items are remembered over middle items.

2. Place your best argument last for a "recency effect," meaning last items are remembered over items in the middle.

3. Middle items in a series are less remembered than those presented first or last, so avoid placing your best argument in the easily overlooked or forgotten middle.

Figure 15.2

Tips for organizing your arguments.

ZUMA Press Inc/Alamy Stock Photo

must be part angel. Not quite. The ethical rules for persuasive speaking allow for critical analysis of arguments and ideas, for profound differences of opinion, for the weighing of evidence and supporting materials, and for the swaying of the audience to your point of view. All these strategies simply work best if you accurately cite your sources and respect them, your audience, and your opponent.

Figure 15.2 gives additional tips for organizing your arguments.

Example Persuasive Presentation

We turn now to an outline for an annotated persuasive presentation that illustrates many of the concepts introduced in the chapter. This outline was written by a student on the legal discrimination of voter fraud laws. She composed this presentation to persuade the audience to change their attitudes, beliefs, and behavior. Read it carefully for its strengths and its weaknesses. What methods does the presenter use to influence listeners? Do the arguments and evidence meet the tests discussed in this chapter? What, if anything, could the presenter have done differently that would have made the message more appealing to you?

Protecting Voting Rights

In 2016, a Wisconsin woman agonized over the 2016 presidential election, not because of who was on the ticket, but because she might be turned away from the polls. As the *New York Times* of November 24, 2017, explains, her only crimes preventing her from voting were her age and the fact that she didn't have a valid photo identification card. At 90 years old, after years of participating devotedly in her civic duty, this American citizen wouldn't be allowed to exercise her right to vote. Thanks to new voter fraud or voter identification legislation, thousands of American citizens have had their right to vote taken away from them. In fact, a 2012 study conducted by the Brennan Center for Justice estimated that at least 21 million people may not

CONTINUED

Narrative attention-getting device

Information attributed to source throughout speech

Use of statistics to establish significance of problem

Thesis

Preview of main points

have the photo ID card they now need in order to vote. By dissecting the issue, we will see how voter fraud laws allow legal discrimination to take place at the polls. Today, we'll address the problems underlying voter fraud laws and discuss solutions to fight for the voices of all Americans. A plastic card should not supersede a constitutional right and a lifetime of service.

This Wisconsin woman was lucky and received the legal help she needed to acquire a photo ID. Others, however, are not nearly as fortunate. Voter fraud laws are problematic because they discriminate against three groups of people: the financially strapped, the elderly, and minorities. First, these laws can prevent those in lower socioeconomic brackets from voting.

Example

Supporters of these laws argue that you only need a driver's license, but as Pamela Moon told NPR on September 7, 2018, she can drive, but since she can't afford a car, she never got a license. Not everyone has a driver's license because not everyone can afford to own, insure, and maintain a vehicle. Although these are the voices legislators need to hear, voter fraud laws literally block them from casting their ballot. Furthermore, as the *Washington Post* of May 23, 2016, reported, elderly Americans struggle to get identification cards because many do not have the birth certificates required by the DMV. The *AARP Bulletin* of August 30, 2012, explains that citizens older than 65 might not have birth certificates because they were born before birth certificates were widespread. Those born at home may not have the documentation needed to renew their license and thus vote.

Internal transition to next subpoint

If discriminating against the financially strapped and elderly isn't enough to illustrate the harm, these laws silence minority voices, too. NPR reported on October 13, 2018, that in North Dakota, Native Americans discovered that since their residences on the reservations did not have a street address, their ID cards could not be used to vote. For minorities, voter fraud laws are also infringing on their 15th Amendment right, which states that voting rights "shall not be denied or abridged by the United States or by any State on account of race, color, or previous condition of servitude." The American Bar Association acknowledged that the required ID cards tend to be the kinds that the middle class and the white population easily access, but that are hard for the elderly and minorities to acquire. As civil rights attorney Deuel Ross told *Wired* of January 4, 2018, "Whether it's intended to harm

600,000 African American and Latino voters or 2 million, our concern is people are passing these laws with the intent to discriminate or the effect of discriminating" (para. 18). Regardless of whether discrimination was intentional, the laws are allowing the privileged to vote while disenfranchising the oppressed.

Furthermore, the new laws are unjustified because available evidence does not support their need. According to PBS *News Hour* from August 3, 2018, the intent of voter ID laws was to prevent voter fraud. However, the Presidential Commission empaneled to explore the problem was unable to document that voter fraud was a problem in the United States. Until it can be established that voter fraud is, indeed, a widespread problem, passing new laws to make it harder to vote is simply not justified. Why would we continue to pass laws to fix a problem that does not exist? These laws are not only unnecessary, but they also diminish people's civil liberties. They should be repealed so that all citizens' rights to vote are protected.

Fortunately, there are solutions that you and I can take to fight for the voting rights of all Americans. First, you can reach out to organizations fighting to get these laws repealed, like the American Civil Liberties Union. Contact Robert Hoffman at rhoffman@aclu.org to show your support and get involved. Second, you can reach out to the grassroots program Spread the Vote, which is helping targeted Americans get the identification cards they need to vote. Volunteer! Donate! Get involved with groups that are making a difference every day. Even if your state doesn't require IDs to vote, help groups like Rock the Vote encourage folks to participate in the process. Third, you can visit congress.gov to learn the identity of our state's senators and representatives, or those from your home state if you are an out-of-state student. I encourage you to contact their offices through email, telephone, or other means and let them know that you are in support of new legislation that eliminates unnecessary barriers to voting and that strongly protects citizens' rights to vote.

> Signposts (numbering) organize ideas

Supporters of voter identification laws claim that they want to prevent fraud, but as you have heard, no evidence of a widespread voter fraud problem exists. In fact, these new laws are only making it harder for the elderly, minorities, and those with low income to vote. There are several steps you can take to protect those rights for yourself and other citizens. Get involved with national organizations, like the American Civil

> Transition to conclusion

> Review of main points

CONTINUED

Liberties Union, and grassroots organizations, or take steps to contact your elected representatives. After considering the people who voter fraud laws disenfranchise and solutions to help those affected vote, we see the truth. It is time these laws are labeled as what they really are—discriminatory—and repealed. You are now equipped to help others fight for their voices. It's not just time to get out the vote. It's time to help people get out of the bureaucratic brambles so that we can all have an equal voice in our democracy.

Call to action

Clincher sentence

References

AARP. (2012, August 30). Can we still vote? *AARP Bulletin*. https://www.aarp.org/politics-society/government-elections/info-01-2012/voter-id-laws-impact-older-americans.html

American Bar Association. (2018, December 12). *Chapter 10: Voter ID as a form of voter suppression*. https://www.americanbar.org/publications/state_local_law_news/2015-16/spring/chapter_10_voter_id_a_form_voter_suppression/

American Civil Liberties Union. (n.d.). *Fighting voter suppression*. https://www.aclu.org/issues/voting-rights/fighting-voter-suppression

Brennan Center for Justice. (2012, October 15). *Voter ID*. https://www.brennancenter.org/analysis/voter-id

Domonoske, C. (2018, October 13). Many native IDs won't be accepted at North Dakota polling places. *NPR*. https://www.npr.org/2018/10/13/657125819/many-native-ids-wont-be-accepted-at-north-dakota-polling-places

Horwitz, S. (2016, May 23). Getting a photo ID so you can vote is easy. Unless you're poor, black, Latino or elderly. *Washington Post*. https://www.washingtonpost.com/politics/courts_law/getting-a-photo-id-so-you-can-vote-is-easy-unless-youre-poor-black-latino-or-elderly/2016/05/23/8d5474ec-20f0-11e6-8690-f14ca9de2972_story.html?utm_term=.89f2f70e50fb

Jaffe, I. (2018, September 7). For older voters, getting the right ID can be especially tough. *NPR*. https://www.npr.org/2018/09/07/644648955/for-older-voters-getting-the-right-id-can-be-especially-tough

Library of Congress. (n.d.). *15th Amendment to the U.S. Constitution*. https://www.loc.gov/rr/program/bib/ourdocs/15thamendment.html

Rock the Vote. (n.d.). *Get ready to vote*. https://www.rockthevote.org/voting-information/

Span, P. (2017, November 24). Older voters stymied by tighter ID requirements. *New York Times.* https://www.nytimes.com/2017/11/24/health/voting-eligibility-elderly.html

Spread the Vote. (n.d.). *Volunteer.* https://www.spreadthevote.org/volunteer/

Lapowsky, I. (2018, January 4). A dead-simple algorithm reveals the true toil of voter ID laws. *Wired.* https://www.wired.com/story/voter-id-law-algorithm/

Villeneuve, M. (2018, August 3). Report: Trump commission did not find widespread voter fraud. *PBS.* https://www.pbs.org/newshour/politics/report-trump-commission-did-not-find-widespread-voter-fraud

How to Resist Persuasion

Listed here are some measures you can take to resist persuasion, not only in public presentations but also on the telephone, in advertising, and when dealing with salespeople:

- *Remember that the best resistance is avoidance.* You do not have to watch or read advertising, go into stores where you do not intend to buy, listen to telemarketers, or watch infomercials.

- *Be skeptical about all messages.* Persuaders who are seeking easy prey look for the uneducated, the desperate, the angry, the very young, the very old, and the unsuspecting. They avoid people who are educated, articulate, cautious, and careful. You should use your knowledge of argumentation, evidence, and proof to analyze claims.

- *Check claims with other, unbiased sources.* A good rule is to verify any persuasive claims with at least two other sources of information. A politician tells you that lower taxes will be good for you. What do the editorials, the political commentators, and the opposition say about that plan? Consumer magazines, especially those that take no advertising, are less likely to be biased, as are news sources that embrace objectivity.

- *Check out the credibility of the source.* Be suspicious if a business is new or changes location often or if a speaker has a questionable reputation for truth or reliability. Customers, institutions, and satisfied audiences will vouch for credible sources. The internet offers ratings of products, businesses, and professionals on websites such as *Yelp, Angi,* and *Consumer Reports.* However, beware because some rating services are sponsored by the vendors being evaluated. In other words, some ranking and rating services are bogus; they are just another attempt to trick you.

- *Be cautious about accepting a persuasive appeal.* Most states have laws that allow even a signed contract to be rejected by the customer in the first 24 to 48 hours—in case you have second thoughts. Accepting claims on impulse is a dangerous practice that you can avoid by never making an important decision in the context of a sales pitch.

- *Question the ethical basis of proposed actions.* Angry people are easy to turn to violence, desperate people willingly consider desperate measures, and frustrated people can easily become an unruly mob. Ask yourself whether the proposed action is self-serving, pits one group against another, or will be good for you when viewed in retrospect.

- *Use your knowledge and experience to analyze persuasive claims.* A claim that sounds too good to be true probably is. If you have a gut feeling that a claim seems wrong, find out why. Use all you know about logic, evidence, and proof to see whether the persuader is drawing a sound conclusion or making an inferential leap that is justified by the evidence. Finally, assume all evidence is open to scrutiny.

- *Use your own values as a check against fraudulent claims.* If someone is trying to get you to do something that runs counter to what you learned, in your home, in the law, in your school, or from your friends, be wary. Sales always enrich the seller but not always the buyer. You can choose to sacrifice, but you should not sacrifice unwittingly. Your values are good protection against those who would cheat you. Ask yourself, "What would my parents, my friends, my neighbors, my professor, or my religious leaders think of this decision?"

- *Check what persuaders say against what they do.* Judge persuaders more by what they do than by what they say. Talk may not be cheap, but words cost less than deeds, and the proof of what people say is in their behavior. We learn to trust people who do what they say; we learn to distrust those who say one thing and do another.

• Learn to be wary about good deals. Use your brain to protect yourself.

Iconotec/Alamy Stock Photo

- *Use your freedom of expression and freedom of choice as protection against unethical persuaders.* In the United States you can hear competing ideas, and the choice to accept or reject them is yours. You can educate yourself about issues and ideas by reading, watching, and listening. Education and learning are powerful protection against persuaders who would take advantage of you. Use your freedoms to help defend yourself.

Now that you know 10 suggestions for resisting persuasion, you can practice the strategies for keeping others from manipulating your mind and picking your pocket.

be ready... for what's next

Inviting Your Audience to Dialogue

The best public speakers are celebrated for their dynamic and engaging speaking styles, in part because they invite people into a conversation. Sharing a personal experience that relates to your topic can help your audience relate to you and open up to your message. Members of an audience who are closed off to you as a speaker are difficult to persuade. A story explaining your extensive experience with a charity you want your audience to get involved with provides ethos; a story about how you or a loved one suffered from using a product you want your audience to discontinue using can provide pathos; and telling a story about the positive effects you experienced after beginning an exercise regimen can support your logical argument that endorphins from exercise reduce stress. If you don't have a personal experience that applies, sharing a friend's story or a hypothetical example can also induce empathy in your audience. In addition, people generally remember stories better than facts and are more likely to take ownership of an idea that is framed as a story. If you are creating a call to action as part of your persuasive presentation, rather than telling your audience, "You should do this," tell a story that positions the call to action as the best thing to do.

Chapter Review & Study Guide

Summary

In this chapter, you learned the following:

1. A persuasive presentation is a message strategically designed to induce change in an audience.

2. Modest changes you can accomplish in a brief presentation represent your immediate purpose, whereas major changes your presentation may contribute to in the future make up your long-range goal.

3. Instead of immediately revealing your purpose in the introduction, as you do in most informative presentations, you may have to delay stating your immediate purpose until you have prepared the way with persuasive strategies.

4. An effective argument consists of a statement of fact, policy, or value backed by supporting material that meets the tests of evidence.

5. You can use *ethos* (source credibility), *pathos* (emotional argument), or *logos* (logical argument) as persuasive strategies in your presentations.

6. The Monroe Motivated Sequence is an appropriate organizational pattern for persuasive presentations, especially when the audience is reluctant to change or to accept a proposed action. It consists of five steps: attention, need, satisfaction, visualization, and action.

7. High ethical standards require you to cite sources accurately, respect your audience, and even respect your opponents.

8. The chapter's annotated, detailed manuscript of a successful persuasive presentation by a student provides a model you can follow in preparing your own presentation.

9. There are many ways to resist persuasion, the most important of which is to avoid placing yourself in a position to be persuaded.

Key Terms

Adoption
Argument
Boomerang effect
Captive audience
Coercion
Deductive argument
Discontinuance
Ethos
Evidence

Fear appeal
Inductive argument
Logos
Manipulation
Micro-persuasion
Monroe Motivated Sequence
Pathos
Persuasive imagery
Persuasive presentation

Proof
Proposition of fact
Proposition of policy
Proposition of value
Rebuttal
Syllogism
Tests of evidence
Voluntary audience

Study Questions

1. The intention of a persuasive presentation is to
   a. inform listeners of a certain topic.
   b. change listeners' minds or behavior.
   c. explain a concept.
   d. describe an important issue.

2. If an audience likes you and your message less after the presentation than they did before, what term correctly describes what has taken place?
   a. source credibility reversal
   b. believability impasse
   c. boomerang effect
   d. continuance cessation

3. When a presenter attempts to convince listeners to stop a current behavior, what has taken place?
   a. discontinuance
   b. adoption
   c. continuance
   d. deterrence

4. If your evidence meets the tests of evidence, it will do all the following *except*
   a. come from unbiased sources.
   b. be consistent with other well-known facts.
   c. overlook counterevidence.
   d. consist of authoritative, valid, and reliable surveys.

5. When resisting persuasion from salespeople and advertisers, you should do all the following *except*

    a. avoid using your own values as a check against fraudulent claims.
    b. listen to all messages while thinking critically.
    c. question the credibility of all sources.
    d. evaluate the ethical basis of proposed actions.

6. Which type of argument uses a series of individual instances that lead to a generalization?

    a. deductive   c. rebuttal
    b. inductive   d. syllogism

7. You can rebut a deductive argument by questioning the

    a. major premise.
    b. clarity of the proposition.
    c. quality of individual instances.
    d. place where the inferential leap occurs.

8. Which of the following statements regarding argument organization is true?

    a. Place your best argument in the middle.
    b. Present one side of an issue to reduce the effects of contrary arguments.
    c. Place your best argument at the beginning or end.
    d. Familiar arguments have more effect than novel arguments.

9. In the Monroe Motivated Sequence, the visualization step includes

    a. gaining and maintaining audience attention.
    b. presenting information or a solution to audience needs.
    c. asking the audience to take specific steps.
    d. demonstrating how the solution will benefit the audience.

10. Which is *not* an ethical standard to follow when preparing and delivering a persuasive presentation?

    a. Accurately cite sources when the words are not your own.
    b. Respect sources of information by revealing their credibility.
    c. Speak truthfully and accurately out of respect for your audience.
    d. Attack your opponent's character instead of the evidence, sources, or logic.

Answers:

1. (b); 2. (c); 3. (a); 4. (c); 5. (a); 6. (b); 7. (a); 8. (c); 9. (d); 10. (d)

Critical Thinking

1. Especially when listening to national-level politicians speak, see whether you can determine the truth and accuracy of what they say. Then visit a fact-checking website, such as Factcheck.org, to see what a politically neutral organization finds accurate about speeches, advertisements, and campaign claims. Were you able to detect any of the inaccuracies that emerge in presentations by politicians in all parties?

2. Over the next week, watch news programs or scan the social media accounts of friends and family members who have different views than you do on social, national, or international issues. What persuasive appeals are being used, and how do you react? Then turn back to the accounts you typically view. How, if at all, are these appeals different or the same?

Sizing Things Up Scoring and Interpretation

Need for Cognition

A key objective in this chapter is to help you think strategically about persuading others. In persuasion literature a number of research studies have explored personality characteristics that influence how people react to persuasive messages. A person's need for cognition addresses the extent to which that person wants to think about information. Those who have a greater need for cognition will react differently to persuasive messages than those who have a lower need for cognition. By using this survey, you can determine your personal need for cognition when being persuaded.

To score the Need for Cognition scale, you should first reverse-code items 2, 3, 5, and 6 (a score of 5 should now be a 1, a score of 4 should now be a 2, and vice versa). Then average responses for all items; higher values indicate a greater need for cognition. Although reliable national norms for this scale have not been identified, an average above the midpoint of 3 would certainly indicate a higher need for cognition, whereas values below the midpoint would indicate a lower need for cognition. As you compare your score with those of your classmates, is your need for cognition higher or lower?

References

1. Reed, R. (2019, January 7). Golden Globes 2019: Read Regina King's speech on improving Hollywood gender gap. *Rolling Stone*. https://www.rollingstone.com/movies/movie-news/golden-globes-regina-king-acceptance-speech-50-percent-women-775642/

2. Kerr, E., & Wood., S. (2002, September 13). See how average student loan debt has changed. *US News and World Report*. https://www.usnews.com/education/best-colleges/paying-for-college/articles/see-how-student-loan-borrowing-has-changed

3. King James Bible (1769/2008).

4. Oxfam International. (2017, January 16). Just 8 men own same wealth as half the world. https://www.oxfam.org/en/pressroom/pressreleases/2017-01-16/just-8-men-own-same-wealth-half-world

5. Vargas, J. A. (2011, June 22). My life as an undocumented immigrant. *New York Times Magazine*.

6. Chen, L. (2005). Persuasion in Chinese culture: A glimpse of the ancient practice in contrast to the West. *Intercultural Communication Studies, 14,* 28–40.

7. Perloff, R. M. (2010). *The dynamics of persuasion: Communication and attitudes in the 21st century* (4th ed.). Routledge.

8. Suter, R. (2022, May 13). How much does a Super Bowl commercial cost? Here's the average breakdown since 1967. *USA Today Ad Meter*. https://admeter.usatoday.com/2022/05/13/super-bowl-commercial-costs-since-1967/

9. Ehninger, D. (1970). Argument as method: Its nature, its limitations, and its uses. *Speech Monographs, 37,* 101–110.

Glossary

A

active listening Involved listening with a purpose.

active perception Perception in which your mind selects, organizes, and interprets that which you sense.

adaptors Nonverbal movements that usually involve the unintended touching or manipulating of our bodies or artifacts to fulfill some physical or psychological need.

adoption Listeners start a new behavior as a result of the persuasive presentation.

affect displays Nonverbal movements of the face and body used to show emotion.

affection The emotion of caring for others and/or being cared for.

affinity bias Tendency to build relationships with people that share similar interests and background.

ageist language Language that denigrates people for being young or old.

aggressiveness The assertion of one's rights at the expense of others and caring about one's own needs but no one else's.

American Sign Language (ASL) A complete language system that uses hand signs coupled with discrete facial expressions and body postures to convey meaning.

analogy A comparison of things in some respects, especially in position or function, that are otherwise dissimilar.

anticipatory socialization The communicative process through which one intentionally and unintentionally learns about occupational choices and sets career expectations.

antonym Defines an idea by opposition.

argument A proposition that asserts some course of action.

argumentativeness The quality or state of being argumentative; synonymous with contentiousness or combativeness.

articulation Coordinating one's mouth, tongue, and teeth to make words understandable to others.

artifacts Ornaments or adornments you display that hold communicative potential.

assigned groups Groups that evolve out of a hierarchy whereby individuals are assigned membership to the group.

asynchronous communication Interactions in which there is a small or even substantial delay, as occurs with email or discussion board posts.

attitude A predisposition to respond favorably or unfavorably to a person, an object, an idea, or an event.

attractiveness A concept that includes physical attractiveness, how desirable a person is to work with, and how much "social value" the person has for others.

attribution bias When we positively evaluate behaviors and situations from people in our in-group and judge those in an out-group more harshly.

audience analysis The collection and interpretation of audience information obtained by observation, inference, research, or questionnaires.

autocratic leaders Leaders who maintain strict control over their group.

automatic attention The instinctive focus we give to stimuli signaling a change in our surroundings, stimuli that we deem important, or stimuli that we perceive to signal danger.

B

bargaining The process in which two or more parties attempt to reach an agreement on what each should give and receive in a transaction between them.

behavioral flexibility The ability to alter behavior to adapt to new situations and to relate in new ways when necessary.

belief A conviction; often thought to be more enduring than an attitude and less enduring than a value.

bibliographic references Complete citations that appear in the "references" or "works cited" section of your speech outline.

bodily movement What the speaker does with his or her entire body during a presentation.

body The largest part of a presentation, which contains the arguments, evidence, and main content.

boomerang effect The audience likes you and your message less after your presentation than they did before.

boundary spanner An individual who shares information between groups and establishes a strategic vision for collaboration.

brainstorming A creative procedure for thinking of as many topics as you can in a limited time.

brakelight function A forewarning to the audience that the end of the presentation is near.

C

captive audience A group consisting of people who did not gather to hear about your particular topic.

cause/effect pattern A method of organization in which the presenter first explains the reasons for an event, a problem, or an issue and then discusses its consequences or results.

celebrity testimony Statements made by a public figure who is known to the audience.

channel The means by which a message moves from the source to the receiver of a message.

chronemics Also called temporal communication; the way people organize and use time and the messages that are created because of their organization and use of that time.

cliché An expression that has lost originality and force through overuse.

closure The tendency to fill in missing information in order to complete an otherwise incomplete figure or statement.

code A systematic arrangement of symbols used to create meanings in the mind of another person or persons.

code sensitivity The ability to use the verbal and nonverbal language appropriate to the cultural norms of the individual with whom you are communicating.

coercion The act of forcing people to think or behave as you wish; not a form of persuasion.

commitment A measure of how much time and effort you put into a cause; your passion and concern about the topic.

common ground The degree to which the speaker's values, beliefs, attitudes, and interests are shared with the audience; an aspect of credibility.

communication The process of using messages to generate shared meaning.

communication accommodation theory Communication accommodation theory is a framework that explains how people adjust their communication style to match the styles of others.

communication apprehension An individual's level of fear or anxiety associated with either real or anticipated communication with another person or persons.

communication competence The ability to effectively exchange meaning through a common system of symbols or behavior.

communication networks Patterns of relationships through which information flows in an organization.

comparison Shows the similarity between something well known and something less known.

competence The degree to which a speaker is perceived as skilled, qualified, experienced, authoritative, reliable, and informed; an aspect of credibility.

complementarity The idea that we sometimes bond with people whose strengths are our weaknesses.

complementary relationships Relationships in which each person supplies something the other person or persons lack.

complementing Using nonverbal and verbal codes to add meaning to each other and to expand the meaning of either message alone.

compliance-gaining Attempts made by a source of messages to influence a target "to perform some desired behavior that the target otherwise might not perform."

compliance-resisting The refusal of targets of influence messages to comply with requests.

conclusion The part that finishes the presentation by fulfilling the four functions of an ending.

concrete language Words and statements that are specific rather than abstract or vague.

confirmation bias When we pay attention to behaviors and ideas that reinforce our existing belief structures.

connotative meaning An individualized or personalized meaning of a word, which may be emotionally laden.

contact theory A theory that explores the conditions under which positive attitudes and behaviors can develop between different social groups.

content curation The collection and storage of documents and other multimedia from the web, covering a specific topic.

context A recurring pattern of behaviors and actions that typically take place in similar settings.

contradicting Sending verbal and nonverbal messages that conflict.

contradictions In dialectic theory, the idea that each person in a relationship might have two opposing desires for maintaining the relationship.

contrast Clarifies by showing differences.

control The ability to influence our environment.

criteria The standards by which a group must judge potential solutions.

critical listening Listening that challenges the speaker's message by evaluating its accuracy, meaningfulness, and utility.

critical thinking Analyzing the speaker, the situation, and the speaker's ideas to make critical judgments about the message being presented.

cultural relativism The belief that another culture should be judged by its own context rather than measured against your culture.

culture A unique combination of rituals, religious beliefs, ways of thinking, and ways of behaving that unify a group of people.

customer service encounter The moment of interaction between the customer and the firm.

D

dating Specifying when you made an observation, since everything changes over time.

deceptive communication The practice of deliberately making somebody believe things that are not true.

decode The process of assigning meaning to others' words in order to translate them into thoughts of your own.

decoding The process of assigning meaning to the idea or thought in a code.

deductive argument A logical structure that uses a general proposition applied to a specific instance to draw a conclusion.

defensiveness The response that occurs when a person feels attacked.

definitions Determinations of meaning through description, simplification, examples, analysis, comparison, explanation, or illustration.

delivery The presentation of a speech using your voice and body to communicate your message.

democratic leaders Leaders who encourage members to participate in group decisions.

demographic analysis The collection and interpretation of data about the characteristics of people.

demonstrating Showing the audience what you are explaining.

denotative meaning The agreed-upon meaning or dictionary meaning of a word.

descriptiveness The practice of describing observed behavior or phenomena instead of offering personal reactions or judgments.

designated leader Someone who has been appointed or elected to a leadership position.

dialectic The tension that exists between two conflicting or interacting forces, elements, or ideas.

dialogue The act of taking part in a conversation, discussion, or negotiation.

direct inference A tentative generalization based on deliberately gathered data.

discontinuance A persuasive purpose rooted in convincing listeners to stop some current behavior.

disinformation The intentional misrepresentation of facts with the intent of polarizing opinions.

diversity Aspects of identity, such as race, ethnicity, gender, economic status, and ability, that are brought together in some way.

dominant culture A cultural identity that gets its power and influence from traditional social structures like politics, religious institutions, schools, and businesses; in the United States the dominant culture is White, male, heterosexual, married, and employed.

downward communication Messages flowing from superiors to subordinates.

dyadic communication Two-person communication.

dynamism The extent to which the speaker is perceived as bold, active, energetic, strong, empathic, and assertive; an aspect of credibility.

E

economic orientation Organizations that manufacture products and/or offer services for consumers.

emblems Nonverbal movements that substitute for words and phrases.

emergent groups Groups resulting from environmental conditions leading to the formation of a cohesive group of individuals.

emergent leader Someone who becomes an informal leader by exerting influence toward achievement of a group's goal but does not hold the formal position or role of leader.

emotional labor Jobs in which employees are expected to display certain feelings in order to satisfy organizational role expectations.

empathic listening Listening with a purpose and attempting to understand another person's perspective.

emphasizing The use of nonverbal cues to strengthen verbal messages.

encode The process of translating your thoughts into words.

encoding The process of translating an idea or thought into a code.

enunciation Combining pronunciation and articulation to produce a word with clarity and distinction.

equity Providing equal opportunities for all people without discriminating on the basis of identity.

ethics A set of moral principles or values.

ethnocentrism The belief that your own group or culture is superior to other groups or cultures.

ethos Called "source credibility" today, the reputation, authority, and integrity of the speaker.

euphemism A more polite, pleasant expression used instead of a socially unacceptable form.

evidence The facts that support a claim.

examples Specific instances used to illustrate your point.

expert testimony Statements made by someone who has special knowledge or expertise about an issue or idea.

explanation A means of idea development that simplifies or clarifies an idea while arousing audience interest.

extemporaneous method A carefully prepared and researched presentation delivered in a conversational style.

extrinsic motivation A method of making information relevant by providing the audience with reasons

beyond the presentation itself for listening to the content of the presentation.

eye contact The extent to which a speaker looks directly at the audience.

F

facial expressions Any nonverbal cues expressed by the speaker's face.

fear appeal Eliciting fear to change behavior.

feedback The receiver's verbal and nonverbal response to the source's message.

figure The focal point of your attention.

first impression An initial opinion about people upon meeting them.

first-person observation An observation based on something that you personally have sensed.

fluency The smoothness of delivery, the flow of words, and the absence of vocalized pauses.

formal communication Messages that follow prescribed channels of communication throughout the organization.

formal role Also called positional role; an assigned role based on an individual's position or title within a group.

frozen evaluation An assessment of a concept that does not change over time.

G

gender identity How you feel about and express your gender.

gender-biased language Language that privileges a certain gender over another.

gestures Movements of the head, arms, and hands to illustrate, emphasize, or signal ideas in a presentation.

ground The background against which your focused attention occurs.

group climate The emotional tone or atmosphere members create within the group.

group conflict An expressed struggle between two or more members of a group.

group culture The socially negotiated system of rules that guide group behavior.

groupthink An unintended outcome of cohesion in which the desire for cohesion and agreement takes precedence over critical analysis and discussion.

H

hearing The act of receiving sound.

heterosexist language Language that implies that everyone is heterosexual.

heuristics Mental shortcuts used to make decisions—for instance, evaluating sources.

horizontal communication Messages between members of an organization who have equal power.

hostile work environment sexual harassment Conditions in the workplace that are sexually offensive, intimidating, or hostile and that affect an individual's ability to perform his or her job.

hurtful messages and events Things partners say and do that create emotional pain or upset.

I

illustrators Nonverbal movements that accompany or reinforce verbal messages.

imagery The use of words that appeal to the senses and create pictures in the mind.

immediacy Communication behaviors intended to create perceptions of psychological closeness with others.

immediate behavioral purposes The actions expected from an audience during and immediately after a presentation.

immediate purpose A statement of what you intend to accomplish in this particular presentation. Also, a highly specific statement using "should be able to" plus an action verb to reveal the purpose of a presentation from the audience's point of view.

impression management Sharing personal details in order to present an idealized self.

impromptu method Delivery of a presentation without notes, plans, or formal preparation; characterized by spontaneity and conversational language.

in-group A group that people belong to that gives them a source of pride, self-esteem, and sense of belonging to a social world.

inclusion The state of being involved with others; a human need.

inclusive communication Reducing barriers so that everyone is included, valued, and has access to the communication situation.

incremental plagiarism The intentional or unintentional use of information from one or more sources without fully divulging how much information is directly quoted.

indexing Identifying the uniqueness of objects, events, and people.

indirect inference A tentative generalization based on observation.

inductive argument A logical structure that provides enough specific instances for the listener to make an inferential leap to a generalization that summarizes the individual instances.

inference A tentative generalization based on some evidence.

inflection The variety or changes in pitch.

informal communication Interactions that do not follow the formal upward and downward structures of the organization but emerge out of less formal interactions among organizational members.

informal role Also called behavioral role; a role that is developed spontaneously within a group.

information literacy The ability to recognize when information is needed and to locate, evaluate, and effectively use the information needed.

information overload Providing much more information than the audience can absorb in terms of amount and complexity.

information relevance The importance, novelty, and usefulness of the information to the audience.

informative content The main points and subpoints, illustrations, and examples used to clarify and inform.

integration orientation Organizations that help mediate and resolve discord among members of society.

interaction management Establishing a smooth pattern of interaction that allows a clear flow between topics and ideas.

intergroup perspective The theory that emphasizes the ways in which people in a social interaction identify and categorize themselves or others in terms of group membership and how these categorizations shape perceptions and interactions with others.

internal references Brief notations indicating a bibliographic reference that contains the details you are using in your speech.

interpersonal communication The process of using messages to generate meaning between at least two people in a situation that allows mutual opportunities for both speaking and listening.

interpersonal relationships Associations between at least two people who are interdependent, who use some consistent patterns of interaction, and who have interacted for an extended period of time.

interpretive perception Perception that involves a blend of internal states and external stimuli.

intersectionality The ways our social identities intersect and overlap, as well as how those with multiple marginalized identities experience systems of oppression and discrimination in multiple ways.

intrapersonal communication The process of using messages to generate meaning within the self.

introduction The first part of your presentation, in which you fulfill the five functions of an introduction.

J

jargon Language particular to a specific profession, work group, or culture and not meant to be understood by outsiders.

job description The responsibilities and scope of a position within a company.

K

keyword outline An outline consisting of important words or phrases to remind you of the content of the presentation.

kinesics The study of bodily movements, including posture, gestures, and facial expressions.

L

laissez-faire leaders Leaders who take almost no initiative in structuring a group discussion.

language A collection of symbols, letters, or words with arbitrary meanings that are governed by rules and used to communicate.

lay testimony Statements made by an ordinary person that substantiate or support what you say.

leadership A process of using communication to influence the behaviors and attitudes of others to meet group goals.

lecture cues Verbal or nonverbal signals that stress points or indicate transitions between ideas during a lecture.

lecture listening The ability to listen to, mentally process, and recall lecture information.

listening The active process of receiving, constructing meaning from, and responding to spoken and/or nonverbal messages. It involves the ability to retain information, as well as to react empathically and/or appreciatively to spoken and/or nonverbal messages.

listening for enjoyment Listening that occurs in situations involving relaxing, fun, or emotionally stimulating information.

logos The use of logical reasoning in an argument.

long-range goal The larger goal or end purpose you have in mind for your presentation.

long-term memory Our permanent storage place for information, including but not limited to past experiences; language; values; knowledge; images of people; memories of sights, sounds, and smells; and even fantasies.

M

main points The most important points in a presentation; indicated by Roman numerals in an outline.

maintenance functions Behaviors that focus on the interpersonal relationships among group members.

manipulation The act of tricking people or using fraudulent means to gain compliance not a form of persuasion.

manuscript method Delivery of a presentation from a script of the entire speech.

mass communication The process of using messages to generate meanings in a mediated system, between a source and a large number of unseen receivers.

meaning The intent of a message by the sender and the interpretation of a message by the receiver.

media convergence The unification of separate channels of communication through new communication technology.

memorized method Delivery of a presentation that has been committed to memory.

mental health Our emotional, psychological, and social well-being that affects how we think, feel, and act.

message The verbal and nonverbal form of the idea, thought, or feeling that one person (the source) wishes to communicate to another person or a group of people (the receivers).

metamorphosis The process of moving beyond the entry phase, gaining skills and confidence in a role, embracing the values of the organization, and beginning to (re)define a role in an organization.

metaphor A figure of speech that likens one thing to another by treating it as if it were that thing.

micro-persuasion An attempt to change others with as few words or symbols as possible as in a tweet.

microaggressions Talk that can send insulting messages that devalue people from marginalized communities.

misinformation Unintentional use of incorrect facts or mischaracterization of facts.

Monroe Motivated Sequence A problem-solving format that encourages an audience to become concerned about an issue; especially appropriate for a persuasive presentation.

N

narrating The oral presentation and interpretation of a story, a description, or an event; includes dramatic reading of prose or poetry.

narratives Stories to illustrate an important point.

noise Any interference in the encoding and decoding processes that reduces message clarity.

nondominant identity A group that exists within a larger, dominant culture and differs from the dominant identities in one or more significant characteristics.

nonverbal codes Messages consisting of symbols that are not words, including nonword vocalizations.

nonverbal communication The process of using messages other than words to create meaning with others.

nonword sounds Sounds like "mmh," "huh," and "ahh," as well as the pauses or the absence of sounds used for effect.

norms Informal rules for group interaction created and sustained through communication.

O

objectics Also called object language; the study of the human use of clothing and artifacts as nonverbal codes.

online communication Use of the Internet, particularly social media and other networking resources, to carry out communication with others.

operational definition A definition that identifies something by revealing how it works, how it is made, or what it consists of.

organization The grouping of stimuli into meaningful units or wholes.

organizational assimilation Using formal and informal communication with others to learn work roles, become accustomed to standard practices, and enact core values of the organization.

organizational communication The ways in which groups of people both maintain structure and order through their symbolic interactions and allow individual actors the freedom to accomplish their goals.

organizational communities Groups of similar businesses or clubs that have common interests and become networked together to provide mutual support and resources.

organizational encounter The formal training, mentorship, and experiences that help someone become familiar with their role within an organization.

organizational patterns Arrangements of the contents of a presentation.

organizations Social collectives, or groups of people, in which activities are coordinated to achieve both individual and collective goals.

out-group A group of people excluded from another group with higher status; a group marginalized by the dominant culture.

outline A written plan that uses symbols, margins, and content to reveal the order, importance, and substance of a presentation.

P

paralinguistic features The nonword sounds and nonword characteristics of language, such as pitch, volume, rate, and quality.

parallel form The consistent use of complete sentences, clauses, phrases, or words in an outline.

paraphrasing Restating another person's message by rephrasing the content or intent of the message.

pathos The use of emotional "proofs" in an argument.

pattern-maintenance orientation Organizations that promote cultural and educational regularity and development within society.

pause The absence of vocal sound used for dramatic effect, transition, or emphasis.

perception The use of the senses to process information about the external environment.

perception checking A process of describing, interpreting, and verifying that helps us understand another person and his or her message more accurately.

perceptual constancy The idea that your past experiences lead you to see the world in a way that is difficult to change; your initial perceptions persist.

personal experience Your own life as a source of information.

personal identity Perception of what makes an individual unique with regard to various personality characteristics, interests, and values.

personal idioms Unique forms of expression and language understood only by individual couples.

personal network A web of contacts and relationships that can help you gain job leads and can provide job referrals.

persuasive imagery The advertiser's method of persuading an audience with fast-paced and dazzling visualization of products.

persuasive presentation A message designed to strategically induce change in an audience.

phatic communication Communication that is used to establish a mood of sociability rather than to communicate important information or ideas.

physical attractiveness The perceived desirability of another person's outward physical appearance.

pitch The highness or lowness of the voice.

plagiarism The intentional use of information from another source without crediting the source.

polarization The division of people into groups that have conflicting views, perspectives, or ideologies and very little common ground.

political orientation Organizations that generate and distribute power and control within society.

positive-thinking approach Using positive thoughts to bolster speaker confidence.

power Interpersonal influence that forms the basis for group leadership.

pragmatics The study of language as it is used in a social context, including its effect on the communicators.

prejudice An unfavorable predisposition about an individual because of that person's membership in a stereotyped group.

problem/solution pattern A method of organization in which the presenter describes an issue and proposes a resolution to that problem.

process An activity, an exchange, or a set of behaviors that occurs over time.

profanity A type of swearing that uses indecent words or phrases.

pronunciation Saying a word correctly or incorrectly.

proof Evidence that the receiver believes.

proposition of fact An assertion that can be proved or disproved as consistent with reality.

proposition of policy A proposal of a new rule.

proposition of value A statement of what we should embrace as important to our culture.

proxemics The study of the human use of space and distance.

proximity The location, distance, or range between persons and things; the principle that objects physically close to each other will be perceived as a unit or group.

public speaking The process of using messages to generate meanings in a situation in which a single speaker transmits a message to a number of receivers.

quality The unique resonance of the voice, such as huskiness, nasality, raspiness, or whininess.

questionnaire A set of written questions developed to obtain demographic and attitudinal information.

quid pro quo sexual harassment A situation in which an employee is offered a reward or is threatened with punishment based on his or her participation in a sexual activity.

R

racist language Language that insults a group because of its race or ethnicity.

rate The pace of your speech.

rebuttal Arguing against someone else's position on an issue.

receiver A message target.

reference librarian A librarian specifically trained to help you find sources of information.

references A list of sources used in a presentation.

reflexivity Being self-aware and learning from interactions with the intent of improving future interactions.

regionalisms Words and phrases specific to a particular region or part of the country.

regulating Using nonverbal codes to monitor and control interactions with others.

regulators Nonverbal movements that control the flow or pace of communication.

relational deterioration The stage in a relationship in which the prior bond disintegrates.

relational development The initial stage in a relationship that moves a couple from meeting to mating.

relational maintenance The stage in a relationship after a couple has bonded and in which they engage in the process of keeping the relationship together.

relationship-oriented groups Groups that are usually long term and exist to meet our needs for inclusion and affection.

relaxation approach Combining deep relaxation with fear-inducing thoughts.

remote delivery method Delivering a presentation through digitally mediated technology.

repeating Sending the same message both verbally and nonverbally.

responsiveness The idea that we tend to select our friends and loved ones from people who demonstrate positive interest in us.

rhetorical questions Questions asked for effect, with no answer expected.

rituals Formalized patterns of actions or words followed regularly.

role The part you play in various social contexts.

rough draft The preliminary organization of the outline of a presentation.

S

Sapir-Whorf hypothesis A theory that our perception of reality is determined by our thought processes, our thought processes are limited by our language, and therefore language shapes our reality and our behaviors.

schemas Organizational "filing systems" for thoughts held in long-term memory.

search engine A program on the Internet that allows users to search for information.

second-person observation A report of what another person observed.

selective attention The tendency, when you expose yourself to information and ideas, to focus on certain cues and ignore others.

selective exposure The tendency to expose yourself to information that reinforces, rather than contradicts, your beliefs or opinions.

selective perception The tendency to see, hear, and believe only what you want to see, hear, and believe.

selective retention The tendency to better remember the things that reinforce your beliefs than those that oppose them.

self-centered functions Behaviors that serve the needs of the individual at the expense of the group.

self-disclosure The process of making intentional revelations about yourself that others would be unlikely to know and that generally constitute private, sensitive, or confidential information.

self-managed approach Reducing the fear of presenting with self-diagnosis and a variety of therapies.

semantics The study of the way humans use language to evoke meaning in others.

sentence outline An outline consisting entirely of complete sentences.

sexual harassment Unwelcome, unsolicited, repeated behavior of a sexual nature.

short-term memory A temporary storage place for information.

signposts Ways in which a presenter signals to an audience where the presentation is going.

silence The lack of sound.

similarity The idea that our friends and loved ones are usually people who like or dislike the same things we do; the principle that elements are grouped together because they share attributes, such as size, color, or shape.

situation The location where communication takes place.

skills approach Reducing fear by systematically improving presenting skills.

slang Informal, casual language used among equals with words typically unsuitable for more formal contexts.

sleeper effect A change of audience opinion caused by the separation of the message content from its source over a period of time.

slide-deck visuals A collection of slides, usually created with a computer program, that are displayed during a presentation.

small-group communication Interaction among three to nine people working together to achieve an interdependent goal.

social identities The social groups you believe you belong to, such as gender, race, or religion.

social identity theory A theoretical framework that explains how individuals form a sense of self and how they categorize themselves and others into social groups.

social media listening The active monitoring of and response to messages on social media platforms by businesses or other types of organizations.

source A message initiator.

source credibility The extent to which the speaker is perceived as competent to make the claims he or she is making.

stakeholders Groups of people who have an interest in the actions of an organization.

statistics Numbers that summarize numerical information or compare quantities.

stereotype A generalization about some group of people that oversimplifies their culture.

stereotyping Making a hasty generalization about a group based on a judgment about an individual from that group.

strategic ambiguity The purposeful use of symbols to allow multiple interpretations of messages.

subjective perception Your uniquely constructed meaning attributed to sensed stimuli.

subpoints The points in a presentation that support the main points; indicated by capital letters in an outline.

substituting Using nonverbal codes instead of verbal codes.

supporting material Information you can use to substantiate your arguments and to clarify your position.

supportive communication Listening with empathy, acknowledging others' feelings, and engaging in dialogue to help others maintain a sense of personal control.

surveys Studies in which a sample of the population is asked a limited number of questions to discover public opinions on issues.

syllogism A logical structure that contains a major premise (a generalization) applied to a particular instance (a minor premise) that leads to a conclusion.

symbolic interactionism The process in which the self develops through the messages and feedback received from others.

symmetrical relationships Relationships in which participants mirror each other or are highly similar.

synchronous communication The instantaneous sending and receiving of messages, as occurs in face-to-face or some text-message interactions.

synonym Defines by using a word similar in meaning to the one you are trying to define.

syntax The way in which words are arranged to form phrases and sentences.

T

tactile communication The use of touch in communication.

task functions Behaviors that are directly relevant to the group's purpose and that affect the group's productivity.

task-oriented groups Also called secondary groups; groups formed for the purpose of completing tasks, such as solving problems or making decisions.

technological convergence The consolidation of voice, data, video, audio, and other channels of communication through smartphones and other devices.

testimonial evidence Written or oral statements of others' experience used by a speaker to substantiate or clarify a point.

tests of evidence Questions that can be used to assess the validity of evidence.

time-sequence pattern A method of organization in which the presenter explains events in chronological order.

Title IX officer The person designated by a college or university (or similar type of organization) to promote compliance with the U.S. Department of Education Title IX requirements, including the investigation of alleged sexual discrimination.

topical-sequence pattern A method of organization that emphasizes the major reasons an audience should accept a point of view by addressing the advantages, disadvantages, qualities, and types of a person, place, or thing.

transition A bridge between sections of a presentation that helps the presenter move smoothly from one idea to another.

trustworthiness The degree to which the speaker is perceived as honest, fair, sincere, friendly, honorable, and kind; an aspect of credibility.

two-sided argument A source advocating one position presents an argument from the opposite viewpoint and then goes on to refute that argument.

U

unconscious bias Unconscious cognitions that engage stereotypes and biases that unknowingly impact our behaviors

upward communication Messages flowing from subordinates to superiors.

V

value A deeply rooted belief that governs our attitude about something.

verbal citations Oral explanations of who the source is, how recent the information is, and what the source's qualifications are.

verbal codes Symbols and their grammatical arrangement, such as languages.

visual resources Any items that can be seen by an audience for the purpose of reinforcing a message.

visualization approach Picturing yourself succeeding.

vocal cues All of the oral aspects of sound except words themselves.

vocal variety Vocal quality, intonation patterns, inflections of pitch, and syllabic duration.

vocalized pauses Breaks in fluency that negatively affect an audience's perception of the speaker's competence and dynamism.

volume The loudness or softness of the voice.

voluntary audience A group that came to hear you, in particular, talk about your topic.

W

within-group diversity The presence of observable and implicit differences among group members.

working memory The part of our short-term memory that interprets and assigns meaning to stimuli we pay attention to.

Index

Please note that **bolded** page numbers indicate defined terms.

interpersonal communication and, 133
selective exposure and, 35
Time
delivery and, 320, 329
nonverbal communication and,
82–83, 91
Time-sequence pattern, **298**
Title VII of the Civil Rights Act, **214**
Titsworth, S., 292
Todd, T., 108
Todoist, **193–194**
Toggl, **194**
Tone of voice, 76
Topic
for informative presentation, 336, 337, 339
for persuasive presentation, 354, 370
Topic selection
adapting your topic in, 243–244
attention-getting strategy and, 290
audience and, 231–235, 245, 289, 291
credibility of (*See* Credibility)
evaluating topics in, 234
narrowing your topic in, 235–236
online brainstorming and, 296
for persuasive presentation, 354
rough draft and, 282
how to select appropriate topic in,
231–235
Topical-sequence pattern, 298, **300**, 362
Touching, 31, 83–85, 91, 111, 237
Toulmin, Stephen, 109, 110
Transitions, 301–303, **302**, 341
Trello, **193**
Trust, 142, **180**, 249, 250
Trustworthiness, **252**, 361
Tulshyan, Ruchika, 63
Turman, Paul, 194
Turnover, 222
Twitter (X)
Boston Strong and, 171
interpersonal communication and, 134
in introduction to communication, 19
micro-persuading with, 356
small groups and, 173
Two-sided argument, **273**

U

Unconscious bias, **163**
Unions, 204

Untamed (Doyle), 44
Upward communication, **205**
U.S. Bureau of Labor Statistics, 114–115
U.S. Census Bureau, 9
U.S. Small Business Administration, 204

V

Values, 239–242, **240**, 357, 370
Vangelisti, A. L., 141
Vargas, José Antonio, 358
Venngage, 330
Verbal citations, **270**
Verbal codes, **12**, 47, 75
Verbal communication, 211
listening and, 112–113
nonverbal communication and, 75–76
workplace communication and, 203
Verbal communication skills, 217
Verbal cues, 5, 41, 136, 143
Verbal feedback, 115
Verbal learners, 348
Verbal responses, 101
Victory Consulting Firm, 314
Video games, 105, 137
Video recordings, 320
Vietnam conflict, 180
Virtual space, 82
Visual aids, 323, 324
Visual information, tips for, 324
Visual learners, 348
Visual resources
defined, **323**
principles to follow when using,
324–330
rough draft and, 282
from the library, 260–262
tips for using, 324
when to use, 323–324
Visualization, 321, 362
Vocabulary comprehension, 118
Vocal aspects of delivery, 314–317
Vocal cues, 85–87, 89
Vocal variety, 89, 91, 252, **316**–317
Vocalized pauses, 86, 313, **315**, 316
Voice, 252, 312, 314, 315, 316–317
Volume, **85**, 86, 91, 112, 314, 315–316
Voluntary audience, **355**
Volunteering, 210
Vye, A., 210